Microsoft®

Distributed Applications with Microsoft® Visual C++® 6.0 MCSD Training Kit

For Exam 70-015

Online Training Solutions, Inc. (OTSI)
Scott F. Wilson

PUBLISHED BY
Microsoft Press
A Division of Microsoft Corporation
One Microsoft Way
Redmond, Washington 98052-6399

Library of Congress Cataloging-in-Publication Data
Distributed Applications with Microsoft Visual C++ 6.0 MCSD Training Kit / Microsoft Corporation.
p. cm.
Includes index.
ISBN 0-7356-0926-8
1. Electronic data processing--Distributed processing. 2. Microsoft Visual C++. I. Microsoft Corporation.
QA76.9.D5 D48556 2000
005.13'3--dc21 00-020244

Printed and bound in the United States of America.

1 2 3 4 5 6 7 8 9 WCWC 5 4 3 2 1 0

Distributed in Canada by Penguin Books Canada Limited.

A CIP catalogue record for this book is available from the British Library.

Microsoft Press books are available through booksellers and distributors worldwide. For further information about international editions, contact your local Microsoft Corporation office or contact Microsoft Press International directly at fax (425) 936-7329. Visit our Web site at mspress.microsoft.com.

Acquisitions Editor: Eric Stroo
Project Editor: Victoria P. Thulman

Contents

About This Book .... **xiii**
Intended Audience xiii
Prerequisites xiv
Course Overview xiv
Getting Started xviii
Using This Book to Prepare for Certification xxiii
Microsoft Certified Professional Program xxix
Technical Support xxx
About the Authors xxxi
Chapter 1 Designing the Application **1**
Lesson 1: Architecture-First Design 2
Architecture-First Design 2
Application Design Principles 4
Lesson Summary 8
Lesson 2: Distributed Application Design 10
Multilayer Design 10
User Interface 14
User Service Layer 15
Business Service Layer 22
Data Service Layer 25
Lesson Summary 35
Review 36
Chapter 2 Development Environment **37**
Lesson 1: Production Channel 38
Details of the Production Channel 39
Lesson Summary 42
Lesson 2: Change Control 43
Change-Control Process 43
Version Control Systems 45
Visual SourceSafe 45
Exploring Features of VSS 51
Lesson Summary 56
Lesson 3: Tools 57
Integrated Development Environment 57
Visual Data Modeling 59

- Visual Modeler ... 62
- Dcomcnfg.exe ... 64
- OLEView ... 68
- Using OLEView to View Installed COM Objects ... 69
- Lesson Summary ... 73

Lab 2: Installing Visual C++ ... 74

Review ... 83

Chapter 3 C++ Development Essentials ... 85

Lesson 1: C++ Libraries ... 86
- Overview of MFC ... 86
- MFC Architecture ... 89
- MFC Library Files ... 99
- Using ATL ... 109
- Using STL ... 111
- Lesson Summary ... 112

Lesson 2: Thread Management ... 113
- Threading Models ... 113
- Apartments ... 114
- In-Process Threads ... 116
- Out-of-Process Threads ... 117
- Lesson Summary ... 118

Lesson 3: Memory Management and System Services ... 119
- Some Basic Concepts ... 119
- Memory Allocation and Management ... 121
- Memory Allocation/Deallocation Examples ... 123
- Resizable Memory Blocks ... 125
- Memory Management Problems and Issues ... 125
- Lesson Summary ... 127

Review ... 129

Chapter 4 Developing User Services ... 131

Lesson 1: Creating Help Systems ... 132
- Help System Considerations ... 132
- WinHelp Files ... 135
- HTML Help ... 136
- Implementing Help Systems ... 137
- Lesson Summary ... 141

Lesson 2: User Interface Navigation ... 142
- Creating Menus with the Menu Editor ... 142
- Creating and Using Toolbars ... 152
- Rebars ... 157

Implementing Status Bars 158
Lesson Summary 161
Lesson 3: User Interface Forms and Dialog Boxes 163
Dialog Boxes 163
Property Sheets 168
Using the CFormView Class 169
Processing and Validating User Input 171
Lesson Summary 175
Lesson 4: Creating and Using ActiveX Controls 176
Using ActiveX Controls 176
Using Event Handlers with Command Messages 179
Creating ActiveX Controls with ATL 180
Creating ActiveX Controls with the Platform SDK 183
Creating ActiveX Controls with MFC 184
Signing an ActiveX Control 194
Downloading an ActiveX Control to the User Interface 195
Lesson Summary 196
Lab 4: Creating a User Interface 197
Exercise 1: Creating a Dynamic Menu 197
Exercise 2: Adding a Modeless Dialog Box 201
Exercise 3: Building an ActiveX Control 210
Review 214
Chapter 5 Building Basic Business Objects 215
Lesson 1: COM Basics 216
The Challenges of Component-Based Applications 216
Coclasses 219
COM Objects 219
COM Components 222
COM Identifiers 223
COM Interfaces 225
COM Security 229
COM Registration 230
COM Support in Distributed Environments 232
Lesson Summary 233
Lesson 2: Visual C++ Classes 235
Implementation Inheritance 240
Allocating and Deallocating Memory in the DLL 244
Interface Inheritance 247
Advantages of Using Interfaces 250
Lesson Summary 255

Lesson 3: Building a COM Component Using the Platform SDK 256
Defining Interfaces with IDL 256
Implementing IUnknown 261
Creating Class Factories 263
COM DLL Entry Points 265
Lesson Summary 269
Lesson 4: Building a COM Component using ATL or MFC 270
Active Template Library 270
Microsoft Foundation Classes 277
Lesson Summary 290
Lab 5: Dissecting ATL 291
Review 298
Chapter 6 Building Advanced Business Objects 301
Lesson 1: Creating Distributed COM Components 302
Configuring DCOM 302
Creating an ATL Out-Of-Process Component 304
Using DCOM Security 306
Registering a DCOM Component 308
Lesson Summary 310
Lesson 2: Creating Multithreaded Components 311
Using Multithreaded Components 311
Creating a Multithreaded Component Using ATL 318
Lesson Summary 319
Lesson 3: Creating Services 320
Creating a Windows NT Service 320
Communicating with Services 324
Managing Services 325
Lesson Summary 325
Lesson 4: Extending Existing COM Components 326
Aggregation 326
Containment 329
Scriptlets 330
Lesson Summary 332
Lesson 5: Creating and Using Active Documents 333
Active Document Containers and Servers 333
Lesson Summary 335
Lesson 6: Using MFC to Create an ISAPI DLL 336
Extending Web Server Capabilities 336
MFC Regular DLLs vs. MFC Extension DLLs 340

Dynamic User Interfaces 341
Lesson Summary 343
Lab 6: Creating an Out-of-Process COM Component 344
Exercise 1: Creating a COM Server 344
Exercise 2: Creating a COM Client 346
Review 348
Chapter 7 Using Microsoft Transaction Services 349
Lesson 1: Transactions and MTS 350
Transactions 350
Coordinating Transactions 351
Transactions and COM 352
What Is MTS? 353
Benefits of Using MTS 353
MTS Structures 357
Lesson Summary 361
Lesson 2: Configuring MTS 362
Installation 362
Configuring Your MTS Server with MTS Explorer 363
Administering Your MTS Server Programmatically 365
Lesson Summary 366
Lesson 3: MTS Objects 367
Designing Objects for MTS 367
Developing Objects for MTS 367
Packaging Objects for MTS 371
Deploying MTS-Based Objects 376
Lesson Summary 379
Lesson 4: Advanced MTS Techniques 380
Role-Based Security 380
Load Balancing 384
Lesson Summary 384
Lesson 5: Creating MTS-Based Applications 386
Controlling the Flow of Transactions 386
Designing with MTS 389
Scaling Applications with MTS 389
Lesson Summary 391
Lab 7: Understanding MTS Activities and Transactions 392
Exercise 1: Putting Everything in Place 392
Exercise 2: Observe How Activities Are Managed 395
Exercise 3: Observe How Transactions Are Managed 397
Review 402

Chapter 8 Microsoft Message Queuing Services 403
Lesson 1: Installing and Configuring MSMQ 404
MSMQ Architecture 405
Installing MSMQ 406
Lesson Summary 410
Lesson 2: Creating and Using Queues 412
COM Objects 412
Creating a Queue 413
Locating a Queue 416
Opening a Queue 418
Sending Messages 419
Receiving Messages 422
Deleting a Queue 427
Lesson Summary 428
Lesson 3: Transactional Queues 429
Transactional Messaging 429
Creating a Transactional Queue 430
Sending and Receiving Messages Within a Transaction 430
Lesson Summary 433
Lab 8: Sending and Receiving Persistent Objects In Messages 434
Exercise 1: Creating a Persistable Object 434
Exercise 2: Sending Messages 438
Exercise 3: Receiving Messages 443
Review 446
Chapter 9 Using Data Access Services 447
Lesson 1: Structured Query Language 448
Basic Concepts 448
Retrieving Data 450
Modifying Data 453
Deleting Data 454
Querying Multiple Tables 456
Summarizing Data 465
Lesson 2: SQL Server 469
Basic Concepts 469
Installing SQL Server 471
Configuring SQL Server 472
Implementing a SQL Server Database 474
Data Integrity 478
Creating and Maintaining Indexes 481

Lesson 3: Data Access Strategies 483
Data Access 483
UDA Technology 483
Fundamental Terms of Data Access 485
Microsoft Data Access Components 487
Using CSocket 489
Choosing the Right Data Access Technology 496
Choosing a Data Access Strategy 498
Lesson Summary 499
Lesson 4: Using ADO 500
Basics of ADO 500
ADO Architecture 501
Guidelines for Choosing ADO as Your Data Access Technology 502
Working with ADO Objects 503
Executing Parameterized Queries with ADO 519
Lesson Summary 523
Lesson 5: Using ODBC 524
ODBC Architecture 524
MFC ODBC Classes 526
Working with ODBC Recordsets 530
Debugging and Error Handling in ODBC Applications 532
Lesson Summary 534
Lesson 6: Using OLE DB 536
Basics of OLE DB 536
OLE DB Architecure 537
OLE DB Physical Architecture 540
OLE DB Consumer Templates 541
Using the CDynamicAccessor Class 545
Creating Parameterized Queries Using CDynamicParameterAccessor .. 547
Lesson Summary 549
Lab 9: Creating an ADO Application 551
Review 555
Chapter 10 Exception Handling 557
Lesson 1: Exceptions 558
Anticipating Program Errors 558
Structured Exception Handling 560
C++ Exception Handling 561
Benign Exceptions 563
Visual C++ Exception Handling Support 563
Lesson Summary 563

Lesson 2: Handling Exceptions and Errors 565
Exceptions and MFC 565
COM Errors 569
Exceptions and Distributed Applications 577
Lesson Summary 577
Lesson 3: Error-Handling Strategies 579
Working with Error Logs 579
Working with MTS 582
Working with MSMQ 587
Working with ADO 588
Handling Exceptions in an ADO Application 589
Lesson Summary 592
Lab 10: Exception Handling in Duwamish Books 593
Exercise 1: Adding Exception Handlers 593
Exercise 2: Rebuilding the D4Cache Project 596
Review 598
Chapter 11 Debugging and Testing 599
Lesson 1: Introduction to Debugging 600
What Is a Debugger? 600
Debug vs. Release 601
MFC Debug Macros 602
Lesson Summary 604
Lesson 2: Using the Integrated Debugger 605
Breakpoints 605
Setting Breakpoints 605
Running the Debugger 609
Debugger Windows 609
Stepping Through Code 611
Edit and Continue 612
Lesson Summary 612
Lesson 3: Debugging COM Objects 614
Debugging Local Objects 615
Debugging Remote Objects 620
Troubleshooting COM Objects 625
Lesson Summary 626
Lesson 4: Dependency Walker 628
What Is a Dependency? 628
Dependency Information 628
Lesson Summary 630

Lesson 5: Spy++ 631
Spy++ Views 631
Viewing Window Messages in Spy++ 634
Lesson Summary 635
Lesson 6: Testing a Distributed Application 636
Glossary of Testing Terms 636
Creating a Test Plan 637
Creating a Test Harness 638
Lesson Summary 639
Lab 11: Debugging a COM Object 640
Exercise 1: Debugging a Local Object 640
Exercise 2: Debugging a Remote Object 643
Exercise 3: Debugging an MTS Object 648
Review 651
Chapter 12 Deploying Distributed Applications 653
Lesson 1: Setup Programs 654
Writing a Setup Program 655
Guidelines for Writing a Setup Program 656
Uninstall Program 657
Adding and Removing Registry Information 657
Cabinet Files 659
Registry Files 660
Adding a Command to the Programs Menu 662
Lesson Summary 666
Lesson 2: Using InstallShield 668
Installing InstallShield 669
Running the InstallShield Tutorial 669
Including and Removing Program Files 670
Creating the Setup.exe Program 671
Lesson Summary 672
Lesson 3: Packaging COM Components 674
Determining Remote Server Names 674
MTS Components 675
Using MSMQ 679
Load Balancing 680
Lesson Summary 680
Lesson 4: Installing COM Components 682
Self-Registering Components 682
Adding Self-Registering Components to an InstallShield Project 683

Registering Remote COM Servers 684
Lesson Summary 684
Lesson 5: Deployment Methods 686
Media-Based Deployment 686
Network-Based Deployment 686
Web-Based Deployment 687
Deployment Checklist 688
Lesson Summary 689
Lesson 6: Zero Administration for Windows 690
Features of ZAW 690
Windows Installer 691
Systems Management Server 692
Zero Administration Kit 692
Lesson Summary 692
Lab 12: Packaging and Deploying a Distributed Application 694
Exercise 1: Building Release Versions of Client2 and Beeper 695
Exercise 2: Creating a Package File for the Beeper Component ... 696
Exercise 3: Creating the InstallShield Project 697
Exercise 4: Modifying the InstallShield Project 700
Exercise 5: Building the Setup Program 704
Exercise 6: Deploying and Testing the Setup Program 706
Review 710
Appendix A Application Design Concepts **711**
Appendix B Review Questions and Answers **771**

Glossary **787**

Index **797**

About This Book

Welcome to *Distributed Applications with Microsoft® Visual C++® 6.0 MCSD Training Kit*. By completing the chapters, practice exercises, and labs in this course, you will acquire the knowledge and skills necessary to develop solutions using Microsoft Visual C++ 6.0.

This book also addresses the objectives of the Microsoft Certified Solution Developer (MCSD) Exam 70-015, providing content that supports the skills measured by the exam. Review questions at the end of each chapter test your knowledge of the chapter material and help you prepare for the 70-015 exam.

Note For more information on becoming a Microsoft Certified Solution Developer, see "Microsoft Certified Professional Program" later in this section.

Intended Audience

This course is designed for students interested in developing their skills in Visual C++ 6.0 while developing distributed applications. These skills include:

- Using the Microsoft Solutions Framework (MSF)
- Building applications with the Microsoft Foundation Classes (MFC)
- Creating user interfaces
- Implementing application behaviors
- Working with persistent data
- Adding database support to applications
- Creating Component Object Model (COM) components and ActiveX controls
- Using MFC and the Active Template Library (ATL)
- Internet programming
- Error handling, debugging, and testing
- Application deployment

Prerequisites

This book assumes that you have a solid working knowledge of C++ application development and are acquainted with but not fully knowledgeable about Microsoft Visual C++ 6.0 and the Microsoft Windows Application Programming Interface (API). Before beginning this self-paced course, you should have:

- A thorough working knowledge of the C++ language as described by the ANSI standard, and an acquaintance with language features such as templates and exception handling
- A good understanding of the principles of object-oriented software development
- A good basic understanding of the operation of a Windows application and the features of the Windows user interface

Course Overview

This course combines text, graphics, and review questions to teach you about designing and implementing distributed applications with Visual C++ 6.0. The course assumes that you will work through the book from beginning to end. However, you can choose a customized track and complete only the sections that interest you. If you choose to customize your course, see the "Before You Begin" section in each chapter for important information regarding prerequisites.

The book is divided into the following chapters:

- **Chapter 1, "Designing the Application"** In this chapter, you will learn about a distributed application design approach that you can use to identify and separate the layers of an application architecture. This approach, based on the Microsoft Solutions Framework (MSF) Application model, can provide your development team with a means to identify and design the application's classes and components.
- **Chapter 2, "Development Environment"** This chapter examines the development environment of the professional developer or development team, and also examines the production channel concept, in which your work moves from initial coding to the production environment in standard, measured steps. In addition, this chapter discusses various aspects of change control, showing you how to manage change to your code even before it enters the production channel, as well as the documentation that should surround your code. Finally, this chapter examines some tools you can use to make these tasks easier and more consistent.
- **Chapter 3, "C++ Development Essentials"** This chapter provides an overview of several essential technologies, including MFC, Active Template Library (ATL) and Standard Template Library (STL). In addition, this chapter covers some programming concepts, including threading and threading models, and memory allocation and management.

- **Chapter 4, "Developing the User Services"** You will begin this chapter by learning user interface techniques with menu systems, toolbars, and tool tips. Additional user interface techniques are implemented using dialogue boxes to present information as well as gather, validate, and process user input. This chapter completes with a discussion on creating and using ActiveX controls.
- **Chapter 5, "Building Basic Business Objects"** In this chapter, you will create several C++ classes using classic C++. After studying some of the problems with the classic C++ architecture, you will convert the classes to COM classes. At the end of that exercise, you will have a COM server written in raw C++. The chapter ends with a discussion of how ATL and MFC simplify the process of building COM servers.
- **Chapter 6, "Building Advanced Business Objects"** This chapter continues our lessons on COM. It begins with more advanced topics of implementing Distributed COM components. To increase the performance of a COM component, we discuss implementing a tread-safe multi-threaded COM component. Additionally, we discuss implementing and packaging COM components as Windows Services. This chapter completes by implementing an ISAPI DLL that dynamically alters web content.
- **Chapter 7, "Using Microsoft Transaction Services"** This chapter discusses transactions and explains how to install and deploy Microsoft Transaction Services (MTS). First, this chapter introduces you to the concept of transactions and describes how MTS serves as an infrastructure for building distributed applications. This chapter then provides an overview of how to install and configure MTS and how to design and create objects for use in MTS. In addition, this chapter introduces you to advanced topics such as security and load balancing, and then concludes with a discussion of design and scalability issues in transaction-based applications.
- **Chapter 8, "Microsoft Message Queuing Services"** This chapter discusses message queues and explains how to install and deploy Microsoft Message Queuing Services (MSMQ). First, this chapter introduces you to the concept of message queues and describes how MSMQ serves as an infrastructure for building distributed applications. This chapter then provides an overview of how to install and configure MSMQ and how to design and create objects for use in MSMQ. This chapter concludes with a discussion of design and scalability issues in message queue-based applications.
- **Chapter 9, "Using Data Access Services"** This chapter begins with an overview of Structured Query Language (SQL). A brief discussion on configuration issues with Microsoft SQL Server is included with discussions on creating, querying, and manipulating relational database tables using SQL, stored procedures, and triggers. Different data access methods are discussed within the context of MFC and ATL including OLEDB, ODBC, ADO, RDO, DAO.
- **Chapter 10, "Exception Handling"** This chapter describes how an application can intelligently respond to many types of errors that can occur during program execution. You will learn about specific types of error events called

exceptions, and how to write programs that are more stable because they monitor exceptions.

- **Chapter 11, "Debugging and Testing"** In this chapter, you will learn about debugging and testing, an essential part of development; they merit as much attention as that given to the designing/coding phase, or more. Generally viewed as less glamorous or interesting than actual coding, debugging and testing often receive inadequate attention due to budget and schedule constraints. However, this lack of attention is almost always false economy; a poorly tested application can cost you in lost revenue, wasted productivity, and strained relations with users.
- **Chapter 12, "Deploying Distributed Applications"** In this chapter, you will learn some of the ways that a Windows application created with Visual C++ can be efficiently deployed. This chapter first presents an overview of deployment methods, focusing on how to write an installation program that copies required files to the user's hard disk. It continues with a discussion on InstallShield, a tool that helps automate the creation of installation programs for Visual C++ projects.
- **Appendix A, "Application Design Concepts"** This appendix serves as additional information for the reader, outside of the exam preparation context. It first presents the concepts of architecture notations such as UML, design patterns, and design antipatterns. It then discusses the implementation of a structured development process and reviews the Unified Process (UP) and the Microsoft Solutions Framework (MSF). It concludes with a detailed process for creating the conceptual, logical, and physical designs of a distributed application including Use Case, Class, and Programming models.
- **Appendix B, "Review Questions and Answers"** This appendix contains the questions from each chapter's review section along with the appropriate answers. These questions serve to reinforce the information within each chapter and are not intended as test review questions.

Features of This Book

The following features are designed to enhance the usefulness of this course:

- Each chapter opens with a Before You Begin section, which prepares you for completing the chapter.
- Each chapter is divided into lessons. Most lessons include hands-on exercises that allow you to practice an associated skill or procedure. Each lesson ends with a short Lesson Summary of the material presented.
- Most lessons contain procedures that give you an opportunity to use the skills presented or explore the part of the application described in the lesson. All procedures are preceded by an arrow symbol.
- The Review section at the end of the chapter lets you test what you have learned in the lesson.

- Appendix A, "Application Design Concepts," contains a detailed distributed application design guide.
- Appendix B, "Review Questions and Answers," contains all of the book's review questions and their corresponding answers.
- The Glossary contains key terms and definitions used in the course.

Conventions Used in This Book

Before you start reading any of the chapters, it is important that you understand the terms and notational conventions used in this book.

Notational Conventions

- *Italic* is used for emphasis when defining new terms. *Italic* is also used for C++ keywords, variable names, function names, placeholders, user input, methods, operators, parameters, and constants.
- Names of files and folders appear in Title Caps. Unless otherwise indicated, you can use all uppercase or lowercase letters when you type a file or folder name in a dialog box or at a command prompt.
- File name extensions appear in all lowercase.
- Dialog box names and options appear in Title Caps, regardless of how they are capitalized on screen.
- Acronyms appear in all uppercase.
- Monospace type represents code samples, examples of screen text, or entries that you might type at a command prompt or in initialization files.
- Square brackets [ ] are used in syntax statements to enclose optional items. For example, [*filename*] in command syntax indicates that you can choose to type a filename with the command. Type only the information within the brackets, not the brackets themselves.

Keyboard Conventions

- A plus sign (+) between two key names means that you must press those keys at the same time. For example, "Press Alt+Tab" means that you hold down Alt while you press Tab.
- A comma (,) between two or more key names means that you must press each of the keys consecutively, not together. For example, "Press Alt, F, X" means that you press and release each key in sequence. "Press Alt+W, L" means that you first press Alt and W together, then release them and press L.
- You can choose menu commands from the keyboard. Press the Alt key to activate the menu bar, and then sequentially press the keys that correspond to the highlighted or underlined letter of the menu name or the command name. For some commands, you can also press a key combination, shown in the menu.

- You can select or clear check boxes or option buttons in dialog boxes from the keyboard. Press the Alt key, and then press the key that corresponds to the underlined letter of the option name. Or you can press Tab until the option is highlighted, and then press the spacebar to select or clear the check box or option button.
- You can cancel the display of a dialog box by pressing the Esc key.

About the Companion CD

The companion CD contains sample exam questions and the files used in the hands-on labs and exercises in the text.

Using the Lab and Lesson Files

The companion CD contains files required to perform the hands-on lab and practice exercises. To copy the files to your hard drive, run the setup.exe program in the \Setup folder on the CD and follow the instructions that appear on your screen.

By default, the lab files are copied to the \DISV\Labs folder. Each chapter in the book has its own subfolder. (For example, material relating to Chapter 1 can be found in \DISV\Labs\Ch01.) Each of these folders might contain subfolders, as required by the particular lab exercises. Files required to complete exercises within a lesson are copied to the \DISV\Lessons folder.

The recommended procedure is to follow the labs in numerical order. None of the labs in this book require that you complete a preceding lab as a prerequisite.

Self Test Software Visual C++ 6.0 Sample Exam

To practice taking a certification exam, you can install the sample exam from Self Test Software (STS) contained on the companion CD. Designed in accordance with the actual Microsoft certification exam, this sample includes questions to help you assess your understanding of the materials presented in this book. Each question includes feedback with an associated course reference so that you can review the material presented. Visit the STS Web site at *www.selftestsoftware.com* for a complete list of available practice exams.

The Self Test Software demonstration for Exam 70-015 is located in the \Exam folder on the companion CD. To install the sample exam on your hard drive, run the mp015.exe program in this folder and follow the instructions that appear on your screen.

Getting Started

This training course is intended to help you prepare for the Microsoft Certified Solution Developer (MCSD) Exam 70-015, "Designing and Implementing Distributed Applications with Microsoft Visual C++ 6.0." To complete the exercises, your computer must meet the following hardware and software requirements.

Hardware Requirements

All hardware should be on the Microsoft Windows 98 or Microsoft Windows NT Hardware Compatibility List.

Computer/Processor	Personal computer with a Pentium-class processor; 166-megahertz (MHz) or higher processor recommended
Memory	24 megabytes (MB) of RAM for Microsoft Windows 95 or later (32 MB recommended); 32 MB for Windows NT 4.0 (64 MB recommended)
Hard Disk Space	Visual C++: 300 MB typical; 360 MB maximum
	Microsoft Developer Network (MSDN): 57 MB typical; 493 MB maximum
	Microsoft Internet Explorer: 43 MB typical; 59 MB maximum
	Windows NT 4.0 Option Pack: 40 MB for Windows 95 or later; 200 MB for Windows NT 4.0
	SQL Server 7.0: 170 MB typical; 266 MB maximum
Drive	CD-ROM drive
Display	VGA or higher-resolution monitor; Super VGA recommended
Operating System	Windows 95, Windows 98, Windows NT Workstation 4.0, or Windows NT Server 4.0 with Service Pack 4 or later
Peripheral/Miscellaneous	Microsoft Mouse or compatible pointing device

Software Requirements

The following software is required to complete the exercises in this course:

- Visual C++ 6.0, Professional or Enterprise Edition
- Microsoft Visual SourceSafe (VSS) Client and Server
- Windows NT 4.0 Option Pack including Microsoft Internet Information Server (IIS) or Microsoft Personal Web Server (PWS)
- SQL Server 7.0
- Internet Explorer 4.01 with Service Pack 2 or later

The above software is not provided on the companion CD.

Installation Instructions

These instructions describe how to install the following software required to complete the exercises and labs in this book:

- Windows NT 4.0 Option Pack
- Internet Information Server 4.0 (if you are running Windows NT 4.0 Server)
  - or -
  Personal Web Server (if you are running Windows NT 4.0 Workstation, Windows 95, or Windows 98)
- SQL Server 7.0 Standard Edition (if you are running Windows NT Server)
  - or -
  SQL Server 7.0 Desktop Edition (if you are running Windows NT Workstation, Windows 95, or Windows 98)

Installing the Windows NT 4.0 Option Pack

The Windows NT 4.0 Option Pack contains Internet Information Server, which can be installed on Windows NT 4.0 Server; and Personal Web Server, which can be installed on Windows NT 4.0 Workstation, Windows 95 or Windows 98. You can download the Windows NT 4.0 Option Pack Setup.exe file from the Web at *http://www.microsoft.com/ntserver/nts/downloads/recommended/nt4optpk/default.asp.*

Note To install all the components of the Windows NT 4.0 Option Pack, networking and the TCP/IP protocol must be installed.

► **To install and configure the Windows NT 4.0 Option Pack including IIS on Windows NT Server 4.0**

1. Download and run the Setup.exe file. If you have Service Pack 4 or later installed, the following message appears: "Setup detected that Windows NT 4.0 SP4 or greater is installed on your machine. We haven't tested this product on SP4. Do you wish to proceed?" Click Yes. If the message appears again, click Yes again.
2. When the Windows NT 4.0 Option Pack Setup window appears, click Next.
3. Click Accept to accept the terms of the license agreement.
4. Select a Typical install. Choose the directories in which to install the files or accept the defaults, and then click Next.
5. For SMTP and NNTP Service Setup, choose the directories you want or accept the defaults, and click Next.
6. Click Finish when the installation is complete.
7. Click Yes to restart the computer and accept the system settings change.

Installing Personal Web Server

Personal Web Server (PWS) comes as a version of the Windows NT 4.0 Option Pack that is configured to install on Windows NT 4.0 Workstation, Windows 95, or Windows 98. You can download the PWS Setup.exe file from the Web at *http://www.microsoft.com/windows/ie/pws/default.htm.*

Note To install all the components of the Personal Web Server, networking and the TCP/IP protocol must be installed.

► **To install and configure Personal Web Server on Windows NT Workstation 4.0**

1. Download and run the Setup.exe file. If you have Service Pack 4 or later installed, the following message appears: "Setup detected that Windows NT 4.0 SP4 or greater is installed on your machine. We haven't tested this product on SP4. Do you wish to proceed?" Click Yes. If the message appears again, click Yes again.
2. When the Windows NT 4.0 Option Pack Setup window appears, click Next.
3. Click Accept to agree to the terms of the license agreement.
4. Select a Typical install. Choose a directory in which to install the Default Web home directory or accept the default, and then click Next.
5. Click Finish when installation is complete.
6. Click Yes to restart the computer and accept the systems settings change.

► **To install and configure Personal Web Server on Windows 95 or Windows 98**

1. Download and run the Setup.exe file.
2. If you are installing on Windows 95, the following message might be displayed: "Setup has installed Winsock2 on your machine and needs to reboot to complete the installation." When prompted to restart your system, click Yes. After your computer restarts, the Personal Web Server Setup window appears.
3. In the Personal Web Server Setup window, click Next.
4. Click Accept to agree to the terms of the license agreement.
5. Select a Typical install. Choose a directory in which to install the Default Web home directory or accept the default, and then click Next.
6. Click Finish when installation is complete.
7. Click Yes to restart the computer and accept the systems settings change.

Installing SQL Server 7.0 Standard Edition

► **To install and configure SQL Server 7.0 Standard Edition on Windows NT Server 4.0**

1. Insert the SQL Server 7.0 CD-ROM. Autorun starts.

2. Select Install SQL Server Components.
3. Select Database Server – Standard Edition.
4. In the Select Install Method window, select the Local installation and click Next.
5. In the Welcome window, click Next.
6. Click Yes to agree to the terms of the license agreement.
7. Complete the User Information section with your name (required) and company information (optional).
8. Select Typical as the Setup Type, set the Destination Folder for Program Files and Data Files to C:\Mssql7, accept the defaults, and click Next.
9. In the Services Accounts window, select Use The Same Account For Each Service. Select Use The Local System Account For Service Settings. Click Next.
10. To start copying files, click Next.
11. Select Per Seat as the licensing mode and click Continue.
12. When the per-seat licensing agreement is displayed, select the I Agree That check box and click OK.
13. After the necessary files are copied to your hard drive, click Finish in the Setup Complete dialog box.
14. Exit the SQL Server setup program.
15. Restart your computer to configure the Data Access Component.

Installing SQL Server 7.0 Desktop Edition

► **To install and configure SQL Server 7.0 Desktop Edition on Windows NT Workstation 4.0**

1. Insert the SQL Server 7.0 CD-ROM. Autorun starts.
2. Select Install SQL Server Components.
3. Select Database Server – Desktop Edition.
4. In the Select Install Method window, select the Local installation and click Next.
5. In the Welcome window, click Next.
6. Click Yes to agree to the terms of the license agreement.
7. Complete the User Information section with your name (required) and company information (optional).
8. Select Typical as the Setup Type, set the Destination Folder for Program Files and Data Files to C:\Mssql7, accept the defaults, and click Next.

9. In the Services Accounts window, select Use The Same Account For Each Service. Select Use The Local System Account For Service Settings and click Next.
10. To start copying files, click Next.
11. After the necessary files are copied to your hard drive, click Finish in the Setup Complete dialog box.
12. Exit the SQL Server setup program.
13. Restart your computer to configure the Data Access Component.

► **To install and configure SQL Server 7.0 Desktop Edition on Windows 95 or Windows 98**

1. Insert the SQL Server 7.0 CD-ROM. Autorun starts.
2. Select Install SQL Server Components.
3. Select Database Server – Desktop Edition.
4. In the Welcome window, click Next.
5. Click Yes to agree to the terms of the license agreement.
6. Complete the User Information section with your name (required) and company information (optional).
7. Select Typical as the Setup Type.
8. Set the Destination Folder for Program Files and Data Files to C:\Mssql7, accept the defaults, and click Next.
9. To start copying files, click Next.
10. When setup is complete, click Yes to restart your computer and then click Finish.

Using This Book to Prepare for Certification

Where to Find Specific Skills in This Book

The following tables provide lists of the skills measured on the Microsoft Certified Solution Developer (MCSD) Exam 70-015 and indicate where in this book you will find the lesson relating to each skill.

Note Exam skills are subject to change without notice and at the sole discretion of Microsoft.

Deriving the Physical Design

Skills measured	Location in book
Explain the elements of an application that is based on the MFC framework.	Chapter 3, Lesson 1
Identify differences between developing an MFC application for Windows NT, Windows 95, and Windows 98.	Chapter 5, Lesson 1 Chapter 6, Lesson 1
Explain when to use the Platform Software Development Kit (SDK) for an MFC application and when to use the functionality provided by the MFC framework.	Chapter 3, Lessons 1, 5 Chapter 9, Lesson 3
Choose whether to use an MFC regular DLL or an MFC extension DLL.	Chapter 6, Lesson 6
Explain how command messages are routed between a user interface object and a handler function.	Chapter 4, Lesson 4
Describe the Document/View architecture.	Chapter 3, Lesson 1
Explain the MFC drawing, printing, and print preview architecture.	Chapter 3, Lesson 1
Explain how the MFC architecture supports multithreading.	Chapter 3, Lesson 2
Evaluate whether access to a database should be encapsulated in an object.	Chapter 1, Lesson 2
Evaluate whether a database should be incorporated in the application.	Chapter 1, Lesson 2 Chapter 9, Lesson 3
Identify which type of library to use. Valid libraries include MFC, ATL, and the SDK.	Chapter 9, Lessons 4-6
Identify which type of object to use. Valid object types include ADO, ODBC, and RDO.	Chapter 9, Lessons 3-6
Design the properties, methods, and events of components.	Chapter 4, Lesson 4 Chapter 5, Lessons 3-4 Chapter 6, Lesson 1 Chapter 7, Lesson 2

Establishing the Development Environment

Skills measured	Location in book
Establish the environment for source-code control by using Visual SourceSafe. Issues include multiple user/multiple location development and versioning of the source code.	Chapter 2, Lessons 1-2
Install the Visual C++ development tools that are necessary for developing a distributed application on various platforms. Platforms include Windows NT Workstation, Windows NT Server, Windows 95, and Windows 98.	Chapter 2, Lesson 3 Lab 2 Chapter 7, Lesson 2
Install server services. Services include MTS, SQL, and MSMQ.	About This Book Chapter 7, Lesson 2 Chapter 8, Lesson 1 Chapter 9, Lesson 2
Configure server services. Services include MTS, SQL, and MSMQ.	Chapter 7, Lesson 2 Chapter 8, Lesson 1 Chapter 9, Lesson 2
Configure a client computer to use an MTS component.	Chapter 7, Lesson 5 Chapter 12, Lesson 3

Creating the User Interface

Skills measured	Location in book
Implement the navigation for the user interface.	Chapter 4, Lesson 2
Create and integrate toolbars in an MFC application.	Chapter 4, Lesson 2
Implement ToolTips for toolbar buttons.	Chapter 4, Lesson 2
Implement and write to the status bar in an MFC application.	Chapter 4, Lesson 2
Given a scenario, select the appropriate options to create a new application by using the MFC AppWizard.	Chapter 4, Lessons 1-2
Create and edit user interface objects by using the resource editors.	Chapter 4, Lesson 2
Create a new class by using ClassWizard.	Chapter 4, Lesson 2
Add member variables by using ClassWizard.	Chapter 4, Lesson 3
Add a message handler for an event by using ClassWizard.	Chapter 4, Lesson 4
Create data input forms and dialog boxes.	Chapter 4, Lesson 3
Create a static menu by using the menu editor.	Chapter 4, Lesson 2
Create a dialog box by using the dialog editor.	Chapter 4, Lesson 3
Create property sheets by using ClassWizard.	Chapter 4, Lesson 3
Create dialog box classes and members by using ClassWizard.	Chapter 4, Lesson 3
Use the *CFormView* class to create a view that contains controls.	Chapter 4, Lesson 3
Validate user input.	Chapter 4, Lesson 3
Validate user input by using DDV.	Chapter 4, Lesson 3
Validate user input by using ClassWizard.	Chapter 4, Lesson 3
Process user input from a form or a dialog box by using DDX.	Chapter 4, Lesson 3
Use an ActiveX user interface control.	Chapter 4, Lesson 4
Insert a control into a project by using the Component Gallery.	Chapter 4, Lesson 4
Handle an event from an ActiveX user interface control.	Chapter 4, Lesson 4
Dynamically create an ActiveX user interface control.	Chapter 4, Lesson 4
Use the MFC AppWizard to create an ISAPI DLL that can dynamically change Web content.	Chapter 6, Lesson 6
Incorporate existing code into an application by using wizards and scriptlets.	Chapter 6, Lesson 4
Create or modify an MFC application to store and retrieve personalized user settings from the registry.	Chapter 6, Lesson 3
Display data from a data source.	Chapter 9, Lesson 3
Implement remote data sources by using *CSocket*.	Chapter 9, Lesson 3
Implement standard serialization by using *Serialize*.	Chapter 9, Lesson 3
Implement persistence by using **CFile**.	Chapter 9, Lesson 3
Display data by using **CArchive**.	Chapter 9, Lesson 3
Connect a recordset to dialog box controls.	Chapter 9, Lesson 4 Lab 9

Skills measured	Location in book
Instantiate and invoke a COM component.	Chapter 4, Lesson 4 Lab 5 Chapter 6, Lessons 1, 4 Chapter 7, Lessons 3-4 Chapter 8, Lesson 2 Chapter 9, Lessons 4-5
Add asynchronous processing.	Chapter 3, Lesson 1 Chapter 6, Lesson 2
Create secondary threads.	Chapter 6, Lesson 2
Download ActiveX user interface controls.	Chapter 4, Lesson 4
Implement online user assistance in an application.	Chapter 4, Lessons 1-2
Implement status bars.	Chapter 4, Lesson 2
Implement ToolTips.	Chapter 4, Lesson 2
Implement context-sensitive Help.	Chapter 4, Lesson 1
Create Help for an application that provides links to a Web page containing Help files.	Chapter 4, Lesson 1
Implement error handling.	Chapter 10, Lessons 1-2
Implement exception handling.	Chapter 10, Lesson 1
Given an error, determine how to handle the error.	Chapter 10, Lesson 2
Use an active document.	Chapter 6, Lesson 5

Creating and Managing COM Components

Skills measured	Location in book
Create a COM component that implements business rules or logic.	Chapter 4, Lesson 4 Chapter 5, Lessons 3-4 Lab 5 Chapter 6, Lesson 1
Create a COM component by using ATL.	Chapter 4, Lesson 4 Chapter 5, Lesson 4
Create a COM component by using the SDK.	Chapter 4, Lesson 4 Chapter 5, Lesson 3
Create a COM component by using MFC.	Chapter 4, Lesson 4 Chapter 5, Lesson 4
Create an ATL COM in-process COM component and an ATL COM client to access it.	Chapter 5, Lesson 4 Lab 5
Create an ATL COM out-of-process COM component and an ATL COM client to access it.	Chapter 6, Lesson 1
Create ActiveX user interface controls.	Chapter 4, Lesson 4
Create an ActiveX user interface control by using ATL.	Chapter 4, Lesson 4
Create an ActiveX user interface control by using the SDK.	Chapter 4, Lesson 4
Create an ActiveX user interface control by using MFC.	Chapter 4, Lesson 4

Skills measured	Location in book
Create a COM component that reuses existing components.	Chapter 6, Lesson 4 Chapter 9, Lesson 4
Explain the difference between aggregation and containment.	Chapter 6, Lesson 4
Add error handling to a COM component.	Chapter 10, Lesson 2
Log errors into an error log.	Chapter 10, Lesson 3
Create and use an active document.	Chapter 6, Lesson 5
Create a COM component that can participate in a transaction.	Chapter 7, Lesson 3 Chapter 9, Lesson 4
Sign a COM component.	Chapter 4, Lesson 4
Debug a COM component.	Chapter 10, Lesson 2 Chapter 11, Lesson 3
Create a COM component that supports apartment-model threading. Models include single-threaded apartment, multithreaded apartment, or both.	Chapter 5, Lessons 3-5 Chapter 6, Lesson 2 Chapter 7, Lesson 3
Create a package by using the MTS Explorer.	Chapter 7, Lesson 3
Add components to the MTS package.	Chapter 7, Lesson 3
Use role-based security to limit use of an MTS package to specific users.	Chapter 7, Lesson 4

Creating Data Services

Skills measured	Location in book
Access and manipulate data by using ad hoc queries. Methods include ODBC, ADO, DAO, RDO, and data source control.	Chapter 9, Lessons 3-6
Access data by using the Stored Procedure model.	Chapter 9, Lesson 1
Manipulate data by using different cursor locations.	Chapter 9, Lesson 4
Manipulate data by using different cursor types.	Chapter 9, Lessons 4-5
Handle database errors.	Chapter 9, Lessons 3, 5
Manage transactions to ensure data consistency and recoverability.	Chapter 7, Lessons 1-3 Chapter 8, Lesson 3 Chapter 9, Lesson 4
Write SQL statements that retrieve and modify data.	Chapter 9, Lesson 1
Write SQL statements that use joins to combine data from multiple tables.	Chapter 9, Lesson 1
Write SQL statements that create views or queries.	Chapter 9, Lesson 2
Use appropriate locking strategies.	Chapter 9, Lesson 4
Implement pessimistic locking.	Chapter 9, Lesson 4
Implement optimistic locking.	Chapter 9, Lesson 4
Create a stored procedure that returns information.	Chapter 9, Lesson 1
Create triggers that implement rules.	Chapter 9, Lesson 1
Create reports that use summary data.	Chapter 9, Lesson 1
Display data in a customized sorted format.	Chapter 9, Lesson 1

Skills measured	Location in book
Create stored procedures to enforce business rules.	Chapter 9, Lesson 1
Create user-defined and system-stored procedures.	Chapter 9, Lesson 1

Creating a Physical Database

Skills measured	Location in book
Implement a data storage architecture by creating and managing files, file groups, and transaction logs.	Chapter 9, Lesson 3
Create databases, and create database tables that enforce data integrity and referential integrity.	Chapter 9, Lesson 2
Create and maintain indexes.	Chapter 9, Lesson 2
Populate the database with data from an external data source.	Chapter 9, Lesson 1

Testing and Debugging the Solution

Skills measured	Location in book
Determine appropriate debugging techniques.	Chapter 11, Lessons 1-2, 4-5
Use library debugging support.	Chapter 11, Lesson 1
Use the IDE.	Chapter 11, Lesson 2
Use Dependency Walker.	Chapter 11, Lesson 4
Use Spy++.	Chapter 11, Lesson 5
Given a scenario, describe the type of debugging support that Visual C++ provides for resolving programming errors.	Chapter 11, Lessons 1–2
Step through code by using the integrated debugger.	Chapter 11, Lesson 2
List and describe the MFC macros that are used to debug applications.	Chapter 11, Lesson 1
Identify and describe the elements of a test plan. Elements include beta testing, regression testing, unit testing, integration testing, and stress testing.	Chapter 2, Lesson 1 Chapter 11, Lesson 6
Evaluate the need for beta testing.	Chapter 11, Lesson 6

Deploying an Application

Skills measured	Location in book
Create a setup program that installs an application and registers the COM components.	Chapter 12, Lesson 1
Register a component that implements DCOM.	Chapter 12, Lessons 3-4
Configure DCOM on the client computer and on the server computer.	Chapter 12, Lessons 3-4
Use .cab files to package and distribute an application.	Chapter 12, Lesson 1
Plan disk-based deployment or CD-based deployment for an application.	Chapter 12, Lesson 5
Plan Web-based deployment for an application.	Chapter 12, Lesson 5
Plan network-based deployment for an application.	Chapter 12, Lesson 5

Skills measured	Location in book
Given a scenario, evaluate the use of Microsoft Systems Management Server as an aid to deploying a solution.	Chapter 12, Lesson 6
Create a setup program that installs an application and allows for the application to be uninstalled.	Chapter 12, Lesson 2
Evaluate Zero Administration for Windows (ZAW) as an aid to deploying a solution.	Chapter 12, Lesson 6

Maintaining and Supporting an Application

Skills measured	Location in book
Implement static load balancing.	Chapter 12, Lesson 3
Fix errors, and take measures to prevent future errors.	Chapter 10, Lessons 1-2 Chapter 11, Lesson 3
Deploy application updates.	Chapter 12, Lesson 5

Microsoft Certified Professional Program

The Microsoft Certified Professional (MCP) program provides the best method to prove your command of current Microsoft products and technologies. Microsoft, an industry leader in certification, is on the forefront of testing methodology. Its exams and corresponding certifications are developed to validate your mastery of critical competencies as you design and develop, or implement and support, solutions with Microsoft products and technologies. Computer professionals who become Microsoft-certified are recognized as experts and are sought after industry-wide.

The MCP program offers eight certifications, based on specific areas of technical expertise:

- **Microsoft Certified Database Administrator (MCDBA)** Demonstrates the ability to derive physical database designs, develop logical data models, create physical databases, create data services by using Transact-SQL, manage and maintain databases, configure and manage security, monitor and optimize databases, and install and configure Microsoft SQL Server.
- **Microsoft Certified Professional (MCP)** Demonstrates in-depth knowledge of at least one Microsoft operating system. Candidates can pass additional Microsoft certification exams to further define their skills with Microsoft BackOffice integrated family of server software products, development tools, or distributed programs.
- **Microsoft Certified Professional—Specialist: Internet (MCP+Internet)** Designates MCPs with a specialty in the Internet, who are qualified to plan security, install and configure server products, manage server resources, extend servers to run CGI scripts or ISAPI scripts, monitor and analyze performance, and troubleshoot problems.

- **Microsoft Certified Professional—Specialist: Site Building (MCP+Site Building)** Designates MCPs with a specialty in site building, who are qualified to plan, build, maintain, and manage Web sites using Microsoft technologies and products. This credential is appropriate for people who manage sophisticated, interactive Web sites that include database connectivity, multimedia, and searchable content.
- **Microsoft Certified Solution Developer (MCSD)** Demonstrates the ability to design and develop Web-based, distributed, and commerce applications with Microsoft development tools, technologies, and platforms, including SQL Server, Microsoft Visual Studio, and Microsoft Transaction Server (MTS).
- **Microsoft Certified Systems Engineer (MCSE)** Demonstrates the ability to effectively plan, implement, maintain, and support information systems in a wide range of computing environments using Windows NT Server and the BackOffice integrated family of server products.
- **Microsoft Certified Systems Engineer—Specialist: Internet (MCSE+Internet)** Designates MCSEs with a specialty in the Internet, who are qualified to enhance, deploy, and manage sophisticated intranet and Internet solutions that include a browser, proxy server, host servers, database, and messaging and commerce components. In addition, an MCSE+Internet-certified professional is able to manage and analyze Web sites.
- **Microsoft Certified Trainer (MCT)** Demonstrates the instructional and technical ability to deliver Microsoft Official Curriculum (MOC) through Microsoft Certified Technical Education Centers (Microsoft CTECs) and Authorized Academic Training Program (AATP) institutions.

Microsoft Certification Benefits

Microsoft certification, one of the most comprehensive certification programs available for assessing and maintaining software-related skills, is a valuable measure of an individual's knowledge and expertise. Microsoft certification is awarded to individuals who have successfully demonstrated their ability to perform specific tasks and implement solutions with Microsoft products. As with any skills assessment and benchmarking measure, certification brings a variety of benefits: to the individual, and to employers and organizations. Not only does certification provide guidance for what an individual should know to be proficient, but it also provides an objective measure for employers to consider when hiring IT professionals.

Technical Support

Every effort has been made to ensure the accuracy of this book and the contents of the companion CD. Microsoft Press provides corrections for books through the World Wide Web at:

http://mspress.microsoft.com/support/

If you have comments, questions, or ideas regarding this book or the companion CD, please send them to Microsoft Press via e-mail to:

tkinput@microsoft.com

or via postal mail to:

Microsoft Press
Attn: Designing and Implementing Distributed Applications with
Microsoft Visual C++ 6.0 MCSD Training Kit Editor
One Microsoft Way
Redmond, WA 98052-6399

Please note that product support is not offered through the above mail addresses.

About the Authors

This course was developed for Microsoft Press by Online Training Solutions, Inc. (OTSI). OTSI is a traditional and online publishing firm dedicated to helping companies identify needs and implement effective solutions, including development tools, training materials, documentation, and Web sites. OTSI brings talent and time-tested expertise to your project, whether delivered online, on CD-ROM, in print, or in the classroom. OTSI has been developing cutting-edge training solutions for many years for clients including Microsoft Corporation and Dun & Bradstreet Business Education Services.

OTSI is the creator of the popular Quick Course® training series, which includes Quick Course books and workbooks, Quick Course Online training, and the Practical Business Series. *Quick Course books and workbooks* offer quality step-by-step, project-based instruction on the most useful features of popular software applications, and are used for instructor-led classes and self-paced training. *Quick Course Online training* offers the same high-quality content in an innovative online viewer, incorporating pre- and post-testing, generic instructions and video demonstrations. The *Practical Business Series* provides modular instruction in the essential skills required to start and operate a small business in the 21st Century, giving entrepreneurs and intrepreneurs the information they need most in order to establish a solid business foundation and turn dreams into reality.

For more information about the products or services offered by OTSI, visit the Web site at *www.otsiweb.com.* For more information about the Quick Course computer training series, visit the Web site at *www.quickcourse.com.* For more information about the Practical Business Series, visit the Web site at *www.PracticalBS.com.*

OTSI produced this course with the assistance of a number of contributing authors. Individuals who participated in the production of this course include:

Lead author, project lead, and courseware designer:

Scott F. Wilson (VOutdoor.com)
scottfwilson@hotmail.com

Contributing authors: Beck Zaratian (Witzend Software)
info1@witzendsoft.com

Jose Mojica
josem@develop.com

Jyothi C M (NIIT)

Vijayalakshmi Narayanaswamy (NIIT)

Bruce Maples

Scott Wilson is the President of VOutdoor.com (*www.voutdoor.com*), a Kentucky-based company that specializes in template-based and customized electronic commerce Web sites. He is the co-author of *Analyzing Requirements and Defining Solution Architectures MCSD Training Kit For Exam 70-100* and of *Desktop Applications with Microsoft Visual C++ 6.0 MCSD Training Kit For Exam 70-016*.

Witzend Software (*www.witzendsoft.com*) is a Seattle-based company that provides custom programming services for firms such as Microsoft. They are specialists in Visual C++, MFC, ATL, and COM.

Jose Mojica is an instructor for DevelopMentor, where he currently teaches COM+ programming for Visual Basic developers. He is the author of *ActiveX Controls with Visual Basic 5.0* and the co-author of *Programming Internet Controls*. His recent articles include "Create a DB App for Windows CE" and "Create ATL Controls More Easily With VB" for *Visual Basic Programmer's Journal*, and "Migrate From C++ to VB" for *Getting Started with Visual Basic*. When he is not writing or teaching he enjoys playing video games with his wife and son in his house in Florida.

NIIT (*www.niit.com*) is a global IT solutions corporation actively involved in creating software solutions and learning solutions for markets worldwide, with presence in over 30 countries.

Bruce Maples is a self-employed consultant and trainer. His work can be seen in *Tech Republic*. He is the co-author of *Analyzing Requirements and Defining Solution Architectures MCSD Training Kit For Exam 70-100*.

CHAPTER 1

Designing the Application

Lesson 1: Architecture-First Design 2

Lesson 2: Distributed Application Design 10

Review 36

About This Chapter

In this chapter, you will learn about a distributed application design approach that you can use to identify and separate the layers of an application architecture. This approach, based on the Microsoft Solutions Framework (MSF) application model, can provide your development team with a means to identify and design the application's classes and components. We discuss applications in terms of five layers: the user interface (UI), user services, business services, data services and a data store. Some information provided about the Application Model is taken from the Microsoft Developers' Network (MSDN) group's *1608: Designing Business Solutions* Course, thus it also serves as an excellent source for additional information on designing distributed applications.

Before You Begin

To complete the lessons in this chapter, you must have:

- A basic understanding of the application development life cycle

Lesson 1: Architecture-First Design

Most successful distributed application projects begin with solid application designs. In this lesson, you will learn the value of making a commitment to an architecture-first project life cycle, and learn what such a commitment entails. In addition, you will learn about the fundamental goal, and also the components, of good architecture-based design.

A true architecture-first design is based on certain principles, including important concepts such as alignment with business goals and the importance of risk management. This lesson takes a look at these principles and their impacts on the design process.

After this lesson, you will be able to:

- Explain an architecture-based application design approach
- Describe key principles of an application design

Estimated lesson time: 30 minutes

Architecture-First Design

For the purposes of this book, *application architecture* is defined as a clear plan for creating an application that achieves business goals and objectives. Such an architecture emphasizes a holistic framework of process, interactivity, and technology, and it is intensely focused on achieving business goals and objectives. An *application architect* is a person who designs and guides an application architecture. Both architecture and architect provide direction for an application's creation.

By concentrating on the essentials of application architecture, an *architecture-first* approach endeavors to achieve results that can be implemented effectively while minimizing complexity. A common example of the need for this type of approach is articulated in a scene from *The Wizard of Oz*:

> *"Follow the yellow brick road!" said the Mayor of Munchkin land.*

Not only did Dorothy and Toto need to know where they were going—to the Emerald City—but they needed a specific path to guide them on their journey. In other words, they needed a plan. Similarly, application developers need to know ahead of time not only what the end product should look like but also the steps involved in creating that product. It is no longer possible to create applications by simply sitting down and writing code.

This example speaks directly to the need for an architecture-first approach to planning, building, and managing almost any business activity. At the heart of an architecture-first approach are simple questions you can ask regarding any project:

- What are the goals for this project?
- Why are those the goals?
- What tasks are necessary to achieve those goals?
- In what order should those tasks be performed?
- How will the team know when those goals have been reached?
- What additional factors need to be considered?

An architecture-first approach strives to answer these questions early in the life cycle of a project, and to continually provide a road map and reference guide throughout the project. Unfortunately, many organizations honor architecture and project planning in word but not in deed. Instead of developing a clear vision of their goals and outlining the tasks needed to achieve them, many organizations simply take any route to project completion, hoping that their eventual destination will be an improvement over where they are now. In addition, many managers feel that they won't be able to finish a project if they take the time to plan ahead. On the contrary, however, time allotted in a project life cycle for planning actually saves time during an application's development, implementation, and deployment.

Note This commitment to planning does not mean that work should not begin until the architecture is established. This book advocates a *plan-while-building* approach. In other words, planning, building, and managing follow one another in an iterative fashion, often overlapping.

Being committed to architecture-first design and practice means that all application development work is based on a coherent, high-level architecture; that the architecture has been worked out before coding work has started; and that the architecture drives the work. When you seriously examine what is involved in a commitment to architecture-first design, you might have second thoughts about your project, which can begin to appear more and more daunting. You might start asking, "Is there any way we can get a handle on this project? And considering the work involved, why should we even try?"

The answer is simple: Every application has its own architecture, whether planned or not. You can assess and plan as needed or fall prey to a random architecture that doesn't necessarily meet your business needs. Only by doing the work involved in planning and building an application architecture can you really gain some control over your projects.

Goal of Architecture-First Design

As noted earlier, providing a direction or goal is an important function of an application architecture. The fundamental goal when developing any architecture is: To provide a logically consistent plan of activities and coordinated projects that guides the progression of an organization's application systems and infrastructure. The plan should move incrementally from the current state to a desired future state based on current and projected business objectives and processes.

Let's examine the elements of this goal in more detail:

- **Logical consistency** Any two or more elements of a sound architecture can always fit together logically.
- **Activities and coordinated projects** An architecture addresses both ongoing activities and future activities. By coordinating the goals and execution of these activities, the implementation time can be decreased and duplicated effort eliminated. Additionally, each system that is developed can be designed to integrate with current and future systems.
- **Progression from current state to desired future state** An architecture does more than simply describe the current project state; it also offers a vision of the desired future state of a project when it is completed or is nearing completion. Most important, the architecture articulates a clear path to move from the current situation to the desired project solution through versioned application releases.
- **Current and projected business objectives and processes** An enterprise architecture plan is ultimately worthless if it is not built upon both current business needs and the projected business plan and processes for a solution to meet such needs.

You should keep these points in mind while considering the details of architecture-based design throughout the rest of this chapter. You should also use these points to analyze the completeness of any architecture plan.

Application Design Principles

The practice of developing software has changed dramatically over the last 20 years. Many traditional management techniques have been updated to reflect recent management experience in developing software. The driving force behind this shift in the software development process has been the desire to develop more features over less time, and as a result, increasing the complexity of software products. Competitive pressures, growing customer influence, constant increases in Information Technology (IT) companies' stock values, and constantly evolving technology have all motivated organizations to streamline their development processes.

Above all, however, the crucial factor behind streamlining development processes is that too many projects have failed. Increasingly, software developers strive to build optimal software—on time and with fewer financial setbacks—that succeeds. The new mantra of developers in the IT industry is "Ship the right product at the right time."

Following this section are application design principles on which to base the development of application's architectures. All of these principles are important to achieve a successful application development process.

Architecture-First

We've already talked about the importance of an architecture-first approach to application development. In *Software Project Management: A Unified Framework* (Addison-Wesley, 1998), Walker Royce states that "architecture-first is a critical theme underlying a successful iterative development process." Using an architecture-first approach achieves a demonstrable balance between the business requirements, architecturally significant design decisions, expected ship dates, and life cycle plans for the product—*before* resources are committed for full-scale development.

When implementing an architecture-first approach, the team can use prototypes and proof-of-concept systems to help determine suitable design decisions. The team must make appropriate tradeoff decisions between resources, ship dates, and features, as well as create a product vision and road map acceptable by all project stakeholders.

Alignment with Organization's Business Goals

Every project must justify its capital resource requirements, and an organization's business goals form the basis of this justification. Thus, the business needs of a project's stakeholders drive the vision and plan for any development project.

A project's return on investment is not always measured in strict financial terms; the project can provide strategic value to an organization, which is difficult to quantify monetarily. However, business values that the project addresses must align with the stated goals of the entire organization hosting the project. As the organization's goals change, the project team must reassess the underlying business goals to confirm that the project is still in alignment with the organization's goals. At the least, the project must not conflict with any new goals that the organization might have developed since the project's inception.

Because business goals are critical to any project's success, the project team should be competent not only in software development, but also in adherence to the organization's goals as a business. Many products have been shelved because they did not meet the organization's business goals, even though they were well written and technically sound. To prevent such disconnection between products and goals, a project team needs to clearly understand the business problem the team is trying to solve.

Product Mindset

The product mindset is not about shipping commercial software products, nor is it about developing applications for internal customers; it's about treating the results of labor as a product. Having a product mindset involves focusing more on execution and the end product of a project rather than on the process of completing the project. The application development process is not unimportant, but should be used to accomplish the end goal and implemented not just for the sake of using a process. Adopting a product mindset implies that everyone on a project team feels responsible for delivering a product—everyone's primary job on the team is to ship the product; all other responsibilities are secondary.

Component-Based Development

Mary Kirtland's book *Designing Component-Based Applications* (Microsoft Press, 1998) summarizes the *component-based* approach, which packages application services into modular elements that are accessible only through a well-known public interface.

Traditionally, an application's services have been exposed through application programming interfaces (APIs). The learning curve is significant for a development team to make effective use of APIs. Object-oriented frameworks are another popular way to expose services, but they also have a significant learning curve. Additionally, object-oriented frameworks are usually specific to one programming language, such as C++.

Components provide a standard model for packaging services and exposing the services to other applications. These components act as "black boxes," hiding all their data and implementation details. Component services are exposed via public interfaces and a common programming model. As an additional advantage, component models provide facilities to enable communication with components regardless of their development language or deployment location.

Design Within Context

Complex applications don't exist in a closed environment; rather, they interact with business needs, network and system infrastructures, data systems, and other applications. Just as applications involve other systems, current and future systems interact with applications. Therefore, applications must be designed to integrate into the entire environment of an enterprise. Project teams must be sure that they understand their products' inherent interactions with and reactions to the environments in which their products will run.

Different Languages for Different Project Phases

Using the appropriate tools at each project phase is a well-recognized best practice in the software industry. Various print and electronic forms can help to communicate business requirements; the Unified Modeling Language (UML), for example, can provide notations for stating requirements and excellent design-modeling capabilities; and programming languages such as Microsoft Visual Basic, C++, and Java can provide robust application development platforms.

Early Product Evaluations

The project team must understand customer interests and help identify and prioritize product features, determining which must appear first and which can wait for a later release.

During the initial project phases, prototypes can be used to give customers, users, and the team a more thorough understanding of the product's features and functions. These prototypes can consist of screens that demonstrate product concepts and system progression. Customers and users will often change their priorities or identify new needs after seeing the prototypes. Such changes usually result from a more thorough understanding on the users' part of what the product can realistically accomplish.

During the middle phases of a project, architects and developers can use proof-of-concept systems to test critical designs before writing or initiating large code segments that rely on unproven designs or technology.

Finally, during the early stages of the deployment process, alpha and beta product releases can help solicit additional input from the stakeholder community. More important, beta product releases address system integration and deployment issues before the development phase has been completed.

Risk Management

Risk is the possibility of suffering loss. For any given project, the loss can be in the form of diminished quality, increased cost, missed deadlines, or complete failure to achieve project goals. Such risks must be addressed, either proactively or reactively. However, good project management *proactively* identifies and manages project risks throughout the entire project life cycle. Managing risks as a formalized process raises awareness of the risks, and provides a common tool set that all project participants can use and review.

A solid risk management process:

- Identifies the risk
- Determines its potential impact on the project
- Determines the probability of occurrence
- Determines risk exposure to the project
- Proactively mitigates the risk
- Designates a contingency plan to be followed if the risk materializes

If the project team practices effective risk management from the beginning of a project, the probability that risks will materialize during the late stages of the project is significantly reduced.

Lesson Summary

Architecture is a coherent, unified technology plan. The goal when developing any architecture is:

> *To provide a logically consistent plan of activities and coordinated projects that guides the progression of an organization's application systems and infrastructure. The plan should move incrementally from the current state to a desired future state based on current and projected business objectives and processes.*

The first requirement of creating a solid application architecture is to make a commitment to architecture-first design. That commitment should be based upon the following software management principles:

- **Architecture-first** Using an architecture-first approach achieves a demonstrable balance among business requirements, architecturally significant design decisions, expected ship dates, and the product's life cycle plans, before resources are committed for full-scale development.
- **Alignment with business goals** Every project must justify its capital resource requirements; an organization's business goals form the basis of this justification. Thus, the vision for each development project is driven by the business needs of the project's stakeholders.
- **Product mindset** Product mindset involves treating the results of labor as a product. Having a product mindset entails focusing more on execution and the end product rather than on the process of completing the project.
- **Component-based development** A component-based approach packages application services into modular elements that are accessible only through a well-known public interface. Components provide a standard model for packaging services and exposing them to other applications. These components act as "black boxes," hiding all their data and implementation details. Component services are exposed via public interfaces and a common programming model. As an additional advantage, component models provide facilities to enable communication with components regardless of their development languages or deployment locations.
- **Design within context** Just as applications involve other systems, current and future systems interact with applications. Therefore, applications must be designed to integrate into the entire enterprise environment.

- **Different languages for different project phases** Using specialized languages for the different phases of development is a well-recognized best practice in the software industry. Such language differentiation enables a project team to apply the most appropriate tools to the tasks at hand.
- **Early product demonstrations** The project team must understand customer interests and help identify and prioritize product features, determining which must appear first, and which can wait for a later release. Early product demonstrations are the best means to ensure that the end product is what the customer wants.
- **Risk management** Risk is the possibility of suffering loss. Good project management proactively identifies and manages project risks throughout a project's entire life cycle. Managing risks as a formalized process raises awareness of the risks and provides a common tool set that all project participants can use and review.

Lesson 2: Distributed Application Design

When designing new applications, you should understand the concept of an application model and its implications. An *application model* is a conceptual view of an application that establishes the definitions, rules, and relationships that will structure the application. It serves as a basis for exchanging ideas during the design of an application.

When you hear the word *house*, you assume without knowing any particulars that the house has an entrance, bedrooms, bathrooms, a kitchen, and so on. Even if a particular house is very different from this model (for example, it might have a sleeping loft instead of bedrooms), the model serves as a starting point for discussing form and function. Similarly an application model describes in general terms what an application is or, more exactly, what people think a typical application is. To enhance communication, an application model needs to be simple and intuitive. The application model shows how the application is structured, not how it will be implemented.

In this lesson, you will learn about the Microsoft Windows Distributed interNet Application (DNA) layers and the MSF Application Model, including the user, business, and data services.

After this lesson, you will be able to:

- Understand the multiple layers in a distributed application design
- Understand the benefits of a multilayer design approach
- Understand the role of the user interface, user service, business service, data service, and data store in application design and implementation

Estimated lesson time: 60 minutes

Multilayer Design

The MSF Application Model provides a multilayer services-based approach to designing and developing software applications. An application can be viewed, at a logical level, as a network of cooperative, distributed, and reusable services that support a business solution. Application services are units of application logic that include methods for implementing an operation, function, or transformation. These services should be accessed through a published interface, should be driven by the interface specification, should focus value toward the consumer or client (not the provider), and should map directly to actions.

The service-based design approach is Microsoft's recommended approach to designing distributed enterprise applications. It aims to:

- Promote a consistent approach to the design and development of client-server applications.
- Provide a standard set of definitions for the application logic in a three-tier application. This is an important aspect of the model. The development community makes continual references to three-tier applications without ever really defining what each tier is, beyond saying they are the separation of user interaction, business logic, and data logic.
- Make it easier to use component technology to implement distributed, multi-tier applications that have the flexibility, scalability, and maintainability needed to address the needs of mission-critical, enterprise-wide applications.
- Shift from the traditional view of monolithic applications that support specific business processes toward the introduction of the concept of systems of interoperable applications built upon a common set of components.
- Describe a way of consistently applying the skills and resources of an application development organization across multiple projects.
- Define a framework for organizing teams, introducing parallelism into the development process, and identifying the required skills.

The MSF Application Model describes applications as using three types of services: user, business, and data. A service is a unit of application logic that implements operations, functions, or transformations applied to objects. Services can enforce business rules, perform calculations or manipulations on data, and expose features for entering, retrieving, viewing, or modifying information.

These services allow for parallel development, better use of technology, easier maintenance and support, and flexibility in distributing the application's services. They can reside anywhere in the environment from a single desktop to servers and clients around the world, and have the following characteristics:

- **User services** Consist of logic that provides an application with its UI. The UI is not necessarily visually conveyed; it can be programmatic, because the user might be a person or another application. User services seek to hide or isolate information views from the application's UI structure.
- **Business services** Consist of logic that controls the sequencing and enforcing of business rules. These services provide transactional integrity as well as transform data into information through the application of business rules.
- **Data services** Consist of logic that provides the lowest visible level of detail used to manipulate data. Data services seek to maintain consistent application data, as well as to separate the application's design and implementation from the location and structure of the data store. Most data services provide the ability to define, create, read, update, and delete data.

In addition to the three fundamental service layers, an application design also includes the UI as a separate design element and the actual data stores as a server-level design element. It also separates the data service layer into the data services components and the data access components. Figure 1.1 illustrates the complete multitier design.

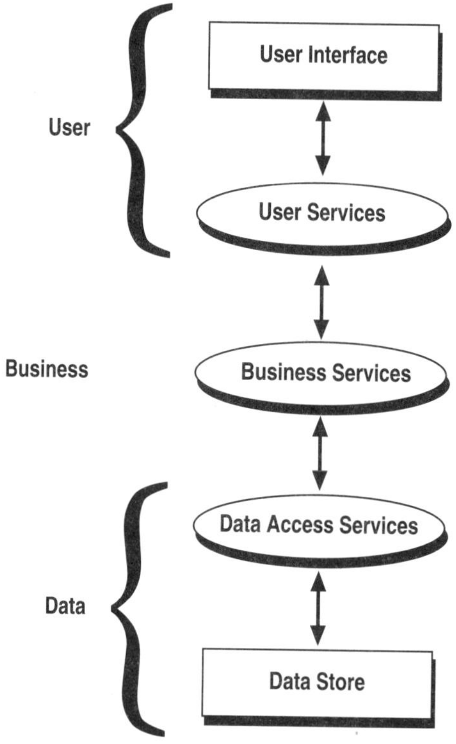

Figure 1.1 Multitier application

Designing Multitier Applications

Using a three-tier, services-based approach for designing and developing software applications and business solutions can create an application as a logical (not physical) network of cooperating services that must function and work together to achieve a common goal.

These services can be distributed across both physical and functional boundaries to support the needs of the solution. The possible breadth of application of each service allows for parallel development, better use of technology, easier maintenance, and increased flexibility in the distribution and deployment of each logical service in the solution.

Some guidelines for designing multitier applications include the following:

- All new applications should be designed using service-layers. This type of structure will lead to applications that can be more easily extended and updated in new versions.
- Distinguishing between the business and data services is especially important. In the past, many designs blurred the line between these two types of services. Separating them in the application design allows for more flexibility during implementation and can also help incorporate important factors such as scalability into an application.
- You should keep in mind the proposed UI when designing user services. Because user services will directly interact with and provide services for the UI, they should work well together, and the combination of the two should provide the necessary functionality.

Learning to design multitier applications can be challenging at first, especially for analysts and developers used to monolithic application design. After the benefits of multitier design become apparent, most developers quickly adopt the concept for all future work—even for stand-alone applications running on a single computer.

Benefits of Multitier Designs

Using a multitier design approach can provide several benefits to the development process and for an organization's enterprise architecture. These benefits include reusability, flexibility of distribution, and parallelism in the design effort, all of which represent a tangible return on investment in the design effort.

- **Reusability** Traditionally, applications have been developed independently, each project focusing exclusively on its own needs. This approach produces applications that provide the required modules of functionality and are easily accessible from other application. Features and informational views that should be consistent across multiple business applications are unlikely to work or look the same. When a business rule or information view changes, each application that works with it has to be modified. Using a services-based, modular approach, developers can design and implement systems whose applications interoperate not only through shared data, but also through shared business logic, running on components located both on application servers and on shared pieces of UI running on a client.
- **Flexibility of distribution** The services-based approach provides maximum flexibility by allowing developers to deploy application logic where it best meets the performance and usage requirements of the application. This approach also supports greater interoperability. With current technologies, services are provided with a transparency of location, enabling them to be distributed in the best configuration for the particular business solution, whether that means all on one client computer or across multiple computers around the world.

- **Parallelism in the development effort** One of the major advantages offered by the service-based approach is the ability to do more than one development task at a time. Because the application model defines an application structure of five distinct pieces, each of these pieces can be worked on in parallel. In the past, with monolithic implementations, development was a serial process because no distinction was made among different types of functionality.

Adoption of this services-based approach can offer these additional key benefits:

- **A consistent approach to application design** Applications are specified and implemented more uniformly, increasing opportunities for reuse and focusing attention on development rather than redefining standards.
- **A model for managing the complexity of distributed application design** Development is split into smaller, more manageable pieces. By implementing a rigorous interface specification, you can assemble the pieces at integration time, providing opportunities for parallel development.
- **More robust applications** Encapsulating behavior on related objects in one component helps isolate problems. After a component has been tested, developers reusing the component can count on the services to be robust.
- **Leveraging of specialized skills and tools** The three categories of service map closely to the three equally important skill sets for client/server application development. The traditional approach to client/server architectures has always separated data from UI and business rules.
- **Easier adoption of new technologies** A distributed, component-based implementation makes it easier to incorporate new client and server technologies. For example, you could develop a new set of user services to incorporate new interaction techniques such as voice recognition or handwriting, without having to reengineer the application's core business services.

User Interface

The UI is the portion of an application that displays and receives information from the application's users. Typically, application users are people who perform particular activities to accomplish their intended work. Although one application could be considered a user of another application, this book primarily considers the UI to be the interaction point for humans, not other applications.

You might be tempted to think that there is no point in designing and creating a UI, figuring that everyone knows how to use a computer. However, a solid UI design and implementation will significantly improve the efficiency and productivity of the application's users.

You might want to bear in mind when designing your application's UI that the interface is distinct from the services that underlie it. The interface has no services of its own, but is merely the code necessary to display the application's information to the user. On the other hand, the user service layer provides the actual manipulation of data to and from the business services layer. This distinction can provide an opportunity for creative problem solving. For example, you could design two different interfaces, one with normal-size screen elements and one with larger elements for visually impaired users, both of which interact with the same user services components.

User Service Layer

The user service layer displays data from business objects, displays data objects to users, and retrieves data from these users. The Microsoft Windows DNA architecture supports a wide range of user service layer architectures, from native Win32 applications to pure Hypertext Markup Language (HTML) Web-based applications. In all cases, the user service layer uses Component Object Model (COM) to access services from business layer components.

Basics of User Service Design

An application's business logic is encapsulated in its business service layer components, rather than in the user service layer. This arrangement makes the business logic easier to reuse if the user service layer needs to be changed. The user service layer communicates with the business logic using COM method calls. The user service layer might also use COM-based Microsoft ActiveX controls to display the actual UI. The same ActiveX controls can be used in native and Web-based applications running on Windows, so it is possible to reuse user service layer code among applications with different types of UIs.

Native Application User Service Layer

Applications that require operating system client support are generally classified as *native applications*. On today's Microsoft Windows platforms, native applications use operating system APIs to provide programmatic functionality. The Win32 API is typically used for 32-bit applications on Windows systems such as Windows 95, Windows 98, Windows NT, and Windows 2000. Thus, if you have a well-defined target desktop, you can create native applications.

Because it encompasses a complete operating system, the Win32 environment allows developers a huge range of local computer control and precise UI capabilities. You can create specialized Win32-based applications and make them available to a large audience. Additional technologies can be incorporated into operating systems and used by application components. Examples of such technologies include the following:

- Microsoft DirectX multimedia
- Open Database Connectivity (ODBC)
- OLE DB for Data Access

Several development tools, such as Visual C++, Visual Basic, and Microsoft Visual J++, can create native applications. In turn, these applications can be compiled and distributed to any number of systems. These languages create truly compiled applications, so if the UI requires a lot of intricate control or has a strong use of graphics, a native application is the ideal choice.

Because application UIs require the use of specific functions from a given operating system, they are generally installed locally. This installation process allows for local high-bandwidth content and remote low-bandwidth content to be mixed during the application's use. For example, Microsoft Office applications can contain 120 megabytes or more of executable files and dynamic-link libraries (DLLs), thus its high-bandwidth content is typically installed locally and its low-bandwidth documents, spreadsheets, and so on, are stored remotely.

Low-bandwidth data files and server applications can transfer much smaller pieces of information, thus saving significant network bandwidth. Because most of the native applications that are created today require installation and configuration on desktop systems, if you will be continually changing the application, or if the application executables are very large, a native application might not be the best choice.

The use of native applications also enables the easy incorporation of significant new technology. For example, the new Extensible Markup Language (XML) parsing capabilities in Microsoft Office 2000 can quickly be added to applications without having to create XML function libraries for each application. Thus, to take full advantage of other native applications that can exist on the desktop, your application should also be a native application to provide the strongest interaction capabilities with other desktop applications.

Web-Based User Service Layer

Web-based UIs offer compelling user service layer features with nearly universal distribution methods and ready-made rendering engines. Freely distributed Web browsers provide easily accessible application interfaces. These interfaces also help make application deployment more efficient. Initial deployment and subsequent upgrading is one of the hardest parts of producing an application. Using Web-based interfaces significantly reduces deployment and application maintenance time because the application doesn't have to be manually distributed to every individual user. Therefore, you should create Web-based applications when distribution, deployment, and continual application maintenance are significant issues.

You should remember that Web-based interfaces are primarily designed as a method of displaying information on a screen. The advent of scripting languages has introduced extensive programmatic and algorithmic capabilities to Web-based interfaces. Web-based navigation can be accomplished by including "hotspots" or links on one page to access and execute additional pages. These links can trigger the execution of code within the page or in a referenced file, as is often the case with new dynamic HTML (DHTML) Web-based interfaces. The control available with Web-based applications has significantly improved with the addition of client-side scripting and DHTML. However, if a lot of screen manipulation or calculations are required, Web-based interfaces are not the most appropriate solution.

Most of today's intranet systems are advanced enough to allow development using HTML 4.0, DHTML, and cascading style sheets. The target coding level will have been identified during the early stages of the development project. All aspects of the application can be tested in a variety of browsers using proof-of-concept systems before the primary application coding is started. A proof-of-concept system is a rough or quickly created application to test an application's look and feel, workflow processes, service layer design, or application tools. Throughout the development of the application, you should consider the range of connection types and determine how graphics, applets, components, and page loading speeds will affect development performance expectations.

Implementing a Web-Based User Service Layer

Like any other enterprise application, an Internet-based application must often generate dynamic displays from one or more data sources. To help with the creation of this type of application, you can use the Active Server Pages (ASP) component of Microsoft Internet Information Server (IIS). With the release of IIS 4, ASP is also integrated with MTS.

Caution A common error made by many new ASP developers is implementing too much business layer logic within ASP scripts. To scale applications and simplify script coding, developers should remember to implement business logic blocks as business-layer COM components.

In an Internet application, a Web browser displays an HTML page-based user service layer. Requests from this layer transmit via Hypertext Transfer Protocol (HTTP) to a Web server. In response to these requests from the client Web browser, ASP pages activate on the Web server. The ASP pages can dynamically generate HTML pages to be returned to the requesting browser. Because these ASP pages can be used to generate UI code to format and control the look and feel of the Web pages, ASP would be considered part of the user service layer.

In addition, the ASP pages can contain server-side script code that implements business logic; thus, ASP pages can be part of the business service layer. However, the ASP pages should contain server-side script code that uses business objects to do much of the work. The business objects might in turn call data access objects to access data sources in the data access service layer. Alternatively, the HTML and client-side script code used to generate the user service layer might be located within the ASP pages. Either way, ASP straddles the line between the user and business service layers.

Combination Native and Web-Based User Service Layer

Applications can contain both native and Web-based UIs; they are not mutually exclusive. The interfaces might be similar, or one might provide specialized functions. Even with two UIs, significant portions of the user services can be shared and reused by both interfaces. This is one of the benefits of creating a user service layer to provide the interaction between the UI and business objects.

Determining the User Services

You should consider the following questions when choosing the architecture for the user service layer:

- Do any application requirements specify the type of UI?
- Do security issues such as firewalls impact communication between user workstations and server-side computers?
- Which operating systems must be supported on user workstations?
- Which Web browsers must be supported?
- Can COM components be installed and run on user workstations?
- Are remote COM components accessible from user workstations?

The answers to these questions will help you determine which type of UI architecture is most appropriate for the application.

Application Requirements

Whether the application will use a native or a Web-based UI might be dictated by business or use requirements for the application, relieving you of responsibility for making this decision. Often, diverse user needs determine the presentation platform that must be implemented. For example, if users must be able to access the application over the Internet, a Web-based architecture is almost always the logical choice. You can write native applications that communicate with server-side code over the Internet; however, users must logically be able to access a particular application through a Web browser to use it over the Internet.

In enterprise applications, application UIs often have some common characteristics. A corporate policy might even dictate the type of interface the application must use. For example, to reduce costs, some organizations have standard UI styles for all their in-house applications.

Many organizations are standardizing with Web-based applications because employees can access Web pages more easily than they can run multiple native applications with which they might not be familiar. Additionally, the cost of maintaining Web-based applications will likely be lower than that of maintaining native applications.

Security Issues

Security issues in three primary areas must be addressed:

- Authentication of users
- Control of access to application components and data
- Encryption of application information

Firewalls and security policies that have an impact on communications between user workstations and server-side computers also have an impact on the architecture choices available to you. Firewall and security issues primarily affect Web-based applications in which users access applications over the Internet. However, similar issues can also apply to applications running on a wide-area network (WAN).

Network traffic from server computers might pass through firewalls that permit only certain communication protocols to access the server. User workstations might need to use proxy servers to access remote computers. In such situations, it might be difficult to use Distributed COM (DCOM) components to communicate between the user and business layers. Although DCOM can work through a firewall, this normally involves modifying the firewall to permit DCOM traffic to pass through. Access through proxy servers presents an additional challenge, because most proxy servers hide user workstation Internet Protocol (IP) addresses. Normally, DCOM network protocols need workstation IP addresses to establish proper communication between workstation and server computers.

Desktop Operating System Constraints

You should determine in the early phases of your project which operating systems must be supported by client-side code. If the user layer needs to run only on Win32 operating systems, all of the technologies discussed in this book are available.

One constraint involves COM's possible unavailability on certain target platforms. If COM is not available, the application cannot use client-side COM objects, nor can it communicate with remote COM objects. Even if you can access COM, DCOM might not be available with such operating systems as Microsoft Windows 3.1 or Macintosh. With Windows 95, DCOM95 must be installed on client computers to use DCOM. If DCOM is unavailable, the application cannot communicate with remote COM objects. In this case, a distributed user layer that uses a server-based ASP page to generate Web pages for a client is probably most suitable.

Another constraint is that COM components are normally distributed as platform-specific binary executables. To use client-side COM objects, components must be available for each target platform. Otherwise, special versions of the user layer must be created that don't use such components.

Finally, UI or Web browsing services supported on different platforms can vary. To work around platform differences for native applications, use a platform-neutral UI framework. To work around platform differences for Web-based applications, it might be necessary to use a restricted subset of HTML and scripting languages. Otherwise, you must write platform-specific user layer applications.

Web Browser Constraints

It might be necessary to support multiple Web browsers even when supporting only a single operating system. When writing a Web-based application, it's important to determine early in the development process which HTML tags, scripting languages, object models, components, and so on are supported by the targeted browsers. Application developers must either find a common feature subset supported by all browsers, or write browser-specific presentation layer applications.

The browser detection capabilities provided with ASP pages in IIS lets developers dynamically generate Web pages that use the highest possible level of browser functionality. Developers can find out which browsers request ASP pages and which feature sets are supported by those browsers. Because the Browser Capabilities component determines supported features using an .ini file indexed by the browser's HTTP user agent string, developers can easily customize the .ini file to provide information about any desired browser features.

Because browsers have different capabilities, deciding which browser(s) to support helps determine how you will implement certain Web features. Different browsers implement slightly different object models, so you will need to watch for incompatibilities among these models that might break the script code. In general, if client-side scripting is being used, European Computer Manufacturers Association (ECMA) script (Microsoft JScript) should be used for browser-neutral applications.

Note Server-side scripts can be written in any scripting language supported by the Web server, because those scripts are never sent to the browser.

It is important for you to recognize which browsers are available to the application's primary users. If the application is to be distributed over a corporate intranet and the organization has implemented a single browser standard, such as Microsoft Internet Explorer 5.0, you can confidently use the innate capabilities of the browser. Otherwise, you might have to design for a much broader range of browser capabilities.

For example, an organization that engages in electronic commerce (e-commerce) cannot afford to turn away customers just because they don't have the latest browser. In such cases, you must design your applications to accommodate older browsers and HTML versions to capture the largest possible user audience.

(This design technique is referred to as *degrading gracefully*.) Users with older browsers should be able to view a text-only version of the site, or at least see a notification that they need to upgrade their browser, along with a link to the appropriate download site.

If you code to the HTML 3.2 standards, you might not have all the layout or data manipulation tools you need. However, your Web pages will work across virtually all platforms, even on mobile operating systems such as Microsoft Windows CE. However, coding with HTML 3.2 does not ensure consistent visual display across platforms or browsers, at least not with pinpoint accuracy. User display sizes can vary from 640 x 480 pixels to 1600 x 1200 pixels, drastically affecting browser window size and thereby affecting on-screen page rendering.

Visual display can also be affected by color depths, which range from 16 colors to millions of colors. The rendering engines themselves visually build pages that can vary by several pixels from browser to browser, with some older browsers not properly rendering certain features at all. You should test your application on every screen size, platform, and browser version possible to work around hurdles posed by HTML 3.2. After this version of HTML renders appropriately on all target systems, developed applications will usually operate smoothly. If you don't know or can't control the variety of platforms and browser versions on which users will run the application, you can't be completely sure how the application's pages will display.

Client-Side COM Components

If the UI is a native application, installing and running COM components on user workstations probably isn't an issue. A Win32 application needs to be installed, but the COM components are simply treated as part of the application's installation routine. Things are somewhat more complicated for Web-based applications. Providing that a particular browser supports client-side COM components, the components usually download and automatically install on users' computers the first time the component is accessed.

ActiveX Controls

ActiveX controls are just self-registering COM components that are typically sent from a Web server to execute on users' desktop with their browser. Some users, or the organizations for which they work, might worry about the security of automatically downloading and installing executable code on client computers. Some users might not allow any components to be downloaded to their computers. If Web-based applications must support such users or organizations, you should not use any client-side COM components (including ActiveX controls) unless the components already exist on the users' computers. Some users want to decide on a case-by-case basis whether to download and install particular components on their computers. In this case, you might choose to use client-side COM components. (Chapter 5 examines ways to make client-side COM components available to user computers.)

DCOM Components

To access remote components, the users' computers must be able to make remote COM calls, using either DCOM or Remote Procedure Calls (RPC) Client-side browsers must also support the creation and scripting of COM objects. In addition, accessing remote components usually requires the installation of some code or registry entries on the users' computers. If an application uses vtable-binding or early-binding to access COM components, proxy/stub DLLs or type libraries must be installed on the users' computers.

Internet and Intranet Connections

If HTML is used for business reasons, the user layer might need to be coded for a variety of browsers. A user layer based on HTML must be served to users through a Transmission Control Protocol/Internet Protocol (TCP/IP) network connection, so development decisions will also be affected by the following:

- Types of connections implemented by users
- Number of connections implemented
- Variety of connection speeds at which users will access the product

An array of connection types with differing bandwidth capabilities are available as follows:

- Analog modems, up to 53 kilobits per second (Kbps) download
- Integrated Services Digital Network (ISDN) modems, up to 112 Kbps download
- Cable modems, up to 10 megabits per second (Mbps) peak during download
- DSL modems, up to 6 Mbps download
- T1 and similar telecom connections, 1.5 Mbps and higher
- Satellite dishes, up to 10 Mbps burst download
- Corporate networks, typically 10 Mbps or 100 Mbps shared Ethernet download

Business Service Layer

Business services are the units of application logic that control the sequencing and enforcement of business rules and the transactional integrity of the operations they perform. Business services transform data into information through the appropriate application of rules.

A goal of a properly designed business service is to isolate business rule enforcement and data transformation logic from service consumers (user and other business services), and from underlying data services. Isolating the business services logic from the user and data services yields the following advantages:

- **Flexibility in deciding how and where to deploy the business services** Possible choices include components on an application server and stored procedures located in the database management system (DBMS) or even on the client.
- **Improved maintainability of business rules and logic** Isolating changes from the application's user and data services allows you to make changes in how business decisions are made, without having to worry about updating or changing the underlying data stores or the client interface.
- **The ability to transparently replace implementations of business services** For example, the set of business rules embodied within a set of business services might vary from country to country; however, the interfaces to those services remain constant throughout their application.

The business service layer is the set of components containing the business object classes delineated during the design process. Of all the objects making up the application, the objects in the business service layer are the most application- and business-specific, because they encapsulate the actual rules and processes needed to run the business. Because of this, business object implementations are often the most valuable part of the development work and, if well designed, can become valuable company assets that can be reused in many applications.

Basics of Business Service Design

As stated earlier, the business service layer is a set of components that implement the classes and methods outlined in the design process. Within Microsoft-specific technologies, those objects will be based on COM.

Note Another leading object model and implementation in the computer industry is Common Object Request Broker Architecture (CORBA). For more information about CORBA, refer to Alan Pope's *The CORBA Reference Guide* (Addison-Wesley, 1998).

COM's essential goal is to let you assemble applications from prebuilt parts, or components, irrespective of component location or the development language used to implement the components. The COM model is defined so that components and applications can evolve independently over time.

The COM programming model is based on objects, interfaces, classes, and components. COM objects are instances of COM classes, which are named implementations of one or more COM interfaces. An interface defines a set of related methods; it represents a contract between the client and the implementer of the interface. All COM interfaces derive from the fundamental interface IUnknown. IUnknown provides object lifetime management and interface navigation features.

COM components are binary units of software that can be used to create COM objects. Components include COM classes, an implementation of a class object used to create instances of each class, and code to create the registry entries needed to locate the classes. Most components available today, including many system services provided by Windows, are Automation-aware components that expose dual interfaces. These components are accessible to almost every development language and programming environment, including scripting languages. COM provides the basic building blocks of the three-service-layer Windows DNA application.

The Windows 95, Windows 98, and Windows NT platforms allow three basic packaging methods for COM components: Windows services, executable files, or DLLs. Components are built as Windows services in situations where the components must always be running, even if no one is logged on to the host computer. Windows executable files are often used where an application provides a UI in addition to furnishing COM objects. Microsoft Word is an example of a COM component built as an executable file. In most other scenarios, components are packaged as DLLs. In particular, most components used to construct three-service layered applications will be packaged as DLLs. The ActiveX controls used in a presentation layer are DLLs, as are all business service components that run within the MTS environment.

Another way to categorize components is by their location relative to the client, as described in the three categories listed as follows:

- **In-process components** These components run within the same process as the client. All in-process components are implemented as DLLs.
- **Local components** Local components run in separate processes, all on the client computer. A local component can be an executable file or a Windows service.
- **Remote components** Remote components operate on computers entirely separate from the client. Remote components can be executable files, Windows services, or DLLs. To run a DLL component remotely, a remote computer would implement a *surrogate process,* or an application run on a remote computer capable of running DLL components. Both COM and MTS provide standard surrogates for DLL components.

Determining the Business Services

Before the business services layer can be implemented, the application's design documents must include a good preliminary specification of the needed main classes (based on the business objects) and how these business objects are to be packaged into components. After the components are designed, implementing them should be a fairly mechanical coding exercise. Nevertheless, you should consider the following key design points:

- Regardless of how the information they use is actually stored, business objects should encapsulate real-world business operations. For example, they should control sequencing and enforcement of business rules, as well as the transactional integrity of the operations they perform.
- Each business object method should perform exactly one unit of work; each unit of work should in turn be implemented in exactly one method.
- Business objects called *directly from* a presentation layer should not retain per-object state across method calls. Business objects called *within* a presentation layer can retain per-object state within a transaction boundary (a boundary between services layers).
- Minimizing network traffic between remote presentation layers and business objects is important; therefore, business objects should be network-friendly.
- Role-based security should be used to restrict access to business objects, because they are the gatekeepers that control data access.
- Transaction models, such as those within Microsoft Transaction Services (MTS), provide a straightforward way of handling errors generated within business object methods.

It is also important to examine each of the objects in the business service layer to ensure that they belong there. You must not let services that are actually user or data services creep into the business service layer. This is particularly true of data services. Developers who are new to n-tier development are often tempted to write data-services and even data-access functionality into their business objects. This practice, though understandable when under a time crunch or when starting out with n-tier design, is to be avoided, because it limits business-object reuse and negates the flexibility advantages of true n-tier design.

Data Service Layer

More than ever, organizations are tasked with providing data in an increasingly diverse manner. Not long ago, most information was held on a mainframe and in various database management systems (DBMSs). Now an organization's important information can also be found in locations such as mail stores, file systems, Web-based text, and graphical files.

Basics of Data Service Design

As organizations seek to gain maximum advantage from data and information distributed throughout their departments and divisions, they can attack the problem of disparate data sources by putting all the data in a single data store. With this *universal storage approach*, a single data store holds any and all kinds of data.

Universal Storage

Universal storage solves the problem of multiple access methods by allowing only one type of data store. However, universal storage presents a huge technical challenge as far as writing a data store that can efficiently store and retrieve any type of data is concerned. Universal storage also fails to address the handling of the existing terabytes of data stored in other locations, because the cost of converting data to the universal store would be enormous. In addition, the possibility of the universal store's single point of failure poses a significant risk.

Realistically, the Microsoft Open Database Connectivity (ODBC) approach of providing a common access method seems more feasible than that of universal storage. However, the common access method must encompass all types of data, rather than limiting itself to relational database tables and Structured Query Language (SQL) queries, as in ODBC.

Application Programming Interfaces

APIs are sets of commands that applications use to request and execute lower-level services performed by a computer's operating system. This section discusses methods of manipulating various data sources through different data access interfaces. Each database vendor provides a vendor-specific API to ease database access. Non-DBMS data can be accessed through data-specific APIs, such as the Windows NT Directory Service API, the Active Directory Services Interface (ADSI), the Messaging API (MAPI) for accessing mail data, and file system APIs. By using a native access method for each data store, developers can use the full power of each store. However, this procedure requires that developers know how to use each access method, and developers must have a detailed understanding of API functions associated with each data store to use API access methods. If developers must maintain access to several data stores, and consequently must learn all the data access methods involved, organizational costs for training alone can become quite high.

Instead of using native data access methods, developers can choose to use a generic, vendor-neutral API such as the ODBC interface. Using this type of interface is advantageous in that you need to learn only one API to access a wide range of DBMSs. Applications can then simultaneously access data from multiple DBMSs.

Universal Data Architecture

The Microsoft Universal Data Architecture (UDA) is designed to provide high-performance access to any type of data—structured or unstructured, relational or nonrelational—stored anywhere in an enterprise. UDA defines a set of COM interfaces that actualize the concept of accessing data. UDA is based on OLE DB, a set of COM interfaces for building database components. OLE DB allows data stores to expose their native functionality without making nonrelational data appear relational. OLE DB also provides a way for generic service components, such as specialized query processors, to augment features of simpler data providers. Because OLE DB is optimized for efficient data access rather than ease of use, UDA also defines an application-level programming interface called Microsoft ActiveX Data Objects (ADO). ADO exposes dual interfaces, so it can easily be used with scripting languages as well as with C++, Visual Basic, and other development languages. Chapter 10 discusses ADO and OLE DB more thoroughly.

UDA is a platform, application, and tools initiative that defines and delivers both standards and technologies tailored to providing enterprise data access. It is a key element in the Microsoft foundation for application development. In addition, UDA provides high-performance access to a variety of information resources, including relational and non-relational data, and an easy-to-use programming interface that is tool-independent and language-independent.

UDA doesn't require expensive and time-consuming movement of data into a single data store, nor does it require commitment to a single vendor's products. UDA features broad industry support and works with all major established database products. UDA has its origins in standard interfaces, such as ODBC, Remote Data Objects (RDO), and Data Access Objects (DAO), but it significantly extends the functionality of these well-known and well-tested technologies.

UDA-Based Access Components

Microsoft Data Access Components (MDAC) provides a UDA implementation that includes ADO as well as an OLE DB provider for ODBC. This capability enables ADO to access any database that has an ODBC driver—in effect, all major database platforms. OLE DB providers are also available for other types of stores, such as the Microsoft Exchange mail store, Windows NT Directory Services, and Microsoft Windows file system using Microsoft Index Server. As shown in Figure 1.2 on the next page, developers can write applications for existing or new data, and for structured or unstructured data, using ADO as the single data access mechanism, regardless of the data's location.

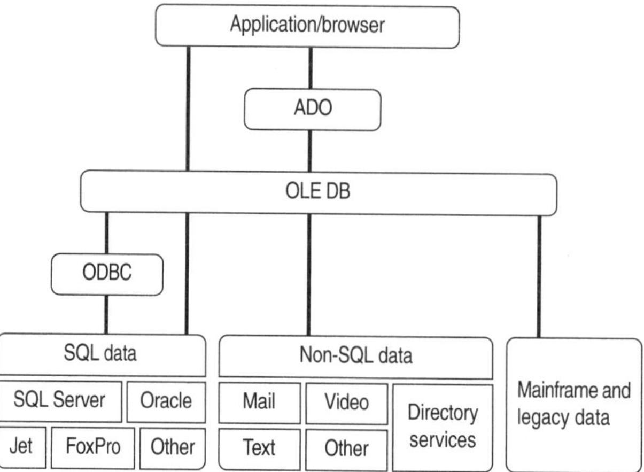

Figure 1.2 Microsoft's UDA design

Determining the Data Services

To achieve the maximum benefit of n-tier design, it is important to classify data services. Strictly speaking there are two separate sub-layers within the data services tier: the data services layer and the data access layer. Although many developers think of these layers as synonymous, they are actually two distinct service layers.

Data services (DS) is the standard Create, Retrieve, Update, Delete (CRUD) data component. This component interfaces with the business services layer, providing that layer with the data services it needs to carry out business functions. In many applications, the DS component or service will also need to provide two additional functions:

- **Manipulate** An extended query function enabling the component to create derived data within a Retrieve. For example, the data store(s) might contain fields for ProductPrice and for SalesTaxRate. The *Manipulate* function could create a SalesTaxAmount field on the fly by multiplying the other two fields.
- **Summarize** Another extended query function enabling the component to create summary information, such as would be used in an Online Analytical Processing (OLAP) application.

It is the task of the DS component to deal with such issues as security and pooling.

Developers can use data rules to provide correct and consistent control of their applications' data access. Furthermore, subsequent applications should be expected to use the data rules set with the initial application, and thereby benefit from the built-in process dependencies and relationships already provided. In general, business rules that perform data access must be designed thoughtfully to provide self-contained, carefully coordinated processes.

Applications typically require data rules under the following circumstances:

- Inserting, updating, deleting, and viewing data
- Validating data
- Controlling data security
- Handling multisource data access
- Providing application-based referential integrity

You can use a data rule each time an application inserts, updates, deletes, or views data. Data rules implemented in this manner provide concise control over data that can be updated. For example, if an application applies new sales orders to an invoice file, a business rule should automatically check the customer's credit limit before accepting and inserting sales order line items and the data rules validate the field types of the sales order line items and insert them into two separate databases using the appropriate tables.

Data integrity is the process of verifying field values and validating related file values. In other words, data integrity verifies that numeric fields are genuinely number-based and within range, and also checks to see if particular relationships exist in their appropriate files. By putting all data validation routines into business rules, applications can guarantee correct data and easily adapt to future requirements.

Applications might require data access security to control access privileges for those permitted to use the applications. Data rules are an excellent way to manage data access privileges.

If a particular application needs to trace a complex chain of records as preparation for a decision process, a business rule can be used to simplify multisource access. Such a data rule would automatically locate all required data stores and repackage them for easy use. For example, suppose an application needs to determine maximum possible payout for a single procedure in a multiline healthcare claim. Inspecting the current line item involves searching the beneficiary's entire claim history for prior use of that line item's identical procedure. Additionally, lifetime and current year-to-date limits must be checked to determine the allowable amount. This multisource access presents an excellent opportunity to create a reusable data rule that consistently and correctly handles the checking process.

One of the most common uses for business rules is handling the referential integrity processes for indexed files. Because indexed files such as those indexed using the virtual storage access method (VSAM) are typically controlled by the data storage engines, an application must provide custom code to handle constraints, foreign key deletions, and other common referential integrity issues. Application-based referential integrity can also be appropriate for relational databases, especially in situations where available triggers, constraints, and stored procedures are either inadequate or too complicated.

These data rules implemented in the DS layer typically use another set of services to access each particular database. Thus, the DS component communicates with the data access (DA) component. The DA component is responsible for actually accessing one or more data stores. It is within the DA component that such technologies as ODBC or OLE DB are used to "get at" the data stores required to service the DS component. In addition, the DA component is responsible for combining data as necessary to present a unified data set to the DS component.

The two components work together to provide a bridge between the business service layer and the actual data stores. They exist to provide maximum flexibility and simplicity. If the data stores change, or new data stores are added, only the DA component must be modified. The DS component and its methods and properties remains unchanged and stable. In addition, as new data technologies become available, they can be implemented in existing applications with a minimum of disruption and recoding.

Writing the standard DS component is covered in many other books and online resources and is a fairly straightforward programming task. The key point to remember is to keep the DS functionality strictly focused on the six methods outlined earlier (CRUD plus *Manipulate* and *Summarize*), and do not allow any DA functionality to invade the DS component. Writing the DA component is a little more complex, however, so we give some pointers in the following section.

Choosing the Right Data Access Technology

Almost all applications require some form of data access. For standalone desktop applications, local data access is typically easy to implement with little or no programming effort. For enterprise applications, data access is considerably more complex, often involving remote data sources with different data formats and storage mechanisms.

The first step is to decide which data access technology to use to build an enterprise application. While making this decision, you need to keep two critical points in mind: the importance of code reuse and the ability to implement the chosen interface. Often, developers implement an exotic data access solution in a quest for better performance or more control, only to create an application that is an expensive maintenance burden. The newer data access technologies typically reduce development time, simplify code, and yet still provide high performance while exposing all required functionality.

You can effectively use virtually all of the Microsoft data access technologies in most situations. Nevertheless, each data access technology has its relative strengths. If your applications require data access, you should understand the unique data access implementation and usage issues specific to each data access method.

When to Use ADO

ADO is Microsoft's latest data access technology. The ADO data access technology and its partner OLE DB comprise the recommended solution for all data access. If your team is developing a new application and planning to use Microsoft technology for data access, you should definitely use ADO and OLE DB.

If you are considering migration to ADO, you have to decide whether the characteristics and benefits of ADO are enough to justify the cost of converting existing software. Older code written in RDO and DAO will not automatically convert to ADO code. However, whatever solutions were previously developed using other data access strategies can definitely be implemented using ADO. In the long run, ADO should be used.

When to Use RDO

If you have an RDO application that works well, you have no reason to change it. If your application needs to be extended to access other kinds of data, you should consider reengineering to use ADO. As mentioned earlier, new applications should use ADO.

When to Use ODBCDirect

ODBCDirect is an acceptable choice if the application must run queries or stored procedures against an ODBC relational database, or if your application needs only the specific capabilities of ODBC, such as batch updates or asynchronous queries. However, every feature in ODBCDirect is also available in ADO.

If you have a working knowledge of ODBCDirect and have large amounts of existing ODBCDirect code, or just need to extend an existing application that already uses it, ODBCDirect will still work for the application. The drawback is that ODBCDirect cannot provide all data access if the application requires other types of non-ODBC data sources. Eventually, you could take advantage of design, coding, and performance benefits provided by ADO.

When to Use ODBC

Several factors influence choosing the ODBC approach, including a requirement of high performance, more granular control over the interface, and a small footprint.

The ODBC API is considerably harder to code than the object-based interfaces, but provides a finer degree of control over the data source. Unlike other data access technologies (such as ADO, RDO, or ODBCDirect), the ODBC API has not been made "bullet proof." Although it's fairly easy to create ODBC errors during development, the ODBC API provides excellent error handling with detailed error messages. In general, developing, debugging, and supporting an ODBC API application requires a tremendous amount of knowledge, experience, and many lines of code. As a general rule, developers prefer to access data by using a simpler, higher-level object interface such as ADO.

ODBC is not suitable for non-relational data such as Indexed Sequential Access Method (ISAM) data because it has no interfaces for seeking records, setting ranges, or browsing indexes. ODBC simply was not designed to access ISAM data. Although you can use the Microsoft Jet ODBC driver to handle ISAM and the native Microsoft Jet engine data, what is really happening is that the Microsoft Jet database engine converts the ISAM data to relational data and then provides limited ISAM functionality. Performance in this situation is slow due to the extra layer imposed by the Microsoft Jet engine.

If the application requires fast access to existing ODBC data, and if you are willing to write many lines of complex code (or already have a log of ODBC code available for reuse), ODBC can be a good choice.

Choosing a Data Access Strategy

You need to consider the following questions before choosing a data access technology:

- **Are you creating a new design, or modifying an existing application that uses obsolete data access technology?** For a modification, it's tempting to continue with the application's former data access methods, which in the short term seems like a reasonable and cost-effective decision. However, the downside involves programming difficulty as the application stretches toward new and different data sources. For a new design, you should use ADO.
- **Where is the data?** Is it on the Web, on a remote server, or simply stored locally on user systems? If the data is simply stored on users' local systems, the need to build a separate server to manage the data might be overkill. If the data is remote, what about connection management? What happens when the application cannot connect? Should the application be using an asynchronous data access technology such as ADO or RDO?
- **What are the developers trained to use?** Do they already have experience with ADO, RDO, or ODBC? Is it worth the modest one-time cost and effort to train the entire staff to use ADO? If you begin using ADO, can developers reasonably anticipate a maintenance cost reduction in the near future?
- **Does an application require data access to both relational and non-relational data sources?** Do you have an OLE DB provider for each source? If so, use ADO.
- **Are you planning to use MTS?** If this is the case, you need to choose one of the data access technologies that can be executed on the server and act as a "resource manager" (an MTS term for a component that implements its set of resource manager interfaces). For example, ADO, RDO, and ODBC can act as MTS resource managers. The DAO interface is not capable of being a resource manger. You should also consider whether the component must be

thread safe, as is the case with ADO and RDO, because this is a requirement for most MTS-managed components if you expect reasonable resource use and performance.

- **Does every application already use the ODBC API?** If you continue with ODBC, how will your applications access other kinds of data sources in the future?

You can use differing data access technologies to implement useful data access and application communication strategies, as listed in Table 1.1.

Table 1.1 Key Characteristics for Data Access Technologies

Best choice is...	If the application requires...	Remarks
ADO	Mainframe data or program	With Microsoft Systems Network Architecture (SNA) Server, you can set up communications OLE DB data providers for mainframe data sources such as Virtual Storage Access Method (VSAM), Customer Information Control System (CICS), Information Management Systems (IMS), and AS/400 files.
	Reengineering	For existing applications, you should consider reengineering with ADO. As an alternative, you could continue with previous data access methods.
	New development	For all new development, you should use ADO data access technology.
	Uniform access to a variety of data sources and data types	ADO is a common interface for all data access requirements.
	Fast development	ADO helps minimize development cost because it is uniform, consistent, and easy to use. You can be trained in its use and benefit continuously thereafter.
	High performance	ADO provides rapid performance.
	Web: IIS ASP	If the application uses IIS with ASP to generate browser-independent HTML from databases, you should use ADO.
OLE DB	Custom file access	You can write custom OLE DB data providers for virtually any data source. ADO can then be used as the data access technology.
RDO	Fast access to existing ODBC data	RDO is fast.
ODBCDirect	Access to ODBC data	ODBCDirect provides a performance improvement over the older DAO data access technology.
ODBC API	Fast access to existing ODBC data	If you are willing to develop and maintain complex code using the ODBC API, this is a good choice.

Completing the Application Model

The terms *multilayer* and *n-tier* don't imply separate computers. The n-tier application architecture promotes scalable applications. To create highly scalable applications, resources such as database connections must be shared. Instead of each client application consuming resources to access data servers directly, client applications communicate with business services. One instance of a business service can support many clients, reducing resource consumption and improving scalability, as shown in Figure 1.3 and Figure 1.4. Because business services do not manage data directly, it's easy to replicate these services to support even more clients.

Services can often be designed and implemented independently of any particular client applications, providing flexibility and the potential for reuse in many applications. By encapsulating application logic behind well-defined public interfaces, you create a body of reusable services that can easily be combined in new ways to create new applications. In addition, common functionality can easily be updated in response to changing business requirements, without impacting the client applications that rely on the functionality. This reduces the management and deployment costs of changing requirements.

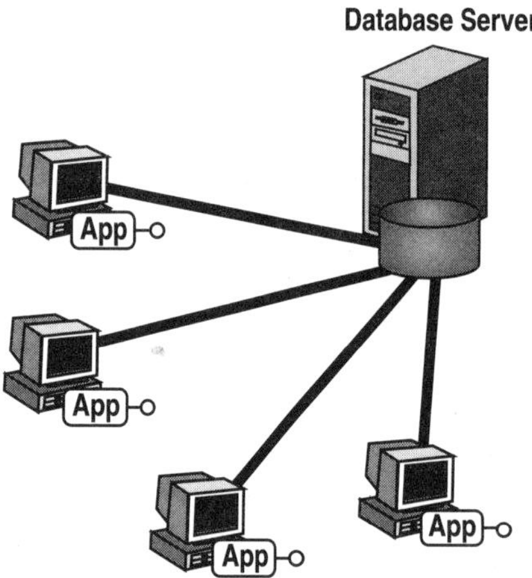

Figure 1.3 Client/server systems

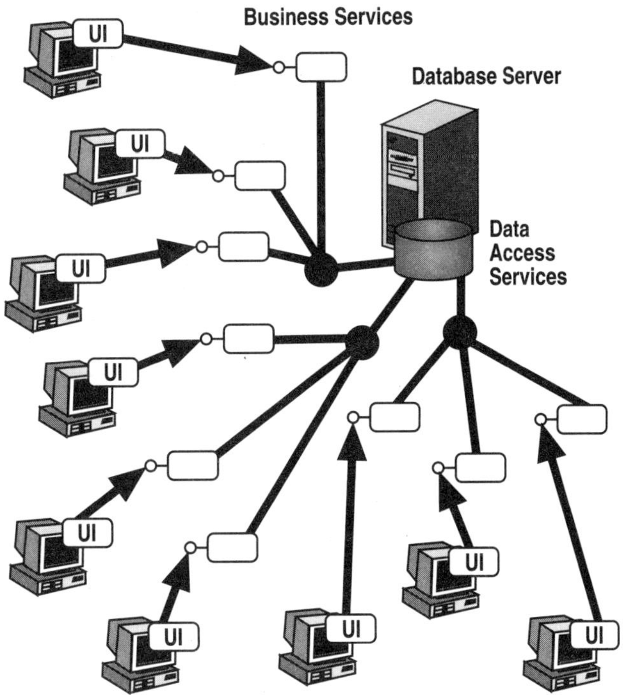

Figure 1.4 N-tier systems

The multilayer application architecture can also help you deal with existing, or legacy, systems. You can "wrap" access to existing systems within business logic, data access, or data store services. Client applications need to worry only about how to access the business logic, not about how to access all the different legacy systems they might rely on. And if the legacy system is modified or replaced, only the wrapper needs to be updated.

Lesson Summary

Application designs can be logically separated into five layers: the UI, user services, business services, data services, and the data stores. This modular design approach allows you to employ different skills, development languages, programming models, and technology features to efficiently implement a distributed application.

Review

The following questions are intended to reinforce key information presented in this chapter. If you are unable to answer a question, review the appropriate lesson and then try answering the question again. Answers to the questions can be found in Appendix B, "Review Questions and Answers," at the back of this book.

1. What is the value of a services-based approach to solution design?

2. What are the service layers of the MSF Application Model?

3. What is the purpose and value of conceptual design?

4. What role can the data service provide within a distributed application?

5. What is the purpose of physical design?

CHAPTER 2

Development Environment

Lesson 1: Production Channel 38

Lesson 2: Change Control 43

Lesson 3: Tools 57

Lab 2: Installing Visual C++ 74

Review 83

About This Chapter

You might be able to "sling code" with the best of them, but you need to be able to do more to be a professional developer. You must be able to test your work without interfering or damaging the work of others. In addition, you must be able to track your work and revert to an earlier version of your code if needed. You must also be able to track the project's documentation so that changes to contracts and specifications are managed and approved as needed. Tracking your work as such in a standardized, straightforward manner protects your own investment in your work as well as the investment of others.

This chapter will examine the development environment of the professional developer or development team and will also examine the production channel concept, in which your work moves from initial coding to the production environment in standard, measured steps. Next, this chapter will discuss various aspects of change control, showing you how to manage changes to your code even before it enters the production channel, as well as the documentation that should surround your code. Finally, you will look at some tools you can use to make these tasks easier and more consistent.

Whether you are a single-person shop or represent a small development team within a larger business or firm doing custom development for your clients, the concepts and techniques explored in this chapter can become part of your daily work habits. Don't make the mistake of failing to build a professional development environment. You should acquire the tools, build your channel, and implement the practices that will ensure your completely and effectively designing your solution.

Before You Begin

To examine some of the systems and tools considered in this chapter, you need to have them installed. Specifically, you should run the following tools:

- Microsoft Visual SourceSafe (VSS) Client
- VSS Server

If you do not have these products installed, you should install them to complete the exercises in this chapter.

Lesson 1: Production Channel

Because current software solutions are complex and critical, your development team must have a solid environment in which to work. Managing your application development environment is often just as important as managing your project. Your development environment—the system of computers and software in which you write code—should be isolated from the working, or *production,* environment of your organization, due to the potential for negative impact both on the organization's daily work and on the direction of the application development.

A critical aspect of management is implementing a change control system, in which you manage changes to the code during both the development and maintenance periods. A change control system ensures that changes to a new application don't adversely affect the organization's production environment and the users that rely on its stability for daily operations.

For example, in the early days of World Wide Web (Web) development, when Web pages usually consisted only of text and pictures, making changes to them was easy. However, current Web pages are much more complex, and many Web sites are full-fledged application environments that must be maintained and available at all times. Downtime on a Web site can result in lost revenues or diminished customer confidence in the Web site's services when customers are unable to access necessary resources. It's no longer acceptable for a Web site to be unavailable while a developer tracks down the change that caused the site to stop working properly, ascertains who made the change and why, and fixes the problem.

Most applications you write will be similar to the previous Web example: complex, multi-user applications that interact with other applications and data. In the development team, you cannot afford downtime caused by poor change management. This lesson will show you how to begin implementing a strong change control system.

After this lesson, you will be able to:

- Describe the production channel, including its four stages and their purposes
- Discuss scaling of the production channel
- List suggested file rights for various roles within the production channel

Estimated lesson time: 30 minutes

Details of the Production Channel

Application projects can undergo at least four distinct stages, which make up a life cycle called the *production channel.* These stages are as follows:

- Development
- Testing
- Certification
- Production

A specified team of people and computer systems supports each of these stages. To ensure that the boundaries between stages remain viable and effective, neither people nor systems should overlap among stages. The team should develop a set of rules to determine when and how specific changes to the application move through the production channel. By following these rules, the team will discover any problems in the testing or certification stage, rather than in the production stage.

Development

The development stage refers to the period of time in which the scope of the project is assessed and coding begins. First and most importantly, you must insist that all changes occur on development computers. If this basic policy is not established before you begin writing any code, the entire production channel process is likely to fail. This policy should not be compromised and should be enforced throughout the organization. You will often be tempted to skirt around the policy when a critical change is necessary or when going through the entire production channel is too inconvenient. However, even the most miniscule change can have unexpected and sometimes destructive consequences. Creating a policy and sticking to it ensures that the entire process is successful.

One way to ensure that changes are made exclusively on development computers is to install development products exclusively on development computers. Thus, when a change is required, you can make the change physically on only a development system, not a testing or certification system. Obviously, this protocol implies separate computers for development, testing, and certification.

Testing

Simply put, the testing stage is concerned with such questions as "Do all the buttons still work?" and "Did fixing the menu bug cause any other menus to stop working?" Each project should have a comprehensive test plan that encompasses major application functionality and ensures that everything in the application works properly. After your development team modifies the application, you should send the changes to the testing team. This transfer of changes might be nothing more than a batch file or a button on a Web page activated by the responsible party with proper access rights to initiate this rollover. From the testing team's perspective, a series of tests determines whether the application is still working properly after changes to it are incorporated.

A key point to remember is that the testing and certification phases should be carried out against each new release candidate of an application. It is sometimes tempting to skip this phase, especially if deadline pressures are high. Experience has shown, however, that any time saved by skipping testing will be lost fixing bugs that would have been caught in this stage. In other words, skipping this stage is false economy.

Certification

When basic testing is complete, the application is rolled over to the certification team. A person or group of people on this team test the application thoroughly to determine whether any bugs or problems remain to be fixed before the application is sent to the production server. Certification testing is much more thorough than the tests carried out by the testing team. Certification testing should include the following:

- **Coverage testing** Attempts to thoroughly test each feature of the product.
- **Usage testing** Validates the application's fulfillment of the use cases and usage scenarios on which the application is based.
- **Performance testing** Checks to see if the application meets its performance targets.

One of the key efforts during this stage is building test cases based on the use case model.

Note A *use case* is defined as a behaviorally related sequence of interactions performed by an actor in a dialogue with a system to provide some measurable value to the actor. In other words, a use case is a prose description of a set of actions, by either a person or a system, that are carried out to achieve some goal or benefit. An example would be a use case for "make a reservation."

A *usage scenario* illustrates a particular instance of a use case and can show either the current state of the process or a desired future state. For example, the "make a reservation" use case might have a number of scenarios, such as "by phone," "in person," and "via the Internet."

The *use case model* is a diagram showing part or all of the use cases for a particular business system, and is used in analyzing and planning software development.

Because the use case model shows the various workflows and activities included in the application, your test cases should test the various activities and workflows described in your use case model. For example, if you have a "Validate credit card" use case, one of your test cases should work through validating a credit card.

The certification team can perform integration checks with other systems that interact with the application, such as applications that share business Component Object Model (COM) objects or the production database. In addition, the certification team can check that the application can handle normal working stress by simulating the loads that are expected in the production environment.

The certification stage concentrates on performance and integration with existing systems. The certification environment should be fully functional, and it should be configured to resemble the production configuration as closely as possible. In particular, it should reproduce any multiple-network protocols, COM transports, domains, or firewalls that restrict access to particular computers. Items such as database connectivity must be configured on the certification servers in the same way they are configured on the production servers.

Production

The project is rolled over to the production server or servers only after the test plan has been completed and the application is proven stable. The advantages of a smoothly operating production channel are greater flexibility and scalability. For example, if certification tests determine that another production server is required to meet demand, the additional server can be configured and added during the production process. Hence, the only modification needed is to configure the application's systems on the new server. In the meantime, your development team might already be working on the next version of the application on the development server.

Lesson Summary

Managing the effects of changed code on your production environment is a critical task. One means of accomplishing this task is to implement the production channel, a four-stage code change and rollout process. The four stages of the production channel are as follows: development (in which all changes are made); testing (in which basic functionality is tested); certification (in which extensive test plans are carried out, including integration testing with an actual replica of the production environment); and production (in which certified code is rolled into the production environment).

Lesson 2: Change Control

When your production channel is set up and functioning, you might be tempted to ignore the larger issue of *change control*. Thorough change control involves both solid *processes* (the standardized means by which you approve and carry out change control) and reliable *systems* (the software and hardware you use when performing change control).

Both processes and systems are important, and both will evolve over time while your organization and your development tools mature. If you have no change control implemented, your first priority is simply to put it in place. In this lesson, you'll learn what to consider when implementing change control, and how to implement it.

After this lesson, you will be able to:

- Discuss the value of a well-conceived change-control process
- List various systems that can aid in executing a change-control process
- Use VSS as a version-control system

Estimated lesson time: 30 minutes

Change-Control Process

Lesson 1 demonstrated how to design and implement a four-stage production channel for your development work. The production channel will serve as the base process for your change-control efforts, but your work cannot stop at the production channel. Ultimately, your goal is to identify, document, and manage every change to all aspects of your development work.

When you work with your development team, your primary task is to approach your work in as professional a manner as possible, with the dual goals of serving both the customers' and your own needs as competently as possible. In other words, you should document the original business case and needs, the solutions you and the customer decided to design and implement, and all information relevant to the project.

You should also capture and document all changes that occur throughout the project—not just to code, but to all artifacts associated with the project. Any business manager of a development project will advise you that nothing is more damaging to the return on investment (ROI) of the project than undocumented requests for changes to specifications. If you have not done a thorough job of change control, you have nothing but the spoken word of your customer vs. the spoken word of your development team or salesperson. Undocumented verbiage is a recipe for an angry customer, an angry development team, a missed schedule, lost profits, or all of the above.

Essentially, you should be able to show a documentation trail for all changes in the business information, project specifications, conceptual–logical–physical designs, component specifications, deployment and packaging design, and performance metrics. In other words, you should *baseline* all artifacts, designs, and code as well as continue to document changes as they occur or are approved. A baseline is a point at which the project stakeholders all agree on a mutually desired solution. It is important to remember that your documentation trail must include any artifact that affects the specifications or design of the application. For example, it would probably be foolish to archive every e-mail sent by every member of a project team, but it would be even more foolish not to document and archive the e-mail authorizing the 25% budget increase you requested! Your change control process must be able to accommodate such artifacts.

Note that part of a complete change control process is a process for approving changes. This means of approval typically is a simple paper or electronic form that outlines the change requested, its impact on the project in terms of time and cost, and the reason for the requested change. Your change-control process should define what types of changes need to be approved, as well as the workflow for getting these changes approved. The decision on whether or not a given change needs to go through the approval process should be based on certain criteria. Examples might include the following:

- The account manager, development manager, and legal department must approve all changes to contracts.
- The program manager, project manager, and development lead must approve all changes to specification documents.
- The enterprise architecture committee must approve changes to business objects.
- UI changes do not need to be approved unless they fall outside the project or corporate UI guidelines.

After you have designed your change-control process, including the approval criteria and workflows, you need to communicate this process to all pertinent parties. Account managers, systems engineers, development managers and staff all need to know what changes can be made on the fly and what changes require approval and process.

A good change control process consists of two parts: the production channel outlined earlier for managing changes to the physical code; and one or more workflows for managing changes to everything outside the code, with approval criteria as needed. You must manage both types of changes to have control over the work.

Version Control Systems

Numerous products exist in the marketplace for managing version control. Some of these products work solely with office suite documents (for example, word processor documents, spreadsheets, and presentations) and cannot manage source code. Other products manage only source code and do not store or aid in storing documents. Some products are integrated into an application's working environment, so that, for instance, when you select Save on the application's File menu if applicable, the version control product manages file saving and captures the latest version automatically.

You can achieve version control in a number of ways, but the two most popular are single-file and multiple-file change control products. In a *multiple-file* change control system, each version of a file is saved separately, and entries for each version are made in a central database. The database is used for retrieving information about the various files and their versions, and for storing the file location of each file. In a *single-file* system, a baseline version of the file is created when the file is first saved; then, as changes are made to the file, the changes are added to the file itself, along with information to allow the system to identify which changes belong to which version. For example, if you choose to use versioning in Microsoft Word, you are using a single-file system.

Most likely, the single-file system will take less storage space. In a small development environment, this benefit might not be a concern; but in a larger development environment, storage space for all of the source code and project documents can become a significant issue, especially when you realize that all of this data needs to be backed up as well.

Integration with the working environment is also a significant consideration when choosing a version control system. If a worker has to save a document to a central storage location, then start up another application and manually type both the changed documents and all pertinent information about the documents and changes, the version control process might become easy to "forget," or prove costly in terms of time.

Included as part of Microsoft Visual Studio, VSS is an ideal version control system that stores only changes to files, so that storage space is more efficiently conserved. VSS is well integrated into the working environment; specifically, it is easy to use, stable, secure, and fast.

Visual SourceSafe

VSS consists of a central database application set up on a server, and client applications that access the central database. VSS is tightly integrated with all of the Visual Studio 6 products, including Microsoft Visual C++. If you are using one of these products, you do not have to run the VSS client separately; instead, it is available directly from within the Visual Studio development environment.

VSS is a project-based system; all files, regardless of file type, are saved within the VSS central database in a project folder. The central database, when viewed from outside VSS, appears as one large database file. When viewed from within either VSS or one of the development tools with which it integrates, the individual project folders, and the files and folders within them, are visible to users, who can manipulate the files and folders in turn. VSS uses a "checkout/checkin" mechanism, thus preventing two users from unintentionally modifying the same file. Additionally, VSS stores all changes made to a file, so it is possible to recover any version of a file or project.

File Management in VSS

When you want to modify a document, you check it out of the VSS database so that you can edit the file. VSS copies the file from the database into a working folder that you have designated in VSS for that file and all files related to it. You can then modify the file. If anyone else attempts to check out this file for editing, VSS generates a message stating the file is already checked out. This simple checkout protocol ensures that conflicts do not arise among multiple users working on the same file. If desired, you can change the project properties to allow multiple checkouts of the same file to different users. Note that multiple users typically cannot check out binary files, although this feature can be overridden.

After you are finished editing the document, you check it back into VSS. This procedure copies the modified document from your working folder into the VSS database, making your changes accessible to other users. VSS stores all the changes that have been made to the document; the most recent copy is always available, but earlier versions can be retrieved as well. The storage technology used by VSS ensures that all versions of a document are available, but uses a minimum of disk space.

If you've made no changes to the file, you can also undo your checkout and return the file to its original state, before you checked it out. If you want to just read a file, and don't need to edit it, you can either get the file in your working folder, or use the View command on the File menu of VSS to view the most recent version of the document.

Project Management in VSS

In terms of VSS, a *project* is a collection of files (any type) that you store in your VSS database. You can add, delete, edit, and share files within and among projects. A project has much in common with an operating system folder, but has better support for file merging, history, and version control.

Your projects exist in a VSS database. Each database is a separate file on the VSS server. It is possible to have multiple VSS databases on the same VSS server, with each database containing different projects. After you have opened a certain VSS database, the client will thereafter open that database automatically;

however, you can open a different database using the Open command on the File menu.

Files are stored in projects in the VSS database. You never work with the master copy of the file that is stored in VSS, except occasionally to examine the file or to compare another copy to it. VSS provides each user with a copy of the file to read or change in the user's working folder. Although you can view a file without a working folder, to actually modify a file within VSS, you must set up a working folder.

Version Control

VSS can maintain multiple versions of a file, including a record of the changes to the file from version to version. Version control addresses the following areas:

- **Team coordination** Makes sure, by default, that only one person at a time is modifying a file. This default prevents files from accidentally being replaced by another user's changes. Your administrator can change this default to allow multiple simultaneous checkouts of a single file, although still preventing overwrites of other changes.
- **Version tracking** Archives and tracks old versions of source code and other files, which can be retrieved for bug tracking and other purposes.
- **Cross-platform development** Tracks portability issues involved in maintaining one code base across multiple development platforms.
- **Reusable or object-oriented code** Tracks which programs use which modules so that code can be reused.

Working Folders

Working folders are where you actually work on files when using VSS. When you either check out or *get* (retrieve a copy of the latest version of) a file, VSS copies the item into your working folder for that project. After you make changes to the file and check it in, VSS copies it from your working folder back into the database. If you perform a get on a file, the copy of the file is yours to keep for reference or backup; it is not recommended that you use this file for primary editing or changes.

Thereafter, VSS manages your working folder by creating folders as needed on your computer when you check files out or perform gets.

Working with VSS Explorer

VSS Explorer displays important status information, such as your current working folder, search criteria, number of files, and so on. Some of this information is shown in file pane column headings, and other information is shown in the status bar at the bottom of the VSS Explorer window. The title bar of VSS Explorer shows the database you are connected to. VSS Explorer uses symbols to provide information about the files and projects, such as check marks to indicate that a file is checked out.

When you start VSS, it first prompts you for your password, if you have set a password. If you have not set a password or are using VSS with integrated network security, you see VSS Explorer. From this Explorer window, you can navigate the VSS database, view your project list, examine file statistics, and execute commands that act on projects and files.

The project pane shows the project list, including the currently open project. The File pane shows the file list, which is a list of all files in the current project. The Results pane displays the results from VSS operations. For example, when you check in a file, this pane shows the name of the file being checked in.

Just beneath the menu bar, the toolbar in VSS Explorer provides command buttons so that you can quickly access the most common VSS commands, such as Get Latest Version and Check Out.

At the bottom of the default VSS Explorer is the Results pane. This pane shows the results of your current VSS operation. As with other Explorer panes, you can resize this pane. You can also eliminate it entirely by clicking the Options command on the Tools menu, clicking the View tab on the SourceSafe Options dialog box that appears, clearing the Show Results Pane check box, and then clicking OK.

Sharing, Branching, and Merging

In VSS, one file can be *shared* among multiple projects. Changes to the file from one project are automatically seen by other projects sharing the file. This encourages code reuse. On the File menu, click Properties, and then click the Links tab on the resulting dialog box to see a list of projects sharing a file.

Once you have shared a file among multiple projects, you might find that you need to change the file in Project A, but you don't want the changes reflected in Project B. In other words, you want to *branch* the file into two separate development paths. VSS keeps track of these branches by tracking the different paths as a project.

Note In non-project-oriented version control systems, branches are tracked through extended version numbers. For example, version 2.3.9.2 is the second revision of the ninth branch of version 2.3. In VSS, however, branches are tracked with different and distinct project names.

Branching a file breaks the shared link, making the file in that project independent of all other projects. The changes you make in the file are not reflected elsewhere, and vice versa. A branch has been created: two files (the file in the project, and its counterpart in other projects) have a shared history up to a certain point, and divergent histories afterwards.

After you branch a file, the Links tab does not show the link that has been broken. Instead, you use the Paths tab (also available from the Properties command on the File menu) to view the branch history of the file.

Merging is the process of combining differences in two or more changed copies of a file into a single, new version of the file. VSS cannot resolve merge conflicts, but can instead present them to you for resolution. You can use two methods for viewing and resolving merge conflicts: *visual merge* and *manual merge*. Visual merge shows the two files being merged in two side-by-side panes, with the differences between the files highlighted. Underneath is a third pane showing the results of the merge. Manual merge, on the other hand, inserts both the original and the changed versions in one file, along with comments indicating which lines are original ones and which lines are changed. Visual merge is usually easier to use, but manual merge makes it possible to keep both sets of code within the file and simply comment out one or the other for testing purposes.

To implement either visual or manual merge, click Options on the Tools menu. In the Options dialog box, click the General tab. In the Use Visual Merge drop-down box, you can select whether or not to use visual merge at all, or to use visual merge only if there are conflicts in the merged copies. (Note that visual merge is chosen by default for all merged files where conflicts are identified.)

VSS Administrator Tool

In addition to supplying the client, VSS also provides an Administrator tool. This tool allows the administrator of the VSS databases to carry out administrative tasks in a graphical environment.

The main Administrator screen shows all users, their default rights, and whether or not they are currently logged on, as shown in Figure 2.1.

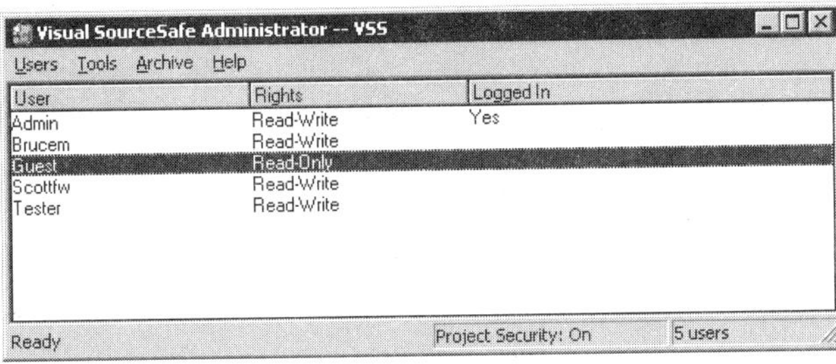

Figure 2.1 Administrator screen in VSS

Several tasks in VSS can be accomplished only by using the Administrator tool. Some of the more important Administrator tasks are turning on and administering project-based security, and archiving the VSS databases.

VSS Security

The default security setting in VSS is for a user to have access to all files in all projects in any database the user can access. If VSS is in use for many persons or projects, you might want to turn on project-based security, so that you can assign rights to users on a per-project basis. To do so, click the Options command on the Tools menu, and in the SourceSafe Options dialog box, select the Enable Project Security check box on the Project Security tab. In this dialog box, as shown in Figure 2.2, you can also set what rights users are given by default.

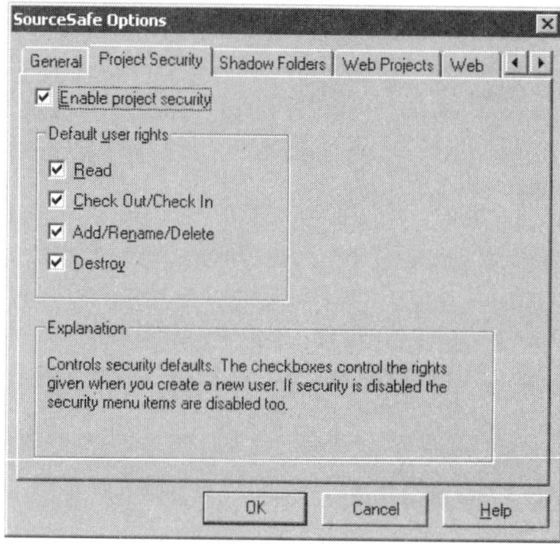

Figure 2.2 Project security rights on SourceSafe Options dialog box

Another setting you might want to implement is to have the VSS server use the user's network name for automatic logon. This setting is under the General tab in the Options dialog box, invoked from the Tools menu, as shown in Figure 2.3.

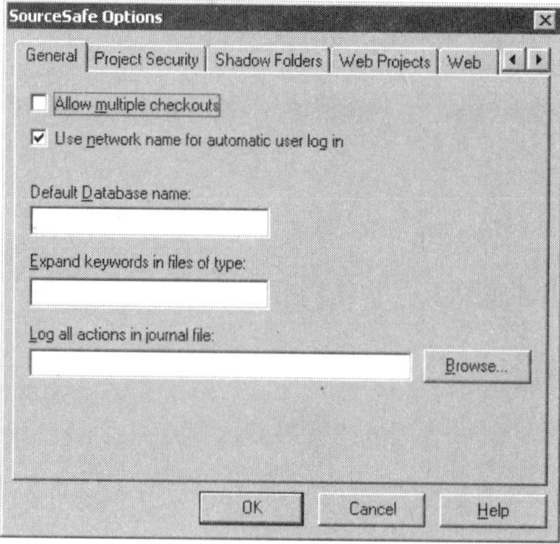

Figure 2.3 Automatic user logon via SourceSafe Options dialog box

After you have turned on project-based security, you can select Rights By Project on the Tools menu, and view the rights each user has for a given project folder, as shown in Figure 2.4.

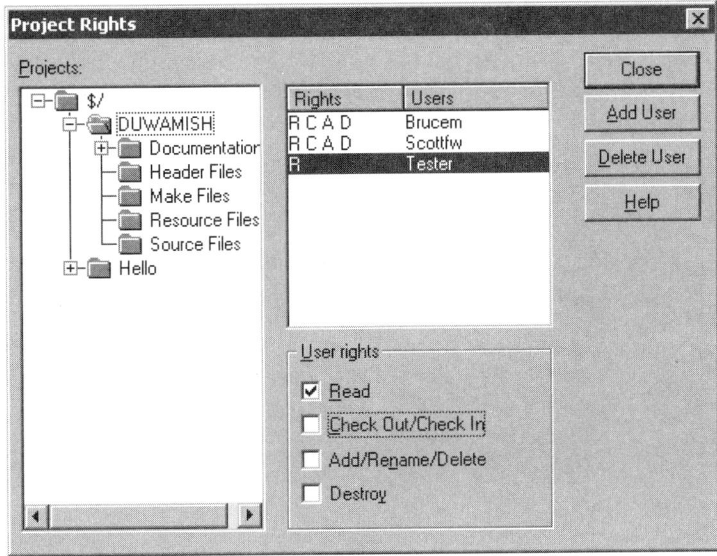

Figure 2.4 Administrator tool's Project Rights dialog box

Archiving in VSS

Periodically, you might want to back up your VSS database or parts of it. You can now archive databases from the VSS Administrator program. In previous versions of VSS, Archive and Restore were only available from the command line.

Archiving allows you to achieve the following:

- Save disk space on your VSS database server.
- Make the Show History command work more quickly.
- Transport files and projects between VSS databases, keeping history information intact.
- Back up all or part of the VSS database to a compressed file.

Exploring Features of VSS

In this practice exercise, you will explore some of the features of VSS, including creating projects, adding files to projects, checking files out and back in, and viewing the history of a file.

1. Start VSS and log on using the dialog box as shown in Figure 2.5.

   If you have never logged on to VSS before, you will be presented with a logon dialog box asking for your user name, password, and the VSS database you want to use. Use the Browse button to find the srcsafe.ini file for the database to which you want to log on.

   Figure 2.5 Logging onto VSS

2. View projects and files.

   After you are logged in, you will see the VSS Explorer window. As you will discover, VSS Explorer works similarly to Microsoft Windows Explorer. On the left is the project pane; on the right is the file list pane; and at the bottom is the results pane. Note that the folders in the project pane have plusses and minuses, indicating whether or not subfolders exist within the folder.

3. Create a project.

   You can use two methods to create a project. The first is to click Create Project on the File menu. This action will create an empty folder underneath the currently selected folder in the project pane. However, if you already have a project folder with subfolders, you can click Add Files on the File menu, browse to that project folder, and select the Recursive check box. (Note that the Recursive check box will appear only if you have selected a folder.) VSS will import all of the folders and files into a new project folder in the VSS database. The new VSS project folder will be named the same as the folder from which you imported the files; if you want, you have the option to change the new folder's name. The new folder will be created under the selected folder in the project pane.

   To create a project using a second method, make sure that the VSS root folder is selected in the Project pane in VSS. Click Add Files on the File menu, and navigate to your CD-ROM drive within which you have placed the CD from this book. Navigate further to this path:

   <<cd drive>>\Duwamish Application\Source Files\Duwamish

Select the Duwamish folder. Be sure that the Recursive check box is checked, and click OK. VSS will create a new Duwamish folder under the $/ root, and then create all the necessary folders under this root and import all the files from the Duwamish folder into the VSS database. VSS will then prompt you to make the folder on the CD-ROM your working folder if you want to do so. Click No, because you want your working folder on your hard drive for the purposes of this exercise.

4. Set a working folder.

   Right-click the new Duwamish folder in the VSS project pane and select Set Working Folder. The Set Working Folder dialog box appears, as shown in Figure 2.6. Decide where you want to put your working folder for the Duwamish files with which you will work later in the book, and navigate to that folder. In that folder, type *Duwamish* at the end of the path in the dialog box and click Create Folder. When the created folder appears in the dialog box, make sure the folder is still selected and click OK.

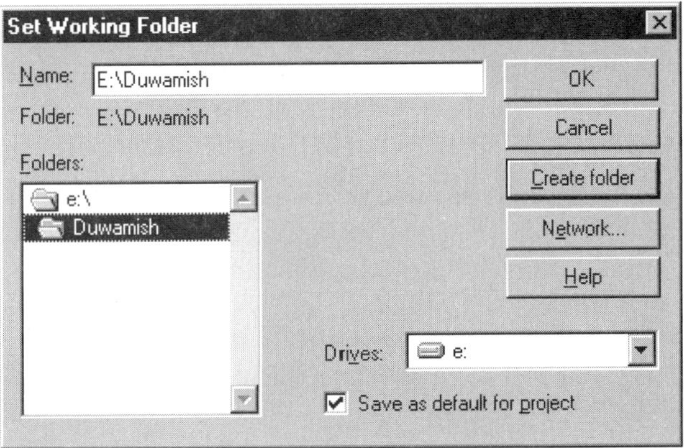

Figure 2.6 Setting a working folder in VSS

5. Add a file.

   You can add a file to a project from any location to which you have access. For this and the following steps, you'll need a simple text file with which to work so you don't change any of the actual Duwamish files. On your hard drive, create a text file with three or four lines of arbitrary text in it. Then, making sure the root Duwamish folder is selected in VSS, select Add Files on the File menu (or click the Add Files button) and add the text file to the root Duwamish folder. You should then see the file listed in VSS as shown in Figure 2.7 on the next page.

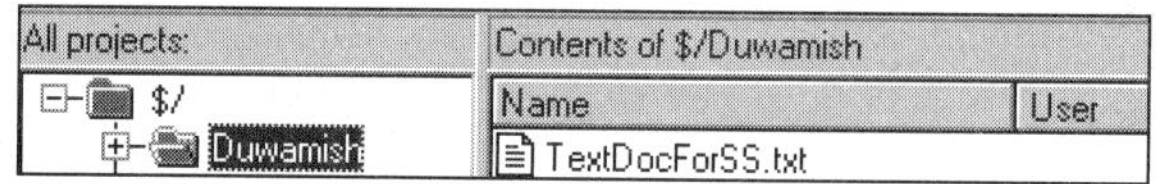

Figure 2.7 File listed in VSS

6. Check out a file and edit it.

   Right-click the text file you just added, and select Edit on the shortcut menu. VSS will prompt you to choose whether you want to edit the file directly in VSS, or copy it to your working folder and mark the file as checked out. Select the second option (check out the file) and click OK. After you click OK, VSS will check out the file, listing your user name and marking the file icon with a red check shown in the file list pane, and then start your text editor. You should see the text editor appear in Notepad.

7. Make changes to the file, save it, and check it back in.

   After you have made some changes to the text file, close your text editor, making sure that you save the text file. Next, right-click the file in VSS and select Check In. You will note that the red check disappears, and no user name is listed as having the file checked out.

8. View the history and differences.

   Right-click the file and select Show History on the shortcut menu. VSS will show you a dialog box listing all the times the file was checked out and back in, as well as the user who last checked out the file. In that dialog box, select the two versions and click the Diff button. You will see a dialog box confirming that you want to compare the two versions of the file. When you click OK, you will see a listing of the differences between the two files.

9. Create a new project.

   Right-click the root VSS folder ($/) and select Create Project. Give the project folder an arbitrary name. An empty folder with the name you provide is added to the database.

10. Share and branch a file at the same time.

    Right-click the new project you just created and select Share on the shortcut menu. In the resulting dialog box, navigate to the Duwamish folder and choose the text file with which you have been working in this exercise. Select the Branch after Share check box (your screen should resemble the dialog box as shown in Figure 2.8), and click OK.

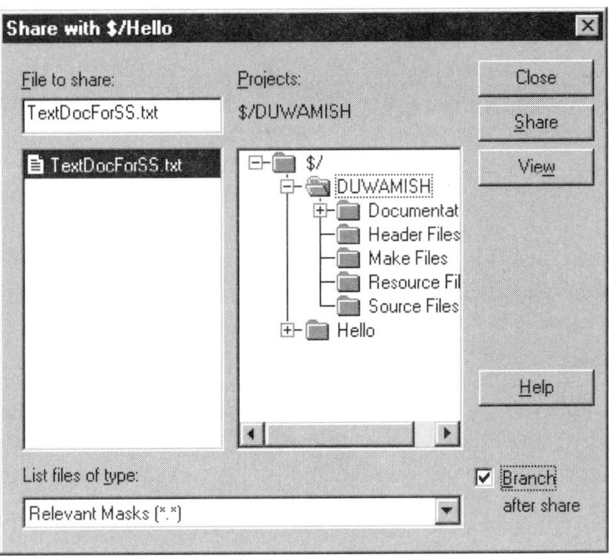

Figure 2.8 Sharing in VSS

11. Log on to a different database.

    If you have more than one database set up in VSS, you can choose which VSS database you want to use. Select Open SourceSafe Database on the File menu. You will see a dialog box similar to the one shown in Figure 2.9. Simply select the database you want to use and click OK.

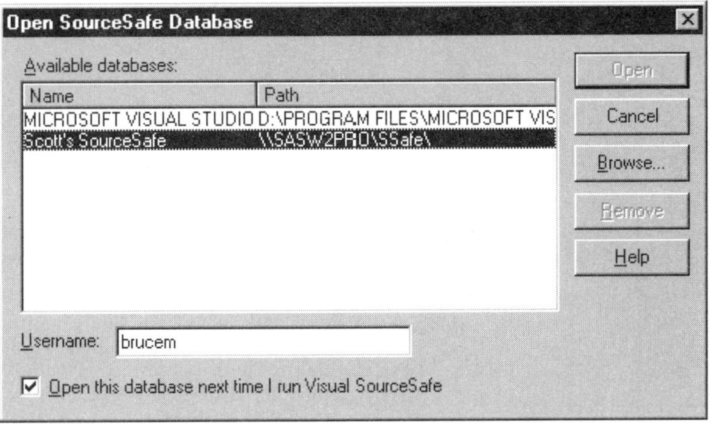

Figure 2.9 Open SourceSafe Database dialog box

Lesson Summary

Designing and implementing a complete change-control process can be a daunting and demanding task, but it is absolutely essential for any development team that wants to be professional and protect the investment in its work.

A complete change control process must contain approval and management workflows for both project artifacts and the physical source code. The process must be documented and include criteria detailing when approval is required before you make changes.

Various systems can make the change-control process easier and less costly to implement. Included in these systems are word processors, electronic mail and groupware, and version control software. A likely candidate for version control software would be VSS, because it is included in Visual Studio and tightly integrated with Visual C++.

Lesson 3: Tools

It is possible for you to write an entire enterprise C++ application using nothing more than a text editor, compiler, and linker. However, you will probably find that it is often most efficient and cost-effective for you to build an enterprise C++ application using an integrated development environment and an appropriate modeling tool.

Tools can save you time and money, and make your application development work both easier and more pleasant. A well-designed tool can pay for itself many times over if you use it appropriately and wisely. However, you should keep in mind that all tools available to you as a C++ developer are worthless unless you put them to sufficient use.

This lesson will examine some of the tools available to you as a professional C++ developer. Used well and wisely, these tools can help you cut even the largest development project down in size.

After this lesson, you will be able to:

- List the features of the Visual C++ Integrated Development Environment (IDE)
- Discuss the basics of data modeling and the advantages of using visual data modeling tools, including Microsoft Visual Modeler
- Understand how to use DCOMCNFG to configure COM over the network
- Understand how to use the OLE/COM Object Viewer (OLEView)

Estimated lesson time: 45 minutes

Integrated Development Environment

Before IDEs were established, most developers relied on a text editor for programming. Finding a good programmer's editor was an ongoing quest; however, even the best editor couldn't save developers from the onerous sequence of editing, saving, closing the editor, running the compiler and linker, noting the bugs, and starting over when changes needed to be made.

More recently in programming use were "integrated development environments," or IDEs. Various vendors touted their IDEs' features, which ranged from a shell command within an editor that ran a special batch file, to having the compiler, linker, and even debugger built into a program editor.

Visual C++ 6.0 shows the natural progression toward having more and more tools and features built into a development program itself. The IDE in Visual C++ provides a broad set of development tools for completing, testing, and refining your program. For example, the Visual C++ IDE includes not only a text editor for writing your code but also resource editors, various build options, an optimizing compiler, an incremental linker, a source code browse window, and an integrated debugger.

For example, Figure 2.10 shows a window with an editor pane on the right, a source code browse window on the left, and an output window at the bottom, with the results of a recent build still visible.

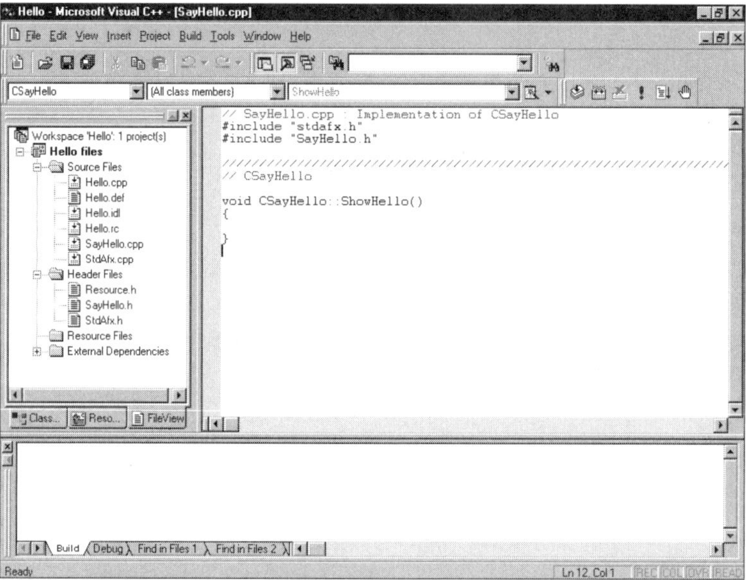

Figure 2.10 Visual C++ IDE

The Visual C++ IDE also includes organizational and helper tools for your various development jobs. The files you create for your program will be organized into a project with its own workspace. When you create a Visual C++ program that uses the Microsoft Foundation Classes (MFC) or the Microsoft Active Template Library (ATL), or when you create a Win32 program or a library, various wizards will help you create project files and starter source files for your program.

Finally, if you have access to VSS as your version control application, you can check your work in and out of the VSS database without leaving the C++ environment, as shown by the Visual C++ Source Control menu in Figure 2.11.

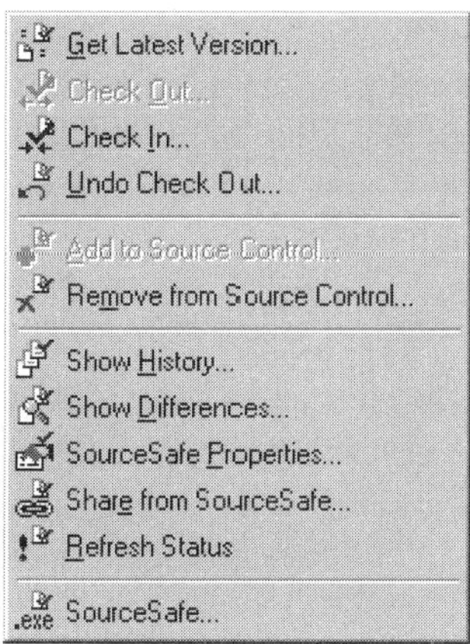

Figure 2.11 Source Control menu in Visual C++

Visual Data Modeling

Many of the applications you design will interact with a database of some sort. In some cases, you can work with an existing database; in others, though, you will have to design your database from scratch. The inexperienced developer begins database design by creating tables and adding fields. The experienced developer begins with *data modeling*.

Data modeling refers to the process of analyzing workflows, use cases, usage scenarios, or other prose material, and deriving a logical data model from that analysis. The input is the various descriptions of the business activities; the output is a logical data model, usually in the form of an *entity-relationship (E/R) diagram*.

Although it is possible, and certainly acceptable, to do such modeling using nothing more than a pencil and a legal pad, in recent years, a number of computer-based tools have emerged to make the modeling task both easier and more attractive. The term *visual data modeling* describes doing data modeling using one or more of these tools. The ER/Win product is a well-known example of a visual data modeling tool. The Visual Modeler tool (discussed as follows) is included with Visual Studio.

As mentioned, data modeling begins with analysis of use cases and usage scenarios upon which the application is based. The goal of this analysis is to identify all of the entities about which you want to store data, their attributes, and the relationships among the various entities.

An *entity* is anything about which data will be collected and stored. An entity can be a person, place, object, or concept. Individual instances of an entity are stored as rows in a table.

If you remember your sixth-grade grammar, you might be thinking "An entity sounds just like a noun." In fact, at the end of the analysis, all of your entities will be nouns. The first step in doing your analysis is to identify all of the nouns in the descriptive prose as potential entities in your database. For example, suppose that one use case stated "A customer buys books from a store." Immediately you can see you have three entities: customer, book, and store. Each of these entities would thus have its own table.

To differentiate among the various instances of each entity, you should implement attributes. An *attribute* is a characteristic of the individual instance of an entity. The easiest way to think of attributes is as adjectives that describe entities as nouns. Attributes are stored in columns in a table. For example, a customer table might look like that as shown in Table 2.1.

Table 2.1 Entities and Attributes

	———Attributes———		
	CustomerID	Name	Address
Instances	25001	Sam Smith	123 4th Street
	25002	Nancy Smith	567 8th Street
	25003	Bill Thomas	The Pines

After you have discovered in your data model all the entities and their attributes, you are ready to look at how the various entities are related. Typically, you will describe these relationships using a verb to link the entities together. In the previous example, you could say "customers *buy* books" as well as "stores *sell* books" (or "books *are sold by* stores" if you choose to describe in the other direction). Again, looking for verbs in the use cases and usage scenarios will give you a good start on your analysis.

However, it is not enough to simply relate two entities. You also have to know exactly how the entities are related. For example, in the example in Table 2.1, can a single customer buy more than one book? Can a book exist if a customer never buys it? Can a customer exist that never buys a book? These real-life questions will ultimately determine the actual relationships in your database. Your goal is to be able to describe each relationship with both a descriptive verb and additional relationship attributes as follows:

- **Cardinality** Specifies the number of instances of an entity that are allowed on each side of a relationship. For example, one customer can buy 0-∞(infinity) books. Cardinality is usually described as one-to-one, one-to-many, or many-to-many.
- **Existence** States whether one entity within a relationship can exist independently of another entity within the relationship, given a specified cardinality. For example, if you decide customers can come into existence only after they have made a purchase, then the purchase entity is mandatory for the customer entity to exist. Existence is described as either mandatory or optional.

E/R Diagram

The output of your analysis is a model known as an E/R diagram. This diagram uses a general syntax to denote the entities, attributes, relationships, cardinality, and existence that comprise the logical data model for a solution.

An entity is represented on the E/R diagram by a rectangle, with its attributes listed inside. For example, a customer entity might be shown as in Figure 2.12.

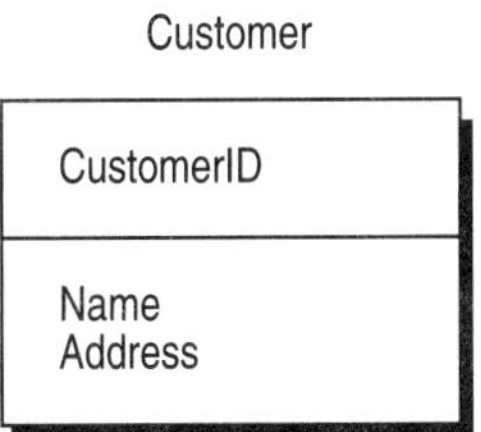

Figure 2.12 Sample customer entity

After all the entities have been defined, you need to tie them together with relationships, which are represented as lines drawn between the entities. Three general types of relationships can exist in an E/R diagram:

- A *one-to-one relationship* is generally represented in an E/R diagram by a line connecting two entities.
- A *one-to-many relationship* is generally represented in an E/R diagram by a connecting line with a dot at one end signifying the child entity.
- A *many-to-many relationship* is usually represented in an E/R diagram by a connecting line with dots at both ends.

The relationship verb is written adjacent to the relationship line in the E/R diagram to specify what the relationship represents.

Cardinality is generally denoted with a number at each end of the relationship line. For example, *1* is written at the end of a one-to-many relationship line to denote the parent side of the relationship, which has exactly one instance; *1.Infinity* is written at the other end to denote the child side of the relationship, which can have more than one instance.

Existence is denoted by the line style. A solid line indicates that a relationship is mandatory, whereas a broken or dashed line indicates that a relationship is optional.

Thus, what might result for a bookstore example is an optional relationship, as shown in Figure 2.13 on the next page.

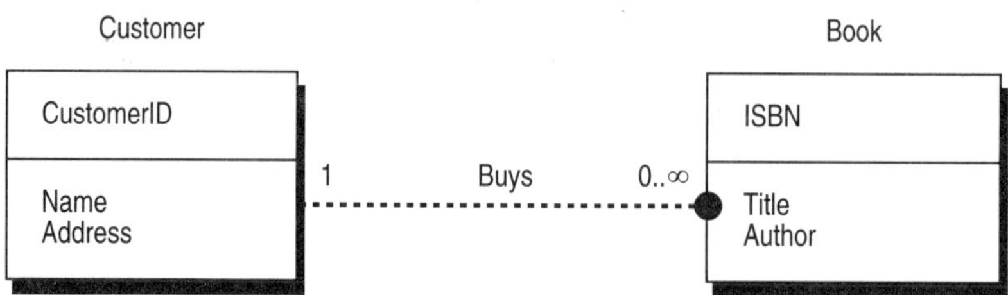

Figure 2.13 Diagram representing an optional relationship

The final phase of the data modeling design task is normalizing the data model. *Normalization* is the process of progressively refining a logical model to eliminate duplicate data from a database. Theorists have devised a set of normalization standards, each standard (or *normal form*) increasingly stringent in what duplicate data it will allow. For most purposes, normalizing a database to third normal form is sufficient.

Why You Should Use Visual Tools

Especially when you are working on a large development project, visual tools can save you a significant amount of time. In addition, most tools are easy to use, with extensive drag-and-drop capabilities and shortcut menus. The printed output is usually quite good, with support for headers and footers, page numbering, styles, and fit-to sizing of drawings. Several tools even support Hypertext Markup Language (HTML) output, so you can store your data model as a Web page or pages.

Finally, some of the more expensive tools let you use your completed logical data model (E/R diagram) as a basis for a complete physical data model, and then will actually implement that physical data model for you in your database of choice. Additionally, some of the tools support *round-trip engineering,* in which any changes made to the physical database can flow back into the physical and logical models, as well as flowing out of the models into the database.

Visual Modeler

Based on a subset of UML, Visual Modeler is a tool for designing n-tier distributed applications, using class and component diagrams. With Visual Modeler, you can visually design models of the classes and components your application needs, then convert these models to Visual C++ code. You can also publish the visual models you create in Microsoft Visual Component Manager so that they can be shared and reused by other developers in your organization.

When implemented with Visual C++, the main feature of Visual Modeler that you will most likely use is its ability to generate *class diagrams*, which represent a design view of the system you are about to develop. Class diagrams are shown through a *model* using a high level of abstraction. Visual Modeler uses a diagram notation that is a subset of the modeling constructs defined by UML.

Note Visual Modeler is not the only visual modeling tool on the market, nor is it the most complete. Such tools as Visio, Rational Rose, and GDPro all do an excellent job of modeling and, in some cases, offer additional features. This book focuses on Visual Modeler because many developers will already have Visual Modeler at hand. Also, Visual Modeler is included with Visual Studio and available to registered Visual C++ users as a download. If you find that modeling becomes an important part of your development process, or you find your modeling work limited somewhat by Visual Modeler, you might want to consider some of these other modeling products.

A model of a system describes a system view on a higher level of abstraction than the source code. Models of complex systems are needed because it is impossible, and not relevant to everyone, to understand all the details of a complex system. By modeling, you can focus on one aspect at a time and also work on a higher level of abstraction. The more complex your system is, the more you need a model.

In Visual Modeler, a system is modeled from three different views, each one with its own purpose:

- **Logical view** Describes the logical structure of the system (the classes and their relationships).
- **Component view** Describes the physical structure of the system (how the system is divided into .exe files and DLLs).
- **Deployment view** Shows the system's nodes and the connections in between and the allocation of processes to nodes.

Several situations occur in the design phase in which using a visual modeling tool such as Visual Modeler has major advantages. The first situation is the early phase, during which you decide what classes you need and how they are related. When the first outline of the object model is stable, you need to specify each class. (Keep in mind that the requirements might still change.) Using Visual Modeler to sketch different solutions and specifying the classes means that:

- It is easier for nondevelopers to understand the system design from your diagram than from the code.
- Your development team has a common diagram notation, which means that everyone on the team understands the diagrams. You can concentrate on what the system is supposed to do, and not how various components of the system are going to be implemented.

- Changing the diagrams and specifications when the requirements change is efficient and quick, compared to the time it takes to rewrite code.
- You can try various design approaches and communicate your ideas among the development team members.

You should use the model when you discuss the system's structure with those who are unfamiliar with your project. You should also use the model when you want new project members to understand the system quickly. Referring to the model during system development gives you a quick overview of how system elements are related.

Visual Modeler includes a number of different diagrams, each used for a different purpose. Most projects would use, at a minimum, the following diagram types:

- **N-tiered diagrams** Illustrate the overall structure of the system. These diagrams support the n-tiered architectural approach used when building applications by separating the system components into three layers of services: User, Business, and Data. The three-tiered model especially supports the creation of large, complex client/server applications. By default, a three-tiered diagram called Three-Tiered Service Model is created at the top level of the Logical View when a new model is opened.
- **Class diagrams** Illustrate a part or an aspect of the model of special interest. For each logical package in the model is a special, automatically created class diagram called Package Overview. A Package Overview diagram illustrates the contents of the package to which it belongs. This diagram is automatically updated when a new class is assigned to or removed from the package.
- **Specifications** Hold all details about the elements in the model. Each class, method, property, or relationship in the model is defined by a specification that is automatically created and updated. The specification is presented in a dialog box with tabs for different aspects. You are also able to define and view the details about a class, method, property, or relationship.

Dcomcnfg.exe

Dcomcnfg.exe is a utility you can use to configure various COM-specific settings in the registry. This configuration utility, dcomcnfg.exe, is included in the Microsoft Windows NT operating system and is used to configure applications to use COM. The dcomcnfg.exe utility is not added to the Start menu or any groups during installation of Microsoft Windows NT 4. An administrator must start it from the Run command on the Start menu.

Dcomcnfg.exe must be used to configure an application's COM properties before the application can use COM to communicate over the network. The Dcomcnfg.exe utility can be used to:

- Make distributed components unavailable for an entire computer or for a specific application. By default, distributed components are available.
- Configure the location of an application.
- Set permissions on server applications, either for all applications or for individual applications.
- Configure the user account that will be used to execute the server application. The client application uses this account to start processes and gain access to resources on the server computer.
- Configure the level of security for connections between applications, for example, using packet encryption.

Both the computers that are running the client and server applications must be configured for a distributed environment with the Dcomcnfg.exe utility as follows:

- **Client application** On the computer that will be running the client application, the administrator must specify the location of the server application. When a COM client application is used, it makes a request to a server application, which could be running on a different computer.
- **Server application** On the computer that will be running the server application, the administrator must specify the user accounts that will have permission to use or start the server application. In addition, it is necessary to specify the user accounts that will be used to run the server application.

When Dcomcnfg.exe starts, it displays the Distributed COM Configuration Properties dialog box. This dialog box has three tabs: Default Security, Default Properties, and Applications.

Default Security

You can use the Default Security tab, as shown in Figure 2.14 on the next page, to specify default permissions for objects on the system. This tab has three sections: Access, Launch, and Configuration. To change a section's defaults, click the corresponding Edit Default button. These default security settings are stored in the registry under HKEY_LOCAL_MACHINE\Software\Microsoft\OLE.

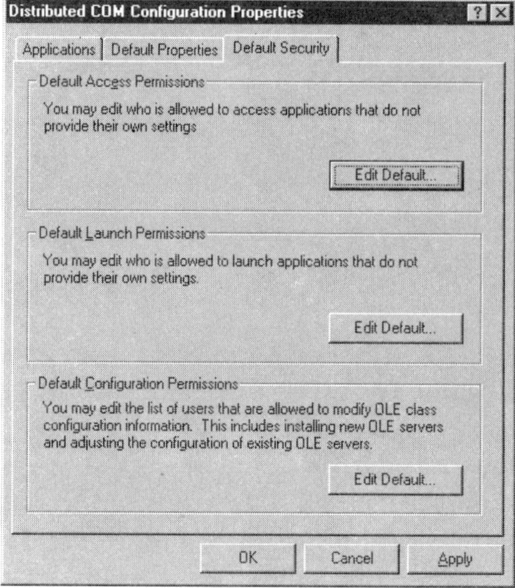

Figure 2.14 Default Security tab

Default Properties

On the Default Properties tab, as shown in Figure 2.15, you must select the Enable Distributed COM on This Computer check box if you want clients on other computers to access COM objects running on this computer. Selecting this option sets the HKEY_LOCAL_MACHINE\Software\Microsoft\OLE \EnableDCOM value to "Y".

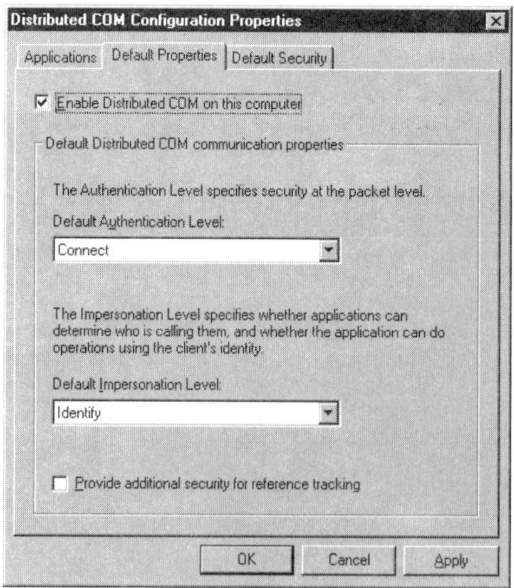

Figure 2.15 Default Properties tab

Applications

You can change the settings for a particular object from the Applications tab, as shown in Figure 2.16. To do so, you select the application from the list and click the Properties button. This action displays the Object Properties dialog box for the selected application.

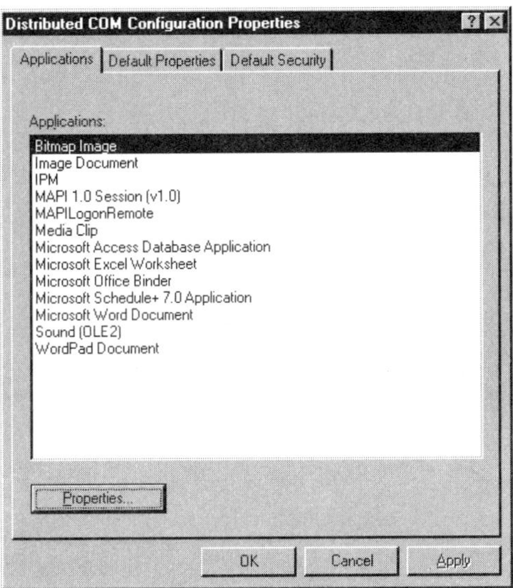

Figure 2.16 Applications tab

The Object Properties dialog box has four tabs:

- **General** Confirms the application with which you are working.
- **Location** Specifies where the application should run when a client calls *CoCreateInstance* with the relevant CLSID. If you select Run Application on the Following Computer check box and type a computer name, a RemoteServerName value is added under the AppID for that application. Clearing the Run Application on This Computer check box renames the LocalService value to _LocalService and renders it unavailable.
- **Security** Contains similarities to the Default Security tab found in the Distributed COM Configuration Properties dialog box, except that these settings apply only to the current application. Again, the settings are stored under the AppID for that object.
- **Identity** Identifies which user account is used to run the application, as shown in Figure 2.17 on the next page.

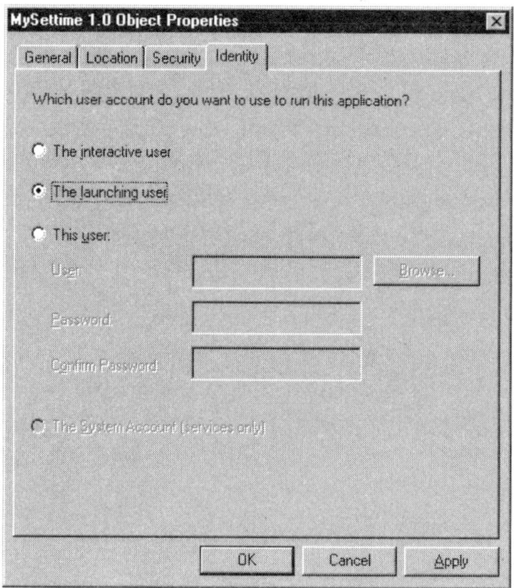

Figure 2.17 Identity tab of the Object Properties dialog box

OLEView

OLEView is an administration and testing tool for developers and power users. Shown in Figure 2.18, OLEView is an alternate means to configure security options for a component. With OLEView, you can achieve the following:

- Browse, in a structured way, all of the COM classes installed on your computer.
- See the registry entries for each class in an easy-to-read format.
- Configure any COM class on your system. This configuration includes Distributed COM (DCOM) activation and security settings.
- Configure system-wide COM settings, including making DCOM available or unavailable.
- Test any COM class by double-clicking its name. The list of interfaces that class supports will be displayed. By double-clicking an interface entry, you can invoke a viewer that will exercise that interface.
- Activate COM classes locally or remotely. This feature is ideal for testing distributed configurations.
- View type-library contents. Use this feature to determine what methods, properties, and events a Microsoft ActiveX control supports.
- Copy a properly formatted OBJECT tag to the clipboard for inserting into an HTML document.

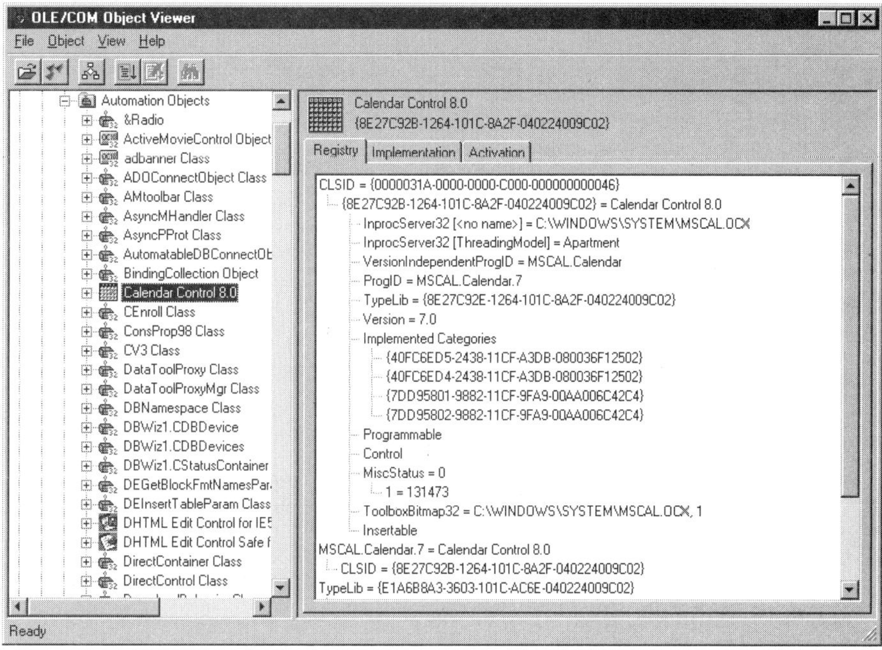

Figure 2.18 OLEView

OLEView provides more information than DCOMCNFG, and you can use it for all the settings done by DCOMCNFG except one: OLEView has no way to set the COM server to RunAs a certain user. The other major difference between DCOMCNFG and OLEView is that DCOMCNFG shows only the servers with AppIDs. OLEView allows the component to use Default Access and Launch permissions, but unlike DCOMCNFG, it doesn't allow the user to modify the Default settings.

In essence, OLEView provides all the functionality provided by clicking the Properties button in the Application tab of DCOMCNFG except for the RunAs identity. OLEView also provides a subset of the Default Properties and Default Security tabs of DCOMCNFG.

Visual Modeler is a modeling tool based on a subset of UML. Visual Modeler can create the class and component models upon which the development project will be based.

Using OLEView to View Installed COM Objects

In this practice exercise, you will use OLEView to look at the COM objects installed on your computer. Note that you must have already installed at least OLEView from Visual Studio or Visual C++ to do this practice.

1. Start OLEView.

   You will usually find OLEView under Programs/Visual C++/Tools/OLE View. You will see the opening dialog shown in Figure 2.19.

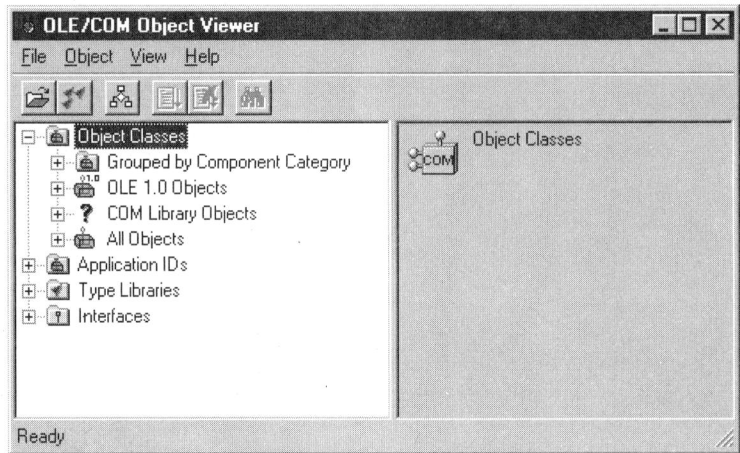

Figure 2.19 Opening OLEView dialog box

2. Select an object to view.

   Expand the Grouped By Component Category group, and then expand Controls. Click various controls until you find one that results in a multi-tab display in the right pane. Figure 2.20 shows the ActiveX Acrobat Reader control.

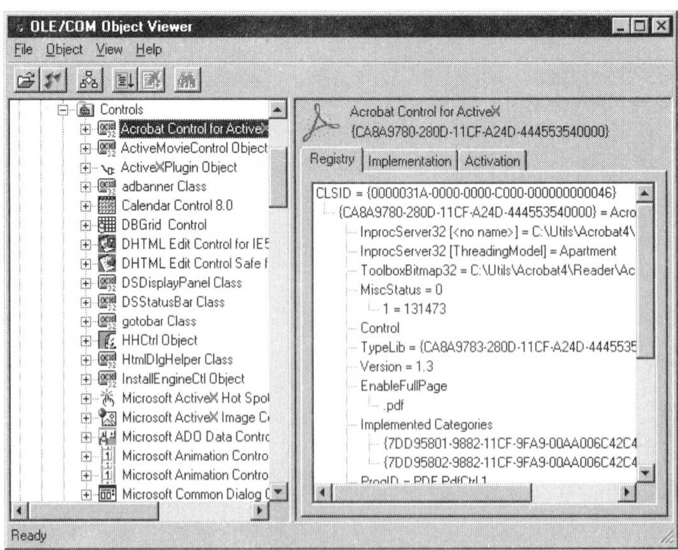

Figure 2.20 ActiveX Reader control

Note The Registry pane first shows all of the pertinent Registry information for this control in a read-only style.

3. Select the Implementation tab.

   On the Implementation tab, various text boxes are available to allow you to edit such settings as the Inproc Server and the Local Server, as needed (see Figure 2.21).

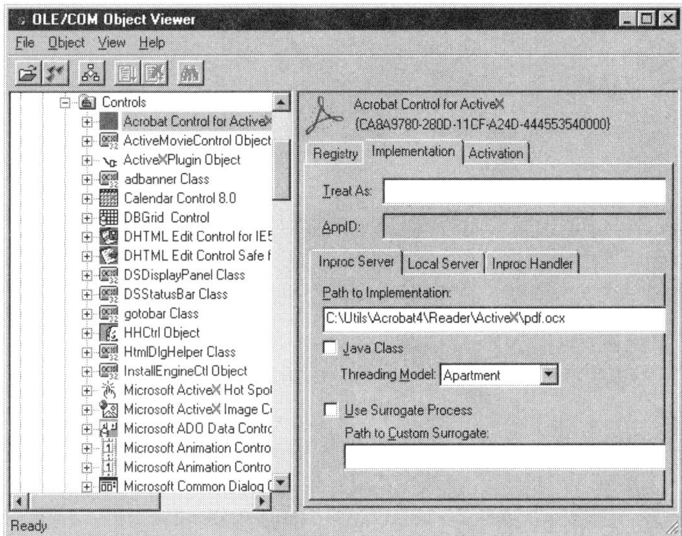

Figure 2.21 Implementation tab for an individual component

   When you look at the Activation tab, you can see that you can define a remote computer for activation of this control, if needed.

4. Expand the view to examine the interfaces.

   Click the plus sign beside the object and you will see the various interfaces for the object (see Figure 2.22, on the next page). Figure 2.22 highlights the IDispatch interface for the Acrobat Reader object.

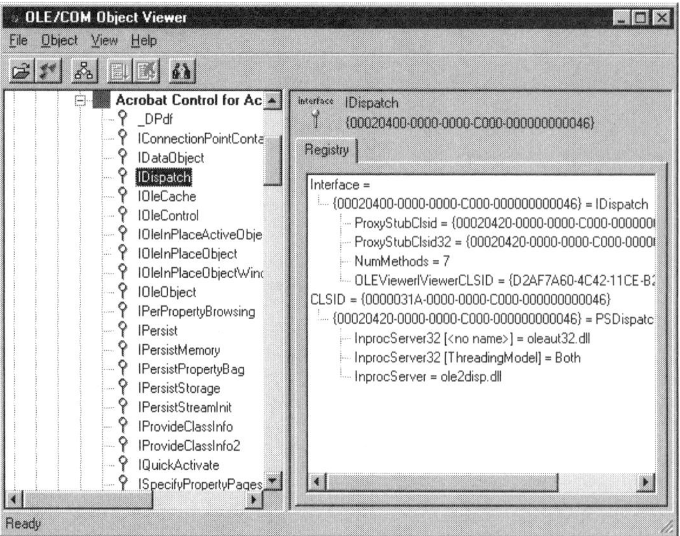

Figure 2.22 IDispatch interface for the Acrobat Reader object

5. Observe the interface's methods and properties.

   Double-click one of the interfaces, select View Type Info, and a dialog box such as the one shown in Figure 2.23 will appear. Spend a few minutes looking at the various methods and properties of the object you have chosen to view. When you are finished, simply close the viewer.

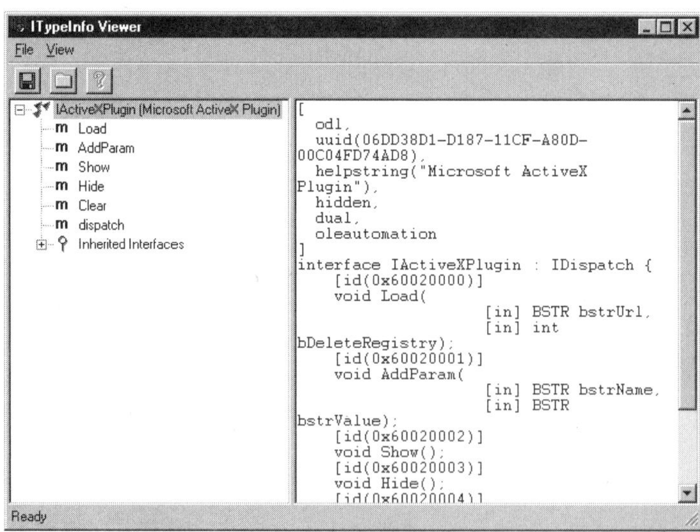

Figure 2.23 TypeInfo for an individual interface

As you can see, OLEView is a powerful tool for both viewing and editing almost every aspect of the OLE and COM components installed on your system. Plan to spend more time exploring all the information it can show you.

Lesson Summary

Tools are an important part of the software development world; they can make your development tasks easier and more efficient. Fortunately, Visual C++ provides a number of excellent tools built into the development environment, as well as others with which it integrates.

This lesson examined the IDE in Visual C++, including the built-in project browser, resource editor, and debugging environment. This lesson also noted how Visual C++ integrates with VSS from within the development environment.

Data modeling and creating E/R diagrams is an important, and often neglected, part of the development process. Data modeling begins with identifying the entities, attributes, and relationships inherent in the business processes that the development project must address. After these data modeling elements have been identified, the E/R diagram can be designed, and later enhanced to show cardinality and existence. Using visual tools to build the E/R diagram can make the work easier to do and read.

Lab 2: Installing Visual C++

In this lab, you will practice installing Visual C++ and the MSDN Library.

Estimated lab time: 30 minutes

1. View the Readme files.

   Insert the installation CD-ROM into your CD-ROM drive. If you have AutoRun available, you will see the initial install screen as shown in Figure 2.24. If AutoRun is not available, browse to the CD-ROM drive and double-click Setup.exe.

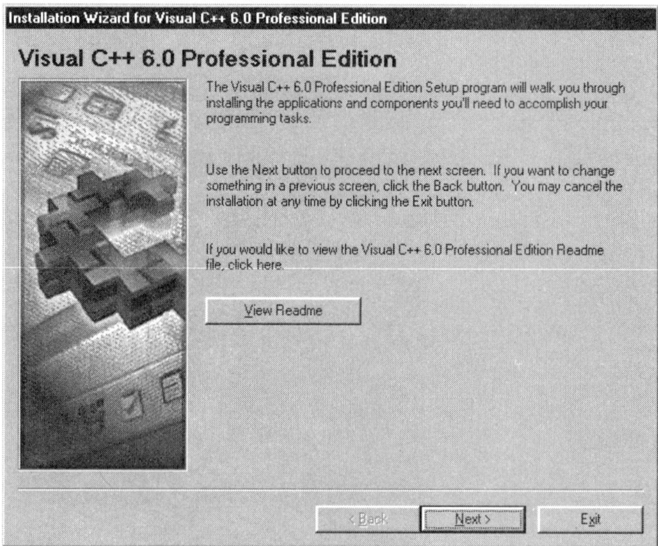

Figure 2.24 Initial Visual C++ install screen

When the Installation Wizard screen appears, click the View Readme button. The Readme files for Visual Studio are in the new HTML Help format. If you do not have a browser installed that is capable of reading this format, you will be prompted to install the version of Microsoft Internet Explorer that comes with Visual Studio. Because all of the Help files for Visual C++ are also in HTML Help format, you will need a browser capable of reading such files.

Note If you have to install Internet Explorer, the Internet Explorer installation routine will restart your computer and then proceed to finish copying files and configuring Internet Explorer. If you have AutoRun available, the Visual Studio or Visual C++ Installation Wizard can also start up. Be sure to let the Internet Explorer installation finish completely before proceeding with the Visual C++ installation.

You will note that the View Readme button takes you to the Visual Studio Readme. This is a "parent" Readme to all the other Readme files that come with Visual Studio. Clicking the various hyperlinks will take you to the other Readme files. Although you might want to scan the Visual Studio Readme, be sure to read thoroughly the Install Readme and the Visual C++ Readme. The Install Readme especially addresses issues you need to understand before proceeding with the installation.

2. Read the End User License Agreement (EULA) and type your product ID number and user information.

   The next two screens take you through the standard EULA and prompt you for your product ID number (found on your CD case) and your user information (name and company). You might want to read some specific clauses in the EULA, especially the ones relating to your license for the product parts that are specific to Windows NT.

3. Install DCOM if necessary.

   If you are installing on a computer that does not have DCOM98, you will be prompted to install it at this time as shown in Figure 2.25. DCOM98 is a required part of Visual C++. If you have to install it, the DCOM installation will reboot your computer, and the Visual C++ installation will resume at the next screen.

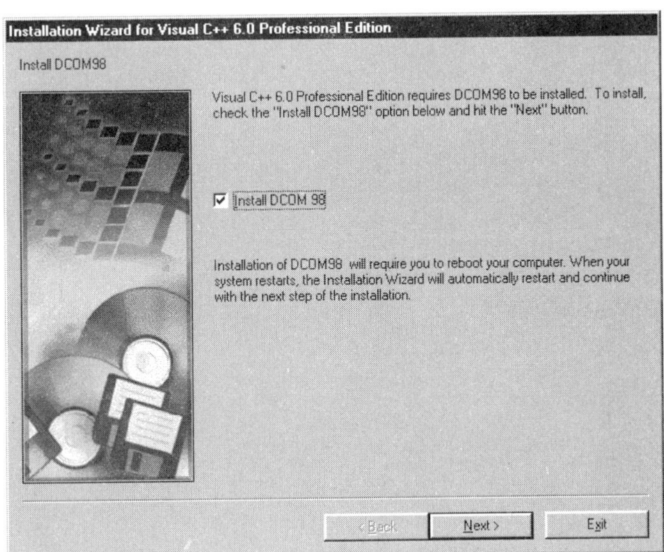

Figure 2.25 Install DCOM 98 dialog box

4. Select a location for the Common Files folder.

The default is under your Program Files folder, but you can browse to another location or create a new folder entirely. Following this procedure, you begin the actual Visual C++ installation.

5. Select the Custom setup option.

   The initial Visual C++ install screen lets you choose between the Typical and the Custom setup. Select Custom so that you can see the various setup options. Note that you can also choose a different location in which to install Visual C++.

6. Examine the Custom setup options.

   In the primary Custom setup dialog box (shown in Figure 2.28), you have various options with accompanying check boxes. Note that the first two choices (Developer Studio and Build Tools) are not optional, even though they appear to be.

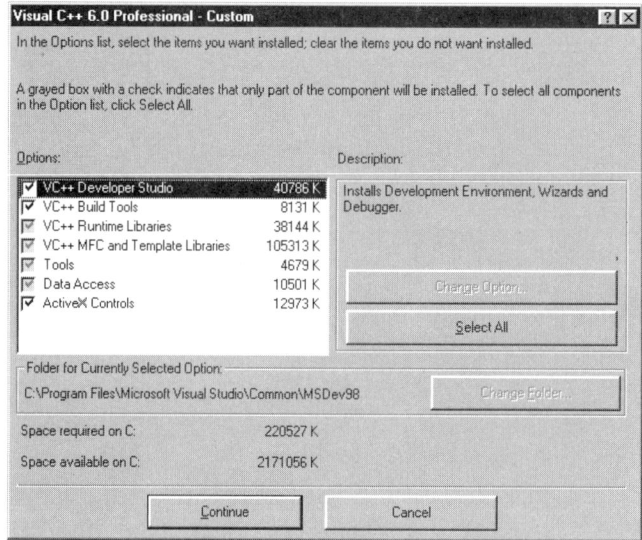

Figure 2.26 Primary Custom setup dialog box

a. Select your run-time libraries.

   When you click the Runtime Libraries option and select Change Option, you can see that the default is to install the static, shared, and single-threaded run-time libraries as shown in Figure 2.27. You can also install the source code for the libraries, but most developers will not need to do so.

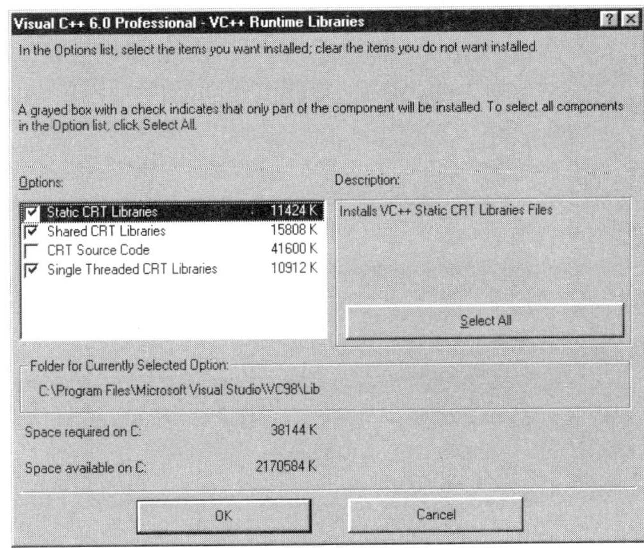

Figure 2.27 Runtime Libraries dialog box

b. Select your MFC and template libraries.

When you select Change Option on the MFC and Template Libraries dialog box (see Figure 2.28), you will note that there are suboptions for the MFC libraries.

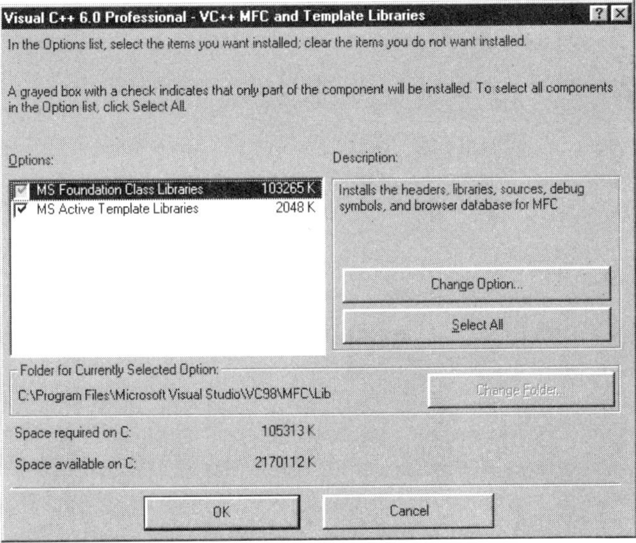

Figure 2.28 MFC and Template Libraries dialog box

c. Select the MFC Libraries option and click Change Option. You will then see the resulting choices shown in Figure 2.29.

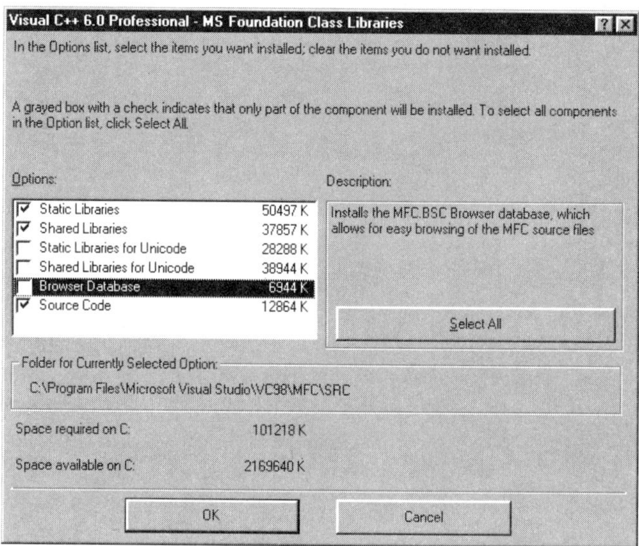

Figure 2.29 MFC Library options

If you are developing applications that require Unicode, you will need to check those libraries, because they are not installed by default. The Browser Database is a handy tool for browsing through the MFC source files, but you can do without it if you are short of disk space. The MFC library source code should be installed if you have room, if for no other reason than the learning you can gain by reading through it.

When you click OK and return to the MFC and Template Libraries dialog box, you must choose whether or not to install ATL. For the purposes of this book, you want to be sure that this option is checked. Note that you must install all or none of ATL; there are no suboptions for it.

d. Select the tools you want to install.

Your next set of options is to determine which tools to install (see Figure 2.30).

All of the tools except the Visual Component Manager are checked by default, and you should install them all. If you have room, it is a good idea to install the Component Manager as well, because it is a useful tool for reusing components from project to project.

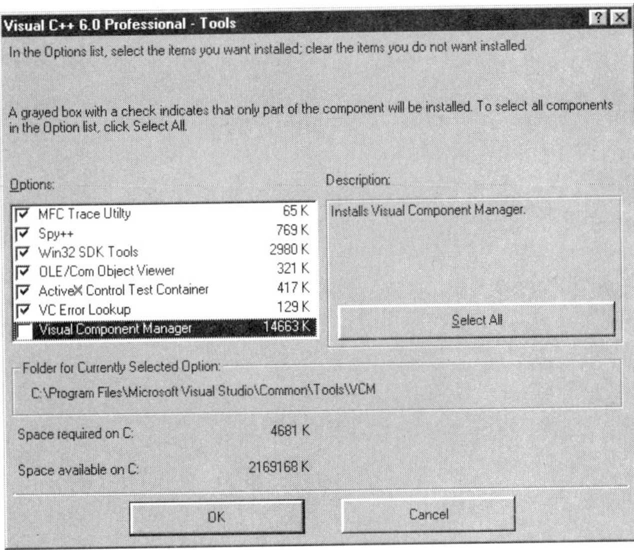

Figure 2.30 Determining which tools to install

e. Select the data access options you need.

When you select Change Option for the Data Access option, you will see the dialog box shown in Figure 2.31.

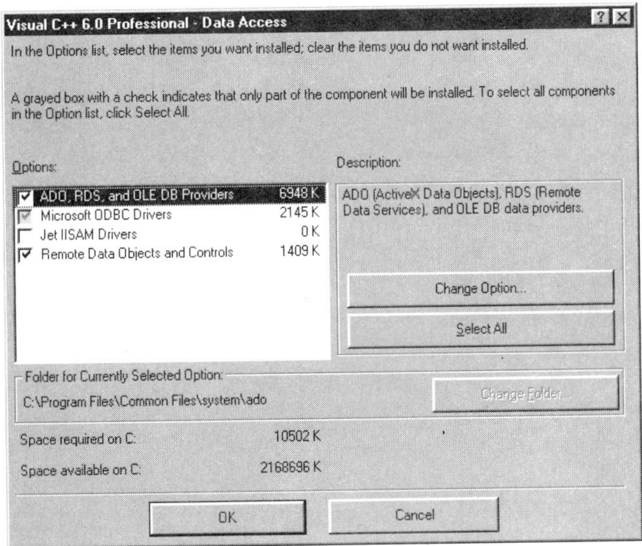

Figure 2.31 Data Access dialog box

As you can see, all of the Microsoft ActiveX Data Objects (ADO), Remote Data Services (RDS), and OLE DB data providers are installed by default. You can select Change Option to view these providers, but you should leave them all selected.

Not all of the Open Database Connectivity (ODBC) drivers, on the other hand, are installed by default. When you select Change Option for these drivers (see Figure 2.32), note that Microsoft SQL Server, Oracle, Access, and Visual FoxPro are checked by default. You might want to uncheck most or all of these, because much of your data access work will be done through ADO.

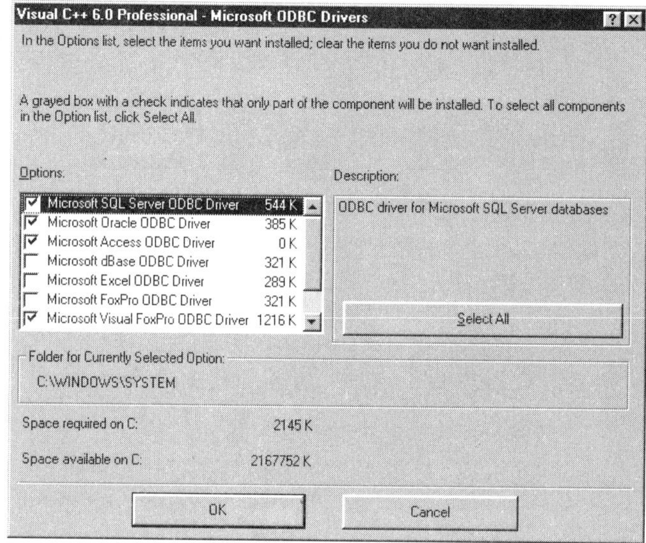

Figure 2.32 Selecting ODBC drivers

Finally, note that none of the Indexed Sequential Access Method (ISAM) drivers are installed by default. The only one of these that you might want to install is the Microsoft Exchange driver, if you plan on accessing the Exchange data store in this manner.

7. Let the Install Wizard proceed with file copying.

   When you have made all the choices you want in the Custom Setup dialog box and clicked OK, the Install Wizard first calculates disk space requirements and tells you if you don't have enough space. Assuming you do, it then proceeds to copy the files you chose to the locations you selected.

8. Install other client tools.

   After the files have been copied, you will see a dialog box that allows you to install other tools. For most installations, the only other tool that will show up in this dialog box is the InstallShield tool. If you want to provide your applications to your users through a professional installation (especially if you want to control where and how the application is installed), you should select InstallShield in the list and click Install. After the installation is complete, the Install Other Tools dialog box will reappear. After you have installed all the client tools you want, click Next.

At this point, you will see the dialog box shown in Figure 2.33, which references a batch file. Although most newer developers will use the build tools from within the IDE, some developers are more comfortable doing a build from the command line. For these developers, the Install Wizard creates a sample batch file that sets the necessary environmental variables.

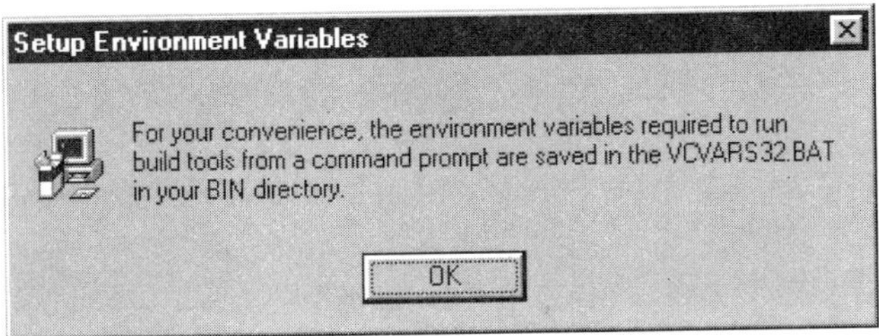

Figure 2.33 Informational dialog box about the batch file that sets environmental variables

9. Restart Windows.

   At this point, the Install Wizard will prompt you to restart. Close your other applications first, and then click Restart Windows.

10. Install MSDN.

    After your computer reboots (assuming you left the CD in the CD-ROM drive) you will see a dialog box prompting you to install the MSDN library. Included in this library is the documentation for Visual C++ as well as sample code, KnowledgeBase articles, and documentation for other tools such as VSS. Make sure the Install MSDN check box is checked, and then click Next. You will see the Welcome screen for MSDN. Click Next, and you will then see the EULA. Click Next yet again, and you will see a dialog box showing you three choices for MSDN setup: Typical, Full, and Custom. The Full installation puts the entire MSDN on your hard drive and takes up to 800 MB of disk space. If you are somewhat limited in disk space (or simply don't want to give up that much space for data you might never use), select either the Custom or Typical installation.

    In the resulting dialog box (see Figure 2.34 on the next page), you can select which parts of the documentation and other library elements you want to install. At a minimum, you should install the Visual C++ documentation. If you have more room, you can choose other components to install. If you are new to component-based system design, it is recommended that you install the Island Hopper sample application.

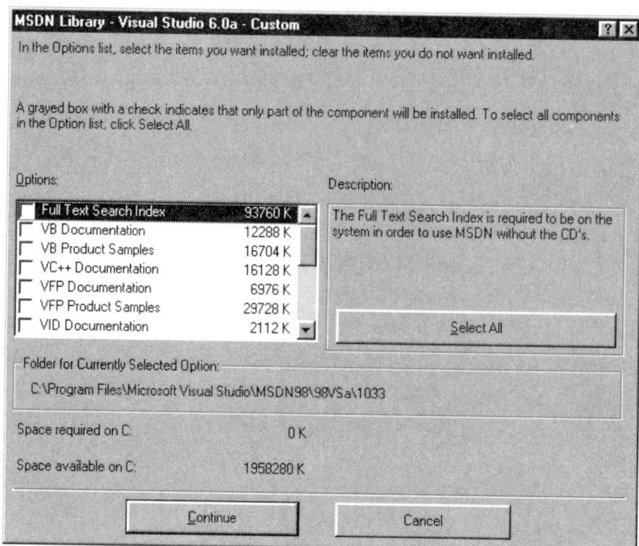

Figure 2.34 Installation choices for the MSDN documentation

11. Finish the installation.

    At this point, you will see the final dialog box, prompting you to register. If you have Web access, you can register over the Web. If you want to register at this time, leave the Register Now check box selected and you will be led through the process. Otherwise, simply clear the check box and click Next or Exit.

Review

The following questions are intended to reinforce key information presented in this chapter. If you are unable to answer a question, review the appropriate lesson and then try answering the question again. Answers to the questions can be found in Appendix B, "Review Questions and Answers," at the back of this book.

1. List the four stages of the production channel and the purpose of each stage.
2. What are the two overall areas of change control?
3. What are some examples of change control systems?
4. What is VSS?
5. What are sharing, branching, and merging in VSS?
6. Where in VSS do you make project-based security available?
7. What does an E/R diagram show?
8. What is Visual Modeler used for?
9. What is DCOMCNFG?
10. What is OLEView?

CHAPTER 3

C++ Development Essentials

Lesson 1: C++ Libraries 86

Lesson 2: Thread Management 113

Lesson 3: Memory Management and System Services 119

Review 129

About This Chapter

This chapter provides an overview of several essential technologies, including MFC, ATL, and Standard Template Library (STL). In addition, this chapter covers some programming concepts, including threading and threading models, and memory allocation and management. By necessity, this chapter provides only an overview; each of these topics is probably worthy of its own book. If the concepts and principles in this chapter seem foreign or especially difficult, you can consult numerous excellent resources, including the technical articles, examples, and tutorials that are included with the Microsoft Visual C++ documentation. A wealth of information on the topics covered in this chapter is also available on the MSDN Web site at *http://msdn.microsoft.com*.

Before You Begin

This chapter assumes that you are familiar with programming in C or C++. Because this chapter is an overview of various development concepts, there are no prerequisites.

Lesson 1: C++ Libraries

In this lesson, you will learn about two important libraries supplied with Visual C++: the MFC library and ATL. You will examine how MFC makes programming Microsoft Windows applications easier, and how ATL is an excellent alternative to MFC for writing COM components with a small memory and code footprint.

After this lesson, you will be able to:

- Describe both MFC and ATL at a general level and give examples of when to use each
- Discuss the document/view approach to application design
- Discuss how to use MFC to program screen access, printing, and print preview
- Describe the purpose and advantages of ATL

Estimated lesson time: 60 minutes

Overview of MFC

MFC is an application framework for programming in Windows. Written in C++, MFC provides much of the code necessary for managing windows, menus, and dialog boxes; performing basic I/O; storing collections of data objects; and so on. All you need to do is add your application-specific code into this framework. Also, given the nature of C++ class programming, it's easy to extend or override the basic functionality that the MFC framework supplies.

The MFC framework is an approach that lets you build upon the existing work of many expert Windows programmers. MFC shortens development time; makes code more portable; provides tremendous support without reducing programming freedom and flexibility; and gives easy access to hard-to-program UI elements and technologies, like Microsoft ActiveX technology, OLE, and Internet programming. Furthermore, MFC simplifies database programming through DAO and ODBC, and network programming through Microsoft Windows Sockets. MFC makes it easy to program features such as property sheets (tabbed dialog boxes); print preview; and floating, customizable toolbars.

Your work with the MFC framework is based largely on a few major classes and several Visual C++ tools. Some of the classes encapsulate a large portion of the Win32 API. Other classes encapsulate application concepts such as documents, views, and the application itself. Still others encapsulate OLE features and ODBC and DAO data-access functionality.

For example, the MFC class CWnd *encapsulates* Win32's window concept. That is, a C++ class named CWnd encapsulates, or "wraps," the HWND handle that represents a Windows window. Likewise, class CDialog encapsulates Win32 dialog boxes.

Encapsulation means that a class contains all the data structures and functions necessary to define and work with an object. The CWnd class contains a member variable of type HWND, and the class's member functions wrap calls to Win32 functions that take HWND as a parameter. The class member functions typically have the same name as the Win32 function they encapsulate.

MFC Limitations

As a general programming framework, MFC can't anticipate every programmer's every need. For example, MFC makes it easy to build the interface for a spreadsheet application, but you must provide all of the important display and computation logic.

Note MFC is not a general function library as is the C run-time library. You cannot simply call MFC class member functions in an otherwise non-MFC context. From within MFC, you can still call Win32 API functions directly, particularly those that MFC does not choose to encapsulate. However, most MFC functions are members of a class, and you must have an object of the class before you can call any of its member functions.

MFC Features

MFC is fairly basic, but it does support you in many specialized ways:

- OLE visual editing
- Microsoft Automation
- ActiveX controls
- Internet programming
- Windows common controls
- DAO database programming
- ODBC database programming
- Multithreaded programming
- Network programming
- Portability

Using MFC Classes to Write Applications for Windows

Taken together, the MFC library classes comprise an application framework—the framework on which you build an application for Windows. At a general level, the framework defines the skeleton of an application and supplies standard UI implementations that can be placed onto the skeleton. Your job as programmer is to fill in the skeleton with the components that are specific to your application. You can get a head start on creating a thorough starter application by using AppWizard to create the files. You use the Visual C++ resource editors to design your UI elements visually, ClassWizard to connect those elements to code, and the class library to implement your application-specific logic.

MFC 3 and later support 32-bit programming for Win32 platforms, including Microsoft Windows 95 and Microsoft Windows NT 3.51 and later. MFC Win32 support includes multithreading. Use version 1.5*x* if you need to do 16-bit programming.

Target Platforms

MFC is the easiest way for you to achieve two kinds of portability:

- Among different operating systems
- Among different processors, such as x86 and DEC Alpha

MFC is designed to wrap your C/C++ applications to work on almost any operating system with little or no modification, including 16-bit and 32-bit Windows and UNIX if a UNIX MFC library is present. MFC is also designed to be completely portable among different processors.

Note If you want to write American National Standards Institute (ANSI) Standard C++ applications, you cannot use the MFC libraries. If you need to write ANSI Standard C++ code, search the MSDN site for "Write Code that Works in the Largest Number of C Compilers" for additional information.

The versions of Visual C++ for Intel x86 and Alpha processors are all based on Windows NT. MFC's job is to make C++ code universal on these platforms by wrapping the system-dependent code such as messages; your applications should port easily among the various platforms. In most cases, a Visual C++ application created in the development environment on one of these platforms can be opened in the development environment on another platform, and the conversion is done automatically.

If you have the UNIX version of MFC on your UNIX system, your Visual C++ applications should port with little difficulty.

If you do not have MFC on your UNIX system, you can still port your Visual C++ applications to UNIX using the Standard C++ libraries and the Visual C++ compiler libraries. Many UNIX functions, such as *open*, *fopen*, *read*, and *write*, are available in the Visual C++ run-time library. Also, a one-to-one mapping of these UNIX APIs to Win32 APIs takes place: *open* to *CreateFile*, *read* to *ReadFile*, *write* to *WriteFile*, *ioctl* to *DeviceIOControl*, *close* to *CloseFile*, and so on. Many of the traditional system calls on which UNIX applications rely are available as Win32 APIs.

MFC Architecture

Within the MFC framework, several key programming architectures are evident. These basic architectures are the basis for most applications created within Visual C++. The basic architectures and systems discussed in this lesson are Messages and Commands, the Document/View architecture, and the Microsoft Windows Graphics Device Interface (GDI).

Messages and Commands

In traditional programs for Windows, Windows messages are often handled in a large switch statement within a window procedure. MFC instead uses *message maps* to map direct messages to distinct class member functions. Message maps are more efficient than creating virtual functions and allow the messages to be handled by the most appropriate C++ object: application, document, view, and so on. You can map a single message or a range of messages, command IDs, or control IDs to class member functions.

MFC defines a standard routing of command messages among the application, frame window, view, and active documents in your program. If necessary, you can override the MFC default route. Message maps also supply a way to update UI objects (such as menus and toolbar buttons), making these objects available or unavailable to suit the current context. Thus, the WM_COMMAND messages—usually generated by menus, toolbar buttons, or accelerators—can use the message-map mechanism.

The easiest way to create these message maps is to use MFC ClassWizard or WizardBar.

Messages

The messages to be processed originate from the operating system and extraneous events. When these messages are initiated, the message loop in the *Run* member function of class CWinApp retrieves queued messages generated by various events. For example, when the user clicks the mouse, Windows sends several mouse-related messages, such as WM_LBUTTONDOWN when the left mouse button is pressed and WM_LBUTTONUP when the left mouse button is released. The MFC framework's implementation of the application message loop then dispatches the message to the appropriate window.

Message Handlers

In MFC, a dedicated *handler* function processes each separate message. Message-handler functions are member functions of a class. This documentation uses the terms *message-handler member function*, *message-handler function*, *message handler*, and *handler* interchangeably. Some kinds of message handlers are also called "command handlers." Writing message handlers accounts for a large proportion of your work in writing a framework application.

What does the handler for a message do? It does whatever you want done in response to that message. ClassWizard will create the handlers for you; however, your job is to fill out the implementation code to perform the appropriate work. You can jump directly from ClassWizard to the handler function's definition in your source files and fill in the handler's code using the Visual C++ source code editor. Alternatively, you can create all of your handlers with ClassWizard, then move to the editor to immediately fill in all functions. You can use all of the facilities of Visual C++ and MFC to write your handlers.

Message Categories

Messages can be separated into three main categories. Each category simply refers to a type of message that is being sent. Message handlers still must be capable of processing the actual messages. The three main categories are:

- **Windows messages** These include primarily those messages beginning with the WM_ prefix, except for WM_COMMAND. Windows and views handle Windows messages. These messages often have parameters that are used in determining how to handle the message.
- **Control notifications** This includes WM_COMMAND notification messages from controls and other child windows to their parent windows. For example, an edit control sends its parent a WM_COMMAND message containing the EN_CHANGE control-notification code when the user has taken an action that might have altered text in the edit control. The window's handler for the message responds to the notification message in an appropriate way, such as retrieving the text in the control. The framework routes control-notification messages like other WM_ messages. One exception, however, is the BN_CLICKED control-notification message sent by buttons when the user clicks them. This message is treated specially as a command message and routed like other commands.
- **Command messages** This includes WM_COMMAND notification messages from UI objects: menus, toolbar buttons, and accelerator keys. The framework processes commands differently from other messages, and they can be handled by more kinds of objects.

Windows handles Windows messages and control notifications for objects of classes derived from class CWnd. This includes CFrameWnd, CMDIFrameWnd, CMDIChildWnd, CView, CDialog, and your own classes derived from these base classes. Such objects encapsulate HWND, a handle to a Windows window.

Command messages can be handled by a wider variety of objects: documents, document templates, and the application object itself in addition to windows and views. When a command directly affects some particular object, it makes sense to have that object handle the command. For example, the Open command on the File menu is logically associated with the application: the application opens a specified document upon receiving the command. Thus the handler for the Open command is a member function of the application class.

Mapping Messages

Each framework class that can receive messages or commands has its own "message map." The framework uses message maps to connect messages and commands to their handler functions. Any class derived from class CCmdTarget can have a message map. In spite of the name "message map," message maps handle both messages and commands—all three categories of messages listed in the preceding section.

UI Objects and Command IDs

Menu commands, toolbar buttons, and accelerator keys are *UI objects* capable of generating commands. Each UI object has an ID. You associate a UI object with a command by assigning the same ID to the object and the command. As explained previously, commands are implemented as special messages. Figure 3.1 shows how the framework manages commands. When a UI object generates a command such as ID_EDIT_CLEAR_ALL, one of the objects in your application handles the command; in Figure 3.1, the *OnEditClearAll* function of the document object is called via the document's message map.

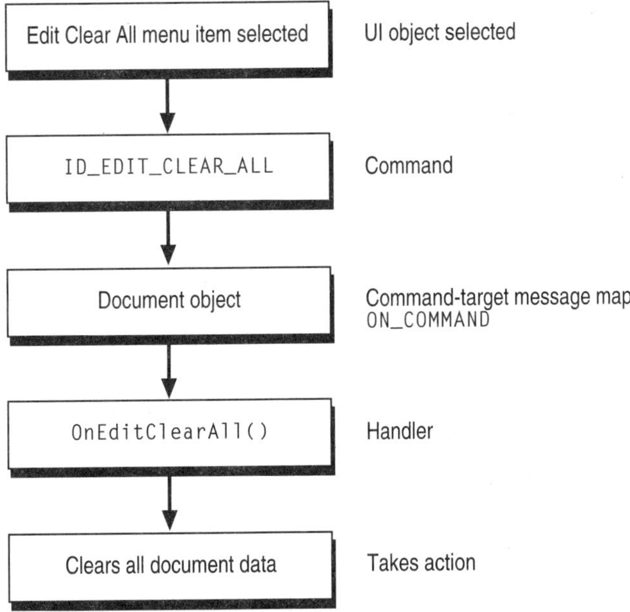

Figure 3.1 Commands in the framework

Figure 3.2 shows how MFC updates UI objects such as menu commands and toolbar buttons. Before a menu drops down, or during the idle loop in the case of toolbar buttons, MFC routes an update command. In Figure 3.2, the document object calls its update command handler, *OnUpdateEditClearAll*, to alternately make the UI object available or unavailable.

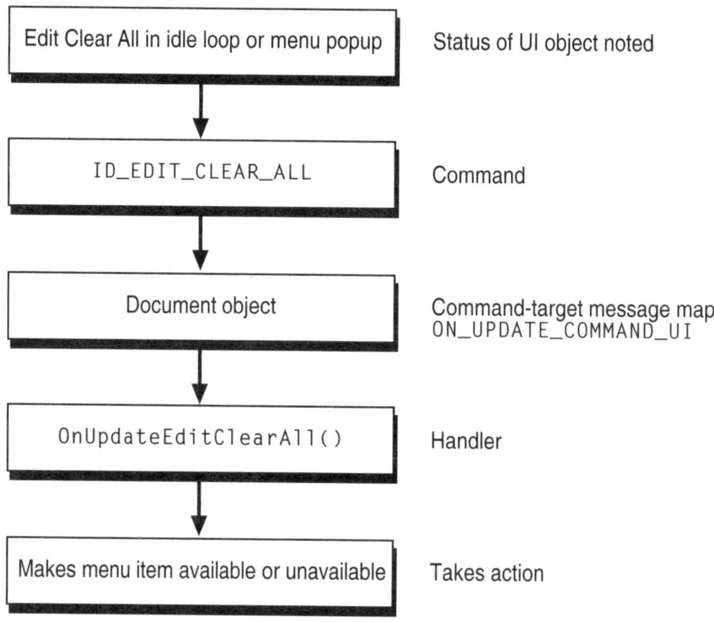

Figure 3.2 Command updating in the framework

Command Targets

Figure 3.1 shows the connection between a UI object, such as a menu command, and the handler function that the framework calls to carry out the resulting command when the object is clicked.

Windows sends messages that are not command messages directly to a window whose handler for the message is then called. However, the framework routes commands to a number of candidate objects—called "command targets"—one of which normally invokes a handler for the command. The handler functions work the same way for both commands and standard Windows messages, but the mechanisms by which they are called are different.

Document/View Architecture

By default, MFC applications use a programming model that separates a program's data from the display of that data and from most user interaction with the data. In this model, an MFC document object reads and writes data to persistent storage. The document can also provide an interface to the data wherever it resides (such as in a database). A separate view object manages data display, from rendering the data in a window to handling user selection and editing of data. The view obtains display data from the document and communicates back to the document any data changes.

Although you can easily override or ignore the document/view separation, compelling reasons encourage you to follow this model in most cases. One of the best reasons is that when you need multiple views of the same document, such as both a spreadsheet and a chart view, the document/view model lets a separate view object represent each view of the data, whereas code common to all views (such as a calculation engine) can reside in the document. The document also takes on the task of updating all views whenever the data changes.

MFC's document/view architecture makes it easy to support multiple views, multiple document types, splitter windows, and other valuable UI features. At the heart of document/view are four key classes:

- **CDocument (or COleDocument)** An object used to store or control your program's data
- **CView (or one of its many derived classes)** An object used to display a document's data and manage user interaction with the data
- **CFrameWnd (or one of its variations)** An object that provides the frame around one or more views of a document
- **CDocTemplate (or CSingleDocTemplate or CMultiDocTemplate)** An object that coordinates one or more existing documents of a given type and manages creating the correct document, view, and frame window objects for that type

The CDocument class provides the basic functionality for programmer-defined document classes. A document represents the unit of data that the user typically opens with the Open command on the File menu and saves with the Save command on the File menu.

The CView class provides the basic functionality for programmer-defined view classes. A view is attached to a document and acts as an intermediary between the document and the user: the view renders an image of the document on the screen and interprets user input as operations upon the document. The view also renders the image for both printing and print preview.

Figure 3.3, at the top of the next page, shows the relationship between a document and its view.

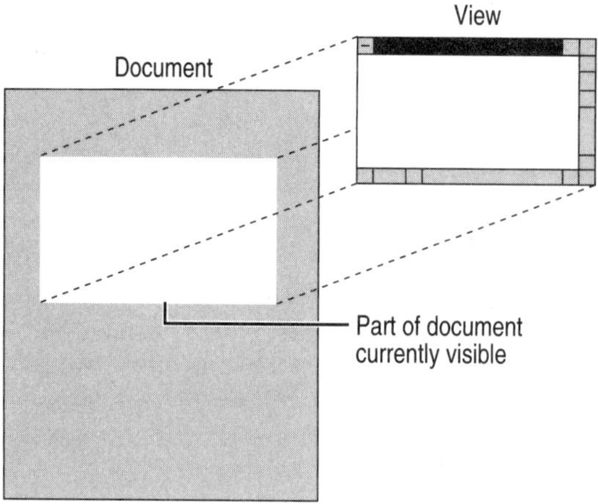

Figure 3.3 Document/view relationship

The document/view implementation in the class library separates the data itself from its display and from user operations on the data. All changes to the data are managed through the document class. The view calls this interface to access and update the data.

A document template creates documents, their associated views, and the frame windows that frame the views. The document template is responsible for creating and managing all documents of one document type.

Gaining Access to Document Data from the View

The view accesses its document's data either with the *GetDocument* function, which returns a pointer to the document, or by making the view class a C++ friend of the document class. The view then uses its access to the data to obtain the data when it is ready to draw or otherwise manipulate it.

For example, from the view's *OnDraw* member function, the view uses *GetDocument* to obtain a document pointer. Next, it uses that pointer to access a *CString* data member in the document. The view passes the string to the *TextOut* function.

User Input to the View

The view might also interpret a mouse click as either selecting or editing data. Similarly it might interpret keystrokes as data entry or editing. Suppose the user types a string in a view that manages text. The view would obtain a pointer to the document and use the pointer to pass the new data to the document, which stores it in a data structure.

Updating Multiple Views of the Same Document

In an application with multiple views of the same document—such as a splitter window in a text editor—the view first passes the new data to the document. Next, it calls the document's *UpdateAllViews* member function, which tells all views of the document to update themselves, reflecting the new data. This synchronizes the views.

Advantages of the Document/View Architecture

The key advantage to using the MFC document/view architecture is that the architecture supports multiple views of the same document particularly well. If you don't need multiple views and the small overhead of document/view is excessive in your application, you can avoid the architecture.

Suppose your application lets users view numerical data in either spreadsheet or chart form. A user might want to see simultaneously both the raw data in spreadsheet form and a chart that results from the data. You display these separate views in separate frame windows or in splitter panes within a single window.

Now suppose the user can edit the data in the spreadsheet and see the changes instantly reflected in the chart. In MFC, the spreadsheet and chart views would each be based on different classes derived from CView. Both views would be associated with a single document object. The document stores the data (or perhaps obtains it from a database). Both views access the document and display the data they retrieve from it.

When a user updates one of the views, that view object calls *CDocument::UpdateAllViews*. That function notifies all of the document's views, and each view updates itself using the latest data from the document. The single call to *UpdateAllViews* synchronizes the different views.

This scenario would be difficult to code without the separation of data from view, particularly if the views stored the data themselves. With document/view, it's easy. The framework does most of the coordination work for you.

Alternatives to the Document/View Architecture

MFC applications normally use the document/view architecture to manage information, file formats, and the visual representation of data to users. For the majority of desktop applications, the document/view architecture is an appropriate and efficient application architecture. This architecture separates data from viewing and, in most cases, simplifies your application and reduces redundant code.

However, the document/view architecture is not appropriate for some situations. Consider the following scenarios:

- If you are porting an application written in C for Windows, you might want to complete your port before adding document/view support to your application.
- If you are writing a lightweight utility, you might find that you can do without the document/view architecture.
- If your original code already mixes data management with data viewing, moving the code to the document/view model is not worth the effort because you must separate the two. You might prefer to leave the code as is.

To create an application that does not use the document/view architecture, clear the Document/View architecture support check box in Step 1 of MFC AppWizard.

Note Dialog box–based applications produced by AppWizard do not use the document/view architecture, so the Document/View Architecture Support check box is unavailable if you select the dialog box application type.

The Visual C++ wizards, as well as the source and dialog editors, work with the generated application just as they would with any other Wizard-generated application. The application can support toolbars, scroll bars, and a status bar; and has an About box. Your application will not register any document templates, and it will not contain a document class.

Note that your generated application has a view class, *CChildView*, derived from CWnd. MFC creates and positions one instance of the view class within the frame windows created by your application. MFC still enforces using a view window, because it simplifies positioning and managing the application's content. You can add painting code to the *OnPaint* member of this class. Your code should add scroll bars to the view rather than to the frame.

Because the document/view architecture provided by MFC is responsible for implementing many of an application's basic features, its absence in your project means that you are responsible for implementing many important features of your application as follows:

- As provided by AppWizard, the menu for your application contains only New and Exit commands on the File menu. The generated menu resource doesn't have an Edit menu and will not support a most-recently used (MRU) list.
- You must add handler functions and implementations for any commands that your application will support, including Open and Save on the File menu. MFC normally provides code to support these features, but that support is tightly bound to the document/view architecture.
- The toolbar for your application, if you requested one, will be minimal.

It is strongly recommended that you use the MFC AppWizard to create applications without the document/view architecture, because AppWizard guarantees a correct MFC architecture. However, if you must avoid using AppWizard, following are several approaches for bypassing the document/view architecture in your code:

- Treat the document as an unused appendage and implement your data management code in the view class, as suggested previously. Overhead for the document is relatively low. A single CDocument object incurs a small amount of overhead by itself, plus the small overhead of CDocument's base classes, CCmdTarget and CObject. Both of the latter classes are small.

  Declared in CDocument are the following:

  - Two CString objects
  - Three BOOLs
  - One CDocTemplate pointer
  - One CPtrList object, which contains a list of the document's views

  Additionally, the document requires the amount of time to create the document object, its view objects, a frame window, and a document template object.

- Treat both the document and view as unused appendages. Put your data management and drawing code in the frame window rather than the view. This approach is closer to the C-language programming model.
- Override the parts of the MFC framework that create the document and view to eliminate creating them at all. The document creation process begins with a call to *CWinApp::AddDocTemplate*. Eliminate that call from your application class's *InitInstance* member function and, instead, create a frame window in *InitInstance* yourself. Put your data management code in your frame window class. This is more work and requires a deeper understanding of the framework, but it frees you entirely of the document/view overhead.

GDI Object

Windows provides a variety of drawing tools to use in *device contexts* (DCs). It provides pens to draw lines, brushes to fill interiors, and fonts to draw text. MFC provides graphic-object classes equivalent to the drawing tools in Windows. Table 3.1, on the next page, shows the available classes and the equivalent Windows GDI handle types.

The general literature on programming for the Windows GDI applies to the MFC classes that encapsulate GDI graphic objects.

Table 3.1 Classes for Windows GDI Objects

Class	Windows handle type
CPen	HPEN
CBrush	HBRUSH
CFont	HFONT
CBitmap	HBITMAP
CPalette	HPALETTE
CRgn	HRGN

Each graphic-object class in the class library has a constructor that allows you to create graphic objects of that class, which you must then initialize with the appropriate create function, such as *CreatePen*.

Each graphic-object class in the class library has a cast operator that will cast an MFC object to the associated Windows handle. The resulting handle is valid until the associated object detaches it. Use the object's *Detach* member function to detach the handle.

The following code casts a CPen object to a Windows handle:

```
CPen myPen;
myPen.CreateSolidPen(PS_COSMETIC, 1, RGB(255,255,0));
HPEN hMyPen = (HPEN) myPen;
```

Process of Creating a Graphic Object in a DC

The following four steps are typically used when you need a graphic object for a drawing operation:

1. Define a graphic object on the stack frame. Initialize the object with the type-specific create function, such as *CreatePen*. Alternatively, initialize the object in the constructor.
2. Select the object into the current DC, saving the original graphic object that was selected previously.
3. When done with the current graphic object, select the original graphic object into the DC to restore its state.
4. Allow the frame-allocated graphic object to be deleted automatically when the scope is exited.

Note If you will be using a graphic object repeatedly, you can allocate it one time and select it into a DC each time it is needed. Be sure to delete the object when you no longer need it.

MFC Library Files

In addition to the basic MFC architectures and wizards, several MFC libraries can provide you with significant help in creating the application. These libraries provide classes and functionality for your application without creating all the code from scratch. In particular, classes are provided to support the typical application features of drawing, printing, and providing print previews.

Drawing, Printing, and Print Preview

In Windows, all graphical output is drawn on a DC virtual drawing area. MFC provides classes to encapsulate the various types of DCs, as well as encapsulations for Windows drawing tools such as bitmaps, brushes, palettes, and pens. These classes encapsulate the different types of DCs available in Windows.

Most of the following classes encapsulate a handle to a Windows DC. A DC is a Windows object that contains information about the drawing attributes of a device such as a display or a printer. All drawing calls are made through a device-context object. Additional classes derived from CDC encapsulate specialized DC functionality, including support for Windows metafiles. Table 3.2 lists the MFC DC classes.

Table 3.2 MFC DC Classes

Class	Description
CDC	The base class for DCs. Used directly for accessing the whole display and for accessing nondisplay contexts such as printers.
CPaintDC	A display context used in *OnPaint* member functions of windows. Automatically calls *BeginPaint* on construction and *EndPaint* on destruction.
CClientDC	A display context for client areas of windows. Used, for example, to draw in an immediate response to mouse events.
CWindowDC	A display context for entire windows, including both the client and nonclient areas.
CMetaFileDC	A DC for Windows metafiles. A Windows metafile contains a sequence of GDI commands that can be replayed to create an image. Calls made to the member functions of CMetaFileDC are recorded in a metafile.

Table 3.3 lists related MFC classes.

Table 3.3 Related MFC Classes

Class	Description
CPoint	Holds coordinate (x, y) pairs.
CSize	Holds distance, relative positions, or paired values.
CRect	Holds coordinates of rectangular areas.
CRgn	Encapsulates a GDI region for manipulating an elliptical, polygonal, or irregular area within a window. Used in conjunction with the clipping member functions in class CDC.
CRectTracker	Displays and handles the UI for resizing and moving rectangular objects.
CColorDialog	Provides a standard dialog box for selecting a color.
CFontDialog	Provides a standard dialog box for selecting a font.
CPrintDialog	Provides a standard dialog box for printing a file.

Table 3.4 lists MFC drawing tool classes. These classes encapsulate drawing tools that are used to draw on a DC.

Table 3.4 MFC Drawing Tool Classes

Class	Description
CGdiObject	The base class for GDI drawing tools.
CBrush	Encapsulates a GDI brush that can be selected as the current brush in a DC. Brushes are used for filling interiors of objects being drawn.
CPen	Encapsulates a GDI pen that can be selected as the current pen in a DC. Pens are used for drawing the border lines of objects.
CFont	Encapsulates a GDI font that can be selected as the current font in a DC.
CBitmap	Encapsulates a GDI bitmap, providing an interface for manipulating bitmaps.
CPalette	Encapsulates a GDI color palette for use as an interface between the application and a color output device such as a display.
CRectTracker	Displays and handles the UI for resizing and moving rectangular objects.

Printing and Print Preview Overview

MFC supports printing and print preview for your program's documents via the class CView. For basic printing and print preview, you can override the view class's *OnDraw* member function. That function can draw to the view on the screen, to a printer DC for an actual printer, or to a DC that simulates your printer on the screen. You can also add code to manage multipage document printing and preview, to paginate your printed documents, and to add headers and footers to them.

Windows implements device-independent display. In MFC, this means that the same drawing calls, in the *OnDraw* member function of your view class, are responsible for drawing on the display and on other devices such as printers. For print preview, the target device is a simulated printer output to the display.

Your Role in Printing vs. the Framework's Role

Your view class has the following responsibilities:

- Inform the framework how many pages are in the document.
- When asked to print a specified page, draw that portion of the document.
- Allocate and deallocate any fonts or other GDI resources needed for printing.
- If necessary, send any escape codes needed to change the printer mode before printing a given page, for example, to change the printing orientation on a per-page basis.

The framework's responsibilities are as follows:

- Display the Print dialog box.
- Create a CDC object for the printer.
- Call the *StartDoc* and *EndDoc* member functions of the CDC object.
- Repeatedly call the *StartPage* member function of the CDC object, inform the view class which page should be printed, and call the *EndPage* member function of the CDC object.
- Call overridable functions in the view at the appropriate times.

How Default Printing Is Done

In MFC applications, the view class has a member function named *OnDraw* that contains all the drawing code. *OnDraw* takes a pointer to a CDC object as a parameter. That CDC object represents the DC to receive the image produced by *OnDraw*. When the window displaying the document receives a WM_PAINT message, the framework calls *OnDraw* and passes it a DC for the screen (a CPaintDC object, to be specific). Accordingly, *OnDraw's* output goes to the screen.

In programming for Windows, sending output to the printer is similar to sending output to the screen. This is because the Windows GDI is hardware-independent. You can use the same GDI functions for screen display or for printing simply by using the appropriate DC. If the CDC object that *OnDraw* receives represents the printer, *OnDraw's* output goes to the printer.

This explains how MFC applications can perform simple printing without requiring extra effort on your part. The framework takes care of displaying the Print dialog box and creating a DC for the printer. When the user selects the Print command from the File menu, the view passes this DC to *OnDraw*, which draws the document on the printer.

However, be aware of some significant differences between printing and screen display. When you print, you have to divide the document into distinct pages and display them one at a time, rather than display whatever portion is visible in a window. As a corollary, you have to be aware of the size of the paper (whether it's letter size, legal size, or an envelope). You might want to print in different orientations, such as landscape or portrait mode. The MFC library can't predict how your application will handle these issues, so it provides a protocol for you to add printing capabilities.

Printing Protocol

To print a multipage document, the framework and view interact in the following manner. First the framework displays the Print dialog box, creates a DC for the printer, and calls the *StartDoc* member function of the CDC object. Then, for each page of the document, the framework calls the *StartPage* member function of the CDC object, instructs the view object to print the page, and calls the *EndPage* member function. If the printer mode must be changed before starting a particular page, the view object sends the appropriate escape code by calling the *Escape* member function of the CDC object. When the entire document has been printed, the framework calls the *EndDoc* member function.

Overriding View Class Functions

The CView class defines several member functions that are called by the framework during printing. By overriding these functions in your view class, you provide the connections between the framework's printing logic and your view class's printing logic. Table 3.5 lists these member functions.

Table 3.5 CView's Overridable Functions for Printing

Function	Reason for overriding
OnPreparePrinting	To insert values in the Print dialog box, especially the length of the document
OnBeginPrinting	To allocate fonts or other GDI resources
OnPrepareDC	To adjust attributes of the DC for a given page, or to do print-time pagination
OnPrint	To print a given page
OnEndPrinting	To deallocate GDI resources

You can do printing-related processing in other functions as well, but the functions listed in Table 3.5 drive the printing process.

Figure 3.4 illustrates the steps involved in the printing process and shows where each of CView's printing member functions are called. (Note that, as cited in the figure, WYSIWYG stands for "what you see is what you get.")

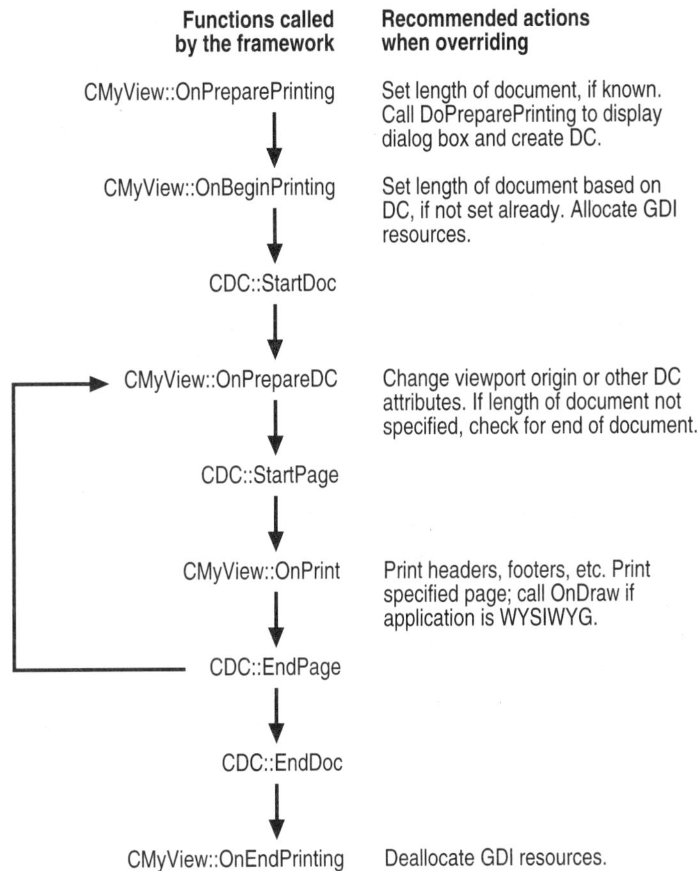
Functions called by the framework
Recommended actions when overriding
CMyView::OnPreparePrinting
Set length of document, if known. Call DoPreparePrinting to display dialog box and create DC.
CMyView::OnBeginPrinting
Set length of document based on DC, if not set already. Allocate GDI resources.
CDC::StartDoc
CMyView::OnPrepareDC
Change viewport origin or other DC attributes. If length of document not specified, check for end of document.
CDC::StartPage
CMyView::OnPrint
Print headers, footers, etc. Print specified page; call OnDraw if application is WYSIWYG.
CDC::EndPage
CDC::EndDoc
CMyView::OnEndPrinting
Deallocate GDI resources.

Figure 3.4 Printing loop

Pagination

The framework stores much of the information about a print job in a CPrintInfo structure. Several of the values in CPrintInfo pertain to pagination; these values are accessible and are shown in Table 3.6, on the next page.

Table 3.6 Page Number Information Stored in CPrintInfo

Member variable or function	Page number referenced
GetMinPage/SetMinPage	First page of document
GetMaxPage/SetMaxPage	Last page of document
GetFromPage	First page to be printed
GetToPage	Last page to be printed
m_nCurPage	Page currently being printed

Page numbers start at 1; that is, the first page is numbered 1, not 0. For more information about these and other members of CPrintInfo, see the *Visual C++ 6.0 Class Library Reference*.

At the beginning of the printing process, the framework calls the view's *OnPreparePrinting* member function, passing a pointer to a CPrintInfo structure. AppWizard provides an implementation of *OnPreparePrinting* that calls *DoPreparePrinting,* another member function of CView. *DoPreparePrinting* is the function that displays the Print dialog box and creates a printer DC.

At this point, the application doesn't know how many pages are in the document. It uses the default values 1 and 0xFFFF for the numbers of the first and last page of the document. If you know how many pages your document has, override *OnPreparePrinting* and call *SetMaxPage* for the CPrintInfo structure before you send it to *DoPreparePrinting*. This lets you specify the length of your document.

DoPreparePrinting then displays the Print dialog box. When it returns, the CPrintInfo structure contains the values specified by the user. If the user wants to print only a selected range of pages, he or she can specify the starting and ending page numbers in the Print dialog box. The framework retrieves these values using the *GetFromPage* and *GetToPage* functions of CPrintInfo. If the user doesn't specify a page range, the framework calls *GetMinPage* and *GetMaxPage* and uses the values returned to print the entire document.

For each page of a document to be printed, the framework calls two member functions in your view class, *OnPrepareDC* and *OnPrint*, and passes each function two parameters: a pointer to a CDC object and a pointer to a CPrintInfo structure. Each time the framework calls *OnPrepareDC* and *OnPrint*, it passes a different value in the *m_nCurPage* member of the CPrintInfo structure. In this way, the framework tells the view which page should be printed.

The *OnPrepareDC* member function is also used for screen display. It makes adjustments to the DC before drawing takes place. *OnPrepareDC* serves a similar role in printing, but a couple of differences exist: first, the CDC object represents a printer DC instead of a screen DC, and second, a CPrintInfo object is passed as a second parameter. (This parameter is NULL when *OnPrepareDC* is called for screen display.) Override *OnPrepareDC* to make adjustments to the DC based on which page is being printed. For example, you can move the viewport origin and the clipping region to ensure that the appropriate portion of the document gets printed.

The *OnPrint* member function performs the actual printing of the page. The *How Default Printing Is Done* subsection shows how the framework calls *OnDraw* with a printer DC to perform printing. More precisely, the framework calls *OnPrint* with a CPrintInfo structure and a DC, and *OnPrint* passes the DC to *OnDraw*. Override *OnPrint* to perform any rendering that should be done only during printing and not for screen display, such as printing headers or footers (see the Printing Headers and Footers subsection for more information). Next, call *OnDraw* from the override of *OnDraw* to do the rendering common to both screen display and printing.

The fact that *OnDraw* does the rendering for both screen display and printing means that your application is a WYSIWYG application. However, suppose you aren't writing a WYSIWYG application. For example, consider a text editor that uses a bold font for printing but displays control codes to indicate bold text on the screen. In such a situation, you use *OnDraw* strictly for screen display. When you override *OnPrint,* substitute the call to *OnDraw* with a call to a separate drawing function. That function draws the document the way it appears on paper, using the attributes that you don't display on the screen.

Printer Pages vs. Document Pages

When you refer to page numbers, it's sometimes necessary to distinguish between the printer's concept of a page and a document's concept of a page. From the point of view of the printer, a page is one sheet of paper. However, one sheet of paper doesn't necessarily equal one page of the document. For example, if you're printing a newsletter, where the sheets are to be folded, one sheet of paper might contain both the first and last pages of the document, side by side. Similarly, if you're printing a spreadsheet, the document doesn't consist of pages at all. Instead, one sheet of paper might contain rows 1 through 20, columns 6 through 10.

All the page numbers in the CPrintInfo structure refer to printer pages. The framework calls *OnPrepareDC* and *OnPrint* one time for each sheet of paper that will pass through the printer. When you override the *OnPreparePrinting* function to specify the length of the document, you must use printer pages. If a one-to-one correspondence exists (that is, one printer page equals one document page), then this is easy. On the other hand, if document pages and printer pages do not directly correspond, you must translate between them. For example, consider printing a spreadsheet. When overriding *OnPreparePrinting,* you must calculate how many sheets of paper will be required to print the entire spreadsheet and then use that value when calling the *SetMaxPage* member function of CPrintInfo. Similarly, when overriding *OnPrepareDC,* you must translate *m_nCurPage* into the range of rows and columns that will appear on that particular sheet and then adjust the viewport origin accordingly.

Print-Time Pagination

In some situations, your view class might not know in advance how long the document is until it has actually been printed. For example, suppose your application isn't WYSIWYG, so a document's length on the screen doesn't correspond to its length when printed.

This causes a problem when you override *OnPreparePrinting* for your view class: you can't pass a value to the *SetMaxPage* function of the CPrintInfo structure, because you don't know the length of a document. If the user doesn't specify a page number to stop at using the Print dialog box, the framework doesn't know when to stop the print loop. The only way to determine when to stop the print loop is to print out the document and see when it ends. Your view class must check for the end of the document during its printing, and then inform the framework when the end is reached.

The framework relies on your view class's *OnPrepareDC* function to tell it when to stop. After each call to *OnPrepareDC,* the framework checks a member of the CPrintInfo structure called *m_bContinuePrinting*. Its default value is TRUE. As long as it remains so, the framework continues the print loop. If it is set to FALSE, the framework stops. To perform print-time pagination, override *OnPrepareDC* to check whether the end of the document has been reached, and set *m_bContinuePrinting* to FALSE when it has.

The default implementation of *OnPrepareDC* sets *m_bContinuePrinting* to FALSE if the current page is greater than 1. In other words, if the length of the document wasn't specified, the framework assumes the document is one page long. You must be careful if you call the base class version of *OnPrepareDC*; you should also not assume that *m_bContinuePrinting* will be TRUE after calling the base class version.

Printing Headers and Footers

When you look at a document on the screen, the name of the document and your current location in the document are commonly displayed in a title bar and a status bar. When looking at a printed copy of a document, you'll find it useful to have the name and page number shown in a header or footer. This is a common way in which even WYSIWYG programs differ in how they perform printing and screen display.

The *OnPrint* member function is the appropriate place to print headers or footers because it is called for each page, and because it is called only for printing, not for screen display. You can define a separate function to print a header or footer, and pass it the printer DC from *OnPrint*. You might need to adjust the window origin or extent before calling *OnDraw* to avoid having the body of the page overlap the header or footer. You might also have to modify *OnDraw* because the amount of the document that fits on the page could be reduced.

One way to compensate for the area taken by the header or footer is to use the *m_rectDraw* member of CPrintInfo. Each time a page is printed, this member is initialized with the usable area of the page. If you print a header or footer before printing the body of the page, you can reduce the size of the rectangle stored in *m_rectDraw* to account for the area taken by the header or footer. Afterwards, *OnPrint* can refer to *m_rectDraw* to find out how much area remains for printing the body of the page.

You cannot print a header, or anything else, from *OnPrepareDC,* because it is called before the *StartPage* member function of CDC has been called. At that point, the printer DC is considered to be at a page boundary. You can perform printing only from the *OnPrint* member function.

Allocating GDI Resources When Printing

Suppose you need to use certain fonts, pens, or other GDI objects for printing, but not for screen display. As a result of the memory that these GDI objects require, it's inefficient to allocate these objects when the application starts up. When not printing a document, the application might need the GDI memory for other purposes. It's more efficient for you to allocate your GDI resources when printing begins, and then delete them when printing ends.

To allocate these GDI objects, override the *OnBeginPrinting* member function. This function is well suited to allocate GDI resources for two reasons: the framework calls this function one time at the beginning of each print job and, unlike *OnPreparePrinting*, this function has access to the CDC object representing the printer device driver. You can store these objects for use during the print job by defining member variables in your view class that point to GDI objects (for example, *CFont* * members, and so on).

To use the GDI objects you've created, select them into the printer DC in the *OnPrint* member function. If you need different GDI objects for different pages of the document, you can examine the *m_nCurPage* member of the *CPrintInfo* structure and select the GDI object accordingly. If you need a GDI object for several consecutive pages, Windows requires that you select it into the DC each time *OnPrint* is called.

To deallocate these GDI objects, override the *OnEndPrinting* member function. The framework calls this function at the end of each print job, giving you the opportunity to deallocate printing-specific GDI objects before the application returns to other tasks.

Print Preview Architecture

Print preview is somewhat different from screen display and printing because, instead of directly drawing an image on a device, the application must simulate the printer using the screen. To accommodate this, the MFC library defines a special class derived from CDC, called CPreviewDC. All CDC objects contain two DCs, but usually they are identical. In a CPreviewDC object, they are different: the first represents the printer being simulated, and the second represents the screen on which output is actually displayed.

Print Preview Process

When a user selects the Print Preview command on the File menu, the framework creates a CPreviewDC object. Whenever your application performs an operation that sets a characteristic of the printer DC, the framework also performs a similar operation on the screen DC. For example, if your application selects a font for printing, the framework selects a font for screen display that simulates the printer font. Whenever your application sends output to the printer, the framework instead sends the output to the screen.

Print preview also differs from printing in that each draws the pages of a document. During printing, the framework continues a print loop until a certain range of pages has been rendered. During print preview, one or two pages are displayed at any time, and then the application waits; no further pages are displayed until the user responds. During print preview, the application must also respond to WM_PAINT messages, just as it does during ordinary screen display.

The *OnPreparePrinting* function is called when preview mode is invoked, just as it is at the beginning of a print job. The CPrintInfo structure passed to the function contains several members, which have values that you can set to adjust certain characteristics of the print preview operation. For example, you can set the *m_nNumPreviewPages* member to specify whether you want to preview the document in one- or two-page mode.

Modifying Print Preview

You can easily modify the behavior and appearance of print preview in a number of ways, including the following:

- By causing the print preview window to display a scroll bar for easy access to any page of the document
- By forcing print preview to maintain the user's position in the document by beginning its display at the current page
- By performing different initializations for print preview and printing
- By setting print preview to display page numbers in your own formats

If you know the document's length, and call *SetMaxPage* with the appropriate value, the framework can use this information in preview mode as well as during actual printing. When the framework knows the length of the document, it can provide the preview window with a scroll bar, allowing a user to page back and forth through the document in preview mode. If you haven't set the length of the document, the framework cannot position the scroll box to indicate the current position, so the framework doesn't add a scroll bar. In this case, the user must use the Next Page and Previous Page buttons on the preview window's control bar to page through the document.

For print preview, you might find it useful to assign a value to the *m_nCurPage* member of CPrintInfo, even though you would never do so for ordinary printing. During ordinary printing, this member carries information from the framework to your view class and causes the framework to instruct the view which page should be printed.

In contrast, when print preview mode is started, the *m_nCurPage* member carries information in the opposite direction: from the view to the framework. The framework uses the value of this member to determine which page should be previewed first. The default value of this member is 1, so the first page of the document is displayed initially. You can override *OnPreparePrinting* to set this member to the number of the page being viewed at the time the Print Preview command was invoked. In this manner, the application maintains the user's current position when moving from normal display mode to print preview mode.

Sometimes you might want *OnPreparePrinting* to perform different initialization depending on whether it is called for a print job or for print preview. You can determine this by examining the *m_bPreview* member variable in the CPrintInfo structure. This member is set to TRUE when print preview is invoked.

The CPrintInfo structure also contains a member named *m_strPageDesc*, which is used to format the strings displayed at the bottom of the screen in single-page and multiple-page modes. By default these strings are of the form "Page *n*" and "Pages *n–m*," but you can modify *m_strPageDesc* from within *OnPreparePrinting* and set the strings to something more elaborate. For additional information, see CPrintInfo in the *Class Library Reference* within the Visual C++ 6 documentation.

Using ATL

ATL is a set of template-based C++ classes with which you can easily create small, fast COM objects. ATL has special support for key COM features including stock implementations of IUnknown, IClassFactory, IClassFactory2 and IDispatch; dual interfaces; standard COM enumerator interfaces; connection points; tear-off interfaces; and ActiveX controls.

You can use ATL code to create single-threaded objects, apartment-model objects, free-threaded model objects, or both free-threaded and apartment-model objects.

Template Libraries vs. Standard C++ Libraries

A template is similar to a macro. As with a macro, invoking a template causes it to expand (with appropriate parameter substitution) to code you have written.

However, a template additionally allows the creation of new classes based on types that you pass as parameters. These new classes implement type-safe ways of performing the operation expressed in your template code.

Template libraries such as ATL differ from traditional C++ class libraries in that they are typically supplied only as source code (or as source code with a little supporting run time) and are not inherently or necessarily hierarchical in nature. Rather than deriving from a class to get the functionality you desire, you instantiate a class from a template.

ATL Features and Limitations

ATL allows you to easily create COM objects, Automation servers, and ActiveX controls. ATL provides built-in support for many fundamental COM interfaces.

ATL is shipped as source code that you include in your application. ATL also makes a DLL available (atl.dll), which contains code that can be shared across components. However, this DLL is not necessary.

When to Use ATL, MFC, or Nothing at All

When developing components and applications, you can choose among three approaches—straight hand-coding, MFC, and ATL.

Advantages and Disadvantages of Hand-Coding

Two primary advantages of expert hand-coding are that the code is lean and tight, and you don't need additional run-time libraries unless you want them. Therefore, if you are a competent C++ programmer writing a COM object, you can be sure when you finish that the footprint of the object is as small as it can be. You also can be sure that it will work exactly as you programmed it.

You should probably not always hand-code your applications, COM objects, and ActiveX controls, largely because you want to finish your projects in a reasonable amount of time. When faced with a choice between hand-coding several thousand lines of code and using a library such as MFC to create those lines of code automatically, most programmers will choose to use the MFC library. Additionally, most libraries have been debugged and tested by scores of programmers, so you can be reasonably sure that the code that MFC creates is stable.

Advantages and Disadvantages of MFC

MFC allows you to create full applications, ActiveX controls, and active documents. As noted previously, MFC can save you countless hours of programming time through its inclusion of standard Windows programming tasks. Because the MFC code has been extensively tested and debugged as mentioned, you can focus your testing and debugging efforts on the non-MFC parts of your code.

The upside of MFC is also its downside. Unfortunately, the multifunctionality of MFC accompanics a fairly large and slow run-time library.

If you have already created a control with MFC, you might want to continue development in MFC. When creating a new control, consider using ATL if you don't need MFC's built-in functionality.

Advantages of ATL

ATL is an excellent compromise between hand-coding and MFC. For a COM object, you must have an implementation for every method of every interface you include in your programs. For a visual ActiveX control, more than 12 interfaces exist, each containing numerous methods. Programming a visual ActiveX control by hand is not a small job. For this control, ATL can create all of these methods and their implementations, without the overhead of the MFC run time and any extraneous code that MFC would include.

Using STL

No discussion of Visual C++ libraries would be complete without a mention of STL. A limitation of C++ has been its lack of common, generic structures for use in programs. As a result, programmers have been reinventing the wheel for years by coding and recoding common tasks such as writing a binary tree.

STL provides C++ programmers with a library of common data structures and fundamental algorithms. Because STL is standardized, programmers can use STL secure in the knowledge that it has been widely tested. It was adopted into the draft standard at the July 14, 1994 ANSI/International Standards Organization (ISO) C++ Standards Committee meeting, and is now included in every major version of C++.

STL is especially useful when combined with ATL. A programmer working with an ATL project might need to add some functionality normally found in MFC. If the functionality is also in STL, it makes more sense to use STL to avoid including MFC in its entire, simply to attain one piece of functionality.

The Visual C++ implementation of STL contains 13 library headers as shown in Table 3.7 on the next page.

Table 3.7 STL Library Headers

Library header	Description
<algorithm>	Numerous templates that implement useful algorithms
<deque>	Template class that implements a deque container
<functional>	Several templates that help construct predicates for the templates defined in <algorithm> and <numeric>
<iterator>	Several templates that help define and manipulate iterators
<list>	Template class that implements a list container
<map>	Template classes that implement associative containers
<memory>	Several templates that allocate and free storage for various container classes
<numeric>	Several templates that implement useful numeric functions
<queue>	Template class that implements a queue container
<set>	Template classes that implement associative containers with unique elements
<stack>	Template class that implements a stack container
<utility>	Several templates of general utility
<vector>	Template class that implements a vector container

Lesson Summary

This lesson examined some of the libraries and templates that ship with Visual C++. Specifically examined was the MFC library; this lesson discussed the advantages and disadvantages of using MFC to build your applications. You considered the document/view architecture for applications, which separates a program's data from the display of that data from most user interaction with the data. You looked at how MFC works with the GDI to manage screen drawing and manipulation, and you also examined how MFC handles printing and print preview.

You then turned your attention to ATL and its strengths and weaknesses with respect to MFC and hand coding. You saw how ATL should usually be your first choice for building COM components, especially when your goal is to produce a component with a small footprint and low overhead.

Finally, you examined STL, included in most C++ products, and the specific implementation of STL within Visual C++.

Lesson 2: Thread Management

It is entirely possible to write numerous lines of code and many applications over time and never have to worry about threading or thread management. However, you will, in your programming career, most likely face a design issue or problem that can be solved only by the intelligent use and management of multiple, concurrent threaded processes. When that time comes, you will be appreciative of the power and flexibility threading can give you.

This chapter will examine the various threading models and apartments you can use in C++. You will also consider various issues related to thread management, including prioritizing, in- or out-of-process threads, and interaction with other systems.

After this lesson, you will be able to:

- Understand the single-threaded apartment (STA) memory model
- Understand the multithreaded apartment (MTA) memory model
- Analyze a programming task and apply the appropriate memory model

Estimated lesson time: 15 minutes

Threading Models

Before you look at the two threading models, you need to be aware of some fundamental terms and concepts.

A *thread* is simply a path of execution through a process. Every process running in Windows has one or more threads of execution. When you create any application in C++, the application automatically has at least one thread. *Multithreaded* refers to a process that has two or more paths of command execution occurring at the same time. *Single-threaded*, on the other hand, refers to a process with only one path of command execution. Keep in mind that the system executes only threads, not processes, even though you might tend to think and talk as if the process is what is being executed.

Multithreaded applications are somewhat more difficult to write, because you must put some thought into how to synchronize the work of the various threads. But as stated in the lesson introduction, certain performance and usability issues can be solved only through the use of multiple threads.

For example, suppose you are writing a word processor, and you want it to be able to print. You write a print routine, test it, and assume that feature is completed. A problem arises when users print a document, and then realize the application is unusable until the print routine finishes and returns. The users complain vociferously as they must wait for the printing to complete before continuing.

Thus, reality points out that a separate thread is needed for the printing process, so processing can be returned to the main application thread as the printing takes place.

To write this new printing thread, the first decision to make is which threading model to use: *UI* or *worker threads.* UI threads are intended for user interaction, whereas worker threads are intended to work in the background without user interaction.

The *UI threading model* creates its own window, and therefore has its own message loop, which is used to communicate with the window. You can choose this threading model for applications that require multiple top-level windows. Windows Explorer actually uses this model whenever a second window is opened—the secondary windows are created as secondary UI threads.

The worker thread, on the other hand, creates no window and therefore has no window message loop. Worker threads are usually easier to program, and will form the bulk of secondary threads used within an application. Their inability to process messages, though, indicates that other communication means are required, which can present certain difficulties unique to worker threads.

One of the key issues in working with threads is *thread synchronization,* also known as writing code where the work of one thread doesn't stomp, obliterate, or otherwise mess up the work of another thread. Whenever two or more threads are working with the same data, you have to synchronize or coordinate their access to that data; otherwise, you risk data corruption, computer failures, or hard-to-find bugs. Though you might think of multiple threads happening concurrently, they actually execute one after another in a round-robin fashion (unless you have multiple processors).

For example, suppose that a worker thread is running a query in the background against a data set. It begins reading in the data rows, but before it can finish, it is interrupted by the scheduler, which switches to the main thread where the user has just deleted a number of rows, some of which have already been read by the worker thread and some of which have not. Without proper synchronization of the two threads, you will either have suspect query results or computer failures. Such bugs can be difficult to track down simply because they will occur seemingly at random, caused solely by the timing of when the thread scheduler decides to switch threads. Your job is to make sure such an instance doesn't happen.

Thus, properly dealing with thread synchronization within your Visual C++ application provides code stability and a reliable, efficient application.

Apartments

Because Microsoft has added more and more threading support to Windows and to various programming languages, many have become concerned about the thread-unaware code that already existed, both in the operating system and in existing applications. To ensure interoperability between thread-unsafe code and the newer multithreaded applications (and components), Microsoft has thus introduced the concept of *apartments*.

An *apartment* is a basic unit of thread safety. Two types of apartments exist: STA and MTA. As the names imply, STAs can have only a single thread executing within the apartment, whereas MTAs can have multiple threads executing within the apartment. In addition, method calls to objects in an STA are automatically *serialized*, or kept in sequence as they come in, whereas calls to objects in an MTA are not.

STAs and MTAs can both be used in a single process; however, you should be aware of rules for doing so. A process must have at least one apartment, either an STA or an MTA. It can have as many STAs as you want, or none at all, but it can have only one MTA.

In the past, the possible combinations of STAs and MTAs within a single process had individual names: single (legacy), apartment, free, and mixed (both). You should be aware of these names, because you will still run across them; however, it is probably better at this point to simply remember the rules about mixing the two apartment types within a single process. Table 3.8 shows these earlier threading model names and the number of each apartment type in each named model.

Table 3.8 Various Threading Model Combinations

Earlier Threading Model Names	STAs	MTAs
Single (Legacy)	1	0
Apartment	1 or more	0
Free	0	1
Mixed (Both)	1 or more	1

STA Model

The STA model is a derivation of earlier Windows coding that was typically thread-unaware. The STA was a step to overcoming the single-threading limitation in that it allowed a given process to have multiple STAs executing at the same time. Currently, if legacy code is called from an application, it automatically runs in a single STA.

The type of apartment to be used is declared when the component is called by using two means. First, if an application initializes COM by calling *CoInitialize(NULL)*, an STA model is automatically used. If the calling application wants to explicitly state the apartment type, it uses *CoInitializeEx* and includes the apartment type as a parameter of the call, either COINIT_APARTMENT-THREADED for an STA or COINIT_MULTI-THREADED for an MTA.

When an STA object is instantiated, the thread that created the object will carry out all method calls to the object. The method calls are passed to the object via window messages; thus, the object must have a message loop using *GetMessage/ DispatchMessage* or other similar code. Note that even though window message queues are used to guarantee serialization, the component does not necessarily have to create a visible window. The first time *CoInitializeEx* is called, the system creates a hidden window for the STA, and then proceeds to use the message queue of this hidden window to synchronize and dispatch messages to the called component. Therefore, if multiple clients make calls to the object, the calls are automatically serialized within the queue, and retrieved in sequence by the server component.

MTA Model

Unlike legacy code, where the use of *CoInitialize* automatically creates an STA, an MTA model must be explicitly created by the use of *CoInitializeEx(NULL, COINIT_MULTI-THREADED)*. The first such call actually creates the MTA; subsequent calls simply join the existing MTA because processes can have only one MTA at a time.

An MTA component does not need a message handling routine, because it does not use messages to receive method calls. Instead, calls to methods within an MTA object are made directly through a vtable.

Because any client can call any method of an MTA object at any time, and because the operating system provides no serialization or synchronization for MTAs, it is the responsibility of the programmer to include thread synchronization routines for all MTA components. The methods available to the programmer include events, critical sections, mutexes, and semaphores.

Threads running within the same MTA can pass interface pointers directly, without worrying about marshalling. (Marshalling must still be used to pass pointers between an MTA and an STA, though.)

In-Process Threads

At this point, you might realize that you didn't declare a threading model within your code. Typically, you simply call *CoInitialize* and proceed. This programming model works if all you have written are in-process components and code.

The apartment models for in-process components are not declared using some form of *CoInitializeEx* simply because the client application will already have initialized COM by the time the object is instantiated. Instead, the component's threading model is set within the registry. Underneath the component's CLSID key, the ThreadingModel value can be set to Apartment, Free, or Both to show which model the component uses. If no ThreadingModel value exists, the component is assumed to be thread-unaware and will have an STA created for it.

Interactions among in-process components can become somewhat complex, depending on the threading model of each component. If the calling client and the in-process server component use the same threading model, calls are passed directly between the two components. On the other hand, if the two components use different threading models, COM must interpose itself between the two components so that concurrency problems do not develop.

Additional issues arise due to the way the objects are instantiated, which varies based on the threading model of both the calling component and the server component. In some cases, a new STA must be created, although in other instances an existing apartment will be used to contain the newly created object. The first STA created in a process is considered the *main STA*; all subsequent calls are then marshaled to this STA. Table 3.9 shows the various combinations of calling and server component threading models and where COM creates the new thread, as well as what access the calling component has to the instantiated object.

Table 3.9 Threading Model Combinations

ThreadingModel value	**Client's Threading Model**		
	Main STA	**STA**	**MTA**
None	Direct access; object instantiated in the main STA.	Proxy access; object instantiated in the main STA.	Proxy access; object instantiated in the main STA. The main STA is created by COM if necessary.
Apartment	Direct access; object instantiated in the main STA.	Direct access; object instantiated in the calling STA.	Proxy access; object instantiated in a new STA created automatically by COM.
Free	Proxy access; object instantiated in the MTA. The MTA is created by COM if necessary.	Proxy access; object instantiated in the MTA. The MTA is created by COM if necessary.	Direct access; object instantiated in the MTA.
Both	Direct access; object instantiated in the main STA.	Direct access; object instantiated in the calling STA.	Direct access; object instantiated in the MTA.

Out-of-Process Threads

Unlike the multiple issues noted previously when calling in-process components, calls among clients and out-of-process components are fairly straightforward. When the client instantiates an object, COM compares the two threading models. COM allows the components to proceed if the two models are the same. If the threading models are different, COM takes on the task of cross-process or cross-computer communication among the components, marshalling and synchronizing the calls as needed. Although this functionality of COM imposes a certain amount of system overhead, this ability of COM to manage interprocess communications nevertheless enables different threading model combinations to work together.

Lesson Summary

This lesson discussed the basic threading models, which you will most likely encounter when creating an application and interacting with COM components. Each different threading model provides its own benefits from the ease of implementation of the STA model to the processing power of an MTA. In addition to the threading model of your application, you must also understand how the application will interact with components. These components can execute within the same process, in-process, in different processes, or on different out-of-process servers.

Lesson 3: Memory Management and System Services

Memory management, although much easier under Visual C++, is still an important skill for programmers to master. The Win32 memory model has eliminated much of the work that was inherent in the 16-bit world, yet you still have memory leaks, general protection faults, and inefficient use of memory.

In this lesson, you will learn about stacks, heaps, and when and how to use each. You will examine memory leaks and what causes them. Finally, you will outline the various system services available under Windows NT, so that you can understand what the operating system provides and how it actually handles your application's memory usage.

After this lesson, you will be able to:

- Describe the difference between stacks and heaps
- Outline what happens when you instantiate a new object
- Determine how and why you would use the *new* and *delete* operators
- List causes of memory leaks and other memory usage problems

Estimated lesson time: 25 minutes

Some Basic Concepts

Before you can understand the finer points of memory allocation, deallocation, and management in C++, you must learn some basic concepts. These concepts include two primary areas of memory you can use, and what happens when you instantiate an object.

Stacks and Heaps

C++ contains two primary memory areas that can be managed from within an application. One of these is the *stack frame,* usually called simply the *stack*. The other is the *free store,* typically called the *heap*.

The stack is an area of memory automatically allocated whenever a function is called. The stack is used for a number of purposes, including holding the values of variables used by the function and storing the memory address of the next execution point of the code that called the function.

The stack is a Last-In/First-Out mechanism, meaning that normally the last values pushed onto the stack must be popped off the stack in sequence. The analogy that is often used is of a stack of dishes: to get to the fourth plate from the top, you must take off the three before it in sequence. The problem with this analogy is that unlike the real-life stack of dishes, where you cannot take one dish out of the middle, a changeable stack pointer working with the stack frame points to the top of the stack.

Essentially, when a function is called within an application, the current execution address of the calling program is pushed onto the stack. If parameters are passed into the function, these values are also pushed onto the stack; and, if variables exist within the function, they are also pushed onto the stack (unless you force the issue, as you'll see later). If the function you have called proceeds to call another function, the process repeats itself: the address, parameters, and variables are pushed onto the stack, before the values from the first function.

When execution returns from a called function, the stack pointer is reset to the location where the prior execution point was stored, making the stack space before the reset location available. In other words, the elements allocated in that stack space are deleted. This process is called *unwinding the stack,* or simply stack unwinding.

You should remember that when a function completes, the stack is unwound and everything put on the stack by that function is deleted. This is why variables are not available after they have gone out of scope—they've been popped off the stack. It is possible to force stack unwinding by enclosing code within nested braces. As a side note, if you create a *static* variable, it doesn't go on the stack.

The other area of memory that can be manipulated within an application is the heap. The heap is reserved for the memory allocation requirements of the application, and is separate from the program code and the stack. The total size of objects allocated on the heap is limited only by the computer system's available virtual memory.

Typical C programs use the functions *malloc* and *free* to allocate and deallocate heap memory. In C++, you use the built-in operators *new* and *delete* to allocate and deallocate objects in heap memory. The *malloc* and *free* functions still exist, but in almost every instance, they should be abandoned in favor of the *new/delete* combination. To further understand the need for *new/delete,* you need to understand what happens when an object is instantiated in C++.

Life of an Object

Much of the programming task in Visual C++ consists of instantiating, managing, and destroying objects. To be effective in the management of memory, you must understand what happens throughout the life of an object.

Whenever an object is instantiated, the class's *constructor* is called. If an explicit constructor was written for the class, that constructor is called. Without an explicit class constructor, the compiler generates a default one for you. This default constructor is then used whenever the object is instantiated. One additional feature of an explicit constructor is it can have arguments, but a default constructor accepts no arguments.

When an object goes out of scope, its *destructor* is automatically called. Again, if an explicit destructor was written, it will be used; if not, a default one will be created and used. Destructors, either explicit or default, never accept arguments.

Because a class can be either derived from another class or included as data members in your class, you should be aware of the chain of construction and destruction. When an object is created for a given class, memory is allocated for all the data members of the class. If a data member is a class, its constructors are called and memory is allocated for its data members as well. Remember that during construction, the data member constructors are called first. Also, when you create an object from a derived class, the memory for the object is set aside, then the base class's constructor is called, then the derived class's constructor. The entire chain is reversed for destruction.

Program efficiency implications exist regarding the way and order that constructors and destructors are coded, but discussing these implications is beyond the scope of this chapter.

Memory Allocation and Management

Basically, you must make a simple decision whenever a variable is dimensioned, a function called, or an object instantiated: Should stack memory or heap memory be used? By default, memory is allocated on the stack. However, when using *new,* memory is instead allocated on the heap. Although you have reasons to do both, you should more closely examine what happens when you use either *new* or *delete*.

When using *new* to allocate memory, the necessary memory is allocated on the heap, and a pointer to the newly allocated memory is returned. The pointer (stored in the pointer variable used in the *new* statement) is then pushed onto the stack. For example, raw storage could be allocated as follows:

```
char* pMyStorage = new char[1024];
```

Alternatively, you could instantiate a new object of the Car class as follows:

```
Car* pMyCar = new Car(color, make, model);
```

In both cases, the pointer is stored on the stack, and in the second case, an explicit constructor for the Car class was used, so arguments could be passed to the constructor.

Whether an object is instantiated on the heap (by using *new*) or on the stack, you do not have to explicitly state how much memory to allocate. The compiler simply looks at the code for the class and allocates enough memory for all the data members and variables within the class. No memory is preallocated for member functions.

Whenever you allocate memory on the heap (by using *new*), you must release that heap memory by using a matching *delete*. Thus, to get rid of your Car object and free up that memory on the heap, the following code could be used:

```
delete pMyCar;
```

The object itself is destroyed from the heap, by the *delete* and the pointer remains on the stack until the function or code block it is in goes out of scope. Most C experts advise following your *delete* call with code to set the pointer to NULL for safety's sake.

What happens if you use *new* without a matching *delete*? The pointer to your allocated memory disappears when it goes out of scope (pops off the stack), but the allocated memory still remains, with no means of accessing it. It cannot be used by anything else, nor can your program use it. Losing heap memory in this manner is called a *memory leak.*

The Debug version of MFC provides modified versions of *new* and *delete***.** When you use these Debug versions, you are able to take advantage of the class library's memory-management debugging enhancements, which can be useful in detecting memory leaks. When building an application with the release version of MFC, the standard versions of the *new* and *delete* operators provide an efficient way to allocate and deallocate memory (the release version of MFC does not provide modified versions of these operators).

Remember, if you do nothing, everything in your code will be created on the stack. To create something on the heap, you must explicitly use *new,* of course with a matching *delete*.

Determining an Allocation Method

Why choose one memory allocation method over another? The primary reason to allow the compiler to allocate memory on the stack is simplicity. Dimension a variable, or instantiate an object, and the compiler does the rest without concerns for memory leaks or memory pointers—clean and simple.

Two primary reasons exist for using *new* to put something on the heap. A subtle reason to use the heap is the size of the memory allocation being made. Remember, if you don't use *new*, the entire entity being allocated is created on the stack, even if it is a large object or array. Because memory for the stack is set aside by the operating system in pages, the operating system can be forced to allocate a new stack page (or even pages). A certain amount of overhead is associated with this stack page allocation, beyond normal stack use, and is greater than allocating the same amount of memory on the heap.

The most common reason to use the heap is control over scope. Remember that if something is created on the stack, it unwinds automatically as soon as the function or variable goes out of scope. On the other hand, if something is created on the heap, a pointer to it is received. Through this pointer, you can give the value of that pointer to another pointer outside the scope of your function or variable, and thus use the entity on the heap after the function or variable goes out of scope.

As a matter of practice, most programmers allow variables to be created on the stack (as long as the variables are not too big), but choose to instantiate all objects on the heap. Not only does this keep the stack space free for the activities it *has* to carry out (such as storing execution addresses), but by using the Debug versions of *new* and *delete*, the compiler automatically checks for *new* and *delete* matches, thus helping to eliminate memory leaks.

Memory Allocation/Deallocation Examples

Following are examples showing how MFC performs frame and heap allocations for each of the three typical kinds of memory allocation as follows:

- An array of bytes
- A data structure
- An object

Allocation of an Array of Bytes

To allocate an array of bytes on the frame, define the array as shown by the following code. The array is automatically deleted and its memory reclaimed when the array variable exits its scope.

```
{
    const int BUFF_SIZE = 128;
    // Allocate on the frame
    char myCharArray[BUFF_SIZE];
    int myIntArray[BUFF_SIZE];
    // Reclaimed when exiting scope
}
```

To allocate an array of bytes (or any primitive data type) on the heap, use the *new* operator with the array syntax shown in this example:

```
const int BUFF_SIZE = 128;
// Allocate on the heap
char* myCharArray = new char[BUFF_SIZE];
int* myIntArray = new int[BUFF_SIZE];
```

To deallocate the arrays from the heap, use the *delete* operator as follows:

```
delete[] myCharArray;
delete[] myIntArray;
```

Be sure to use *delete[]* (with brackets) to delete an array from the heap. Otherwise, all you will do is delete the first element of the array.

Allocation of a Data Structure

To allocate a data structure on the frame, define the structure variable as follows:

```
struct MyStructType {int topScore;};
void SomeFunc(void)
{
    // Frame allocation
    MyStructType myStruct;

    // Use the struct
    myStruct.topScore = 297;

    // Reclaimed when exiting scope
}
```

The memory occupied by the structure is reclaimed when it exits its scope.

To allocate data structures on the heap, use *new* to allocate data structures on the heap and *delete* to deallocate them, as shown by the following examples:

```
// Heap allocation
MyStructType* myStruct = new MyStructType;

// Use the struct through the pointer ...
myStruct->topScore = 297;

delete myStruct;
```

Allocation of an Object

To allocate an object on the frame, declare the object as follows:

```
{
CPerson myPerson;
    // Automatic constructor call here

myPerson.SomeMemberFunction();
    // Use the object

}
```

The destructor for the object is automatically invoked when the object exits its scope.

To allocate an object on the heap, use the *new* operator, which returns a pointer to the object, to allocate objects on the heap. Use the *delete* operator to delete them.

The following heap and frame examples assume that the CPerson constructor takes no arguments.

```
// Automatic constructor call here
CPerson* myPerson = new CPerson;

myPerson->SomeMemberFunction();
    // Use the object

delete myPerson;
    // Destructor invoked during delete
```

If the argument for the CPerson constructor is a pointer to char, the statement for frame allocation is as follows:

```
CPerson myPerson("Joe Smith");
```

The statement for heap allocation is as follows:

```
CPerson* MyPerson = new CPerson("Joe Smith");
```

Resizable Memory Blocks

The *new* and *delete* operators are good for allocating and deallocating fixed-size memory blocks and objects. Occasionally, an application might need resizable memory blocks. For this, you must use the standard C run-time library functions *malloc*, *realloc*, and *free* to manage resizable memory blocks on the heap.

Important Mixing the *new* and *delete* operators with the resizable memory-allocation functions on the same memory block will result in corrupted memory in the Debug version of MFC. You should not use *realloc* on a memory block allocated with *new*. Likewise, you should not allocate a memory block with the *new* operator and delete it with *free*, nor should you use the *delete* operator on a block of memory allocated with *malloc*.

Memory Management Problems and Issues

One of the biggest memory management issues involves *memory leaks*. As explained previously, a memory leak occurs whenever your program allocates memory on the heap, and then does something to lose or change the pointer to the allocated memory, thus losing connection to the memory block. The lost memory was allocated to your application, so that no other application can access it; your program can't access the memory, thus your application can't use it either. The memory is simply lost. If an application does this one time with a small amount of memory, the leak might not be especially harmful or even noticeable. On the other hand, if an application executes this leak repeatedly, it will eventually cause a problem, even if the size of the leak is small.

Often, programmers test with only a small data set, or for only a short time, small memory leaks don't become apparent during testing. Only when your program is used over time do the leaks show up.

Common causes of memory leaks include the following:

- **Calling *new* and never calling *delete*** If *delete* is never called, the variable simply goes out of scope and the pointer is lost.
- **Changing variables storing pointer values** Changing a pointer kept in a variable without deleting the original memory to which the pointer was pointing.
- **Mismatching versions of *new* and *delete*** Arrays created with *new* requires *delete[]*, not just *delete*.
- **Forgetting to properly dereference a pointer** Changing a pointer's address rather than changing the data to which it points will lose access to the data.
- **Throwing an exception before reaching the *delete*** Exceptions before a *delete* create a memory leak, even if the exception is handled gracefully.

You must keep your memory usage in the back of your mind whenever you are coding your error-trapping routines.

Other Memory Problems

Although memory leaks are often the most insidious memory problems you will confront, they are certainly not the only ones. Following are several memory issues that you might confront from time to time:

- **Forgetting to allocate memory at all** For instance, you create a pointer, but don't then use *new* to actually create an object in memory for the pointer to point to.
- **Going out of bounds on an array** For example, an array has 10 elements, and you try to get the value of element 20. Forgetting that the first element in an array is number 0 often causes this mistake.
- **Forgetting to walk the "chain of destruction" that occurs whenever an object is destroyed** If the object has members that are also objects, their destructors will also be called, sometimes leading to unwanted results.

- **Going out of bounds when putting something into a variable or buffer** For instance, you dimension a char with a size of 5, then try to load "Hello!" into it.
- **Assuming that memory actually got allocated** It is just good practice to include exception handling code to deal with an allocation that fails.

Lesson Summary

In this lesson, you learned that, in C++, you can manage two primary memory areas from within your program—the stack frame, or stack; and the free store, or heap. The stack frame is an area of memory that is automatically allocated whenever a function is called. The stack is used for a number of purposes, including holding the values of variables used by the function and storing the memory address of the next execution point of the code that called the function. When a function completes, the stack is unwound and everything put on the stack by that function is deleted.

The heap is reserved for the memory allocation needs of the program. It is an area apart from the program code and the stack. In C++, you use the built-in operators *new* and *delete* to allocate and deallocate objects in heap memory.

Whenever you instantiate an object, the class's *constructor* is called. If you have explicitly written a constructor for the class, that constructor is called. If your class does not have an explicit constructor, the compiler generates a default one for you, which is then used whenever the object is instantiated. When an object goes out of scope, its *destructor* is automatically called. Again, if you have included an explicit destructor, it will be used; if not, a default one will be created and used.

This lesson discussed either allowing the compiler to automatically allocate memory on the stack, or choosing to allocate memory on the heap by using *new*. The primary reason to allow the compiler to allocate memory on the stack is that it is simple. Dimension your variable or instantiate your object, and let the compiler do the rest. You don't have to worry about memory leaks or pointers—clean and simple.

The most common reason you would choose to use the heap is the control over scope that it can give you. Remember that if you create something on the stack, it unwinds automatically as soon as the function or variable goes out of scope, and you can do nothing about it. On the other hand, if you create something on the heap, you receive a pointer to it. If you can get the value of that pointer to another pointer outside the scope of your function or variable, you can use the entity on the heap after your function or variable goes out of scope.

This lesson also took a look at memory management problems and issues. One of the biggest memory management issues involves memory leaks. A memory leak occurs whenever your program allocates memory on the heap, and then does something to lose or change the pointer to the allocated memory, thus losing connection to the memory block. The memory is allocated to your program, so that no other program can use it; however, your program can't communicate with the memory, so your program can't use it either. The memory is simply lost.

Finally, this lesson examined the various system that Windows NT provides, including:

- **System services** Windows 32-bit applications run in separate application spaces to ensure that separate applications are protected from one another at all times.
- **Memory management** Windows NT provides each application with its own memory space and simplifies allocation and deallocation of memory.
- **Virtual memory services** An application does not directly access memory hardware; Windows NT manages the memory between physical memory and virtual memory stored on the hard drive.
- **File caching** Windows NT provides and manages file caching capabilities, thus keeping frequently accessed files stored in memory.

Review

The following questions are intended to reinforce key information presented in this chapter. If you are unable to answer a question, review the appropriate lesson and then try answering the question again. Answers to the questions can be found in Appendix B, "Review Questions and Answers," at the back of this book.

1. What is the MFC document/view architecture?

2. How can the *OnDraw* member function be used with printing and print preview?

3. Within thread management, what is an apartment?

4. Within thread management, what is an STA?

5. Within thread management, what is an MTA?

6. Within memory management, what is a stack frame?

7. Within memory management, what is a heap?

8. What are three common problems that cause memory leaks within an application?

CHAPTER 4

Developing User Services

Lesson 1: Creating Help Systems 132

Lesson 2: User Interface Navigation 142

Lesson 3: User Interface Forms and Dialog Boxes 163

Lesson 4: Creating and Using ActiveX Controls 176

Lab 4: Creating a User Interface 197

Review 214

About This Chapter

In this chapter, you will learn about creating various user interface (UI) controls in a Microsoft Windows application. These resources form the basis of the UI and simplify processes for users. You will also learn about help systems, a crucial but often neglected part of application development.

Before You Begin

To complete the lessons in this chapter, you must have installed the Microsoft Visual C++ development tools as described in Lab 2. You should also be somewhat familiar with the MFC document/view architecture.

Lesson 1: Creating Help Systems

An online help system is an important part of an application. Programmers often neglect online help systems, because implementing them is generally difficult.

Visual C++ simplifies the process of creating help systems by writing some of the help text for you.

After this lesson, you will be able to:

- Understand the different types of help systems
- Distinguish between various help system files
- Create an HTML Help system by using AppWizard

Estimated lesson time: 25 minutes

Help System Considerations

To design a simple, user-friendly help system, you should consider the types of help support that you can provide in your application. Help systems can be categorized based on the following:

- Types of help.
- The method used to invoke help files. For example, in a Windows environment, you can invoke help by clicking the Help icon or pressing F1.
- The appearance of a help system.

Help System Types

Help systems generally can be subcategorized into context-sensitive help, task-oriented help, reference help, and wizards. This section will examine each type of help system in brief.

Context-Sensitive Help

Context-sensitive help is used to display information about objects on the screen. Such objects include the controls in property pages and dialog boxes. Context-sensitive help is also used to answer questions such as "what does a button do?" In a Windows environment, a user can activate context-sensitive help by pressing the F1 key. In addition, right-clicking an item and then clicking the What's This? command can display context-sensitive help.

Task-Oriented Help

Task-oriented help explains how to accomplish a certain task, such as printing a document. This type of help must be included in applications that are used to perform a variety of tasks. You can use task-oriented help to provide beginning or novice users with an overview of steps involved in a complex task.

Reference Help

Reference help serves as a source for looking up information such as parameters, commands, or syntax. Reference help is intended for advanced users, such as programmers, who refer to parameters or syntax when writing programs.

Wizards

Wizards provide assistance to a user required to complete a task or a procedure. For example, AppWizard in Visual C++ assists the user to create a new project. A wizard hides the complexity of accomplishing a task by accepting simple details from a user, and then accomplishes the task based on the information that the user provides. You can use wizards in your application to help a user accomplish tasks that otherwise require considerable time and effort.

WinHelp Categories

Based on their appearances, Windows help systems can be categorized into the Help Topics dialog box, secondary help window, and pop-up window.

Help Topics Dialog Box

A Help Topics dialog box lets users scroll through an index, provides users with a table of contents, and allows users to search for specific words and phrases. Figure 4.1 shows an example of a Help Topics dialog box.

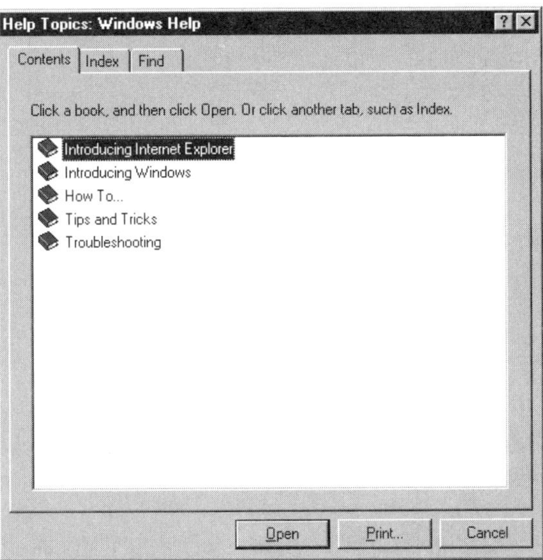

Figure 4.1 Help Topics dialog box

Secondary Help Window

A secondary help window has buttons such as Help Topics, Back, and Options. You can also resize secondary help windows. Figure 4.2 shows an example of such a help window.

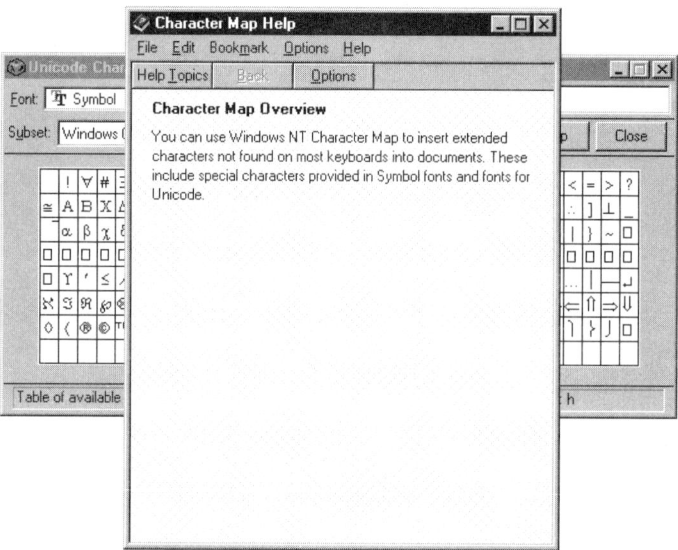

Figure 4.2 Secondary help window

Pop-Up Help Window

Pop-up help windows are smaller than ordinary help windows. They disappear when the user clicks anywhere on the screen. Figure 4.3 shows a sample pop-up help window.

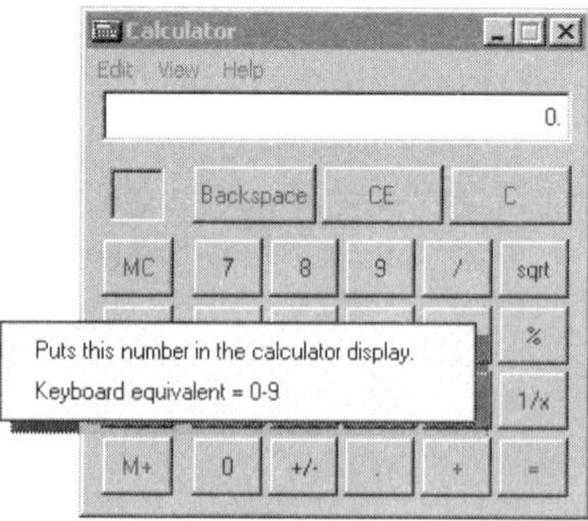

Figure 4.3 Pop-up help window

WinHelp Files

A WinHelp system for an application consists of a number of files. These files are compiled to form the Help file for the application.

.hlp

The file that users view within an application is a help file with the .hlp extension. This file contains the text and graphics to communicate online information about an application. An .hlp file contains one or more topics that a user can select by clicking hot spots in the help file. A user can either perform a keyword search or browse through topics. The help text for each help topic is contained in the text files with the .rtf extension covered later in this section. These files are in Rich Text Format (RTF) and contain encoded, formatted text for easy transfer among applications. In the case of creating HTML help, the compiled file has a .chm extension (.chm files are discussed later in the chapter).

.hm

The help map (.hm) file contains the help topic IDs corresponding to IDs of dialog boxes, menu commands, and other resources. Help topic IDs are the connections between your help text and help system. These IDs allow the help system to link a topic to a resource and display context-sensitive help for the resource. For example, to display context-sensitive help for a check box, the resource ID of the check box is mapped to the topic ID of the text file. This information is contained in the help map file.

.bmp

A help file can contain graphic files that are usually stored as bitmap files with the .bmp extension.

.cnt

A file with the extension .cnt has a table of contents used to create a Contents tab in a help system. The .cnt file creates the hierarchy of help topics that appears on the Contents tab of a help file. This file provides the structure for the Contents window in Windows Help.

.hpj

The help project file has the .hpj extension, and is used to compile the .hlp file. This file combines .hm and .rtf files to create an .hlp file when compiled.

.rtf

An .rtf file provides the structure for the Contents window in Windows Help. It contains the graphic images of a help topic. The .rtf file also maps the help topics IDs with resource IDs in addition to containing the text for each help topic.

HTML Help

In addition to creating WinHelp, you can create online help systems using Microsoft HTML Help, which is the standard help system for the Windows platform. Authors can use HTML Help to create online help for a software application or to create content for a multimedia title or Web site. Developers can use the HTML Help API to program a host application or hook up context-sensitive help to an application. You can use HTML Help to create a normal window or pop-up windows for your help system or Web site.

Note HTML Help pop-up windows are text-only and cannot contain formatted text, links to other topics, or links to images.

HTML Help Tools

In this section, you will examine the tools that Microsoft HTML Help provides.

HTML Help Workshop (Hhw.exe)

HTML Help Workshop is a help authoring tool that provides an easy-to-use graphical interface for creating HTML Help files, including Help project files, HTML topic files, contents files, and index files.

HTML Help ActiveX Control (HHCtrl.ocx)

This tool can be used for inserting features such as help navigation and secondary window functionality into an HTML file.

HTML Help Java Applet (HHCtrl.class and associated .class files)

These tools provide you with the facility to insert help navigation and secondary window functionality into an HTML page in case you want to use Java applets instead of a Microsoft ActiveX control.

HTML Help Image Editor (Flash.exe)

The Microsoft HTML Help Image Editor is used to create screenshots; convert, edit, and view image files; and browse thumbnail images.

HTML Help Authoring Guide

The HTML Help Authoring Guide provides online details for using HTML Help Workshop and designing a Help system. In addition, the guide provides a complete HtmlHelp API reference for developers and an HTML tag reference for authors.

HTML Help Viewer (Hh.exe)

HTML Help Viewer is the tool that displays and runs your help system. The help topics displayed in the HTML Help Viewer can use the HTML Help ActiveX control for navigational elements such as a table of contents, index, full-text search, or related topic jumps specified by the author that will be part of the help system.

Along with these tools, HTML Help provides two important features:

- The ability to convert existing Windows Help files to HTML Help files.
- The ability to compress your HTML files while compiling them into a single file. This feature greatly reduces the amount of disk space required for your HTML files and simplifies distribution. A compiled HTML Help file (.chm) plays the same role as a compiled Windows Help file (.hlp).

HTML Help Files

An HTML Help file is a combination of various files, reviewed in the following subsections.

.chm

The compiled HTML Help file has a .chm extension. This file contains the text and graphics to communicate online information about an application. HTML Help Workshop creates the .chm file when the HTML Help project file is compiled. This text file combines all the elements of a help project.

.htm or .html

The topic files in an HTML Help project, which contain the text for each help topic, are in HTML format and have an .htm extension or an .html extension.

.hhc

The HTML Help contents file, which has an .hhc extension, contains the topic titles for the table of contents in the help file.

.hhk

The HTML Help index file has an .hhk extension and contains the keywords for the index of the help file.

Implementing Help Systems

In MFC applications, you can provide two types of help: WinHelp and HTML Help. Until recently, all Windows applications used the WinHelp help system. However, Microsoft is currently using HTML Help systems in its latest applications and operating systems.

AppWizard creates a WinHelp help system if you select the Context-Sensitive Help check box while creating an application. You can later add your topic files to your WinHelp system as the files become available for use.

Creating a Compiled HTML Help File

You can create an HTML Help file by using HTML Help Workshop, which is shipped with Microsoft Visual Studio 6. To install the HTML Help Workshop, run Htmlhelp.exe, which is in the \HtmlHelp subdirectory on Disk 1 of your Visual Studio CD-ROMs.

► **To create an HTML Help file named TestHelp that is based on existing HTML files**

1. Start HTML Help Workshop.
2. Click New on the File menu.
3. In the New dialog box, select Project and click OK to create a new HTML Help project file.
4. A New Project wizard appears, helping you create an HTML Help project. You can also convert an existing WinHelp project into an HTML Help project by selecting the Convert WinHelp Project check box. To continue with the creation of a new HTML Help project, click Next.
5. HTML Help Workshop creates a help project file with an .hhp extension. This file is then compiled to form the help file, which has a .chm extension.
6. Type a location and a name for the project, and then click Next to open the New Project—Existing Files dialog box.
7. If you have already created the HTML, index, and contents files for the project, you can use the New Project—Existing Files dialog box to include the files in your help project. You can also add these files later. To add an HTML file to the project, select the HTML Files check box and click Next.
8. The New Project wizard displays a list in which you can add or remove HTML files. To add an HTML file, click Add.
9. Select the HTML file that you want in the New Project wizard's list. Click Next.
10. To create the help project, click Finish.
11. To compile the project, select compile from the File menu.
12. In the Create a Compiled File dialog box, click Compile. After it compiles successfully, the HTML Help Workshop will create a compiled HTML Help file with a .chm extension.

Adding HTML Help File Support to Visual C++ MFC Applications

By default, projects created in Visual C++ include support for WinHelp files. You can also include support for an HTML Help file by including the htmlhelp.lib and htmlhelp.h files from the HTML Help Workshop in your project.

► **To add HTML Help file support to an MFC project**

1. Start Visual C++ 6.0 and open the MFC project using the Open command on the File menu.
2. To add the htmlhelp.lib and htmlhelp.h files, edit the project's settings. To edit the project's settings, click Settings on the Project menu.
3. The Project Settings dialog box displays the project name and files in the left pane, and the project options in the right pane. To specify a library file to be included while linking, click the Link tab.
4. To specify input libraries, select the Input option from the Category drop-down list.
5. In the Object/Library Modules text box, specify the name of any object file or standard library to be used by the linker. Add *htmlhelp.lib* as a standard library.
6. Type the location of the library file in the Additional Library Path text box, which by default is *C:\Program Files\HTML Help Workshop*.
7. After specifying the library path, you will include the C++ header files. To specify additional include directories, click the C/C++ tab.
8. Select Preprocessor in the Category drop-down list.
9. You can specify the path to the directories containing the include files in the Additional Include Directories field. To specify the path to the htmlhelp.h file, type the path, which by default is *C:\Program Files\HTML Help Workshop* and click OK.
10. You now need to include the htmlhelp.h file in the application. You can do this by adding the header file to the StdAfx.h file. To include the header file htmlhelp.h, type the line *#include <htmlhelp.h>* and compile the project.

You have just added HTML help file support to an MFC application.

Adding Context-Sensitive Help to MFC Applications

Context-sensitive help is used to describe an object on the screen, including controls in property pages and dialog boxes. You can include context-sensitive help in your applications to make them user-friendly. Users can usually invoke context-sensitive help by pressing the F1 key.

► **To implement context-sensitive help to an MFC application**

1. To implement context-sensitive help for a resource, it is first necessary to create a text file containing the help text. Each resource should have a topic

associated with it. This text file should be included in the help project of the application. Format the topics as follows:

```
.topic 1
help text for control 1
.topic 2
help text for control 2
...
```

2. You now need to create a two-dimensional array that maps control IDs to help IDs (topic numbers). The array contains pairs of numbers; the first number is a resource ID and the second is a topic number from the context-sensitive help text file. If you do not want a specific resource to have context-sensitive help, type *–1* for its topic number. The following code is an example array for a single resource:

```
static DWORD myHelpArray[] = {IDC_CHECK1,1,0,0};
```

Note The last pair of numbers in the array should be 0,0.

---

3. Use ClassWizard to implement a message handler for the WM_HELPINFO message. This message will allow the user to press F1 to get context-sensitive help. Open ClassWizard by pressing CTRL+W.
4. To add the message handler for the WM_HELPINFO message, double-click the WM_HELPINFO option.
5. To edit the message handler for the WM_HELPINFO message, click the Edit Code button.
6. Edit the handler for the WM_HELPINFO message in the source file. In this handler, you will use the *HtmlHelp* function to call the .chm file when the user presses the F1 key. The code for the handler should look somewhat like the following:

```
if (pHelpInfo->iContextType == HELPINFO_WINDOW)
{
    return HtmlHelp((HWND)pHelpInfo->hItemHandle,
        "help.chm::/help.txt",
        HH_TP_HELP_WM_HELP,
        (DWORD)(LPVOID)myHelpArray) != NULL;
}
return TRUE;
```

7. When you are done, you can compile and execute the application.

Adding Links to the Web

In MFC applications, you can include HTML Help files. An advantage of using these files is that you can provide links to the files on the Web. You can create links to the Web-based help files and provide users with the latest help information about your applications.

► **To add a link from the word WebHelp to a file on the Web**

1. Open the HTML file that you want to provide a link to the Web.
2. Insert the word *WebHelp* and add an anchor cross-reference link from the word to a Web-based help file. The user will be able to click the link to access the Web page.
3. Save the HTML file and compile the HTML Help file. When you compile the HTML Help file, you will notice that the word WebHelp displays as hypertext. You can access the Web-based help file by clicking the WebHelp hyperlink.

Lesson Summary

In this lesson, you learned about various types of help systems, which are an important part of any Windows application. For most application developers, adding help for an application is their last task, because creating help files can be time-consuming. Visual C++ makes it easy to create help files.

Before you create a help file for your application, you will need to decide what type of help files to implement in the different sections of the application. You can implement pop-up windows, help topics dialog boxes and secondary help windows. You will also have to decide when to invoke the help files—when the F1 key is pressed or when a question button is clicked, and so on.

Once you have decided what type of help system is required for the application, you can create a simple, graphical, user-friendly help system and link it to your application. You can create WinHelp or HTML Help files using HTML Help Workshop. HTML Help provides most of the WinHelp features and adds support for HTML, ActiveX, Java, and HTML image formats. You can also add context-sensitive help to the application.

Lesson 2: User Interface Navigation

Navigating through UIs should be easy. This is an important aspect to be kept in mind by all application developers. To ease application development, Visual C++ provides various built-in classes to create UI elements, including menus, status bars, toolbars, and ToolTips. This lesson will discuss how to create such elements.

After this lesson, you will be able to:

- Create a static menu by using the menu editor
- Create and integrate toolbars in an MFC application
- Implement ToolTips for toolbar buttons
- Implement status bars

Estimated lesson time: 75 minutes

Creating Menus with the Menu Editor

Menus allow users to navigate high-level UI structures quickly. Menus have menu bars, menu items, and menu commands. Menu commands themselves can have submenus and can be made unavailable. Menus can also be checked and treated as radio controls.

You can easily create and maintain menu resources using the menu editor. The menu editor lets you add and remove menu headers and menu commands in a "what you see is what you get" (WYSIWYG) manner.

Adding New Menu Resources

When you create a single-document interface (SDI) or multiple-document interface (MDI) application using AppWizard, a default menu is created. This menu has an ID IDR_MAINFRAME. As a result, you will get an initial default menu from the view with an ID of IDR_MAINFRAME. If you want to add additional menus, you can add them by using the resource editor.

To determine whether to use an SDI or MDI architecture, keep in mind that the SDI architecture allows a user to work with only one document at a time. However, the MDI architecture allows a user to work with multiple documents at a time, with each document containing its own window.

► **To add a new menu resource**

1. Open a new or existing project in Visual C++ 6.0.
2. Display the project resources by clicking the ResourceView tab.
3. Right-click the top-level item and select the Insert option from the shortcut menu to display the Insert Resource dialog box, as shown in Figure 4.4.

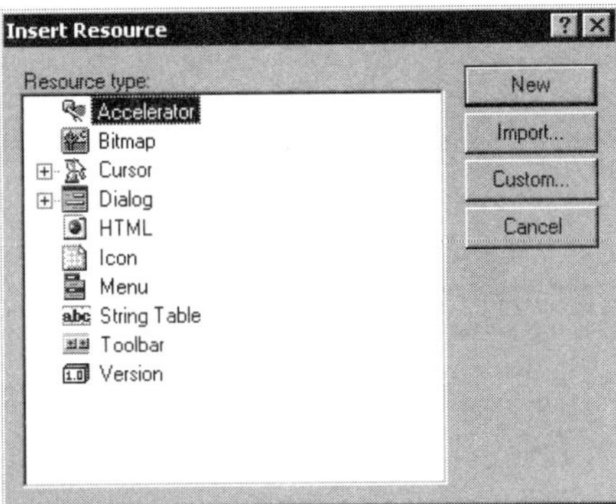

Figure 4.4 Insert Resource dialog box

4. Select Menu from the list of new resource types.
5. Click the New button to insert the new menu resource. Notice in Figure 4.5 that a new menu template appears under the Menu resources.

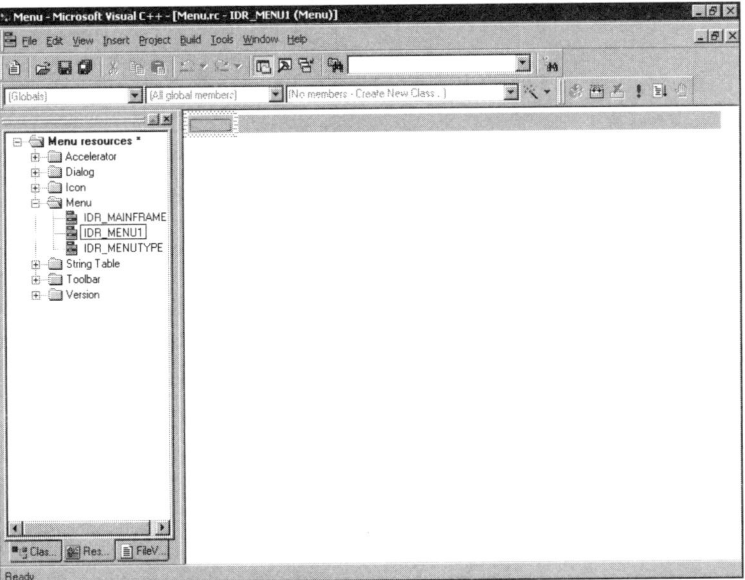

Figure 4.5 New menu template

6. Right-click the menu editor window and select Properties from the shortcut menu to display the Menu Item Properties dialog box, as shown in Figure 4.6 on the next page.

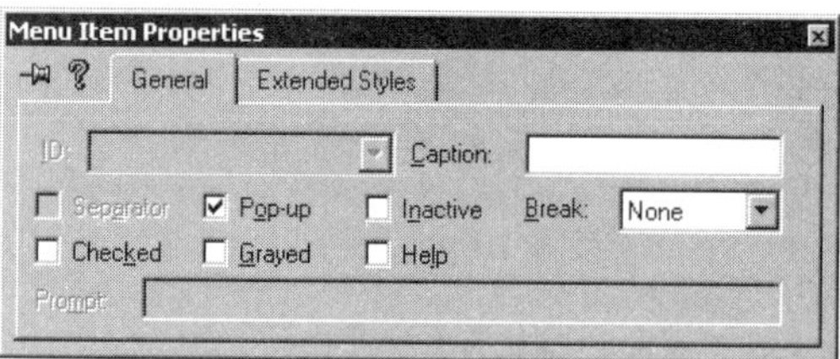

Figure 4.6 Menu Item Properties dialog box

7. You can now change the default ID name to a more appropriate name for your dialog box.

Adding Menus

After you have inserted a menu resource, you can add or edit menu headers in the menu editor window.

► **To insert a new menu**

1. Double-click the menu resource in the ResourceView pane. The menu appears in the menu editor window.
2. Click the menu header on the menu bar to select it. When selected, a white border appears around the menu header's rectangle, as shown in Figure 4.7.

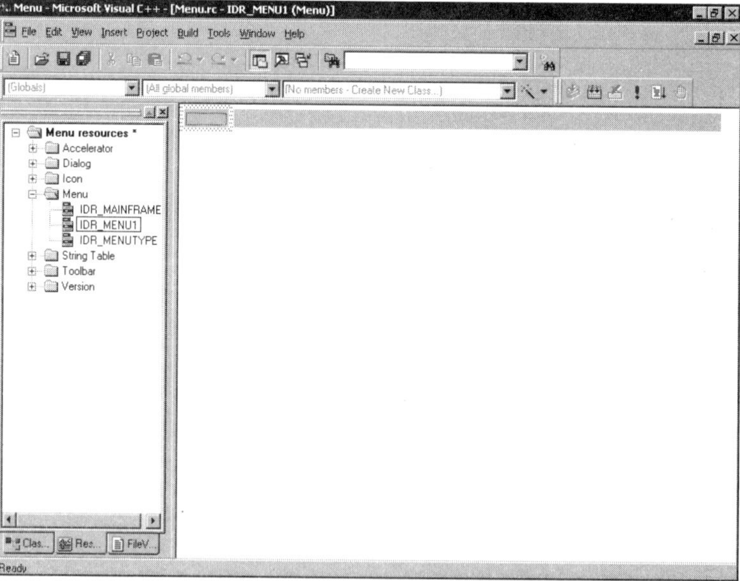

Figure 4.7 Selected menu

3. To add a new menu header, click the blank rectangle and type the name of the new menu header. The text for the new header name appears in the rectangle as you type. Also, a Menu Item Properties dialog box appears, as shown in Figure 4.8, along with a menu command box beneath the menu header.

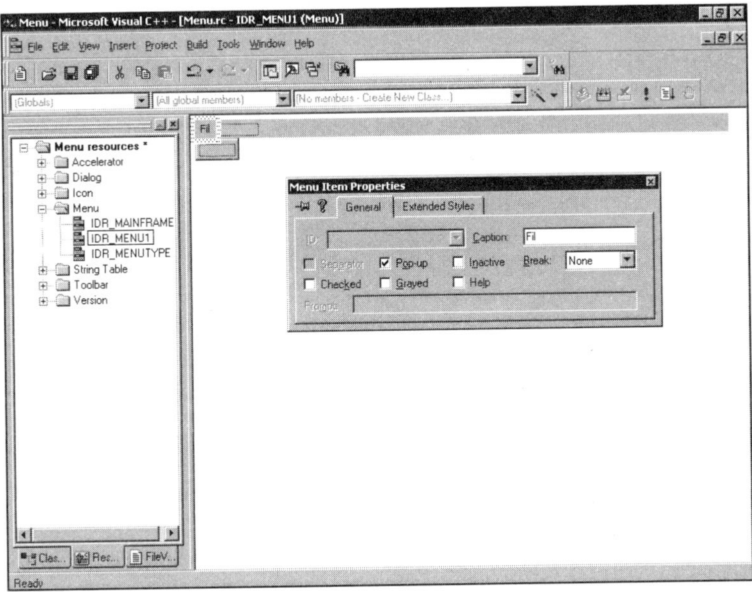

Figure 4.8 Another perspective of Menu Item Properties dialog box

4. Select any required property flags for the new menu header.
5. Press ENTER to complete the new menu header insertion.
6. Repeat steps 2 to 5 to add more menu headers.
7. Rearrange the order of the menu headers by dragging and dropping them in the desired location.

Adding Menu Commands

After adding menu headers, you can add menu commands within the headers.

► **To add a new menu command**

1. Select the menu header that will contain the new menu command, and then select the blank rectangle that appears.
2. Type the name of the new menu command. The name should appear in the rectangle as you type; also, the Menu Item Properties dialog box appears.
3. You can also add *separators* for the menu commands. For example, to specify a separator option, select the Separator check box from the Menu Item Properties dialog box.

4. In addition, you can specify the text that should appear in the status bar when the menu is active. This text can be added to the Prompt edit box.
5. You can also add a second string to the Prompt edit box after the first that will appear in a ToolTip over an associated toolbar icon. The strings are separated with a \n newline character. For example, to specify the status bar description of the menu as "Edit Text" and the ToolTip as "Edit," type *Edit Text\nEdit.*
6. Click the ID combo box. A default menu ID appears, based on the menu command and header name. If necessary, change this default ID for your application.
7. As you can with menu headers, you can drag and drop the new menu command into any position in the menu.

Assigning Command IDs

If you want to assign an existing ID to a menu command, you can select the appropriate ID from the ID combo box. This is helpful in case you want to share IDs among different menu resources. For example, your application might have two File menus: a standard File menu and an advanced File menu with additional commands. Because the commands on the standard menu have the same functionality as their counterparts on the advanced menu, you can assign a common ID to the shared commands. The shared IDs allow your program to call a single document-based handler function.

Creating Cascading Menu Commands

A *cascading menu* is a secondary menu or submenu that appears when a menu option is selected from a parent menu. A triangular arrow next to the parent item in the menu indicates a cascading menu. Cascading menus are useful because they can be used to display menu commands hierarchically.

There is no actual limit to the number of menus that you can nest by cascading, but UI guidelines suggest that you use no more than four levels of nesting. You can create submenu commands that act as header items in that they invoke another list of menu commands.

► **To create a cascading menu**

1. Add a new menu command using the steps provided in the Adding Menu Commands section.
2. Select the Pop-Up check box in the Menu Item Properties dialog box to set the pop-up property for that menu command.

You can now insert new submenu commands of that menu command as you would normal menu commands. These submenu commands can also be cascading menus to form yet another sublevel menu, if required.

Adding Shortcuts

You can insert shortcut characters in the menu command text. To do so, insert an ampersand character (&) before the desired shortcut character. When you display the menu command, the shortcut character will be underlined and the corresponding key will automatically work as a shortcut to that menu command.

For example, if you wanted to make the S of My Shortcut a shortcut key, you would type the menu caption as My &Shortcut, which would be displayed as My Shortcut.

If you actually want an ampersand character to be displayed as part of the command, you must use two ampersands together. Thus, My && Am&persand will display the text: My & Ampersand.

Handling Menu Commands

You can use ClassWizard to create menu command handlers. These handlers will create a message map entry for a Windows WM_COMMAND from your menu command with the ID of the selected menu command. When a user selects the menu command, Windows passes a WM_COMMAND message to the application window that owns the menu; your application will route the message to the associated handler function if your message map contains a corresponding message map entry.

Adding a Menu Command Handler Function

To add functionality to the newly added menu command, you will need to add a command *handler function* that will execute the code associated with the menu command. You can implement a handler function in any class in which objects will receive the menu selection command message when the command is selected. Typically, the object would be either your document that supports the views, or the specific view that implements the menu option. You can also handle the menu option in the application or frame window classes.

The best guide as to where to implement the handler function is to consider where it is more appropriate in terms of accessing data and methods that it needs from the various application objects. You can use ClassWizard to add this handler.

► **To add a menu command handler function using ClassWizard**

1. Select the menu command for which you want to add a handler function.
2. Select ClassWizard from the View menu (or press CTRL+W). You should see the menu command ID selected in the Object IDs list of the ClassWizard screen.
3. The destination class for your new handler function appears in the Class Name combo box. If the resource doesn't have a class, you'll see the Adding

a Class dialog box shown in Figure 4.9. You can select the required implementation class.

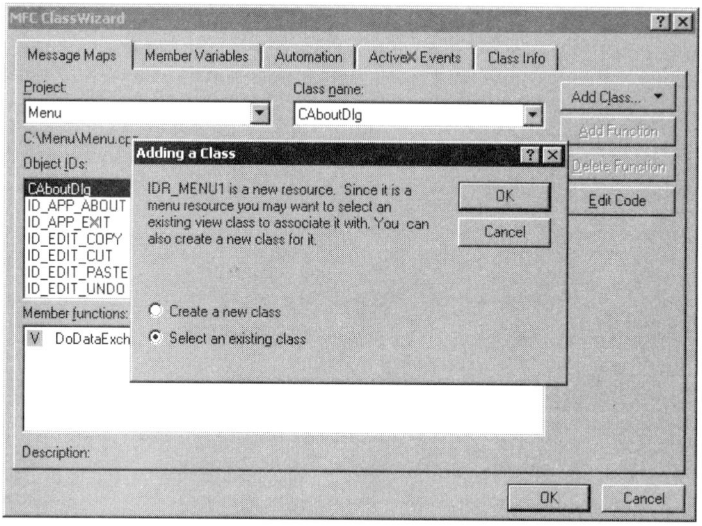

Figure 4.9 MFC ClassWizard—Adding A Class dialog box

4. Double-click the COMMAND message shown in the Messages list box to invoke the Add Member Function dialog box.
5. The default handler function name is based on the resource ID of the menu command. You can modify this name in the Member Function Name edit box before creating the new handler function.
6. Click OK to add the new member function. The new member function appears in the Member Functions list at the bottom of the ClassWizard dialog box.
7. You can edit the code of the new member function by clicking the Edit Code button. When you have added the new handler function, you can add your application-specific implementation code. For example, the following menu handler displays a message box indicating that the menu command has been selected:

```
void CSDIMenu::OnMymenu()
{
    AfxMessageBox("You have selected the first menu item");
}
```

Adding a Command UI Handler Function

You can also add command UI handler functions to your code. These functions are responsible for the appearance, style, and behavior of each specific menu command. Before the menu appears, the corresponding UI handler functions are called to let your application make each command available or unavailable, add or remove check marks, or change the command's text.

You can change these various UI attributes by calling the access functions of a CCmdUI object associated with the menu command. Whenever your UI handler function is called, it will be passed a pointer to a CCmdUI object.

For example, the following UI handler makes the menu command available so that a user can select it. It accomplishes this task by calling the *Enable* function of the CCmdUI object pointed to by the pCmdUI pointer, as shown in the following code:

```
void CSDIMenu::OnUpdateItem(CCmdUI* pCmdUI)
{
    pCmdUI->Enable(TRUE);
}
```

Making Menus Available or Unavailable

You can make menus available or unavailable by calling the CCmdUI object's *Enable* function. If you pass a TRUE value to this function, the menu is available; otherwise, the menu option will be unavailable and grayed out.

You could maintain this grayed state by setting a Boolean member variable embedded in the class and passing it to the *Enable* function of the CCmdUI object when your UI handler function is called with a line such as the following:

```
pCCmdUI->Enable(m_bMySubItemEnableStatus);
```

By maintaining the state of *m_bMySubItemEnableStatus* in your application, the menu command can correspondingly be made available or unavailable.

Setting or Clearing a Check Mark

You can display a check mark next to a menu command. You can set the status of the check mark by calling the CCmdUI object's *SetCheck* function. Passing 0 (FALSE) to *SetCheck* will clear the check mark and passing 1 (TRUE) will set the check mark. To maintain the status of the check mark, you can use a Boolean variable.

You could create a simple toggle switch on a menu command. Selecting the menu command would let the user toggle the check mark on and off. You could implement this toggle switch with the following code:

```
void CSDIMenu::OnUpdateItem()
{
    // Toggle the current state
    m_nToggleState = m_nToggleState == 0 ? 1 : 0;
```

```
    // Make the menu command available
    pCmdUI->Enable(TRUE);
    // Set the current toggle state
    pCmdUI->SetCheck(m_nToggleState);
}
```

In the previous code, both the command and the command UI message handler are used in combination to implement the toggle switch. The message command handler function *OnUpdateItem* maintains the state of the toggle in the *m_nToggleState* member variable. This member variable could be defined in the class definition as a simple integer as follows:

```
int m_nToggleState;
```

The UI handler ensures that calling the CCmdUI object's *Enable* function always makes the menu command available.

When you call the CCmdUI object's *SetCheck* function in the previous code, you update the current toggle state to the menu command by setting or clearing the check mark status. *SetCheck* is passed the *m_nToggleState* variable to either set or clear the check mark, depending on the value of *m_nToggleState*.

Changing the Menu Text Dynamically

You can also use the command UI handler function to change the menu command text by passing a new text string to the CCmdUI object's *SetText* function. The menu will then be changed to the new text string, including any shortcut codes set by the ampersand symbol (&).

For example, you could make the menu command text in the previous toggle example change the menu text to display On or Off, depending on the toggle state. This can be accomplished by adding the following line to the end of the UI handler function:

```
pCmdUI->SetText(m_nToggleState ? "&On":"O&ff");
```

Adding Shortcut Menus

A *shortcut menu* is a menu that pops up on the screen when a user right-clicks an application object. The user can then select menu commands specific to the application object from the menu. You can add a new menu resource to appear as the shortcut menu.

You can implement shortcut menus in your application by adding a handler for the Windows WM_CONTEXTMENU message. This message is passed to your application when the user right-clicks anywhere within an application window.

In the handler function, you can load the appropriate menu resource and then start the shortcut menu by calling the *TrackPopupMenu* function. You can add menu command handler functions as you normally would to implement the menu command functionality.

You can add a handler for the WM_CONTEXTMENU shortcut menu message with the steps in the following procedure.

► **To add a shortcut menu handler function**

1. In the ClassView tab, right-click the class to which you want to add the new shortcut menu.
2. Click the Add Windows Message Handler command from the shortcut menu. The New Windows Message And Event Handlers dialog box appears.
3. Select the WM_CONTEXTMENU message from the New Windows Messages/Events list and click the Add And Edit button to add a new handler function for the shortcut menu message.
4. Add your application code to the default implementation of the *OnContextMenu* handler function.

Creating and Accessing Menu Objects

MFC provides the CMenu class that wraps an underlying Windows menu handle (HMENU) and simplifies menu operations. You can use CMenu to programmatically build your own menus, or you can dynamically add and remove menu commands from existing menus. CMenu has a host of member functions that handle every aspect of menu display and manipulation.

Initializing the CMenu Object

Before you can use a declared new CMenu object, you must initialize it by either loading the menu command from a menu resource template, by creating a new menu, or by attaching an existing Windows menu handle to the menu.

- **Loading the menu from a menu resource template** Using the *LoadMenu* member function, you can load a menu by passing the resource ID of the required menu.
- **Creating a new menu** The *CreateMenu* function will dynamically create a new Windows menu resource with no menu commands. You can add menu commands dynamically to the new menu.
- **Attaching an existing menu** You can call *Attach* to attach an existing Windows menu to the CMenu object by passing the HMENU handle to the existing Windows menu. You can obtain this handle from an associated CWnd by calling the window object's *GetMenu* function. When you have finished manipulating the menu, you can detach it from your CMenu object by calling *Detach*.

After you have initialized the CMenu object, you can add, remove, or modify the menu commands to suit the needs of your application.

Dynamically Adding Menu Commands

New menu commands can be added to a menu at run-time by calling either *AppendMenu* or *InsertMenu,* depending on whether the menu command should be added to the end of the menu or inserted into the menu at a specific position.

The *AppendMenu* function needs three parameters. The first mandatory parameter is a flag value that specifies the new menu command type and a combination of menu style values. The second parameter requires you to pass an ID for command messages or the HMENU handle of a shortcut menu if the MF_POPUP flag is specified. You can pass a string pointer for the third parameter for the menu command text.

The *InsertMenu* function has four parameters and lets you insert the new menu command at a specific position, or before a menu command with a specific ID. If you want to specify the position by index, pass the position as a zero-based offset to the first parameter, and include the MF_BYPOSITION flag with your flag values passed to the flag's parameter.

To insert the new menu command before the existing menu command, with a specific ID, pass the ID as the first parameter and include the MF_BYCOMMAND flag with your flag parameter value. The other three parameters are identical to *AppendMenu* parameters.

You can also modify the menu commands while they are displayed, or if they are valid objects, by calling the *ModifyMenu* function. To remove menu commands from a CMenu object, you can use the *RemoveMenu* function.

Deleting Menus

Before exiting, an application must free system resources associated with a menu if the menu is not assigned to a window. An application frees a menu by calling the *DestroyMenu* member function.

Creating and Using Toolbars

A *toolbar* is a window that contains one or more rows of command buttons. These command buttons provide a quick way for a user to perform a task. Toolbar buttons frequently duplicate much of the functionality of menus.

Toolbar button graphics are based on a single bitmap that contains a row of button images.

Creating Toolbars

In Visual C++, you use Toolbar Editor to create and manipulate toolbars.

► **To create a toolbar**

1. Select the ResourceView pane to display the project resources.
2. Right-click the top-level folder and select the Insert option from shortcut menu. The Insert Resource dialog box appears.
3. Select Toolbar from the list of new resource types.
4. Insert the new toolbar resource by clicking the New button. Shown in Figure 4.10, the new toolbar is listed in the Toolbar folder under Toolbar Resources, and it appears in the editor window along with a blank button.

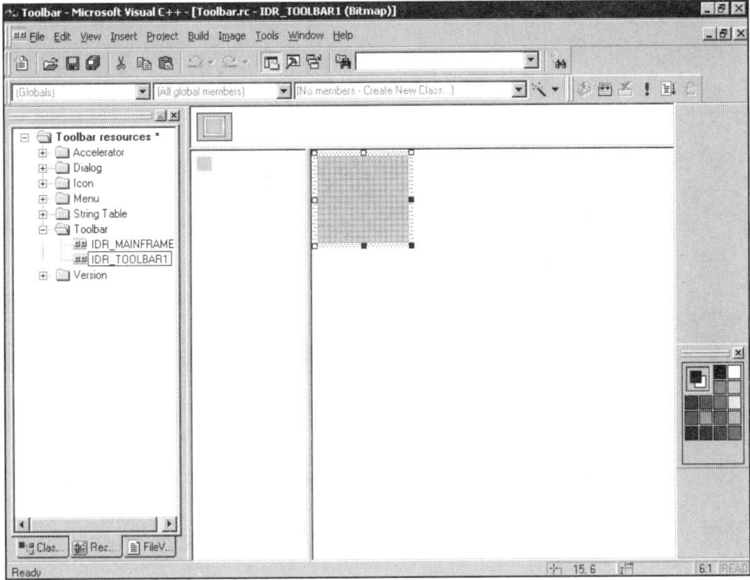

Figure 4.10 New toolbar

5. You can now specify the properties for the toolbar. Right-click the toolbar resource and click the Properties command on the shortcut menu to display the Toolbar properties.

6. Change the default IDD_resource ID name to a more appropriate name for your toolbar.
7. Resize the blank toolbar to change the default size of the toolbar and its buttons.

You are ready to edit the blank toolbar and insert new buttons as appropriate.

► **To add buttons to the new toolbar**

1. Select the blank button in the toolbar and edit the button's bitmap. When editing the toolbar button, you will notice that a new blank button appears to the right of the button that you are currently editing.
2. For each new button, you should set a command ID and prompt string. Select each button and press ALT+ENTER to invoke the Toolbar Button Properties dialog box.
3. Set the command ID to a unique value by typing a new ID identifier into the ID combo box. You can also specify an existing ID for the toolbar button.
4. As you could with menu commands, you can type a string, to be displayed in the status line, in the Prompt edit box. You can also add a ToolTip by adding the ToolTip string after the \n separator code in the Prompt edit box.
5. The toolbar button will appear when you build and run the program. However, the button is unavailable and grayed out until you add a handler function. For information on adding handler functions, refer to the previous section, Adding a Menu Command Handler Function.
6. When you have inserted the toolbar button and handler function, you can add your application-specific code to run when a user clicks a button. You can also share the handler function with a menu command ID, as is often done by developers when the toolbar provides a shortcut for a menu command.
7. Repeat steps 2 through 6 for adding additional buttons to the toolbar.

CToolBar Class

After you have typed the appropriate IDs for the toolbar buttons, you can use ClassWizard to create a class (based on the CToolBar class) for the toolbar. MFC handles the buttons' response functions, but at times you might want to change the toolbar's default behavior or appearance. In these cases, you can use the member functions of the CToolBar class. Table 4.1 provides some functions of the CToolBar class and their descriptions.

Table 4.1 Member Functions of the CToolBar Class

Function	Description
CommandToIndex	Retrieves the index of the button that has the specified ID
Create	Creates a toolbar
GetButtonInfo	Retrieves information about the button
GetButtonStyle	Retrieves information about the button style
GetButtonText	Retrieves the button's text
GetItemID	Obtains the ID of the button at the specified index
GetItemRect	Obtains the display rectangle for the item at the specified index
GetToolBarCtrl	Retrieves a reference to the CToolBarCtrl object represented by the CToolBar object
LoadBitmap	Loads the images for the toolbar's buttons
LoadToolBar	Loads the toolbar resource
SetBitmap	Sets a new button image
SetButtonInfo	Sets the ID, style, and image number for a button
SetButtons	Sets the IDs for the toolbar's buttons
SetButtonStyle	Sets the style for the button
SetButtonText	Sets the text for the button
SetHeight	Sets the height for the toolbar
SetSizes	Sets the size for the toolbar's buttons

Normally, you will not need to call any of the CToolBar functions. However, in cases where you receive some unusual results, you might have to use these functions. For example, if the default height of the toolbar is not suited for your application, you will need to call the *SetHeight* function.

Additional Toolbar Functionality

When you use MFC AppWizard to create an application, it creates a default toolbar (IDR_MAINFRAME) and adds it to your application. The MFC framework provides the default functionality for the toolbar.

Making Docking Available in a Frame Window

The MFC Library supports *dockable toolbars*, which can be attached to any side of its parent window, or which can float in their own miniframe windows. By default, AppWizard creates a dockable toolbar. You can manually add the code necessary for a dockable toolbar to your application.

► **To make docking available in your application**

1. Make docking for the frame window available by using the *CFrameWnd::EnableDocking* function. This function takes a *DWORD* parameter, which is a set of style bits indicating which side of the frame window will accept docking. The values you can pass to this function and their descriptions are provided in Table 4.2.

   Table 4.2 DWORD Values and Their Descriptions

Function	Description
CBRS_ALIGN_TOP	Allows docking at the top of the client area
CBRS_ALIGN_BOTTOM	Allows docking at the bottom of the client area
CBRS_ALIGN_LEFT	Allows docking on the left side of the client area
CBRS_ALIGN_RIGHT	Allows docking on the right side of the client area
CBRS_ALIGN_ANY	Allows docking on any side of the client area

   If you pass 0, the control bar will not dock.

2. Make docking available for the toolbar by using the *CControlBar::EnableDocking* function. This function also takes a *DWORD* parameter that has the same possible values as the *CFrameWnd::EnableDocking* function. (You must call *CControlBar::EnableDocking* for each toolbar that you want to be able to dock.)

If the code for any of these functions is missing, your application displays a standard toolbar.

Creating ToolTips for Toolbars

In most applications, toolbars provide some basic help and hints to a user in the form of *ToolTips*. ToolTips are small pop-up windows that appear for a predefined interval when the user places the mouse pointer over a UI element such as an icon or a toolbar button. Typically, a ToolTip contains a short line of descriptive text about the associated UI element.

► **To create a ToolTip for a toolbar button**

1. Double-click the toolbar button. The Toolbar Button Properties dialog box appears.
2. Specify the description for the toolbar button followed by a newline (\n) character and the ToolTip in the Prompt text box. For example, to specify the description of the toolbar button as "Cut the picture" and the ToolTip as "Cut," type *Cut the picture\nCut*.

You can now compile and execute the project.

Rebars

Simple to create, a *rebar* is a toolbar that can contain controls other than the toolbar buttons. An example of a rebar appears on the Microsoft Internet Explorer toolbar.

► **To create a project that uses a rebar**

1. Start AppWizard and create an MFC AppWizard project named MyRebar.
2. Accept the default settings on each step, and then click Finish.
3. When the project is created, double-click CMainFrame in ClassView to edit the header file. You will have to add the following code in MainFrm.h to add the rebar as a public member variable:

   ```
   CReBar m_rebarobj;
   ```

4. For this test run, add a check box to the bar. The CButton class is designed for check boxes, radio buttons, and command buttons, all with slightly different styles. The code to declare a check box is listed as follows:

   ```
   CButton m_check;
   ```

5. Create and initialize the rebar in the *OnCreate* function of the mainframe class. The code for this function will look similar to the following:

   ```
   if (!m_rebar.Create(this))
   {
       TRACE0("Cannot create rebar\n");
       return -1;
   }
   ```

6. The check box control requires a resource ID. When you create a control with the dialog editor, the name you provide the control is automatically associated with a number. However, when creating the check box using code, you will need to specify the resource ID. You can specify the code in the Resource Symbols dialog box.
7. To specify the resource ID for the check box, click the Resource Symbols command on the View menu.
8. Click the New button.
9. Specify the resource ID as IDC_CHECK1.
10. The Value field displays a value for the resource ID. Accept the default value and click OK.
11. Close the Resource Symbols dialog box.

12. Add code to create and initialize the check box in the *OnCreate* function. The code resembles the following:

```
if (!m_check.Create("Checked", WS_CHILD|WS_VISIBLE
|BS_AUTOCHECHBOX, CRect(0,0,50,50), this,
IDC_CHECK1))
{
    TRACE0("Cannot create check box \n");
    return -1;
}
```

13. Add the check box and the band to the rebar by using the *AddBar* function. The *AddBar* function requires four parameters: a pointer to the control that will be added, some text to put next to it, a pointer to a bitmap to use for the background image on the rebar, and a rebar style. Table 4.3 provides a description for each rebar style.

Table 4.3 Rebar Style Parameters and Their Descriptions

Function	Description
RBBS_BREAK	Places the band on a new line even if there is room for the band at the end of an existing line
RBBS_CHILDEDGE	Places the band against a child window of the frame
RBBS_FIXEDBMP	Prevents the movement of the bitmap if the user resizes the band
RBBS_FIXEDSIZE	Prevents the user from resizing the band
RBBS_GRIPPERALWAYS	Ensures that the sizing wrinkles are present on the rebar
RBBS_HIDDEN	Hides the band
RBBS_NOGRIPPER	Suppresses the sizing wrinkles
RBBS_NOVERT	Hides the band when the rebar is vertical
RBBS_VARIABLEHEIGHT	Allows resizing of the band

The code to add the band and check box to the rebar is listed as follows:

```
m_rebarobj.AddBar(&m_check, "My First Rebar", NULL,
RBBS_BREAK);
```

Implementing Status Bars

A *status bar* is a Windows control used to display text at the bottom of an application's main frame window. The status bar has several parts, which are called *panes*. The panes display information about the status of the application and the system. These panes include indicators for the keys such as CAPS LOCK and NUM LOCK, as shown in the WordPad window in Figure 4.11. The panes also include a message area for displaying the status text and command descriptions.

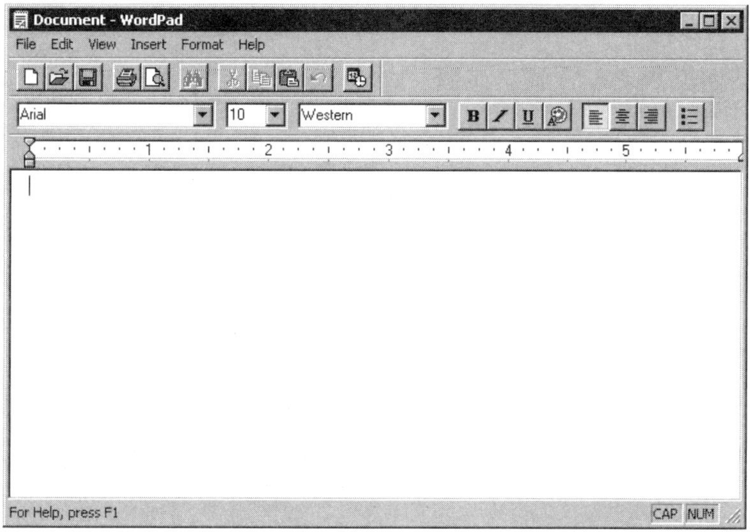

Figure 4.11 WordPad window

By default, AppWizard creates a standard status bar that you can manually customize.

► **To create a status bar with left and right panes**

1. Create a command ID for the status bar by clicking the Resource Symbols command on the View menu. The Resource Symbols dialog box displays the currently defined symbols for the resources of your application.
2. To add a new resource symbol, click the New button to open the New Symbol dialog box.
3. Specify an ID, such as ID_MYLEFTPANE or ID_MYRIGHTPANE, for the button in the Name text box and click OK.
4. Close the Resource Symbols dialog box by clicking Close.
5. Click the ResourceView tab in the Workspace window.
6. Double-click the String Table folder.
7. Double-click the String Table option.
8. The String Table Editor appears. To insert a string, click the New String command on the Insert menu.
9. Specify the command ID for the position of a pane in the ID combo box. For example, to specify a right pane, you would type *ID_INDICATOR_RIGHT*. For a left pane, type *ID_INDICATOR_LEFT*.

10. You also need to specify the pane's position in the Caption text box. Type *LEFT* for a left pane or *RIGHT* for a right pane.

11. The MFC framework uses an array of IDs to determine the locations of the panes to be displayed. This array is passed as an argument to the *SetIndicators* member function of the status bar, which is called in the *OnCreate* function of the CMainFrame class. The code for the array holding the IDs is found in the MainFrame.cpp file, as follows:

```
static UNIT indicators[] =
{
    ID_SEPARATOR,
    ID_INDICATOR_CAPS,
    ID_INDICATOR_NUM,
    ID_INDICATOR_SCRL
};
```

You can edit the code in the MainFrame.cpp file for modifying status bar information, as you'll see in the next section.

Creating Command Update Handlers for the Panes

To make the new panes in a status bar available, you must create a command update handler for the new panes. However, ClassWizard does not allow you to specify handlers for status bar messages, so you must manually add handler entries to the message map and then add the code for the handlers.

► **To add command update handlers for the panes**

1. Open the MainFrm.h header file. This file contains the message map entries.
2. Add the entries for the new handlers to the message map to associate the command ID with the handler in the MainFrm.cpp source file. The code will then resemble the following:

```
protected:
//{{AFX_MSG(CMainFrame)
    afx_msg int OnCreate(LPCREATESTRUCT
    lpCreateStruct);
//}}AFX_MSG
afx_msg void OnUpdateMyLeftPane(CCmdUI *pCmdUI);
afx_msg void OnUpdateMyRightPane(CCmdUI *pCmdUI);
DECLARE_MESSAGE_MAP
```

3. Add the handler to the source message map to associate the command ID with the handler. The modified code resembles the following:

```
BEGIN_MESSGE_MAP(CMainFrame, CframeWnd)
//{{AFX_MSG_MAP(CMainFrame)
    ON_WM_CREATE
//}}AFX_MSG_MAP
```

```
ON_UPDATE_COMMAND_UI(ID_MYLEFTPANE, OnUpdateMyLeftPane)
ON_UPDATE_COMMAND_UI(ID_MYRIGHTPANE, OnUpdateMyRightPane)
END_MESSAGE_MAP
```

3. To set up the status bar, you can use the main frame window's *OnCreate* function.

Some additional status bar member functions are listed in Table 4.4.

Table 4.4 Member Functions of the CStatusBar Class

Function	Description
CommandToIndex	Retrieves the index of the specified indicator
Create	Creates a status bar
GetItemID	Obtains the ID of the indicator at the specified index
GetItemRect	Obtains the display rectangle for the item at the specified index
GetPaneInfo	Obtains information about a pane
GetPaneStyle	Retrieves a pane style
GetPaneText	Obtains indicator text
GetStatusBarCtrl	Retrieves a reference to the CStatusBarCtrl object represented by the CStatusBar object
SetIndicators	Sets the IDs for the indicators
SetPaneInfo	Sets the ID, width, and style for the pane
SetPaneText	Sets the text for the pane
SetPaneStyle	Sets the style for the pane

Lesson Summary

This lesson covered various resource elements such as menus, toolbars, and status bars. Visual C++ provides wizards and classes to allow you to create resource elements. The wizards provide a guided tour for creating and modifying the resource elements. These elements form the basis of navigation in Windows applications; simple and easy navigation across an application is the most attractive point of Windows applications.

Menus offer a convenient and consistent way to group commands and an easy way for users to access them. Menus allow you to arrange commands in a logical, easy-to-find fashion. With the Menu editor, you can create and edit menus by working directly with a menu bar that closely resembles the one in your finished application. Menu Editor allows you to create standard menus and commands, move menus and commands from one place to another, and edit the properties of menu items. To provide functionality to the menus, you will need to add handler functions by using MFC ClassWizard, which guides you through this process.

The CMenu class helps in adding functionality to menus in your application. The CToolBar and CStatusBar classes provide various member functions that you can use in case you confront a problem in implementing a toolbar or a status bar.

Toolbars form an integral part of any GUI application. Recall that a toolbar is a window that contains one or more rows of command buttons. The toolbar editor enables you to create toolbar resources and convert bitmaps into toolbar resources. You can link toolbar buttons to code using ClassWizard, or add ToolTips to your toolbars. For handling toolbar button responses, you can use the methods provided by the CToolBar class. You can also make a toolbar dockable, which will allow it to be attached to any side of its parent window, or float in its own mini-frame window.

Rebars are toolbars that contain controls other than the toolbar buttons. You can create these by using the MFC AppWizard. Status bars are objects that sit at the bottom of an application window. The status of various keys such as the Caps Lock and the Num Lock keys are displayed on the status bar. You can create status bars using the MFC AppWizard. The CStatusBar class provides various methods that make it very easy to work with status bars. For example, the *Create* method allows you to create a status bar for the application window. Other methods include *SetPaneStyle*, *GetPaneStyle*, *GetPaneText*, *SetPaneText* and *GetStatusBarCtrl*, which you can use to work with the status bar.

Lesson 3: User Interface Forms and Dialog Boxes

Dialog boxes are used by nearly every application. MFC provides various classes that enable you to create dialog boxes quickly and easily. MFC also allows you to create form views. A *form* is a dialog box with controls that display related information about an underlying object. For example, a database might display information about a customer, such as the first name, last name, phone number, and so on, in a form. The database user can use the form to access and change the customer's data.

After this lesson, you will be able to:

- Create a dialog box using the dialog editor
- Create dialog box classes and members by using ClassWizard
- Create property sheets by using ClassWizard
- Use the CFormView class to create a form
- Validate user input by using Microsoft dialog data validation (DDV)
- Use ClassWizard to restrict user input to a specified range
- Process user input from a form or a dialog box by using Microsoft Dialog Data Exchange (DDX)

Estimated lesson time: 60 minutes

Dialog Boxes

A dialog box contains controls to accept and handle user inputs. It provides a means for users to type data, and it usually appears in response to selecting a menu command.

Dialog boxes are derived from the CDialog base class. The CDialog class provides an interface for managing dialog boxes. The CDialog class is used to manage two kinds of dialog boxes—*modal* and *modeless*.

Modal Dialog Box

When using a modal dialog box, a user cannot work in the same UI thread until the modal dialog box is closed. When open, the modal dialog box is always on the top of all other windows in an application. A user can move to other windows in the application only after closing the modal dialog box. An example of a modal dialog box is the Print dialog box, shown in Figure 4.12.

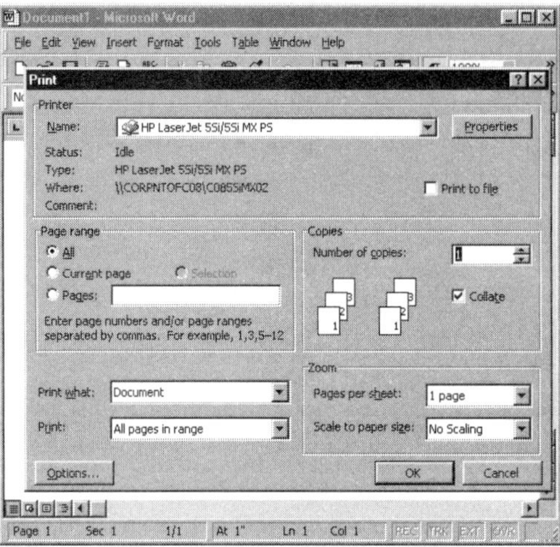

Figure 4.12 Print dialog box—modal

The modal dialog box appears at run time when you call the *DoModal* dialog class member function. This function returns the control back to the parent window only when the user closes the dialog box.

Two variations of modal dialog boxes exist: *application modal* and *system modal*. In an application modal dialog box, a user can interact with other applications that are open but cannot move to other windows in the application when the dialog box is active. In a system modal dialog box, users cannot perform any action on any application on the system without closing the dialog box.

Modeless Dialog Box

A modeless dialog box allows a user to perform other activities in the parent window of an application when the dialog box is open. An example of a modeless dialog box is the Find and Replace dialog box in Microsoft Word, as shown in Figure 4.13.

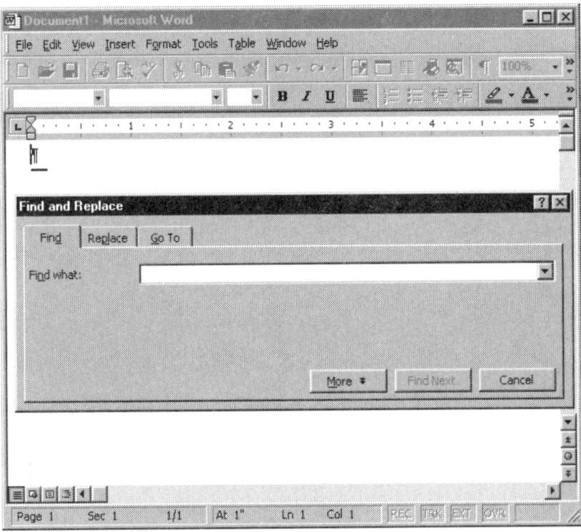

Figure 4.13 Find and Replace dialog box—modeless

The modeless dialog box appears at run time when you call the *Create* function instead of the *DoModal* function. The *Create* function allows the user to move to the parent window while the dialog box is still active.

Creating Dialog Boxes

Visual Studio provides a dialog template that serves as the basic interface for a dialog box. By default, the template provides a window with a caption, a Close button, and OK and Cancel buttons. You add controls to the dialog box and add code to your application to complete the functionality of the dialog box.

However, you can customize the dialog box to suit your requirements. First, you should create a new dialog template.

► **To create a dialog template**

1. Click the Resource command on the Insert menu. The Insert Resource dialog box appears.
2. Select the Dialog option in the Resource Type list box, and click New.
3. To add any controls to the dialog template, drag and drop the controls you want from the Controls toolbar to the new dialog template. To accept user inputs for processing data, the dialog template should contain any necessary controls such as edit boxes, list boxes, radio buttons, check boxes and static text.
4. To display the Dialog Properties dialog box, right-click anywhere in the dialog template except on the OK or Cancel button and click the Properties command on the shortcut menu.
5. Specify the caption of the dialog template.

6. Specify the ID for the dialog template. If the dialog template ID is associated with the class of the dialog box, then you would specify the CLSID.
7. Add controls to the dialog box by dragging and dropping them from the Controls toolbar onto the dialog box. For example, to add a check box control, you would drag the check box from the Controls toolbar and drop it on the dialog box where you require it. Similarly, you can add an edit text box or other controls.
8. You will then need to specify IDs for the controls you've added by using the control properties dialog box. (Right-click a control and select Properties from the shortcut menu to open the Control Properties dialog box.)

Associating a Dialog Template with a Class

After a dialog template is created, you will need to associate the dialog template with a class. The classes in the following procedure are derived from the CDialog base class.

► **To associate a dialog template with the CTest class**

1. Click the ClassWizard command on the View menu to open the MFC ClassWizard dialog box. The Adding a Class dialog box also appears.
2. By default, the Create a New Class radio button is selected in the Adding a Class dialog box. Confirm the creation of a new class by clicking the OK button.
3. Specify a name for the new class in the Name box of the New Class dialog box that appears and click OK.

The name that you specify for the class results in creating the corresponding source and header files. For example, if you specify the name of the class as CDialogClass, then ClassWizard will create DialogClass.cpp and DialogClass.h and add them to your project.

Adding Member Variables to Dialog Box Controls

To allow a dialog box to accept user inputs in its various controls, you need to add member variables to the dialog box control.

► **To add a member variable to a dialog box control**

1. If ClassWizard isn't open, click the ClassWizard command on the View menu and click the Member Variables tab.
2. Select the control for which you want to create a member variable, and then click the Add Variable button to open the Add Member Variable dialog box.
3. Type the member variable's name in the Member Variable Name box.
4. The Category drop-down list displays two options: Value and Control.

The Value option is selected for standard Windows controls. This option creates a variable that contains the text or the status of a control that the user has typed. Selecting the Value option ensures that variable data is added to the data type that you will select in the Variable Type drop-down list.

The Control option is selected to create a control variable that allows you to access the control. For the control option, the Variable Type drop-down list has only one option available: the BOOL option, which contains either a TRUE or FALSE value. The variable type of a check box control is always BOOL because a check box can be either selected or cleared.

5. Finally, select the member variable's type in the Variable Type drop-down list and click OK.
6. You can repeat steps 2 to 5 for adding more member variables.

Displaying a Dialog Box

After you've created the dialog template, its controls, its associated classes, and a menu command that will open the dialog box, display the dialog box.

► **To display a modal dialog box**

1. If ClassWizard isn't open, click the ClassWizard command on the View menu, and click the Message Maps tab.
2. In the Object IDs list, select the object ID of the menu command that will open the dialog box.
3. Select the COMMAND option in the Messages list box.
4. Click the Add Function button, and then click OK to open the Add Member Function dialog box.
5. Type a name for the handler function and click OK.
6. To write code for displaying the dialog box, click the Edit Code button.
7. Write code to create an object of the associated class and call the object's *DoModal* function. The code would look similar to the following code for a simple message box that contains both an OK button and a Cancel button:

```
CDialogClass obj1;
CString msg;
if (obj1.DoModal() == IDOK)
{
    msg = "You clicked OK";
}
else
{
    msg = "You clicked Cancel";
}
AfxMessageBox(msg);
```

8. You will also need to include the header file for the class in the MainFrm.cpp file.

Property Sheets

Although you can distribute data across various dialog boxes, you can also group a number of related dialog boxes into a single dialog box. After you have grouped the dialog boxes, each dialog box appears in the form of a page. Each page is called a *property page*; a group of such property pages is a *property sheet*. Property sheets provide a user-friendly environment in your application. Because a property sheet is an actual dialog box, it can be either modal or modeless.

Creating Property Sheets

You can create property sheets using the CPropertySheet class, which is derived from the CWnd class.

► **To create a property sheet**

1. Open an existing dialog template that you want to convert to a property sheet in the dialog editor; or create a dialog box by using the dialog editor. (To create a dialog box, refer to the Dialog Boxes section.)
2. Delete existing OK and Cancel buttons by selecting them and pressing the DELETE key.
3. Use the Properties dialog box to change the dialog box's caption to the title you would like to appear on the tab in the property sheet.
4. Use the Styles property page to modify the style for the page.
5. Place the controls for the page by dragging and dropping them from the Controls toolbar.
6. Associate a new class with the property page by clicking ClassWizard on the View menu.
7. Specify a class name in ClassWizard's Name text box.
8. Specify CPropertyPage as the base class for the new class in ClassWizard's Base class drop-down list.

Repeat steps 1 through 8 for each dialog box that will appear in the property sheet.

Creating a Property Sheet Class

You also need to create a class for your property sheet.

► **To create a property sheet class**

1. Click ClassWizard on the View menu.
2. Click the Add Class button. The New Class dialog box appears.
3. Type the new class name in the Name text box.
4. Specify CPropertySheet as the base class for the new class from the Base class drop-down list, and click OK.

Displaying a Property Sheet

The final step in the creation of property sheets is to display the sheet at run time.

► **To display a property sheet**

1. Click the ClassView tab and expand the classes folder to display the list of classes.
2. Double-click the entry for the property sheet class to open its header file. Add include statements for the header files of each property page, and add data members for the property pages, as shown in the following code:

```
CNewPage m_newpage1;
```

3. Open the implementation file for the property sheet and write the code to add the property page to the property sheet. The easiest way to add the property pages is to use the *AddPage* function in the property sheet's constructors, as demonstrated in the following code:

```
AddPage(&m_newpage1);
```

4. Add the code to initialize and call the property sheet's *DoModal* function, as follows:

```
CPropSheet prop("New Sheet", this, 0);
int result = prop.DoModal();
```

Using the CFormView Class

CFormView is the base class for all forms. This class provides a window in which the client area contains dialog box controls. These controls support typing in, viewing, or altering data that you would usually find in a form-based, data-access application.

The CFormView class:

- Permits the creation of form-based documents in an application that accepts user input

- Is associated with a dialog box resource that defines the characteristics and layout of the frame
- Contains the controls that accept user input
- Supports DDV and DDX functions
- Receives command messages for menu commands and toolbar messages from the application framework

Creating a Form View

You use the CFormView class to create form-based documents with edit boxes and other dialog box controls in an application. You can create a form-based application using AppWizard.

► **To create a form view using AppWizard**

1. Start Microsoft Visual C++ and click the New command on the File menu.
2. Click the Projects tab and select the MFC AppWizard (.exe) option.
3. Type the project name and click OK.
4. The MFC AppWizard—Step 1 dialog box appears. For this project, select the Single Document radio button and click Next.
5. You don't need any database support for this project, so accept the default settings and click Next.
6. Accept the default compound document and automation support and click Next.
7. Accept the default settings and click Next.
8. Accept the default settings again and click Next.
9. The MFC AppWizard—Step 6 dialog box appears. Because this application will be form-based, the base class you will use for the CProjView class is CFormView. Select CFormView from the Base Class drop-down list box.
10. Click Finish, and then click OK.
11. Add controls to the form by dragging control icons from the Controls toolbar and dropping them into the form.

You have just created a new form-based project; the form template appears in the dialog editor.

► **To create a new form in an application**

1. Click New Form on the Insert menu.
2. The CFormView class is selected as the base class by default in the New Form dialog box. Type a name for your form in the text box. The default dialog box ID is based on the name you typed in the Name text box; you can specify a different ID if you want.

When you run an application that contains more than one form, the application displays the New dialog box. The New dialog box lists each form in the application; select the form you want the application to use and click OK.

Processing and Validating User Input

Data processing and validation are extremely important tasks in most applications. Determining whether the data entered is valid and then processing it is an intricate part of application development. To ease the data processing and validation tasks, MFC provides DDX and DDV functions. This section discusses these functions.

Introduction to DDX and DDV

You can create a dialog box class that collects and validates the dialog box data by using custom message handlers. However, MFC provides two routines, DDX and DDV, for data exchange and validation. These routines can be used repeatedly in your projects.

You can use DDX to initialize the controls in your dialog box and gather data typed in by a user. With DDV, you can easily validate data entry in a dialog box.

Using ClassWizard to create data members, set their data types, and specify validation rules will allow you to take advantage of DDX and DDV.

Note To use DDX, you must define member variables in the dialog box, form view, or record view class; and associate each of them with a dialog box control. Set the initial values of the dialog box's member variables in the *OnInitDialog* handler or the dialog box constructor.

During data exchange and validation, a series of events for processing and validating user inputs take place as follows:

1. An application invokes the DDX mechanism to transfer the values of the member variables to the dialog box controls when a dialog box opens. These controls appear along with the dialog box in response to either the *DoModal* or the *Create* function.
2. The default implementation of *OnInitDialog* in the CDialog class calls the *UpdateData* member function of the CWnd class to initialize dialog box controls. DDX transfers values from the controls to member variables when a user confirms the changes.
3. *UpdateData* sets up a CDataExchange object and calls the *DoDataExchange* member function of the class to carry out the data exchange. *UpdateData*

works in both the left and right directions as specified by the *BOOL* parameter passed to it. The CDataExchange object passed to *UpdateData* represents the context of the exchange. Each DDX function can exchange data in both the left and right directions based on the context supplied by the CDataExchange argument. *DoDataExchange* accepts an argument of the CDataExchange type.

4. Data validation takes place when you specify data validation rules by calling DDV functions. If the value typed by a user at run time exceeds the specified range, the framework automatically displays a message box prompting the user to retype the value. The validation of DDX variables occurs after the user clicks the Confirmation button.

Using DDX Functions

You can take a closer look at these data validation lines by examining the contents of a *DoDataExchange* function. Consider the example of validating the name and age of a customer. The code will look similar to the following:

```
void CmyDlg::DoDataExchange(CDataExchange* pDX)
{
    CDialog::DoDataExchange(pDX);
    //{{AFX_DATA_MAP(CmyDlg)
        DDX_Text(pDX, IDC_AGE, m_nAge);
        DDX_Text(pDX, IDC_NAME, m_Name);
    //}}AFX_DATA_MAP
}
```

In this code, a pDX pointer to a CDataExchange object is passed to the *DoDataExchange* function. The CDataExchange object holds the details associated with the direction and target window for the data transfer. The pDX pointer is then passed along with a dialog box ID and associated member variable to the *DDX_Text* function to implement the data transfer. Several of these *DDX_* functions handle the various types of controls and datatypes. ClassWizard automatically adds code lines for you between the *//AFX_DATA_MAP* comments when you map a member variable to a control from ClassWizard's Member Variable tab. You can also add your own entries manually at the end of the *DoDataExchange* function after ClassWizard's map.

These functions then interrogate the passed CDataExchange object pointer to determine the transfer direction, held in its *m_bSaveAndValidate* member. You can check this flag and perform specific tasks depending on the transfer direction with a line such as the following:

```
if (pDX -> m_bSaveAndValidate == TRUE)
```

A list of the more common DDX functions is provided in Table 4.5.

Table 4.5 DDX Functions and Their Control Types

Function	Control Type	Associated Datatypes
DDX_Text	Edit box	BYTE, short, int, UINT, long, DWORD, String, LPTSTR, float, double, COleCurrency, COleDateTime
DDX_Check	Check box	int
DDX_Radio	Radio button	int
DDX_LBString	Drop list box	CString
DDX_LBStringExact	Drop list box	CString
DDX_CBString	Combo box	CString
DDX_CBStringExact	Combo box	CString
DDX_LBIndex	Drop list box index	int
DDX_CBIndex	Combo box index	int
DDX_Scroll	Scroll bar	int

Using DDV Functions

When you add some types of mapped member variables to a dialog box with ClassWizard, such as edit box to CString or int datatypes, you can also supply optional validation parameters. You can set these parameters using the Member Variables tab of ClassWizard. The validation options are at the bottom of the tab. For example, when you map a CString to an edit control, you can supply a maximum character length to limit the length of the input string that the user types.

When you add validation rules, ClassWizard generates the corresponding DDV calls in the *DoDataExchange* function. For example, if you type the validation for ages as being between 18 and 65, the validation rule will produce the following DDV_ line:

```
DDV_MinMaxInt(pDX, m_nage, 18, 65);
```

The DDV function call will appear directly after the corresponding DDX call so that the value of *m_nage* is up-to-date before the validation is performed. If the entered range fails the validation check, the user is informed with an appropriate message box and the *UpdateData* call that initiates the exchange will return a FALSE value indicating validation failure.

The available DDV validation functions are listed in Table 4.6 on the following page. These functions can be used with any control map that supports the appropriate applicable data type, such as edit controls and radio groups.

Table 4.6 DDV Functions and Their Descriptions

DDV Function Name	Data type	Description
DDV_MaxChars	char	Limits the number of characters to specified range
DDV_MinMaxByte	byte	Limits the number to specified range
DDV_MinMaxDouble	double	Limits the number to specified range
DDV_MinMaxDWord	DWord	Limits the number to specified range
DDV_MinMaxFloat	float	Limits the number to specified range
DDV_MinMaxInt	int	Limits the number to specified range
DDV_MinMaxLong	long	Limits the number to specified range
DDV_MinMaxUnsigned	unsigned	Limits the number to specified range

Creating Custom Validation Functions

If you want your application to include validation capabilities that are not part of standard DDV, such as checking whether an edit control contains data, you will need to write the appropriate code. To do this, you must write a function that accepts the pointer to the CDataExchange object (pDX), a reference to the mapped variable to be tested, and any additional custom parameters you might need.

The first condition your custom validation function must check is that the CDataExchange object is in save and validate mode. You can do this by checking that *pDX->m_bSaveAndValidate* is TRUE. If this flag is not TRUE, the controls are being initialized from the member variables; thus, no validation checks are required and your function should just return. Otherwise, you should validate the mapped member variable according to your custom criteria.

If the mapped variable is valid, your function can return normally; otherwise, you should display a prompting message box and call *Fail* on the CDataExchange object pointer pDX to inform the calling *UpdateData* that validation has failed.

For example, if you wanted to extend the age checking so that 40-year olds are not valid, you might write a validation function as follows:

```
void DDV_ValidateAge(CDataExchange* pDX, int& nAgeValid)
{
    if (pDX -> m_bSaveAndValidate && (nAgeValid < 18 ||
    nAgeValid > 65 || nAgeValid == 40))
    {
        AfxMessageBox("Ages must be between 18 and 65
        but cannot be 40");
        pDX->Fail;
    }
}
```

Because the *nAgeValid* parameter is a reference to the calling mapped variable, you could optionally reset the value to a valid default if you find it to be incorrect.

The custom *DDV_ValidateAge* function could then be called from the *DoDataExchange* function after you have used the corresponding DDX function to update the member variable with a call as follows:

```
DDV_ValidateAge(pDX, m_nage);
```

Your custom validation should now accept age values between 18 and 65, but excluding 40.

Lesson Summary

In this lesson, you learned that dialog boxes are most commonly used for data input and validation. To ease the process of creating and managing dialog boxes, Visual C++ provides the CDialog class, which is used to manage modal and modeless dialog boxes. Creating either type of dialog boxes involves creating dialog templates, adding controls, associating the dialog boxes with classes, and writing code to display the dialog boxes at run time.

This lesson also covered how to create property sheets and forms, which can provide a user-friendly environment in your applications. Visual C++ provides the CPropertySheet class to create and work with property sheets. You can use MFC ClassWizard to manage your property sheets. Regarding forms, the CFormView class is the base class used to create form views. You can create form-based applications using the MFC AppWizard.

In addition, this lesson covered performing validations using the DDV and DDX functions. You can validate data using ClassWizard, or you can create custom validation functions.

Lesson 4: Creating and Using ActiveX Controls

ActiveX controls are built on COM. With ActiveX technology, reusability of components has become extraordinarily easy. Visual C++ supports creation of ActiveX controls and also provides a set of ActiveX controls.

In this lesson, you will learn about the various tools that can be used to create ActiveX controls, and also use ActiveX controls in your applications.

After this lesson, you will be able to:

- Use ActiveX controls in existing applications
- Create ActiveX controls using ATL, MFC, and the Microsoft Platform Software Development Kit (SDK)
- Download an ActiveX control
- Sign an ActiveX control

Estimated lesson time: 45 minutes

Using ActiveX Controls

ActiveX controls are basically COM in-process servers that provide quick and easy integration into applications. This section will cover the steps to include ActiveX controls from the Component Gallery into your applications.

Component Gallery

The Component Gallery is a collection of components that you can import into an application to enhance its features.

► **To display ActiveX controls in the Component Gallery**

1. Click Add to Project on the Project menu.
2. Select the Components and Controls menu command, as shown in Figure 4.14.

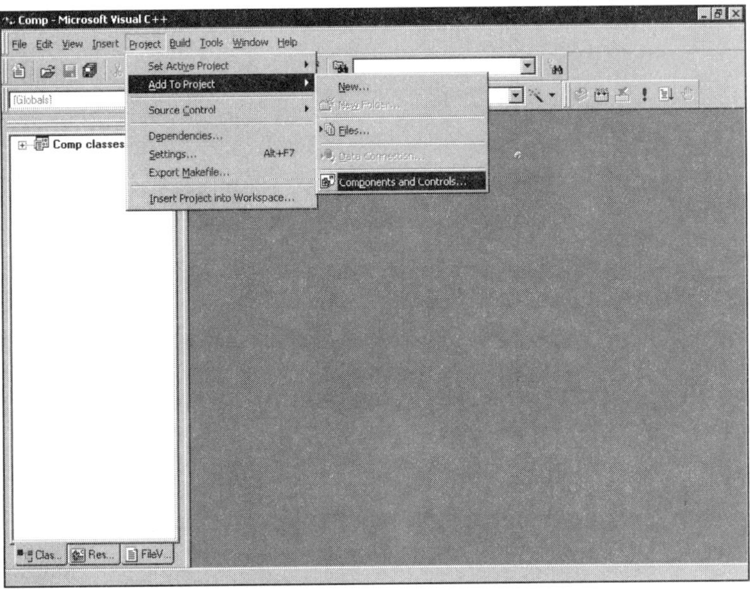

Figure 4.14 Components and Controls menu command

3. Open the Registered ActiveX Controls folder from the Components and Controls Gallery.
4. A list of ActiveX controls appears in the Components And Controls Gallery dialog box, which is shown in Figure 4.15. Notice that the controls are displayed as shortcuts and the path of the code for ActiveX controls appears in the Path To Control box.

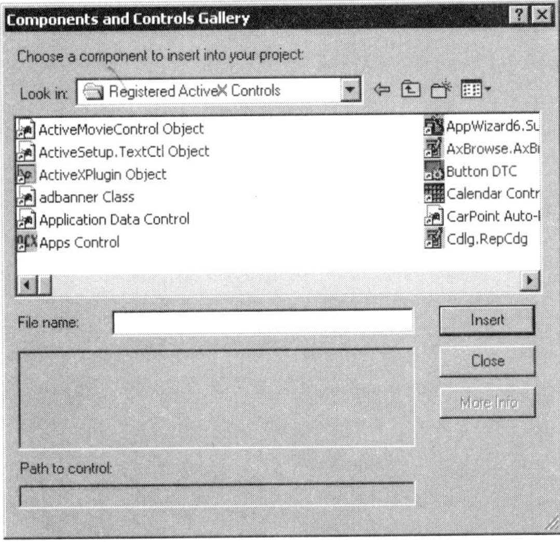

Figure 4.15 Components and Controls Gallery dialog box

Notice that all ActiveX controls are .ocx and DLL files. Therefore, to distribute an application that you create, you will need to package the ActiveX control files along with the application. Also, you will need to register the DLLs. To register a DLL or .ocx file, you can use the regsvr32.exe file.

The syntax for registering a DLL or .ocx file is as follows:

```
regsvr32 <path of the DLL or .ocx>
```

The controls available as part of the Component Gallery are already registered. Therefore, when using these controls in your application, you will not need to register them. You can view details about most controls by selecting the control and clicking the More Info button.

► **To add the Calendar control to an application**

1. Click Calendar Control 8.0.
2. Click Insert. When the Insert This Component? alert message shown in Figure 4.16 appears, click OK.

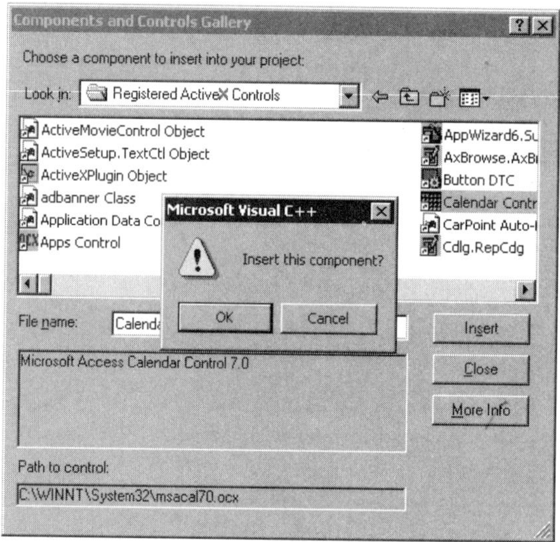

Figure 4.16 Insert This Component? alert message

3. The Confirm Classes dialog box appears, as shown in Figure 4.17. This dialog box provides a list of filenames to be added to the project for implementing the dispatch classes needed for the control. Although the original filenames typically are retained, you can rename the files if you want.

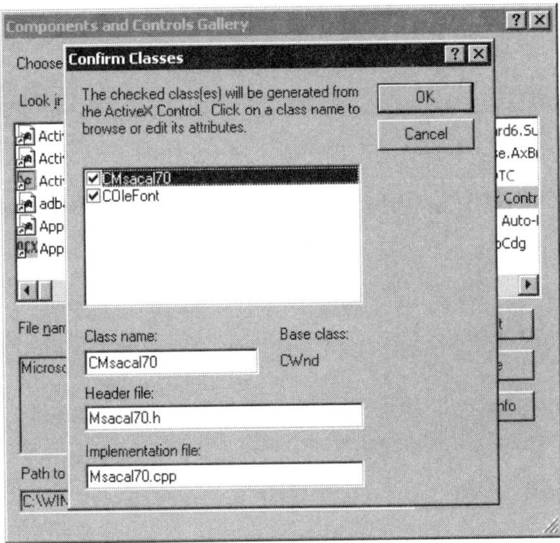

Figure 4.17 Confirm Classes dialog box

4. When you are done with your changes, or if you want to accept the default settings, click OK. Visible in the ClassView pane, the new classes and their files will be added to the project. You can drag and add a control to the dialog box as you would any other control.

Using Event Handlers with Command Messages

Using event handlers, you can allow ActiveX controls to trap the change in the state of a control. You can add event handlers to trap ActiveX control state by using ClassWizard.

► **To add an event handler to the application to trap the selection of a date in the Calendar control**

1. Start ClassWizard by pressing CTRL+W. Click the Member Variables tab and add a member variable for the Calendar control.
2. Click the Message Maps tab. To display the object IDs, select the object containing the Calendar control from the Class Name combo box.
3. Select the ID of the Calendar control from the list of object IDs for adding an event handler for the Calendar control.
4. On the list of messages, double-click the Click message to show the Add Member Function dialog box.
5. The *OnClickCalendar* function is selected by default. Accept the selection and click OK.
6. To edit the event handler function, click the Edit Code button.

7. To allow the function to trap a click or a date change in the Calendar control, you can use the *GetValue* and *SetWindowText* functions, as shown in the following code:

```
void CTestCal::OnClickCalendar()
{
    COleDateTime dtChooseDate(m_Calendar.GetValue44);
    SetWindowText(dtChooseDate.Format
    ("Selected Date %#x"));
}
```

8. In the previous code, the *GetValue* function retrieves the current selected date from the control. If you double-click the *GetValue* function under the CCalendar class in the ClassView pane, you will see that the *GetValue* function returns a VARIANT. The code for the *GetValue* function is listed as follows:

```
VARIANT CCalendar::GetValue()
{
    VARIANT result;
    InvokeHelper(0xc, DISPATCH_PROPERTYGET,
    VT_VARIANT,(void*)&result, NULL);
    return result;
}
```

Creating ActiveX Controls with ATL

Small-sized ActiveX controls are popular among Web designers. Fortunately, Visual C++ provides ATL for the development of these small components.

ATL provides an extensive set of C++ class templates designed for the development of server objects that can be embedded in an application through COM services.

A COM component will need to implement the IUnknown interface to operate as an ActiveX control. In addition, it should be embeddable and self-registering. Typically, an ActiveX control maintains a set of data, fires events, and supports many interfaces with which a client application can successfully interact.

ATL incorporates a number of techniques that help reduce executable size, but implementing the interfaces listed in Table 4.7 on the next page requires a lot of code. The only way to reduce the code is to use COM programming without the benefit of ATL or any other support library.

Table 4.7 ATL Interfaces and Their Descriptions

ATL Interface	Description
IClassFactory	Instantiates a requested class object and returns a pointer to the object. A class identifier registered in the system registry identifies this object.
IClassFactory2	Adds licensing support to the control.
IConnectionPoint	Implemented by controls that support the IConnection-Point container.
IConnectionPointContainer	Required by controls that fire events. This interface enumerates the events that a control object can fire for a client.
IDataObject	Required by controls that transfer data to a container in some way, such as through a file.
IDispatch	Implemented by controls that have custom methods or properties, which a client can access through *IDispatch::Invoke*.
IOleInPlaceActiveObject	Implemented by controls that provide a UI and support IOleInPlaceObject.
IOleInPlaceObject	Implemented by controls that can be activated in place and that provide their own UI.
IOleObject	Required for communication with the client site of a control, except through events.
IPersistStorage	Implemented by controls that can save to and load from an IStorage instance provided by the container.
IProvideClassInfo	Required by controls that contain type library information.
IViewObject2	Required by visible controls that display a window.

Other than the size, another benefit of using ATL to create ActiveX controls is that it can produce components that require neither MFC nor the C run-time library. Some components can be distributed over the Internet as stand-alone entities that do not rely on availability of other support files on a computer.

Furthermore, ATL produces a single representative class for each class object that the control contains. The class derives from all the interfaces that the object supports. ATL provides the same result with more flexibility by using multiple inheritance, in which the class is derived from several base classes.

The greatest benefit of ATL is the library's implementation code for many COM interfaces that controls generally support. As a collection of class templates, the library code saves you from having to write your own code to support common interfaces.

Along with the library code, ATL provides an AppWizard that gets started on a server project, and another wizard that generates class code for the ActiveX control.

▶ To create an ATL ActiveX control

1. Click New on the File menu.
2. Click the Projects tab. Select ATL COM AppWizard, as shown in Figure 4.18.

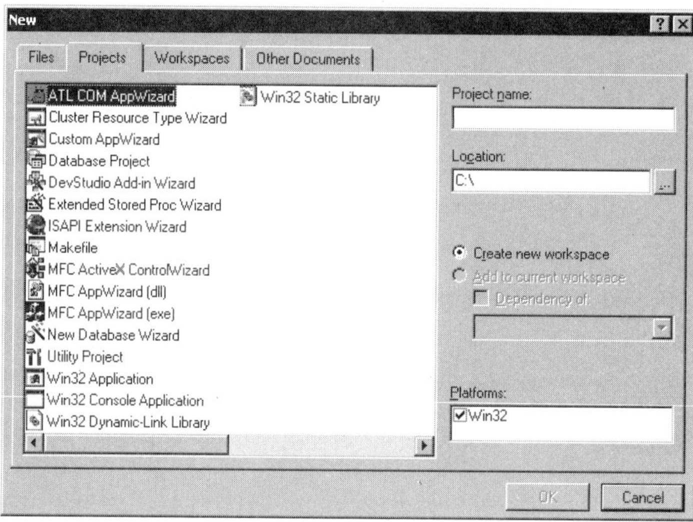

Figure 4.18 ATL COM AppWizard list option

3. Type a name for the project in the Project Name text box. (For this exercise, type *ATLControl* as the project name.) Click OK, and the ATL COM AppWizard—Step 1 of 1 dialog box appears.
4. Accept the default settings for the basic structure of the control by clicking the Finish button.
5. The specifications for the project appear. Accept the specifications by clicking OK.
6. The wizard creates the component without any initial COM objects. It is necessary to specify the category of the object that you will add to this project. You can do this by clicking New ATL Object on the Insert menu.
7. The ATL Object Wizard dialog box displays the four ATL object categories that can be inserted into the project. When you select a category, the icons of the ATL objects under that category are displayed in the Objects list box. Select the Controls category to create an ActiveX control.
8. The icons of the ATL objects under the Controls category appear. To allow the ActiveX control you create to be used on the Internet, you must make sure that the control supports all types of interface containers. Select the Full Control object type and click Next.

9. Select the Names tab and type *MyControl* as the short name of the control in the Short Name text box.
10. Specify the threading model, interface, and aggregation details for the control in the Attributes property page. Threading models are covered in Chapter 6, "Building Advanced Business Objects."
11. You can now build the MyControl ActiveX control project. Make sure that you register the control before you use it.

Creating ActiveX Controls with the Platform SDK

Many applications need to reuse ActiveX controls. ActiveX controls that are easily implemented and maintained are in great demand. You can easily create such controls by using the Platform SDK.

To create ActiveX controls using the SDK, you will need the BaseCtl framework. This framework provides small, self-sufficient, and lightweight controls that are not dependent on associated DLLs.

► **To create an ActiveX control using the SDK**

1. Design the ActiveX controls framework, which implements the core functionality in the CAutomationObject and COleControl C++ classes. (Recall that all C++ objects inherit from CUnknownObject, which provides the support for aggregation. You can download the framework from the MSDN Web site at *http://msdn.microsoft.com.*)

   The ActiveX controls framework provides the basic code, which can be modified to suit the individual application requirements. The framework has a fixed directory structure, and contains the FrameWrk, IELnk, IEMIME, Include, Lib, ToDoSvr and WebImage directories.

   The FrameWrk and Include directories contain the core code for writing an ActiveX control. The FrameWrk directory contains the core functionality in the COleControl class, which compiles into a static library (.lib) form. The Include directory contains the header files.
2. Declare a new object. The object should inherit the functionality from the COleControl class. Derived from CWnd, COleControl is a powerful base class used for developing ActiveX controls. This class inherits all the functionality of a window object and has the additional functionality specific to ActiveX.
3. Ensure that the object inherits the functionality of a Microsoft Automation interface, such as IMyControl. An Automation interface describes the properties and methods for the control.
4. Implement the virtual methods of COleControl, which are declared as pure. The virtual methods of COleControl are *WindowProc, LoadBinaryState,* and *OnDraw*. *WindowProc* is an application-defined method that processes the

messages sent to a window. The WNDPROC type defines a pointer to this callback method. *WindowProc* is a placeholder for the application-defined function name. *LoadBinaryState* is called to restore the settings of each control bar of the frame window. *OnDraw* is another important method, called by the framework to draw the OLE control in the specified bounding rectangle using the specified device context. *OnDraw* is typically called for screen display. Following is an example of the *OnDraw* method syntax:

```
OnDraw(CDC* pDC, const CRect& rcBounds, const Crect&
rcInvalid);
```

Table 4.8 lists *OnDraw* methods and their descriptions.

Table 4.8 *OnDraw* Methods and Their Descriptions

Method	Description
PDC	Screen device context.
rcBounds	Target device context.
rcInvalid	Actual rectangle that is invalid. In some cases, the *rcInvalid* parameter value will be smaller than the *rcBounds* parameter value.

5. Create a new object to implement a property page. The new object inherits from CPropertyPage. The new object must implement *DialogProc*. You can also implement automation objects and collections by declaring a new object that inherits from CAutomationObject.
6. Describe all your objects in a file, because an ActiveX control is an in-process OLE server. This file will also contain a table, which contains all the objects and their information. In addition, the file must also contain the information on the type of localization the server is to use and the type of licensing support that is required.
7. Describe the interfaces and event interfaces in a resource file. It is also necessary to describe linking information in another file and define all the GUIDs that are declared.

Creating ActiveX Controls with MFC

MFC ActiveX ControlWizard is a special type of AppWizard. You can invoke this wizard from the Projects tab. In the following procedure, you will learn how to start ControlWizard for creating an ActiveX framework for an ActiveX project, Test, with ActiveX ControlWizard.

► **To start ControlWizard**

1. Click New on the File menu.
2. Click the Projects tab and select MFC ActiveX ControlWizard, as shown in Figure 4.19.

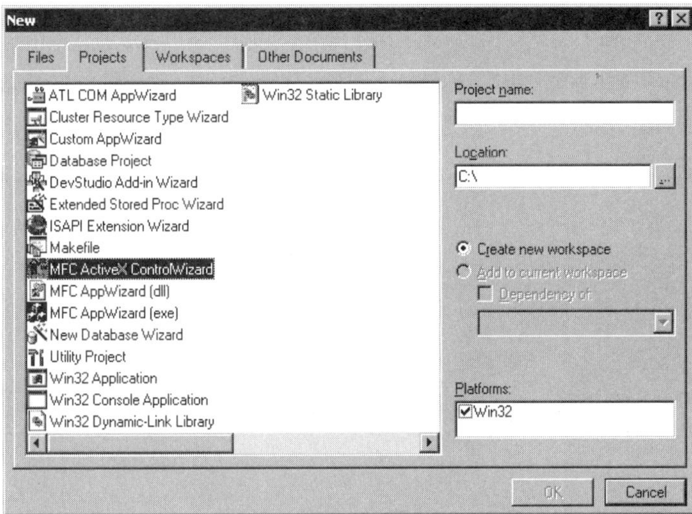

Figure 4.19 MFC ActiveX ControlWizard list option

3. Type *Test* as the name of the project and click OK.

The first screen for ControlWizard is displayed.

Specifying the Number of Controls, Licensing, and Help

The first step of ControlWizard lets you add various levels of support to the new ActiveX control project, shown in Figure 4.20.

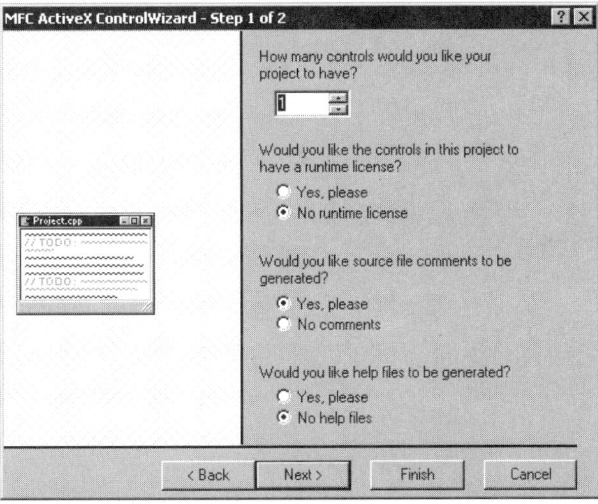

Figure 4.20 MFC ActiveX ControlWizard—Step 1 of 2

The first question is, "How many controls would you like your project to have?" A single ActiveX control implementation file can support multiple ActiveX controls, so the wizard wants to know if you would like to generate your project to have more than one control. If you pick a number larger than one here, ControlWizard will emit multiple COleControl-derived classes in your project but will create only one project workspace file.

If you put more than one control in a project, you will inherently require the user to load all of the controls, even when they only need one. This means that if there is a chance that the user might not need all the controls you have to offer, you are probably better off putting them in separate projects.

If you have controls which will always, or at least usually, be used together, it is a good idea to make sure they live in the same project, because this will greatly improve the instantiation time for the controls. COM will not have to load a whole module, get it hooked up and initialize it, before other controls in the same module are available for use.

The "Would you like the controls in this project to have a runtime license?" question allows you to add support for license validation. If you answer yes to this question, a license-checking function will be added to your classes and a default .lic license file will be generated. Your control can then be distributed only with a valid license file.

The next question, "Would you like source file comments to be generated?" allows you to add source code comments to the framework.

The last question is "Would you like Help files to be generated?" If you answer affirmatively, the wizard will produce context-sensitive help for your control. You will get a rudimentary help file, and ControlWizard will ensure that code lands in your project to make your control sensitive to the F1 key when it is appropriate.

The second page of MFC ActiveX ControlWizard provides more options. These options are used for specifying the class names and usage options.

The first of these options lets you override the default file and class names for the control selected in the combo box. When you click the Edit Names button, you will see a list of files and class names that will be generated for that control.

There is a class for the control CTestCtrl, and a class for its associated property page CTestPropPage. Because ActiveX controls are COM/OLE objects, you will see the associated Type Name and Type ID listed on the right side of the Edit Names dialog box. These names are available in Microsoft Visual Basic Scripting Edition (VBScript), or other languages that want to use the ActiveX control. You can change any of these class, file, or type names at this point.

If you close this dialog box and return to the MFC ActiveX ControlWizard—Step 2 of 2, you will see a list of features available to the control, shown in Figure 4.21.

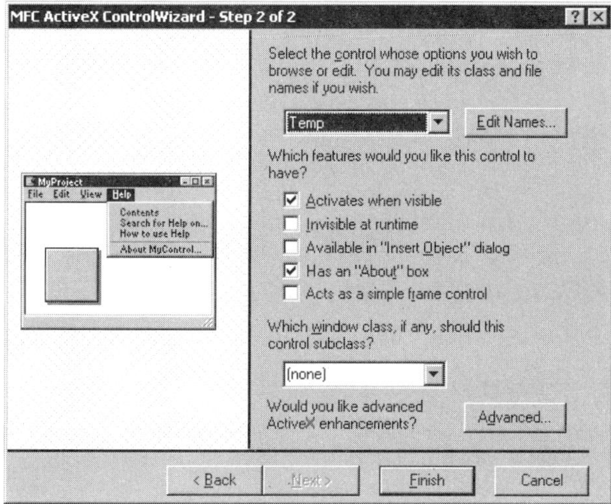

Figure 4.21 MFC ActiveX ControlWizard—Step 2 of 2

Following are options that you can select in Control Wizard's second step:

- **Activates When Visible** This option is normally checked and requests that the control container automatically activate the control when it becomes visible.
- **Invisible At Runtime** You can write ActiveX controls that do not actually display anything, but can be included in OLE containers to add some functionality.
- **Available In "Insert Object" Dialog** If you select this option, the control will automatically register itself with COM as an insertable item. In other words, the control's registry entry will have the Insertable key. The presence or absence of this setting is a design decision that you can implement at your discretion. If you activate the option, the user will be able to insert the control in any ActiveX control container. If you turn it off, the control can only be used in containers that search the registry specifically for ActiveX controls. Most developers leave this option off; your users might become confused if they insert your controls in applications that cannot work with controls.
- **Has An "About" Box** With an About box, you can give information such as the name and version of the control. This box is connected to a method that will allow the control's container to display the box, which can be modified

to your requirements. This option makes it easy to add this common feature to your control.

- **Acts As A Simple Frame Control** This option sets the status information that allows this control to contain other Windows controls. Basically, ActiveX controls are *disassociated;* in other words, one control does not recognize the existence of any other. However, you might want to implement some control that has influence over other controls, such as a group box. Such controls should be built with the Acts As a Simple Frame Control option. These controls will implement an ISimpleFrameSite interface for their container. The container will listen to this interface; the control should use it to let the container preview any Windows messages the control receives. The container can react as it sees fit, even snatching the message away from the control to abort the processing of the message.

Subclassing a Control

You can use the last combo box on the page to pick a control from which you want to subclass the ActiveX control. This feature lets you extend the Windows control functionality. For example, if you are improving the standard scroll bar, you could subclass from the scroll bar to build upon the scroll bar functionality.

Using Advanced ActiveX Features

You can click the Advanced button to display the Advanced ActiveX features, as shown in Figure 4.22.

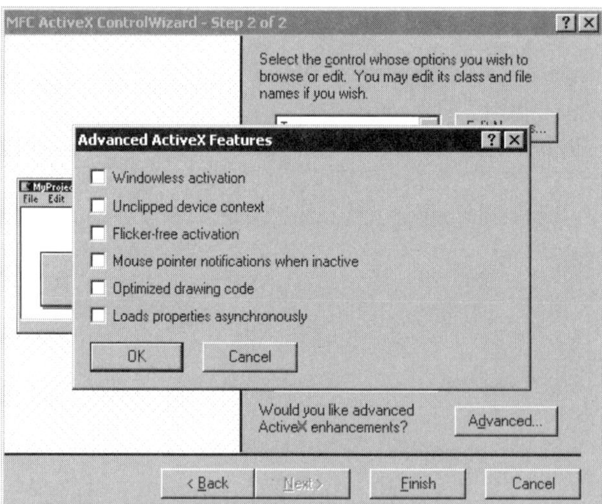

Figure 4.22 Advanced ActiveX features

These features let you set the following options:

- **Windowless Activation** Set this option so that your control uses the containers window rather than a window of its own that is faster but requires some work to implement.
- **Unclipped Device Context** If your control is well-behaved and will not draw outside its own region, this option will provide a small speed gain.
- **Flicker-Free Activation** Controls normally redraw themselves when activated or deactivated, but if there is no difference in the display of both states, you can check this flag to cancel the redraw requests.
- **Mouse Pointer Notifications When Inactive** Setting this option allows an interface to process mouse movement notification even when the control is inactive.
- **Optimized Drawing Code** Some containers might support a mode that preserves the handles for the GDI objects used in the controls. You can test this, and if drawing code is supported, write drawing code that reuses these handles.
- **Loads Properties Asynchronously** If your control is embedded in a Web page, you can implement asynchronous downloading to get the UI running as soon as possible. You can leave images and other properties that are slower to download and less important until the more important properties have loaded.

What's In the Project?

When you have used MFC ActiveX ControlWizard to create your project, you will find it is a little different from most of the projects we have built so far. Your control project builds to a file with the .ocx extension; this file is really just a DLL.

The DLL implements one or more COleControl-derived classes. This MFC class provides you with just about everything you need to implement an ActiveX control; you just need to plug in your own painting code and any accessories you might want to add.

COleControl Module

COleControl is the backbone of each control in your project; you can have more than one COleControl-derived class if you have more than one control in your project, but your control module will only have a single instance of COleControlModule of your control.

Events

A function of any ActiveX control is to communicate with its container; ActiveX controls use *events* to do so. Events are of two types, *custom events* and *stock events*.

Custom Events

The COleControl class does not automatically fire custom events. A custom event recognizes an action determined by the control. The event map entries for custom events are represented by the EVENT_CUSTOM macro.

Stock Events

The COleControl class automatically fires stock events. The COleControl class contains predefined member functions that fire events resulting from common actions.

Some common actions implemented by COleControl include single-click and double-click events on the control, keyboard events, and the changes in the state of the mouse buttons. The event map entries for stock events are always preceded by the prefix EVENT_STOCK.

► **To add a stock event that will fire the single-click event for the ActiveX control by using MFC**

1. Open the ActiveX control project to which you want to add the stock event.
2. Start ClassWizard.
3. In the ActiveX Events tab, select the control's class from the Class name box.
4. Click Add Event, and select one of the stock events from the External name box.
5. To specify a single-click event for the control, select the Click option from the External name drop-down list. When you select an event, the Stock radio button in the Implementation group box automatically becomes selected, because the Click event is a stock event.
6. Confirm your selection by clicking OK. You added the Click stock event to the ActiveX control. It is always useful to test the functionality of the event. To do this, you can use the ActiveX Control Test Container window.
7. The ActiveX Control Test Container window displays the control to which you added the Click stock event. If you click the control, the event name will appear in the result pane of the window.

Creating Property Pages

ActiveX control property pages allow you to display and alter a control's properties without affecting the control container displaying the control. These property pages will work with any type of container control. You can also use the property pages to provide a dialog box-type interface for setting properties.

Implementing the Default Property Page

When you create an ActiveX control by using ControlWizard, the template provides for one default property page. This template includes both an empty property page resource and the code to invoke the property page.

A property page appears as a tabbed page on a dialog box that acts much like a standard dialog box. You can add controls to the default property page, and add more pages to suit the needs of your ActiveX control. You can view the default property page for any ActiveX control by selecting Properties from the shortcut menu for the control.

► **To add a control to a property page**

1. Open the appropriate property page template in the Dialog section of the ResourceView tab.
2. Add a control to the template that will be associated with a control property.
3. Start ClassWizard to add a member variable to hold the property value.
4. Click the Member Variables tab.
5. Select the control for which the member variable is to be added from the Control IDs list and click Add Variable.
6. Specify the member variable name in the Add Member Variable dialog box.
7. Set the category to value and ensure that the variable type is accurate.
8. In the Optional Property Name combo box, type the name of the ActiveX control property associated with this variable, or select a stock property and click OK.

ClassWizard declares and initializes member variables. Next, it adds an appropriate entry to the *DoDataExchange* function to transfer information between the member variables and the controls, as appropriate.

Exchanging Data Between Controls and Property Pages

DoDataExchange is designed to transfer data between controls on the property page and the member variables in the property page class to link property page values with the actual values of properties in the ActiveX control. The DDX group of functions handles these transfers. You must map the appropriate property page fields to their respective control properties to establish links. This allows the property page object to get and set control properties, as would an ActiveX container.

Use the *DoDataExchange* function for property page (DDP) functions to map property page fields to control properties. DDP functions work much like DDX functions used in standard MFC dialog boxes, with one exception: in addition to the reference to a member variable, DDP functions take the name of the control property. Following is a typical entry in the *DoDataExchange* function for a property page:

```
DDP_Text(pDX, IDC_CAPTION, m_caption, _T("Caption"));
```

This function associates the property page's *m_caption* member variable with the Caption property of the ActiveX control. Table 4.9 describes the DDP functions available in MFC.

Table 4.9 DDP Functions and Their Purposes

DDP Function	Purpose
DDP_CBIndex	Links the selected string's index in a combo box with a control property.
DDP_CBString	Links the selected string in a combo box with a control property. The selected string can begin with the same letters as the property's value, but does not need to fully match it.
DDP_CBStringExact	Links the selected string in a combo box with a control property. The selected string and the property's string value must match exactly.
DDP_Check	Links a check box with a control property.
DDP_LBIndex	Links the selected string's index in a list box with a control property.
DDP_LBString	Links the selected string in a list box with a control property. The selected string can begin with the same letters as the property's value, but need not match it exactly.
DDP_LBStringExact	Links the selected string in a list box with a control property. The selected string and the property's string value must match exactly.
DDP_Radio	Links a radio button with a control property.
DDP_Text	Links text with a control property.

Your property page's *DoDataExchange* function includes a call to DDP_Processing to complete the transfer of data to the control.

Adding Stock Property Pages

To invoke a stock property page, update the control's property page macro set in the property page map by:

- Adding a PROPPAGEID entry with the appropriate CLSID for the stock property page, as shown in Table 4.10
- Incrementing the number of property pages in the BEGIN_PROPPAGEIDS macro

Table 4.10 Stock Property Pages and Their CLSIDs

Stock property page	CLSID
Font chooser	CLSID_CFontPropPage
Picture chooser	CLSID_CPicturePropPage
Color chooser	CLSID_CColorPropPage

The following code contains a property page macro set that uses the color chooser property page for a sample Clock control:

```
BEGIN_PROPPAGEIDS(CClockCtrl, 4)
    PROPPAGEID(CClockPropPage::guid)
    PROPPAGEID(CAlarmPropPage::guid)
    PROPPAGEID(CLSID_CColorPropPage)
END_PROPPAGEIDS(CClockCtrl)
```

Adding Custom Property Pages

You can also add custom property pages to your ActiveX control. You first need to create the dialog box resource for your property page, as demonstrated in the following procedure.

► **To create the dialog box resource for the property page**

1. Create a new dialog box resource using the resource editor.
2. Name the dialog box *IDD_PROPPAGE_Xxxx* (where "Xxxx" is a name that describes the topic of the property page).
3. Set the dialog box style to create a child window with a thin border. Make sure the Titlebar and Visible options are cleared.
4. Size the dialog box. Although not mandatory, this step will eliminate compiler warnings that the property page is a nonstandard size.

Note If you create your property page using the IDD_OLE_PROPPAGE_SMALL or IDD_OLE_PROPPAGE_LARGE templates, the resource editor will set the size and properties appropriately.

► **To create the new property page class**

1. Start ClassWizard and click Create A New Class.
2. Provide the name for the new class and ensure that COlePropertyPage is the base class. Click OK and close ClassWizard.

► **To associate a property page name and caption**

1. Use the string table editor to add an entry for the property page name. For example, the ID could be IDS_ALARM_PPG and the Alarm Property Page string.
2. Use the string table editor to add an entry for the property page caption that will be displayed on the page's tab. For example, use IDS_ALARM_PPG_CAPTION for the ID and Alarm for the string.
3. Use the property page name to register the property page. In the *UpdateRegistry* function in your property page class, update the *AfxOleRegisterPropertyPage* function to use your property page name ID as the last parameter. This will update the registry so that the property page can be properly invoked when requested.
4. Make the caption available by modifying the property page constructor to pass the caption ID to the COlePropertyPage base class.

► **To add the property page to the control's property page list**

1. Update the macro block in the control class's property page to use the new property page.
2. Add a new PROPPAGEID entry for the new property page.
3. Increment the number of property pages in the BEGIN_PROPPAGEIDS macro.

The following code shows how to add the custom Alarm page to the Clock control:

```
BEGIN_PROPPAGEIDS(CClockCtrl, 3)
    PROPPAGEID(CClockPropPage::guid)
    PROPPAGEID(CAlarmPropPage::guid)
END_PROPPAGEIDS(CClockCtrl)
```

Signing an ActiveX Control

ActiveX controls can be distributed over the Internet or intranets. To distribute an ActiveX component over the Internet, it must be signed. Signing is accomplished using the SIGNCODE utility, such as the one that ships with Microsoft Visual J++. Users who want to use signed ActiveX controls can download and install these components from the Internet and intranets.

Typically, signing a component means packaging and distributing the component to use Internet Component Download. Internet Component Download is a service that is provided by Internet Explorer 3 and later. The service allows users to download and install signed components.

► **To sign an ActiveX control**

1. Create the .cab file for the ActiveX control. Next, sign the control by using the SIGNCODE utility.
2. When you start the SIGNCODE utility, the Code Signing Wizard appears. Click Next.
3. Specify the name and location of the .cab file of the ActiveX control.
4. When you sign a component, a certificate is generated. Type the name of the control on the certificate.
5. You can also specify a filename or Uniform Resource Locator (URL) that contains information about the control that you are signing.
6. The next screen displays the different cryptographic providers that are installed on the computer. You can select any one of the providers from the list.
7. Type the Software Publishing Credentials (SPC) and private key names. SPC is a type of file under which a component is signed.
8. A browser generates a *private key,* or a file that is packaged along with the certificate. Typically, this file has the .pvk extension. You must store this file in a safe location.
9. Certificate information about the ActiveX control appears. Click Next.
10. To sign the control, click the Sign button.

Downloading an ActiveX Control to the User Interface

Many sites on the Internet provide ready-to-use ActiveX controls. To use these controls, you can download the controls and register them directly onto your computer.

► **To download an ActiveX control from the Internet**

1. Download the .zip file for the ActiveX control that you want from the Internet to the hard disk of your computer.
2. Unzip the files and then register the control through the Visual C++ Integrated Development Environment (IDE). Open the control in Visual C++ IDE by clicking Open on the File menu.
3. The Open dialog box appears. By default, the dialog box looks for C++ files. The ActiveX control files have the .ocx extension. Therefore, you will need to change the entry in the Files of Type drop-down list box to Executable Files. Open the ActiveX control file.

4. To begin registering the downloaded control, click Register Control on the Tools menu.
5. The RegSvr32 message box displays the successful registration of the control file. To close the message box, click OK.
6. When the control is registered, you can insert it into your applications by double-clicking the control's icon in the Control box.

Lesson Summary

In this lesson, you learned that ActiveX controls are basically COM in-process servers that can be used to provide additional functionality to applications. You can add ActiveX controls to your applications from the Components Gallery in Visual C++. Adding event handlers allows you to provide functionality to ActiveX controls.

You also learned how to create ActiveX controls using MFC, the SDK, and ATL. Creating ActiveX controls using MFC is the easiest method. However, if you want to achieve small file images, you should create ActiveX controls using ATL.

Additionally, this lesson examined signing and downloading ActiveX controls, processes made simple when you use Visual C++.

Lab 4: Creating a User Interface

In this lab, you will gain hands-on experience in creating a UI using the Visual C++ ClassWizard and AppWizard. You will also create an ActiveX control using MFC.

After completing this lab, you will be able to:

- Create a dynamic menu
- Add a modeless dialog box
- Build an ActiveX control

Estimated lab time: 60 minutes

Exercise 1: Creating a Dynamic Menu

In this exercise, you will add items to a menu dynamically.

When a user selects the Extra Colors menu command that you'll create in this exercise, your application will add the items Cyan, Purple, and Yellow to the Colors menu.

► **Consolidate the command range**

1. Open Dynamenu.dsw and then open the DynaView.cpp file and edit the message map of the view class to map the commands with their respective member functions, as follows:

```
ON_COMMAND(ID_OPTIONS_EXTRACOLORS,
OnOptionsExtracolors)
ON_COMMAND(ID_OPTIONS_STANDARDCOLORS,
OnOptionsStdcolors)
ON_COMMAND_RANGE(ID_COLORS_CYAN, ID_COLORS_YELLOW,
OnColors)
ON_COMMAND_RANGE(ID_COLORS_BLACK, ID_COLORS_BLUE,
OnColors)
```

2. Open the file DynaView.h and add the following code to the section under generated message map functions:

```
afx_msg void OnOptionsExtracolors();
afx_msg void OnColors(UINT nUID);
afx_msg void OnUpdateColors(CCmdUI* pCmdUI);
afx_msg void OnUpdateOptions(CCmdUI* pCmdUI);
afx_msg void OnOptionsStdcolors();
```

► Add menu commands dynamically

1. Open DynaView.cpp and write the following code to add menu commands to the Colors menu when the Extra Colors item is selected:

```
void CMenusDynamicView::OnOptionsExtracolors()
{
    CMenu *pAddinMenu, *pTopMenu;

    // To append to the Colors menu, a pointer is
    // required. Obtain a pointer to the top-level menu.
    pTopMenu = AfxGetMainWnd()->GetMenu();

    // Colors is the 3rd menu, but that's #2 in a
    // 0-based system.
    pAddinMenu = pTopMenu->GetSubMenu(2);
    ASSERT(pAddinMenu != NULL);

    // First, add a separator to separate the
    // default menus from the dynamic menus
    pAddinMenu->AppendMenu(MF_SEPARATOR);

    // Append the three menu commands. They will generate
    // consecutive command IDs.
    CString prompt;
    for (int i = 0; i < 3; i++)
    {
        prompt.LoadString(ID_COLORS_CYAN + i);
        pAddinMenu->AppendMenu(MF_STRING,
            ID_COLORS_CYAN + i, prompt);
    }
}
```

2. Add strings to the string table to store the menu command labels shown in Table 4.11.

Table 4.11 Menu Command Labels

ID	Caption
ID_COLORS_PURPLE	&Purple
ID_COLORS_CYAN	&Cyan
ID_COLORS_YELLOW	&Yellow

► Implement the *OnColors* function

The next step is to write a command handler for the dynamic menu. The following code can be added to handle the commands that are generated by the additional menus:

```
void CMenusDynamicView::OnColors(UINT nUID)
{
    CMenusDynamicDoc* pDoc = GetDocument();
    ASSERT_VALID(pDoc);

    pDoc->SetColor(IDtoColorRef(nUID));
    Invalidate();
}
```

► Implement the *OnOptionsStdcolors* function

When the user selects the Standard Colors menu command, you need to set the menu back to the standard options that were available before the menu commands were added. Write code for the *OnOptionsStdcolors* function as follows:

```
void CMenusDynamicView::OnOptionsStdcolors()
{
    CMenu *pAddinMenu, *pTopMenu;

    // Obtain a pointer to the top-level menu
    pTopMenu = AfxGetMainWnd()->GetMenu();

    pAddinMenu = pTopMenu->GetSubMenu(2);
    int i = pAddinMenu->GetMenuItemCount();
    if (8 == i)
    {
        i--;
        while(i > 3)
        {
            pAddinMenu->RemoveMenu(i, MF_BYPOSITION);
            i--;
        }
    }
    // Finally, force a redraw;
    CMenusDynamicDoc* pDoc = GetDocument();
    pDoc->SetColor(BLACK);
    Invalidate();
}
```

► Add update handlers

1. To include update handlers for the menus, you need to add the following code in the view's message map.

```
ON_UPDATE_COMMAND_UI_RANGE(ID_COLORS_CYAN,
    ID_COLORS_YELLOW, OnUpdateColors)
ON_UPDATE_COMMAND_UI_RANGE(ID_COLORS_BLACK,
    ID_COLORS_BLUE, OnUpdateColors)
ON_UPDATE_COMMAND_UI(ID_OPTIONS_EXTRACOLORS, OnUpdateOptions)
ON_UPDATE_COMMAND_UI(ID_OPTIONS_STANDARDCOLORS, OnUpdateOptions)
```

2. Write the code for the *OnUpdateColors* handler to check the selected color in the Colors menu as follows:

```
void CMenusDynamicView::OnUpdateColors(CCmdUI* pCmdUI)
{
    CMenusDynamicDoc* pDoc = GetDocument();
    ASSERT_VALID(pDoc);

    pCmdUI->SetCheck(pDoc->GetColor() ==
        IDtoColorRef(pCmdUI->m_nID));
}
```

3. Write the code for the *OnUpdateOptions* handler to verify the selected menu command in the Options menu:

```
void CMenusDynamicView::OnUpdateOptions(CCmdUI* pCmdUI)
{
    CMenu *pAddinMenu, *pTopMenu;
    pTopMenu = AfxGetMainWnd()->GetMenu();
    pAddinMenu = pTopMenu->GetSubMenu(2);

    switch (pCmdUI->m_nUID)
    {
        case ID_OPTIONS_EXTRACOLORS:
            pCmdUI->Enable(pAddinMenu
            ->GetMenuItemCount() == 4);
            break;
        case ID_OPTIONS_STANDARDCOLORS:
            pCmdUI->Enable(pAddinMenu
            ->GetMenuItemCount() != 4);
    }
}
```

4. Save DynaView.cpp. Build Dynamenu and run it. Changing the selection in the Options menu will dynamically modify the menu commands available in the Colors menu. See the companion CD for the completed exercise.

Exercise 2: Adding a Modeless Dialog Box

In this exercise, you will perform the following actions for adding a modeless dialog box:

- Create the dialog template
- Implement the dialog class
- Integrate the dialog box into an application

Creating the Dialog Template

Begin this part of the exercise by starting a new project. On the Resource toolbar, click the New Dialog button to create a dialog template. Set the Caption and ID properties of the dialog box shown in Table 4.12.

Table 4.12 Caption and ID Properties of a Dialog Box

Property	Value
Caption	Find Difference
ID	IDD_NEXTDIFF

► **Add controls to the dialog template**

Open the IDD_NEXTDIFF dialog box resource. Add the controls shown in Table 4.13 to the dialog template.

Table 4.13 Controls to Add to the Dialog Template

Control type	ID	Caption
Default command button (already added)	IDOK	Find Next
Command button (already added)	IDCANCEL	Cancel
Group box	IDC_STATIC	Find
Option button	IDC_RADIO_NEXTDIFF	&Next Difference
Option button	IDC_RADIO_NEXTEQUAL	Next &Equal Sequence
Group box	IDC_STATIC	Direction
Option button	IDC_RADIO_UP	&Up
Option button	IDC_RADIO_DOWN	&Down

► **Group controls on the dialog template**

1. Right-click the Next Differences option button and click Properties.
2. Select the Group check box.

3. Perform the same steps to select the Group check box for the Up option button.
4. Double-click the Find Next button and click its Group box.
5. Save the dialog template.

► **Set the tab order for the controls on the dialog template**

1. Click Tab Order on the Layout menu. The property page is hidden. Currently, the dialog editor displays a number for each control in the dialog box template. By default, the numbers indicate the order in which each control was added to the template. Note that when you set the tab order, the OK button automatically has the Default Button option selected.
2. Click the controls in the required order. Set the tab order shown in Figure 4.23.

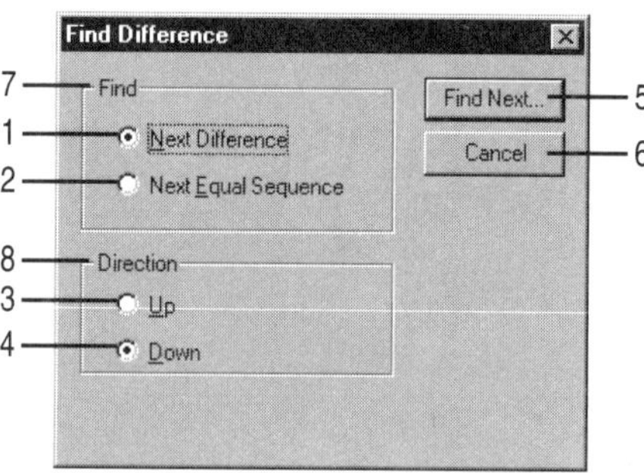

Figure 4.23 Tab order

3. To end the tab-ordering operation, click inside the dialog editor window, but outside the dialog box resource.

► **Check and save your file**

1. Test the dialog template by clicking Test on the Dialog toolbar.
2. Save the current file when you are satisfied with your work.

► **Create a dialog box class using ClassWizard**

1. Make sure the dialog editor for the IDD_NEXTDIFF dialog box resource is open.
2. Invoke ClassWizard by selecting it in the View menu. ClassWizard should automatically display the Adding a Class dialog box.
3. To create a new class, click Create a New Class and click OK. The New Class dialog box appears.
4. In the Name box of the New Class dialog box, type *CFindDiff* for the name of the associated C++ dialog class.

5. In the Base Class drop-down list, click CDialog. The Dialog ID drop-down list should already be set to IDD_NEXTDIFF.
6. Shorten the file names FindDifferenceDialog.cpp and FindDifference-Dialog.h to FindDiff.cpp and FindDiff.h by using the Change button and its dialog box, and then click OK.
7. When you are finished, click OK in the New Class dialog box.
8. Click OK in the MFC ClassWizard dialog box.

Implementing the Dialog Class

Having created the dialog template, you are now ready to implement the dialog class CFindDiff in this portion of the exercise. Because you are creating a modeless dialog box, you can query controls directly.

► **Set up members for control states in the dialog box**

1. Open the FindDiff.h file.
2. Create member variables to determine whether you want the dialog box to terminate or to find the next difference, as shown in the following code:

```
protected:
    BOOL m_bTerminate;
    BOOL m_bFindNext;
```

3. Declare member functions to return the internal state of the application as follows:

```
public:
    BOOL IsTerminating() const;
    BOOL SearchDown() const;
    BOOL FindDifference () const;
    BOOL FindNext() const;
```

4. Preceding the CFindDiff class, add the following constant:

```
const char* const FINDDIFF_MSGSTRING = "diffapp_FindDifference";
```

5. Save FindDiff.h.
6. Open the file FindDiff.cpp.
7. Implement the *CFindDifferenceDialog::IsTerminating* function to return *m_bTerminating* as follows:

```
BOOL CFindDiff::IsTerminating() const
{
    return m_bTerminating;
}
```

8. Implement *CFindDifferenceDialog::SearchDown* to return the state of the Search Down option button as follows:

```
BOOL CFindDifferenceDialog::SearchDown() const
{
    return(IsDlgButtonChecked(IDC_RADIO_DOWN));
}
```

9. Implement *CFindDifferenceDialog::FindDifference* to return the state of the Next Difference option button as follows:

```
BOOL CFindDifferenceDialog::FindDifference() const
{
    return(IsDlgButtonChecked(IDC_RADIO_NEXTDIFF));
}
```

10. Implement *CFindDifferenceDialog::FindNext* to return *m_bFindNext* as follows:

```
BOOL CFindDifferenceDialog::FindNext() const
{
    return m_bFindNext;
}
```

11. Save FindDiff.cpp.

► Implement the Find Next button handler

When the main application window is notified that the user has clicked a button, it will query the dialog box about the action. You could use the *WPARAM* parameter of the message to pass this information, but this would entail a more complicated maintenance scheme.

1. Open FindDiff.h.
2. Define a constant string for the name of the message as follows:

```
const char* const FINDDIFF_MSGSTRING = "diffapp_FindDifference";
```

3. Save FindDiff.h.
4. Invoke ClassWizard.
5. Create a handler for BN_CLICKED on the IDOK button. Give it the name *OnFindNext*.
6. In the *OnFindNext* function, set *m_bFindNext* to TRUE.

```
m_bFindNext = TRUE;
```

7. Send the private message to the parent of the dialog box with a pointer to the dialog box object in LPARAM.

```
GetParent()->SendMessage(::RegisterWindowMessage
(FINDDIFF_MSGSTRING), 0, LPARAM)this);
```

8. Reset *m_bFindNext* to FALSE.

► **Implement dialog box initialization**

1. In the constructor, initialize *m_bTerminating* as follows:

```
CFindDifferenceDialog::CFindDifferenceDialog
(CWnd* pParent /*=NULL*/)
    :CDialog(CFindDifferenceDialog::IDD, pParent)
{
    // {{AFX_DATA_INIT(CFindDifferenceDialog)
    // }}AFX_DATA_INIT
    m_bTerminating = FALSE;
m_bFindNext = FALSE;
}
```

2. Invoke ClassWizard. Create handlers for the WM_INITDIALOG and *Create* messages and click OK.
3. In the *OnInitDialog* handler, add the following code to click the Next Difference and Down option buttons as follows:

```
BOOL CFindDifferenceDialog::OnInitDialog()
{
    CDialog::OnInitDialog();
    CheckDlgButton(IDC_RADIO_NEXTDIFF, TRUE);
    CheckDlgButton(IDC_RADIO_DOWN, TRUE);
    return TRUE;
}
```

4. Delete the parameters from the *Create* handler. Because all the members are set up in *CDialog::CDialog*, the call to the *Create* handler should look as follows:

```
BOOL CFindDiff::Create()
{
    return CDialog::Create (m_lpszTemplateName, m_pParentWnd);
}
```

5. Save FindDiff.cpp.
6. In the FindDiff.h file, remove the parameters from *Create*.
7. Save FindDiff.h.

► **Implement dialog box shutdown**

1. Use ClassWizard to create handlers for the BN_CLICKED message on the IDCANCEL object (*OnCancel*) and the *PostNcDestroy* message on the CFindDiff object. When finished, click OK.
2. Edit the code for *CFindDiff::OnCancel*. Use *CWnd::DestroyWindow* to close the window when the Cancel button is clicked, as follows:

```
void    ::OnCancel
{
    DestroyWindow();
}
```

3. Edit the code for *CFindDifferenceDialog::PostNcDestroy*. CWnd sends *PostNcDestroy* after the window has been destroyed. Because your window no longer exists, you cannot follow your window tree with *CWnd::GetParent*. You will use the stored *m_pParentWnd* handler to communicate with the parent window. Set the *m_bTerminating* member to TRUE, and then send the message to your parent window as follows:

```
m_bTerminating = TRUE;
m_pParentWnd->SendMessage(
    ::RegisterWindowMessage(FINDDIFF_MSGSTRING),
    0, (LPARAM)this);
```

4. As the last step, delete your object. Add this code to *CFindDiff::PostNcDestroy*:

```
delete this;
```

5. Save FindDiff.cpp and build your project. See the companion CD for the completed exercise.

Integrating the Dialog Box into an Application

In this portion of the exercise, you will write the code to provide functionality to the dialog box. This code is placed in the CMainFrame class.

► **Resolve dependencies on CDifferenceDialog in Mainfrm.h**

First you will add reference to CFindDifferenceDialog class in MainFrm.h. You will also need to include FindDiff.h in any file that includes MainFrm.h prior to that include. Add the include statements to the MainFrm.cpp, DiffView.cpp, DiffDoc.cpp, and Diff.cpp files.

► **Add menu items to the IDR_MAINFRAME menu**

1. Open the IDR_MAINFRAME menu.
2. Add a separator to the end of the Edit menu.
3. Add the two menu items provided in Table 4.14 after the separator.

Table 4.14 Menu Items and Their Captions

ID	Caption
ID_EDIT_FIND	&Find...
ID_EDIT_FINDDIFF	Find &Difference...

4. Save Diff.rc.

► **Integrate CFindDifferenceDialog into CMainFrame**

1. Open MainFrm.h.
2. Declare a pointer to a *CFindDifferenceDialog* object in the protected implementation section as follows:

```
CFindDifferenceDialog*m_pFindDiffDlg;
```

3. Declare a handler for the FINDDIFF_MSGSTRING registered message before DECLARE_MESSAGE_MAP as follows:

```
afx_msg LRESULT OnFindDifferenceCmd (WPARAM, LPARAM lParam);
```

4. Declare a member function to find the next difference as follows:

```
void OnFindNextDifference(BOOL bSearchDown, BOOL bNextDifference);
```

5. Save MainFrm.h.
6. Open MainFrm.cpp.
7. Initialize a variable to hold the ID of the registered message as follows:

```
static const UINT nMsgFindDifference =
::RegisterWindowMessage(FINDDIFF_MSGSTRING);
```

8. Add the following code to map the message to CMainFrame:

```
ON_REGISTERED_MESSAGE (nMsgFindDifference, OnFindDifferenceCmd)
```

9. Using ClassWizard, add a command handler for ID_EDIT_FINDDIFF (*OnEditFindDiff*).
10. Set *m_pFindDiffDlg* to NULL in the constructor.

► **Implement the menu handler for ID_EDIT_FINDDIFF**

1. Edit the code for *CMainFrame::OnEditFindDiff* to check if the dialog box is already displayed, as the following code demonstrates:

```
if(m_pFindDiffDlg == NULL)
```

2. Construct a dynamic *CFindDifferenceDialog* instance and assign the pointer to *m_pFindDiffDlg* if the dialog box is not already displayed, as follows:

```
m_pFindDiffDlg = new CFindDifferenceDialog(this);
```

3. Call *CFindDifferenceDialog::Create* to initialize it, as follows:

```
if(m_pFindDiffDlg)
{
    m_pFindDiffDlg->Create();
}
```

4. Display the dialog window by adding the following code:

```
if(m_pFindDiffDlg)
{
    m_pFindDiffDlg->SetActiveWindow();
    m_pFindDiffDlg->ShowWindow(SW_SHOW);
}
```

► **Implement a handler for the registered message**

1. In the MainFrm.cpp file, define *CMainFrame::OnFindDifferenceCmd* as follows:

```
LRESULT CMainFrame::OnFindDifferenceCmd
(WPARAM, LPARAM lParam)
```

2. Cast LPARAM to a pointer to *CfindDifferenceDialog* as follows:

```
CFindDifferenceDialog* pDialog =
(CFindDifferenceDialog *)lParam;
```

3. The dialog box sends its message when the Find Next button is clicked, or when the dialog box is closing. In the latter case, clear *m_pFindDiffDlg*, as shown in the following code:

```
if (pDialog->IsTerminating())
{
    m_pFindDiffDlg = NULL;
}
```

4. When the Find Next button is clicked, check the state of the option buttons and dispatch to *CMainFrame::OnFindNextDifference*, as follows:

```
else if (pDialog->FindNext())
{
OnFindNextDifference(pDialog->SearchDown(), pDialog-
>FindDifference());
}
```

5. Return 0 for the message.
6. Save MainFrm.cpp.

► **Implement visual feedback**

1. In the MainFrm.cpp file, define *CMainFrame::OnFindNextDifference* as follows:

```
void CMainFrame::OnFindNextDifference
(BOOL bSearchDown, BOOL bNextDifference)
```

2. Get the active view, as demonstrated in the following code:

```
CDiffView * pView = (CDiffView *)GetActiveView();
if(pView)
{
```

3. Find out which line (if any) is currently highlighted, as follows:

```
int nLineCnt = pView->GetRichEditCtrl().GetLineCount();
LONG lStart = 0;
LONG lEnd = 0;
pView->GetRichEditCtrl().GetSel(lStart, lEnd);
```

4. Add the following code to any location in the window:

```
int nNewLine;
if(bSearchDown)
{
nNewLine = lCurLine + (rand() % (nLineCnt-lCurLine)+1);
}
else
{
    nNewLine = rand() % (lCurLine+1) + 1;
}
```

5. Add the following code to find the starting and ending characters of that line and select them:

```
lStart = pView->GetRichEditCtrl().LineIndex(nNewLine);
lEnd = lStart + pView->GetRichEditCtrl().
LineLength(nNewLine); pView->GetRichEditCtrl().
SetSel(lStart, lEnd);
```

6. Add the following code to use the status bar text to show the current option:

```
if (bNextDifference)
{
    m_wndStatusBar.SetWindowText(_T("Found next
    difference"));
}
else
{
    m_wndStatusBar.SetWindowText(_T("Found next equal
    run"));
}
```

7. Save MainFrm.cpp.

► **Build and test the application**

Build the application. Select menu items in the Edit menu, set the focus in either pane, and find the next difference between the files either forward or backward.

Exercise 3: Building an ActiveX Control

In this exercise, you will create an ActiveX control. You will use an existing device-independent bitmap (DIB) class. After you create the control, you will test the control by using the ActiveX Control Test Container.

► **Build the framework control**

1. Start Visual Studio 6.
2. On the File menu, click New. The New dialog box appears.
3. On the Projects tab, click MFC ActiveX ControlWizard, set the project name to PalView and click OK to start MFC ActiveX ControlWizard.
4. In Step 1 of ControlWizard, create one control, leave the other options at their default settings, and click Next.
5. In Step 2 of ControlWizard, accept the default settings for all options and click Finish.
6. The New Project Information dialog box appears. Click OK to create the project.

7. On the Project menu, click Add to Project, and then click Files.
8. Insert the files Dib.cpp and DibPal.cpp from the companion CD into the project. The CDIB class creates a DIB from an existing bitmap file, and the CDIBPal class uses this information to determine the colors used to create the bitmap.

► **Integrate CDIBPal into the CPalViewCtrl control**

1. Right-click CPalViewCtrl in ClassView and add a protected member variable. The protected member variable will be defined as follows:

```
CDIBPal*    m_pDibPal;
```

2. This pointer will be used to refer to the CDIBPal object. Open the file PalViewCtl.cpp.
3. Include the files Dib.h and DibPal.h before the file PalViewCtl.h.
4. Update the constructor to initialize the *m_pDibPal* message to NULL.
5. Update the destructor to delete *m_pDibPal* if it exists.

► **Update the *CPalViewCtrl::OnDraw* function to use the *CDibPal::Draw* function**

1. Modify *CPalViewCtrl::OnDraw* to use *CDibPal::OnDraw* if CDibPal has been instantiated, as follows:

```
if(NULL != m_pDibPal)
    m_pDibPal->Draw(pdc, rcBounds, TRUE);
```

2. Otherwise, fill the control with a white brush as shown in the following code:

```
else
    pdc->FillRect(rcBounds, CBrush::FromHandle
        ((HBRUSH)GetStockObject(WHITE_BRUSH)));
```

3. Save PalViewCtl.cpp.

► **Add a function to extract the palette from a DIB file**

1. Right-click CPalViewCtl in ClassView and add a protected member function as follows:

```
void ExtractPalFromDIBFile(LPCTSTR lpszFileSpec)
```

The function will be used to extract the color palette from the DIB file.

2. Add the following local variables to the implementation of *ExtractPalFromDIBFile*:

```
CDIB Dib;  //use to load DIB
CFile DibFile;  //use to open bitmap file
```

3. Open the bitmap file, using the path stored in *lpszFileSpec* as follows:

```
if(DibFile.Open(lpszFileSpec, CFile::modeRead))
{
```

4. Copy the file into a CDIB instance as follows:

```
if(Dib.Load(&DibFile))
(
```

5. Create a palette and extract the color table from the DIB into the palette as follows:

```
CDIBPal* pTemp = new CDIBPal;
ASSERT(pTemp != NULL);
if(pTemp->Create(&Dib))
(
```

6. Add the following code to delete the instance of CDIBPal, if it exists:

```
if(NULL != m_pDibPal)
{
    delete m_pDibPal;
    m_pDibPal = NULL;
}
```

7. Assign the palette you created to *m_pDibPal* as follows:

```
m_pDibPal = pTemp;
```

8. Draw the palette in three-dimensional style as follows:

```
m_pDibPal->SetDraw3D(TRUE);

delete pTemp;
```

9. Add three closing braces for the *if* statements and then save PalViewCtl.cpp.

▶ **Add DibFileName property**

1. In ClassWizard, click the Automation tab and make sure the Class Name drop-down list is set to CPalViewCtrl.
2. Click the Add Property button. The Add Property dialog box appears.
3. Create a new DibFileName property, using the following settings:
   - **External name** DibFileName
   - **Type** CString
   - **Variable name** *m_dibFileName*
   - **Notification function** *OnDibFileNameChanged*

4. In PalViewCtl.cpp, modify the new *OnDibFileNameChanged* function to extract the palette from DibFileName and repaint the control by calling *ExtractPalFromDIBFile* and *InvalidateControl.*
5. In the constructor, initialize *m_dibFileName* as follows:

```
m_dibFileName = _T ("");
```

► **Build and run the control using the ActiveX Control Test Container**

1. Save all files and build the file PalView.ocx.
2. Visual Studio provides a test container for ActiveX controls. To run the test container, click ActiveX Control Test Container on the Tools menu.
3. On the Edit menu, click Insert New Control.
4. In the Insert Control dialog box, select PalView Control and click OK.
5. Resize the control to an appropriate size.
6. On the Edit menu, click Properties.
7. The Properties dialog box appears. Because you have not implemented a property sheet for this control, invoking Properties displays only the blank default property sheet provided by ControlWizard.

Review

The following questions are intended to reinforce key information presented in this chapter. If you are unable to answer a question, review the appropriate lesson and then try answering the question again. Answers to the questions can be found in Appendix B, "Review Questions and Answers," at the back of this book.

1. Which function adds menu commands to a cascading menu?

2. To create a dockable toolbar, which steps must you complete?

3. How do you invoke modal and modeless dialog boxes?

4. Which function adds controls to a rebar?

CHAPTER 5

Building Basic Business Objects

Lesson 1: COM Basics 216

Lesson 2: Visual C++ Classes 235

Lesson 3: Building a COM Component Using the Platform SDK 256

Lesson 4: Building a COM Component Using ATL or MFC 270

Lab 5: Dissecting ATL 291

Review 298

About This Chapter

In this chapter, you will learn the basics of Microsoft's Component Object Model (COM). COM serves as a binary standard for creating components. Using a binary standard means that different programming languages will know how to communicate with your components. You will also learn about COM's interface and methods, as well as how COM can be distributed across a network as Distributed COM (DCOM). In additional lessons, you will put the basic COM concepts you learn into practice. You will create several C++ classes using classic C++. After studying some of the problems with the architecture, you will convert the classes to COM classes. At the end of that exercise you will have a COM server written in raw C++. The chapter ends with a discussion of how ATL and MFC simplify the process of building COM servers.

Before You Begin

To complete the lessons in this chapter, you will need to have Microsoft Visual C++ 6.0 installed and configured.

Lesson 1: COM Basics

At the heart of developing distributed applications is how code segments and their corresponding application logic communicate with other code segments. An application is typically separated into discrete blocks of code that perform a particular type of work. The individual working units must fit together and communicate to perform the overall work of the application. To simplify this communication between code segments, as well as standardize how these code segments communicate with the operating system, Microsoft developed the COM specification. You'll further explore why a specification standard is needed, as well as how the COM specification affects an application's design.

After this lesson, you will be able to:

- Describe the rationale for an object communication standard
- List the differences between COM classes (coclasses), objects, and components
- Identify a COM component's required interface

Estimated lesson time: 50 mInutes

The Challenges of Component-Based Applications

One of the fundamental goals of COM is to enable developers to create applications assembled from prebuilt parts known as *components*. Component-based applications must meet several technical challenges by being able to:

- Locate and execute components on a computer or network
- Interact with a computer's operating system
- Be accessible to and from other applications
- Be language independent
- Maintain component version control

First your application must be able to locate a component on a computer or network and then be able to execute that component. The component that must be located is the binary file, stored by the operating system with a particular name. If a standard mechanism for locating these various components does not exist, the programming overhead costs of learning to use components is very high. Additionally, the costs and inconsistencies of coding logic to locate multiple components from different sources would present significant barriers to reusing prebuilt components.

When your application has located the components, you must make sure that the operating system recognizes how to execute them; thus, the services of the operating system must have a known and common technique to load components into the client computer's memory.

The second technical challenge is to provide standards for the application to interact with the components when they have been loaded into a computer's memory. If no standards exist, the overhead cost of learning how to use such objects creates a barrier to reusing code. This lesson refers to the components as *objects* at this point, because they have been loaded into a computer's memory. Ideally, a standard mechanism for object interaction would not distinguish the location of any given object, whether the object exists within its own application's process, within another process on the application's host computer, or within a different process on another computer altogether. Interprocess and remote communications usually require tremendously complex coding within an application. Providing standards for object interaction allows application and component developers to spend less time creating such complex code. In addition, different operating systems must also support your application. Thus, by creating an application based on components that can be used on different operating systems, such as Microsoft Windows 95, Microsoft Windows 98, Microsoft Windows NT, and Microsoft Windows 2000, the application gains cross-platform support and a wider distribution base.

Third, component-based applications must be accessible to and from other applications. To further the concept of application reuse, the components that are created must be commonly accessible from other applications, without learning multiple proprietary programming interfaces. To promote reuse, access to an application's components should be simple and easy to use.

The fourth technical challenge is executing true language independence, a complex challenge for any object model. Every element involved in a particular object—memory allocation, method names, parameter types, calling conventions, and so on—must be defined in such a way that the object can be created in one programming language and used by another. You should not need to spend valuable time or energy worrying about which programming languages or tools are used to create a desired component. Without wide support from development languages and tools, many different models would fragment the component market. This fragmentation raises the costs of identifying, purchasing, and developing components that are operable only in certain environments. Thus, the goal of language independence is the ability to create a component in your language of choice and to interact with any existing component regardless of the language used.

Finally, an ongoing challenge is the ability to maintain the potential to create newer versions of applications and components. Applications developed at different times can implement similar components, and thus cause potential usage conflicts when running on a given computer. Because developers continue to upgrade components to maintain and improve functionality, version compatibility must be maintained between old and new versions of the components.

COM was designed to address each of these challenges. The successful evolution of COM has brought added functionality and helped to solve some of the increasingly complex issues of distributed computing. This success is rooted in the fact that COM is a binary standard.

COM as a Binary Standard

COM is a binary standard for object interaction. It addresses many component challenges because it is both specification-based and implementation-based.

COM is specification-based in that it defines objects in a manner independent of language and location. It also defines how to locate and identify components and how to create objects. A COM component's interface can be recognized with the Interface Definition Language (IDL) or equivalent header file or type library.

COM is implementation-based in that it provides system services that locate components and load them into memory. Additionally COM defines the exact binary representation of an interface. Any programming language or tool that supports COM must create object interfaces that correspond to this standard binary representation.

COM, OLE, and ActiveX

You might be more familiar with OLE and Microsoft ActiveX than with COM. You might also be confused as to which technologies these terms refer and how they are related. This wouldn't be surprising: Microsoft has changed its definitions of these terms over the past couple of years, even though the technologies themselves have not changed. Following is a quick run-down:

- **COM** The fundamental component object model, introduced in 1992. The COM (as well as the DCOM and COM+) specification is available on the Microsoft Web site at *http://www.microsoft.com/com/resources/specs.asp*, and only those items defined in the specification are part of COM proper.
- **OLE** Built on top of COM and the mechanism used for compound documents. An example of using OLE is when a Microsoft Excel spreadsheet is inserted into a Word document.
- **ActiveX** Originally introduced with Microsoft's COM-based Internet technologies in 1996; essentially a marketing label used to identify these technologies. Later, COM-based technologies were grouped under the ActiveX umbrella, causing some confusion. Currently, the term ActiveX refers only to ActiveX controls, a specific technology built on top of COM for programmatic controls. When you put a control on a Microsoft Visual Basic form or embed an <OBJECT> tag in an HTML page, you use ActiveX controls.

Coclasses

All COM objects are instances of coclasses. A coclass is simply a named implementation of one or more COM interfaces. A coclass is named using a class identifier (CLSID), which is a type of *globally unique identifier* (GUID, pronounced "goo-id" or "gwid"). Like *interface identifiers* (IIDs), CLSIDs are guaranteed to be unique but are difficult to use. Therefore, coclasses can also have string names, called *programmatic identifiers* (ProgID).

Every coclass has an associated *class object,* also known as a class factory, which has the ability to create instances of a single coclass. The COM specification defines a standard API function for creating class objects (*CoGetClassObject*), and a standard interface for communicating with class objects (IClassFactory). Thus, clients need only one mechanism to create any type of COM object.

The most important method of IClassFactory is *CreateInstance*, which creates an object and returns a specified interface pointer. A client can create a COM object simply by calling *CoGetClassObject* to capture an IClassFactory interface pointer. The client can hold on to the pointer to IClassFactory and then call *CreateInstance* each time it needs a COM object. Most of the time, the client is only interested in creating one or two instances of an object, and does not need to hold on to the IClassFactory pointer. Thus, a client can create such an object by calling IClassFactory *CreateInstance* to send an interface pointer to the object, then releasing the IClassFactory interface pointer. Because this procedure occurs often in COM applications, COM provides a wrapper function that lets you perform this procedure with one call: *CoCreateInstanceEx*.

Coclasses differ from most language-based classes in that when an object has been created its class is irrelevant to the client. All interaction with the object occurs through public interface pointers, which don't recognize the private implementation class used to create the object. This rigorous separation of interface and implementation is a key feature of COM. Thus, its standard published interface and "black box" implementation concept greatly simplifies the client coding effort because the client does not need to know how the component works, just that it does work.

COM Objects

Object is one of the most overloaded terms in programming. As with most object-oriented models, COM objects are run-time instances of a particular class, with the class representing a real-world entity. For example, based on their characteristics, classes could define a Customer, Order, or SalesTaxCalculator. Thus, each Customer object would represent a specific instance of a real-world customer; each Order object would represent a specific instance of an order; and so on.

An object usually contains an identity, a state, and a type of behavior. *Identity* is the unique name or label distinguishing one object from another; *state* represents data associated with a particular object and *behavior* is a set of methods called to query or manipulate an object's state.

To help clarify these concepts, you should examine C++ objects, which are run-time instances of C++ classes. A C++ class defines member variables and methods that apply only to objects of this particular class. Upon an object's creation, a contiguous block of memory becomes allocated for member variables; in effect, the allocated memory's address becomes the object's identity and the memory block's contents become the object's state. Elsewhere in memory, method implementation code defines the object's behavior.

Most language-based object models are similar to that of C++, but the COM object model is somewhat different. Recall that two challenges faced by COM are language and location independence. When you begin to examine interprocess and remote communications, you might find that memory addresses are not sufficient to identify objects. In addition, compatibility among all programming languages and tools, regarding memory layout for object member variables, is nearly impossible.

Accounting for these potential complications, COM approaches objects in a different manner than C++. In COM, the notion of an object's public interface and its implementation are completely separate. Applications can interact with COM objects only through the object's public interfaces using a COM-defined interface pointer. Because all interactions must go through the interface pointer, COM ignores an object's state location and memory management. Additionally, because an interface pointer is the only means through which an application references a given object, the object's identity must relate to that pointer.

Interface Pointers and vtables

The client's interface pointer is actually a pointer to a table of more pointers. The table of pointers is called the *vtable*. Each pointer in the vtable points to the binary code for an interface method in exactly the same manner as in a C++ virtual function table.

A specific pointer to a vtable is appropriately called a *vtable pointer*. Each COM object contains a vtable pointer for each interface it supports. A client requesting an interface pointer to an object obtains *a pointer to an appropriate vtable pointer*, not the vtable pointer itself. The vtable pointer needs an additional pointer to support an interface because the component needs a way to identify the object on which it should be working.

When a COM object is created, a single block of memory is usually allocated for both vtable pointers, as well as any internal data members that the object needs. The component recognizes the relationship between the locations of both the vtable pointer and the object's entire memory block; thus, this component can identify its appropriate object. By using the interface pointer, COM further specifies that the first parameter passed to each method call is a pointer to the particular object mentioned.

Fortunately, most COM-supportive programming languages and tools automatically map interface pointers and vtables to equivalent concepts in the languages themselves. For example, C++ interfaces are equivalent to abstract base classes. These interfaces can be implemented by deriving a particular class from the abstract base class. Calling COM methods through an interface pointer is exactly like calling C++ methods through an object pointer.

As another example, Visual Basic interfaces are almost completely hidden within the Visual Basic language itself. Using the *Implements* keyword (and thereby implementing the interface's methods) you can implement an interface. To use a COM object, you should declare an interface type object variable, create the object, and make function calls as normal.

Combined with a common interpretation of interface definitions, the binary standard for interfaces provides language independence as well as the potential for complete location independence. You should ideally make in-process, interprocess, and remote calls identical on the client computer. Within a single process, the interface pointer can direct itself to the original vtable pointer and call methods directly. Although such a technique probably wouldn't work across different processes or computers, the interface pointer could be redirected to point to a proxy vtable pointer. The client-side proxy would presumably recognize methods in which to make interprocess or remote calls to an equivalent server-side object, or stub object; in turn, that particular object would make in-process calls to the original object. To clients and components, method calls would appear identical.

Managing Object Lifetimes

Assuming that an object has been created on a client computer holding an interface pointer to the object, it seems logical that this object could be destroyed on the client on which it was created. However, the process of destroying an object that is no longer needed is complicated. For instance, one client can use *QueryInterface* to obtain multiple interface pointers to a single object. This client might not be able to track when it has finished using all interface pointers needed to safely destroy the object. Another client could potentially need to use the object after it was marked for deletion. No single client can distinguish when all clients have finished using the object except the object itself—with some assistance from each client.

To address the issues involved in destroying an object, IUnknown provides *object lifetime management,* commonly referred to as reference counting—which tracks the number of clients using an interface. When a new interface pointer to an object is created, the object's reference count must be incremented by calling *IUnknown::AddRef*. A client computer that has finished using an interface pointer calls *IUnknown::Release* to *decrement* the object's reference count. When the reference count is set to zero, the object destroys itself upon determining that its use is complete. Hence the object lifetime management feature neatly solves the problems of both a single client with multiple interface pointers as well as multiple independent clients. With this feature implemented, the client computer's only tasks are to create an object to get an interface pointer, use the pointer to make method calls, and release the pointer using *IUnknown::Release*.

COM Components

A *COM component* is a binary unit of software you can use to create COM objects. For a given CLSID, a component will include the coclass, the code to implement the class object, and usually the code needed to create appropriate entries in a system registry.

Note Although components are sometimes called servers, this chapter avoids confusion with server computers by maintaining the original term as *component*.

The Windows 95, Windows 98, and Windows NT platforms allow three basic packaging methods for COM components:

- **Windows services** Components are built as Windows services in situations where the components must always be running, even if no one is logged on to the host computer.
- **Executable files** Windows executable files are often used where an application provides a UI in addition to furnishing COM objects. Microsoft Word is an example of a COM component built as an executable file.
- **DLLs** In most other scenarios, components are packaged as DLLs. In particular, most components used to construct multilayered applications will be packaged as DLLs. The Microsoft ActiveX controls used in a presentation layer are DLLs, as are all business service components that run within the MTS environment.

Another way to categorize components is by their location relative to the client, as described in these three categories:

- **In-process components** These components run within the same process as the client. All in-process components are implemented as DLLs.
- **Local components** Local components run in separate processes, all on the client computer. A local component can be an executable file or a Windows service.

- **Remote components** Remote components operate on computers entirely separate from the client. Remote components can be executable files, Windows services, or DLLs. To run a DLL component remotely, a remote computer would implement a *surrogate process,* or an application run on a remote computer capable of running DLL components. Both COM and MTS provide standard surrogates for DLL components: Dllhost.exe and Mtx.exe respectively.

The remainder of this lesson relates to COM and will focus on components implemented as DLLs, because these components are most prevalent in n-tier, or service-layered, applications.

DLL Component Structure

In addition to implementing coclasses and class objects provided by all types of components, DLL components are expected to implement four well-known entry points as follows:

- *DllGetClassObject* returns an interface pointer to a class object for a specified component-implemented CLSID.
- *DllCanUnloadNow* indicates whether any objects created by a component are still active. If so, the DLL needs to remain in memory; otherwise, the DLL can be unloaded, allowing for computer resource conservation.
- *DllRegisterServer* writes all registry entries required for all coclasses implemented in the component.
- *DllUnregisterServer* removes all registry entries created by *DllRegisterServer.*

The COM system services call *DllGetClassObject* and *DllCanUnloadNow;* applications should never need to call these functions directly. Installation programs and developer tools usually call *DllRegisterServer* and *DllUnregisterServer.*

COM Identifiers

Unique COM identifiers are needed to locate components and to reference each interface. Using a string identifier to provide a unique identifier to cite each interface could cause several problems.

For example, it is difficult to guarantee the selection of a truly unique identifier. Even when a naming convention is imposed, another developer might use the same identifier for a different purpose. To guarantee uniqueness, a central authority could issue prefixes—for example, one prefix per company. However, each company would then need a central registry of names to prevent duplicates within the company. To impose such a method on string identifiers is unnecessarily complicated.

Instead of using string identifiers, COM implements GUIDs, which are 128-bit system-generated integers that uniquely identify components. The algorithm used to generate GUIDs is statistically guaranteed to generate unique identification numbers.

Note According to the COM specification, GUIDs can be generated at the rate of 10,000,000 per second per computer for the next 3,240 years without risk of duplication.

You can generate GUIDs by using a tool such as Guidgen.exe, which accompanies Microsoft Visual C++ and the Microsoft Platform SDK. Guidgen.exe calls the system API function *CoCreateGuid* to generate the GUID, then provides several output options. For example, the following GUID was generated using the *static const* output option, and is suitable for inclusion in a C++ source file:

```
// {45D3F4B0-DB76-11d1-AA06-0040052510F1}
static const GUID GUID_Sample =
{0x45d3f4b0, 0xdb76, 0x11d1,
    {0xaa, 0x6, 0x0, 0x40, 0x5, 0x25, 0x10, 0xf1}};
```

The first line in the code example shown previously is a comment demonstrating how a GUID appears in string form; GUIDs are normally presented to users in this string form. The remaining lines in this code example define the GUID as a constant that you can use in C++ code.

Note Most development tools automate the process of creating skeleton COM components. Such tools also generate appropriate GUIDs for developers in a format that the skeleton COM code can recognize.

Every interface is identified by a GUID. Whenever you need to uniquely identify an interface to COM, you use its GUID, which is, in this case, called an interface identification (IID). The IID can be complex numerical figures such as {45D3F4B0-DB76-11d1-AA06-0040052510F1} or {45D3F4B1-DB76-11d1-AA06-0040052510F1}.

To simplify IID standards for use in source code, every interface should also have a string name. Conventionally, these string names usually begin with the letter "I"—for example, IComputeSalesTax. String names aren't guaranteed to be unique, but it's unlikely that two different interfaces with an identical string name would be used in one source code file.

COM Interfaces

Understanding interfaces is essential to understanding COM. A *COM interface* is a collection of logically related operations that define a particular behavior. When you define an interface, you provide specifications only for a set of operations, but not for implementations. Interface definitions represent a contract between a caller and an implementer. If a component implements a particular interface, the caller can expect the component to obey the interface specification. Such a specification includes a strict definition of interface method syntax, as well as a definition of interface semantics.

To be defined as a COM interface, an interface must satisfy the following requirements:

- A unique identifier must identify the interface.
- The interface must ultimately derive from the special interface IUnknown.
- When published, the interface must be immutable. In other words, the interface can't be changed.

IUnknown (composed of *QueryInterface*, *AddRef*, and *Release)* is the *standard interface* developed by Microsoft for use with COM—to be a COM object your interface must implement IUnknown. Interfaces that you develop are known as *custom interfaces.*

IUnknown Interface

To actually be a part of COM, a COM object must always publicly inherit the IUnknown interface, as demonstrated in the following line of code:

```
class IMove : public IUnknown
```

By inheriting from IUnknown in your code, you add the COM functionality to the class you are building. In fact, at a fundamental level, a C++ object combined with IUnknown comprises a COM object. The IUnknown interface is critical because it provides these three methods, and also defines fundamental behavior for COM interfaces. Clients can rely on this fundamental behavior because all COM interfaces derive from IUnknown. IUnknown helps resolve the technical challenge of providing a standard means to interact with objects, and additionally provides four important features: *object identity*, *interface navigation, interface versioning,* and *object lifetime management.*

After you have built your COM component using IUnknown along with your custom interfaces, a client must be able to access the component. Ideally, the client would be able to determine the features and functions of your component, because the client doesn't have or want access to your source code, only to your components functionality. To find out what your component can do, the client must accomplish two things:

1. Start COM. All client applications that intend to use COM must first initialize the COM library by calling the *CoInitialize/CoInitializeEx* function. (Almost all of the built-in COM functions begin with *Co*.)
2. Instantiate an instance of your coclass to create the actual COM object with which the client will communicate. You achieve this by calling *CoCreate-Instance/CoCreateInstanceEx*, and passing the class identifier (or CLSID) of the desired class. *CoCreateInstance* then searches the CLSID section of the registry to find the component containing the particular class. The *CoCreate-Instance* function includes other parameters that determine, for instance, whether the object will run in-process or out-of-process.

If both of these functions have completed successfully, the client application should have a pointer to the interface requested in CoCreateInstance. Through the pointer, though, the client can use the *QueryInterface* method of IUnknown to obtain pointers to other interfaces the object supports.

QueryInterface Method

By inheriting from IUnknown when you wrote your class, you automatically included the three methods of the IUnknown interface: *QueryInterface*, *AddRef*, and *Release*. A client application can call *QueryInterface* to determine if the COM object supports other interfaces, as demonstrated in the following code fragment:

```
hr = pUnknown->QueryInterface(IID_IMove,
(void**)&pMove);
```

The first parameter is the IID of the interface you are seeking, which is typically defined within the file generated by the Microsoft IDL generator. If the IMove interface is found in the object, a pointer to the IMove interface is returned in the second parameter. It is also important to know that *AddRef* is also called when *QueryInterface* is called, thus the object's reference count is also increased.

AddRef and *Release* Methods

Because numerous client applications (which might or might not be aware of one another) can call a given COM object when it is instantiated, you must find a function to recognize when an object that is no longer needed can be safely destroyed in memory. The *AddRef* and *Release* methods of IUnknown accomplish this function, and are also used for reference counting.

For a given interface pointer, you must call *AddRef* before calling any other methods, and call *Release* when the interface pointer is no longer needed by the client. When the reference count reaches zero, the object will be destroyed.

Note that it is the responsibility of the COM server to increase the reference count of the object automatically upon creation. Therefore, you do not have to call AddRef explicitly after using CoCreateInstance.

Automation and IDispatch

For a client to talk to a custom interface it must have knowledge of the vtable layout of that interface at design time—this is called early-binding. However, there are times when a client may need to talk to a COM interface at run time without having had prior knowledge of the vtable's layout of the interface—this is called late-binding. An example of a client that may need this functionality is Microsoft Internet Explorer. An HTML document can contain Microsoft Visual Basic Scripting Edition (VBScript) code to tell Internet Explorer to create a COM object, and call some of its methods. There is no possible way for Internet Explorer to have knowledge at design time (when it was compiled by Microsoft) of every interface in every object that an HTML document may call at run time. To make late-binding possible, Microsoft introduced IDispatch. With IDispatch a client only needs to know the vtable layout of one interface: IDispatch. The IDispatch interface has two key methods that enable a client to make a method call in a generic fashion at run time, namely *GetIDsOfNames* and *Invoke*. Consider a client making a method call in VBScript. For example:

```
Dim obj
Set obj = CreateObject("HelloServer.HelloServer")
obj.SayHello("Joe")
```

When Internet Explorer encounters the *SayHello* method call, it obtains a pointer to the object's IDispatch interface, then calls *GetIDsOfNames* passing the method name (*SayHello*) as one of the parameters. *GetIDsOfNames* tells Internet Explorer if the method is supported and provides Internet Explorer with an ID number for the method. This ID number is a programmer-assigned number for the method. After obtaining the ID number for the method, Internet Explorer calls the *Invoke* method, passing the ID number for the method and an array of VARIANTs containing the parameters for the function call.

The greatest disadvantage of IDispatch is that calling IDispatch consumes more time than directly manipulating the custom interfaces. As you can see, it takes two method calls to IDispatch for every call made by the client. Because it takes longer to use IDispatch it is best to provide a custom interface for clients that can use early binding. A technique that some developers use is to derive their interfaces from IDispatch and mark them as dual in the IDL file. Marking an interface as dual tells a client that reads the type library that the interface supports both vtable binding and IDispatch binding. However, it does not make sense to have more than one interface derived from IDispatch and marked as dual per coclass. This is because a single IDispatch implementation is sufficient to enable a client to make any method call the coclass supports. Just like IDispatch is needed at run time when the client does not have foreknowledge of an object's interface, there also needs to be a mechanism for creating an object for which the CLSID is not known ahead of time. You have already learned that by using *CoCreateInstance* a client can create an instance of a COM object. The first parameter to *CoCreateInstance* is the CLSID of the coclass you wish to create. We have already mentioned that along with a CLSID a developer may assign to the object a *ProgID*. (The ProgID is a string name composed usually of Company Name, dot, coclass name.) A scripting client can use the CLSIDFromProgID API to get the CLSID of a particular coclass before creating it.

Regardless of the method used for creating the object and interacting with it, the creation and initialization of the object on the COM server code is usually done through the IClassFactory interface.

IClassFactory

One of the key attributes of COM is *location transparency*. In other words, a client instantiating and using a COM object should not recognize the object's location, nor should the object's location bear any weight on the client's implementation of the object. If the component containing the class is running in a separate memory space, or even on a remote computer, a reliable means of locating the correct component and then instantiating an object of the desired class must be in place. To ensure this reliability, you must build the IClassFactory interface into your class. As mentioned, the IClassFactory interface actually instantiates an object from your class internally, when instructed to do so.

Versioning Interfaces

Because components and applications can be built and published independently, an interface that has been published is immutable—no changes to syntax or semantics are allowed. Changing a published interface is not permitted; even changes to an interface's number of methods could cause client programs to fail. For instance, a new client application could erroneously read an interface as containing five methods, and unsuccessfully attempt to call an obsolete component containing only four methods, thus a program error would occur. COM interfaces are therefore immutable to avoid such conflicts.

Because an interface cannot be changed, a new interface must actually be defined to "version" an interface. Existing clients are probably incompatible with new interfaces, because the original interface continues to exist. Therefore, these clients are unaffected by whether or not components implement the interfaces. New clients can implement support for new interfaces and access new features when the clients communicate with new components. If a new client happens to access an older component, it can use *QueryInterface* to safely detect that the component does not support the new interface and avoid using the new features.

In summary, when a COM interface is defined, it cannot be changed. Thus, to create a new version, you should add the new interface to the component to ensure maintaining the previous interface.

COM Security

The COM security model defines a standard means for COM objects to interact with operating system-provided security services. The COM security model is independent of the specific security services that might be available.

COM security primarily addresses two issues: who is allowed to launch components, and how calls are secured through interface pointers by providing activation security and call security.

Activation Security

The server computer's Service Control Manager (SCM) applies activation security whenever it receives a request to activate an object. *Activating* an object means either creating a new object or getting an interface pointer to a published object, such as a registered class object or an object in the running object table. This book will not cover published objects, but instead will focus on activation security as it applies to creating new objects.

The SCM uses information in the registry (or information obtained dynamically from published objects) to determine whether an activation request should be allowed. First, the SCM checks a computer-wide setting to determine whether any remote activation requests are permitted. If the computer-wide check succeeds, the SCM looks for component-specific security settings.

In essence, the registry can contain an access control list (ACL) that indicates which users can activate specific components. The SCM checks the client's identity against the ACL to decide whether the activation request can proceed. If no component-specific setting is available, the SCM looks at a default ACL.

If the access check succeeds, the SCM will launch the component, if necessary, and activate the object; otherwise access is denied. The SCM uses information in the registry to determine the security context and user identity, which the object should use to run. This identity becomes the client identity for any activation requests the object might make.

Call Security

When an interface pointer to an object is obtained, a client can make calls to the object. COM also applies security to each method call through an interface pointer. Per-call security has two separate aspects. The first aspect is caller authentication and authorization, which is virtually identical to the activation security check described in the previous section, except that a different ACL is used and the component and client have moderate control over how often the check is performed. The other aspect relates to data integrity and privacy—that is, ensuring that network packets containing COM method calls have not been violated, and also preventing data in the packets from being read during transmission.

Performing security checks on every method call can have considerable overhead costs and involve unnecessary and redundant work. Thus, COM lets applications configure when and how to apply per-call security. Both client and server applications can establish process-wide defaults for per-call security by calling the *CoInitializeSecurity* function. Settings involved in calling this function include an ACL for authorization checks and an authentication level that determines how often authentication is performed, as well as whether data integrity and/or privacy should be enforced. If an application does not explicitly call *CoInitializeSecurity,* the COM run time will call this function, using information from the registry and on the application's behalf, before any objects are activated. As with activation security settings, COM will first look for component-specific settings; if COM does not find any component-specific settings, the default settings for COM components are applied.

In addition to setting per-call security at a process level, applications and components can tune security settings on individual interfaces and method calls using the standard IClientSecurity and IServerSecurity interfaces. Using these interfaces represents a more advanced technique than those found in this book. For additional information, refer to the books by Guy Eddon and Henry Eddon, *Inside Distributed COM* (Microsoft Press, 1998) and *Inside COM+* (Microsoft Press, 1999). For many applications, process-wide settings are sufficient. As this chapter later discusses, MTS offers a role-based security abstraction on top of the COM security model that further simplifies securing access to components.

COM Registration

To anyone familiar with COM, it is an understatement to say that COM relies on the registry. Indeed, without the registry, COM simply cannot operate. COM uses the registry to locate components, based on their CLSID, to store data about type libraries, to store ProgIDs, and so on.

Security Registration

COM security relies on a number of registry entries. On Microsoft Windows and Windows NT, these settings are usually configured using the DCOM configuration tool, Dcomcnfg.exe. Dcomcnfg.exe lets developers set computer-wide and per-application settings involving actual registry keys. Several key DCOM settings can be configured at the computer level, and are stored as values under the registry key HKEY_LOCAL_MACHINE\Software\Microsoft\Ole. Dcomcnfg.exe also allows settings for specific applications to be specified. In COM, an application is nothing more than an identified process that hosts one or more components. Applications are identified by GUIDs called AppIDs.

With the AppID key in place, Dcomcnfg.exe can be used to establish security settings on a per-application basis. These settings will be used if the application does not call *CoInitializeSecurity* explicitly. The settings are stored as named values under the HKEY_CLASSES_ROOT\APPID\{appid-guid} registry key for the application on the server computer.

Note If you do not have an AppID, Dcomcnfg.exe will create one for you. Dcomcnfg.exe will use the GUID of the first CLSID it finds belonging to the server.

Registration Settings

In addition to security settings, the registry also contains information about the component's location. On the server computer, this information is usually written to the registry by the component when it is installed. All that's needed on the server computer is the path to the COM component, stored under the InprocServer32 (for DLL servers) or LocalServer32 key (for EXE servers) for each CLSID. If the component runs as a service, some additional entries are needed.

It is also necessary to put information in the registry of remote client computers for those computers to be able to request remote objects, unless client applications are written to specify the server computer name when *CoCreateInstanceEx* is called. In particular, the client computer needs an AppID with a RemoteServerName value. The client might also need registry entries for proxy/stub DLLs used to marshal interfaces exposed by the objects, depending on whether custom marshaling is required or not. The remote component itself can't write the registry information because it isn't installed on the client computer.

Two common ways exist to create the client-side registry entries on Windows computers. If no proxy/stub DLLs are required by the component, a .reg file containing the registry settings can be distributed to client computers and merged into the local registry. Otherwise, an installation program can be distributed that would write appropriate registry entries and install any proxy/stub DLLs required for the components to work correctly. In some cases, the installation program or .reg file will create the AppID key, but it won't specify where the component is. If this is the case, Dcomcnfg.exe can be used on the client to set the AppID's RemoteServerName value.

COM Support in Distributed Environments

Although running COM components on a single computer, whether in-process or out-of-process, is a major step toward reusable components and modularity, there is another aspect of COM that is truly changing the face and style of business application development. That breakthrough technology is DCOM.

DCOM enables components to be called and run not only in a separate process, but also on a separate computer. This computer can be on the local area network (LAN), or it can be across the continent. As long as the calling client can communicate with the component via a network, and the component is on a computer that supports DCOM, the functionality of that component is available anywhere on that network.

Application developers can thus split their applications into a number of components, each of which runs on a separate computer. This remote activation is accomplished via the proxy/stub technology discussed previously, Remote Procedure Calls. The beauty of DCOM is that the client calls the remote component exactly as it would for an in-process component, and DCOM takes care of the details of finding the remote component and activating it.

Remote Activation and Marshaling

Recall the three types of COM components: in-process, local, and remote. If the component is called in-process, the passing of data and pointers is not a problem, because both the client application and the component providing the service run in the same memory space. What do you do, though, if the object is called out-of-process, either local or remote? A valid interface pointer in one process is undecipherable to another process. You must thus find a way to communicate between processes, and when communication is established, to pass meaningful data back and forth. This process is *marshaling*.

To enable a client in one process to talk with a component in another process, you use a *stub and proxy* system. In this system, the proxy is loaded into the client's address space, acting as a proxy for the actual component and receiving the calls from the client, which it then forwards on to the stub. The stub is loaded into the address space of the component and receives the calls from the proxy, which it then passes to the component. The stub then takes the return values from the component, passes them to the proxy, which passes them to the client.

There are three ways to marshal an interface in COM. One way is to take advantage of the universal marshaler, or type library marshaler. The type library marshaler can marshal any interface that is OLEAUTOMATION compatible. This means that your interface must return HRESULTS, and use parameters that are compatible with the C++ VARIANT structure. The interface must also be part of the type library. To make the interface part of the type library you can add the oleautomation attribute to the interface declaration as follows:

```
[object,
    oleautomation,
    uuid(3A93E7C0-C768-11D3-88FB-0080C8BA8841)]
```

You can also use the dual attribute if the interface is derived from IDispatch. Another way to make the interface part of the type library is to simply declare it within the library block of the IDL file.

Then you must register the type library. The type library can be registered with the RegisterTypeLib API. It can be installed on a client's computer as part of the server EXE (included as a resource), or as a separate TLB file. Remember that the TLB file is generated by the MIDL compiler.

The second way to marshal the interface is to create a proxy/stub DLL. The source code for this DLL is generated by the MIDL compiler. If you generate your project with the ATL wizard, the wizard will create the necessary project files to compile the source generated by MIDL. You then have to register the proxy/stub DLL on both the server and client computers (if they are not the same computer). This option is known as *standard marshaling*.

When using standard marshaling, it is recommended that the stub-and-proxy code be built as a separate component rather than simply part of the client and server components. If the proxy is built into the client and other clients want to access the proxy to talk to the server component, they will be unable to do so. On the other hand, if the proxy is its own DLL, it can be called and loaded by as many different client applications as needed to communicate with the server component.

The third option is to do custom marshaling. Custom marshaling involves implementing the IMarshal interface in your component. When COM needs to marshal your interface it first asks through *QueryInterface* if your object supports the IMarshal interface. If you implement this interface you are telling COM that you want to be in charge of packaging and unpackaging the parameters and return values of every COM call made to your interface.

Lesson Summary

In this lesson, you examined COM as a binary standard for object interaction. You looked at coclasses, which are simply named implementations of one or more COM interfaces, and at how COM separates an object's public interface and its implementation.

You learned that the IUnknown interface must be present in every coclass, and how IUnknown provides three fundamental methods—*QueryInterface*, *AddRef*, and *Release*—to enable clients to communicate with a COM component and to manage the lifetime of the object. Other COM objects locate a given coclass based on its identifiers in the registry, then uses *CoCreateInstance* to instantiate an object of that class.

When you looked at the COM security model, you saw that it defines a standard means for COM objects to interact with operating system-provided security services. COM security primarily addresses two issues: who is allowed to launch components, and how calls are secured through interface pointers by providing activation security and call security.

You also looked at the important topics of registration and marshaling, and how COM makes it possible for components on completely separate computers to interact across a network. This remote activation capability is one of the key ingredients of distributed application design.

Lesson 2: Visual C++ Classes

If you have decided to use Visual C++ as your development environment, your business code will most likely be found in *classes*. Classes are the primary building blocks of C++ applications.

It is common for enterprise development teams to use more than one development language to provide distributed solutions. Visual C++ offers a great range of features; this development package is particularly strong in the area of middle-tier component development. However, when developing interfaces, a particular project can call for the ease of use of Microsoft Visual Basic, or even the cross-platform capabilities of Java. That is why, at times, you will find references to these languages throughout the book. When appropriate, the chapters will show you techniques in C++ that would make integration with these other languages easier.

After this lesson, you will be able to:

- Identify the differences between implementation inheritance and interface inheritance
- Understand the problems with leaving the allocation and deallocation of exported classes to the client
- Describe how virtual functions work, and how abstract classes are used in creating upgradeable components

Estimated lesson time: 30 minutes

Note You will find the code for this lesson in the Lessons\Ch05\Lesson2 folder on the companion CD.

When classes need to be shared among applications, developers can take one of several approaches. One approach is to share the source files among the projects. The source can be compiled into each executable or DLL that needs the component. The advantage of this approach is that it creates few dependencies in each executable, but there are problems with this approach. One problem is that the size of each compiled program is larger, because each program must compile all of the source code. Another problem is that of maintenance. Whenever the code in one of the shared classes changes, each compiled program must be updated. If all of the programs aren't updated, some projects might end up with older versions of the class.

To solve this problem, you can create a static library that contains the source code for the shared components. Although this approach is less likely to result in having different versions of the source code in various projects, it does not solve the problems of bloating and having to recompile each project every time the source code changes.

Another solution to address the size and versioning problems is to use DLLs, which allow compiled programs to share components. The source code does not need to be compiled into the program, which means that each executable will be smaller. It also means that the changes to the code are made in only one place, and each compiled program will pick up the change without problems.

Other problems with sharing components do not have to do with the mechanism for sharing, but rather with C++ compilers. You will learn about these problems later in the chapter. Following are some common goals that developers should keep in mind when building their components:

- Components should be reusable. One of the primary goals of C++ classes is to allow a developer to inherit functionality from other classes. Any mechanism used, should allow functionality inheritance.
- Components should be easy to upgrade. It is important to be able to replace the DLL in the field without having to recompile and redistribute all of the programs that use it.
- Components should be useable by clients written in different compilers or languages. Most development teams use one compiler, but it is not uncommon for development teams to purchase components from other vendors. It is also not uncommon to have clients written in Visual Basic or HTML, and to have middle-tier components written in C++.

Going on the principle that it is a sounder approach to build DLLs than to share source code, and keeping in mind the goals presented, you will build a C++ project with several classes, and two client programs to take advantage of these shared classes. The application you will create is a bank application. The DLL will have three classes as follows:

- The CAccount class will serve as the base class for two other accounts, CChecking and CSavings. CAccount has two methods—*Deposit* and *Withdraw*—and one property, Balance. In this chapter, the term *property* is used for a set of functions (*Get* and *Set*) whose sole purpose is to get and set the value of a member variable.
- The CChecking class derives from CAccount, and has another property named LastCheckNumber.
- The CSavings class also derives from CAccount and has an extra property named InterestRate.

Table 5.1 summarizes the methods and properties of each class.

Table 5.1 Bank Application Shared Classes

Class	Return value	Method name and parameters
CAccount	BOOL	Deposit(double Amount)
CAccount	BOOL	Withdraw(double Amount)
CAccount	double	GetBalance
CAccount	void	SetBalance(double Amount)
CChecking	short	GetLastCheckNumber
CChecking	void	SetLastCheckNumber(short LastCheckNumber)
CSavings	double	GetInterestRate
CSavings	void	SetInterestRate(double Amount)

► **To create the BankMiddle DLL**

1. Start Visual C++ 6.0.
2. On the File menu, click New. The New dialog box appears, as shown in Figure 5.1.

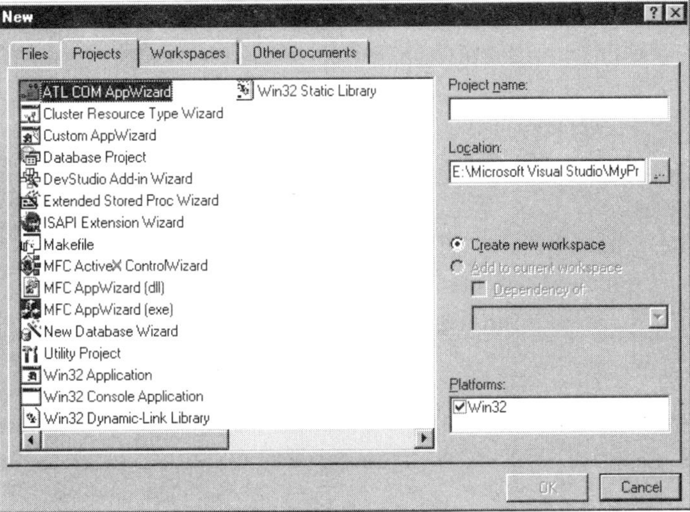

Figure 5.1 New dialog box

3. Select Win32 Dynamic-Link Library. Type *BankMiddle* for the project name, and click OK to open the Win32 Dynamic-Link Library Project Wizard.

4. In the Win32 Dynamic-Link Library dialog box, choose A Simple DLL Project (shown in Figure 5.2), and click Finish. Click OK in the New Project Information dialog box to generate the project.

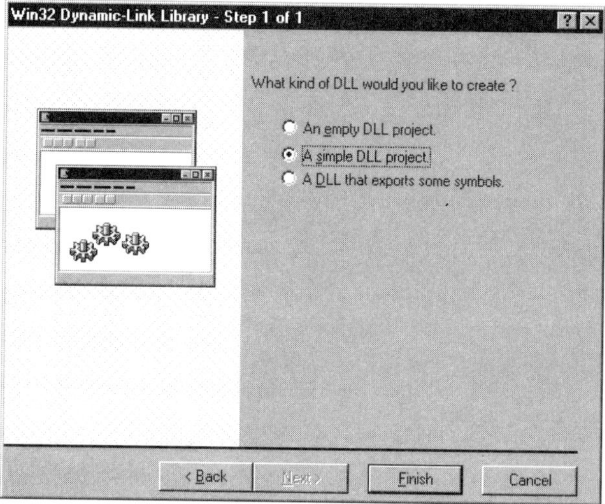

Figure 5.2 Win32 Dynamic-Link Library Project Wizard

Your project should now contain three files: BankMiddle.cpp, StdAfx.h, and StdAfx.cpp. You will now create the classes for your project, beginning with the CAccount class.

► **To create the BankMiddle CAccount class**

1. On the Insert menu, click New Class.
2. Type *CAccount* for the class name and click OK.

   Study the code that was generated. The New Class Wizard has added two files: Account.cpp and Account.h. The header file contains the declaration for CAccount. The wizard has added the default constructor and destructor declarations. Notice that the destructor has been declared as virtual, as shown in the following code:

```
class CAccount
{
public:
    CAccount();
    virtual ~CAccount();
};
```

   You should remove the *virtual* keyword. You do not need to have a virtual destructor yet, because you do not have virtual functions. (You will learn about virtual functions later in this chapter.) Making the destructor virtual adds the baggage of a vtable, as will be discussed later in this chapter.

3. Add declarations to the CAccount header file Account.h as follows:

```
private:
    double m_dBalance;
protected:
    // This function can be used only by derived classes
    void SetBalance(double dAmount);
public:
    BOOL Deposit(double dAmount);
    BOOL Withdraw(double dAmount);
    double GetBalance();
```

The preceding code shows one private member variable, one protected function, and three public functions. The private member *m_dBalance* keeps track of the balance. The functions *Deposit* and *Withdraw* add or subtract money to the balance respectively. These two functions return TRUE if the function is successful. The function *GetBalance* returns the value *m_dBalance*, and the function *SetBalance* sets the value of *m_dBalance*. The implementation of these functions is as follows:

```
CAccount::CAccount() :
m_dBalance(0)
{
}
CAccount::~CAccount()
{
}
BOOL CAccount::Deposit(double dAmount)
{
    m_dBalance += dAmount;
    return TRUE;
}
BOOL CAccount::Withdraw(double dAmount)
{
    if (m_dBalance > dAmount)
    {
        m_dBalance -= dAmount;
        return TRUE;
    }
    else
        return FALSE;
}
double CAccount::GetBalance()
{
    return m_dBalance;
}
void CAccount::SetBalance(double dAmount)
{
    m_dBalance = dAmount;
}
```

4. Replace the existing code in your Account.cpp file with the code shown in step 3. Now that the base class is in place, you will create the derived classes.

Implementation Inheritance

Inheritance is the mechanism by which one class gains the functionality of another. The class that provides the functionality is called the *base class*; the class that obtains and extends the functionality is called the *derived class*. In the bank application, the CChecking and CSavings classes inherit the methods of the CAccount class. In essence, CChecking and CSavings classes are types of accounts, with a few variations (CChecking has a LastCheckNumber property and CSavings has an InterestRate property).

► **To create the derived classes**

1. On the Insert menu, click New Class.
2. Type *CChecking* in the Class Name box.
3. Type *CAccount* in the Derived From field of the Base Class(es) box, and leave the As input field set to Public. Click OK.
4. Repeat the process for the CSavings class.
5. Remove the virtual keyword from the destructors for CChecking and CSavings because they are not going to be used yet.
6. Table 5.1 illustrated that the CChecking class has an extra property named LastCheckNumber, and that the CSavings class has an extra property named InterestRate. The declaration and implementation for both properties is shown next. Add the following code to the Savings and Checking files as indicated in the comments:

```
// Add the following code to the savings.h file
private:
    double m_dInterestRate;

public:
    void SetInterestRate(double NewRate);
    double GetInterestRate();

// Add the following code to the savings.cpp file
void CSavings::SetInterestRate(double NewRate)
{
    m_dInterestRate = NewRate;
}
double CSavings::GetInterestRate()
{
    return m_dInterestRate;
}
```

```
// Add the following code to the checking.h file
private:
    int m_iLastCheckNumber;
public:
    void SetLastCheckNumber(int LastCheckNumber);
    int GetLastCheckNumber();

// Add the following code to the checking.cpp file
void CChecking::SetLastCheckNumber(int LastCheckNumber)
{
    m_iLastCheckNumber = LastCheckNumber;
}
int CChecking::GetLastCheckNumber()
{
    return m_iLastCheckNumber;
}
```

7. Build the BankMiddle DLL.

Next you will create a simple client program that uses the DLL.

► **To create a client program**

1. On the File menu, click New.
2. On the Projects tab, select Win32 Console Application. Type *BankFront* as the project name and click OK. You will see the dialog box shown in Figure 5.3.

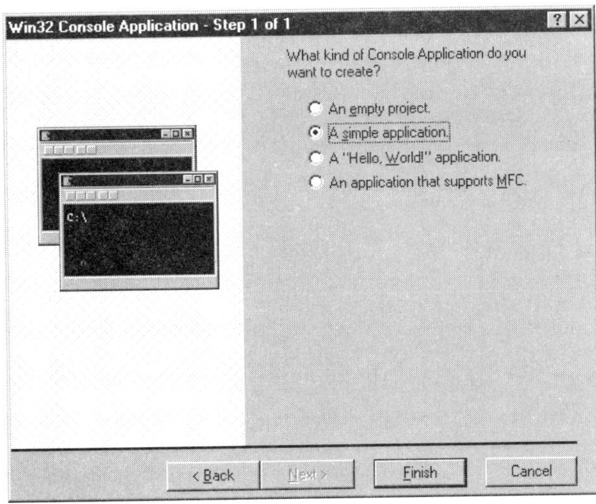

Figure 5.3 Win32 Console Application Wizard

3. In the Win32 Console Application Wizard dialog box, choose A Simple Application. Click Finish, and then click OK. The project should now contain three files: BankFront.cpp, StdAfx.h and StdAfx.cpp.

4. Before you can finish the client program, however, you must make a change to the DLL project. If you have been following each step carefully, you will notice that currently you have no way to access the classes in the DLLs—none of the classes have been exported. You will now expose the derived classes, CSavings and CChecking. To do so, you must add the compiler directive __declspec(dllexport) to the CAccount class declaration in the BankMiddle project as follows:

   ```
   class __declspec(dllexport) CSavings : public CAccount
   ```

   Because the client application will need to read the declaration as __declspec(dllimport) instead of __declspec(dllexport), you can use a macro to switch the direction of the export depending on who is using it.

5. Create a new header file to include the macro definition, and all header files that the client application is going to need to use the classes. Create the file Bank-Middle.h and add the following code to the file:

   ```
   #ifdef BANKMIDDLE_EXPORTS
   #define BANKMIDDLE_API __declspec(dllexport)
   #else
   #define BANKMIDDLE_API __declspec(dllimport)
   #endif

   #include "checking.h"
   #include "savings.h"
   ```

6. You must also add the previous macro definition to the BankMiddle's stdafx.h file. Then modify the declaration of the CChecking and CSavings classes as
   follows:

   ```
   class BANKMIDDLE_API CChecking : public CAccount
   class BANKMIDDLE_API CSavings : public CAccount
   ```

7. For the macro to work properly, you must define BANKMIDDLE_EXPORTS in the list of preprocessor definitions for the BankMiddle project, and not for the client project. To define the symbol in the BankMiddle project, click Settings on the Project menu. On the C++ tab, select the Preprocessor category (from the Category drop down box). Be sure *BANKMIDDLE_EXPORTS* appears in the processor definitions text box.

8. Build the BankMiddle DLL project again, and ignore the two warnings for now.

9. Now you are going to use the CChecking class in the BankFront project. In the file StdAfx.h, add the following declarations:

```
#include <stdio.h>
#include <windows.h>
```

10. Modify the file BankFront.cpp file as follows:

```
#include "stdafx.h"
#include <conio.h>
#include <iostream.h>
#include "..\BankMiddle\BankMiddle.h"
int main(int argc, char* argv[])
{
    CChecking *PersonalChecking = new CChecking();
    PersonalChecking->Deposit(500.00);
    printf("balance=%f\n",
        PersonalChecking->GetBalance());
    PersonalChecking->SetLastCheckNumber(100);
    printf("last check number=%i\n",
        PersonalChecking->GetLastCheckNumber());
    PersonalChecking->Withdraw(250.85);
    printf("balance=%f\n",
        PersonalChecking->GetBalance());
    delete PersonalChecking;
    while (!_kbhit());
    return 0;
}
```

11. You will also need to link BankMiddle.lib. On the Project menu, click Settings. On the Link tab, select Input for the category from the Category drop-down box. In the Object/Library Modules text box, add *bankmiddle.lib* to the list of input libraries. Next, type *..\BankMiddle\debug* (or *..\BankMiddle\release* if looking at release properties) in the Additional Library Path text box and click OK.

When you attempt to build your project, the build will fail. The linker will tell you that you do not have the symbols Deposit, GetBalance, and Withdraw defined. This happens because the methods are in the CAccount class, and the CAccount class is not one of the exported classes. The intent was to force clients to use one of the derived classes and not the base class directly. The solution is to export the CAccount class as well using the BANKMIDDLE_API macro. (Simply change the class declaration to class BANKMIDDLE_API CAccount and recompile the BankMiddle project.) Making this change will allow you to compile and execute the BankFront program. Before running the client program, make sure that the client program and the DLL are in the same directory. The sample code for this chapter included in the \Labs\Ch05 directory copies both the executable and the DLL to a bin directory in a post-build step.

The output of this program should resemble the output in Figure 5.4.

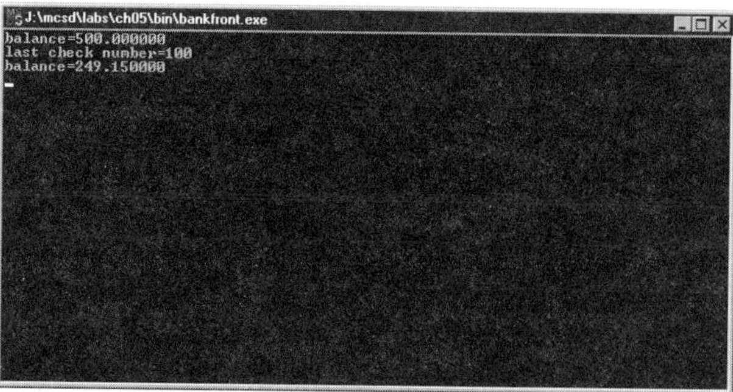

Figure 5.4 Output of the BankFront program

Allocating and Deallocating Memory in the DLL

For now, this chapter will put aside the problem of giving clients unwanted access to the base class and discuss a larger problem with the current architecture if the base class code needs to change. For example, suppose that the CAccount class needs to keep track of whether or not an initial deposit has been made. You create a member variable for the CAccount class and add it to the header file as follows:

► **To track whether an initial deposit has been made**

1. Add the following code to the Account.h header file.

```
private:
    BOOL m_bIsInitialDeposit;
```

2. Add the following code to your Account.cpp file to use the new member variable as follows:

```
CAccount::CAccount() :
m_dBalance(0),
m_bIsInitialDeposit(0)
{
}

CAccount::~CAccount()
{
}

BOOL CAccount::Deposit(double dAmount)
{
    if (m_dBalance == 0)
        m_bIsInitialDeposit=TRUE;
```

```
    else
        m_bIsInitialDeposit=FALSE;

    m_dBalance += dAmount;
    return true;
}
```

3. Recompile your DLL project. Notice that no changes have been made to the signature of the methods. The only change is that a new private member variable, *m_bIsInitialDeposit,* has been introduced. The code for the *Deposit* function has been modified to use this new value. At first glance, these changes do not seem to impact the client program. However, try running the client program again without recompiling it. As soon as the client program deletes the instance of the class, the program displays the debug error shown in Figure 5.5.

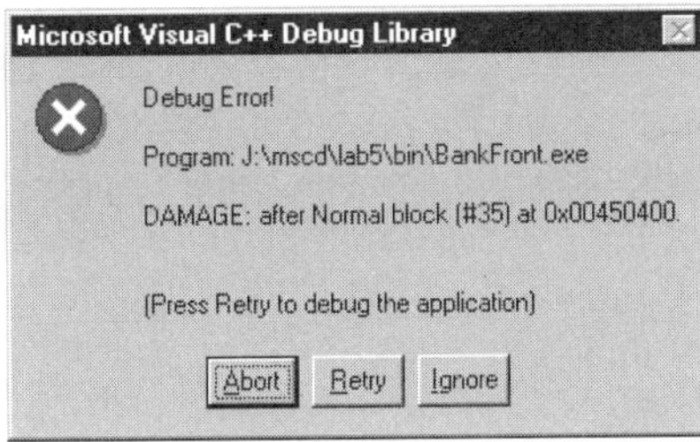

Figure 5.5 BankFront debug error

A problem exists in that the client application creates and destroys instances of the class in the DLL. In other words, the client program must know ahead of time how much memory it needs to allocate and release for the exported classes. The client program knows how much memory to allocate and release by reading the import library.

When you added a member variable to the CAccount class, although the change did not seem to affect the way that clients would use the derived classes, the change did affect the memory requirements for each derived class. Because the client program was not recompiled, the changes to the import library were not included. As a result, the client program allocated too little space for the CChecking class.

Therefore, when the client executed the *Deposit* method, and this method changed the value of the new member variable, data was written to a memory location outside the boundaries of CChecking. The debugger realized that your class had written to a memory location that did not belong to you, and it presented you with an error.

4. The DLL should allocate and destroy its exported classes. To allow the client to create instances of each class, you must add an exported function to create each class. Add the following code to the BankMiddle.cpp file:

```
long BANKMIDDLE_API CreateCheckingAccount(CChecking **ppChecking)
{
    *ppChecking = new CChecking();
    return 0;
}

long BANKMIDDLE_API CreateSavingsAccount(CSavings **ppSavings)
{
    *ppSavings = new CSavings();
    return 0;
}
```

5. Make sure that you include the header files Checking.h and Savings.h in the BankMiddle.cpp file. You must tell the client application about the *CreateCheckingAccount* and *CreateSavingsAccount* functions by declaring them in the BankMiddle.h file. In addition, you must implement a mechanism for deleting an instance of the class. To implement a delete mechanism, you can add a Delete function to each exported class (CChecking and CSavings), as shown in the following code:

```
// Add the Delete declaration to the Checking.h file
// Do the same to the CSavings class
public:
    void Delete();
// Add the Delete implementation to the Checking.cpp
// file. Do the same to the CSavings class
void CChecking::Delete()
{
    delete this;
}
```

6. Comment out the code that declares and uses the *m_bIsInitialDeposit* code in the CAccount class, and recompile the BankMiddle.dll. Then modify the code in the BankFront client to use the new creation and deletion methods, and recompile as follows:

```
int main(int argc, char* argv[])
{
    CChecking *PersonalChecking;
    CreateCheckingAccount(&PersonalChecking);
    PersonalChecking->Deposit(500.00);
    printf("balance=%f\n",
        PersonalChecking->GetBalance());
    PersonalChecking->SetLastCheckNumber(100);
```

```
    printf("last check number=%i\n",
        PersonalChecking->GetLastCheckNumber());
    PersonalChecking->Withdraw(250.85);
    printf("balance=%f\n",
        PersonalChecking->GetBalance());
    PersonalChecking->Delete();
    while (!_kbhit());
    return 0;
}
```

7. Run the client program; it should work correctly. If you go back to the DLL and uncomment the code that declares and uses the *m_bIsInitialDeposit* code in CAccount and recompile it, then run the client program without recompiling it; everything should still work correctly.

Interface Inheritance

Suppose that you are asked to write a function to transfer money from one account to another. Rather than writing four different functions to cover all possible transfer combinations (checking to savings, savings to checking, checking to checking and savings to savings), write one general function that takes two arguments, both of type CAccount. Because your account classes are derived from CAccount, this task can be accomplished quite simply, using the code as follows. Add this code to BankMiddle.h and BankMiddle.cpp as indicated in the code comments:

```
// Add this declaration to the BankMiddle.h file
BOOL BANKMIDDLE_API TransferMoney(CAccount *Acc1,
    CAccount *Acc2,double Amount);
// Add this implementation to the BankMiddle.cpp file
BOOL BANKMIDDLE_API TransferMoney(CAccount *Acc1,
    CAccount *Acc2,double Amount)
{
    BOOL bContinue = Acc1->Withdraw(Amount);
    if (bContinue)
        bContinue = Acc2->Deposit(Amount);
    return bContinue;
}
```

Modify the client application to use this new function as follows:

```
int main(int argc, char* argv[])
{
    CChecking *PersonalChecking;
    CreateCheckingAccount(&PersonalChecking);
    CSavings *InterestSavings;
    CreateSavingsAccount(&InterestSavings);
    PersonalChecking->Deposit(500.00);
```

```
        TransferMoney(PersonalChecking,InterestSavings,
        350.25);
        printf("balance checking=%f\n",
            PersonalChecking->GetBalance());
        printf("balance savings=%f\n",
            InterestSavings->GetBalance());
        PersonalChecking->Delete();
        InterestSavings->Delete();
        while (!_kbhit());
        return 0;
    }
```

The client program creates two accounts: Personal Checking and Interest Savings. The program then deposits $500 into checking and transfers $350.25 to savings. The last task the program performs is to print the balance for each account. Recompile both the DLL and the client program, and verify that it functions correctly.

Suppose that you are now asked to add one more requirement—for all accounts except checking, a transfer is not allowed if the withdrawal would create a negative account balance. In other words, savings accounts must contain enough money to cover the transfer. However, checking accounts can be overdrawn up to $1,000. The default implementation of the *Withdraw* method does not allow the withdrawal if there are insufficient funds in the account. Therefore, the *Withdraw* function must be modified to work differently in the CChecking class than in the other classes.

Your first action might be to override the *Withdraw* function in the CChecking class as follows:

```
//Add this code to Checking.h
BOOL CChecking::Withdraw(double dAmount);

//Add this code to Checking.cpp
BOOL CChecking::Withdraw(double dAmount)
{
    if ((GetBalance() - dAmount) > -1000)
    {
        SetBalance(GetBalance()-dAmount);
        return TRUE;
    }
    else
        return FALSE;
}
```

However, overriding the function is not enough. If you change the client code slightly so that the Transfer line attempts to transfer more money than what is available (but within the $1,000 buffer), you will notice that the code does not behave as expected—the transfer will fail. Add the previous code to the

CChecking class and change the client code as follows, recompile the client, and try the program, as follows:

```
PersonalChecking->Deposit(500.00);
TransferMoney(PersonalChecking,InterestSavings,1000);
printf("balance checking=%f\n",
    PersonalChecking->GetBalance());
printf("balance savings=%f\n",
    InterestSavings->GetBalance());
```

After the preceding code executes, the checking account balance will remain at $500, and the savings account balance will be $0. The expected result was for the checking account to have a balance of –$500 and the savings account to have a balance of $1,000. The *TransferMoney* function accepts parameters of CAccount. The current code executes the *Withdraw* function of the CAccount class, not the *Withdraw* function of the derived class. C++ has a mechanism for changing this behavior. By declaring *Withdraw* to be a *virtual function*, the compiler creates a virtual function table (vtable) for the class. Figure 5.6 is a visual representation of the vtable.

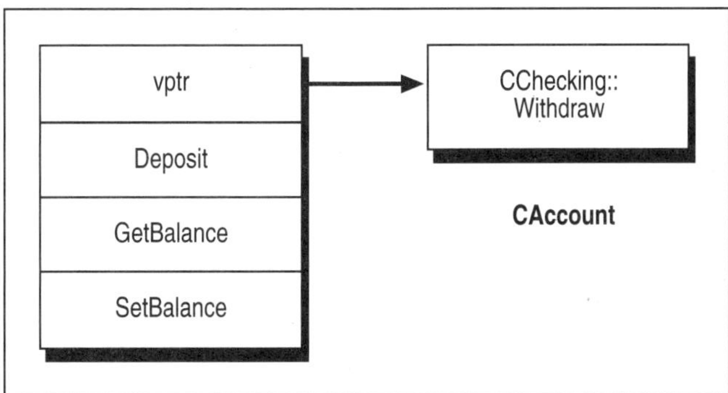

Figure 5.6 The vtable mechanism

The vtable maintains a list of pointers to virtual functions. At run time, the program refers to the vtable to determine which implementation of the function to run. Change the declaration of the *Withdraw* method in Account.h to virtual as follows:

```
virtual BOOL Withdraw(double dAmount);
```

Recompile the BankMiddle DLL and retry the client program. The output should now be –$500 for checking and $1,000 for savings, as expected. When the client program passes an instance of the CChecking account to the *TransferMoney* function, the vtable entry for *Withdraw* in CAccount is set to point to the implementation in the CChecking class.

Note When using virtual functions, it is best to make your destructors virtual as well. Therefore, you might want to go back to each class and change the declaration of the destructors back to virtual.

The primary benefit of the inheritance mechanism you have been using thus far is that the derived classes inherit all the functionality of the base class. For example, the derived classes did not have to write their own *Deposit*, *GetBalance*, and *SetBalance* functions. By deriving the classes from CAccount, they obtained this functionality for free.

However, there are some problems with this mechanism. First, to export the classes, you need to make each class declaration available to the client. Although the DLL provides a mechanism for creating instances of each derived class, nothing is really stopping a client from creating the classes directly. Second, an even greater problem is upgradability. If you needed to add a parameter to the *Deposit* function of the CChecking account, every program would need to be recompiled. Third, different compilers handle inheritance differently; for example, derived classes created with Visual C++ cannot be used in a client written in Sybase's Watcom C++.

A class has two main characteristics: one is the signature of the functions; the other is the implementation. The problems stated previously stem from the fact that the definition of the signatures is combined with the implementation of the functions. There is no mechanism in the current architecture for extending a class definition without changing the class implementation.

Advantages of Using Interfaces

C++ provides a mechanism for separating the definition or interface of the class from the implementation. The mechanism involves a specialized form of virtual functions called *pure virtual functions*, or virtual functions not implemented in the class. These functions provide a function signature that other classes must implement. The fact that there is no implementation in the class for the function means that you must inherit from the class—the class cannot be instantiated.

An *interface* is a class that has only pure virtual functions. An interface does not have any implementation code; it rather serves as a definition for a class. To see the advantages of using interfaces, you will define some interfaces and modify your existing classes to use them. Begin by adding the following declarations to the MiddleBank.h file:

```
struct IAccount
{
    virtual BOOL Deposit(double dAmount)=0;
    virtual BOOL Withdraw(double dAmount)=0;
    virtual double GetBalance()=0;
};
```

```
struct IChecking : IAccount
{
    virtual void SetLastCheckNumber
        (int LastCheckNumber)=0;
    virtual int GetLastCheckNumber()=0;
    //ideally Delete would be part of another interface
    //that ISavings would derive from
    virtual void Delete()=0;
};

struct ISavings : IAccount
{
    virtual void SetInterestRate(double NewRate)=0;
    virtual double GetInterestRate()=0;
    //ideally Delete would be part of another interface
    //that ISavings would derive from
    virtual void Delete()=0; };
```

The preceding code defines three interfaces: IAccount, ISavings, and IChecking. ISavings and IChecking are derived from IAccount. These three interfaces contain no implementation code whatsoever; they only define the signature of the functions.

Note Interfaces are usually defined as struct instead of class so that every function declaration is automatically public. Otherwise, there is no difference between the two.

The client application will work with pointers to these three interfaces. To obtain an instance of a class, the client cannot create one of the interfaces. They are *abstract* (noncreatable) classes. Instead, the client will call the *CreateSavingsAccount* or *CreateCheckingAccount* functions. Your job is to provide instances of classes derived from these interfaces. In essence, you must provide a class that implements all the methods in the interface. The following code illustrates an example of this (do not add this code to your project):

```
class CCheckingImpl : public IChecking
{
    // Methods in IAccount
    // Methods in IChecking

};
```

Note The phrase Impl is used in the class name to denote a class that serves as an implementation class for an interface.

In the preceding example, the CCheckingImpl class must implement not only the IChecking interface methods but also the IAccount methods. This is because IChecking is derived from IAccount. However, it would not make sense to implement all the methods of IAccount in both CChecking and CSavings. In other words, you do not want to use interfaces at the expense of implementation inheritance.

To implement the methods in IAccount, you cannot simply derive CAccount from IAccount and then derive your CChecking or CSavings class from it, because CChecking must also derive from IChecking, which in turn derives from IAccount. The compiler would notify you of having ambiguous declarations.

However, you can use implementation inheritance at the same time as interface inheritance by using a *template class*. With a template class, you can write a class definition that provides implementation for different interfaces. You derive your CChecking class and CSavings class not from the interface directly, but from a template that provides the implementation for the members of IAccount.

For this implementation to work, the template definition must have IChecking or ISavings in the inheritance map, as demonstrated in the following code. In the Accounts.h file, replace your definition of CAccount with the following:

```
#include "bankmiddle.h"
template<class IT>
class CAccountImpl : public IT
{
private:
    double m_dBalance;
    BOOL m_bIsInitialDeposit;
protected:
    void SetBalance(double dAmount)
    {
        // Use previous implementation
    }
public:
    CAccountImpl() :
    m_dBalance(0),
    m_bIsInitialDeposit(0)
    {
    }
    ~CAccountImpl()
    {
    }
    BOOL Deposit(double dAmount)
```

```
    {
        // Use previous implementation
    }
    BOOL Withdraw(double dAmount)
    {
        // Use previous implementation
    }
    double GetBalance()
    {
        // Use previous implementation
    }
};
```

To fully understand how this mechanism works, modify the declarations of the CChecking and CSavings classes in Checking.h and Savings.h as follows:

```
class CChecking : public CAccountImpl<IChecking>
class CSavings : public CAccountImpl<ISavings>
```

Other than these changes, the CChecking and CSavings classes remain the same. The classes are derived from the template class. The interface they intend to implement is passed as part of the template parameter. The template class uses this parameter to derive the base class from the appropriate interface. In other words, the CChecking class will be derived from CAccountImpl, which is derived from IChecking, which is derived from IAccount. Figure 5.7 illustrates the derivation hierarchy.

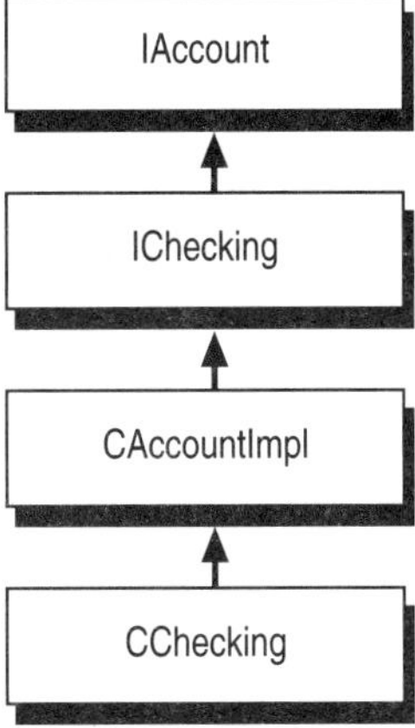

Figure 5.7 Inheritance hierarchy in the CChecking class

As Figure 5.7 demonstrates, using the template class makes it possible to use implementation inheritance at the same time as interface inheritance.

Modify the DLL entry functions in both BankMiddle.h and BankMiddle.cpp to use the interfaces instead of the implementation classes, as shown in the following code:

```
long BANKMIDDLE_API CreateCheckingAccount(IChecking **ppChecking);
long BANKMIDDLE_API CreateSavingsAccount(ISavings **ppSavings);
BOOL BANKMIDDLE_API TransferMoney(IAccount *Acc1,
    IAccount *Acc2,double Amount);
```

► **To compile the DLL properly**

1. Remove *#include "checking.h"* and *#include "savings.h"* from BankMiddle.h.
2. Add *#include "bankmiddle.h"* to BankMiddle.cpp.
3. Remove BANKMIDDLE_API from the class declarations in CChecking and CSavings (checking.h and savings.h).
4. Surround the interface declarations in BankMiddle.h with *#ifndef _BANKMIDDLEINTERFACES_* to ensure that the declarations are only included once. To do this, add the following code:

   ```
   #ifndef _BANKMIDDLEINTERFACES_
   #define _BANKMIDDLEINTERFACES_
   // place interface definitions here
   #endif
   ```

   If you are unsure, consult the BankMiddle.h source code included with this chapter in the Labs\Ch05\Lesson1\Interfaceinheritance\Bankmiddle directory on the companion CD.
5. Remove Account.cpp from the project.

   Compile the new DLL and modify the client code to use the interfaces, as follows:

   ```
   IChecking *PersonalChecking;
   CreateCheckingAccount(&PersonalChecking);
   ISavings *InterestSavings;
   CreateSavingsAccount(&InterestSavings);
   ```

Using interfaces instead of implementation classes offers several advantages as follows:

- The classes can be used from clients written in different compilers. The way that virtually every Windows compiler implements vtables is the same.
- The client no longer has access to the base classes. This mechanism also allows the DLL to control all aspects of creation and destruction of the derived classes.

- None of the classes need to be exported. The import library contains the declarations for only three functions: *CreateCheckingAccount*, *Create-SavingsAccount*, and *TransferMoney*.
- The implementation classes can be enhanced without having to recompile the clients. The client can remain constant as long as *CreateCheckingAccount* returns an instance of a class that implements the IChecking interface. It does not matter if it is not the CChecking class. It also does not matter whether CChecking implements many interfaces. The client only deals with the IChecking interface definition.

Lesson Summary

In this lesson, you reviewed the concepts of building business components in C++. You learned that in C++ programs, business logic is often implemented in classes. You then built a middle-tier DLL that exposed several C++ classes. Additionally, you learned how to write a base class and create derived classes from it. You then wrote a simple client application to use the classes in the DLL.

After attempting to enhance the classes in the DLL, you found that the DLL must allocate and destroy the classes. Therefore, you created functions for creating the classes, and you implemented a Delete mechanism in each class. After that, you learned about how virtual functions work, and how the compiler creates a vtable. You then used the vtable mechanism to create pure virtual (abstract) classes.

These classes allowed you to define abstract classes, called interfaces, which served as definitions for the functions in each class. Separating the interface from the implementation solved a number of problems, including compiler independence and upgradability. To use implementation inheritance in conjunction with interface inheritance, you used template classes.

You have now learned the basics of designing business objects using C++ without using any class libraries. In the next lesson, you will learn how to convert your classes to coclasses.

Lesson 3: Building a COM Component Using the Platform SDK

In Lesson 1, you learned about COM. So far in this chapter, you have learned about building components using C++ without COM. However, COM bases its architecture on many of the principles you used in Lesson 2. In this lesson, you will convert the BankMiddle component into a COM in-process server.

After this lesson, you will be able to:

- Write a COM in-process server from scratch in plain C++

Estimated lesson time: 60 minutes

Note You will find the code for this lesson in the Lessons\Ch05\Lesson3 folder on the companion CD.

Defining Interfaces with IDL

In Lesson 2, you learned that interfaces allow you to separate the definition of a class from the implementation details. COM uses the same principle to achieve its goal of language independence. A cursory examination of interfaces defined in various programming languages shows that it is possible to correctly define the same interface in a number of ways, depending on the language used. Because interfaces are supposed to be immutable, this possibility creates a problem: a single interface cannot have multiple legal definitions.

To remedy this problem, IDL was developed by the Open Software Foundation as part of its Remote Procedure Call (RPC) package. IDL is not a part of COM; rather it is a standard language used to define interfaces that is supported across programming languages. Standardizing with IDL to define COM interfaces, Microsoft includes its Microsoft IDL (MIDL) compiler (midl.exe) in many of its programming products. Microsoft has also made some extensions to IDL to support COM more fully. Your first step in COM programming should be to write your class's interface definitions in IDL.

In Lesson 1, you learned that all interfaces in COM are derived from IUnknown. In fact, one of the few definitions consistent throughout COM, ActiveX, and OLE is that an interface must ultimately derive from IUnknown. Your interfaces must derive either from IUnknown, or from an interface that derives from IUnknown. You will now declare the interfaces for the BankMiddle classes in IDL.

▶ To create an IDL file for the BankMiddle project

1. On the File menu, click New.
2. In the New dialog box, select C++ Source File and type *BankMiddle.idl* as the file name. Click OK.
3. Insert the following code to import COM type declarations and interface definition files:

```
import "oaidl.idl";
import "ocidl.idl";

// The import command works like #include except that
// it will ignore any procedure prototypes
```

Now that you have an IDL file with the declaration files in place, add code to define each interface. Each interface definition requires an interface attribute. (Note that brackets surround attributes in IDL.) The interface attribute contains the keyword *object* followed by the universally unique identifier (UUID) for the interface. Without the object attribute, the MIDL compiler assumes the interface is a Distributed Computing Environment, Remote Procedure Calls (DCE-RPC) interface.

The interface attribute is followed by the interface name and the interface from which it derives. An interface can only derive from one other interface. COM interfaces must derive from IUnknown or from another interface that derives from IUnknown. Add the following code to the BankMiddle.idl file to define the three interfaces in the BankMiddle project:

```
[
    object,
        uuid(418F4021-A18E-11D3-820C-0050BAA1DBA9),
        oleautomation
]
interface IAccount : IUnknown
{
    HRESULT Deposit([in] double dAmount);
    HRESULT Withdraw([in] double dAmount);
    [propget] HRESULT Balance([out, retval] double *pVal);
};
[
    object,
        uuid(C9862970-A191-11d3-820C-0050BAA1DBA9),
        oleautomation
]
interface IChecking : IAccount
```

```
{
    [propget] HRESULT LastCheckNumber([out, retval] short *pVal);
    [propput] HRESULT LastCheckNumber([in] short newVal);
};

[
    object,
        uuid(18BBBB90-A192-11d3-820C-0050BAA1DBA9),
        oleautomation
]
interface ISavings : IAccount
{
    [propget] HRESULT InterestRate([out, retval] double *pVal);
    [propput] HRESULT InterestRate([in] double newVal);
};
```

If you study the interface attributes in the previous code, you will notice the use of the *oleautomation* keyword. The oleautomation attribute enforces the use of Automation parameter types in the interface. Automation parameter types are defined in the VARIANT structure definition (see the Platform SDK Help documentation for more information on Automation parameter types).

It is important to limit your parameter types to Automation types if your interfaces are going to be used by Visual Basic or scripting clients. Keeping the parameters to Automation types also makes it possible for the type library marshaler to work.

Another benefit of using oleautomation is that it tells the type library to add the interface definitions to the registry when the type library is registered. The type library is registered with the *RegisterTypeLib* function.

As you can see, some of the functions also have attributes. In particular are functions with the [propget] and [propput] attributes. These attributes make the compiler treat the functions as properties. The generated header file will contain the functions *get_InterestRate* and *put_InterestRate*. These attributes also allow Visual Basic to treat the function pair as a property.

Notice that parameters also have attributes: [in], [out], and [retval]. The specifics of these attributes are described in detail in the MIDL Language Reference Help file included with Platform SDK Help. For this example, it is sufficient to know that [in] means the parameter is sent in by value, and [out] means the parameter is sent in by reference and will be modified by the function. The [retval] attribute is for Visual Basic clients; it tells Visual Basic to treat the parameter as the return value for the function. This means that a Visual Basic programmer can write code as follows:

```
Dim lc As Long
lc = obj.LastCheckNumber()
```

When the interfaces are in place, it is useful to add a library block to your DLL. Having a library block means that MIDL will generate a type library, which is needed for two main reasons as follows:

- The type library marshaler uses the type library to marshal the interfaces.
- The type library provides the interface declarations in a format that other languages such as Visual Basic and Java can read.

To add a library block, add the following code to your IDL file:

```
[
    uuid(418F4013-A18E-11D3-820C-0050BAA1DBA9),
        version(1.0),
        helpstring("BankMiddle 1.0 Type Library")
]
library BANKMIDDLEATLLib
{
    importlib("stdole32.tlb");
    importlib("stdole2.tlb");
};
```

Library blocks also have attributes; one attribute that is required is the UUID—type libraries have their own GUIDs. In the preceding code, the library block does not add much benefit, because only interfaces declared or referenced from within the library block will appear in the type library. You can enhance the type library by defining coclasses. As you might recall from Lesson 1, coclasses are descriptors for the types of objects that your DLL is exposing. Coclasses give languages such as Visual Basic information about what interfaces each class supports. Add the following code to the library block in your IDL file:

```
[
    uuid(418F4022-A18E-11D3-820C-0050BAA1DBA9),
        helpstring("Account Class")
]
coclass Checking
{
    [default] interface IChecking;
};

[
    uuid(861C3350-A192-11d3-820C-0050BAA1DBA9),
        helpstring("Account Class")
]
coclass Savings
{
    [default] interface ISavings;
};
```

Your IDL file now contains all the essential parts, and is ready to compile after you change a few MIDL compiler settings.

► **To change the MIDL compiler settings for your IDL file**

1. Right-click the BankMiddle.idl file in the workspace window.
2. On the shortcut menu, click Settings.
3. Adjust your settings to resemble those shown in Figure 5.8.

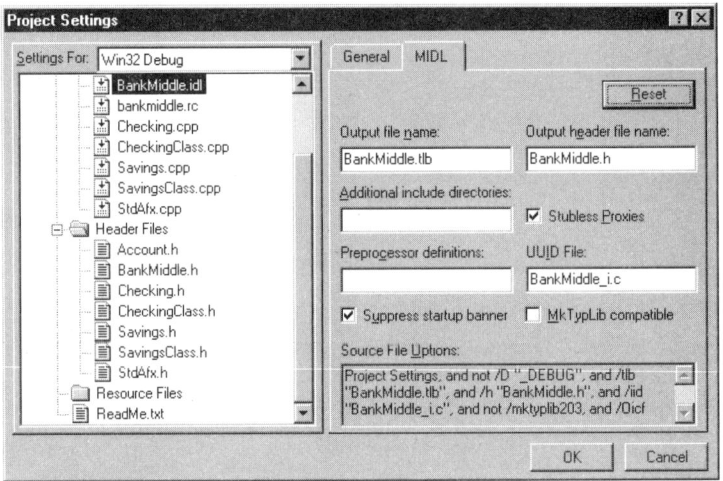

Figure 5.8 MIDL compiler settings

The important settings in the Project Settings dialog box are Output File Name, which is the name of the type library file to create; Output Header File Name, which is the header file with the interface declarations that MIDL will generate; and UUID File, which defines IID structures to contain the GUIDs for each interface, co-class, and library block. You should clear the MkTypLib Compatible check box, because this is only for legacy Object Description Language (ODL) files.

MIDL will generate the three files specified in the Project Settings dialog box, along with files to create a proxy/stub DLL. In this chapter, you will not create the proxy/stub DLL; instead, you will use the type library marshaler.

Before continuing with the COM-specific tasks of building the BankMiddle server, you must change some of the interface declarations in each of the classes in the project to be more in line with typical COM components. If you look carefully at the interface definitions you will notice that all return values that used to be BOOL have been changed to HRESULTs. In fact, all return values are now HRESULTs. *HRESULTs* are long values that communicate error conditions. Throwing exceptions is also compiler-dependent, so to make COM truly compiler-independent, error values are reported though return codes. A discussion of all method changes is beyond the scope of this chapter. Refer to the source code included with this chapter to see the changes that have been made to each function signature. The function signatures now return HRESULTS. Functions that previously returned BOOLs now return S_OK for TRUE, and S_FALSE for FALSE. Functions that previously returned a value now have a parameter that acts as the placeholder for the return value. Also, integer types have been changed to short to be compatible with Visual Basic and scripting languages.

Implementing IUnknown

Lesson 2 identified the need for a create-and-delete mechanism to replace direct creation and destruction in the client code. IUnknown provides this mechanism, and also provides the mechanism for asking an object if it implements a certain interface: *QueryInterface*.

Each class that is exposed to the client, including CChecking and CSavings, will implement IUnknown. The following code implements the IUnknown methods in the CChecking account. Add this code to your DLL, and then copy the code into the CSavings class.

► **To implement the IUnknown methods**

1. Add the following declarations to the Checking.h file:

```
private:
    long m_lCount;
public:
    // IUnknown methods
    STDMETHODIMP QueryInterface(REFIID riid, void **ppv);
    STDMETHODIMP_(ULONG) AddRef(void);
    STDMETHODIMP_(ULONG) Release(void);
```

2. Add the following implementation to the Checking.cpp file:

```
// IUnknown methods
STDMETHODIMP CChecking::QueryInterface(REFIID riid, void **ppv)
{
    if (riid == IID_IUnknown || riid == IID_IChecking)
        *ppv = static_cast<IChecking*>(this);
    else if (riid == IID_IAccount)
        *ppv = static_cast<IAccount*>(this);
    else
    {
        *ppv = NULL;
        return E_NOINTERFACE;
    }
```

```
        reinterpret_cast<IUnknown*>(*ppv)->AddRef();
        return S_OK;
    }
    STDMETHODIMP_(ULONG) CChecking::AddRef(void)
    {
        return ++m_lCount;
    }
    STDMETHODIMP_(ULONG) CChecking::Release(void)
    {
        ULONG lCount = --m_lCount;
        if (lCount == 0)
            delete this;
        return lCount;
    }
```

3. Do not forget to initialize the *m_lCount* variable in the constructor so that the constructor looks as follows:

```
CChecking::CChecking() :
m_lCount(0)
{
}
```

4. Repeat the process for the CSavings class.

AddRef, *Release*, and *QueryInterface* Functions

The implementations of *AddRef* and *Release* are straightforward. *AddRef* increases the count; *Release* decreases the count. The *Release* function creates a local variable to store the count before deleting the class. This is because the function needs to return the count when it is done, but if the class is deleted, it will not be able to use the *m_lCount* member variable. The *QueryInterface* function is also straightforward. *QueryInterface* basically casts the instance of the object (the THIS pointer) to the requested interface.

With a few modifications to BankMiddle.cpp and to StdAfx.h, you should be able to compile your project. It is not yet a full COM server, but it is at a state in which you can compile the project. Add a header file that defines a number of COM APIs and structures to the StdAfx.h file as follows:

```
#include <objbase.h>
```

Add the following two header files to BankMiddle.cpp:

```
#include "BankMiddle.h"
#include "BankMiddle_i.c"
```

These header files include the declarations for the interfaces and the IID structures.

Creating Class Factories

In Lesson 1, you learned about class factories. When a client requests to create a coclass through *CoGetClassObject,* or *CoCreateInstance,* the SCM enters the COM DLL through a specific entry point, *DllGetClassObject,* and asks for a pointer to a class that supports the IClassFactory interface. This class is a singleton class whose sole purpose is to create instances of a particular implementation class. (A *singleton* is an object that is the one and only one instance of its class.)

► **To create class factories for your classes**

Add two classes that implement IClassFactory as follows:

1. On the Insert menu, click New Class.
2. Type *CCheckingClass* as the class name, and *IClassFactory* in the Derived From field. Click OK. You will receive a warning that the wizard cannot find the header file that contains the IClassFactory definition. Click OK.
3. Add the following declarations in the CheckingClass.h header file for the IClassFactory methods:

```
// IClassFactory methods
STDMETHODIMP CreateInstance(IUnknown *pUnkOuter, REFIID
    riid, void **ppv);
STDMETHODIMP LockServer(BOOL bLock);
```

4. Add the following declarations in the CheckingClass.h header file for the IUnknown methods (remember that every interface derives from IUnknown):

```
// IUnknown methods
STDMETHODIMP QueryInterface(REFIID riid, void **ppv);
STDMETHODIMP_(ULONG) AddRef(void);
STDMETHODIMP_(ULONG) Release(void);
```

5. Write code to implement these methods. You have seen the standard implementation for IUnknown in the previous section. However, because ClassFactory is a singleton class, COM rules say you can optimize *AddRef* and *Release* slightly. The CCheckingClass (ClassFactory) will be created when the DLL is first loaded into memory, and destroyed when the DLL is unloaded. In other words, you never want to delete it as the result of a *Release.* COM rules state that, for classes where the client does not determine life management, you can simply return arbitrary values for *AddRef* and *Release.* COM rules also state that clients should not count on these return values to be accurate. Therefore, the implementation code for *AddRef* and *Release* for this class simply returns 5 and 2 (two arbitrary values), respectively.

6. Add the following code, showing the implementation of the *QueryInterface* methods, to the CheckingClass.cpp file:

```
// IUnknown methods
STDMETHODIMP CCheckingClass::QueryInterface(REFIID riid, void **ppv)
{
    if (riid == IID_IClassFactory || riid == IID_IUnknown)
        *ppv = static_cast<IClassFactory*>(this);
    else
        return (*ppv = 0), E_NOINTERFACE;
    reinterpret_cast<IUnknown*>(this)->AddRef();
    return S_OK;
}
STDMETHODIMP_(ULONG) CCheckingClass::AddRef(void)
{
    return 2;
}
STDMETHODIMP_(ULONG) CCheckingClass::Release(void)
{
    return 1;
}
```

7. Now you must implement the methods in IClassFactory. For now, you will implement only one of the methods, *CreateInstance*. The other method, *LockServer,* will be discussed later in this lesson. The *CreateInstance* function does exactly what the name implies—it creates instances of a class. The CCheckingClass class factory creates instances of the CChecking class. The following code shows you how to implement the *CreateInstance* method:

```
STDMETHODIMP CCheckingClass::CreateInstance(IUnknown *pUnkOuter,
    REFIID riid, void **ppv)
{
    if (ppv == 0)
        return E_POINTER;
    *ppv = 0;
    if (pUnkOuter)
        return CLASS_E_NOAGGREGATION;
    CChecking *pObj = new CChecking();
    if (!pObj)
        return E_OUTOFMEMORY;
    pObj->AddRef();
    HRESULT hr = pObj->QueryInterface(riid, ppv);
    pObj->Release();
    return hr;
}
```

At the heart of the *CreateInstance* implementation are the lines that create an instance of the class and call *QueryInterface* on the created class, as shown in the next code fragment. To optimize the creation process, a client can request a specific interface. *AddRef* and *Release* surround the *QueryInterface* method, stabilize the reference count in the class, and use the standard deleting mechanism if the class does not support the requested interface.

When the class is created, the reference count is zero. *AddRef* increases the count to one. If *QueryInterface* succeeds, *QueryInterface* in the class will increase the reference count to two. In that case, *Release* in the *CreateInstance* function puts the reference count back to one (which is the correct number of references to the class). If *QueryInterface* fails, then *Release* in the *CreateInstance* function puts the reference count down to zero, and the class gets deleted. Consider the following code:

```
CChecking *pObj = new CChecking();
pObj->AddRef();
HRESULT hr = pObj->QueryInterface(riid, ppv);
pObj->Release();
```

The rest of the code checks for different error conditions. One interesting error condition is CLASS_E_NOAGGREGATION. If you study the *CreateInstance* function parameters, you will notice that the first parameter is *pUnkOuter*. This parameter is used for aggregation. *Aggregation* is a specialized form of containment in which an object can use another compiled object for aiding it in implementing some interfaces (Lesson 3 will briefly re-mention aggregation). Your class does not support aggregation, so if this parameter is not NULL, you should return CLASS_E_NOAGGREGATION.

8. Add the *LockServer* function to your implementation file, CheckingClass.cpp (you will complete this function in the next section):

```
STDMETHODIMP CCheckingClass::LockServer(BOOL bLock)
{
    return S_OK;
}
```

9. Create another class factory for the CSavings class. If you need help with this step, you can refer to the source code for the CSavingsClass class in CSavingsClass.cpp and CSavingsClass.h.

COM DLL Entry Points

Every COM DLL has four entry points: *DllRegisterServer*, *DllUnregisterServer*, *DllGetClassObject*, and *DllCanUnloadNow*.

DllRegisterServer and *DllUnregisterServer*

The code for *DllRegisterServer* and *DllUnregisterServer* is not presented in great detail in the text for this chapter. The implementation of these two functions involves putting the necessary keys into the registry at the time that *DllRegisterServer* is called, and removing the keys from the registry when *DllUnregisterServer* is called. What you need to know is what keys to put in and remove from the registry.

Each coclass defined in the type library has a GUID assigned to it. GUIDs for coclasses are called *class identifiers* (*CLSIDs*). To register your class, add your CLSID to HKEY_CLASSES_ROOT\CLSID. Under the CLSID for your class you must create a subkey called InProcServer32. This key stores the path to the COM DLL that exports that class, and also marks the threading model that your class supports. (You learned about threading models in Chapter 3.) Under your CLSID, you can also specify a programmatic identifier (ProgID) subkey. The ProgID is a name such as BankMiddle.CheckingClass that a client can use to locate your CLSID. The ProgID is essential if your class will be used from scripting clients.

Information about each interface in the type library must also be added to the registry. This is done in the case of BankMiddle because we are going to use the type library marshaler. The type library marshaler looks at the interface definitions to learn how to package and unpackage the parameters and return values for each method call. Registering each interface is done automatically by registering the type library itself. Registering the type library marshaler is done with a COM API function: *RegisterTypeLib*.

DllGetClassObject

Perhaps the most important entry point is *DllGetClassObject*, the function that the SCM calls to obtain an instance of your class factory, and from that point creates instances of your implementation class. Add the following code to BankMiddle.cpp to implement this function in your BankMiddle server:

```
CCheckingClass g_checkingclass;
STDAPI DllGetClassObject(REFCLSID rclsid, REFIID riid, void **ppv)
{
    *ppv = 0;
    if (rclsid == CLSID_Checking)
        return g_checkingclass.QueryInterface(riid, ppv);
    else
        return CLASS_E_CLASSNOTAVAILABLE;
}
```

This function replaces the *CreateCheckingAccount* and *CreateSavingsAccount* functions, which allowed the C++ DLL to handle class creation. The code defines a global instance of the CCheckingClass—the class factory for CChecking. When the client wants to create an instance of the CChecking class, it requests the class by its Class ID. The *DllGetClassObject* function checks the CLSID specified in the *rclsid* parameter. If this value matches one of the exported classes, the function succeeds. If the CLSID cannot be matched to one of the exported classes, the function returns CLASS_E_CLASSNOTAVAILABLE. If a match is made, the function calls the *QueryInterface* method of the global class. The *QueryInterface* function essentially casts the global class to the requested interface (normally IClassFactory) and returns a pointer to it. The outcome is that the SCM will obtain a pointer to the class factory interface and return it to the client. The client can use this to create instances of the implementation class.

DllCanUnloadNow

The last entry point is *DllCanUnloadNow*. One goal in COM is for clients to be able to unload DLLs that are no longer in use.

A client can call the COM function *CoFreeUnusedLibraries* to unload any COM DLLs from memory that are no longer needed. When *CoFreeUnusedLibraries* is called, COM asks your DLL if it is able to unload at this time. It is your responsibility to answer no (S_FALSE) if any outstanding references to your objects exist. If there are no outstanding references, you can return S_OK, and COM will unload your DLL. The implementation of this function involves examining the value of a global variable that keeps track of outstanding references. It is similar to the variable used in reference counting when implementing IUnknown, except that this variable keeps track of all references throughout the DLL.

To implement this function, use the following code:

```
STDAPI DllCanUnloadNow(void)
{
    return g_cLocks ? S_FALSE : S_OK;
}
```

Declare a global variable in your BankMiddle.cpp file to keep the reference count, and include two functions that can add and subtract references as follows:

```
LONG g_cLocks = 0;
void LockModule(void)
{
    InterlockedIncrement(&g_cLocks);
}
void UnlockModule(void)
{
    InterlockedDecrement(&g_cLocks);
}
```

You can call these functions at key points throughout your DLL to make sure the reference counting is maintained. The most reliable way to know when a reference to one of your objects is outstanding is by increasing the count each time *AddRef* is called in any of your objects, and likewise decreasing the count each time *Release* is called. You must also adjust the count in the *LockServer* method in each of the ClassFactory implementations as follows:

```
STDMETHODIMP CCheckingClass::LockServer(BOOL bLock)
{
    if (bLock)
        LockModule();
    else
        UnlockModule();
    return S_OK;
}
```

After you have implemented all the preceding functions, recompile your project. You have just built a COM server with only Platform SDK functions.

To test the COM version of the DLL you will need to modify the client program so that it also uses COM.

► **To modify the client program so that it uses COM**

1. Using the previous version of BankFront, include the BankMiddle_i.c file that contains the CLSID and IID declarations for the classes and interfaces in BankMiddle. (This file was generated by MIDL after compiling the IDL file.) To do this, add the following to BankFront.cpp:

   ```
   #include "..\..\BankMiddle\BankMiddle_i.c"
   ```

2. Call *CoInitialize* before any COM calls and call *CoUninitialize* before the program ends. *CoInitialize* is a COM API function that must be called before any COM API executes. Add the following code to your client:

   ```
   int main(int argc, char* argv[])
   {
       CoInitialize(NULL);
       // Code that uses COM objects goes here
       CoUninitialize();
   }
   ```

3. Instead of CreateCheckingAccount or CreateSavingsAccount, use CoCreate-Instance as follows:

   ```
   IChecking *PersonalChecking;
   HRESULT hr =
       CoCreateInstance(CLSID_Checking,NULL,CLSCTX_ALL,
       IID_IChecking,(void **)&PersonalChecking);
   ```

```
if (FAILED(hr))
    return hr;

ISavings *InterestSavings;
hr = CoCreateInstance(CLSID_Savings,NULL,CLSCTX_ALL,
    IID_ISavings,(void **)&InterestSavings);

if (FAILED(hr))
    return hr;
```

4. Use the *Release* function instead of *Delete* as follows:

```
PersonalChecking->Release();
InterestSavings->Release();
```

5. Change the *GetBalance* function to *get_Balance*. Because *get_Balance* now takes in a double parameter, you must declare a variable of type double and use it as the parameter. This change also affects the call to the *printf* function. The *get_Balance* changes are as follows:

```
double dTotal=0;
PersonalChecking->get_Balance(&dTotal);
printf("balance checking=%f\n",dTotal);
InterestSavings->get_Balance(&dTotal);
printf("balance savings=%f\n",dTotal);
```

You should now have all the code to create a client that uses COM to create the classes in the BankMiddle server.

Lesson Summary

In this lesson, you learned how to create an in-process COM server using the Platform SDK. You started by defining the interfaces using IDL. After defining COM-like interfaces (using HRESULTs), you modified the function signatures in the implementation classes to match the new COM-like signatures. You then implemented IUnknown in each class and created class factories for each implementation class. Creating a class factory involved creating a new class that derived from IClassFactory. The final step was to implement the four entry points to COM DLLs.

Lesson 4: Building a COM Component Using ATL or MFC

A lot of the code in Lesson 2 was repetitive; only a few ways exist to implement IUnknown in your classes. The code to implement IClassFactory is essentially the same for every class, and the same is true for the COM DLL entry points. All this code defines the infrastructure for your server, and only deals with the COM aspects of your server—not with the business logic itself. Ideally, you should not have to write this code; your time should be devoted to writing business logic. For this reason, Microsoft has provided two class libraries that provide this infrastructure code for you: MFC and ATL.

After this lesson, you will be able to:

- Describe the differences between the Platform SDK, ATL, and MFC approaches to building a COM component
- Decide when to use ATL versus MFC for building COM component
- Write a COM component using ATL
- Write a COM component using MFC

Estimated lesson time: 60 minutes

Note You will find the code for this lesson in the Lessons\Ch05\Lesson4 folder on the companion CD.

Active Template Library

As you learned in Lesson 2, a workaround for using implementation inheritance with interface inheritance is to use template classes. This is the goal of Active Template Library (ATL); all the boilerplate code to implement IUnknown, class factories, COM entry points, and so on is provided for you in ATL template classes from which you can derive. ATL was designed to be a lightweight library; although it does not attempt to hide COM details in any way, ATL provides default implementations for common tasks.

As you will see later, MFC takes a different approach—it attempts to hide COM details so that you can create components without ever having to see an IUnknown implementation. ATL was originally designed to allow developers to create ActiveX controls for the Internet. ATL helps you create fast, small, COM servers with few or no dependencies.

You will first learn how to create the BankMiddle DLL in ATL.

► To create an ATL DLL in-process server

1. On the File menu, click New.
2. On the Projects tab, click ATL COM AppWizard. Type *BankMiddleATL* for the project name, and click OK. Figure 5.9 shows the ATL COM AppWizard.

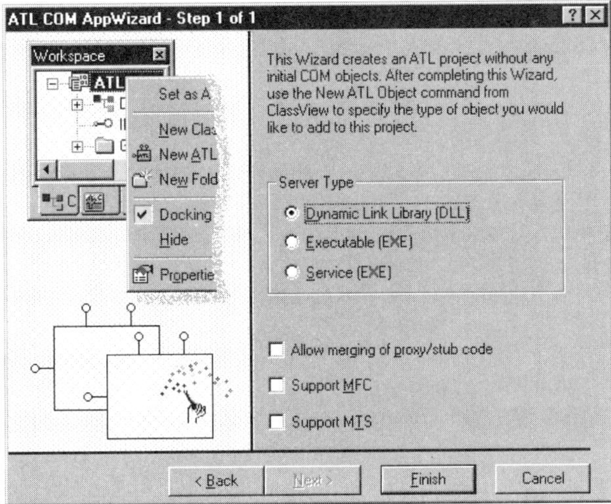

Figure 5.9 ATL COM AppWizard

3. The wizard can create three types of COM servers: a DLL, an executable file, and a service. In-process servers are DLLs, so select Dynamic Link Library (DLL). You can leave the other options unselected. The Allow Merging of Proxy/Stub Code option lets you decide if you want the proxy/stub code needed for marshaling to be part of the same DLL or a separate DLL. (Traditionally, the proxy/stub code is part of a separate DLL.) Selecting this option allows you to ship one DLL instead of two, but it also means that your DLL will be larger. In the case of BankMiddle, you will leave marshaling to the type library marshaler; it does not make sense to merge the proxy/stub code into the DLL.
4. The second check box asks if you want to use MFC. If you have a particular need for using MFC in your server—for example, if part of your business logic is already using MFC—then you need to select this option. Adding MFC means that your ATL component will be larger and have dependencies on the MFC libraries.
5. The last option, Support MTS, appears at first to be a feature that automatically makes your component run in an MTS environment. Actually, this option simply links two MTS libraries, Mtx.lib and Mtxguid.lib, to your project. You will learn more about what these libraries do in Chapter 7.
6. Click Finish, and then click OK.

The ATL COM AppWizard has created the shell code for your in-process COM server. It has also created a .cpp file using the name of your project (in this case, BankMiddleATL.cpp) that contains the code to implement the four COM DLL entry points: *DllRegisterServer, DllUnregisterServer, DllCanUnloadNow,* and *DllGetClassObject*.

DllRegisterServer and *DllUnregisterServer*

If you examine the code for *DllRegisterServer* and *DllUnregisterServer,* you will see the following:

```
/////////////////////////////////////////////////////////////////////////////
// DllRegisterServer adds entries to the system registry
STDAPI DllRegisterServer(void)
{
    // Registers object, typelib and all interfaces in typelib
    return _Module.RegisterServer(TRUE);
}
/////////////////////////////////////////////////////////////////////////////
// DllUnregisterServer removes entries from the system registry
STDAPI DllUnregisterServer(void)
{
    return _Module.UnregisterServer(TRUE);
}
```

The *_Module* variable is declared within the same files as follows:

```
CComModule _Module;
```

The CComModule class contains a number of functions, including *Register-Server* and *UnregisterServer*. This class is also responsible for keeping track of the outstanding references to your component (lock count) and of your DLL's INSTANCE handle (hInstance). If you are writing the implementation for the DLL entry points in ATL without the wizard, ATL counts on you to declare the *_Module* instance. *DllRegisterServer* and *DllUnregisterServer* use a COM object called the Registrar, included in ATL.DLL, that is able to parse a script found in an .rgs file. Three .rgs files are included as resources in your DLL. You will study the preceding code later in this section.

DllCanUnloadNow

The code for implementing *DllCanUnloadNow* is as follows:

```
////////////////////////////////////////////////////////////////////////////
// Used to determine whether the DLL can be unloaded by OLE
STDAPI DllCanUnloadNow(void)
{
    return (_Module.GetLockCount()==0) ? S_OK : S_FALSE;
}
```

DllCanUnloadNow reports whether or not clients still have outstanding references to the server. As mentioned previously, CComModule keeps track of how many locks have been placed on the server. CComModule provides two functions to increase and decrease the lock count: *Lock* and *Unlock*. ATL calls the *Lock* function (increasing the count) when a client creates an instance of your object, and calls the *Unlock* function (decreasing the count) when a client destroys your object.

DllGetClassObject

To fully understand how *DllGetClassObject* works, it is best to add some objects to your server.

► **To add the Checking object to your COM server**

1. On the Insert menu, click New ATL Object. Figure 5.10 shows the ATL Object Wizard.

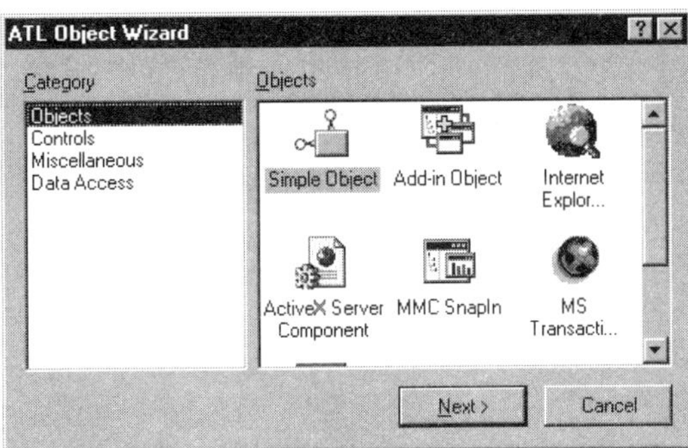

Figure 5.10 ATL Object Wizard

The ATL documentation included with the MSDN Library that ships with Visual Studio contains a document titled Adding Objects And Controls that explains in detail each of the object types. The most important object types are Simple Object and Full Control. Simple Object generates a COM object with the minimum set of interfaces required for a class to be a COM object, and perhaps to be used from a scripting client (as you will see shortly). Full Control (in the Controls category) provides you with an object that has all the interfaces typically necessary to turn a class into an ActiveX control that can be dropped into an ActiveX container (such as a Visual Basic form).

2. For the Checking class, select Simple Object and click Next. The ATL Object Wizard Properties screen will appear, as shown in Figure 5.11.

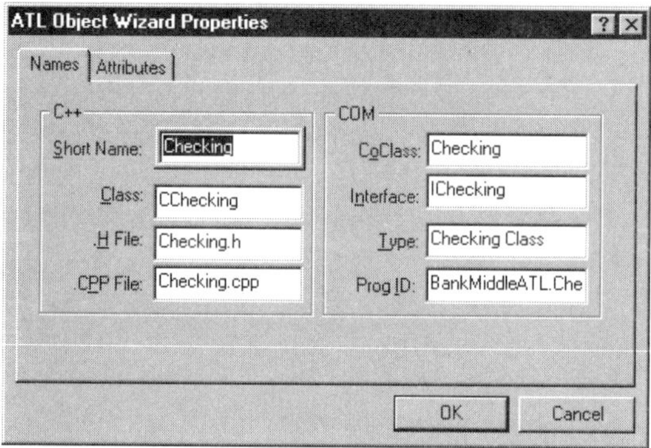

Figure 5.11 ATL Object Wizard Properties screen

3. Type *Checking* in the Short Name box. The wizard automatically fills in the rest of the input fields. The left side of the dialog box shows the C++ properties: source file name, header file name, and class name. The right side of the dialog box shows the COM-specific properties. COM properties include CoClass Name, Interface Name, Type (object short description), and ProgID (the name that scripting clients will use to create an instance of your object).
4. The dialog box has another tab titled Attributes. The Attributes tab lets you set the threading model for your object (single, apartment, both, or free), and the type of interface (dual, which is a type of interface derived from IDispatch that adds support for scripting clients, and custom, which is an interface derived from IUnknown).

Note It is a misconception that Visual Basic requires IDispatch support. Visual Basic is able to perform vtable binding directly to custom interfaces.

5. The aggregation property adds or removes support for aggregation. Aggregation is a specialized type of containment in which two objects present themselves to the client as one object. The object that is being aggregated must accept a pointer to the aggregator and let the aggregator handle *QueryInterface, AddRef,* and *Release*. If you select Yes, your object will have support for this type of creation without impacting the way you write your implementation code. Select Apartment threading, Custom interface, and Yes for aggregation. (Although aggregation will not come into play in our project, it is not a bad idea to normally select Yes.) Click OK.

The wizard has created two other source files: Checking.h and Checking.cpp. Checking.cpp currently contains no source code. Checking.h contains a class declaration for your CChecking class as shown in the following code:

```
class ATL_NO_VTABLE CChecking :
    public CComObjectRootEx<CComSingleThreadModel>,
    public CComCoClass<CChecking, &CLSID_Checking>,
    public IChecking
```

If you had selected Dual instead of Custom for the interface you would see the following line of code instead of IChecking:

```
public IDispatchImpl<IChecking, &IID_IChecking,
    &LIBID_BANKMIDDLEATLLib>
```

In the preceding code, you can see that your class is derived from two other templatized classes: CComObjectRootEx and CComCoClass. The CComObjectRootEx class has a default implementation for reference counting; CComCoClass provides a default ClassFactory class that will be handed out to clients (among other things), and IDispatchImpl adds a default implementation for the members of the IDispatch interface necessary for scripting clients.

ATL offers a default implementation for *QueryInterface*. If you look at the declaration of CChecking in the Checking.h file, you will find a code block for the *interface map,* an array declaration that lists all the interfaces that your object supports.

The wizard also adds a new resource to your DLL project: Checking.rgs. This file contains the script that the Registrar object will use to register your component.

If you take a look back at the BankMiddleATL.cpp file, you will see that the ATL Object Wizard made one minor modification, as shown in the following code:

```
BEGIN_OBJECT_MAP(ObjectMap)
OBJECT_ENTRY(CLSID_Checking, CChecking)
END_OBJECT_MAP()
```

The wizard has added an entry to what is known as the *object map*. The object map is an array, with entries that match a particular CLSID to a series of ATL-generated functions in your class that handle updating the registry for your particular object and creating your object, among other tasks. Following is a code representation of the *DllGetClassObject* function:

```
/////////////////////////////////////////////////////////////////////////////
// Returns a class factory to create an object of the requested type

STDAPI DllGetClassObject(REFCLSID rclsid, REFIID riid, LPVOID* ppv)
{
    return _Module.GetClassObject(rclsid, riid, ppv);
}
```

When the SCM requests a class instance, the ATL code looks for the CLSID in the object map, then (in the default case) it calls a static member function of your class: *CreateInstance*. You won't find *CreateInstance* in the header of your class—it is a member of CComCoClass, which is a base class for your class. CComCoClass creates an instance of the CComClassFactory, which is a class that implements IClassFactory and uses the object map to create instances of your class, and hands this class to the SCM.

The only task left to perform is adding properties and methods to your object.

► **To add a property or method to your object**

1. Select the class view in your workspace window.
2. Select the interface that you want to add a member to (notice that the workspace window displays both the class and the interface separately). Right-click the interface and select either Add Method or Add Property. Add Property will add two functions with the propget and propput attributes mentioned earlier. Add a property to the CChecking class, as shown in Figure 5.12.

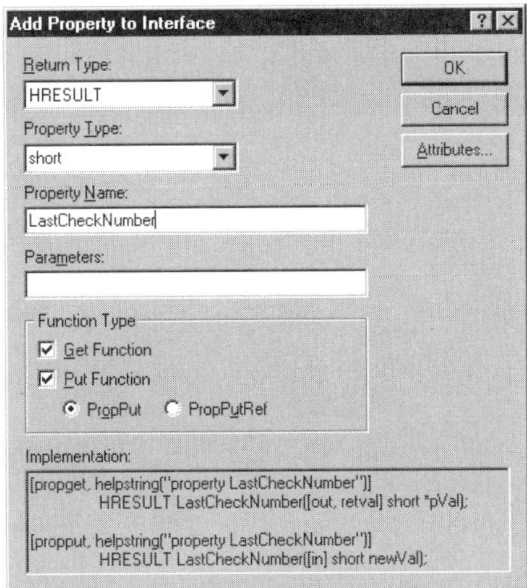

Figure 5.12 Adding a property to the CChecking class

3. In the Add Property To Interface dialog box, type LastCheckNumber for the Property Name. Then, select (or type) *short* in the Property Type combo box. The type for the property is not the return value for the function, which is always *HRESULT,* but the type of the *[out,retval]* parameter in the function. Remember that, with the attributes propget and propput, and with a parameter marked as *[out,retval],* Visual Basic can present the function as a property to programmers. When specifying properties or methods that have parameters, you must type each parameter along with the [in], [out], or [in,out] attributes.
4. Click OK.

   The wizard adds the function declarations to the IDL file and to the header and implementation files for the class.

Compile your project—you now have a fully functional COM server with a creatable class that has one method. All this was done with a few mouse clicks and the ATL wizards. In Lab 5, you will use ATL to create a simple COM component. You will also replace each of the templates and macros for Platform SDK functions.

Microsoft Foundation Classes

Another alternative for creating COM servers more easily is using MFC. MFC was developed before ATL, so this option is considered legacy to a number of COM developers. However, MFC does provide an easy way to create COM objects especially if you already have business logic in MFC.

So far you have seen how to implement interfaces in a class using inheritance. In all the previous COM examples in this chapter, when a client creates an instance of the CChecking class and requests the IAccount interface through *QueryInterface*, the function returns a reference to itself. The code for *QueryInterface* simply casts the THIS pointer to the requested interface. This is possible because CChecking is derived from IAccount.

There is another way to support an interface—composition. In composition you build classes to implement certain interfaces. Then when the client requests an interface with *QueryInterface* you give them a reference to one of the implementer classes. There is, however, one rule in COM that is critical to uphold—whenever a client requests IUnknown, you must give them the same reference. IUnknown in COM is not just for reference counting (in fact as you saw in the implementation in the class factory it was not for reference counting at all). IUnknown is ultimately used for identity. The way you know if COM object A is the same as COM object B is to add *QueryInterface* to both objects for IUnknown and compare the pointers. If they are equal then the two objects are in fact the same object instance.

Suppose that you have two interfaces: IAccount and ISaveToDisk. You are already familiar with the IAccount interface from previous lessons. The ISaveToDisk interface has one method: *Save(BSTR Location).* The purpose of this interface is to persist the state of an account class. It is then perfectly conceivable for a class to want to support both interfaces. It is also understandable that the two interfaces are separate, because they do not share a common goal. If you want your implementation class to support both interfaces, one way to do it is to derive a class, CChecking for example, from both IAccount and ISaveToDisk. When the client requests one of the interfaces, you would simply cast the THIS pointer to the requested interface and hand the result to the client, as follows:

```
class CChecking : public IAccount,
public ISaveToDisk
{
    STDMETHODIMP QueryInterface(REFIID riid, void **ppv)
    {
        if (riid == IAccount)
            *ppv = (IAccount *)this;
        else if (riid == ISaveToDisk)
            *ppv = (ISaveToDisk *)this;

        //the rest of the code is omitted for the
            sake of simplicity
    }
}
```

Another way to support the interfaces is to create individual classes for each interface as follows (from now own, this book will refer to these two classes as the interface implementers):

```
class IAccountImpl : public IAccount
{
public:
    // IUnknown methods
    STDMETHODIMP QueryInterface(REFIID riid, void **ppv);
    STDMETHODIMP_(ULONG) AddRef(void);
    STDMETHODIMP_(ULONG) Release(void);

    // IAccount methods
    STDMETHODIMP Deposit(double dAmount);
    STDMETHODIMP Withdraw(double dAmount);
    STDMETHODIMP get_Balance(double *pVal);
};

class ISaveToDiskImpl : public ISaveToDisk
{
public:
    // IUnknown methods
    STDMETHODIMP QueryInterface(REFIID riid, void **ppv);
    STDMETHODIMP_(ULONG) AddRef(void);
    STDMETHODIMP_(ULONG) Release(void);

    // ISaveToDisk
    STDMETHODIMP Save(BSTR Location);

};
```

Then you could create a container class CChecking with a method similar to *QueryInterface* that would be in charge of handing references to each implementer class as clients requested the implemented interface. The code for this class would be as follows:

```
class CChecking
{
    IAccountImpl m_pIAccountImpl;
    ISaveToDiskImpl m_pSaveToDiskImpl;

    STDMETHODIMP InternalQueryInterface(REFIID riid, void **ppv)
    {
        if (riid == IID_IUnknown)
            *ppv = (IUnknown *)&m_pIAccountImpl;
        if (riid == IID_IAccount)
            *ppv = (IAccount *)&m_pIAccountImpl;
        else if (riid == IID_ISaveToDisk)
            *ppv = (ISaveToDisk *)&m_pSaveToDiskImpl;
```

```
        // the rest of the code is omitted for the
            sake of simplicity
    }
};
```

The problem with the previous code is that when the client has a pointer to *m_pIAccountImpl*, he or she is able to call *QueryInterface* on that object directly; the same is true for the m_pSaveToDiskImpl class. The *QueryInterface* implementation for *m_pIAccount* and for *m_pSaveToDiskImpl* must return the same reference when asked for IUnknown, as you learned earlier. What's more, if a client has a pointer to *m_pSaveToDiskImpl* and requests the IAccount interface from it, the client will expect the interface to be supported. In other words, *QueryInterface* for the ISaveToDiskImpl class must in a sense know about the IAccountImpl class and vice versa. You would also have a problem with reference counting—both implementer classes must work together as a unit. The solution is for the implementer objects to simply forward each call to IUnknown to the parent class. The parent class can then administer all the methods in IUnknown properly. You should thus rewrite the container class and interface implementers in such a way that the implementers can access the parent class. Consider the following code:

```
class CChecking
{
    class IAccountImpl : public IAccount
    {
    public:
        // keep a reference back to the parent
        CChecking *m_pParent;

        // IUnknown methods
        STDMETHODIMP QueryInterface(REFIID riid, void **ppv);
        STDMETHODIMP_(ULONG) AddRef(void);
        STDMETHODIMP_(ULONG) Release(void);

        // IAccount methods
        STDMETHODIMP Deposit(double dAmount);
        STDMETHODIMP Withdraw(double dAmount);
        STDMETHODIMP get_Balance(double *pVal);
    };
    class ISaveToDiskImpl : public ISaveToDisk
    {
    public:
        // keep a reference back to the parent
        CChecking *m_pParent;

        // IUnknown methods
        STDMETHODIMP QueryInterface(REFIID riid, void **ppv);
        STDMETHODIMP_(ULONG) AddRef(void);
        STDMETHODIMP_(ULONG) Release(void);
```

```
    // ISaveToDisk
    STDMETHODIMP Save(BSTR Location);
};

private:
    IAccountImpl m_pIAccountImpl;
    ISaveToDiskImpl m_pISaveToDiskImpl;
    long m_lRefCount; //used for reference counting

    // Constructor
    CChecking()
    {
        m_lRefCount = 0;
        m_pIAccountImpl.m_pParent = this;
        m_pISaveToDiskImpl.m_pParent = this;
    }

    //Functions to manage IUnknown methods
    STDMETHODIMP InternalQueryInterface(REFIID riid, void **ppv);
    STDMETHODIMP_(ULONG) InternalAddRef(void);
    STDMETHODIMP_(ULONG) InternalRelease(void);
};
```

The CChecking class serves as a container for two nested classes, IAccountImpl, and ISaveToDiskImpl. The main thing to notice is that the IAccountImpl and ISaveToDiskImpl classes have an *m_pParent* member variable that stores a pointer to the container class CChecking. The CChecking class serving as the parent sets each of the *m_pParent* variables to itself in its constructor, as shown in the following code:

```
// Constructor
CChecking()
{
    m_lRefCount = 0;
    m_pIAccountImpl.m_pParent = this;
    m_pISaveToDiskImpl.m_pParent = this;
}
```

Whenever the client makes a call to one of the methods in IUnknown in one of the implementer classes, the classes use the m_pParent pointer to forward the call back to the Parent class. The following code shows you how this is done in IAccountImpl, the same code applies to ISaveToDiskImpl:

```
STDMETHODIMP
CChecking::IAccountImpl::QueryInterface(REFIID riid, void **ppv)
{
    return m_pParent->QueryInterface(riid,ppv);
}
```

```
STDMETHODIMP_(ULONG) CChecking::IAccountImpl::AddRef()
{
    return m_pParent->AddRef();
}

STDMETHODIMP_(ULONG) CChecking::IAccountImpl::Release()
{
    return m_pParent->Release();
}
```

The CChecking parent class implements the methods of IUnknown as usual, except that as in the previous example it returns references to the implementer classes in *QueryInterface*. The following code shows you how CChecking implements the methods in IUnknown:

```
STDMETHODIMP CChecking::InternalQueryInterface(REFIID
riid, void **ppv)
{
    *ppv = NULL;

    if (riid == IID_IUnknown)
        *ppv = (IUnknown *)&m_pIAccountImpl;
    else if (riid == IID_IAccount)
        *ppv = (IAccount *)&m_pIAccountImpl;
    else if (riid == IID_ISaveToDisk)
        *ppv = (ISaveToDisk)&m_pISaveToDiskImpl;
}

STDMETHODIMP_(ULONG) CChecking::InternalAddRef()
{
    return m_lRefCount;
}

STDMETHODIMP_(ULONG) CChecking::InternalRelease()
{
    long lCount = --m_lRegCount;
    if (lCount == 0)
        delete this;
    return lCount;
}
```

You might have noticed that the CChecking class names the methods in IUnknown *InternalQueryInterface*, *InternalAddRef*, and *InternalRelease*. Why does the class not use the standard IUnknown methods? If you notice, the CChecking class is not derived from IUnknown. It does not need to be a COM object. If a client requests to create the CChecking class, our server creates a class factory, CCheckingClass for example, that implements IClassFactory and gives this to the client. The client then calls the *CreateInstance* method of

IClassFactory. You wil recall from Lesson 3 that implementing *CreateInstance* creates an object and then calls *QueryInterface* on the object as follows:

```
CChecking *pobj = new CChecking();
pobj->AddRef();
hr = pobj->QueryInterface(iid,ppv);
pobj->Release();
```

The pointer that the client receives comes from the *QueryInterface* function. In the case of CChecking this would be a pointer to *m_pIAccountImpl* or *m_pISaveToDiskImpl*. The client never gets a reference to CChecking directly. Therefore, CChecking does not need to implement IUnknown. In fact, the code in the *CreateInstance* function of the CChecking class factory could be rewritten as follows:

```
CChecking *pobj = new CChecking();
pobj->InternalAddRef();
hr = pobj->InternalQueryInterface(iid,ppv);
pobj->InternalRelease();
```

As you can see, the CChecking class supports both IAccount and ISaveToDisk with the aid of composition. Composition is done in this case by creating two nested classes—IAccountImpl and ISaveToDiskImpl. You learned previously that an ATL component uses inheritance to provide interface implementations. MFC uses composition.

MFC uses a series of macros to simplify the creation of nested classes. One set of important macros is BEGIN_INTERFACE_PART and END_INTERFACE_PART. Take a look at the CChecking class using the MFC macros to declare the IAccountImpl and ISaveToDiskImpl nested classes as follows:

```
class CChecking : public CCmdTarget
{
// Interface Maps
protected:
    // The rest of the code is omitted for the
        sake of simplicity

    //IAccount implementation
    BEGIN_INTERFACE_PART(IAccountImpl, IAccount)
        STDMETHOD(Deposit)(double dAmount);
        STDMETHOD(Withdraw)(double dAmount);
        STDMETHOD(Balance)(double *pVal);
    END_INTERFACE_PART(IAccountImpl)
    //ISaveToDisk implementation
    BEGIN_INTERFACE_PART(ISaveToDiskImpl, ISaveToDisk)
        STDMETHOD(SaveToDisk)(BSTR location);
    END_INTERFACE_PART(ISaveToDiskImpl)
};
```

The BEGIN_INTERFACE_PART and END_INTERFACE_PART macros declare a nested class within the parent class CChecking. The nested classes will be named XIAccountImpl, and CXISaveToDiskImpl, respectively. The classes are declared with the BEGIN_INTERFACE_PART macro. The macro expands to the following:

```
class XIAccountImpl  : public IAccount
{
public:
    STDMETHOD_(ULONG, AddRef)();
    STDMETHOD_(ULONG, Release)();
    STDMETHOD(QueryInterface)(REFIID iid,
    LPVOID* ppvObj);
```

Between BEGIN_INTERFACE_PART and END_INTERFACE_PART are the method definitions for each function in the respective interfaces. The END_INTERFACE_PART macro translates to the following:

```
} m_xIAccountImpl;
friend class XIAccountImpl;
```

As you can scc, thc END_INTERFACE_PART completes the nested class declaration and creates a member variable for each nested class. For composition to be fully functional a few other elements must be added. One of the elements missing is for the container class CChecking to manage the methods in IUnknown. The MFC class CCmdTarget provides the default implementation for these methods. The CChecking class is derived from CCmdTarget because CCmdTarget contains default implementations for the methods in IUnknown in three functions—*InternalQueryInterface, InternalAddRef,* and *InternalRelease*. You might recall that *InternalQueryInterface* must hand out references to the nested classes that implement the requested interfaces. Therefore, you must tell *InternalQueryInterface* about the member variables that instantiate the nested classes. This is done with the aid of three other macros—BEGIN_INTERFACE_MAP, INTERFACE_PART, and END_INTERFACE_MAP.

In the implementation file for CChecking, you would then add an interface map as follows:

```
BEGIN_INTERFACE_MAP(CChecking, CCmdTarget)
    INTERFACE_PART(CChecking,IID_IAccount,IAccountImpl)
    INTERFACE_PART(CChecking,IID_ISaveToDisk,ISaveToDiskImpl)
END_INTERFACE_MAP()
```

When CCmdTarget receives a request for *QueryInterface,* it looks up the requested IID in the interface map and returns a pointer to the contained class that implements it. You will still need to implement each method in the contained classes including the IUnknown methods, because the BEGIN_INTERFACE_PART/END_INTERFACE_PART macros only add declarations for the IUnknown interface for each contained class. The following code shows you the signature for the Deposit method of the IAccount interface in the CChecking MFC class:

```
STDMETHODIMP CChecking::XIAccountImpl::Deposit()
{
    return S_OK;
}
```

Remember from the previous discussion that each IUnknown method implementation in the nested class must forward the call to the container class. This was done earlier by introducing a member variable *m_pParent* in each nested class to contain a pointer to the parent class. However, in MFC this is done a little bit differently. With the aid of the METHOD_PROLOGUE macro, a nested class can gain access to the parent class. The METHOD_PROLOGUE calculates the location of the parent class in memory using the following formula. The following code shows what the METHOD_PROLOGUE macro translates to in the case of XIAccountImpl:

```
CChecking* pThis = ((CChecking*)((BYTE*)this -
    offsetof(CChecking, m_xIAccountImpl)));
```

You would therefore use these macros in the implementation of the IUnknown methods as follows:

```
STDMETHODIMP CChecking::XIAccountImpl::QueryInterface(REFIID riid,
    void **ppv)
{
    METHOD_PROLOGUE(CChecking,IAccountImpl)
    return pThis->ExternalQueryInterface(&riid,ppv);
}

STDMETHODIMP_(ULONG) CChecking::XIAccountImpl::AddRef()
{
    METHOD_PROLOGUE(CChecking,IAccountImpl)
    return pThis->ExternalAddRef();
}

STDMETHODIMP_(ULONG) CChecking::XIAccountImpl::Release()
{
    METHOD_PROLOGUE(CChecking,IAccountImpl)
    return pThis->ExternalRelease();
}
```

For more details on how to implement these methods, consult the documentation that accompanies Microsoft Visual Studio.

Now that you know the approach that MFC uses for creating COM objects, you are ready to use the MFC AppWizard to build an MFC COM project.

► To create an in-process COM server

1. On the File menu, select New, and then select MFC AppWizard (DLL) on the Projects menu. Type *BankMiddleMFC* as the Project Name, and click OK. The MFC AppWizard appears, as shown in Figure 5.13.

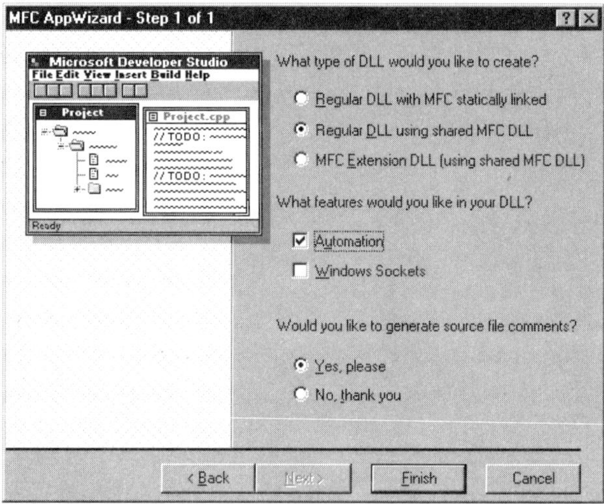

Figure 5.13 MFC AppWizard

2. In the MFC AppWizard dialog box, select the Automation check box. Selecting this option will cause the wizard to automatically add implementation for the four COM DLL entry points. For a class to be a COM class in MFC, it must be derived directly or indirectly from CCmdTarget. CCmdTarget has a default implementation for IUnknown that uses the nested mechanism described previously. (You can use CWnd as your base class, because this class is derived from CCmdTarget.)
3. Click Finish. The New Project Information dialog box appears. Click OK.
4. On the Insert menu, choose New Class. You will see the New Class dialog box, shown in Figure 5.14.

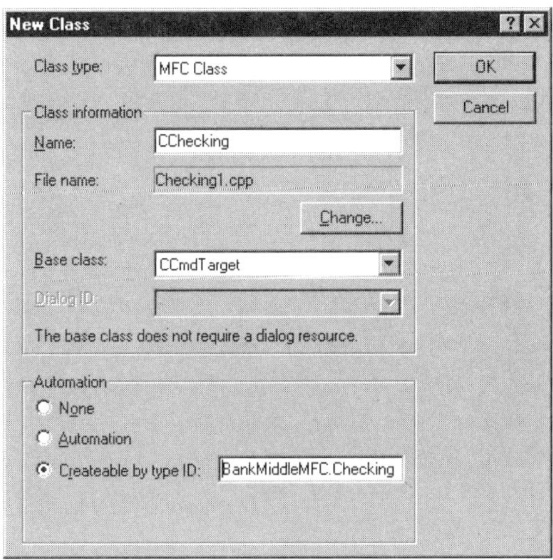

Figure 5.14 New Class dialog box

5. The class type will default to MFC Class. Type *CChecking* as the class name.
6. In the Base Class drop-down list, select CCmdTarget. You will see that the wizard has made several properties available in the bottom half of the dialog box. If you want the client to be used from scripting clients, you can choose Automation. The Creatable By Type ID option adds the macro to your class to declare a class factory function for your class. When you have made your selections, click OK. Choose Creatable By Type ID and use the default value for this setting. Click OK. You should now have two new files: Checking.cpp and Checking.h.
7. Add the interface definitions for IAccount and ISaveToDisk to the .odl file. The .odl file is the equivalent of the .idl file in the previous projects. Add to this file the following declarations within the library block:

```
[
    object,
    uuid(418F4021-A18E-11D3-820C-0050BAA1DBA9),
    oleautomation
]
interface IAccount : IUnknown
{
    HRESULT Deposit([in] double dAmount);
    HRESULT Withdraw([in] double dAmount);
    [propget] HRESULT Balance([out, retval] double *pVal);
};
[
    object,
    uuid (D588AF50-B48C-11d3-822A-0050BAA1DBA9),
```

```
    oleautomation
]
interface ISaveToDisk : IUnknown
{
    HRESULT Save([in] BSTR FileName);
};
```

8. In the Checking.h file, add the declaration for the nested classes. This is done with the aid of the BEGIN_INTERFACE_PART and END_INTERFACE_PART macros.

```
// IAccount implementation
BEGIN_INTERFACE_PART(IAccountImpl, IAccount)
    STDMETHOD(Deposit)(double dAmount);
    STDMETHOD(Withdraw)(double dAmount);
    STDMETHOD(get_Balance)(double *pVal);
END_INTERFACE_PART(IAccountImpl)

//ISaveToDisk implementation
BEGIN_INTERFACE_PART(ISaveToDiskImpl, ISaveToDisk)
    STDMETHOD(Save)(BSTR location);
END_INTERFACE_PART(ISaveToDiskImpl)
```

9. In the Checking.cpp file, add the Interface map definition. This is done with the aid of the BEGIN_INTERFACE_MAP, INTERFACE_PART, and END_INTERFACE_MAP macros as follows:

```
BEGIN_INTERFACE_MAP(CChecking, CCmdTarget)
    INTERFACE_PART(CChecking,IID_IChecking, Dispatch)
    INTERFACE_PART(CChecking,IID_IAccount,IAccountImpl)
    INTERFACE_PART(CChecking,IID_ISaveToDisk,ISaveToDiskImpl)
END_INTERFACE_MAP()
```

10. Implement the methods for each nested class including the methods for IUnknown. In the IUnknown methods use METHOD_PROLOGUE to find the parent class in memory. Next, forward the calls to the parent as follows:

```
// *** IAccount ***
STDMETHODIMP CChecking::XIAccountImpl::Deposit(double dAmount)
{
    //the implementation has been left out for the
        sake of simplicity
    return S_OK;
}
STDMETHODIMP CChecking::XIAccountImpl::Withdraw(double Amount)
{
    // the implementation has been left out for the
        sake of simplicity
    return S_OK;
}
```

```
STDMETHODIMP CChecking::XIAccountImpl::get_Balance(double *pVal)
{
    //the implementation has been left out for the
        sake of simplicity
    return S_OK;
}

// IUnknown methods
STDMETHODIMP CChecking::XIAccountImpl::QueryInterface
    (REFIID riid, void **ppv)
{
    METHOD_PROLOGUE(CChecking,IAccountImpl)
        return pThis->ExternalQueryInterface(&riid,ppv);
}

STDMETHODIMP_(ULONG) CChecking::XIAccountImpl::AddRef(void)
{
    METHOD_PROLOGUE(CChecking,IAccountImpl)
        return pThis->ExternalAddRef();
}
STDMETHODIMP_(ULONG) CChecking::XIAccountImpl::Release(void)
{
    METHOD_PROLOGUE(CChecking,IAccountImpl)
        return pThis->ExternalRelease();
}

// *** ISaveToDisk ***
STDMETHODIMP CChecking::XISaveToDiskImpl::Save(BSTR FileName)
{
    // the implementation has been left out for the
        sake of simplicity
    return S_OK;
}

// IUnknown methods
STDMETHODIMP CChecking::XISaveToDiskImpl::QueryInterface
    (REFIID riid, void **ppv)
{
    METHOD_PROLOGUE(CChecking,IAccountImpl)
        return pThis->ExternalQueryInterface(&riid,ppv);
}

STDMETHODIMP_(ULONG)
Checking::XISaveToDiskImpl::AddRef(void)
{
    METHOD_PROLOGUE(CChecking,IAccountImpl)
        return pThis->ExternalAddRef();
}
```

```
STDMETHODIMP_(ULONG) CChecking::XISaveToDiskImpl::Release(void)
{
    METHOD_PROLOGUE(CChecking,IAccountImpl)
        return pThis->ExternalRelease();
}
```

You should now know all of the necessary steps for building COM classes in MFC.

Lesson Summary

In the previous lesson, you learned how to create COM objects from scratch. After doing so, you then learned that a lot of the code used is boilerplate code that can be copied and pasted without many modifications into other projects. Microsoft provides this boilerplate code in both ATL and MFC. ATL was designed with the goal of creating thin and fast COM servers with few dependencies. MFC was created primarily to serve as a code library for creating full-fledged business applications. Both libraries use different approaches to building COM objects that implement several interfaces. ATL uses inheritance whereas MFC uses composition with nested classes.

Lab 5: Dissecting ATL

In this lab, you will first create a component using ATL, and then remove all traces of ATL to end up with a Platform SDK equivalent of your component. The purpose of this lab is to understand each aspect of a simple COM server.

Estimated lab time: 60 minutes

Exercise 1: Creating the ATL Server

This chapter discussed objects in terms of business applications; this exercise uses the object Dog.

Note You will find the code for this exercise in the Labs\Ch05\Ex01 folder on the companion CD.

► Create the ATL server

1. On the File menu, click New.
2. On the Projects tab, select ATL COM AppWizard. Type *DogServer* as the project name, and click OK.
3. In the ATL COM AppWizard dialog box, retain the default settings and click Finish, and then click OK. You should now have the shell for your COM server.
4. On the Insert menu, click New ATL Object, select Simple Object, and click Next.
5. In the ATL Object Wizard Properties dialog box, type *Dog* as the short name. On the Attributes tab, select Custom for the interface type (it is best to not implement the methods for IDispatch for the moment), and click OK. Your server now has one object: Dog.
6. In the Class view of your project workspace, right-click the IDog interface entry and select Add Method from the shortcut menu.
7. In the Add Method To Interface dialog box, type *Bark* as the method name. The *Bark* method will have one parameter: *Times*. Type the parameter for the object as follows: *[in] short nTimes*. Click OK. The wizard will add the declaration to the IDL file as well as to the header file and the implementation file for Dog.
8. In the implementation file, Dog.cpp, type the following code for the *Bark* method:

```
STDMETHODIMP CDog::Bark(short nTimes)
{
    for (int i=1;  i  <= nTimes; i++)
        MessageBox(NULL,"Woof!","Dog",MB_OK);

    return S_OK;
}
```

You now have a method named *Bark* that displays a message box a variable number of times.

9. Build your COM server.

Exercise 2: Creating a Client Program

In this exercise, you will create a test client program. The easiest way to do this is to create a console application.

Note You will find the code for this exercise in the Labs\Ch05\Ex02 folder on the companion CD.

► **Create a client program**

1. On the File menu, click New.
2. On the Projects tab, select Win32 Console Application. Type *DogOwner* as the project name, and click OK.
3. In the Win32 Console Application, select A Simple Application, click Finish, and then click OK.
4. In the StdAfx.h file, add support for COM by adding the following #include statements:

```
#include <windows.h>
#include <objbase.h>
```

5. In the DogOwner.cpp file, add support for the *printf* and *kbhit* functions by adding the following #include statements:

```
#include <conio.h>
#include <stdio.h>
#include <iostream.h>
```

   In the same file, add the declarations for the Dog class:

```
#include "..\DogServer\DogServer.h"
#include "..\DogServer\DogServer_i.c"
```

6. In the *main* function, add the following code to create an instance of Dog and make the dog bark:

```
HRESULT hr;
hr = CoInitialize(NULL);
if (FAILED(hr))
    return hr;
IDog *pDog=NULL;
hr =CoCreateInstance
    (CLSID_Dog,NULL,CLSCTX_ALL,IID_IDog,(void **)&pDog);
if (FAILED(hr))
    return hr;
```

```
printf ("Dog created successfully.\n");
hr = pDog->Bark(5);
if (FAILED(hr))
    return hr;
printf ("Dog finished barking.\n");
pDog->Release();
printf ("Dog destroyed\n");
while (!_kbhit());
CoUninitialize();
```

7. Build and test the client program. You should be able to create instances of your Dog, and make it bark.

Exercise 3: Removing ATL

You will now remove the ATL-created code from your project. Start by removing the ATL base classes from the CDog class.

Note You will find the code for this exercise in the Labs\Ch05\Ex03 folder on the companion CD.

▶ **Remove ATL from the CDog class**

1. In the inheritance list for CDog (in the declaration of CDog in Dog.h), remove all the base classes, and derive the class from IDog as follows:

```
class CDog : public IDog
```

2. Add the following declarations for the IUnknown interface to your header file:

```
private:
    long   m_lRefCount;
public:
    // IUnknown methods
    STDMETHODIMP QueryInterface(REFIID riid, void **ppv);
    STDMETHODIMP_(ULONG) AddRef(void);
    STDMETHODIMP_(ULONG) Release(void);
```

3. Add the following code to implement the IUnknown interface to your implementation file, Dog.cpp:

```
// IUnknown methods
extern void LockModule();
extern void UnlockModule();

STDMETHODIMP CDog::QueryInterface(REFIID riid, void **ppv)
{
    if (riid == IID_IUnknown || riid == IID_IDog)
```

```
        *ppv = static_cast<IDog*>(this);
    else
    {
        *ppv = NULL;
        return E_NOINTERFACE;
    }
    reinterpret_cast<IUnknown*>(*ppv)->AddRef();
    return S_OK;
}
STDMETHODIMP_(ULONG) CDog::AddRef(void)
{
    LockModule();
    return ++m_lRefCount;
}
STDMETHODIMP_(ULONG) CDog::Release(void)
{
    ULONG lRefCount = --m_lRefCount;
    if (lRefCount == 0)
        delete this;
    UnlockModule();
    return lRefCount;
}
```

Notice that the implementations of *LockModule* and *UnlockModule* have not been provided—they will be provided later when you modify the four COM DLL entry points.

4. Remove all other ATL macros from the header file, including the interface map and resource macros. Also remove ATL_NOVTABLE from the class declaration. This macro tells the compiler not to create a vtable for instances of the class. Our class needs a vtable.

You should now have a Dog class that does not have any ATL. The next step is to create a class factory for CDog.

► Create a ClassFactory class for CDog

1. Add the following CDogClass declaration to the Dog.h file:

```
class CDogClass : public IClassFactory
{
};
```

2. Implement IUnknown for the CDogClass class. Add the function declarations to the class definition as follows:

```
// IUnknown methods
STDMETHODIMP QueryInterface(REFIID riid, void **ppv);
STDMETHODIMP_(ULONG) AddRef(void);
STDMETHODIMP_(ULONG) Release(void);
```

3. Add the implementation for the IUnknown methods to the Dog.cpp file as follows:

```
STDMETHODIMP CDogClass::QueryInterface(REFIID riid, void **ppv)
{
    if (riid == IID_IUnknown || riid == IID_IClassFactory)
        *ppv = static_cast<IClassFactory*>(this);
    else
    {
        *ppv = NULL;
        return E_NOINTERFACE;
    }

    reinterpret_cast<IUnknown*>(*ppv)->AddRef();
    return S_OK;
}

STDMETHODIMP_(ULONG) CDogClass::AddRef(void)
{
    return 2;
}

STDMETHODIMP_(ULONG) CDogClass::Release(void)
{
    return 3;
}
```

4. Add the following method declarations for the IClassFactory interface:

```
// IClassFactory methods
STDMETHODIMP CreateInstance(IUnknown *pUnkOuter,
REFIID riid, void **ppv);
STDMETHODIMP LockServer(BOOL bLock);
```

5. Add the following implementation for these methods to the Dog.cpp file:

```
STDMETHODIMP CDogClass::CreateInstance(IUnknown
*pUnkOuter, REFIID riid, void **ppv)
{
    if (ppv == 0)
        return E_POINTER;
    *ppv = 0;
    if (pUnkOuter)
        return CLASS_E_NOAGGREGATION;
    CDog *pObj = new CDog();
    if (!pObj)
        return E_OUTOFMEMORY;
    pObj->AddRef();
    HRESULT hr = pObj->QueryInterface(riid, ppv);
    pObj->Release();
```

```
        return hr;
    }
    STDMETHODIMP CDogClass::LockServer(BOOL bLock)
    {
        if (bLock)
            LockModule();
        else
            UnlockModule();
        return S_OK;
    }
```

You should now have a ClassFactory for CDog in place. The next task is to eliminate ATL from the four COM DLL entry points. Begin with *DllCanUnloadNow*.

► Implement the COM DLL entry points

1. To implement the *DllCanUnloadNow* method, you must declare a global variable to keep track of outstanding references to your objects, and implement the *LockModule* and *UnlockModule* functions. Add the following code to the DogServer.cpp file:

```
LONG g_cLocks = 0;
void LockModule(void)
{
    InterlockedIncrement(&g_cLocks);
}
void UnlockModule(void)
{
    InterlockedDecrement(&g_cLocks);
}
```

2. Modify the code in *DllCanUnloadNow* to the following:

```
STDAPI DllCanUnloadNow(void)
{
return g_cLocks ? S_FALSE : S_OK;
}
```

3. When this code is in place, you can change the implementation for the *DllGetClassObject* function. To do so, you must declare a global variable to contain an instance of the CDogClass class (CDog class factory). Add the following code to your DogServer.cpp file:

```
CDogClass g_dogclass;
```

4. Modify the *DllGetClassObject* function as follows:

```
STDAPI DllGetClassObject(REFCLSID rclsid,
    REFIID riid,
    void **ppv)
{
    *ppv = 0;
    if (rclsid == CLSID_Dog)
        return g_dogclass.QueryInterface(riid, ppv);
    else
        return CLASS_E_CLASSNOTAVAILABLE;
}
```

In the Labs\Ch05\Exercise3 folder on the companion CD, you will find a file called register.txt. This file contains the implementations for *DllRegisterServer*, and *DllUnregisterServer*. This file also contains code for *DllMain* that is needed for registration to work. Simply copy this code to your project.

5. Remove the OBJECT_MAP macros and the CComModule declaration from DogServer.cpp.
6. Build the DLL project.
7. Run the DogOwner.exe client to test the project. The program should run without needing to be rebuilt.

You should now have a DogServer COM DLL that uses only Platform SDK functions. If you run the DogOwner client program you will notice that it runs as before without modifications.

Review

The following questions are intended to reinforce key information presented in this chapter. If you are unable to answer a question, review the appropriate lesson and then try answering the question again. Answers to the questions can be found in Appendix B, "Review Questions and Answers," at the back of this book.

1. What is a COM coclass?

2. What is a COM object?

3. What is a COM component?

4. What are the four interfaces that every COM class must implement?

5. True or false: allocating and deallocating instances of an exported class is the job of the client; it should not be left to the server.

6. What method do C++ programmers use to separate the interface declaration from the implementation?

7. What is a good method for using implementation inheritance at the same time as interface inheritance?

8. What are the four entry points to a COM DLL?

9. True or false: *AddRef* and *Release* must always return an accurate count of an object's outstanding references.

10. Can ATL only be used to create in-process servers?

CHAPTER 6

Building Advanced Business Objects

Lesson 1: Creating Distributed COM Components 302

Lesson 2: Creating Multithreaded Components 311

Lesson 3: Creating Services 320

Lesson 4: Extending Existing COM Components 326

Lesson 5: Creating and Using Active Documents 333

Lesson 6: Using MFC to Create an ISAPI DLL 336

Lab 6: Creating an Out-of-Process COM Component 344

Review 348

About This Chapter

This chapter provides you with some advanced Microsoft Visual C++ concepts, including DCOM and multithreading, that are currently gaining popularity. In addition, you will learn about Microsoft Windows NT services.

Before You Begin

To complete the lessons in this chapter, you must have read Chapter 5, which provides information about COM concepts and creating COM components, as well as threading models, ATL, and MFC.

Lesson 1: Creating Distributed COM Components

Distributed COM (DCOM) is a process for using COM servers over a network so that you can place the client and the server on different computers. DCOM works with all types of servers: basic, Microsoft Automation, and Microsoft ActiveX.

DCOM adds three major features to COM, all of which are involved with networking. They include remote server usage, security protection and location transparency. A brief description of each of these features is given in Table 6.1.

Table 6.1 DCOM Features and Their Descriptions

Feature	Description
Remote server usage	With DCOM, any type of server can be created on a remote computer and used there.
Security protection	DCOM supports several types and levels of security, permitting limitations on which computers can run which clients with which servers.
Location transparency	Through the registry's AppID system, DCOM permits legacy clients not available for DCOM to still use remote servers and security.

After this lesson, you will be able to:

- Configure DCOM on a computer
- Create an out-of-process COM component
- Use DCOM security
- Register a DCOM component

Estimated lesson time: 35 minutes

Configuring DCOM

Configuring DCOM on computers is important for running the components. This section discusses configuring DCOM on different platforms.

DCOM Support for Microsoft Windows 98

In Windows 98, DCOM is an integral part of the operating system that allows users to take advantage of all DCOM features without any additional installation steps. Therefore, you would not need to redistribute DCOM98 with your applications.

DCOM Support for Microsoft Windows 95

Because Windows 95 doesn't include integrated support for DCOM, users must first install Dcom95.exe before installing DCOM-based applications. In some cases, application developers will redistribute Dcom95.exe as part of their applications' setup programs. Microsoft allows redistribution of Dcom95.exe to ensure that it is available for DCOM-based applications.

Installing DCOM on Windows 95

You can install DCOM for Windows 95 by using the Dcom95.exe distribution executable file. (You can download the file from the OLE Development section of the Microsoft Web site at *http://msdn.microsoft.com/library/default.htm*). When you run this executable file, DCOM will be automatically installed on your system. During installation, DCOM for Windows 95 will back up all the system files that it replaces. The backup files will allow the system to be restored to the original condition in case you uninstall DCOM in the future. Keep in mind that you'll need to reboot the system before you can use DCOM.

After installation, the only DCOM utility that a user application can directly access is a configuration utility called Dcomcnfg.exe. Dcomcnfg.exe is coded in such a way that it will not start if user authentication against a computer with Microsoft Windows NT Server is not configured for your system.

Besides Dcomcnfg.exe, DCOM for Windows 95 installs two additional system executables: Rpcss.exe and Dllhost.exe. Rpcss.exe is the DCOM-enhanced Service Control Manager (SCM). The Dllhost.exe utility surrogate allows in-process COM servers to be executed out-of-process or remotely across the network.

Testing DCOM with Windows NT 4

You can test DCOM on Windows NT 4 systems. On a Windows NT system, full launch and access security support is provided. Also, Windows NT 4 offers automatic launch service. Besides supporting in-process and local servers, Windows NT 4 also supports COM servers executing in the form of a native Windows NT Service. However, you must ensure that you have Service Pack 2 (or later) installed on your system.

Dcomcnfg.exe on Windows NT 4 will allow you to adjust the registry entries and security permissions, and so on. For your casual testing, you should make the security and permission checking support unavailable by setting the default values as shown in the following code:

```
Default Authentication Level = None
Default Impersonation Level = Anonymous
```

This procedure puts your system at the same level of accessibility as computers using Windows 95.

Creating an ATL Out-Of-Process Component

ATL is predominantly a technology for creating COM components. Creating COM servers using ATL is very easy and does not require you to write a lot of code, thanks to the combination of wizard-generated code and the library code provided by ATL.

COM Server Types

COM is an industry standard built into many operating systems and compilers. COM components implement communication between client applications and server applications.

COM servers are designed to provide services to client applications. These servers are classified based on server location in relation to the client application. A COM server can occupy the same address space as the client application. Alternatively, a COM server can occupy a separate address space from the client application or on a remote computer. For example, a UI component should reside as close to an individual client as possible. On the other hand, a component that supplies statistical calculations of remote data should reside on a remote computer.

Depending on the server's location, a component is classified as either an *in-process* or *out-of-process* server. The server's location thus can greatly affect the client application's performance.

An in-process server is usually implemented as a COM DLL. COM DLLs are also called ActiveX DLLs. An in-process server and the client application share the same address space. As a result, calls are made directly between the two components, providing efficient communication between both server and client. A disadvantage of using an in-process server is that it is not fault-tolerant, implying that the entire host process will fail when the DLL fails. Such a failure occurs because the DLL resides in the same address space as its client application.

An out-of-process server is usually implemented as a COM executable. This executable file runs in its own address space on either the same or a separate computer. The method calls between client and server must be marshaled between processes. This implies that parameters and return values need to be packaged and sent across process boundaries. An advantage of an out-of-process COM server is that faults are limited to the COM out-of-process server. If the COM out-of-process server fails, other processes in the system will continue to operate.

Creating an Out-of-Process COM Server

COM servers contain COM components that are designed to provide services to the client application. COM servers are classified based on the server's location in relation to the client application.

► **To create an out-of-process COM server**

1. Select New from the Microsoft Visual Studio File menu, click the Projects tab of the New dialog box, and select ATL COM AppWizard.
2. Type the project's name in the Project Name text box, and then click OK.
3. The ATL COM AppWizard—Step 1 Of 1 dialog box appears. The server type will determine the option that you should select in the Server Type group box. To create an out-of-process server, select the Executable (EXE) option.
4. To complete the procedure for creating the component's basic structure, click Finish. The specifications of the new project appear.
5. Accept the default specifications by clicking OK.
6. Choose the New ATL Object command from the Insert menu. Different categories of objects appear in the ATL Object Wizard dialog box.
7. The ATL Object Wizard dialog box displays four categories of ATL objects that can be inserted into a project: Objects, Controls, Miscellaneous, and Data Access. When you select a category, the icons of the ATL objects for that category appear in the Objects list. For the purposes of this lesson, select the Objects category, click the Simple Object icon, and then click Next to create a simple object.
8. Type a name for the object in the Short Name text box, and then click OK.
9. The interface for the new object appears on the ClassView tab of Visual Studio's Project Workspace window. To add a property to the interface, right-click the interface and choose Add Property from the shortcut menu. Fill in the information for the new property in the Add Property To Interface dialog box and click OK.
10. To add a method to the interface, right-click the interface and choose Add Method from the shortcut menu. Fill in the information for the new method in the Add Method To Interface dialog box and click OK.

COM Client Creation

COM clients are required in order to access the components of a COM server. You can use one COM client to access components of both in-process and out-of-process servers.

► **To create a COM client that can access an ATL COM server**

1. Choose New from the Visual Studio File menu, click the Projects tab of the New dialog box, and select MFC AppWizard (EXE).
2. Type the project's name in the Project Name text box, and then click OK.
3. The MFC AppWizard—Step 1 dialog box appears. For the purposes of this lesson, click the Dialog Based radio button, and then click Next.

4. To allow the client application to manipulate the server application data, select the Automation check box.
5. Accept the default automation settings that appear, and click the Finish button.
6. When the new project specifications appear, click OK to accept them.
7. You can now add functionality to the client application. You will need to include in the StdAfx.h file the path of the COM server that the client will access. When you have finished creating the COM client, you can add any method or function to the client application using the same procedure as for an out-of-process COM server.

Using DCOM Security

DCOM systems include substantial security features. The most important aspects of DCOM security providers include the authentication process and access vs. launch permissions. By default, DCOM uses the Windows NT security features.

Typically, a computer running Windows NT is used by multiple clients to access resources and applications. To access the Windows NT resources and applications, users must have access permissions. However, DCOM requires the users to have a *launch permission*, which allows users to start a given COM server on their own. This is less common, so it requires intervention by a Windows NT administrator to make sure that everything works correctly.

Using DCOM, you can apply security to launch and access DCOM components. You can apply security in two ways: *declaratively* and *programmatically*. When you apply declarative security, the security settings are held as part of the COM server's registry values. These values are available in the AppID for the component server. As a result, declarative security does not allow for security on a fine-grained, per-coclass or per-object call basis. For per-coclass or per-object call security, you need to apply security programmatically.

If you use ATL for DCOM components, ATL assumes that you will apply declarative security.

Authentication

Authentication is a mechanism for verifying a user's identity. Windows NT and Microsoft Windows 2000 perform authentication by using a challenge-response scheme where passwords are passed over the network in an encrypted form to prevent the passwords from being obtained illegally. If the information entered by the user matches the information stored on the domain controller, the controller applies the user's security permissions to the client computer. The network administrator grants these security permissions.

You can implement authentication under the following circumstances:

- When a client first connects
- When a method call is made
- On every data packet passed from a client to the server computer

---

Note The Default Properties tab of the Dcomcnfg.exe utility allows you to set the default authentication level for all COM servers on your computer.

You might decide to turn off authentication entirely, but this is not advisable. Note that the default authentication level is applied only when there is not a server-specific value.

In addition to authentication levels, you can increase security by using the *impersonation level*, which is available only on Windows NT. If available on a sufficient level, a component can get the identity of a connected client and use the impersonation-level identity to access the server. The impersonation options are as follows:

- **Anonymous** With this option, the client's identity is not available to the server.
- **Delegate** Selecting this option will permit the component to impersonate the client to call a remote component; this component will get the security of the original client.
- **Identify** This option allows the component to impersonate the client only for the purposes of obtaining an identity.
- **Impersonate** With this option, the component can impersonate the client to access secured components.

Authorization

Authorization is the process of validating whether or not a user is allowed to perform a task. COM applies authorization to two tasks: *launching* and *accessing* a server. Default authorization can be applied through the Default Security tab of the Dcomcnfg.exe utility. The values specified on this tab are used whenever a server does not have a list of authorized accounts.

Dcomcnfg.exe

Dcomcnfg.exe is used to specify the authentication and authorization levels for a DCOM component. Dcomcnfg.exe provides four tabs to configure a DCOM component, as follows:

- **Applications** Lists all the servers that have an entry in the AppID key. If this tab cannot find the descriptive name of a server, it will give the first coclass it can find that uses the AppID. However, be aware that the settings on this tab are applied to the AppID, but not to a coclass. You can double-click an entry to change the security settings for that server.
- **General** Provides information about the server, including the server file and details about whether an executable file, service, or surrogate will be used.
- **Location** Used to set the RemoteServerName value.
- **Security** Allows you to specify the user accounts that are authorized to launch and access the server.

You will now examine the Security tab in detail.

Security Tab

Using this tab, you can edit the custom access permissions, as demonstrated in the following procedure.

► **To specify the permission for launching a server**

1. Click Use Custom Launch Permissions.
2. Click Edit. A standard Windows NT dialog box appears; this dialog box displays the accounts and account groups that can launch the server. You can edit these values to allow the required users to launch the server. User accounts are added from lists of accounts obtained from the local Windows NT computer and any domain in which the computer can be a member.

Registering a DCOM Component

When you install and configure a remote COM server, you can trick COM into DCOM by using Regedit.exe to modify the local server's keys and the AppID key of the local registry.

Registering a Server for Remote Access

Regedit.exe is located in the Windows\System directory in Windows 95 and Windows 98, and in the Windows directory (usually C:\Winnt) in Windows NT 4 and Windows 2000. To start it, either locate the executable from Windows Explorer or use the Start menu's Run dialog box.

Getting DCOM to use a remote rather than local computer for a given COM server is easy. You simply need to add a specific subkey to the component's basic registry key entry. DCOM requires an AppID value beneath a COM server's CLSID key in order to register a server for remote access. The AppID value's data is a GUID that also appears as a subkey under the HKEY_CLASSES_ROOT\AppID key.

The AppID subkey is used to control configuration options for a single executable. Because an executable can serve several coclasses, the configurations applied to the AppID key will affect all the coclasses.

► **To register a local COM server**

1. Obtain the registry format of the GUID for the COM server in question.
2. After you have located the proper GUID entry using Regedit.exe, click the New Key menu command on the Edit menu to place a subkey under it named AppID. This key will appear with a default value of an empty string.
3. Obtain a unique GUID value to use as the link between this server and the DCOM system. To create a GUID that is guaranteed to be unique, use the Guidgen.exe application found in the Microsoft Visual Studio 98\Common\Tools subdirectory of the Microsoft Visual Studio installation. Make sure that the Registry Format radio button is selected, click New GUID, and then click Copy to place a copy of the new GUID to the Clipboard.
4. Activate your Regedit.exe window.
5. Click the default value under the AppID you created in step 2.
6. Choose Modify from the Edit menu.
7. The Edit String dialog box appears. Right-click the Value Data box and choose Paste from the shortcut menu. The GUID that is copied from GUIDGEN will appear in the proper format.
8. Click OK to set the default value for the AppID key.

► **To add an AppID key**

1. Choose Find from Regedit.exe's Edit menu and use the Find dialog box to locate the AppID main key.
2. Choose New Key from the Edit menu and add a new key named with the same GUID value that you used for the default value of the AppID key in the previous procedure.
3. Under this key, create a blank string key named DllSurrogate, and a string key named RemoteServerName that contains the value of the remote server that you want to use.
4. To allow security for the remote server, type *AccessPermission* and *LaunchPermission* as the values with multi-string types.

5. Type the list of authorized users and domains into the appropriate values with the multistring editor.
6. Close Regedit.exe and reboot the computer.
7. When your local client attempts to connect to the supposedly local COM server, it will use DCOM and connect to the remote one instead.

Lesson Summary

In this lesson, you learned that you can install DCOM on systems running Windows 95 by using Dcom95.exe; DCOM is already installed on Windows 98. You also learned that DCOM components are basically out-of-process components that you can create using either MFC or ATL.

If you use ATL, you can provide DCOM components with security levels only declaratively. You can use Dcomcnfg.exe to configure the DCOM components. You can use Regedit.exe to manipulate the registry for making a COM component act as a DCOM component.

Lesson 2: Creating Multithreaded Components

With the advent of Windows 95 and Windows NT, multithreading has become a common feature of graphical user interface (GUI) applications. You can use either MFC or ATL to create multithreaded components. This lesson delves into the creation of multithreaded components.

After this lesson, you will be able to:

- Create secondary threads using MFC
- Create threads using ATL

Estimated lesson time: 30 minutes

Using Multithreaded Components

Threads can be categorized as either primary or secondary threads. In the applications that you create, you can dedicate the primary program thread to process messages so that the program can respond quickly to commands and other events. To carry out multiple tasks, you can use a secondary thread, which will allow you to perform any lengthy task, such as drawing complex graphics that would otherwise block program message processing if performed by the primary thread.

Creating Secondary Threads

Starting a secondary program thread is relatively quick and consumes little memory. In addition, all threads within a program run within the same memory space and own the same set of Windows resources; consequently, they can easily share memory variables and Windows objects such as windows, pens, memory allocations, DCs, and so on. In this section, you will learn to create secondary threads using MFC.

To use multithreading in an MFC program, you must ensure that the Use Run-Time Library project setting has an appropriate value for multithreading. A new project has an appropriate setting by default; you can change the value of this setting if you do not want to accept the default setting.

► **To reset project settings**

1. Choose Settings from the Project menu.
2. In the Project Settings dialog box, select the project name in the list of projects.
3. Click the C/C++ tab and select Code Generation in the Category list.

4. To set the release project configuration, select either Multithreaded or Multithreaded DLL in the Use Run-Time Library list.
5. To set the debug configuration, select Debug Multithreaded or Debug Multithreaded DLL in the Use Run-Time Library list.

To start a new thread in your program, you can call the global MFC function *AfxBeginThread*. *AfxBeginThread* starts the new thread and allows it to run along with the thread that called *AfxBeginThread* to create the new thread. *AfxBeginThread* has the following form:

```
CWinThread* AfxBeginThread
    (AFX_THREADPROC pfnThreadProc,
    LPAVOID pParam,
    int nPriority = THREAD_PRIORITY_NORMAL,
    UINT nStackSize = 0,
    DWORD dwCreateFlags = 0,
LPSECURITY_ATTRIBUTES lpSecurityAttrs = NULL);
```

AfxBeginThread takes six parameters. The first parameter, *pfnThreadProc*, specifies the thread function. The new thread begins by executing this function. When the thread function returns, the new thread is terminated.

The second parameter is *pParam*. This parameter specifies the value to be passed to the thread function. You must define the thread function so that it has the following form:

```
UNIT ThreadFunction(LPVOID pParam);
```

Notice that the thread function returns a UINT value; this value is known as the *exit code*, which you will learn about later in this chapter. Normally, the thread function returns the value 0 to indicate a normal exit; however, you can use any return value convention you want, because the value is read and interpreted only by your own code.

The last four *AfxBeginThread* parameters have default values, which you can generally accept. The *nPriority* parameter specifies the priority of the new thread. The priority of a thread determines how frequently the thread is allowed to run when the operating system switches control from thread to thread. If the thread must perform its task quickly and respond to events efficiently, you should assign it a relatively high priority. The default value THREAD_PRIORITY_NORMAL assigns the thread an average priority and suits most purposes. Table 6.2 provides additional thread priority values and their adjustments.

Table 6.2 Thread Priority Values and Their Adjustments

Thread priority class	Priority adjustment
THREAD_PRIORITY_ ABOVE_NORMAL	One more than the base priority for the process
THREAD_PRIORITY_ BELOW_NORMAL	One less than the base priority for the process
THREAD_PRIORITY_ HIGHEST	Two above the base priority for the process
THREAD_PRIORITY_ IDLE	A base priority level of 1 for IDLE_PRIORITY_CLASS, BELOW_NORMAL_PRIORITY_CLASS, NORMAL_ PRIORITY_CLASS, ABOVE_NORMAL_PRIORITY_ CLASS or HIGH_PRIORITY_CLASS processes, and a score of 16 for REALTIME_PRIORITY_CLASS processes
THREAD_PRIORITY_ LOWEST	Two points below the normal priority for the priority class
THREAD_PRIORITY_ NORMAL	Exactly the base priority score
THREAD_PRIORITY_ TIME_CRITICAL	Indicates a base priority of 15 for IDLE_PRIORITY_ CLASS, BELOW_NORMAL_PRIORITY_CLASS, NORMAL_PRIORITY_CLASS or HIGH_PRIORITY_ CLASS processes, and a base priority level of 31 for REALTIME_PRIORITY_CLASS processes

Related to the thread priority is a process priority level. The various process priority levels and their base priorities are shown in Table 6.3.

Table 6.3 Process Priority Values and Their Base Priorities

Process priority class	Base priority
REALTIME_PRIORITY_ CLASS	24
HIGH_PRIORITY_CLASS	13
NORMAL_PRIORITY_ CLASS	9 if the thread has a window in the foreground, or 7 if it has a window in the background
IDLE_PRIORITY_CLASS	4

The last parameter to *AfxBeginThread* is *dwCreateFlags*. If *dwCreateFlags* is assigned a value 0, the new thread begins running immediately. If assigned CREATE_SUSPENDED, the new thread will not start running until you call *CWinThread::ResumeThread*. You can almost always assign the default values to the *nStackSize* and *lpSecurityAttrs* parameters, which specify the thread's stack size and security attributes.

The following example code starts a new thread, which executes *MultiThreadFnc* and any related functions *MultiThreadFnc* calls.

```
UNIT MultiThreadFnc (LPVOID pParam)
{
// statements and function calls to be executed by the new thread
return 0; // terminate the thread and return 0
exit code
}

void MultiThreadSomeFnc (void)
{
//
int Code = 1;
CWinThread *PWinThread;
PWinThread = AfxBeginThread(MultiThreadFnc, &Code);
//
}
```

Terminating a Thread

To terminate a thread, you can use one of two methods. The first method is to return to the thread function by passing back the desired exit code. This method is the most effective way to end a thread. The stack that the thread uses is deallocated, and all automatic data objects that the thread has created will be properly destroyed.

The second method is to call the *AfxEndThread* function with the desired exit code as follows:

```
void AfxEndThread (UINT nExitCode);
```

Calling *AfxEndThread* is a convenient way to immediately end a thread from within a nested function. Using this method, the thread stack will be deallocated, but destructors for automatic objects created by the thread will not be called.

Both methods for stopping a thread must be performed by the thread itself. If you want to terminate a thread from a second thread, the MSDN Library documentation recommends having the second thread signal the thread that you want to end, requesting it to terminate itself.

Managing the Thread

AfxBeginThread returns a pointer to a CWinThread object. You can use this pointer to manage the new thread. You can call the CWinThread member function *SuspendThread* to temporarily stop the thread from running, as shown in the following line of code:

```
PWinThread->SuspendThread();
```

You can call *CWinThread::ResumeThread* to rerun the thread as follows:

```
PWinThread->ResumeThread();
```

You can change the thread's priority from the level it was initially assigned in the *AfxBeginThread* call by calling *CWinThread::SetThreadPriority*. For example, the following code raises a thread's priority from the default level as shown:

```
PWinThread->SetThreadPriority(THREAD_PRIORITY_ABOVE_NORMAL);
```

You can obtain the thread's current priority level by calling *CWinThread::GetThreadPriority*.

Also, you can call the Win32 API function *GetExitCodeThread* to determine whether the thread is still running and, if it has stopped running, to obtain its exit code. You must assign the first *GetExitCodeThread* parameter the Windows handle for the thread, which is stored in the CWinThread data member *m_hThread* as demonstrated in the following code:

```
DWORD ExitCode;
::GetExitCodeThread
// Windows handle for thread
(PWinThread->m_hThread,
// address of DWORD variable to receive exit code
&ExitCode);
if (ExitCode == STILL_ACTIVE)
// thread is still running
else
// thread has terminated and ExitCode contains its exit code
```

GetExitCodeThread assigns a value to the *DWORD* variable, which has an address that you can pass as the second parameter. If the thread is still running, it assigns this variable the value STILL_ACTIVE; if the thread has terminated, it assigns the variable the thread's exit code.

When you are done using the thread object, you should explicitly delete it. The syntax is shown as follows:

```
delete PWinThread;
```

Synchronizing Threads

For 32-bit programs running with Windows 95 or later, or with Windows NT, multithreading is preemptive, and threads run asynchronously. This can be problematic if two or more threads try to access a shared resource, such as a global variable. Consider two threads executing a block of code, which increments a global counter and then prints out the new counter value as shown in the following code:

```
// Declared globally:
int cnt = 0;
//

// Function that is executed by two threads:
void ThreadSharedFnc()
{
    //
    ++cnt;
    cout << cnt <  \n';
    //
}
```

If this function is called repeatedly, printing a series of consecutive integer values starting with 1 is expected to result. However, because the code is executed by two threads, you might encounter the following series of problems:

1. The first thread increments cnt.
2. The first thread is preempted and the second thread receives control.
3. The second thread increments cnt and prints the new value.
4. The first thread again receives control, and then prints the same value just printed by the second thread; the value it should have printed is skipped.

To prevent these errors, you will need to synchronize the action of the threads. Fortunately, the Win32 API provides a variety of synchronization objects that you can use to synchronize the actions of separate threads. Using these objects, you can perform various types of synchronization as follows:

- You can prevent more than one thread from accessing a resource at the same time.
- You can limit the number of threads that can simultaneously access a resource.
- You can perform other types of signaling among threads.

One of the common synchronization objects is the *mutex*. The name of this synchronization object derives from the expression *mutual exclusion*. This object is used for limiting access to a given resource to a single thread at a time.

To use a mutex, the first step is to call the Win32 API function *CreateMutex* to create a mutex synchronization object. *CreateMutex* has the following form:

```
HANDLE CreateMutex(
    // Pointer to security attributes
    LPSECURITY_ATTRIBUTES lpMutexAttributes,
    // Flag for initial ownership
    BOOL bInitialOwner,
    // Pointer to mutex-object name
    LPCTSTR lpName
);
```

The *CreateMutex* function takes three parameters. The first parameter specifies the security attributes of the mutex. You can pass NULL to assign it default security attributes and make the mutex handle noninheritable.

The second parameter specifies the initial state of the mutex; passing FALSE creates a mutex that is initially signaled. The third parameter specifies the name of the mutex. *CreateMutex* returns a handle, which the threads in the program use for referring to the mutex.

The next step is to add a call to the *WaitForSingleObject* Win32 API function to the beginning of any block of code that accesses the resource you want to protect, and to add a call to the *ReleaseMutex* Win32 API function to the end of each of these blocks. For example, you could prevent more than one thread from simultaneously accessing the global counter in the example just given, by implementing the following code:

```
::WaitForSingleObject
(HMutex, INFINITE);
++cnt;
cout << cnt << \n';
::ReleaseMutex(HMutex);
```

A mutex can be in one of the two states: *signaled* or *nonsignaled*. Normally, a newly created mutex is signaled. If the mutex in the previous code is signaled when a thread calls *WaitForSingleObject*, this function changes the mutex to the nonsignaled state and returns immediately. The thread proceeds to execute the protected block of code and then calls *ReleaseMutex*, which sets the mutex back to signaled. If the mutex is nonsignaled when a thread calls *WaitForSingleObject*, *WaitForSingleObject* waits until the mutex becomes signaled and then sets the mutex to nonsignaled and returns. The overall result is that only one thread at a time can execute the protected block of code. Note that when a synchronization object is nonsignaled, it is also owned by the thread that caused it to become nonsignaled.

The first parameter passed to *WaitForSingleObject* and *ReleaseMutex* is the mutex handle returned by *CreateMutex*. *WaitForSingleObject* takes the time-out period, in milliseconds, as its second parameter. After waiting for the specified time-out period, *WaitForSingleObject* will return even if the mutex has not become signaled. However, most programs assign this parameter the special value INFINITE, which causes *WaitForSingleObject* to wait as long as necessary for the mutex to become signaled.

If your program has finished using a mutex, it can call the Win32API function *CloseHandle* to close the mutex handle. The folllowing call would close the mutex handle used in the previous examples:

```
::CloseHandle (HMutex);
```

If you do not call *CloseHandle*, the system will automatically close the handle when the program exits. When all handles for a given object have been closed, the system releases the object and frees the memory it consumes.

Creating a Multithreaded Component Using ATL

You can create multithreaded components using ATL. ATL supports all the threading models (STA and MTA). You can ensure that the threading models can interact directly with your ATL code.

► **To ensure that the threading model interacts with your ATL code**

1. Select the threading model from the Attributes tab provided by the Object Wizard.

When you create a new coclass, you have the choice of setting the threading model. The value that you set has two main effects: it sets the threading model class used as the template parameter to CComObjectRootEx, and it sets the ThreadingModel registry entry in the RGS file.

CComObjectRootEx is the base class used to handle the IUnknown methods of your generated class, and is therefore responsible for reference counting. If you pick Single or Apartment, CComObjectRootEx<CComSingleThreadModel> is used as the base class. If you pick Both or Free, CComObjectRootEx<CComMultiThreadModel> is used.

CComSingleThreadModel is used to implement *AddRef* and *Release* with the *increment* and *decrement* operators. The CComMultiThreadModel class ensures that *AddRef* and *Release* are implemented using *InterlockedIncrement* and *InterlockedDecrement*, thus preventing concurrent access to the reference count when it is being changed.

Global Threading Model

The global threading model for an ATL project is defined in StdAfx.h by one of the following symbols:

- _ATL_SINGLE_THREADED
- _ATL_APARTMENT_THREADED
- _ATL_FREE_THREADED

The default setting is _ATL_APARTMENT_THREADED.

These symbols are used to typedef one of the threading model classes to CComObjectThreadModel and CComGlobalsThreadModel, as the following code, taken from Atlbase.h, demonstrates:

```
#if defined(_ATL_SINGLE_THREADED)
    typedef CcomSingleThreadModel
    CComObjectThreadModel;
    typedef CcomSingleThreadModel
    CComGlobalsThreadModel;
#elif defined(_ATL_APARTMENT_THREADED)
    typedef CcomSingleThreadModel
    CComObjectThreadModel;
    typedef CcomMultiThreadModel
    CComGlobalsThreadModel;
#else
    typedef CComMultiThreadModel CComObjectThreadModel;
    typedef CcomMultiThreadModel
    CComGlobalsThreadModel;
#endif
```

Lesson Summary

In this lesson, you learned that multithreading has become an integral part of GUI application development. You learned that you can code for multithreading using MFC or ATL.

You also learned that you can use *AfxBeginThread* and *AfxEndThread* functions to start and end a thread. You can use additional functions, such as *WaitForSingleObject*, *CreateMutex*, and *ReleaseMutex*, to synchronize threads.

Lesson 3: Creating Services

A Windows NT service is a program that runs whenever the computer is running the operating system. Such a service does not require a user to be logged on. When using Windows NT, you need services to perform user-independent tasks, such as directory replication and process monitoring. With Visual C++, creating a Windows NT service is easy.

After this lesson, you will be able to:

- Create Windows NT services
- Communicate with Windows NT services
- Manage Windows NT services

Estimated lesson time: 10 minutes

Creating a Windows NT Service

Although creating a service for Windows NT is not particularly hard, it involves more than simply creating service code. In addition, you must write code to perform the following:

- Reporting warnings and errors in the system or application logs.
- Controlling the service through either a separate application or Control Panel applet. This involves implementing a communication mechanism for your service.
- Installing and removing the service from the operating system.

Writing the Service Code

A service contains three major functions, as follows:

- A *main function* is the entry point of the code. Use a main function to parse any command-line arguments and get the service installed, removed, started, and so on.
- A function that provides the entry point for the actual service code.
- A function that processes command messages from the service manager.

Service Callback Functions

Because the actual service code and the command message processing functions are called from the system, they must conform to the parameter-passing scheme and calling convention of the operating system. In other words, the functions cannot simply be member functions of a C++ class. Following is code used to create a service:

```
class CNTService
{
    [...]
    // static data
    static CNTService* m_pThis;
    [...]
};
```

To initialize the m_pThis pointer, you should implement the following code:

```
CNTService::CNTService(const char* szServiceName)
{
    // Copy the address of the current object
    so you can access it from the static member
    callback functions.
    // m_pThis = this;
    [...]
}
```

If you want to create the simplest possible service, you need to override only *CNTService::Run*, which is the function for which you write the code to perform whatever task your service provides. You also need to implement the main function. If your service needs to perform some initialization, such as reading data from the registry, it also needs to override *CNTService::OnInit*. If you need to be able to send command messages to your service, you can use the *ControlService* system function and handle the requests in the service by overriding *CNTService::OnUserControl*.

Using CNTService in Your Application

You can derive a new class from CNTService, as shown in the following code:

```
// myservice.h
#include "ntservice.h"
class CMyService : public CNTService
{
public:
    CMyService();
    virtual BOOL OnInit();
        virtual void Run();
        virtual BOOL OnUserControl(DWORD dwOpcode);
        void SaveStatus();
    // Control parameters
    int m_iStartParam;
    int m_iIncParam;
    // Current state
    int m_iState;
};
```

CMyService overrides *OnInit*, *Run*, and *OnUserControl* from CNTService. In addition, it has a function called *SaveStatus* that is used to write data to the registry, and also some member variables to hold the current state.

Implementing the Main Function

Having derived your class from CNTService, you can implement the main function in a simple manner, as follows:

```
int main(int argc, char* argv[])
{
    // Create the service object.
    CMyService MyService;

    // Parse for standard arguments (install,
    uninstall, version, and so on)
    if (!MyService.ParseStandardArgs(argc, argv)) {

        //
//
        //
        MyService.StartService();
    }

return MyService.m_Status.dwWin32ExitCode;
}
```

When you have created an instance of the CMyService class, you will need to have a constructor that sets the initial state and name of the service, as shown in the following code:

```
CMyService::CMyService()
:CNTService("NT Service Demonstration")
{
    m_iStartParam = 0;
    m_iIncParam = 1;
    m_iState = m_iStartParam;
}
```

A call is then made to *ParseStandardArgs* to see if the command line contains a request to install the service (-i), remove it (-u), or report its version number (-v). *CNTService::ParseStandardArgs* calls *CNTService::IsInstalled*, *CNTService::Install*, and *CNTService::Uninstall* to process these requests. If no recognizable command-line arguments are found, the code assumes that the SCM is trying to start the service, and therefore calls *StartService*. This function does not return until the service stops running. The call to *DebugBreak* causes a break in the debugger when the service is first started. When you are done debugging the code, you can comment out or delete this line.

Writing Your Service Code

In this section, you will learn how to write the code that actually implements your service.

Initialization

The parameters corresponding to the services are stored in HKEY_LOCAL_MACHINE\SYSTEM\CurrentControlSet\Services in the registry. To initialize your service, you will need to read the parameters from this location, as demonstrated in the following code:

```
BOOL CMyService::OnInit()
{
    // Read the registry parameters.
        // Try opening the registry key:
        // HKEY_LOCAL_MACHINE\SYSTEM\
        CurrentControlSet\Services\<AppName>\
        Parameters
        HKEY hkey;
    char szKey[1024];
    strcpy(szKey,
    "SYSTEM\\CurrentControlSet\\Services\\");
    strcat(szKey, m_szServiceName);
    strcat(szKey, "\\Parameters");
        if (RegOpenKeyEx(HKEY_LOCAL_MACHINE,
                szKey,
                0,
                KEY_QUERY_VALUE,
                &hkey) == ERROR_SUCCESS) {
        // You are installed
        DWORD dwType = 0;
        DWORD dwSize = sizeof(m_iStartParam);
        RegQueryValueEx(hkey,
                "Start",
                NULL,
                &dwType,
                (BYTE*)&m_iStartParam,
                &dwSize);
        dwSize = sizeof(m_iIncParam);
        RegQueryValueEx(hkey,
                "Inc",
                NULL,
                &dwType,
                (BYTE*)&m_iIncParam,
                &dwSize);
        RegCloseKey(hkey);
    }

    // Set the initial state
```

```
    m_iState = m_iStartParam;

    return TRUE;
}
```

After you have implemented the service parameters, you are ready to run the service.

Running the Service

The main body of the service code is executed when the *Run* function is called, as shown in the following code:

```
void CMyService::Run()
{
    while (m_bIsRunning) {

    // Sleep for a while
        DebugMsg("My service is sleeping (%lu)...",
        m_iState);
        Sleep(1000);

    // Update the current state
    m_iState += m_iIncParam;
    }
}
```

Note that the *Run* function does not exit until the service is stopped. The *CNTService::m_bIsRunning* flag is set to FALSE when you make a request to stop the service. You can also override *OnStop* or *OnShutdown* if you need to perform cleanup when your service terminates.

Communicating with Services

Communicating with services is an important component to be taken care of in application development. You can use the ControSerivce system function to enable this.

ControlService

You can communicate with your service using named pipes, thought transference, sticky notes, and so on. However, for simple requests, the *ControlService* system function is easy to use. CNTService provides a handler for nonstandard messages that are sent through the *ControlService* function, as shown in the following code:

```
BOOL CMyService::OnUserControl(DWORD dwOpcode)
{
    switch (dwOpcode) {
    case SERVICE_CONTROL_USER + 0:

        // Save the current status in the registry
        SaveStatus();
        return TRUE;

    default:
        break;
    }
    return FALSE;  // Say not handled
}
```

As shown in the previous code, *SaveStatus* is a local function that saves the service state in the registry.

Managing Services

Managing services involves installing and removing services. Visual C++ provides built-in functions to perform these tasks.

Installing and Removing the Service

Installing the service is handled by *CNTService::Install*, which registers the service with the Windows NT service manager and makes entries in the registry to support logging messages when the service is running.

Removing the service is handled by *CNTService::Uninstall*, which simply informs the service manager that the service is no longer required. *CNTService::Uninstall* does not remove the actual service executable file.

Lesson Summary

In this lesson, you learned to create, communicate with, and manage Windows NT services with the ease of using Visual C++. The CNTService class acts as the base class for creating all Windows NT services.

Lesson 4: Extending Existing COM Components

COM enables you to reuse code by inheriting it from an interface or an implementation. Reusing code saves time and minimizes the errors in an application.

To create a COM component that reuses an existing component, COM uses the aggregation and containment techniques. This section will focus on these concepts.

After this lesson, you will be able to:

- Understand the difference between aggregation and containment
- Understand the steps to implement aggregation and containment for reusing existing COM components

Estimated lesson time: 20 minutes

Aggregation

Aggregation is a reuse technique in which the outer object exposes the interfaces of the inner object directly and makes it seem like the interfaces are part of the outer object. As a result, the interfaces of the inner object are exposed directly to the client rather than through the interface stubs. Therefore, there is no overhead of forwarding calls to the inner object. This reuse technique is useful when the outer object delegates every interface call to the same interface of the inner object.

Aggregation is very simple to implement with the exception of implementing the three IUnknown functions: *QueryInterface*, *AddRef*, and *Release*. The catch is that from the client's perspective, any IUnknown function on the outer object must affect the outer object. This implies that *AddRef* and *Release* affect the outer object and *QueryInterface* exposes all the interfaces available on the outer object. However, if the outer object simply exposes an inner object's interface as its own, the behavior of the IUnknown members of the inner object will differ from that of the outer object. This is not acceptable.

The solution is that aggregation requires an explicit implementation of IUnknown on the inner object and delegation of the IUnknown methods of any other interface to the outer object's IUnknown methods. In addition, the outer object stores a reference to the IUnknown interface of the inner object.

Aggregation Process

For aggregation to work, the inner object must be written to support aggregation.

1. First, the outer object calls the *CoCreateInstance* function to create the inner object.

   In the call to *CoCreateInstance*, the outer object passes a pointer to its IUnknown interface and requests the IUnknown interface of the inner object.
2. Then, on receiving a request from a client for an interface implemented by the inner object, the outer object queries the inner object for the interface and passes the pointer returned by the inner object to the client.
3. If the client calls *QueryInterface* using the pointer to an interface of the inner object, the inner object forwards the call to the IUnknown interface of the outer object through the stored pointer to the IUnknown interface of the outer object.

   This results in the client seeing only the IUnknown interface of the outer object and not that of the inner object. The client is unaware of the existence of the inner object. From the client's perspective, the outer object implements all interfaces.

Controlling Unknown

The IUnknown interface of the outer object is known as the controlling unknown because all IUnknown method calls by the client are routed to the implementation of the outer object of the IUnknown interface.

The outer object is responsible for determining if a pointer should be returned to the inner object or it should be forwarded to the *QueryInterface* call to an inner object. In addition, the inner object is unaware of calls to *AddRef* and *Release* that are made through pointers to interfaces implemented by the outer object. Therefore, the inner object cannot control the lifetime of the entire object and must delegate calls to *AddRef* and *Release* to the outer object's IUnknown interface.

Implementing Aggregation

To implement aggregation, you can use ATL because it provides a series of macros to implement outer and inner objects.

Implementing the Outer Object

To implement an outer object, ATL places the DECLARE_GET_CONTROLLING_UNKNOWN macro in the object class file and defines the function *GetControllingUnknown*. This function provides the controlling unknown to the inner object.

► **To implement an outer object**

1. Declare the DECLARE_GET_CONTROLLING_UNKNOWN macro.
2. Override the *FinalConstruct* and *FinalRelease* methods.
   - In the *FinalConstruct* method, call *CoCreateInstance* by passing the CLSID of the inner object that you want to create and by requesting a returned pointer back from IUnknown. You will also be required to call the *GetControllingUnknown* function to provide the inner class with the controlling IUnknown pointer.
   - In the *FinalRelease* method, release the inner object's IUnknown.
3. Add an entry for the COM_INTERFACE_ENTRY_AGGREGATE macro to the COM map. The COM_INTERFACE_ENTRY_AGGREGATE macro adds an appropriate entry to the *QueryInterface* function of the outer object. This macro will need to be added to the COM map for each interface delegated to the inner object.
4. Add the interface definition for the inner object to the .idl file of the outer object. Reference that interface in the coclass.
5. Make the inner object's interface available to the .idl file of the outer object by using the importlib statement.
6. Add the interface of the inner class to the coclass definition.
7. Get the CLSID and IID of the inner class.
8. Add a public IUnknown pointer and initialize it in the constructor.
9. The *QueryInterface* function of the outer object has to be aware of inner object interfaces when they are aggregated, as shown in the following code:

```
COuter::QueryInterface(REFIID riid, void ** pp)
{
    if ((IID_IUnknown == riid) ||
    (IID_IDispatch == riid))
    {
        *pp = this;
        return S_OK;
    }
    else
    {
        return m_pIn->QueryInterface(riid, pp);
    }
}
```

Implementing the Inner Object

To implement an inner object, you will need to add the DECLARE_AGGREGATABLE macro to the class definition. This macro is automatically added to CComCoClass if you use the ATL Object Wizard and choose Aggregation.

Creating a Client

A client that is using an aggregated object needs to obtain a pointer to the inner object and calls the appropriate interface methods.

The following code illustrates how a Microsoft Visual C++ client accesses the methods of the two objects, Animal and Canine:

```
ICaninePtr pDog;
HRESULT hrs = pDog.CreateInstance(CLSID_Canine);
pDog->Bite();
IAnimalPtr pAnimal;
pAnimal = pDog; //obtains a pointer to the inner object, Animal
pAnimal->Teeth(15);
long height = pAnimal->GetHeight();
```

Containment

Containment is a common method of object reuse in COM. Containment is a client-object relationship where the outer object uses the inner object without changing the functions and methods of the inner object.

How Containment Works

Containment works in the following manner:

1. The client application calls the *CoCreateInstance* function to create an outer object.
2. The outer object in turn calls the *CoCreateInstance* function to create the inner object instance. When the inner object is created, the outer object exposes a stub interface for each interface of the inner object.
3. The stub interface forwards all the method calls to the inner object, except for the methods of the IUnknown interface. For example, when the calls are made to the *QueryInterface* method, they are directed by the stub interface to the controlling IUnknown interface. Directing calls to the controlling IUnknown interface will ensure that the inner object is isolated from the requests for outer object interfaces. It also ensures that reference counting is handled only by the outer object.

Implementing Containment

To implement containment, you need to enable the outer object to support containment.

► **To implement the outer object**

1. As with aggregation, you will need to override the *FinalConstruct* and *FinalRelease* methods.
2. Add an entry for the macro COM_INTERFACE_ENTRY2 to the COM map.
3. Modify the .idl file of the outer object. The procedure is exactly the same as that for aggregation. For detailed steps, review the Implementing Aggregation section earlier in this lesson.
4. Include the header file of the inner object and add the interface to the multiple inheritance list.
5. You can either write the stub code for the inner object's interfaces on a per-method basis or use the Implement Interface Wizard for generating the stub code for the methods. To invoke the Implement Interface Wizard:

   - Right-click the outer object in ClassView and select Implement Interface.
   - From the type library of the inner object, select the desired interfaces.

Scriptlets

A scriptlet is a software component that contains script code. It includes information that allows you to work with the scriptlet as a control. For example, you can access and set the properties of a scriptlet and call its methods from an application. Scriptlets consist of an HTML page and some script code. Scriptlets are identified by CLSIDs and need to be registered on the system before being incorporated in your application. To use scriptlets, you need Internet Explorer 4 or later.

Benefits of Using Scriptlets

A scriptlet provides various benefits to application developers and script authors. Scriptlets provide script authors with the ability to create controls and access to a broad range of system services, such as ODBC connections and file management.

In addition, a scriptlet is easy to create and maintain because it is small. Scriptlets can be created by using Web scripting languages, such as VBScript, ECMAScript and JavaScript.

Types of Scriptlets

You can create two types of scriptlets—Dynamic HTML (DHTML) scriptlets and Server scriptlets. A DHTML scriptlet is a Web page based on DHTML. You can use a DHTML scriptlet as a control in any application that supports controls.

Server scriptlets serve as COM components. Server scriptlets contain only script code. They do not contain any HTML or other user interface elements. You can use Server scriptlets as COM components in applications such as IIS, Microsoft Windows Scripting Host (WSH), and any other application that can support COM components.

► To add a scriptlet in your application

1. Create a scriptlet container object in your application and set its Name property. The container object creates a window for the scriptlet. The scriptlet container object also provides you with the interface to set the properties of the DHTML, call its methods and respond to its events.
2. Next, set the URL property of the scriptlet container object to the URL of the scriptlet that you want to use. Consider URL = file:///Script\Clock.htm. The URL points to the file Clock.htm that must reside in the /Script directory on the current drive.

► To create an instance of a scriptlet

There are a variety of options available for creating an instance of a scriptlet. These are dependent on the host application, the type of scriptlet you are using and the deployment location of the scriptlet.

The main criterion for selecting an option is whether you want to create a local instance or a remote instance of the scriptlet.

1. If the scriptlet is installed on the same computer as the host application, you can register the scriptlet in the host application.
2. If you create an instance of the scriptlet and change the .sct file while using that instance, your instance of the component is not updated. To update it, you need to create a new instance of the scriptlet.

When the scriptlet is installed on the same computer as the host application, you can register the scriptlet on the host application. To register a scriptlet, you should perform the following actions:

1. Make sure the scriptlet run-time Scrobj.dll is available and registered on your computer.
2. Right-click the scriptlet, which is a .sct file, and then select the Register option.
3. Specify the command regsvr32 file:\\myserver\newscriptlet.sct. In the command, newscriptlet is the name of the scriptlet.

Lesson Summary

In this lesson, you learned about the methods that can be applied for using existing COM components within new COM components. These methods are aggregation and containment. Aggregation is very simple to implement with the exception of implementing the three IUnknown functions—*QueryInterface*, *AddRef*, and *Release*—while containment is one of the most frequently used methods. Containment uses a stub interface for the outer object that interacts with the inner object interfaces. In aggregation, however, there is no stub interface.

You also learned about using scriptlets in your applications to significantly reduce the development time for dynamic Web pages and server objects and let others reuse your code more efficiently.

Lesson 5: Creating and Using Active Documents

Active documents extend the compound document technology of OLE. The extensions are in the form of additional interfaces that manage views, so that objects can function within containers and retain control over their display and printing functions. This process makes it possible to display documents both in foreign frames, such as the Microsoft Office Binder or Microsoft Internet Explorer, and in native frames, such as the product's own view ports. This section will discuss how to create active documents and use them in other applications.

After this lesson, you will be able to:

- Create and use an active document

Estimated lesson time: 15 minutes

Active Document Containers and Servers

Active document applications can function as active document containers and active document servers.

Active Document Containment

Active document containment is a technology that provides a single application frame for working with documents, irrelevant of the document type. Unlike OLE technology, with active document containment, you activate an entire document within the context of a single frame.

Active document containment is implemented as a set of extensions to OLE documents. The extensions are additional interfaces that allow an embeddable, in-place object to represent an entire document instead of a single piece of embedded content. Active document containment uses a container that provides the display space for active documents, and servers that provide the user interface and manipulation capabilities for the active documents themselves.

Active Document Containers

An active document container is an application that hosts active documents. An active document container allows the server to merge its menus and add any other user interface components within the view area of the container. This allows the container to host any number of different active documents while maintaining the same user interface. For example, users of an active document container application can create active documents using their favorite applications, yet the users can manage the resulting project as a single entity, which can be uniquely named, saved, printed, and so on. MFC provides full support for active document containers in the COleDocObjectItem class. You can use the MFC

AppWizard to create an active document container by selecting the active document container check box in step 3 of the MFC AppWizard.

Active Document Servers

An active document server is an OLE local server that supports one or more active document classes. Each of these classes in turn supports the extension interfaces that allow the object to be activated in a suitable container.

The active document server provides user interface components, including menus, toolbars, status bars and scroll bars. This allows programmers to host an active document server by a number of different active document containers while maintaining the same user interface.

MFC implements active document servers with document/view interfaces, command dispatch maps, printing, menu management, and registry management.

Creating Active Documents

Using Visual C++, you can create applications that act both as an active document container and an active document server. Creating such an application ensures that the basic user interface features and the functionality of the document application are part of the same application.

To create an active document application, you can use MFC AppWizard.

► **To create an active document application that is both a container and a server**

1. Start Visual C++.
2. Select New from the File menu.
3. The New dialog box appears. Click the Projects tab and select the MFC AppWizard (EXE) option.
4. In the Project Name text box specify a name of the Project; then click the OK button to confirm the project name.
5. The MFC AppWizard—Step 1 Of 6 dialog box appears. In this dialog box, you can specify whether you want to create an SDI or an MDI application. You can also specify whether your application will support the MFC Document/View architecture. After specifying these details, click Next.
6. The MFC AppWizard—Step 2 Of 6 dialog box appears, where you can specify the database support your application will provide. Make your selection and click Next.
7. The MFC AppWizard—Step 3 Of 6 dialog box appears. To specify that the application should act both as a server and a container, click the Both Container And Server radio button.

8. Since your application should act as both a container and a server, click the Active Document Server check box and the Active Document Container check box.
9. Your application must also contain automation support. Automation support enables the application to manipulate the objects of another application. To include automation support for the application, click the Automation check box.
10. To proceed, click Next.
11. The MFC AppWizard—Step 4 of 6 dialog box appears. This dialog box contains an Advanced button. Clicking this button opens the Advanced Options dialog box, where you must specify the default extension for the files that are generated by your application. Type a default extension and close the Advanced Options dialog box.
12. To generate the project files, click Finish. The New Project Information dialog box appears. The dialog box displays the specifications with which the MFC AppWizard will create the new skeleton project. Close the dialog box by clicking OK.

You can now compile and run the active document application.

Lesson Summary

To summarize, active document containment is a technology that provides a single application frame for working with documents, regardless of the document type. You can create active document applications using MFC.

Lesson 6: Using MFC to Create an ISAPI DLL

Internet Server Application Program Interface (ISAPI) extensions extend the capabilities of your Web server. MFC makes it easy to create ISAPI extensions. This lesson discusses how you can create ISAPI DLLs using MFC. You will also learn about when you should use the regular DLL and when to use an extension DLL.

After this lesson, you will be able to:

- Use the MFC AppWizard to create an ISAPI DLL that can dynamically change Web content
- Choose whether to use an MFC regular DLL or an MFC extension DLL

Estimated lesson time: 25 minutes

Extending Web Server Capabilities

To extend the capabilities of your Web server, such as counting the number of users for an application or authenticating users, you can use ISAPI extensions.

ISAPI Extensions

ISAPI extensions are of two types, ISAPI server extensions and ISAPI filters. Both ISAPI server extensions and the ISAPI filter are DLLs.

Both the ISAPI server extension and filter DLLs can work only from a server that is ISAPI-compliant, such as Internet Information Services (IIS).

ISAPI Server Extensions

An ISAPI server extension is a DLL that can be loaded and called by an HTTP server. It can perform Internet business transactions, such as order entry. ISAPI server extensions are invoked by a user from a Web page, and are similar to the Common Gateway Interface (CGI) applications. An ISAPI server extension runs in response to a GET request or a POST request from a browser. The browser can pass parameters to the program. The parameters are often the responses of the browser user through controls such as edit controls or list boxes. The ISAPI server extension returns the HTML code based on those responses.

ISAPI Filters

An ISAPI filter is a DLL that runs on an ISAPI-enabled HTTP server to filter data traveling to and from the server. This enables the server to perform tasks, such as specialized logging.

To use ISAPI filter DLLs, you must be able to change the registry of the server on which you host the Web pages. An ISAPI filter DLL is loaded when the WWW service is started. The filter is then in the loop for all HTTP requests. This enables you to read and change any data that is transmitted to or from the server.

ISAPI Classes

ISAPI filters and server extensions are derived from five MFC ISAPI classes: CHttpServer, CHttpFilter, CHttpServerContext, CHttpFilterContext and CHtmlStream. These classes form the source for creating an ISAPI filter or server extension.

CHttpServer

The CHttpServer class along with the CHttpServerContext class provides a means to extend the functionality of an ISAPI-compliant Web server. The CHttpServer class wraps the ISAPI functionality and can process various types of client requests, including extension DLLs.

When an ISAPI-compliant Web server receives a request from a client browser, a CHttpServer object is created and initialized and a CHttpServerContext object is created. Only one instance of CHttpServer may exist for a module. However, one CHttpServerContext object is created for each call made to the server.

Since the CHttpServer object uses multiple CHttpServerContext objects to run in separate threads, it allows simultaneous, multiple calls to the CHttpServer object by different client connections. The communication between the CHttpServer object and the client or the server happens via the CHttpServerContext object.

When the server loads the CHttpServer object, it calls the server extension DLL at the entry point *GetExtensionVersion* for obtaining the version number of the specification on which the extension is based.

The *HttpExtensionProc* member function of CHttpServer is called for every client request. The default implementation of *HttpExtensionProc* reads the client data and decides what action needs to be taken. You can override this member function to customize the implementation.

Other CHttpServer member functions process the client request, format the responses and correspond with the client. When a CHttpServer object receives a client command, the parse maps associate the command to its class member function and parameters. Only one parse map is created for each CHttpServer object.

CHttpFilter

The CHttpFilter class creates and manages an HTTP filter object with CHttpFilterContext. An HTTP filter is a replaceable DLL that the server calls on every HTTP request. When the filter is loaded, it informs the server about the type of events it can process. Whenever the selected event occurs, the filter is called to process that event.

CHttpServerContext

The CHttpServerContext class provides the tools that a CHttpServer object needs for processing data that a client sends to the HTTP server. For example, when an IIS receives a request from a client browser, a CHttpServer object is created and initialized and a CHttpServerContext object is created. Since the server extension DLL processes the requests, it uses CHttpServerContext member functions to perform tasks.

A CHttpServerContext object exists separately from a CHttpServer object in order to enable multithreading. Only one CHttpServer exists in a module; however, a server might be required to process multiple client requests simultaneously. CHttpServer creates a CHttpServerContext for each request to handle the multiple requests. CHttpServer uses multiple CHttpServerContext objects to run in separate threads. When there are different client connections, this design allows simultaneous, multiple calls to the CHttpServer object.

CHttpFilterContext

CHttpFilterContext provides the tools that a CHttpFilter object needs to process data that passes through the filter. When the filter receives a request, a CHttpFilter object is created and initialized and a CHttpFilterContext object is created. As the filter processes requests, it uses CHttpFilterContext member functions to perform tasks. A CHttpFilterContext object exists separately from a CHttpFilter object in order to allow multithreading. Only one CHttpFilter object exists in a module. This filter might be required to process multiple client requests simultaneously. CHttpFilter will create a CHttpFilterContext for each request to handle these multiple requests. A CHttpFilter uses multiple CHttpFilterContext objects to run in separate threads. This design allows simultaneous, multiple calls to the CHttpFilter object when there are different client connections.

CHtmlStream

CHtmlStream is a class that manages in-memory HTML. HTML memory files are useful for temporarily storing raw bytes or serialized objects before their transmission. CHtmlStream is used to store data in a temporary buffer before sending out the data. The data stored in a CHtmlStream memory file cannot be read.

CHtmlStream objects are usually created automatically and handed to the application by *CHttpServer::ConstructStream* member function. However, you can override the *CHttpServer::ConstructStream* member function and provide your own functionality. CHtmlStream objects can automatically allocate their own memory, or you can attach your own memory block to the CHtmlStream object by calling the *Attach* member function. The memory will be automatically deleted upon destruction of the CHtmlStream object if the memory was originally allocated by the CHtmlStream object. Otherwise, you should manually deallocate the memory you attached to the object. CHtmlStream uses the run-time library functions *malloc*, *realloc*, and *free* to allocate, reallocate and deallocate memory, respectively. It uses the intrinsic *memcpy* function to block copy memory when increasing the buffer.

Creating ISAPI Extensions and Filters

You can create ISAPI server extensions and filters with MFC. The only requirement is that the Internet server software that you have should be ISAPI-compliant.

When you use ISAPI Extension Wizard to create an MFC DLL program, you obtain a working starter DLL program.

The MFC starter program will include C++ source (.cpp) files, resource (.rc) files, header (.h) files, a project (.dsp) file and a project workspace (.dsw) file. The code generated in these starter files is based on MFC and provides the classes that wrap ISAPI to create and handle ISAPI server extensions and filters.

► **To create an ISAPI extension:**

1. Start Microsoft Visual C++.
2. Select New from the File menu.
3. The New dialog box appears. Click the Projects tab and select the ISAPI Extension Wizard option.
4. Specify a name for the DLL in the Project Name text box and click OK.
5. The ISAPI Extension Wizard—Step 1 of 1 dialog box appears. Accept the default selections and click Finish.
6. The New Project Information dialog box with the details about the project is displayed. Click OK to let AppWizard create your project.
7. The next step in creating an ISAPI server extension DLL is to add your functions. For each function, write a parse map entry for the required and optional parameters. A parse map consists of code written by you, which enables a CHttpServer-derived object to map client requests to its member functions. If you want to perform custom processing, override the *CHttpExtensionProc* function.
8. Build the project and copy the .dll file into a directory onto the Web server. Ensure that the directory offers EXECUTE privileges to the users of your server and that you install the correct MFC DLLs in the \<Windows>\SYSTEM directory of the server.

MFC Regular DLLs vs. MFC Extension DLLs

A DLL is a set of routines that can be called from a program. DLLs are loaded and linked to your application at run time. DLLs facilitate sharing data and code; multiple applications can simultaneously access the contents of a single copy of a DLL in memory. Microsoft Windows itself is made up of three distinct DLLs: User32.DLL, Kernel32.DLL and GDI32.DLL.

A DLL is compiled to load at a preferred base address for system memory. In case of an address conflict between two DLLs, both DLL files are mapped to the same virtual memory address.

DLLs are useful in writing modular software and can save you time when you're developing applications. MFC provides for two types of DLLs: MFC regular DLLs and MFC extension DLLs. There are certain differences between these two types of DLLs.

MFC Regular DLL

MFC regular DLLs are subdivided into two categories, statically linked and dynamically linked.

MFC Regular Statically Linked DLL

An MFC regular statically linked DLL uses MFC internally. The exported functions in the DLL can either be called by MFC or non-MFC executables. This kind of a DLL is built using the static link library of MFC. Functions are usually exported from these DLLs by using the standard C interface.

A statically linked regular DLL may be used by client executables written in any language that supports the use of DLLs. This implies that it does not necessarily need a client created using MFC. Also, a separate version of the static link libraries is not required for regular Visual C++ DLLs.

There are certain requirements for implementing a regular statically linked DLL:

- This type of DLL must instantiate a class derived from CWinApp.
- An MFC regular statically linked DLL uses the *DllMain* provided by MFC. As a result, the _USRDLL system variable must be defined on the compiler command line.
- Regular statically linked DLLs must have a CWinApp-derived class and a single object of that application class as that of an MFC application.
- To pass pointers to the MFC objects or MFC-derived objects between the calling executable and the DLL, you must build an extension DLL.

MFC Regular Dynamically Linked DLL

An MFC regular DLL that is statically linked to MFC cannot dynamically link to shared MFC DLLs. However, this type of DLL is dynamically bound to the application like any other DLL.

As the name suggests, an MFC regular dynamically linked DLL is built using the DLL version of MFC. The MFC import library linked to a regular dynamically linked DLL is the same as that used for extension DLLs or for the applications that use the MFC DLL.

MFC Extension DLLs

An MFC extension DLL implements reusable classes derived from the existing MFC classes. Extension MFC DLLs are built using the dynamic-link library of MFC. MFC executables, which are either applications or regular DLLs and are built with the shared version of the MFC DLL, can use an extension DLL.

You can use the MFC extension DLLs to derive new custom classes from MFC and then offer this extended version of MFC to the applications that call your DLL. Extension DLLs can also be used for passing MFC-derived objects between the application and the DLL. The member functions associated with the passed object exist in the module where the object was created. MFC extension DLLs also allow you to pass the MFC or MFC-derived object pointers between an application and the DLL it loads. This is because member functions are exported when using the shared DLL version of MFC DLLs.

A requirement for an MFC extension DLL to work is that the client EXE must be an MFC application compiled with the system variable _AFXDLL defined. Further, an MFC extension DLL must be compiled with the _AFXEXT system variable defined. This will ensure that the proper declarations are called from MFC header files. In addition, MFC extension DLLs must not instantiate a class derived from CWinApp. These DLLs must rely on the client application or the DLL to provide a CWinApp object unlike the regular DLLs. Extension DLLs, however, must provide a *DllMain* function and perform any necessary initialization in the function. An extension DLL does not have a built-in CWinApp-derived object. As a result, it has to work with the CWinApp-derived object of the client application.

Dynamic User Interfaces

Different users have different interface preferences such as the position of the toolbar. To ensure that the interface visible to users is dynamic and customizable according to their preferences, you may need to modify the registry. MFC provides a set of registry access functions, which makes it very easy to make changes to the registry from an application.

MFC Functions

Consider a text-processing application, TextWriter, that stores the most recent font and point size in the registry. The registry structure, which is displayed, is based on certain assumptions—that the program name forms the root of the key and that the application maintains two hierarchy levels below the name.

The function *SetRegistryKey* enables an MFC application to use the registry. You call this function from the InitInstance member function of your CWinApp-derived class. The *SetRegistryKey* function takes a string parameter. This string parameter establishes the top level hierarchy for the application.

The last two levels of the hierarchy, called the heading name and the entry name, are defined by four functions: *GetProfileInt*, *WriteProfileInt*, *GetProfileString*, and *WriteProfileString*. These functions treat the registry data as either CString objects or unsigned integers. All the functions require a heading name and an entry name as parameters.

Consider the following example in which the heading name is Text Formatting and the entry names are Font and Points. To use the registry access functions for setting these values as the default in the TextWriter application, you will first need to have a pointer to the application object. The global function *AfxGetApp* provides the necessary pointer. You can make the registry entry for the above settings using the following code:

```
AfxGetApp()->WriteProfileString("Text Formatting",
    "Font", "Times Roman"); , AfxGetApp()
    ->WriteProfileString("Text Formatting", "Points", 10);
```

Creating a Dynamic User Interface

As a programmer, you can ensure that the interface visible to the user is dynamic and customizable according to their preferences. You can use the registry access functions that MFC provides to accomplish this task.

▶ **To create a dynamic user interface**

1. Open the implementation file for the CMainFrame class.
2. To enable an application to store and retrieve personalized user settings from the registry, override the *OnDestroy* function.
3. Create an object of WINDOWPLACEMENT that will store the information about window placement on the screen and add the code to store the length of the structure.
4. Next, to obtain the current window state and placement, type *BOOL bRet=GetWindowPlacement(&wndp1);*, where wndp1 is the WINDOW-PLACEMENT object. You can then add the code to identify whether or not the *GetWindowPlacement* function successfully returned the current window state and placement using the if...else statements.

5. Type *AfxGetApp->WriteProfileString("Window Size", "Rect", strText);* to write the values of the current window state and placement in the registry.
6. To ensure that the values of the window state and placement are stored in the registry, it is necessary that the application also reads from the registry when creating the window. To do this, you will need to override the *ActivateFrame* function.
7. Next, to enable the application to retrieve the values from the registry, type *strText=AfxGetApp->GetProfileString("Window Size", "Rect");*

Lesson Summary

ISAPI extensions can be categorized as servers and filters. Using MFC, you can create these extensions for your applications. To create ISAPI server and filter extensions, MFC contains built-in classes that eases the creation of the extensions.

This lesson also covered the two types of MFC DLLs: regular DLLs and extension DLLs. Ideally, you should use regular DLLs when you have applications that are created using software other than MFC and use extension DLLs with applications created using MFC.

Finally, you learned about creating dynamic UIs. MFC provides functions that are used to create dynamic UIs by performing read/writes to the registry. These functions enable you to write applications in which users can determine the appearance of a user interface according to their preferences.

Lab 6: Creating an Out-of-Process COM Component

In this lab, you will gain hands-on experience in creating an out-of-process component using ATL.

Estimated lab time: 15 minutes

Exercise 1: Creating a COM Server

In this exercise, you will create an out-of-process COM server named COM_Server that will contain the components to accept two numbers and calculate their product.

► **Create an out-of-process COM server**

1. Choose New from the Visual Studio File menu, click the Projects tab of the New dialog box, and select ATL COM AppWizard.
2. Type *Servers* for the name of the project in the Project Name text box, and click OK.
3. The ATL COM AppWizard—Step 1 Of 1 dialog box appears. The server type will determine the option that should be selected in the Server Type box. To create an out-of-process server, select the Executable (EXE) option.
4. To complete the procedure for creating the basic structure of the component, click Finish.
5. The new project specifications appear; accept these specifications by clicking OK.
6. Choose the New ATL Object command from the Insert menu to open the ATL Object Wizard dialog box. Four different categories of objects that can be inserted into a project appear in the ATL Object Wizard dialog box.
7. In the ATL Object Wizard dialog box, select the Objects category. The icons of the ATL objects under that category appear in the Objects list.
8. For this exercise, click the Simple Object icon, and then click Next to create a simple COM server.
9. Type *Component1* for the component name in the Short Name text box, and then click OK.
10. In this lesson, we'll add properties and methods to accept two long integers and calculate their product. Start by right-clicking the interface for the new object in the ClassView tab of Visual Studio's Project workspace window and choose Add Property from the shortcut menu that appears.

11. The Add Property To Interface dialog box appears. Because you will use the property to accept a long integer for multiplication, type *long* as the property type, and then press the Tab key.
12. Type *Val1* as the first property's name.
13. Close the Add Property To Interface dialog box by clicking OK.
14. You will use a second property to accept another long integer for calculating the product. Right-click on the interface and choose Add Property from the shortcut menu, then add this property by typing *long* as the property's type and pressing the Tab key.
15. Type *Val2* as the second property's name, and click OK.
16. After adding the properties, you need to add the method to calculate the product of the two numbers and display it. Right-click the interface and click Add Method on the shortcut menu that appears.
17. Type *Product* as the method name, and press the Tab key.
18. The method must return a value that is a product of the two parameters. The parameter to be used for this purpose should be named **Prod*. To do this, type *[out, retval] long *Prod* in the Parameters text box and click OK.
19. Complete the code to allow these properties to accept values and the method to calculate the sum and print it. Open the Component1.cpp file and edit the *get_Val1* function. To assign the value to the Val1 property, add the line **pVal = Val1*. The function should look like the following:

```
STDMETHODIMP CComponent1::get_Val1(long *pVal)
{
    // TODO: Add your implementation code here
    *pVal = Val1;
    return S_OK;
}
```

20. Edit the *get_Val2* function to assign the value to the Val2 property. The function should look like the following:

```
STDMETHODIMP CComponent1::get_Val2(long *pVal)
{
    // TODO: Add your implementation code here
    *pVal = Val2;
    return S_OK;
}
```

21. Edit the *put_Val1* function to store the value of the Val1 property. The function should look like the following:

```
STDMETHODIMP CComponent1::put_Val1(long newVal)
{
    // TODO: Add your implementation code here
    Val1 = newVal;
    return S_OK;
}
```

22. Edit the *put_Val2* function to store the new value in the Val2 property. The function should look like the following:

```
STDMETHODIMP CComponent1::put_Val2(long newVal)
{
    // TODO: Add your implementation code here
    Val2 = newVal;
    return S_OK;
}
```

23. Now edit the *STDMETHODIMP CComponent1::Product* function to calculate the product of the two numbers and assign the value of the product to the **Prod* parameter The function should look like the following:

```
STDMETHODIMP CComponent1::Product(long *Prod)
{
    // TODO: Add your implementation code here
    *Prod = Val1 * Val2;
    return S_OK;
}
```

24. Add the declarations for Val1 and Val2 to Component1.h and build the project.

Exercise 2: Creating a COM Client

In this exercise, you will create a COM client called Client that can access an ATL COM server.

► **Create a COM client that can access an ATL COM server**

1. To start the procedure for creating a COM client, choose New from the Visual Studio File menu, click the Projects tab of the New dialog box, and select MFC AppWizard (EXE).
2. Type *Client* in the Project Name text box, and click OK.
3. The MFC AppWizard—Step 1 dialog box appears. To use a dialog box to accept the two numbers and display their product, select the Dialog Based radio button, and then click Next.

4. To allow the client application to manipulate the data of the server application, select the Automation check box.
5. Accept the default automation settings that appear and click the Finish button.
6. To accept the specifications of the new project that appear, click OK.
7. Add functionality to the client application. Because the client application is dialog box-based, you need to add the required controls in the dialog box that will appear. In the following steps, you will add three edit box controls, two static text boxes, and one button control in the dialog box. You will use the client to access the COM server components that can accept two numbers, calculate their product, and display the product on the screen.
8. Include the path of the COM server that the client will access in the StdAfx.h file. The statement should look similar to the following:

```
#import "..\Servers\Servers.tlb" no_namespace
named_guids
```

9. Create a smart pointer to access the COM server by overloading the *pointer-dereference* (->) operator. Type the code for creating the smart pointer that you will use to access the COM server, and add this code to the *OnAdd* function. An example of this code can be found in the Ch06\Exercise6.2 folder on the companion CD.
10. Declare three variables of the type integer to store the values of the two numbers and their product.
11. The variable n1 will store the number that is typed in the IDC_EDIT1 edit box.
12. The variable n2 will store the number that is typed in the IDC_EDIT2 edit box.
13. Declare the ptr pointer to store the memory address of the variables.
14. Initialize the value of ptr.
15. Call the *put_Val1* function with *n1* as the parameter.
16. Call the *put_Val2* function with *n2* as the parameter.
17. Store the value of the product that is returned by the *prod* function.

Review

The following questions are intended to reinforce key information presented in this chapter. If you are unable to answer a question, review the appropriate lesson and then try answering the question again. Answers to the questions can be found in Appendix B, "Review Questions and Answers," at the back of this book.

1. Which function is used to create a mutex synchronization?

2. Which files does Dcom95.exe install on a computer?

3. Which class forms the base for creating Windows NT services?

4. To register a server for remote access, what part of the registry do you need to modify?

CHAPTER 7

Using Microsoft Transaction Services

Lesson 1: Transactions and MTS 350

Lesson 2: Configuring MTS 362

Lesson 3: MTS Objects 367

Lesson 4: Advanced MTS Techniques 380

Lesson 5: Creating MTS-Based Applications 386

Lab 7: Understanding MTS Activities and Transactions 392

Review 402

About This Chapter

This chapter discusses transactions and explains how to install and deploy Microsoft Transaction Services (MTS). First, this chapter introduces you to the concept of transactions and describes how MTS serves as an infrastructure for building distributed applications. This chapter then provides an overview of how to install and configure MTS and how to design and create objects for use in MTS. In addition, this chapter introduces you to advanced topics such as security and load balancing, and then concludes with a discussion of design and scalability issues in transaction-based applications.

Before You Begin

To complete the lessons in this chapter, you must have:

- Read Chapter 1, which provides an overview of distributed applications design.
- Read Chapters 5 and 6, which discuss how to build COM objects.

Lesson 1: Transactions and MTS

In this lesson, you will learn about transactions from the real-world and programming perspectives. You will also learn about MTS.

After this lesson, you will be able to:

- Explain transactions and their properties
- Describe MTS and the benefits of using it
- Identify the various objects in the MTS object hierarchy

Estimated lesson time: 30 minutes

Transactions

In the real world, a *transaction* typically involves the exchange of at least two items, such as payment in exchange for goods (or services). For example, when a customer buys a book at a bookstore, the customer exchanges payment (cash, check, or credit card) for a book. A sales receipt is generated, providing a record for both the customer and the store, indicating that the transaction was completed successfully. Figure 7.1 illustrates the details of this type of transaction.

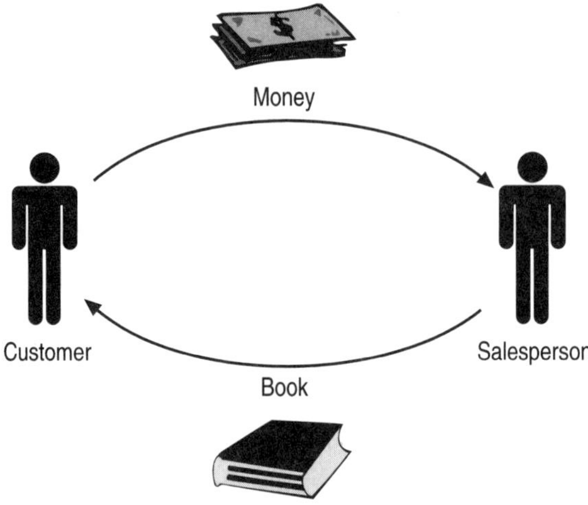

Figure 7.1 Real-world transaction

In database applications, a *transaction* is an action taken by a program that affects at least two pieces of shared data bound by a business rule. For example, in a client/server database application, a business rule might state that for each item removed from an inventory table in a relational database, a record for the money received must be added to one of the accounts tables in that database or in another database.

From a programming perspective, transactions must follow four criteria, known as the ACID rules. According to the principles of ACID, transactions must be:

- **Atomic** Transactions must be all-or-nothing operations. For example, if inventory is depleted, an increase in revenue must occur. The application cannot simply deplete inventory without adding revenue. Along the same lines, the application cannot add revenue and not deplete inventory. Changes are permanent only when all the pieces have completed successfully.
- **Consistent** After a transaction completes, the data in the database must be valid as specified by the rules of referential integrity. This means that even if individual changes break the database rules, when all updates have been made the data must be valid.
- **Isolated** Multiple transactions occurring simultaneously must affect the data as if all transactions were running one at a time and in sequence. A transaction is not allowed to use the uncommitted changes of another transaction. If transaction A, for example, depletes the number of books in inventory, transaction B cannot use the uncommitted total of books until transaction A is finalized.
- **Durable** All commits in a transaction are final. After a program receives confirmation that a transaction has succeeded, if the operating system crashes or the network dies, when the system is restored the changes must remain.

Coordinating Transactions

A common problem with distributed applications is coordinating transactions involving more than one data source in multiple servers that might be vastly different from one another. For transactions to be atomic, the servers must be coordinated. In other words, one server cannot be triggered to commit a transaction, only to discover that another server cannot continue the transaction. For a transaction to complete successfully, the servers must both commit the transaction. To accomplish this, transaction systems employ the services of a transaction manager that executes a protocol known as the *two-phase commit*, illustrated in Figure 7.2 on the next page.

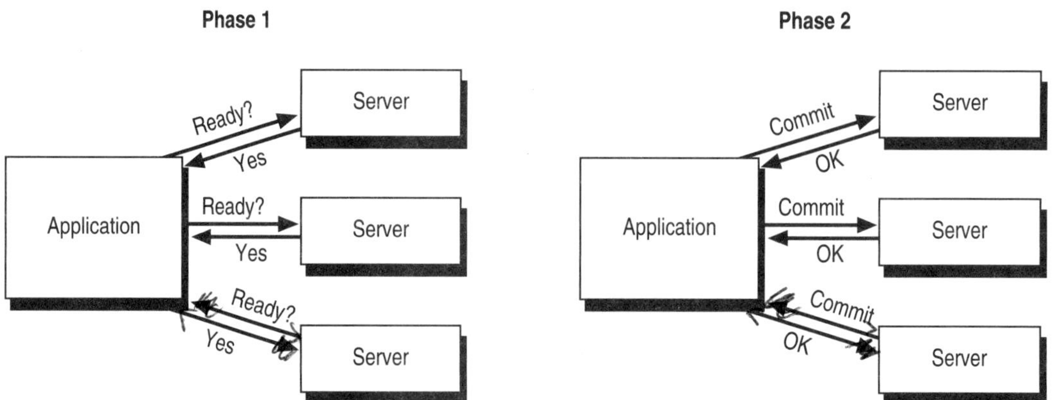

Figure 7.2 The two-phase commit method

The two-phase commit is a protocol in which, prior to committing a transaction, a data source or *resource manager* is asked whether it is ready to commit. After all the RMs reply positively, they are all instructed to commit.

The term *resource manager* denotes a system that manages durable data (or resources). An example of a resource is a database. The Microsoft SQL Server is an example of a resource manager. Other examples of resources include message queues, files, and so on.

To simplify coordinating transactions using the two-phase commit, you can use Microsoft Distributed Transaction Coordinator (MS DTC). MS DTC was first shipped in April 1996 with SQL Server 6.5. Later, MS DTC was separated from the SQL Server, and is now part of the Microsoft Windows NT core services. MS DTC coordinates transactions that occur across multiple resource managers, which can operate on separate computers.

Transactions and COM

In the past, organizations created fat clients or two-tier solutions around specific database systems. In a client/server system, the database resided on a server computer and clients connected to the server via the network. Clients ran applications that contained code to display data and code to manipulate the data directly with the database system following a particular set of rules (business rules). These applications normally accessed the database server through a series of proprietary API functions designed for that particular database. These APIs often offered methods to begin, commit and abort transactions. Thus, the client determined the length of a transaction.

Fat clients use a lot of memory, drive space, and have many dependencies. To improve performance and scalability, the fat client was split to allow it to run from different computers. The database manipulation code and business rules code were separated from the front end and became known as the middle tier. Developers in Windows environments turned to COM as the standard for building middle-tier components.

With COM, you can create separate components that specialize in multiple business tasks. For example, an application can have one component for updating inventory, another for calculating commissions, and so on. However, it is difficult to coordinate transactions among different COM objects, especially if these transactions involve multiple databases in more than one server.

To make it easier to write middle tiers in COM, Microsoft introduced MTS.

What Is MTS?

MTS is a container for COM-based middle-tier components. MTS serves as a transaction processing (TP) monitor. A TP monitor is a piece of software that manages transactions. TP monitors facilitate the implementation of the ACID rules and use transaction managers to execute the two-phase commit protocol in transactional distributed applications. In short, a TP monitor is the software location in which transactions occur—think of it as the marketplace. MTS enlists the services of MS DTC to coordinate transactions among COM objects that might involve different database resources in various computers.

MTS also serves as an *object request broker* (ORB). An ORB is a piece of software that can manage the lifetime of middle-tier components.

You will learn in this section, however, that MTS is much more than a TP monitor and an ORB. In many ways MTS is an enhancement to classic COM.

Benefits of Using MTS

So far this lesson has defined MTS in terms of transaction processing (after all, the product is called Transaction Services). However, MTS can do much more than help coordinate transactions. MTS can enhance and change the way that components behave.

To provide many of its services seamlessly, MTS uses a mechanism known as *interception*. Interception allows MTS to monitor every call made into an object before and after the call occurs. You will learn more about interception later in this lesson.

Because MTS can monitor and intercept calls, it can perform many more functions than just coordinating transactions. For example, MTS uses interception to implement a role-based security mechanism more sophisticated than that provided by DCOM. Intercepting the calls allows MTS to block calls made from clients that do not have permission to use the object. This feature of MTS minimizes the need for the component to handle DCOM security APIs directly. You can simply use MTS Explorer to create security groupings (or *roles*) and assign these groupings to different interfaces in a component. MTS Explorer is illustrated in Figure 7.3 and is discussed in detail in Lesson 2.

Role-based security is one example of how the behavior of a component or even an application can be affected by changing a few settings with MTS Explorer without modifying the actual component. This type of configuration in which external attributes control a component's behavior is *declarative programming*. A COM object that lives in MTS, and thus can have its behavior modified by declarative properties, is said to be a configured component.

Because MTS hosts COM objects and can use interception to control the behavior of those objects, MTS provides you with several benefits as discussed in the following sections.

Surrogate Process for Components

MTS eliminates the need to create out-of-process servers (such as Microsoft ActiveX executables). COM objects that reside in MTS are always part of in-process servers (ActiveX DLLs). When a client instantiates a COM object found in a different computer, MTS launches a surrogate process (Mtx.exe) to host the COM objects that communicate with the client. For a complete discussion of surrogates, refer to the MSDN ActiveX SDK documentation.

Note COM ships with another surrogate process called Dllhost.exe.

Role-Based Security

MTS eliminates the need to access COM security APIs directly. In addition, MTS enhances the security model provided by DCOM. In a default configuration of DCOM, you can control launching and access security only for a group of components declared to be part of one application under an AppID. In the MTS environment, you can create groupings (or roles) that can be assigned to each component within an application, and even to each interface within a component.

Note In COM+, you can also assign roles to each method within an interface.

Just-In-Time Activation

Because MTS can intercept calls to each configured component, MTS can delay activation of an object when one of its methods is being called for the first time. You will learn about this functionality, called Just-In-Time (JIT) activation, in Lesson 3.

MTS Explorer

MTS Explorer is a user-friendly tool that allows you to configure COM objects running under MTS (see Figure 7.3).

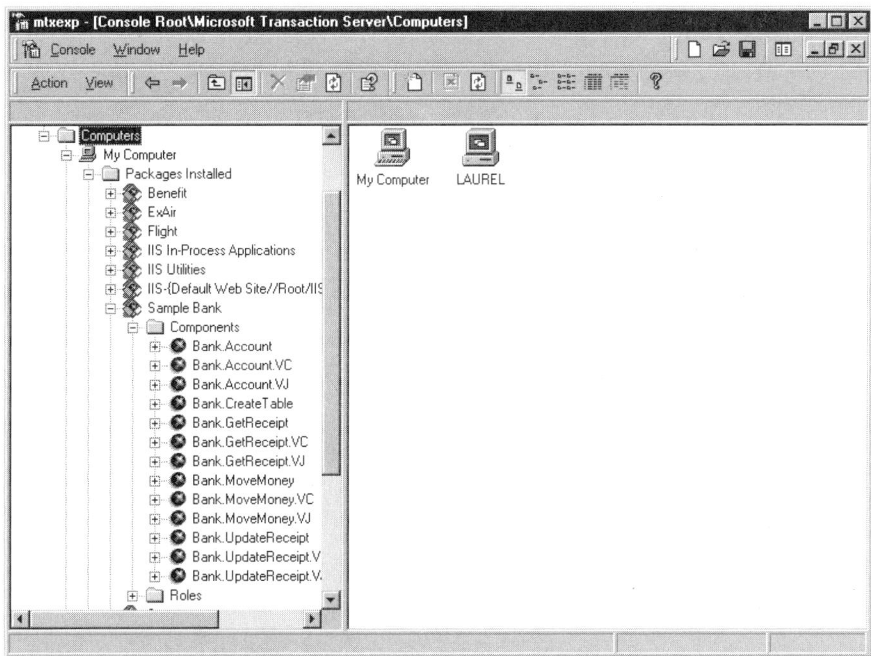

Figure 7.3 MTS Explorer

The UI of this tool is much easier to use and more robust than Dcomcnfg.exe, the tool used to configure DCOM servers, shown in Figure 7.4 on the next page.

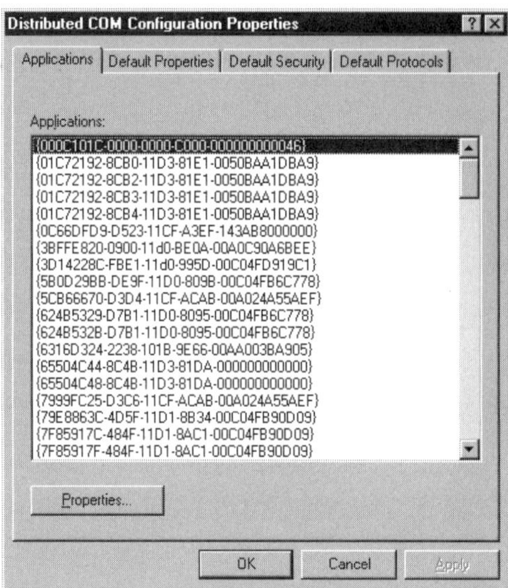

Figure 7.4 Dcomcnfg.exe tool

Transaction Coordination

As mentioned, one of the main jobs of MTS is to coordinate transactions among components. MTS uses a "democratic" system of transactions. In other words, objects are not able to explicitly begin, commit, or abort a transaction. Instead, objects vote on whether the transaction should continue. The client originates the transaction when it makes a call to the first component marked as transactional. You will learn more about transaction coordination in Lesson 3.

Integration with Microsoft Internet Information Server

Although not discussed in detail in this chapter, Microsoft Internet Information Server (IIS) is tightly integrated with MTS. An Active Server Page (ASP) can participate in a transaction, simply by specifying *Transaction=required* in its header, as shown in the following code:

```
<%@ TRANSACTION=Required LANGUAGE="VBScript" %>
```

Integration with Microsoft Message Queuing Services

As you will learn in the next chapter, Microsoft Message Queuing Services (MSMQ) is a means for distributed applications to communicate through messaging. An application can send and receive an MSMQ message as part of a transaction. For example, an object might send a message, but the message will not be truly sent until the transaction has been committed.

Now that you are aware of the benefits of using MTS, take a look at how MTS is organized.

MTS Structures

This section explains the hierarchy of MTS objects and how MTS works internally. Figure 7.5 illustrates the three main structures defined by MTS: packages, objects, and roles.

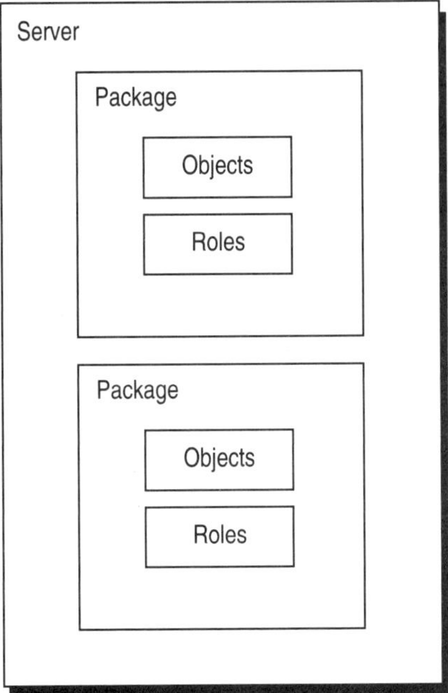

Figure 7.5 MTS catalog contains packages, objects, and roles

Packages

A *package* is a group of objects with a common goal; a package can often be considered to be the middle tier of an application. Two types of packages—server and library—exist in MTS. A *server* package runs in its own process; a *library* package is loaded into the process space of the client.

Note In COM+, packages are known as applications.

An object cannot be part of more than one package. As mentioned, MTS provides a surrogate process Mtx.exe to host COM objects found in a DLL. When you add a COM class to a server package, MTS modifies the registry settings for that class. As you learned in Chapter 5, COM classes store configuration settings in the registry under HKEY_CLASSES_ROOT\CLSID.

Each coclass has a GUID, also known as a CLSID. When a client wants to create a class, it invokes the COM API *CoCreateInstance* or *CoGetClassObject*. *CoCreateInstance* and *CoGetClassObject* use the SCM to get an instance of the class. A client specifies in the APIs what class to create with a CLSID. The SCM looks through the registry for that particular CLSID, and when it finds the CLSID, it looks in the InProcServer32 subkey for the name and path of the DLL that contains the class. The SCM then loads the DLL, and calls into a well-known entry point, *DllGetClassObject*.

The *DllGetClassObject* function gives the SCM a pointer to the intended class. When you create a package and add your components to this package, MTS changes the value of the InProcServer32 key. If the component is added to a server package, MTS deletes the value in the InProcServer32 subkey and adds a LocalServer32 subkey. (The LocalServer32 subkey specifies the path to out-of-process servers.) In the LocalServer32 subkey, MTS will write code similar to the following:

```
D:\WINNT\System32\mtx.exe  /p:{4B118EAB-8BA8-11D3-81D8-000000000000}
```

The first half of the string is the name and path to the MTS surrogate process (Mtx.exe). The second half of the string is a command line argument for the executable—it specifies the GUID for the package that contains the original server name. In other words, clients are able to continue requesting the same CLSID, and the application will transparently instantiate the object in the MTS surrogate process. MTS also adds the package GUID to the registry under HKEY_LOCAL_MACHINE\SOFTWARE\Microsoft\Transaction Server\Packages.

In the example shown, the exact package entry would be *HKEY_LOCAL_MACHINE\SOFTWARE\Microsoft\Transaction Server\Packages\{4B118EAB-8BA8-11D3-81D8-000000000000}*. Under this key, you will find all configuration settings for the package, and a component subkey with additional subkeys for each component in the package. Figure 7.6 illustrates the steps of activating a server package.

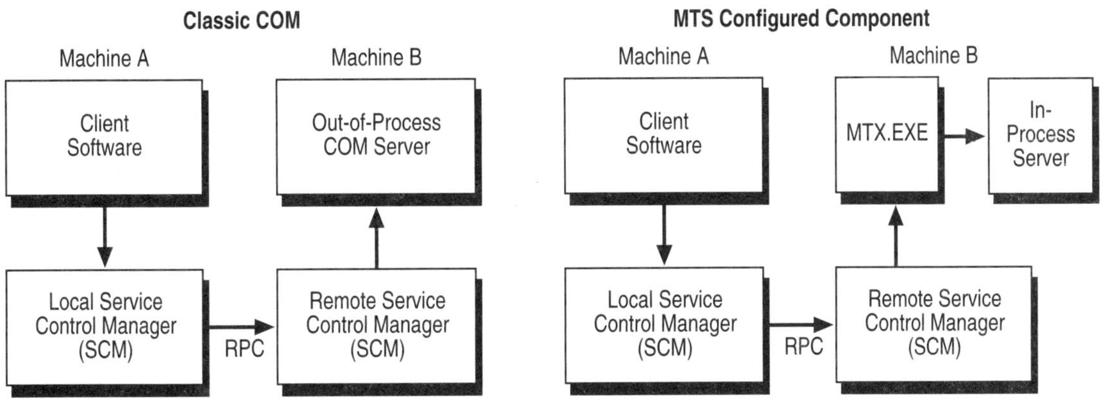

Figure 7.6 How activation occurs in both classic COM and MTS

In addition to creating instances of the requested COM object, Mtx.exe loads the MTS Executive (Mtxex.dll). The MTS Executive (or MTS run-time) is in charge of creating a context wrapper for your object. You will learn more about context wrappers in the next section.

Note If the component is added to a library package, MTS changes the value of InProcServer32 to point to the MTS executive (Mtxex.dll).

Components and Context

Packages store components. An MTS component is equivalent to a COM class or coclass. An MTS object is the in-memory instance of an MTS component. Before MTS creates an object it creates a context wrapper for the object (MTS destroys the context wrapper before it destroys the object). The context wrapper contains information about the object's execution environment—it stores security settings, transaction information, and so on. MTS inserts the context wrapper between the stub (in the proxy/stub layer) and the object. With the context wrapper in place, MTS can intercept each call made to the object both before and after it takes place. For all practical purposes, think of the context as the place where an MTS object lives.

In Lesson 3, you will learn how to ensure that the relationship between the context wrapper and object is maintained at all times. To take full advantage of MTS, you will also learn how to get access to your object's context wrapper and invoke its methods. Each object instance from an MTS configured component (MTS component) has a context wrapper associated with it. Each object has at most one context wrapper associated with it. Object instances from non-configured components (non-MTS components) created by configured components do not have their own context wrappers but can access the context wrapper of their creator.

Activities

An *activity* is a group of objects that have the same concurrency requirements. In MTS 2, only one concurrency model that cannot be set through properties exists. (This aspect of MTS 2 will become more important in Microsoft Windows 2000 with COM+, because an administrator might change an object's concurrency requirements.) The only concurrency model MTS 2 supports is serialized; only one client can make a call into an activity at a time. MTS begins a new activity when a client creates a new MTS object. The client creating the object is called the base client; the object that the base client creates to begin the activity is known as the root of the activity. The root object can invite other objects to be part of the same activity with a special MTS API function, *CreateInstance* (you will learn how to do this later). *CreateInstance* is a function in the IObjectContext interface. Henceforth, any other object in the activity can use this API to invite other objects into the activity. An activity can involve components from one or more packages, and even from components in packages in other computers. Only objects in the same activity can participate in the same transaction. Figure 7.7 illustrates the relationship among objects, context wrappers, activities, and packages. In viewing this figure, think of the context wrapper as shielding the object from the outside world.

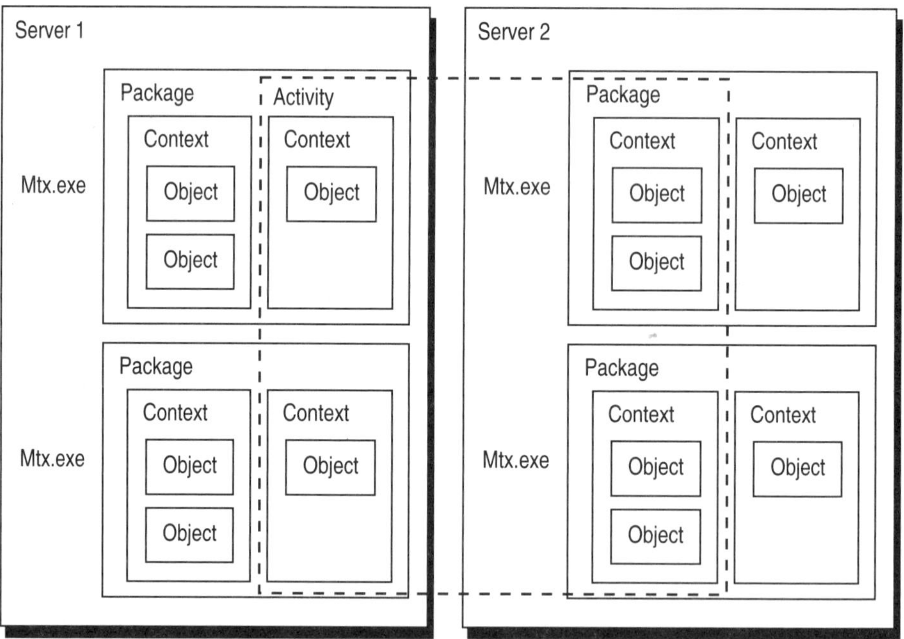

Figure 7.7 Objects, context wrappers, activities, and packages

Roles

An examination of the MTS structures would not be complete without discussing roles. As mentioned earlier, roles are user-defined groups that define user access to a package, component, or interface. In Lesson 2, you will learn how to create a role and assign it to a package, a component, or an interface.

Lesson Summary

In programming, transactions are actions that affect shared data. A transaction must follow the ACID rules: atomic, consistent, isolated, and durable. When more than one database system is involved in a transaction, transaction systems use an algorithm known as the two-phase commit. It is difficult to build an infrastructure to make COM components available to share a transaction, to guarantee the ACID rules, and to use the two-phase commit algorithm by hand. Microsoft provides that infrastructure through MTS, which serves as a TP monitor—software that can manage the flow of a transaction; and serves as an ORB—software that can create and manage the lifetime of middle-tier components.

MTS uses interception to monitor all calls going to and from an object. By using interception, MTS is able to provide its clients with more services than just transaction management. For example, interception allows MTS to provide role-based security. As mentioned earlier, components residing in MTS are configured components. MTS uses declarative attributes to change the behavior of an object. MTS provides interception by inserting a context wrapper object between the stub and the object. Objects that have the same concurrency requirements run as part of an activity.

Lesson 2: Configuring MTS

In this lesson, you will learn how to install and configure MTS.

After this lesson, you will be able to:

- Install MTS in different versions of Windows
- Make security available in the application package
- Write scripts to configure the server programmatically

Estimated lesson time: 20 minutes

Installation

To install MTS, use the Microsoft Windows NT 4 Option Pack. The Windows NT 4 Option Pack is available through a variety of sources. You can download it from Microsoft's Web site (*http://www.microsoft.com/ntserver/nts/downloads/recommended/nt4optpk/default.asp*). It is also included with Microsoft Visual Studio 6.0 Enterprise Edition. The Windows NT 4 Option Pack is available for three Windows operating systems: Microsoft Windows 95/98, Microsoft Windows NT Workstation 4, and Microsoft Windows NT Server 4. If you are using the option pack included with Visual Studio Enterprise Edition, you will find the files in the Ntoptpak directory on the CD-ROM labeled CD-2. In that directory, you will find a subdirectory called X86, which in turn contains three subdirectories: Win.95, Winnt.srv, and Winnt.wks. In each of these three subdirectories is a Setup.exe program, which you should run as appropriate for each platform.

The Windows NT 4 Option Pack requires that you install Microsoft Internet Explorer 4.01 or later. MTS also requires DCOM.

Note If you are unsure whether you have DCOM installed in your computer, attempt to run the DCOM configuration management tool called Dcomcnfg.exe. This file is available only when DCOM is present in the computer.

To use Windows 95, install DCOM support. Windows NT 4 and Windows 98 already support DCOM. However, you should make sure that you have the latest version of DCOM installed. To get the latest DCOM support for Windows 95, visit Microsoft's Web site at *http://download.microsoft.com/msdownload/dcom/95/x86/en/dcom95.exe*. For Windows 98, use *http://download.microsoft.com/msdownload/dcom/98/x86/en/dcom98.exe*. For Windows NT, make sure to install the latest service pack. At the time of this writing the latest service pack is Service Pack 6b, and it is available through *http://www.microsoft.com/ntserver/nts/downloads/recommended/sp6/*.

If you are installing under Windows NT 4 with Service Pack 4 or later, you will receive a warning message that reads: "Setup detected that Windows NT 4 SP4 or greater is installed on your computer. We haven't tested this product on SP4. Do you want to proceed?" Click Yes. The warning message might appear again. If so, click Yes. You should see the Microsoft Windows NT 4 Option Pack splash screen listing all the software that is included in the pack. Click the Next button. The second dialog box is the license agreement; you must click Accept to continue. You will then see the Select Components dialog box, shown in Figure 7.8.

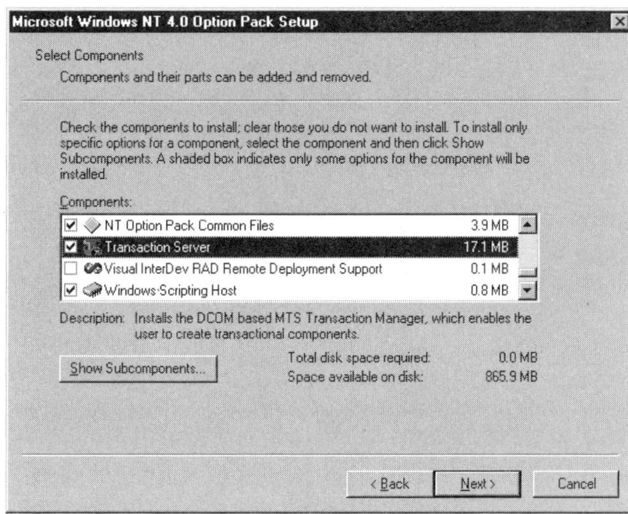

Figure 7.8 Select Components dialog box

Select Transaction Server, click Show Subcomponents, and then select Transaction Server Development. The latter option will install examples, among other features, of how to use the MTS administration objects. (You will learn about these later in this lesson.) Aside from doing a full installation of MTS, you might want to select Windows Scripting Host (WSH). WSH will allow you to test programmatic administration of the server.

After you complete your installation, you can run MTS Explorer by clicking Start, pointing to Programs, pointing to Windows NT 4 Option Pack, and then selecting MTS Explorer.

Configuring Your MTS Server with MTS Explorer

There are normally two types of environments for MTS: production and development. When configuring the server in a production environment you might want to restrict the users who can modify properties for a component. MTS provides a system package that you can configure to restrict access to various features in the server. This package has two predefined roles: Administrator and

Reader. However, these two roles do not have any users assigned to them. In a production environment you will want to assign users to these roles and ensure that security is turned on for this package.

▶ **To ensure that security is active**

1. Start MTS Explorer.
2. In the left pane, open the Packages Installed folder under My Computer.
3. Right-click the System package, and then select Properties.
4. Click the Security tab, and then select the Enable Authorization Checking check box. (See Figure 7.9.)

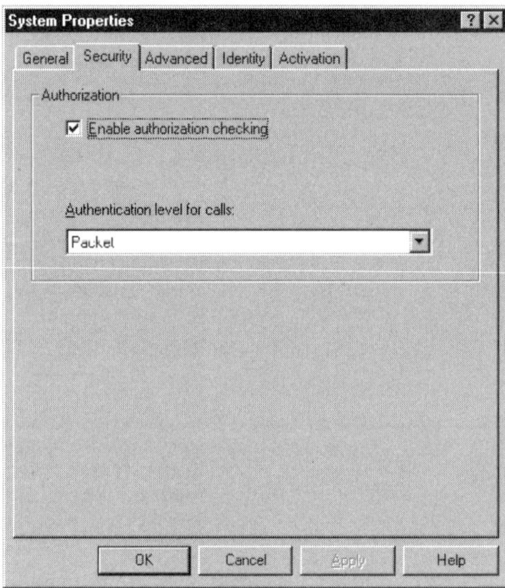

Figure 7.9 System package properties

By default, your MTS Explorer is set to view only the properties for the current computer. However, you can administer another computer's MTS settings on a network through a single computer.

▶ **To view another computer in MTS Explorer**

1. Right-click the Computers folder, point to New, and then select Computer.
2. In the Add Computer dialog box, type the name of the computer that you want to administer and click OK. You must have access to this computer, and you must be a member of Reader to view settings, or Administrator to change properties.

Note You cannot remotely administer a computer running Windows 95 from a computer running Windows NT.

Administering Your MTS Server Programmatically

MTS provides a series of scriptable objects that allow you to administer your server programmatically. These objects are based on IDispatch, and although it is definitely possible to use Visual C++ to write programs to use these objects, most people will agree that using the IDispatch interface is best left to scripting clients. The MTS administration objects are as follows:

- **Catalog** Root object that allows you to connect to a local or remote catalog and retrieve a collection
- **CatalogObject** Allows you to get and set object properties
- **CatalogCollection** Enumerates, adds, deletes, and modifies catalog objects
- **PackageUtil** Allows you to install and export a package
- **ComponentUtil** Installs a component in a specific collection and imports components registered as in-process servers
- **RemoteComponentUtil** Allows you to pull remote components from a package on a remote server
- **RoleAssociationUtil** Associates roles with a component or interface

(Consult the MTS Help file that is installed with MTS for a complete list of methods for each object.)

The following script creates a new package named mcsdpackage in the Packages Installed folder. This example is written in Microsoft Visual Basic Scripting Edition (VBScript). The code first creates an instance of the Catalog object and uses the *GetCollection* method to retrieve the Packages collection. The code then calls the *Add* method of the collection.

To run this code with WSH installed, type the code into a Notepad file and save it with a .vbs extension. To run it, double-click the file.

```
' First, create the catalog object
Dim catalog
Set catalog = CreateObject("MTSAdmin.Catalog.1")

' Next, get the packages collection
Dim packages
Set packages = catalog.GetCollection("Packages")
packages.Populate
```

```
' Add a new package
Dim newPackage
Set newPackage = packages.Add
newPackage.Value("Name") = "mcsdpackage"

' Commit new package
packages.SaveChanges

' Refresh packages
packages.Populate
```

Lesson Summary

MTS is included with the Windows NT 4 Option Pack. You can install the option pack in Windows 95/98, Windows NT 4 Workstation, or Windows NT 4 Server. MTS requires DCOM. When using MTS in a production environment it is a good idea to restrict access to configuration settings in the server. You do this by adding users to the Administrator's role in the system package. You can configure other servers from a single computer. MTS provides a set of objects that allow you to administer a server using scripts.

Lesson 3: MTS Objects

In this lesson, you will learn how to design, develop, and deploy components for MTS.

After this lesson, you will be able to:

- Identify the requirements for objects to run in MTS
- Create a server and add components that are context-aware
- Create packages for hosting MTS components
- Export packages and deploy them in other servers and client computers

Estimated lesson time: 45 minutes

Designing Objects for MTS

It is difficult to give general guidelines for building middle-tier components because they vary depending on each situation. However, you can follow several tips that should apply to most projects.

First, when creating components for database applications, you should not attempt to do the work of the database in your middle-tier components. Database work, such as searching for a record and joining two tables, is best done with queries.

Second, you should not attempt to write general-purpose components that work inside as well as outside MTS. As explained in Lesson 1, MTS creates a context wrapper for each object. MTS objects can gain access to the context wrapper and obtain various properties. For instance, if your object is dependent on MTS running on a transaction, you should first verify that the administrator has not changed the configuration of your object before you change the database. Similarly, if your object must have tight security, you should be aware that an administrator could turn off security for your package. You must check the context to ensure that security is indeed turned on. You will learn more about these operations in Lesson 4. MTS objects also follow a different lifetime path than classic COM objects, you will learn about this also in Lesson 4.

Developing Objects for MTS

MTS components are COM classes that have the following requirements:

- MTS components must reside within in-process servers.
- Classes must implement *IClassFactory*.
- Type-library marshaling or standard fully interpreted marshaling must be used.
- All component interfaces and coclasses must be included in the type library.

In-Process Server Location

MTS requires that objects exist in in-process servers (DLLs). MTS objects can exist inside a library package or a server package. When a client asks MTS to create an object in a library package, the objects are loaded into the address space of the client. When the client asks MTS to create an object in a server package, MTS loads the objects into the address space of an MTS-provided surrogate Mtx.exe. If you are used to creating out-of-process servers, consider that the code necessary to run an out-of-process server is usually insignificant when compared to the business code in your component. MTS handles the infrastructure needed to run your component.

IClassFactory Implementation

Every COM DLL has a standard entry point called *DllGetClassObject* that COM uses to obtain an instance of a COM class. This class must implement IClassFactory. MTS will create objects using the *IClassFactory::CreateInstance* method.

Type-Library or Standard Fully-Interpreted Marshaling

An object can use one of two marshaling mechanisms: type-library marshaling or standard marshaling. MTS does not allow custom marshaling. If a proxy-stub DLL is required, the DLL source must be generated with the /Oicf MIDL compiler flag. This will generate a proxy-stub DLL that is "fully-interpreted." Also, if you use a proxy-stub DLL, the source must be generated with MIDL 3.00.44 or later, and you must link the DLL with the Mtxih.lib library provided by MTS. The Mtxih.lib library must be the first file that you link into your proxy-stub DLL.

Component Interfaces and Coclasses in a Type Library

MTS reads a server's type library to display the names of the classes, interfaces, and methods in MTS Explorer.

► **To create an MTS-compatible COM server with ATL**

1. Open Visual C++ 6.0. On the File menu, click New.
2. On the Projects tab of the New dialog box, select ATL COM AppWizard, type a name for the project, and click OK.
3. In the ATL COM AppWizard, select Dynamic Link Library (DLL) under Server Type and select the Support MTS check box.
4. Click Finish, and then click OK.

Projects generated with this procedure add two libraries to the linking step aside from the "traditional libraries." The two libraries are Mtx.lib (which is an import library for the MTS run time, Mtxex.dll, containing various MTS API functions such as *CreateInstance* and *SafeRef*) and Mtxguid.lib (which contains all the

GUIDs for the various classes and interfaces in MTS). In addition, the project is linked with the Delayimp.lib library. This library allows the server to delay-load a DLL, in this case Mtxex.dll. A small problem with the project files generated is that it adds the self-registration step as a custom build step, which is not desirable because registering the server will change the registry settings back to their original state (prior to adding the DLL to a package).

► To create COM objects that can access their context wrapper objects

The ATL Object Wizard allows you to create COM objects that are MTS compatible and that can take advantage of MTS run-time features. You do this by selecting MS Transaction Server Component from the Objects group in the ATL Object Wizard. However, if you want to modify an existing component to run in MTS, you can replicate the features of the ATL Object Wizard by performing the following steps:

1. Start with the equivalent of an ATL simple object shown in the previous code.
2. Add the following code: *#include <mtx.h>*
3. Add the macro DECLARE_NOT_AGGREGATABLE inside your class declaration in the header file for your class. MTS classes cannot be aggregatable.

By including Mtx.h you gain access to several MTS API functions and several MTS interface definitions. One of these API functions is *GetObjectContext*. With this API, you can reach the context wrapper object associated with your object instance. The use of this API is shown in the following code:

```
IObjectContext *pObjectContext = NULL;
HRESULT hr = GetObjectContext(&pObjectContext);
if (SUCCEEDED(hr))
{
    // do something with the context wrapper here
    ...
    // release the context wrapper when done
    pObjectContext->Release();
}
```

For MTS to do its magic, it must perform interception. As you already know, interception occurs through the context wrapper. The client talks to the context wrapper and thinks of the context wrapper as the object. It is important that a client, or even another object, never gets a reference to your object directly, thus bypassing the context wrapper and interception. Therefore, never send a reference to your object to another object. For example, consider an example in which your object is implementing a callback interface, as follows:

```
ISomeObject *pObject;
HRESULT hr = CreateSomeObject(&pObject);
pObject->RegisterCallback(this);
```

The last line in the previous code is sending a direct reference to the object. Instead, you must use the *SafeRef* function. *SafeRef* gives you a reference to the context wrapper. You would then hand this reference to the client or other objects. The following code shows the correct way to share your object in a callback:

```
ISomeObject *pObject = NULL;
HRESULT hr = CreateSomeObject(&pObject);
IMyInterface *pIMe = NULL;
pIMe = SafeRef(IID_IMyInterface, (IUnknown*)this);
pObject->RegisterCallback(pIMe);
```

MTS 2 uses a feature known as Just-In-Time (JIT) activation. In JIT when a client creates an object, MTS creates the object and a context wrapper. It inserts the wrapper between the stub and the object, but does not bind the context wrapper to the object until activation. Activation occurs when the client makes its first method call. In the same fashion, before an object is destroyed, MTS performs deactivation. In deactivation, MTS destroys the context wrapper. Next, the object is destroyed.

JIT implies that all objects in MTS 2 have four phases in their life cycle: creation, activation, deactivation, and destruction. Therefore, in MTS 2, creation and destruction occur as they do without MTS; in other words, your object is created when another developer creates your object, and destroyed when all references are released. However, the object cannot gain access to the context wrapper until activation.

Similarly, an object cannot gain access to the context wrapper in its destructor because the context wrapper has already been disconnected at that point. (MTS 2 makes virtually no distinction between deactivation and destruction, except that the context wrapper is still available in the deactivation phase.) COM+ introduces the concept of *object pooling,* in which an object can control whether releasing all references truly deletes the object, or whether the object is instead stored in an object pool. To know when your object is activated and deactivated, implement the IObjectControl interface as follows.

► **To implement IObjectControl for receiving JIT notifications**

1. Add IObjectControl to your inheritance list of your MTS-compatible class.
2. Add the interface to your query interface map as follows: *COM_INTERFACE_ENTRY(IObjectControl)*
3. Implement the three methods in IObjectControl—*Activate*, *CanBePooled*, and *Deactivate*:

```
HRESULT Ctestobj1::Activate()
{
}
```

```
BOOL Ctestobj1::CanBePooled()
{
    return FALSE;
}

void Ctestobj1::Deactivate()
{
}
```

Object pooling is not available in MTS 2; therefore, the previous code should return FALSE.

Note In reality, you can also return TRUE. Some people suggest answering TRUE so that object pooling can start working as soon as it is available. However, this is not recommended unless the implications of object pooling have been carefully considered.

Table 7.1 shows the order of life-management events in your objects.

Table 7.1 Order of Life-Management Events in Objects

Phase	Context Wrapper
Constructor	Not Available
FinalConstruct	Not Available
Activate	Available
Method Call	Available
Deactivate	Available
FinalRelease	Not Available
Destructor	Not Available

Packaging Objects for MTS

After you have created your middle-tier components, you will want to create packages to host your components.

► **To create a package in MTS**

1. In MTS Explorer, open the Computers branch.
2. Open the computer branch where you want the package to be installed.
3. Right-click the Packages Installed branch, point to New on the shortcut menu, and then click Package. The Package Wizard dialog box appears, as shown in Figure 7.10 on the next page.

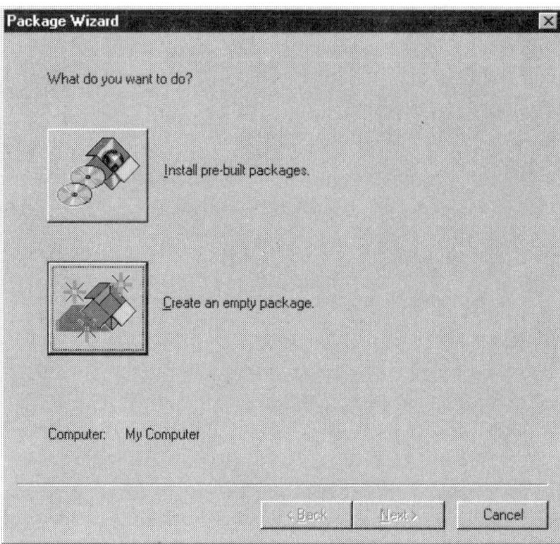

Figure 7.10 Package Wizard dialog box

4. Click the Create An Empty Package button. (You will learn how the Install Pre-Built Packages button is used in the "Importing a Package" section.)
5. Type a name for the new package (the name can include spaces). Click Next.
6. Set the package identity. You can change the identity later in the Package Properties dialog box. During development, you want to use the Interactive User. This setting uses the credentials of the logged on user. A side effect of using the Interactive User is that all output appears in the current WinStation. A problem with this setting is that it requires someone to be logged on for the package to execute.
7. In a production environment, you should select the This User option. When you select This User, you can type in a particular user's credentials, which will be implemented when the server needs to access shared resources such as files. Be aware that you should never display output with this setting. The output will not appear in the current WinStation. For example, if you attempt to display a message box, the message would not be visible and your program will appear frozen as it waits for user interaction.
8. Click Finish.

Adding Objects to a Package

Although you can add objects to a package using a variety of mechanisms, you can most easily accomplish this by using a drag-and-drop operation to move the DLL that contains the classes into the Components folder underneath your package.

► To add objects to a package using drag-and-drop

1. Make sure the Components folder is selected.
2. In Windows Explorer, drag the DLL file into the right pane of the MTS Explorer window. MTS will add all the objects described in the type library.

You can also add objects to a package without drag-and-drop.

► To add classes to the package without a drag-and-drop operation

1. Expand the package branch where you want to insert components. Right-click the Components folder, point to New on the shortcut menu, and then select Component. The Component Wizard dialog box appears, as shown in Figure 7.11.

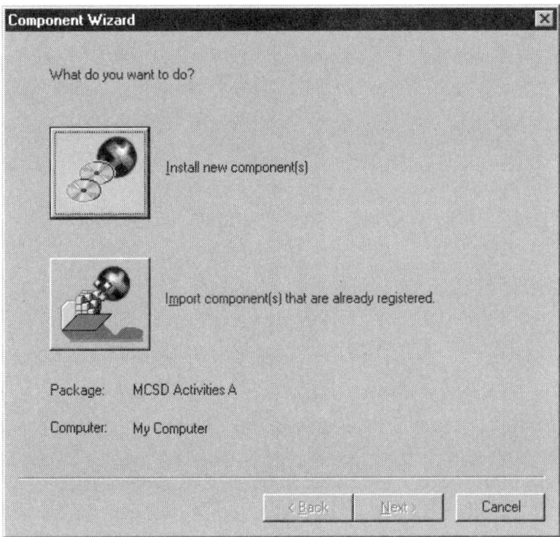

Figure 7.11 Component Wizard dialog box

2. Click Install New Component(s) if you want to add every component in a certain DLL. This option is similar to using the drag-and-drop operation and does not require that the DLL be preregistered.
3. If you want to select a component by its ProgID from the list of registered components, click Import Component(s) That Are Already Registered. This procedure is the only way to add individual components from a DLL. Use this method if you want to add some components to one package and some components to another package.

When creating packages, make sure to add any type libraries on which your objects depend, as well as your proxy-stub DLL if you need one. This will come in handy when deploying your package on another computer.

Package Properties

A package has many properties of which you need to be aware. You can right-click a package and select Properties from the shortcut menu to view the Package Properties dialog box, shown in Figure 7.12.

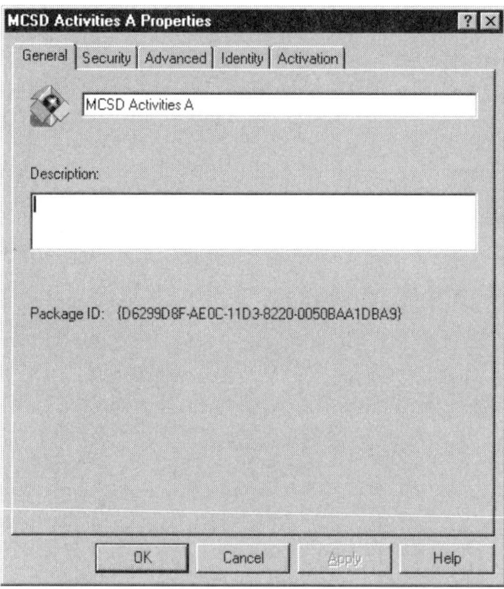

Figure 7.12 Package Properties dialog box

On the General tab, notice that you can type a description for a package. This is useful when importing a package in another computer. The Security tab contains a check box for enabling security for a package. Notice that the default is No Security. This tab also contains the authentication level for calls made between a client and a package. You will learn more about authentication level settings in Lesson 4.

The Advanced tab provides a setting called Server Process Shutdown, which is used to determine when to shut down the server process. This is an optimization in MTS that you can use after all references to your objects have been released. After the server has deleted all instances of objects in a package, the server will remain loaded for the amount of time specified in the Server Process Shutdown setting. This improves performance for clients initiating a conversation with the server within the specified amount of time.

Note During development, you should set the Server Process Shutdown setting as low as possible, because you will be unable to rebuild your code when the server is running and the server DLL is loaded.

The Advanced tab also has two permission settings: Disable Deletion and Disable Changes. By enabling these settings you are locking the package from users of MTS explorer. If you make the Disable Changes option available, users will not be able to modify this package. All the options in the property dialog box except for the permission settings will be made unavailable. To make modifications later, you must unlock the package; clearing the permission options unlocks the package.

The Identity tab allows you to choose the Security Identifier (SID) that MTS will use when accessing shared resources, such as files on the network. This is the user ID and password that your server will impersonate when making outbound calls. For example, your code might access files on another computer. You might use a specific user ID and password to access that other computer, or you might use the interactive user—the user currently logged on. However, your server might not have anyone logged on, which will render your server unusable; or the logged-on user might not have security to access the shared resource. Therefore, in a production environment, you should use a specific user with enough security to reach shared resources.

Probably the most important property you can set for a package is the activation type, found on the Activation tab. The choices are Library Package or Server Package. A library package is simply a package to be used in-process. A server package is one that will be loaded into the MTS surrogate process Mtx.exe. A library package has a few limitations over a server package; the most notable is that library packages do not control security. The process that is loading them determines their security.

Object Properties

Objects also have a series of declarative properties. Perhaps the most important of these properties is *transaction support*. Transactional applications will be explained in greater detail in Lesson 5. For now, this section will discuss how each of the properties affects how the object will participate in transactions.

You might recall from Lesson 1 that MTS is in charge of initiating a transaction and calling on the services of MS DTC to enlist resource managers and control the flow of the transaction. Components dictate when MTS starts a transaction through declarative settings. An administrator can change the transaction requirements of a component by changing the Transaction properties of the component. To do so, right-click the component you want to modify and select Properties on the shortcut menu. Next, click the Transactions tab. On the Transactions tab, you can choose from four options: Requires A Transaction, Requires A New Transaction, Supports Transactions, and Does Not Support Transactions. MTS starts a transaction when an object marked as Requires A New Transaction or Requires A Transaction is created and activated (after the first method call). The object that makes MTS begin the transaction is known as the *root* of the transactions.

Other objects can participate in the same transaction if they are created from within an object already in the transaction. For an object to participate in the same transaction, it must be part of the same activity. In other words, it must be created with the *CreateInstance* function of the IContextObject interface. The component must also be marked as Requires A Transaction or Supports Transactions. If the secondary component is marked as Requires A New Transaction, MTS will create a new transaction for the object; the object will not be able to participate in the transaction of the creator. Components marked as Does Not Support Transactions cannot participate in the same transaction.

As you can see, changing the Transaction property setting in a component can have a huge impact on how your application behaves. Just imagine what would happen if you had coded object B with the idea that it would be in the same transaction as object A, and an MTS administrator decided to mark object B as Requires A New Transaction. You cannot do much to prevent an administrator from doing this. However, you can set a default transaction setting for each of your components in the type library. To do so, first include the file Mtxattr.h in the top of your IDL file as follows:

```
#include <mtxattr.h>
```

This file declares certain attributes that you can use as coclass attributes. These attributes are: TRANSACTION_REQUIRED, TRANSACTION_SUPPORTED, TRANSACTION_NOT_SUPPORTED, and TRANSACTION_REQUIRES_NEW. To use these attributes, simply add them to the coclass attributes as follows:

```
[
    uuid(01C72192-8CB0-11D3-81E1-0050BAA1DBA9),
    helpstring("ctxobj1 Class"),
    TRANSACTION_REQUIRED
]
coclass ctxobj1
{
    [default] interface Ictxobj1;
};
```

These attributes do not prevent an administrator from changing the property; they only give MTS the default transaction setting for the component. That is, when the component is added to a package, the transaction setting will be set according to the default setting.

Deploying MTS-Based Objects

MTS provides a mechanism for exporting a package definition along with its components and importing the package in another server. MTS also provides a way to generate a setup program that will install the necessary registry information to activate a server component into client computers that do not have MTS installed.

Note A client machine does not need to have the DLLs that implement the server objects installed in order to create instances of the objects, nor does it need MTS installed. The only things the client requires are the class ID GUID (CLSID) and the interface GUIDs (IIDs) in the registry. If the interfaces in the server components were designed to take advantage of the type library marshaler, then you must register the type library, not only in the server's machine, but also in the client's machine. If, however, the server components require standard marshaling with a proxy/stub DLL, then you must register the proxy/stub DLL instead on both machines. The setup program generated from exporting the package takes care of installing the type library, or the proxy/stub DLL, and adding the necessary keys to the registry. It creates a subdirectory called Remote Applications under the Program Files directory and there installs the type library or proxy/stub DLL. However, in the case where the server has the type library embedded as a resource in the DLL, make sure to also add to the package the type library file (TLB) as a separate DLL. Otherwise, MTS will add the server files to the client setup instead of simply adding the type library file.

Exporting a Package

After you are ready to move your application to a production server, you will want to export your package.

► **To export a package**

1. In MTS Explorer, right-click the package you want to export, and select Export. The Export Package dialog box appears, as shown in Figure 7.13.

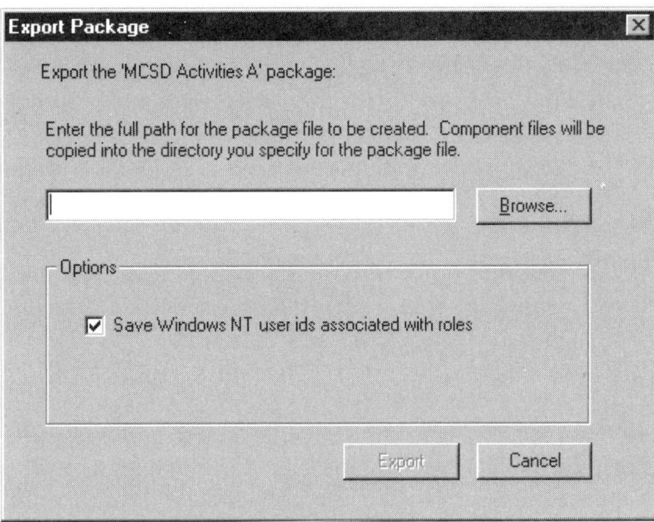

Figure 7.13 Export Package dialog box

2. Type the exact path and name for the package. If you want to export the user IDs for each role, select the Save Windows NT User IDs Associated With Roles check box. This check box refers only to the users in the roles. If you do not select this check box, the role information will still be exported, but the actual user IDs within the role will not be included. This is normally what you want to do when moving from development to deployment. Click Export.
3. If this is not the first time you're exporting a package to the same location, the Overwrite Files dialog box will prompt you to overwrite the old package and DLL. Click OK.
4. The Export Package dialog box closes. When the export is complete, MTS Explorer reappears with a message box telling you that the package was exported successfully. Click OK.

You should now have an exported package in a .pak file. The .pak file is a text file containing the settings necessary to recreate the package in another server.

Importing a Package

After exporting the package you can import it into another MTS server.

► **To import a package into another MTS server**

1. In MTS Explorer, open the Computers branch, and then open My Computer.
2. Right-click the Packages Installed folder, point to New on the shortcut menu, and then select Package. The Package Wizard dialog box appears.
3. Instead of clicking the Create An Empty Package button, click the Install Pre-Built Packages button. The Select Package Files dialog box appears.
4. Click the Add button, locate the package you want to install, and then click Next.
5. In the Set Package Identity dialog box, specify the account under which the package will run. Remember that when you are developing, it is more convenient to select Interactive User, but in a production environment, you will want to select This User and specify the user's credentials. Click Next.
6. In the Installation Options dialog box, type the directory where you want to copy the component files. This directory is the location in which the components will be registered. Click Finish.

Many times, you might want to distribute an application with a UI to the clients, but not install the server components. For example, it does not make sense to install all the components on each client computer. All that is needed in client applications is the registry information for the classes in a package. When you export a package, MTS creates a client subdirectory that contains a small executable that simply writes the registry information to the client computer.

Lesson Summary

In this lesson, you learned the requirements for building MTS COM objects. You learned that MTS objects reside within in-process servers, implement *IClassFactory*, have fully-interpreted proxies, and must include information about their coclasses and interfaces in the type library. You learned how to create the server shell for an MTS server with ATL. You also learned how to add code to an existing object to communicate with the MTS executive. An object hosted in MTS can reach its context wrapper with *GetObjectContext*.

This lesson also discussed JIT and how to get notifications from MTS as to when your object is being activated and deactivated. These notifications come through the IObjectControl interface. You learned how to create a package to host your object, and how to add your object to the package. You also learned about the properties of a package, and the properties of an object. One of the most important properties in an object is the Transaction property setting. An administrator can affect how a component works within a transaction by changing this setting. A programmer can suggest the default transaction setting for each class by adding transaction attributes to each coclass definition.

MTS provides a mechanism to export a package and import it into another MTS server. This wizard also generates a client setup program for adding the necessary registry keys to the client's computer to access the server.

Lesson 4: Advanced MTS Techniques

In this lesson, you will learn some advanced topics dealing with MTS. In particular, you will learn about role-based security and load balancing.

After this lesson, you will be able to:

- Set up roles and control security at the component and interface level
- Programmatically control security at the method level
- Understand load balancing and potential problems involved in performing load balancing with MTS

Estimated lesson time: 30 minutes

Role-Based Security

MTS security is built on top of DCOM, so it is no surprise that many of its elements are based on DCOM paradigms. However, MTS extends DCOM security by doing two things. First, because MTS provides a container application (Mtx.exe) it takes charge of controlling security for out-of-process activation and allows programmers to worry less about programming directly to the COM security APIs. Second, because MTS provides more security checkpoints, it provides higher granularity in security. DCOM provides only two security checkpoints: launching the server and accessing the server. In addition to those two levels, MTS provides checkpoints at the component level and the interface level. What's more, MTS provides several simple methods for extending security to the method level.

Making Security Available for a Package and a Component

A role is a group of users. Roles are assigned on a per-package basis. When you create a new package, security is unavailable by default. You can make security available for a package or for a component by performing the following steps.

► **To make security available for a package**

1. In MTS Explorer, right-click the package and select Properties on the shortcut menu. The Properties dialog box appears.
2. On the Security tab, select the Enable Authorization Checking check box and click OK.

► **To make security available for a component**

1. In MTS Explorer, right-click the component and select Properties on the shortcut menu. The Properties dialog box appears.
2. On the Security tab, select the Enable Authorization Checking check box and click OK.

Note Security checking is available by default at the component level. In other words, as soon as you make security available at the package level, you must create roles and assign them to each component. Otherwise, every user will be denied permission to the package.

Creating a Role for a Package

Under DCOM, security is affected programmatically per process. The same is true under MTS; each package is run in a separate process. If you view the Task Manager, you will see that each time a client instantiates a component in a different package, MTS runs a separate instance of Mtx.exe (the surrogate process for the component). Because each package runs in a different process, roles are created in a per-package basis. This is also the reason why a library package cannot use the MTS role-based security. A library package loads in the process space of the caller, and is then bound to the process' security model. Therefore, this library package can be secured or unsecured. A library package is secured when the Mtx.exe process loads it; that is, when the package is created by an MTS COM object. A non-MTS process that creates a library package automatically renders it unsecured.

► **To create a role for a package**

1. In MTS Explorer, select and open the package for which you want to set up roles.
2. Right-click the Roles folder, point to New on the shortcut menu, and then select Role.
3. In the New Role dialog box, type the role's name and click OK.
4. Open the New Role branch. Right-click the Users folder, point to New on the shortcut menu, and then select User.
5. You will be presented with the Add Users And Groups To Role dialog box. Select the users you want to add to the role and click OK. You can add individual users or Windows NT security groups.

Assigning a Role to a Component or an Interface

After you have created a role, you can assign the role to specific components and interfaces in a package.

► **To assign a role to a component or an interface**

1. In MTS Explorer, select and open the object for which you want to assign roles.
2. Right-click the Role Membership folder, point to New on the shortcut menu, and then select Role.
3. The Select Roles dialog box containing a list of all the package roles appears. Select as many roles as you want, and click OK.

Affecting Security Programmatically

MTS also allows you to programmatically control security at the method level. To do so, you can use two methods in the IObjectContext interface: *IsSecurityEnabled* and *IsCallerInRole*. *IsSecurityEnabled* helps you decide if security is activated for this package. If security is not activated, this function returns FALSE. This function is important for two reasons. First, if you are working in a library package, the function returns TRUE if the package was loaded from within an MTS object living inside Mtx.exe, and it returns FALSE if a client outside MTS created the component directly. Second, when security is turned off for a package, *IsCallerInRole* always returns TRUE. Therefore, before using *IsCallerInRole*, you must check to see if security is available.

The following code shows you how to test for security at the method level:

```
HRESULT MyObj::SecuredMethod()
{
    IObjectContext *pContext=NULL;
    HRESULT hr = GetObjectContext(&pContext);
    if (SUCCEEDED(hr))
    {
        if (!pContext->IsInTransaction())
        return E_ACCESSDENIED;

    BSTR bstrAdmin = SysAllocString(L"Admins");
    BOOL bInRole=FALSE;
    if (!pContext->IsCallerInRole(bstrAdmin,&bInRole))
    {
        SysFreeString(bstrAdmin);
        return E_ACCESSDENIED;
    }

        pContext->Release();
    }

    // Add your security code here
    return S_OK;
}
```

Direct Caller vs. Original Caller

MTS performs role-based security when a client outside MTS communicates with an object inside MTS. When an object inside MTS makes a method call on another MTS object, MTS does not check security. Consider an example where a client has access to method1 in objectA, but does not have access to method1 in objectB. If the client calls method1 in objectA, objectA has access to method1 in objectB and could potentially call it. Because MTS does not check security for MTS objects calling other MTS objects, the client will not be stopped from performing this type of sequence. This could pose a security problem.

However, MTS does provide several APIs to help you determine the identity of a client. MTS distinguishes between the original caller (the client that accessed the first COM object in the chain) and the direct caller (the caller that made the method call). You can obtain the security identifiers for both the Original Caller and the Direct Caller using the methods in the ISecurityProperty interface. This interface has five methods: *GetDirectCreatorSID, GetOriginalCreatorSID, GetDirectCallerSID, GetOriginalCallerSID,* and *ReleaseSID*. To reach this interface, call *QueryInterface* on the context object.

The following code demonstrates how to use the ISecurityProperty interface:

```
IObjectContext* pContext = NULL;
ISecurityProperty* pISecProp = NULL;
PSID pSid = NULL;
HRESULT hr = S_OK;

// Get the object context
hr = GetObjectContext(&pContext);

if (SUCCEEDED(hr))
{
    // Get a reference to the ISecurityProperty
    interface
    hr = pContext->QueryInterface(
          IID_ISecurityProperty,
          (void**)&pISecProp);

    // Obtain the creator's security ID
    hr = pISecProp->GetDirectCreatorSID(&pSid);

    // Add your security code here

    // Release the security ID
    pISecProp->ReleaseSID(pSid);

    // Release the interface
    pISecProp->Release();
```

```
    // Release the context
    pContext->Release();
}
```

Load Balancing

This section discusses *load balancing*, and suggests an algorithm for programmatically performing load balancing.

The basic goal behind load balancing is to improve server performance. Performance can be measured in many ways, but for the sake of this discussion, it means two things: more users and faster response.

There are two types of load balancing: dynamic and static. *Dynamic load balancing* occurs when the operating system can choose, based on performance statistics, which server will be most suited to run the components requested by the client. *Static load balancing* occurs when a program determines which server should handle a request based on fixed quantities (for example, if there are more than 50 users making requests, then use server B).

Because MTS and Windows NT Server 4 cannot perform dynamic load balancing, the simplest way to perform load balancing is to make your distributed applications more scalable by having multiple servers export the same package and then letting the clients decide on which server they want to run. A more complicated and robust technique might involve creating a load balancing package. Using this technique, every client communicates with the load balancing package. The load balancing package's job is to then create instances of middle-tier components based on either an algorithm or a round-robin approach.

Microsoft offers several products that can help with load balancing, including Microsoft Cluster Server (MSCS). MSCS allows several Windows NT Enterprise Server computers to act as a single unit. Although a full discussion of MSCS is beyond the scope of this chapter, you can find more information about this product by visiting the Microsoft Web site *www.microsoft.com/Windows/server/Technical/management/ClusterArch.asp*.

Lesson Summary

MTS extends DCOM security in two ways: first, it suppresses the need in many cases to use COM security APIs; second, it adds more granularity by offering more than the two security checkpoints offered by DCOM. MTS uses the concept of roles, or groups of users, to manage security. You can assign roles to packages, objects, and interfaces. MTS also provides a mechanism for programmatically handling security. With the *IsCallerInRole* and the *IsSecurityEnabled* methods, you can control which users can access a particular method. MTS makes a distinction between the client that first initiated the call chain (original caller) and the client that is next to last in the call chain (direct caller). In addition, MTS provides an interface, ISecurityProperty, to allow you to reach this information.

MTS does not perform dynamic load balancing. If you want to perform load balancing, you must use static load balancing. Microsoft offers enhancements to Windows NT Server to provide more thorough resource management.

Lesson 5: Creating MTS-Based Applications

In this lesson, you will learn the essentials of creating transaction services-based applications using MTS.

After this lesson, you will be able to:

- Understand how transactions flow through activities
- Control the outcome of a transaction programmatically
- Design a system optimized for performance

Estimated lesson time: 45 minutes

Controlling the Flow of Transactions

One of the key goals in transaction-based applications is to perform a transaction as quickly as possible. When the transaction is occurring, database systems place locks on the data to prevent other applications from looking at intermediate data. Locking prevents concurrency, which is a detriment to scalability. To improve scalability, you must design your objects so that they do not spend much time in the actual transaction.

Two aspects determine the longevity of a transaction. One involves the interception mechanism in MTS, specifically JIT. The other involves the timeout feature in MTS that automatically aborts a transaction in a specified amount of time. To understand these two forces, you must first understand how transactions operate in MTS.

In Lesson 1, you learned about context wrappers and about activities. Recall that activities are groups of objects with the same concurrency requirements. In MTS 2, when a base client creates an MTS object, MTS creates a new activity and puts the object instance in it. This object can in turn invite other objects to be part of the activity using the *CreateInstance* function in the IObjectContext interface (recall that you obtain IObjectContext from the *GetObjectContext* API).

Also, remember that only objects that are part of the same activity can vote on a transaction. Transactions have a single entry point and begin when an object marked as Requires A Transaction or Requires A New Transaction is activated.

You might recall also from Lesson 1 that an object is activated when a client makes the first method call. Thus, an object is first created when the client requests to create the object, but is not activated until the first method call. The vote an object makes is stored in the context wrapper. Therefore, voting begins when the object is activated and ends when the object is deactivated.

When the root of the transaction is destroyed, MTS will either commit the transaction or abort it. If an object needs to be part of the transaction more accurately, it must be created from within the first object and it must be invited into the same activity. Because MTS 2 was built after COM was released, an object in an activity cannot use the standard COM APIs to create an MTS component within the same activity. If you were to use *CoGetClassObject* or *CoCreateInstance* the object would be part of a separate activity. To create an object that is part of the same activity, use the *CreateInstance* method in the IObjectContext interface. The following example shows how to invite an object CLSID_FriendObject into the same activity.

```
IObjectContext *pContext;
HRESULT hr = GetObjectContext(&pContext);

if (SUCCEEDED(hr))
{
    IFriendObject *pFriendObject;
    pContext->CreateInstance(CLSID_FriendObject,
    __uuidof(pFriendObject),
    (void **)&pFriendObject);
}
```

When an object's context wrapper is gone, the vote cannot be changed. A context wrapper keeps track of the vote status on what is commonly called the "happy" flag. A vote of yes means the object is "happy," a vote of "no" means the object is "unhappy." If the context wrapper gets destroyed in an unhappy state, the transaction will be doomed. Two styles of voting can occur. One style is to make a temporary vote, another style is to make a final vote. With a temporary vote an object is indicating that it can change its mind ("I'm unhappy but perhaps if you make another method call, I can be persuaded to be happy"). With a permanent style an object says "I'm unhappy (or happy) and there is nothing anyone can do to change my mind." The object controls the state of happiness by calling one of two methods in the IObjectContext interface: *EnableCommit* and *DisableCommit*. *EnableCommit* sets the state of the "happy" flag to happy, and *DisableCommit* sets the state to unhappy. The following code shows how to call these methods:

```
IObjectContext *pContext;
HRESULT hr = GetObjectContext(&pContext);

if (SUCCEEDED(hr))
{
    pContext->EnableCommit();
    pContext->Release();
}
```

EnableCommit and *DisableCommit* do a temporary vote—they do not affect the lifetime of the context wrapper, they only affect the state of the happy bit. If the object is destroyed and the context wrapper with it then at that point the last vote will be final.

If your object reaches a state in which it is definitely done with its part of the transaction, the object can request deactivation from MTS. As a result, the object will also be destroyed. Remember that the transaction does not end until the root object is deactivated. However, when a subordinate object is destroyed, the object notifies the application that it has completed voting. To deactivate itself, an object can call one of two methods in the IObjectContext interface: *SetComplete* or *SetAbort*. *SetComplete* and *SetAbort* tell MTS that the object has completed doing its job.

In other words, when the method call finishes and passes through the context wrapper, MTS will deactivate the context wrapper and destroy the object. *SetComplete* tells MTS that it wants to be deactivated in a happy state; *SetAbort* tells MTS that it wants to be deactivated in an unhappy state. Deactivation occurs when the call returns through the context wrapper. The following code demonstrates calling the *SetComplete* method:

```
IObjectContext *pContext;
HRESULT hr = GetObjectContext(&pContext);

if (SUCCEEDED(hr))
{
    pContext->SetComplete();
    pContext->Release();
}
```

Note In COM+, the object will have a choice to be destroyed or pooled.

Based on the previous rules for voting, you can infer the following rules:

- If an object says that it is unhappy with *DisableCommit,* it can change its mind and become happy with *EnableCommit*. An object can change its mind until it is destroyed.
- If one object calls *SetAbort* within a method call and does not change its mind, ending the method call with *SetComplete,* for example, when the call ends and goes through the context wrapper MTS will destroy the object and the transaction will be doomed.
- If the root object is destroyed, any objects that are part of the transaction will also be destroyed.

Designing with MTS

Many developers like to call *SetAbort* at the beginning of the method code, then call *SetComplete* when they are sure the code has executed properly. In this way, if an unexpected error occurs and the method exits prematurely, changes will not be committed.

This lesson introduced the notion that a goal is to spend as little time as possible in a transaction. When designing your application, you should observe the following guidelines.

First, try to use *SetComplete* and *SetAbort* instead of *EnableCommit* and *DisableCommit*. Using *SetComplete* and *SetAbort* could mean that your object would be continually destroyed and recreated on a per-call basis. This could have an enormous impact on your system—your objects will be stateless. (In fact, you should write your object with the assumption that it will be stateless. Write any initialization code in the *Activate* method, perform your operation in the method call, and clean up in the *Deactivate* method.)

Second, after a subordinate object is destroyed in an unhappy state, either explicitly with *SetAbort* or implicitly when all of its references are gone, the transaction will be doomed. There is no point in continuing it; therefore, to make the system perform as quickly as possible, you should eliminate the root object as soon as you have determined that the transaction is doomed in the root object. Similarly, you should almost never call *EnableCommit* or *DisableCommit* from within the root object. It is not good design practice for middle-tier components to let the client make the decision of when the transaction will end.

If you call *EnableCommit* instead of *SetComplete*, the transaction continues until the client eliminates all references to the object. Letting the client decide means the system will perform slower and that the transaction has a greater chance of failing. This is because MTS sets a timeout for transactions. If you were to return a code to the client so that the client could make a decision, the system might timeout before the user gets around to answering. Instead, you should let the transaction fail, and return an error code indicating that the user should retry the operation. A well-designed UI should allow the user to retry a transaction without having to retype all the information, or to type in a compensating transaction if an error was committed.

Scaling Applications with MTS

When people use the term "scaling an application," they usually mean adding more users. Computers can handle only a certain number of users running concurrently. The answer to adding more users after a certain time is to add more servers. In MTS applications, it is possible to run certain components in separate computers. You might have noticed from looking at the *CreateInstance* method in IObjectContext that there is no way to specify a server computer where the object should be created. It is possible, however, to create objects from another server and have them be part of the same activity. To do so, you must tell one MTS server through MTS Explorer that the object is going to be created remotely. You can do so in the manner as demonstrated in the following subsections.

Remote Administration

An administrator can tell MTS Explorer to execute various components remotely.

► **To run components remotely with MTS Explorer**

1. Ensure that the remote computer is a Windows NT 4 Workstation or Server and that it has MTS installed.
2. Verify that the Packages directory under the MTS installation directory on the remote computer is shared with read access to the administrator.
3. The package must be installed in the remote computer. If you are exporting from your local computer, use the package exporting procedure described in Lesson 3 in the "Deploying MTS-Based Objects" section.
4. The component you are configuring to run remotely must not be installed in the local computer.
5. Right-click the Remote Components folder in the local computer, point to New on the shortcut menu, and then select Remote Components. The Remote Components dialog box appears, as Figure 7.14 shows.

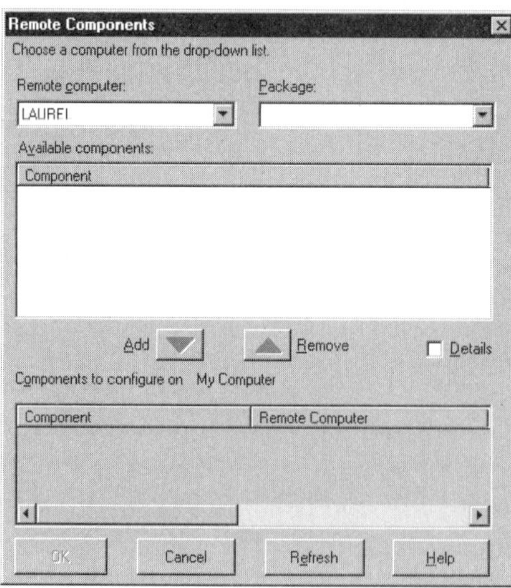

Figure 7.14 Remote Components dialog box

6. Select the computer in which you want to run the component, and the package you want to use. The Remote Components dialog box lists the components in the package. Click the components you want to use, and then click Add.

Lesson Summary

MTS uses a transactional system in which components can vote on the outcome of a transaction. A transaction occurs within the confines of an activity. Only components in the same activity can participate in the transaction. To ensure that a subordinate component becomes part of the same activity, use the *CreateInstance* method of the IObjectContext interface. If you were to use *CoCreateInstance,* MTS would treat the request as a separate client and the object would become part of a different activity. Objects can vote on the outcome of a transaction using four methods: *EnableCommit, DisableCommit, SetComplete* and *SetAbort*. *SetComplete* and *SetAbort* also tell the system to deactivate the component when the method call completed. When designing a distributed application, always try to destroy the components as soon as possible so that you can ensure a higher level of concurrency.

Lab 7: Understanding MTS Activities and Transactions

In this lab, you will gain a perspective on how MTS manages transactions. In particular, this lab is designed to show you how MTS uses activities, how objects work together in an activity, and how an object votes on the outcome of a transaction.

Rather than learning specifics of database access or about OLE DB's participation in a transaction, your goal in completing this lab is to understand how objects are activated and deactivated, and how the objects work together in an activity. At the end of this lab, you should be able to determine when two objects will become part of the same activity, and when the objects will become deactivated.

This lab is mostly about observing—nearly all the code is provided to you on the companion CD.

Estimated lab time: 45 minutes

Exercise 1: Putting Everything in Place

In this exercise, you will ensure that all the tools are in place for you to observe how MTS operates. You will first make sure that your computer is able to run a tool called MTS Spy. This tool can report different activities in an MTS server. Next, you will import a package into your MTS server and run the client application provided.

MTS Spy is included with the companion CD that accompanies this book. This tool consists of two components, Mtsspy.exe and Mtsspyctl.dll, both of which are available in the Labs\Ch07\Mtsspy folder on the companion CD.

The purpose of MTS Spy is to report events from an MTS server, such as when activities are formed, when a method call occurs, when MTS begins and ends a transaction, and so on. To learn more about how the tool works, look for the topic "How MTS Spy Works" in the MTS SDK documentation.

Note MTS Spy currently works only on Windows NT computers because it is built for Unicode, which is not supported in Windows 98.

Your first task is to register the Mtsspyctl.dll control and ensure that Mtsspy.exe is running properly.

► **To make sure MTS Spy is working properly**

1. Register the Mtsspyctl.dll component. To register it, use Regsvr32.exe as with any other control. For example, on the Start menu, click Run and type *e:\regsvr32 mtsspyctl.dll*, where *e* is your CD-ROM drive.

2. Run the file Mtsspy.exe. An example of MTS Spy in action is shown in Figure 7.15.

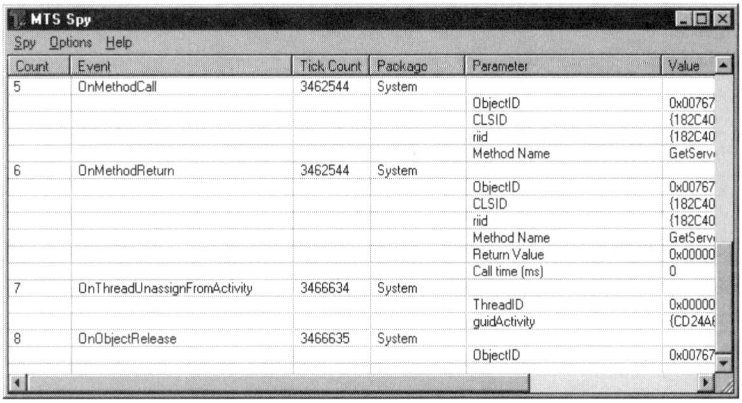

Figure 7.15 MTS Spy tool

Next, you will create a package called MCSD ActivitiesA. This package will contain two components: mtscomp1 and mtscomp2. Both of these components are provided for you as well. You will find the package definition as activitiesA.pak in the Labs\Ch07\ActivitiesA folder on the companion CD. Your next task is to import this package into MTS Explorer.

► **To import the package into MTS Explorer**

1. Run MTS Explorer by clicking Start; pointing to Programs, Windows NT 4 Option Pack, and Microsoft Transaction Server; and then clicking Transaction Server Explorer.
2. Expand the Microsoft Transaction Server, Computers, My Computer, and Packages Installed branches. These branches are visible in the MTS Explorer window's left pane.
3. Right-click the Packages Installed branch and click Package on the New menu. The Package Wizard appears.
4. Click the Install Pre-Built Packages button.
5. On the Select Package Files dialog box, click the Add button and locate the file ActivitiesA.pak. Click Next twice, and then click Finish to accept the default settings.

You should now have the MCSD ActivitiesA package installed. If you examine the package, you will find the two components mtscomp1 and mtscomp2. The mtscomp1 component has one method—*CreateAndDestroy2*. This method creates an instance of mtscomp2 and calls mtscomp2's *SayHello* method.

The *SayHello* method simply displays a message box with the words "Hello World!" Next, *SayHello* proceeds to release the object. The *CreateAndDestroy2* method has one input parameter, *VARIANT_BOOL bUseCreateInstance*. This parameter tells the function whether to use the *IObjectContext::CreateInstance* function or the classic COM function *CoCreateInstance* to create the mtscomp2 object. You will find the source code for this function in the Labs\Ch07\ActivitiesA\Source\Mtsactivities folder on the companion CD.

In the Labs\Ch07\ActivitiesA\Source\Vbclient folder on the companion CD, you will find a client program, Client1.exe, that you can use to exercise the components. The purpose of the client program, which is written in Visual Basic, is to create an instance of the mtscomp1 component and to call its *CreateAndDestroy* method. Figure 7.16 shows the client program.

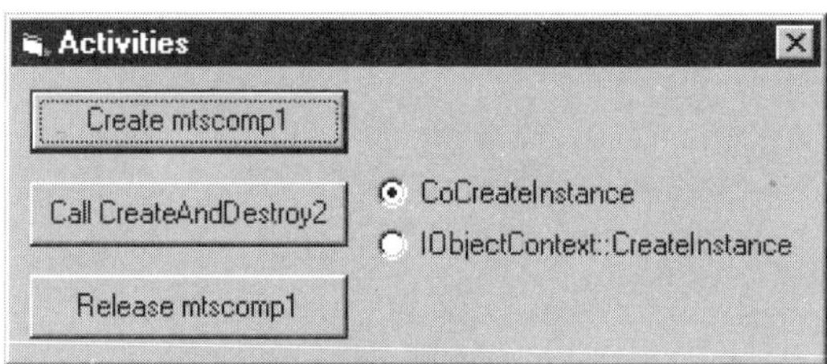

Figure 7.16 Client1 program

As shown, the program has three buttons: Create Mtscomp1, Call CreateAndDestroy2, and Release Mtscomp1. Next to the Call CreateAndDestroy2 button are two option buttons for selecting the method of creating mtscomp2—CoCreateInstance and IObjectContext::CreateInstance.

Run the Mtsspy.exe program, and then run the Client1.exe program. Now exercise the client program one time to make sure that MTS Spy is properly logging events. Click the Create Mtscomp1 button in the program, and then click the Release Mtscomp1 button. Although you will not yet see any output, MTS Spy logs events only for packages that are running.

By creating and destroying the object one time, MTS Spy will let the package continue to run. Remember that MTS can keep a package running for a specific amount of time even after all references to all of its objects have been released. The amount of time that MTS keeps the package running is dictated by the Shutdown After Being Idle For X Minutes option on the Advanced tab of the Package Properties dialog box.

Next, in the MTS Spy tool, click Select Packages on the Spy menu. The Select Events dialog box appears as shown in Figure 7.17.

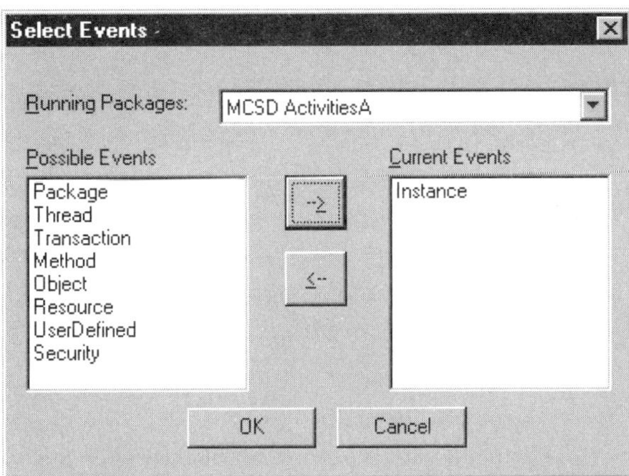

Figure 7.17 Select Events dialog box in MTS Spy

Select the MCSD ActivitiesA package from the drop-down list. Select all the events in the Possible Events list and click OK. Click the Create Mtscomp1 and Release Mtscomp1 buttons again. You should see a series of events displayed in the MTS Spy window. You now have all the tools in place to experiment with activities as follows.

Exercise 2: Observe How Activities Are Managed

In this exercise, you will run through different scenarios of creation for the mtscomp2 component, and observe whether mtscomp1 and mtscomp2 terminate in the same activity or in different activities.

Clear the output in the MTS Spy window by selecting Clear All Events from the Spy menu. For this exercise, it will be easier if you monitor only Instance events from the server. Therefore, when you select the MCSD ActivitiesA package in the Select Packages dialog box, only select to monitor the Instance event. Ideally, you want to determine whether mtscomp1 and mtscomp2 share the same activity. You do this by comparing the Activity GUID that MTS assigns to each object as they are created. MTS will report this Activity GUID as each object is created. If the GUIDs match, then the two objects are in the same activity; otherwise, they exist in different activities.

You can also get the Activity GUID from the context wrapper object programmatically. To do so, obtain a reference to the context wrapper with *GetObjectContext,* then call *QueryInterface* to obtain a pointer to the IObjectContextActivity interface. This interface is defined in the Mtx.h header file. Use the *GetActivityID* method in the IObjectContextActivity interface to get the Activity GUID for the object. Record the outcome of the following different scenarios.

Scenario 1: Both Components in the Same Package

For this scenario, click the Create Mtscomp1 button, and then click the Call CreateAndDestroy2 button with the CoCreateInstance option selected. Finally, click the Release Mtscomp1 button. The MTS Spy window should record four events: *OnObjectCreate* (for mtscomp1), *OnObjectCreate* (for mtscomp2), *OnObjectRelease* (for mtscomp2), and *OnObjectRelease* (for mtscomp1). If you closely examine the Activity GUIDs for both *OnObjectCreate* events, you will notice that they are different because the objects are in different activities.

Repeat the procedure, but this time select IObjectContext::CreateInstance. The Activity GUIDs should match, indicating that the objects are in the same activity.

Scenario 2: Components in Separate Packages

To test this scenario, create a new package and move mtscomp2 to it.

► **To create a new package and move mtscomp2 to it**

1. Right-click the Packages Installed branch in MTS Explorer. On the shortcut menu, point to New and then click Package. The Package Wizard appears.
2. Click the Create An Empty Package button, and type *MCSD ActivitiesB* for the package name. Click Next, and then click Finish to accept the default options.
3. In the component list for the MCSD ActivitiesA package, right-click the mtscomp2 component (mtsactivities.mtscomp2.1). On the shortcut menu, click Move. The Move Components dialog box appears. Select the MCSD ActivitiesB package and click OK. A dialog box appears, prompting you to make sure you want to move this package. Click Yes.

You now have a new package, MCSD ActivitiesB, that hosts the mtscomp2 object. Run through the same series of tests as you did in Scenario 1. Note that this time, you need to monitor the events for two packages. Therefore, click all three buttons in the client program to make both packages active. Next, monitor the Instance event for both packages by clicking Select Packages on the Spy menu.

Click the buttons in the client program as you did previously, first with the CoCreateInstance option selected, and then with the IObjectContext::CreateInstance option selected.

You should notice that, as before, the objects are in different activities when *CoCreateInstance* is used, and in the same activity when *IObjectContext::CreateInstance* is used—it does not matter that the components are in separate packages.

Differences do exist between Scenario 1 and Scenario 2, but not in the way that MTS places the components into activities. You can see a major difference between the two situations if you were to run Task Manager and examine the process list for Mtx.exe.

In Scenario 1, both objects exist inside the same process, although in Scenario 2, each object exists in a separate process. In other words, you should see one instance of Mtx.exe (actually two instances because you will also see one for the system package that is always running if MTS Explorer is simultaneously running) in Scenario 1 and two instances of Mtx.exe in Scenario 2.

Scenario 3: Components in Separate Packages in Separate Computers

In this scenario, you will test creation with packages in different computers. This procedure is not required, because few people will most likely have the necessary hardware and software configuration to try it. You will need two machines with MTS installed; one of the machines must be running Windows NT Workstation 4.0 or Windows NT Server 4.0. The machine running Windows NT will serve as the remote server. Also, make sure that MTS Spy is installed on both machines.

As explained earlier, it is possible to run components in other computers. To do so, you would export MCSD ActivitiesB package from the MTS server on one computer and import the package into the MTS server on another computer. Then you would delete it from the first MTS server. You would then make sure that the Catalogs folder was shared from the second MTS server, and in the first MTS server you would add mtscomp2 as a new remote component. This procedure was explained in detail earlier in the chapter.

After you have added the mtscomp2 component as a remote component, you could run through the scenario again. However, you must be able to run MTS Spy on both computers. Thereafter, you would run through the creation steps one time to make sure the packages are active on both computers. Next, you would select MCSD ActivitiesA package from MTS Spy in Server 1, and select MCSD ActivitiesB package from MTS Spy in Server 2. Finally, you would run the test as before, first with *CoCreateInstance,* and then with *IObjectContext::CreateInstance*.

You should obtain the same results as you did in the previous two scenarios: *CoCreateInstance* results in different activities; *IObjectContext::CreateInstance* result in the same activity.

Exercise 3: Observe How Transactions Are Managed

You have already seen how two components can partake in the same activity. You might recall that, in MTS 2, this is required for the objects to share in a transaction. In this exercise, you will learn when MTS begins and ends a transaction. You will also study how each component can affect the outcome of a transaction.

To test the various transaction scenarios, begin by creating a new package. Your first task in this exercise is to import the Transactions.pak package (found in the

\Labs\Ch07\Transactions folder on the companion CD) into MTS Explorer. You should already be familiar with this procedure. After importing the package, you should see the new package name MCSD Transactions. In the package, you should see two components: mtstran1 and mtstran2.

The mtstran1 component is intentionally the root object in the transaction. If you look at the transaction properties for each component, you will notice that mtstran1 is marked as Requires A Transaction, and mtstran2 is marked as Supports Transactions.

The mtstran1 component has a single method called *Begin*. This method makes the object display a Manage Mtstran2 dialog box (see Figure 7.18).

Figure 7.18 Manage Mtstran2 dialog box displayed when the *Begin* method is invoked

The purpose of this dialog box is to control the creation of the secondary object mtstran2. Using the dialog box, you can create mtstran2, call its *SayHello* method, and release mtstran2. Note that the creation of mtstran2 occurs with the *IObjectContext::CreateInstance* method, which places the secondary object in the same activity as the first.

The mtstran2 component has only one method: *SayHello*. This method displays a message box with the famous phrase "Hello World." Immediately after the function displays Hello World, and just before the *SayHello* method finishes, the method displays a Transaction Vote dialog box (see Figure 7.19). With this dialog box, you are able to vote on the outcome of the transaction. Your choices are EnableCommit, DisableCommit, SetComplete, and SetAbort. Be aware that as you select each option the respective command executes immediately.

In this way, you are able to see if each method has an immediate effect or not. After you are done voting, control returns to the Manage mtstrans2 dialog box. Using this dialog box, you can continue making method calls, or choose to release the object. When you are done making changes to the secondary object, you can click Done to exit the dialog box. At this point, you are again presented with the Transaction Vote dialog box, although this time the root object, mtstran1, gets to cast a vote.

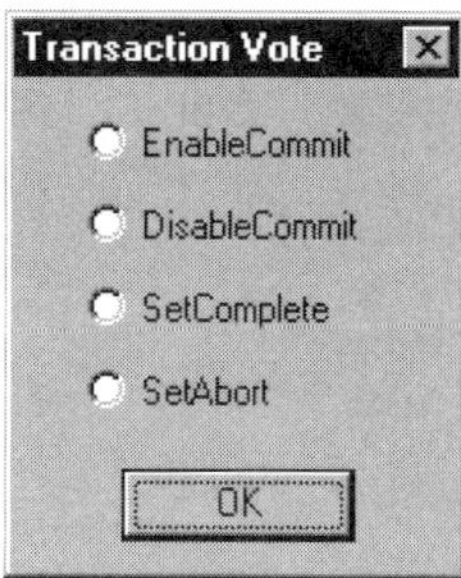

Figure 7.19 Transaction Vote dialog box

Again, you will want to use MTS Spy to monitor the creation and destruction of the objects. Therefore, you should monitor Instance events. You should also monitor Object events. This option will cause MTS Spy to report when objects become activated and deactivated as well. You can also monitor Transaction events with MTS Spy; however, you can more easily monitor such events with MTS Explorer. To monitor events with MTS Explorer, simply click the Transaction Statistics node under My Computer in the left pane of the MTS Explorer window. As Figure 7.20 shows, the Transactions Statistics dialog box appears.

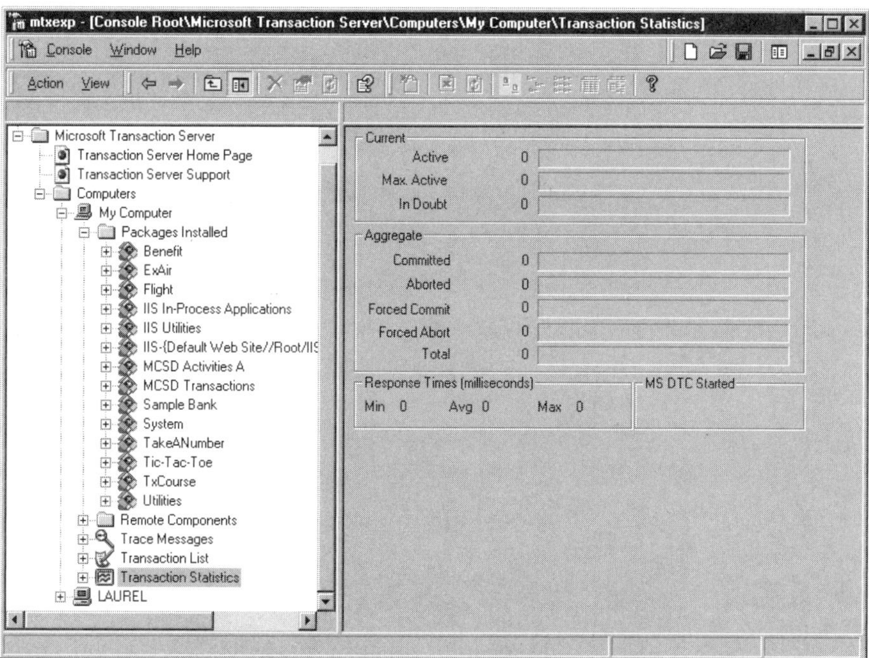

Figure 7.20 Transactions Statistics dialog box in MTS Explorer

This dialog box reports a count of active transactions as well as a count of the total transactions committed and aborted.

With MTS Spy and the Transaction Statistics window, you have everything in place to run a few tests. To create an instance of the root object, use the client program, Client2.exe, found in the Labs\Ch07\Transactions folder on the companion CD. You can see what this program looks like in Figure 7.21.

Figure 7.21 client2.exe

As was Client1.exe, this program was written in Visual Basic. This program has three buttons: Create mtstran1, Call mtstran1::Begin, and Release mtstran1.

Run the Client2.exe program, and click the Create mtstran1 button, followed by the Release mtstran1 button. Remember that the purpose of this step is to activate the package, so that it can be selected from the MTS Spy program. After you have activated the package, select the MCSD Transactions package for monitoring in MTS Spy. Select to see the Instance and Object events of the package.

Click the Create Mtstran1 button again. You should see an event in the MTS Spy program indicating that the object was indeed created. The transaction has not been started because activation has not occurred. Activation occurs with the first method call. Click the Call Mtstran1::Begin button. You should see that one active transaction appears in the Transaction Statistics window.

At this point, the Manage Mtstran2 dialog box should appear. Click the Create Mtstran2 button. Again, you should see an event reported in MTS Spy indicating that the second object was created. Click the Call Mtstran2::SayHello button. You should see a message box with the words Hello World! When you click OK, the Transaction Vote dialog box will appear.

In the Transaction Vote dialog box, you can choose how mtstran2 votes on the transaction. Select EnableCommit and click OK. Control returns to the Manage mtstran2 dialog box. Click Done. You should now see the Transaction Vote dialog box again, this time for mtstran1. Click EnableCommit and click OK. Notice that the transaction is still active, because the context wrapper has not yet been destroyed.

Return to Client2.exe, click the Release mtstran1 button, and reexamine the Transaction Statistics dialog box. The dialog box should now report 0 Active Transactions and 1 Committed Transactions. If you take too long to release the mtstran1 in the Client2.exe program, one transaction would appear as aborted. This occurs because MTS transactions have a default timeout period of 60 seconds. If nothing has happened after 60 seconds, the transaction automatically aborts. As you can see, the client should not control when the transaction ends—imagine what would happen if the operator clicked the Call Mtstran1::Begin button and then left the computer idle. In this case, the transaction would fail.

Next, repeat this procedure, except this time do not select EnableCommit, but choose SetComplete, at both voting stages (mtstran2 and mtstran1). When you choose SetComplete in mtstran2 and click OK, and as soon as the method call ends, you will see an event in MTS Spy denoting that the object has been deactivated. This event will also occur when the root, mtstran1, object votes *SetComplete* and exits the *Begin* method. However, if you look at the Transaction Statistics window, you will notice that the transaction was committed immediately. With this approach, the root component had control over when the transaction was committed or aborted.

Run through the procedure one more time, except this time select SetAbort at the first voting stage (mtstran2), and select SetComplete at the second (mtstran1). You should see that the transaction was aborted.

In addition to the three scenarios in this exercise, you should experiment with as many of your own scenarios as you can, and be sure to record your findings.

Review

The following questions are intended to reinforce key information presented in this chapter. If you are unable to answer a question, review the appropriate lesson and then try answering the question again. Answers to the questions can be found in Appendix B, "Review Questions and Answers," at the back of this book.

1. What are the four rules that all transactions must follow?

2. What is the technique that the context wrapper uses to do preprocessing and postprocessing of every call into an object?

3. In MTS 2, can two objects created by two separate base clients ever take part in the same transaction?

4. What are the four stages of an MTS object's life cycle?

5. True or false: Two MTS components in different computers cannot be part of the same activity because you must use *IObjectContext::CreateInstance* to do so, and you cannot specify a remote computer name with this function.

6. True or false: If you call *SetAbort* within a method call, the transaction is doomed immediately, and nothing can be done to make it succeed.

CHAPTER 8

Microsoft Message Queuing Services

Lesson 1: Installing and Configuring MSMQ 404

Lesson 2: Creating and Using Queues 412

Lesson 3: Transactional Queues 429

Lab 8: Sending and Receiving Persistent Objects In Messages 434

Review 446

About This Chapter

In Chapter 7, you learned that MTS provides a mechanism by which clients can communicate with middle-tier components. A client that wants to communicate with an MTS application remotely uses DCOM (a protocol built on Remote Procedure Calls, or RPCs) to start the MTS surrogate Mtx.exe server and invoke methods on the components in an MTS package.

All of these technologies—MTS, DCOM, and RPC—have one thing in common: they are synchronous in nature. As you might recall, synchronous communication typically involves two entities: a client and a server. For the two entities to communicate, a link must be established. A client must find a specific server, and both client and server must be available at all times. After the client makes a method call to the server, it must wait until the server is done processing the call to get a response.

These systems provide the benefit that calls are guaranteed to be handled in real time, and often sequentially. Synchronous calls also have the advantage of being atomic—that is, when a call finishes, and a client receives a successful return code, the client knows that the server handled the call. Unfortunately, synchronous communication can often be inconvenient. Types of applications in which a connection to the server is not always possible, or in which information needs to be passed and control must return to a client immediately, require *asynchronous* communication.

Asynchronous communication is the core of Microsoft Message Queuing Services (MSMQ), which introduces a middle entity to act as an intermediary between client and server—e-mail. With MSMQ, programs create, locate, and use *queues* (repositories of messages) to send and receive *messages* from one another. In terms of MSMQ, a *message* is an array of bytes that can take the form of legible text (such as "At what time do you arrive?"), database information (such as "WorkOrder=32,Shop=ELEC"), or a binary stream (such as the contents of a .wav file). Important in MSMQ is that both sender and reader know the exact format of the message.

In this chapter, you will learn about MSMQ. You will first learn how to install MSMQ, and set up the various computers in a network according to the MSMQ architecture. You will also learn how to create, manage, and locate queues; as well as send and receive messages. Finally, you will learn how to create transactional queues, and send and receive messages within transactions.

Before You Begin

To complete the lessons in this chapter, you must have:

- Read Chapters 5 and 6 which discuss how to build COM objects
- Read Chapters 7 for an overview of how transactions work

Lesson 1: Installing and Configuring MSMQ

In this lesson, you will learn how to install and structure computers in a network to fit the MSMQ design. Before you begin installation, be aware that you can choose between two different versions of MSMQ: *standard* or *enhanced*. Standard MSMQ is virtually identical to its enhanced counterpart with the exception of two important differences, as follows:

- Standard MSMQ has a limit of 25 concurrent connections at each *primary site controller* (PSC). This lesson will explain PSCs in greater detail, but for now, you should consider PSC generally as a computer that can run Microsoft Windows NT Server.
- Enhanced MSMQ includes the Connector Server, an MSMQ-specific feature that provides a way for MSMQ to interact with non-Microsoft messaging systems, such as the IBM MQSeries.

The enhanced version of MSMQ is available on the second of the Microsoft Windows NT Server 4 Enterprise Edition installation CDs. You can install enhanced MSMQ to take advantage of unlimited concurrent connections as well as the MSMQ Connector Server. Be aware that the standard version of MSMQ is upgraded regularly, whereas enhanced MSMQ is not.

To take advantage of the latest bug fixes and updates to MSMQ and still preserve the features of the enhanced version, you can opt to install enhanced MSMQ initially and simply add standard MSMQ over your initial installation as standard MSMQ becomes upgraded. However, you need only the standard version of MSMQ to complete this chapter successfully.

After this lesson, you will be able to:

- Install MSMQ
- Explain how each computer in a network can fit in the MSMQ architecture

Estimated lesson time: 30 minutes

MSMQ Architecture

Before you begin installing MSMQ, you should be familiar with the particular elements and concepts of this messaging service and the features that MSMQ offers. For instance, MSMQ considers computers to be either servers or clients; both are part of the MSMQ *enterprise*, which is analogous to a corporation or similar organization. Although it is possible for MSMQ to communicate from one enterprise to another, MSMQ is rather designed to handle all communication within a single enterprise.

Within the MSMQ enterprise, computers are grouped into *sites,* or physical subdivisions or branches. MSMQ assumes that communication within computers in a single site is fast, as it is in LANs, whereas communication with other sites is slow and costly, as it is in wide area networks (WANs). Computers within a site do not need to use the same network protocol. Each enterprise needs at least one server computer to act as the primary enterprise controller (PEC), and each site needs at least one server to act as a PSC. The PEC also acts as the PSC of the site in which the server resides.

The PEC creates a database called MSMQ Information Store (MQIS). MQIS is a Microsoft SQL Server database that stores configuration settings relating to the enterprise, and certification keys used to authenticate messages. Each PSC also creates an MQIS for the site to store site-specific configuration information, as well as a list of all the queues in the site. The PEC stores a master copy of the MQIS and replicates it across each PSC. A program can locate a certain queue in a site with the aid of MQIS; Lesson 2 explains this procedure in greater detail.

Sites can optionally have *backup site controllers* (BSCs), which maintain read-only copies of the site's MQIS and can provide MQIS information when the PSC is overloaded or offline. Because the PEC, PSC, and BSCs create a SQL Server database, Microsoft SQL Server 6.5 or later must be installed in each of these computers. To communicate among computers with different protocols, an administrator might choose to add *routing servers*. The function of routing servers is to transfer messages among computers with different protocols. Because routing servers do not create an MQIS, they do not require SQL Server. Computers that use the same networking protocol and are on the same subnet should instead be made part of the same connected network (CN).

MSMQ recognizes two types of client computers: *independent* and *dependent*. Independent clients can create local queues, as well as send and receive messages. However, because they cannot store a copy of MQIS, independent clients are unable to browse or configure queues while they are disconnected from an MSMQ enterprise. This is the most preferable situation for clients that are not always going to be connected to a site, because an application might send messages to a queue and have MSMQ store them locally until the client computer is connected to the network. Dependent clients can send and receive messages only when the clients are connected to a site.

Installing MSMQ

This lesson's introduction provided location details for installing enhanced MSMQ if you choose to do so. As mentioned, however, standard MSMQ is sufficient for completing the exercises in this chapter. The standard version of MSMQ is available in the Microsoft Windows NT 4 Option Pack, which can be downloaded from the Microsoft Web site at *http://www.microsoft.com/ntserver/nts/downloads/recommended/NT4OptPk/default.asp*. The Windows NT 4 Option Pack is available for three Windows operating systems: Microsoft Windows 95/98, Microsoft Windows NT Workstation 4, and Windows NT Server 4.

Standard MSMQ is also included with Microsoft Visual Studio Enterprise Edition. If you are using this installation, you will find the files in the Ntoptpak directory in the second CD. In the Ntoptpak directory, you will find a subdirectory called X86, which in turn contains three subdirectories: Win.95, Winnt.srv, and Winnt.wks. In each of these three subdirectories is a Setup.exe program, which should run as appropriate for each platform.

► **To install the standard version of MSMQ**

1. Run the appropriate setup program. If you are installing in Windows NT 4 with Service Pack 5 or later, you will receive a warning message that reads, "Setup detected that Windows NT 4 SP 4 or greater is installed in your computer. You haven't tested this product on SP 4. Do you want to proceed?" Click Yes.
2. You should see the Windows NT Option Pack 4 splash screen listing all of the software included in the option pack. Click the Next button.
3. The second dialog box is the license agreement; you must click Accept to continue.

4. You will then be prompted to select components, as shown in Figure 8.1.

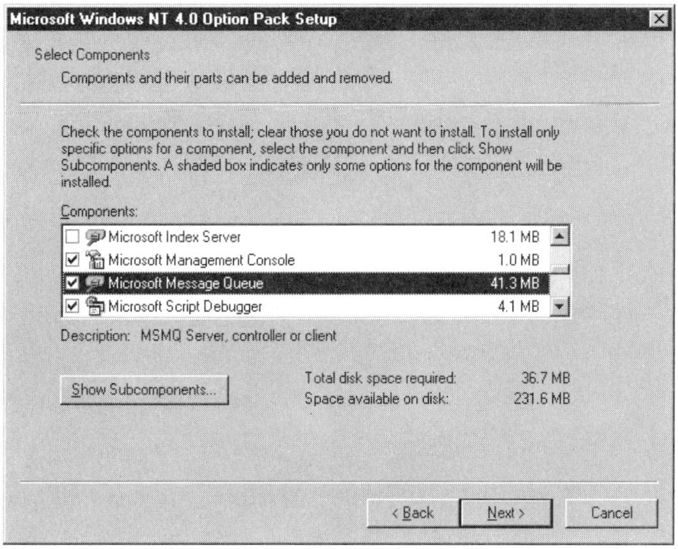

Microsoft Windows NT 4.0 Option Pack Setup

Select Components

Components and their parts can be added and removed.

Check the components to install; clear those you do not want to install. To install only specific options for a component, select the component and then click Show Subcomponents. A shaded box indicates only some options for the component will be installed.

Components:

- [ ] Microsoft Index Server 18.1 MB
- [x] Microsoft Management Console 1.0 MB
- [x] Microsoft Message Queue 41.3 MB
- [x] Microsoft Script Debugger 4.1 MB

Description: MSMQ Server, controller or client

Show Subcomponents...

Total disk space required: 36.7 MB

Space available on disk: 231.6 MB

< Back | Next > | Cancel

Figure 8.1 Selecting components

5. Select Microsoft Message Queue (and any other options you want to install) from the list and click Next. The next screen prompts you to select the type of MSMQ client or server to install (see Figure 8.2).

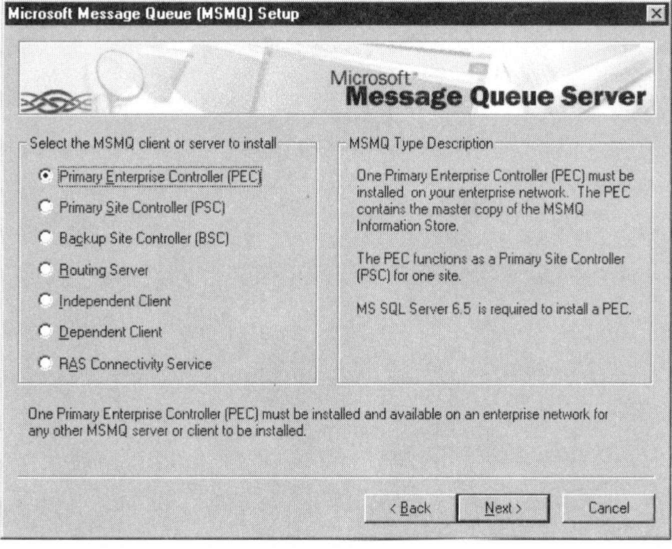

Figure 8.2 Selecting the MSMQ client or server to install

6. Select Primary Enterprise Controller if this is your first time installing MSMQ, and then click Next. You should see the dialog box shown in Figure 8.3.

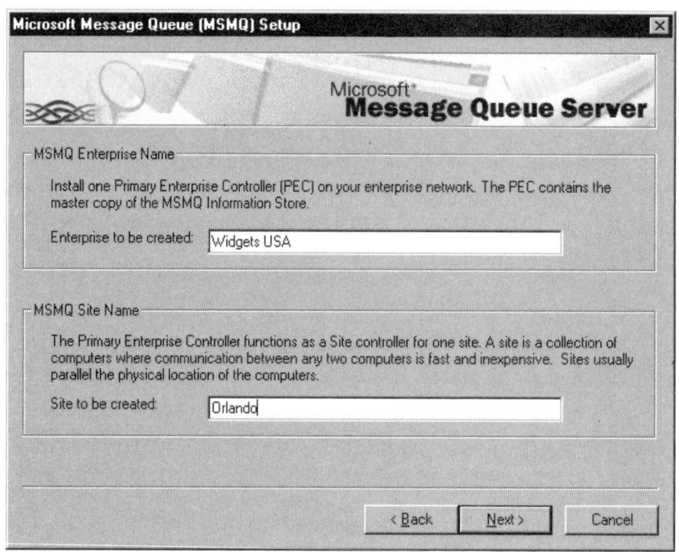

Figure 8.3 MSMQ setup for PEC

7. Type the name for your enterprise, which would most likely be your company's name. For the lab in this chapter, you might want to call the enterprise Widgets USA, the name Figure 8.3 uses as an example.
8. Type a site name. The PEC also serves as the PSC for one site. Again, for the lab, you might want to call the site Orlando as shown in Figure 8.3. Click Next.
9. Select the location for the MSMQ files in the next dialog box, shown in Figure 8.4. The location you choose will be the default location for the database files for the MQIS unless you change the MQIS option in the dialog box. Click Next, and the setup program will install the necessary files.

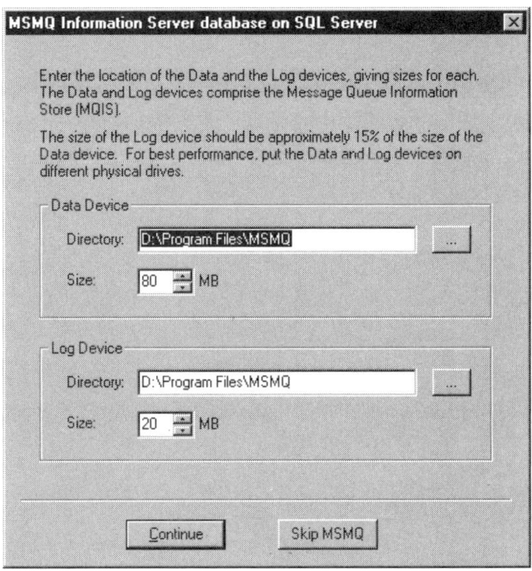

Figure 8.4 MSMQ Information Server database on SQL Server dialog box

10. Type the respective locations for the MQIS files and the log device; sample paths are shown in Figure 8.4. Remember that MQIS only stores configuration information, but not actual messages. Click Continue. You should see the MSMQ Connected Networks dialog box shown in Figure 8.5.

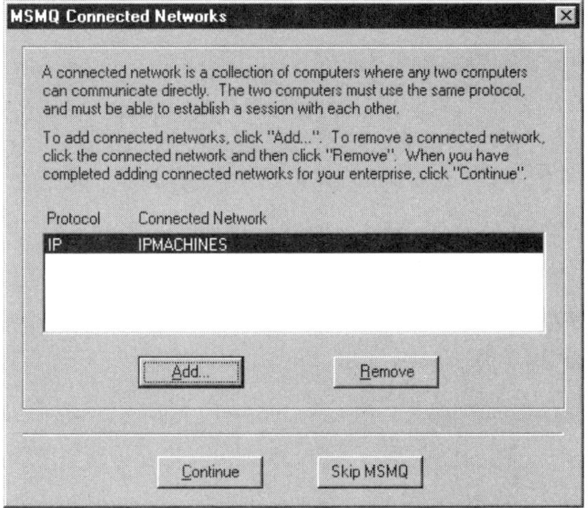

Figure 8.5 MSMQ Connected Networks dialog box

11. The MSMQ Connected Networks dialog box prompts you to create a list of connected networks. As the dialog box reads, a *connected network* is a series of computers that uses the same network protocol for communicating. Connected networks are independent of site boundaries—that is, computers from different sites can share in the same connected network. This dialog box does not ask you to list all the computers, only to create a group name to which you will add computers later, and to specify the protocol they will use. You can choose from two protocols: IP or Internetwork Packet Exchange (IPX). Click the Add button to create a new group name. Select its protocol and click Continue. The installation process should now be complete.

To make sure that the installation worked correctly, open MSMQ Explorer by clicking Start; pointing to Programs, Windows NT 4 Option Pack, and Microsoft Message Queue; and clicking Explorer. You should see the MSMQ Explorer window, shown in Figure 8.6.

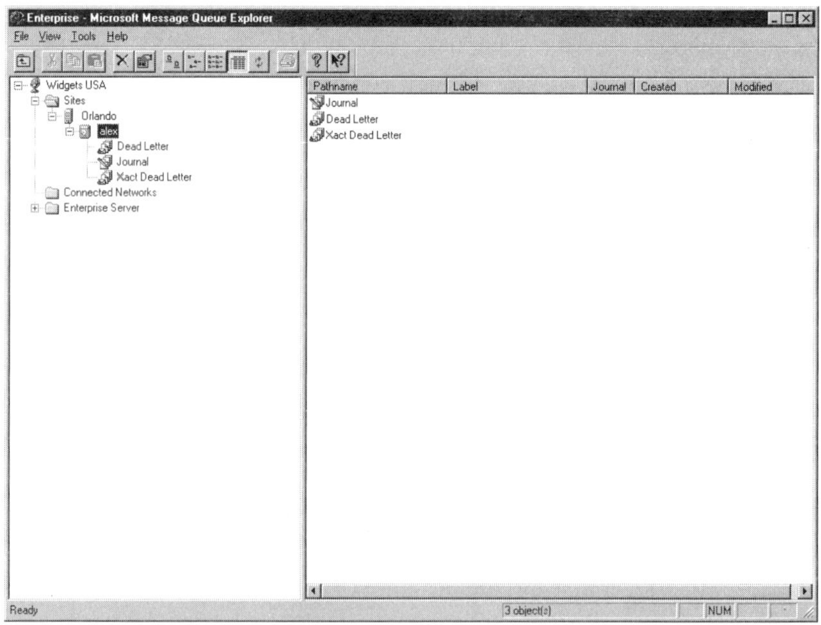

Figure 8.6 MSMQ Explorer window

Lesson Summary

In this lesson, you learned that MSMQ computers can act as either servers or clients. You learned that every MSMQ enterprise needs a PEC, and that MSMQ enterprises are divided into sites, which are managed by PSCs.

Communication among computers in the same site is assumed to be fast, whereas such communication in different sites is assumed to be slow and costly. Computers in the enterprise that communicate with the same protocol are grouped into a connected network. When implementing MSMQ, connected networks can choose from two protocols: IP or IPX. MSMQ servers store management information in MQIS, a SQL Server database.

If you followed the steps in the lesson's installation procedure correctly, you should have set up an enterprise, Widgets USA, containing one site, Orlando. In the next lesson, you will learn how to create, locate, open, and destroy queues; and send and receive messages from a queue.

Lesson 2: Creating and Using Queues

Two APIs are available for writing MSMQ applications: a COM-based API and a C-based API. Using the C-based API can render slightly more power and flexibility at the cost of ease of use. To avoid redundancy by showing both methods, this lesson focuses solely on using the COM-based API to create and use queues in MSMQ.

After this lesson, you will be able to:

- Create, locate, open, and delete queues
- Send and receive messages

Estimated lesson time: 45 minutes

COM Objects

Nine COM interfaces are available for writing MSMQ applications. Three of these—IMSMQTransaction, IMSMQCoordinatedTransactionDispenser, and IMSMQTransactionDispenser—are discussed in the next lesson, which also examines transactional queues. This lesson explains the remaining six interfaces as follows:

- **IMSMQQuery** Use this interface to locate a group of queues that meet a certain criteria.
- **IMSMQQueueInfo** This interface represents a message queue manager, and also allows you to access the properties of a queue. Use this interface to create and open queues.
- **IMSMQQueue** This interface represents a message queue. With this interface, you are able to receive messages from a queue.
- **IMSMQMessage** Use this interface to set and retrieve the contents of a message.
- **IMSMQQueueInfos** This interface provides a user with a collection of IMSMQQueueInfo interfaces obtained from the IMSMQQuery interface.
- **IMSMQEvent** This interface allows you to receive messages asynchronously.

The previous six interfaces are implemented in the Mqoa.dll COM server. To use them in a C++ program, include the Mqoai.h header file (which contains the interface definitions) into your project.

Creating a Queue

You can create a message queue using either MSMQ Explorer or create the queue programmatically. Most of the time, administrators create queues using MSMQ Explorer.

► **To create a message queue with MSMQ Explorer**

1. Open MSMQ Explorer by clicking Start; pointing to Programs, Windows NT 4 Option Pack, and Microsoft Message Queue; and then clicking Explorer.
2. Expand the main Sites branch, and select a site at which you want to create the queue. Expand the branch of your chosen site, and select the site server in which you want to host the queue.
3. Right-click the computer on which you wish to create the queue, and select New from the shortcut menu. The Queue Name dialog box appears, as shown in Figure 8.7.

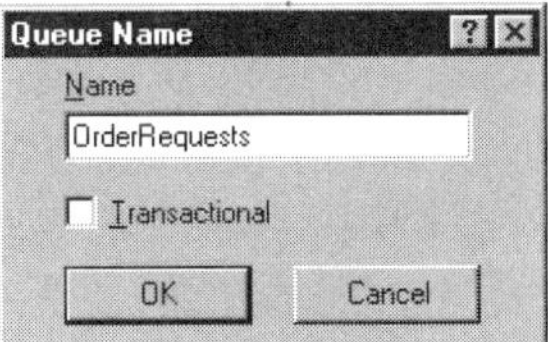

Figure 8.7 Queue Name dialog box

4. Type *OrderRequests* in the Name text field for the queue's name, and leave the Transactional check box under the Name field clear. Be aware that this attribute cannot be changed; therefore, designate the queue as non-transactional (default). (Transactional queues will be explained in detail in Lesson 3.)
5. Click OK. You should see the new queue in the list of queues for the site server you chose in step 2.

To look at your new queue's properties, right-click the newly created queue and select Properties from the shortcut menu. The OrderRequests Queue Properties dialog box, shown in Figure 8.8 on the next page, appears.

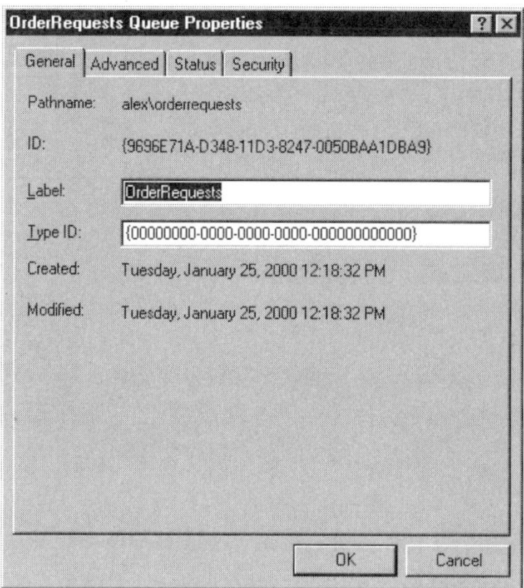

Figure 8.8 OrderRequests Queue Properties dialog box

When you create a queue, the Mqsvc.exe service creates a file to store messages for that queue under the *local queue storage* (LQS). You can find the LQS in the directory where you installed MSMQ in the Storage\Lqs subdirectory. In this directory, you will find a file for each queue that MSMQ creates. The name of each file is a GUID that the MSMQ manager assigns to the queue. You can see the GUID for the queue you created in the ID field on the General tab of the dialog box shown in Figure 8.8. This ID is the name that the MSMQ manager uses to refer to the queue.

When you create a queue, MSMQ assigns a path for the queue. The *path* is the computer name, a backslash, and the name of the queue (for example, Alex\OrderRequests). You can create two types of queues: *public* and *private*.

When the queue is public, as is the OrderRequests queue you created, MSMQ adds a record to the queue table of the MQIS database. In this table, MSMQ stores the ID of the queue and a wide string representation of the path. A client can locate a queue by using the path as long as the computer in which it is running has access to MQIS. MSMQ looks up the path in the queue table to find the ID name of the queue.

Private queues are named as such because they cannot be located with a path; MSMQ does not create an entry in the MQIS for private queues. A client must know the queue's ID to communicate with a private queue. It is easier to create a private queue programmatically than with MSMQ Explorer, but possible by using the latter.

Also in the General tab of your queue's Queue Properties dialog box is the *Type ID,* which is a programmer-assigned GUID used to group queues of similar functionality. You can also locate a queue by its Type ID; the next section will cover locating queues in greater detail.

To create a queue programmatically, you must use the *Create* method of the IMSMQQueueInfo interface. The *Create* method has the following signature:

```
STDMETHODIMP Create(VARIANT FAR* IsTransactional,
    VARIANT FAR* IsWorldReadable);
```

The *IsTransactional* parameter determines whether the queue will be transactional. (Lesson 3 will explain transactional queues in greater detail.) If set to TRUE, the *IsWorldReadable* parameter allows other clients to read from the queue. The default setting for *IsWorldReadable* is FALSE, which requires that only the creator of the queue can read from the queue; other clients can only send messages from the queue.

In addition, you must create an instance of the MSMQQueueInfo object (CLSID_MSMQQueueInfo) with *CoCreateInstance* and obtain a reference to the IMSMQQueueInfo (IID_IMSMQQueueInfo) interface. Next, you must set the path for the queue using the *put_Path* function of the IMSMQQueueInfo interface. This will instruct MSMQ where to create the queue and whether the queue is public or private. You can optionally specify a label for the queue and a Type ID for the queue using the *put_Label* and *put_ServiceTypeGuid* functions, respectively. The following code shows you how to create a queue using the COM APIs:

```
hr = CoCreateInstance(CLSID_MSMQQueueInfo,
    NULL,
    CLSCTX_ALL,
    IID_IMSMQQueueInfo,
    (void **)&pInfo);

if (SUCCEEDED(hr))
{
    CComBSTR bstrPath(L"Alex\\OrderRequests");
    pInfo->put_Path(bstrPath);

    CComBSTR bstrLabel(L"Order Requests");
    pInfo->put_Label(bstrLabel);

    CComVariant vaTransactional(VARIANT_FALSE);
    CComVariant vaIsWorldReadable(VARIANT_TRUE);

    hr = pInfo->Create(&vaTransactional,
        &vaIsWorldReadable);
```

```
    if  (SUCCEEDED(hr))
        MessageBox(NULL,
            _T("Order Requests Creation Succeeded"),
            _T("MSMQ Client"),
            MB_OK);
    else
        MessageBox(NULL,
            _T("Order Requests Creation Failed"),
            _T("MSMQ Client"),
            MB_OK);

    pInfo->Release();
}
```

Note The previous code makes use of the CComBSTR and CComVariant helper classes, both of which are ATL classes. To use these classes, simply include the Objbase.h file in your project.

To see the newly-created queue in your MSMQ Explorer, click the Refresh command on the View menu.

To create a private queue, use the same method as previously described, except that you type *$private* between the computer and queue names in the path (for example, Jose\Private$\OrderRequests).

Locating a Queue

The COM APIs allow you to locate a specific queue with the help of MQIS. To locate a queue, MSMQ provides the IMSMQQuery interface. This interface has a single method, *LookupQueue*, shown in the following code:

```
STDMETHODIMP LookupQueue(
    VARIANT *QueueGuid,
    VARIANT *ServiceTypeGuid,
    VARIANT *Label,
    VARIANT *CreateTime,
    VARIANT *ModifyTime,
    VARIANT *RelServiceType,
    VARIANT *RelLabel,
    VARIANT *RelCreateTime,
    VARIANT *RelModifyTime,
    IMSMQQueueInfos **ppqinfos);
```

The *QueueGuid* parameter allows you to search for a queue by its ID number. This search should return at most one matching queue, because queue IDs are unique. The *LookupQueue* method accepts four additional parameters that define the search criteria: *ServiceTypeGuid*, *Label*, *CreateTime*, and *ModifyTime*.

Note You cannot pass NULL for any of the parameters in this method; doing so will make your program fail. To pass an empty parameter, you must send in a VARIANT structure marked as an optional parameter. The code that follows Table 8.1 shows you how to perform this action. For more information on passing empty parameters, refer to the article titled *SAMPLE: OPTARG: Optional Parameters with Automation.* (This article is included on the Microsoft Developer Network CDs. You can also find it by searching the Microsoft Knowledge Base at *http://search.support.microsoft.com/kb.*)

The next four parameters (*RelServiceType*, *RelLabel*, *RelCreateTime*, and *RelModifyTime*) allow you to control how *LookupQueue* will treat each of the search parameters. The possible values for the *Rel* parameters are shown in Table 8.1.

Table 8.1 *Rel* Parameters and Their Possible Values

Parameter	Value
REL_NOP	Ignore the search parameter
REL_EQ	Look for a value equal to the search parameter
REL_NEQ	Look for a value not equal to the search parameter
REL_LT	Look for a value less than the search parameter
REL_GT	Look for a value greater than the search parameter
REL_LE	Look for a value less than or equal to the search parameter
REL_GE	Look for a value greater than or equal to the search parameter

The last parameter in the *LookupQueue* is the *output* parameter. *LookupQueue* returns a pointer to the IMSMQQueueInfos interface. Notice that this interface name ends with Infos instead of Info to denote a collection of QueueInfo objects. The collection interface allows you to navigate through a series of the QueueInfo objects that match the search criteria. The following code demonstrates how to search for a particular queue by its label:

```
IMSMQQuery *pQuery;

hr = CoCreateInstance(CLSID_MSMQQuery,
    NULL,
    CLSCTX_ALL,
    IID_IMSMQQuery,
    (void **)&pQuery);

if (SUCCEEDED(hr))
{
    IMSMQQueueInfos *pInfoColl;

    // Create an optional parameter
    CComVariant *vtNull = new CComVariant();
    vtNull->vt = VT_ERROR;
    vtNull->scode= DISP_E_PARAMNOTFOUND;
```

```
        hr  =  pQuery->LookupQueue(vtNull,
        vtNull,
        &CComVariant(L"Order Requests"),
        vtNull,
        vtNull,
        vtNull,
        &CComVariant(REL_EQ),
        vtNull,
        vtNull,
        &pInfoColl);
        delete vtNull;

        if (SUCCEEDED(hr))
        {
            hr = pInfoColl->Next(&pInfo);

            if (SUCCEEDED(hr))
        {
            BSTR sQueueGuid;
            pInfo->get_QueueGuid(&sQueueGuid);
        }
        }
}
```

The previous code illustrates how to search for a queue by its label name. When you have the appropriate IMSMQQueueInfo instance, you can open the queue by calling the *Open* method.

Opening a Queue

To open a queue, use the *Open* method in the IMSMQQueueInfo interface. The *Open* method has the following signature:

```
STDMETHODIMP Open(long Access,
    long ShareMode,
    IMSMQQueue ** ppq);
```

In addition to the two parameters in the *Open* method, you must also set the FormatName property of the IMSMQQueueInfo interface to open a queue. The *format name* is simply the word *public* or *private,* followed by an equal sign, followed by the ID number of the queue. An example of a format name is *public=0199594D-C9E2-11D3-8909-0080C8BA8841*. You can obtain this number in one of two ways, as follows:

- If creating the queue programmatically, you can call the *Refresh* method of the IMSMQQueueInfo interface immediately afterward. This will cause the interface to refresh its FormatName property with the values assigned by MSMQ.

- You can search for the query with MSMQQuery, as demonstrated previously. When you find the queue you need, the IMSMQQueueInfo will already have the FormatName property populated.

The *Open* method has two parameters: *Access* and *ShareMode*. The *Access* parameter lets you specify your intentions with the queue by using three options: sending messages (MQ_SEND_ACCESS), peeking at messages (MQ_PEEK_ACCESS), or receiving messages (MQ_RECEIVE_ACCESS). You should keep in mind that you cannot send and receive messages with the same instance of the IMSMQQueue interface. However, you can open the queue twice—once for reading and once for writing. If you open the query for peeking at messages, messages are not removed from the queue. If you open the queue for receiving, you can choose to remove messages from the queue or to leave them in the queue (peek).

The *Open* method's second parameter, *ShareMode*, has two options: MQ_DENY_NONE or MQ_DENY_RECEIVE_SHARE. If you open the queue for sending or peeking, you must set access to MQ_DENY_NONE, the default option, which allows other processes to read from the queue. When opening the queue for receiving, you can also specify MQ_DENY_NONE; otherwise, you can specify MQ_DENY_RECEIVE_SHARE, which only gives access for receiving messages to the process that issued the *Open* call.

The *Open* method returns an instance of the IMSMQQueue interface. You can use this interface to receive messages. You must use this interface also for sending messages, albeit indirectly. The following code shows you how to open the OrderRequests queue for sending messages:

```
IMSMQQueue *ordersq;
hr = pInfo->Open(MQ_SEND_ACCESS,MQ_DENY_NONE,&ordersq);
```

Sending Messages

Sending messages is not done through the IMSMQQueue interface, but rather through the IMSMQMessage interface. Sending a message first involves creating an instance of the message object, then calling the message's *Send* method and passing an instance of the IMSMQQueue interface that was previously opened as the first parameter. This approach gives you the flexibility of sending the same message to multiple queues at multiple times.

The IMSMQMessage interface contains too many properties for this book to devote adequate time to each. Instead, this section shows the minimum number of properties necessary to send a message. Your first step in sending a message is to get a reference to an instance of the IMSMQMessage interface, by using *CoCreateInstance* with the CLSID_MSMQMessage CLSID. When you have a pointer to IMSMQMessage, you can set the contents of the message by setting the value of the Body property.

To accomplish this action, use the *put_Body* function in IMSMQMessage. This function accepts a VARIANT; therefore, anything that you can put into a VARIANT structure can be sent as part of the message. What you can include in your VARIANT are integers, longs, BSTRs, as well as more complex data types such as SAFEARRAYS. Furthermore, you can also store references to an object in either the IDispatch or IUnknown interfaces of the VARIANT structure. The object for which you store references must support a persistent interface such as IPersistStream or IPersistStorage.

When MSMQ detects that the body of the message contains a reference to a COM object, it calls the object's IPersistStream interface and writes the stream into the message body. MSMQ also stores the CLSID of the object in the stream—*GetCLSID* is a function in both IPersistStream and IPersistStorage. The receiving client must have the object's definition in its registry. When the receiving program reads the message, MSMQ creates an instance of the object using the CLSID stored in the message, and then recreates the object's state from the data in the message.

The following code illustrates how to send a message (note that the message contains a reference to an order object):

```
// First, create the message object
IMSMQMessage *pMsg;
hr = CoCreateInstance(CLSID_MSMQMessage,
    NULL,
    CLSCTX_ALL,
    IID_IMSMQMessage,
    (void **) &pMsg);

// Next, create the object that will store the order
information
IOrderInfo *pOrderInfo;
hr = CoCreateInstance(CLSID_OrderInfo,
    NULL,
    CLSCTX_ALL,
    IID_IOrderInfo,
    (void **)&pOrderInfo);

if (SUCCEEDED(hr))
{
    // Set the properties of the order information object
    pOrderInfo->put_InvoiceNo(1000);
    pOrderInfo->put_LastName(CComBSTR("Mojica"));
    pOrderInfo->put_FirstName(CComBSTR("Jose"));

    VARIANT vaBody;
    VariantInit(&vaBody);
    vaBody.vt = VT_DISPATCH;
    pOrderInfo->QueryInterface(IID_IDispatch,
```

```
    (void     **)&vaBody.pdispVal);

    // Set the message properties
    hr = pMsg->put_Label(CComBSTR("Order"));
    hr = pMsg->put_Body(vaBody);

    // Send the message
    hr = pMsg->Send(ordersq,vtNull);

    pMsg->Release();
    pOrderInfo->Release();
}
```

Two other important properties of a message are its label and priority. The label property allows you to assign a name to your message. Keep in mind that only a label assigned by you has meaning to other programs that read this label. The label property has the following signature:

```
STDMETHODIMP put_Label(BSTR bstrLabel);
```

Perhaps the most important property in IMSMQMessage (aside from Body) is a message's priority, which represents a numeral from 0 to 7. The lower the number, the less important the message is. Messages with higher priority numbers are inserted in the queue before messages with lower priority. Messages with equal priority are simply placed in the order in which they were received. The signature for this property is as follows:

```
STDMETHODIMP put_Priority(long lPriority);
```

To set the priority level, you can use a value from MQ_MIN_PRIORITY=0 through MQ_MAX_PRIORITY=7.

When the sending application intends for the receiving program to send a response as the result of receiving a message, the sending application can set the message's ResponseQueueInfo property. This property receives a pointer to an IMSMQQueueInfo interface. In this manner, a sender can create a queue to receive responses. After creating the queue (or locating the queue, if it already exists), the sender will have a pointer to an IMSMQQueueInfo interface. The sender then sets the ResponseQueueInfo property using the *putref_ResponseQueueInfo* function.

When the receiving application receives the message, that application is responsible for determining if the ResponseQueueInfo property has been set. If it has, the application should open the queue specified in ResponseQueueInfo for sending messages, and send a response message.

The body of the message is determined by both the sending and receiving applications. A standard in MSMQ programming is to use the original message's property CorrelationId when sending a response message. The application sending a response message should set the CorrelationId property in IMSMQ-Message to the message's ID number. MSMQ assigns a GUID to each message as it is sent. This GUID is stored in the id property. Therefore, the application sending the original message can obtain the id property after calling the *Send* function (at which point MSMQ assigns the GUID to the message). When receiving a response message, the application can look at the contents of the CorrelationId property, and then associate the response with the original message ID.

A sender can also specify two properties—MaxTimeToReachQueue and MaxTimeToReceive—that determine when a message has expired. Both of these properties allow you to specify an expiration time, which you specify in seconds. The MaxTimeToReachQueue gives you a time limit in which the message must arrive at the destination queue. A message travels from one server to another in the enterprise until it reaches the queue. If the message does not reach the queue within the specified amount of time, MSMQ places the message in a *dead letters* queue, which is a special system queue that MSMQ creates whenever you add a server to your enterprise.

Receiving Messages

Receiving a message essentially involves removing the message from the message queue. However, you can make a request to MSMQ to only provide you with the information stored in a message without removing it from the queue; this procedure is called *peeking*. Later, you will examine peeking more fully; first, however, this section will provide you with an overview of how MSMQ allows messages to be received.

In Chapter 7 and at the beginning of this chapter, you learned that messages can be received synchronously or asynchronously. In MSMQ, you can allow synchronous message retrieval through the IMSMQQueue interface with the *Receive* method. The *Receive* method has the following signature:

```
STDMETHODIMP Receive(VARIANT* Transaction,
    VARIANT* WantDestinationQueue,
    VARIANT* WantBody,
    VARIANT* ReceiveTimeout,
    IMSMQMessage **ppmsg);
```

The purpose of the *Receive* function is to receive a reference to the IMSMQ-Message interface. In the previous section, you learned that the IMSMQMessage interface has a *put_Body* function that allows you to set the contents of the message. To retrieve the contents of the message, use the *get_Body* function instead. The *get_Body* function returns a VARIANT structure with the data contents of the message. If the contents refer to an object, the VARIANT structure will store a pointer to an IUnknown interface. MSMQ recreates the object from the CLSID, and populates its member variables by calling IPersistStream's *Load* method.

Receiving a message synchronously is a timed operation. You can specify how long you want to wait for a message using the *ReceiveTimeout* parameter. You can use the *INFINITE* constant if you want to wait an undetermined amount of time for a message. The first parameter, *Transaction*, informs MSMQ if the receive operation is to be part of a transaction. Lesson 3 will discuss this parameter in greater detail.

Additional parameters used for synchronous message receiving are TRUE/FALSE parameters. When *WantDestinationQueue* is set to VARIANT_TRUE (stored in a VARIANT structure), MSMQ populates the *DestinationQueueInfo* parameter of the IMSMQMessage interface (use *get_DestinationQueueInfo* to retrieve it). The *DestinationQueueInfo* stores a pointer to an IMSMQQueueInfo interface—in this case, the interface stores information about the queue for which the message was intended. MSMQ sets the *DestinationQueueInfo* parameter in the IMSMQMessage interface whenever a message is sent. This is particularly useful if the message delivery time expired (recall the MaxTimeToReachQueue property) and the message was transferred to a dead letters queue.

The *WantBody* parameter tells MSMQ whether you want to retrieve the body contents of the message. If you do not need the contents of the body, then you should set this parameter to VARIANT_FALSE to improve the performance of receiving the message.

The *Receive* method extracts the first message in the message queue. If you want to study the message contents without removing it from the queue, you can implement peeking by using the *Peek* function. The *Peek* function has the following signature:

```
STDMETHODIMP Peek(VARIANT* WantDestinationQueue,
    VARIANT* WantBody,
    VARIANT* ReceiveTimeout,
    IMSMQMessage**ppmsg);
```

As you might notice, the *Peek* function has the same signature as the *Receive* function (except that it lacks the first parameter in *Receive(VARIANT* Transaction)*). The purpose of each parameter is the same as in *Receive*. The only difference is that a call to *Peek* does not remove the message from the queue.

When you open a queue with the *Open* method in MSMQQueueInfo, MSMQ creates a cursor for the queue. A cursor is a placeholder that indicates the current message within the queue. *Receive* and *Peek* both retrieve information from the first message. These two functions, when called, place the cursor position at the top of the queue. You can advance the cursor by calling the *PeekNext* function, which has the following signature:

```
STDMETHODIMP PeekNext(VARIANT* WantDestinationQueue,
    VARIANT* WantBody,
    VARIANT* ReceiveTimeout,
    IMSMQMessage** ppmsg)
```

This function has the same signature as *Peek*, except that *PeekNext* moves the cursor location to the next message in the queue first, and then either retrieves information for the next message (if one exists), or waits until a new message arrives. If the cursor no longer points at the first message in the queue, and you want to retrieve the message, you cannot use *Receive* because, as mentioned earlier, this method places the cursor at the top of the queue. However, MSMQ provides the *ReceiveCurrent* function as an alternative to remedy this conflict. Use *ReceiveCurrent* to retrieve the message at the current cursor location. The signature for this function is as follows:

```
STDMETHODIMP ReceiveCurrent(VARIANT* Transaction,
    VARIANT* WantDestinationQueue,
    VARIANT* WantBody,
    VARIANT* ReceiveTimeout,
    IMSMQMessage** ppmsg);
```

When receiving with the *Receive* function and examining with the *Peek* method, the operation for the messages is synchronous—the program will pause until either a message is received or the operation exceeds the amount specified in the *ReceiveTimout* parameter.

The actual sending and receiving of messages is an asynchronous operation—the sender does not have to be connected to the receiver in order to communicate with it. This is because the sender communicates with a message queue and not with the receiver. The sender does not have to wait until the receiver receives the message to continue executing the rest of the program. So far, you have seen that the receiving program does have to wait for the message queue to contain a message (as a synchronous operation). But it is also possible to receive messages asynchronously by making a request to MSMQ to notify you when a new message arrives. Receiving messages asynchronously is somewhat complex, because the COM interface for MSMQ was designed to be used with scripting clients. Thus, receiving a notification has to be done through connection point objects. In addition, because scripting clients support only the IDispatch interface, your event sink (the class that will receive notifications from MSMQ) must be derived from IDispatch.

To receive messages asynchronously, you must first create a COM class that implements IDispatch. The easiest way to do this using the ATL Object Wizard is to insert a new simple object into your project. Set the interface parameter in the wizard to *Dual*, which will produce an interface derived from IDispatch.

This procedure will also provide you with a class implementation derived from IDispatchImpl. When you have generated the source code with the wizard, you must add the following to your class:

```
[id(0), helpstring("method Arrived")] HRESULT
Arrived([in] IDispatch *Queue, [in] long Cursor);

[id(1), helpstring("method ArrivedError")] HRESULT
ArrivedError([in] IDispatch * Queue,[in] long
ErrorCode,[in] long Cursor);
```

Make sure to match the id attributes with the previous declaration—MSMQ does not ask for a DispID dynamically like other clients using IDispatch. A scripting client normally calls the *GetIDsOfNames* method in IDispatch to obtain a DispID of a member function based on its name. MSMQ assumes that the *Arrived* method has a DispID of 0.

After adding the two methods to the interface definition and implementing them, you must modify the interface map of the class to map the DIID__DMSMQEventEvents GUID to the IDispatch interface. MSMQ does a *QueryInterface* for this GUID when connecting your class to the event connection point (explained later in this section), shown in the following code:

```
BEGIN_COM_MAP(CSendOrderReceive)
    COM_INTERFACE_ENTRY(ISendOrderReceive)
    COM_INTERFACE_ENTRY(IDispatch)
    COM_INTERFACE_ENTRY_IID(DIID__DMSMQEventEvents,
        IDispatch)END_COM_MAP()
```

When you have a class derived from IDispatch that implements the *Arrived* and *ArrivedError* methods, and supports the DIID__DMSMQEventEvents GUID, you are ready to ask for events by using connection point objects, provided by MSMQ. To ask MSMQ for notifications, first create an instance of the MSMQEvent object, and then obtain a pointer to the IMSMQEvent interface as follows:

```
IMSMQEvent *event;
HRESULT hr = S_OK;
hr = CoCreateInstance(CLSID_MSMQEvent,
    NULL,
    CLSCTX_ALL,
    IID_IMSMQEvent,
    (void **)&event);
```

The MSMQEvent object implements the IConnectionPointContainer interface. Obtain a pointer to this interface, and then call the *FindConnectionPoint* method in the interface. The first parameter in this method is the GUID of the connection point interface for which you are searching. The GUID you need is DIID__DMSMQEventEvents. The second parameter is an *out* parameter; it will contain a pointer to an IConnectionPoint interface if the call is successful. Use the pointer to IConnectionPoint to connect your event sink class with the MSMQ event source, by first calling the *Advise* method of the IConnectionPoint interface, and then passing a reference to the IUnknown interface of your event sink class. You will learn more about this process in Lab 8.

The following code shows the entire process of connecting an event sink class to the appropriate connection point. The code uses a smart pointer to make the job easier, shown as follows:

```
CComQIPtr<IConnectionPointContainer> pContainer = event;

if (pContainer)
{
    CComQIPtr<IConnectionPoint> cp;
    pContainer->FindConnectionPoint(
        DIID__DMSMQEventEvents,&cp);
    if (cp)
    {
        cp->Advise(rcv.GetUnknown(),&dwCookie);
    }
}
```

In the previous example, the *rcv* parameter in the *Advise* call is an instance of the event sink class. The code in this section so far only helps you create an event sink class, and then shows you how to create an instance of the MSMQEvent class and connect the two classes with the connection point mechanism. You still have to tell MSMQ that you want to receive notifications by using the *EnableNotification* method of the IMSMQQueue interface. The *EnableNotification* method has the following signature:

```
STDMETHODIMP EnableNotification(IMSMQEvent* Event,
    VARIANT* Cursor,
    VARIANT* ReceiveTimeout)
```

The first parameter is a pointer to an IMSMQEvent interface. This is the class you learned about earlier—the class with the connection point. The second parameter is *Cursor*. The *Cursor* parameter is used to tell MSMQ the position within the queue from which you want to receive messages. This parameter contains three possible values, shown as follows:

```
MQMSG_FIRST=0,
MQMSG_CURRENT = 1,
MQMSG_NEXT = 2
```

The first time you call the *EnableNotification* method, use the MQMSG_FIRST cursor position to ask MSMQ if the queue contains any messages. If it does, MSMQ will call the *Arrived* method of your event sink class. It will also place the cursor (position marker) to the first message. You can then ask MSMQ to notify you if another message arrives and is placed in the same location

(MQMSG_CURRENT) or if the new message was placed after the current location (MQMSG_NEXT).

The following code demonstrates how to use the *EnableNotification* method:

```
hr = pOrderRequestQueue->EnableNotification(
    event,&CComVariant(MQMSG_FIRST),
    &CComVariant((long)INFINITE));
```

Making this call will not pause execution of the program; the caller can continue executing the rest of the code. When a message arrives, MSMQ will call the *Arrived* method in the event sink class, shown as follows:

```
STDMETHODIMP Arrived(IDispatch *Queue, long Cursor)
{
    return S_OK;
}
```

This method reports the queue that contains the message in the first parameter, *Queue*. This report might seem unusual, because you have to call *EnableNotification* on a particular queue anyway. Additionally, you could receive notifications from more than one queue in the same event sink class by creating multiple Event objects and connecting all to a single event sink class.

When you receive a notification that a message has arrived, you must call *EnableNotification* again to continue receiving messages.

Deleting a Queue

You can delete a queue by using MSMQ Explorer or coding programmatically. To delete it with MSMQ Explorer, simply locate the queue in the left pane. You might need to open the Sites branch, the branch for your particular site, and then the branch for the computer within the site that contains the queue. When you locate the queue, right-click the queue name and select Delete from the shortcut menu. MSMQ Explorer will prompt you to confirm the deletion; simply click Yes to complete the deletion. Remember that MSMQ assigns a GUID to each queue. If you delete a queue and recreate it with the same name, the queue will have a different ID.

You can delete a queue programmatically using the *Delete* method of the IMSMQQueue interface. The *Delete* method has the following signature:

```
STDMETHODIMP Delete();
```

This function takes no parameters, and has no output parameters (except the standard HRESULT return value).

Instead of deleting a queue, you might want only to purge all the messages from a queue, by using MSMQ Explorer. In MSMQ Explorer, locate the queue, right-click the queue name in the left pane, and select Purge from the shortcut menu. When you are prompted to confirm the purge, click Yes, and MSMQ will delete all the messages from the queue.

To perform purges programmatically requires a bit of ingenuity because no programmatic purge command exists per se. However, you can call the *Receive* method until no more messages are left in the queue. Remember that *Receive* extracts the first message in the queue, but be sure that you don't use the INFINITE value for the *timeout* parameter, or the program will halt when no other messages remain in the queue.

Lesson Summary

In this lesson, you learned the basics of sending and receiving messages. You learned how to create a queue, first using MSMQ Explorer, and then using the IMSMQQueueInfo interface when creating a queue programmatically. You also learned that queues have an id property, a GUID that MSMQ assigns to the queue.

When creating a queue, you learned that you also create a path for the queue, by first specifying the name of the server at which you want to create the queue, and then specifying the name of the actual queue. MSMQ stores paths in MQIS; you can have MSMQ use MQIS to translate a certain path to an ID number.

In addition, you learned how to locate a queue using the IMSMQQuery interface. This interface allows you to specify search criteria, and returns a collection of IMSMQQueueInfo objects (IMSMQQueueInfos).

When you locate a queue, you can open it with the *IMSMQQueueInfo::Open* function. At the time you open the queue, you must specify if you want to send messages to or retrieve messages from the queue. To send messages to a queue, you must first create an MSMQMessage object and set the Body property of the object. Next, you must call the *Send* function.

Receiving messages is done through the IMSMQQueue interface and its *Receive* function, which removes messages from the queue. You can also peek at messages, although allow them to remain in the queue, with the *Peek* function.

You can receive messages synchronously or asynchronously. Receiving messages asynchronously involves creating an Event object and connecting to it through a connection point.

Lesson 3: Transactional Queues

So far in this chapter, you have learned how to create, locate, open, and delete queues. You also learned how you can both send messages to or receive messages from an opened queue. In this lesson, you will learn how to send and receive messages within the confines of a transaction.

After this lesson, you will be able to:

- Create transactional queues
- Send and receive messages during a transaction

Estimated lesson time: 30 minutes

Transactional Messaging

The methods that you have learned so far for creating queues and sending and receiving messages suffer from several problems. First, the underlying mechanism that MSMQ uses for sending the messages does not guarantee that the same message will be delivered more than once. Also, messages might not be received in the order in which they were sent.

In addition, applications must be able to send a number of messages at the same time as a unit. For example, for an order system, you must send two messages: one to charge the client and one to deplete inventory. Both messages must be delivered; if one is delivered, but one is not, the order system fails; these messages must be processed as one unit.

You can solve such problems using *transactional messaging,* which guarantees the following:

- Messages are placed in the queue in the order in which they were sent; such messages are sent exactly once.
- Messages sent within a transaction are all sent as a unit.
- Messages received within a transaction are all received as a unit.

MSMQ is able to work with three different transaction coordinators: the MSMQ internal transaction coordinator, Microsoft Distributed Transaction Coordinator (MS DTC) directly, or MS DTC though a transaction managed by MTS.

Creating a Transactional Queue

Transactional messages can be sent or received only from transactional queues. In the previous lesson, you learned how to create a nontransactional queue through either MSMQ Explorer or hard coding; you can use these methods to create a transactional queue as well.

► **To create a transactional queue using MSMQ Explorer**

1. In the MSMQ Explorer window, select the server in which you want to create the queue, and right-click the server icon.
2. Point to New and then select Queue from the shortcut menu. You will be prompted with the Queue Name dialog box, shown previously in Figure 8.7.
3. Type a name for the queue as you did when creating a nontransactional queue in the previous lesson. Select the Transactional check box and click OK.

Remember from the previous lesson that when you have created a queue and marked it as either transactional or nontransactional, you cannot change the queue's properties.

You can also create a transactional queue programmatically. To create a queue programmatically, you must use the *Create* method of the IMSMQQueueInfo interface. The *Create* method has the following signature:

```
STDMETHODIMP Create(VARIANT FAR* IsTransactional,
VARIANT FAR* IsWorldReadable);
```

Set the first parameter, *IsTransactional*, to VARIANT_TRUE. For example, your code might read, *&CComVariant(VARIANT_TRUE)*. The second parameter, *IsWorldReadable*, works the same way as with nontransactional queues (refer to Lesson 2 for a review).

Sending and Receiving Messages Within a Transaction

When you have a transactional queue from which to send and receive messages, you must decide which transactional coordinator system to use. You can use one of three systems: the internal coordinator that MSMQ provides, MS DTC, or an MTS transaction already in progress.

Using the MSMQ Internal Transaction Coordinator

The first step in sending or receiving a transactional message using the internal transaction coordinator is to create an instance of the MSMQTransactionDispenser object. You must obtain a reference to the IMSMQTransactionDispenser interface, and then call the *BeginTransaction* method of this interface. The *BeginTransaction* method returns a pointer to the IMSMQTransaction interface. Use this interface pointer as the second parameter in the *Send* function of the

IMSMQMessage interface, or in the *Receive* function of the IMSMQQueue interface. The messages are not sent or received until you complete the transaction by calling the *Commit* method in the IMSMQTransaction interface, as demonstrated in the following code:

```
IMSMQTransactionDispenser *pDispenser;

hr = CoCreateInstance(CLSID_MSMQTransactionDispenser,
    ULL,
    LSCTX_ALL,
    ID_IMSMQTransactionDispenser,
    void **)&pDispenser);
```

Create an instance of the MSMQTransactionDispenser object using *CoCreate-Instance*. Ask for a pointer to the IMSMQTransactionDispenser interface. Next, initiate the transaction by calling the *BeginTransaction* method of the IMSMQ-TransactionDispenser interface, using the following code:

```
IMSMQTransaction *pTransaction;
hr = pDispenser->BeginTransaction(&pTransaction);
```

The *BeginTransaction* function returns a pointer to an IMSMQTransaction interface. Use this interface pointer whenever you send or receive messages.

To send messages within a transaction, use the following code:

```
hr = pOrderMsg->Send(pOrderRequestQueue1,
    &CComVariant(pTransaction));
hr = pOrderMsg->Send(pOrderRequestQueue2,
    &CComVariant(pTransaction));
hr = pOrderMsg->Send(pOrderRequestQueue3,
    &CComVariant(pTransaction));
```

The previous code sends the same message to three separate queues, all of which are transactional. The messages will not be sent until the transaction is committed with the *Commit* function in the IMSMQTransaction interface, as follows:

```
pTransaction->Commit(&CComVariant(0),
    &CComVariant(0),
    &CComVariant(0));
```

The first and third parameters are reserved for use by MS DTC when you use MS DTC as your transaction coordinator. The second parameter allows you to specify whether you want the commit to occur either asynchronously, with XACTTC_ASYNC (execution of the program continues before messages are sent); or synchronously, with XACTTC_SYNCPHASEONE (the commit does not return until all messages have been sent).

Receiving messages within a transaction is done in exactly the same fashion, except that you use the *Receive* method of the IMSMQQueue interface. The first parameter in this function is a pointer to the IMSMQTransaction interface. Therefore, to receive messages within a transaction, write the following:

```
hr = pOrderQueue->Receive(&CComVariant(pTransaction)...)
```

The message information is read immediately, but the messages are not removed from the queue until the *Commit* takes place.

Using MS DTC as Your Transaction Coordinator

Sending messages using the internal transaction coordinator offers the best performance; however, this option does not allow you to integrate with other transaction coordinators. You learned in Chapter 7 that MTS as well as other Microsoft packages, such as SQL Server, use MS DTC for coordinating transactions.

By using MS DTC, MSMQ messages can run in conjunction with SQL Server queries (for example, through ADO). The outcome of the transaction will determine the fate of both the Queries and the messages. To use MS DTC as the transaction coordinator use the IMSMQCoordinatedTransactionDispenser interface. Just as in the case of the IMSMQTransactionDispenser interface, this interface has a method called *BeginTransaction* that returns a pointer to an IMSMQ-Transaction interface. Use this pointer to send and receive messages with the *Send* and *Receive* methods, in exactly the same fashion as with the internal coordinator.

Sending Messages within MTS Transactions

In Chapter 7, you learned that transaction programming with MTS is somewhat different from traditional transaction programming. The main difference is that objects do not begin transactions explicitly. Instead, objects are marked as transactional through the settings in MTS Explorer. When a client creates an object that is marked as requiring a transaction, MTS initiates the transaction with MS DTC. MTS objects then vote on the outcome of the transaction (for more information, see Chapter 7).

You can instruct MSMQ to use an MS DTC transaction already in progress when sending or receiving messages from within an MTS object. Previously, you created an object that served as a transaction dispenser, and called *BeginTransaction* to obtain a pointer to the IMSMQTransaction interface. When sending messages within MTS transactions, MTS has already started the transaction; therefore, you do not have to create a transaction dispenser or call *BeginTransaction*. MSMQ is able to use the existing transaction by allowing you to send in a special value, MQ_MTS_TRANSACTION, instead of a pointer to the IMSMQTransaction interface when sending and receiving messages. To use this value when sending messages, implement the following code:

```
hr   =   pOrderMsg->Send(pOrderRequestQueue1,
    &CComVariant(MQ_MTS_TRANSACTION));
```

As you can see, the MQ_MTS_TRANSACTION parameter is sent as the second parameter in the *Send* function. In the previous example, you specified a pointer to an IMSMQTransaction interface instead. Whether the messages are sent or not depends on the outcome of the transaction, which is determined by how the objects vote in the transaction.

Lesson Summary

Transactional messaging has several advantages over nontransactional messaging. With transactional messaging, messages are guaranteed to be delivered in order and exactly once. To send and receive messages within a transaction, you must first create a transactional queue. Transactional queues are created either programmatically with the *IMSMQQueueInfo::Create* method, or nonprogrammatically with MSMQ Explorer.

To send and receive transactional messages, you must first choose the transactional coordinator you want to employ. MSMQ supports three transaction coordinators: the internal transaction coordinator, MS DTC, or an MTS transaction already in progress.

To send a message or receive messages within an internal transaction, you first create and instance of the IMSMQTransactionDispenser object. Next, call the *BeginTransaction* function in the interface to obtain a pointer to the IMSMQTransaction interface. Use this pointer as the second parameter in the *Send* function, or the first parameter of the *Receive* function.

To send a message or receive a message within an MS DTC coordinated transaction, create an instance of the IMSMQCoordinatedTransactionDispenser. Use the *BeginTransaction* function of this interface to begin a transaction and obtain a pointer to the IMSMQTransaction interface. Finally, use this pointer as the transaction parameter in the *Send* and *Receive* functions.

To send and receive messages within an MTS transaction, send *&CComVariant(MQ_MTS_TRANSACTION)* in the transaction parameter of the *Send* and *Receive* functions.

In the lab for this chapter, you will send and receive messages that transfer the contents of a persistable COM object.

Lab 8: Sending and Receiving Persistent Objects In Messages

In this lab, you will create a COM object with support for IPersistStream, and also send and receive messages that contain a persisted state of the object. In addition, you will also locate and open a queue, and send and receive messages.

Estimated lab time: 60 minutes

Exercise 1: Creating a Persistable Object

In this exercise, you will create the OrderInfo COM object, which will contain three properties: InvoiceNo, LastName and FirstName. This object will represent invoice information in a tracking system. In the next exercise, you will create a message queue programmatically, and send order requests in messages containing the persisted state of your OrderInfo object.

► **Create a persistable COM object in ATL**

1. Select New from the File menu. The New dialog box appears.
2. Click the Projects tab, select ATL COM AppWizard, type *OrderObjects* as the project name, and then click OK. In ATL COM AppWizard, click Finish to select the default values. Click OK in the New Project Information dialog box.
3. From the Insert menu, select New ATL Object. Select Simple Object from the ATL Object Wizard and click Next. Type *InvoiceInfo* as the object's short name. Click OK to generate the code.
4. Add a few properties to the InvoiceInfo object. In the ClassView of your Project Workspace window, right-click the IInvoiceInfo interface and select Add Property from the shortcut menu.
5. When the Add Property dialog box appears, type *long* for the property type and *InvoiceNo* for the property name. You can leave all the other settings as their default values. Click OK, and then add two more properties in the same fashion. Create a LastName property and a FirstName property, both of type BSTR.
6. Implement the properties in your object. The properties only need to store the appropriate values and report them when requested. Add three member variables as private to your InvoiceInfo.h file, and add code to your InvoiceInfo.cpp file as follows:

```
private:
    long m_lInvoiceNo;
    BSTR m_sLastName;
    BSTR m_sFirstName;
```

```
// Initialize the variables in the object's
constructor, as follows:

CInvoiceInfo():
m_lInvoiceNo(0),
m_sLastName(NULL),
m_sFirstName(NULL)
{
}

// Modify the code in your InvoiceInfo.cpp to store
and report the property values, as follows:

STDMETHODIMP CInvoiceInfo::get_InvoiceNo(long *pVal)
{
    *pVal = m_lInvoiceNo;
    return S_OK;
}

STDMETHODIMP CInvoiceInfo::put_InvoiceNo(long newVal)
{
    m_lInvoiceNo = newVal;
    return S_OK;
}

STDMETHODIMP CInvoiceInfo::get_LastName(BSTR *pVal)
{
    *pVal = m_sLastName;
    return S_OK;
}

STDMETHODIMP CInvoiceInfo::put_LastName(BSTR newVal)
{
    m_sLastName = newVal;
    return S_OK;
}

STDMETHODIMP CInvoiceInfo::get_FirstName(BSTR *pVal)
{
    *pVal = m_sFirstName;
    return S_OK;
}

STDMETHODIMP CInvoiceInfo::put_FirstName(BSTR newVal)
{
    m_sFirstName = newVal;
    return S_OK;
}
```

7. With the properties implemented, add support for IPersistStream. Although template implementation helper for IPersistStream is not available, IPersistStreamInit does have such a helper. Because the vtables are identical between IPersistStream and IPersistStreamInit (except for one extra method in IPersistStreamInit), you can use the IPersistStreamInitImpl helper template.
8. Derive your class from IPersistStreamInitImpl as follows (take care to make the appropriate changes to InvoiceInfo.h):

```
class ATL_NO_VTABLE CInvoiceInfo:
    public CComObjectRootEx<CComSingleThreadModel>,
    public CComCoClass<CInvoiceInfo,
        &CLSID_InvoiceInfo>,
    public IDispatchImpl<IInvoiceInfo,
        &IID_IInvoiceInfo,
        &LIBID_ORDEROBJECTSLib>,
        public IPersistStreamInitImpl<CInvoiceInfo>
```

9. Add IPersistStream to the interface map. You should also add IPersist to the interface map, and optionally you can add IPersistStreamInit. This interface is readily available for your use when you implement IPersistStreamInitImpl. Make the following changes to the interface map in your INVOICEINFO.H header file:

```
BEGIN_COM_MAP(CInvoiceInfo)
    COM_INTERFACE_ENTRY(IInvoiceInfo)
    COM_INTERFACE_ENTRY(IDispatch)
    COM_INTERFACE_ENTRY(IPersistStreamInit)
    COM_INTERFACE_ENTRY2(IPersistStream,
        IPersistStreamInit)
    COM_INTERFACE_ENTRY2(IPersist,IPersistStreamInit)
END_COM_MAP()
```

10. The IPersistStreamInitImpl interface requires that you declare a property map. A property map is an array of properties. IPersistStreamInitImpl looks at this property map when it writes the property contents to the stream, and reads from the stream. To declare a property map, add the following code to the public section of your class declaration:

```
BEGIN_PROP_MAP(CInvoiceInfo)
    PROP_ENTRY("InvoiceNo",1,CLSID_NULL)
    PROP_ENTRY("LastName",2,CLSID_NULL)
    PROP_ENTRY("FirstName",3,CLSID_NULL)
END_PROP_MAP()
```

11. If you examine the property map, you will notice that the entries have three parameters. The firs parameter is a string name for the property. You can assign any name to this parameter that you want—this name does not have to match the property name.

    The second parameter is the PropID for the property. PropIDs are defined in the Interface Definition Language (IDL) file. If you look at the interface definition in the OrderObjects.idl file, you will find that each property declaration is preceded with an ID attribute—for example: *[... id(1) ...] HRESULT InvoiceNo()*. Use this ID number in the second parameter of the PROP_ENTRY macro.

    The third parameter is the CLSID of a property page that you can use to change this property value. Keep in mind that this parameter doesn't normally apply to property pages, which only apply to the context of ActiveX controls. Use CLSID_NULL for the last parameter.

12. In addition to adding a property map, you must declare the *BOOL m_bRequiresSave* variable. The template needs this variable to tell it when the properties need to be persisted. Clients using IPersistStream might ask the object if the properties need persisting by calling the *IsDirty* method of the interface. The implementation returns the value of the *m_bRequiresSave* variable; you should set *m_bRequiresSave* to TRUE if any of the properties have changed in value. Place the following declaration as a public member of your class:

```
public:
    BOOL m_bRequiresSave;
```

13. You must make the template recognize when to set this value to TRUE. You should set *m_bRequiresSave* to TRUE in each of your *put** property functions. The code below shows you how this is done in the LastName property. Make the same change to the other *put* functions as demonstrated in the following:

```
STDMETHODIMP CInvoiceInfo::put_LastName(BSTR newVal)
{
    m_sLastName = newVal;
    m_bRequiresSave=TRUE;
    return S_OK;
}
```

14. Also, make sure to initialize the *m_bRequiresSave* variable to TRUE in the class constructor.

15. The implementation of IPersistStreamInit returns E_NOTIMPL for one of its crucial members: *GetSizeMax*. Although some clients do not rely on this E_NOTIMPL value, MSMQ does. You must return the number of bytes that you have placed into the stream. Add the following code to the header file:

```
STDMETHOD(GetSizeMax)(ULARGE_INTEGER FAR* pcbSize)
{
    pcbSize->LowPart = sizeof(DWORD)+
        sizeof(long)+
        sizeof(WCHAR)*wcslen(m_sLastName)+
        sizeof(WCHAR)*wcslen(m_sFirstName);
    pcbSize->HighPart = 0L;
    return NOERROR;
}
```

16. Build your project.

Exercise 2: Sending Messages

If you followed all the instructions in the previous exercise, you should have set up an enterprise in MSMQ Explorer, along with a single site, Orlando. The Orlando site should contain one computer, yours; your computer should in turn have one queue: OrderRequests. If you did not create the queue, do not worry about creating it by hand; your program will check if the queue exists, and create it for you if you haven't created a queue previously.

A Microsoft Visual Basic client, which you can use to send messages, is available in the Labs\Ch08 folder on the companion CD. This client program has only the visual interface implementation for invoking a *Send* function in a COM object that you will create.

Figure 8.9 shows the Order Requests (Sender) dialog box of the Visual Basic client program.

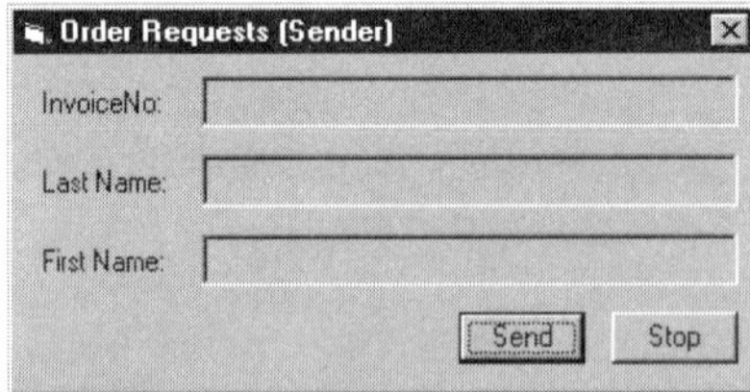

Figure 8.9 Order Requests (Sender) dialog box

If you study the visual interface of this dialog box, you will notice that it has two buttons: Send and Stop. The source code for this project is included in the Labs\Ch08 folder on the companion CD. The Send button simply creates an instance of a COM object you will provide with a single interface and two methods—*Send* and *Receive*. The *Send* method will accept three parameters: *InvoiceNo*, *LastName*, and *FirstName*.

The client program will continue to send messages every 10 seconds, but you can click the Stop button to stop it at any time. Later, you will complete the COM object that will do the actual sending and receiving of the messages. The skeleton for the project is included in the Before subdirectory of the OrderExchange directory, in the Labs\Ch08 directory on the companion CD. The OrderExchange project contains the ATL code to implement the OrderExchangeObj object, which has the *Send* and *Receive* methods explained earlier. Your job in this part is to add code to the *Send* method to actually send the message.

▶ **Send messages by implementing the *Send* method**

1. Open the OrderExchangeObj.cpp file. In this file, you will find the skeleton for the *Send* method with a comment that reads: "Insert your code for Part 2 here."
2. The first step is to include the Mqoai.h file in the OrderExchange.cpp. This file contains the COM API interface declarations for MSMQ objects. Before including this file, you must also include <initguid.h>. Your code should look as follows:

```
#include <initguid.h>
#include <mqoai.h>
```

3. Locate the queue for sending messages. If you cannot find the queue, you will simply create one. When you find the queue, open it for sending messages. Create an instance of the MSMQQuery object, and add the following code to the *Send* function as follows:

```
IMSMQQuery *pQuery = NULL;
HRESULT hr = CoCreateInstance(CLSID_MSMQQuery,
    NULL,
    CLSCTX_ALL,
    IID_IMSMQQuery,
    (void **)&pQuery);

if (FAILED(hr))
{
    // Generate a COM exception and exit
    return E_FAIL;
}
```

4. Notice that the previous code uses *CoCreateInstance* to create an instance of the MSMQQuery object. *CoCreateInstance* returns an HRESULT. As a standard, you should check the HRESULT throughout this code for failure after each call; however, returning rich error information to the client is left as an

exercise for you to do at your leisure. Use the *LookupQueue* function in the MSMQQuery interface, and search for a queue with a label that reads, "OrderRequests." Type the following code:

```
// Create an optional parameter
CComVariant *vtNull = new CComVariant();
vtNull->vt = VT_ERROR;
vtNull->scode= DISP_E_PARAMNOTFOUND;

IMSMQQueueInfos *pInfoColl;
hr = pQuery->LookupQueue(vtNull,
    vtNull,
    &CComVariant(L"Order Requests"),
    vtNull,
    vtNull,
    vtNull,
    &CComVariant(REL_EQ),
    vtNull,
    vtNull,
    &pInfoColl);

pQuery->Release();

if (FAILED(hr))
{
    // Generate a COM exception and exit
    return E_FAIL;
}

IMSMQQueueInfo *pOrderRequestInfo;
hr = pInfoColl->Next(&pOrderRequestInfo);
pInfoColl->Release();
```

5. The previous code executes the *LookupQueue* function, which returns a collection of MSMQQueueInfo objects in the *pInfoColl* variable. Use this collection to navigate through the queues that match the criteria. You should find only one in your current scenario, because you have created only one queue. If the queue exists, the *pOrderRequestInfo* parameter should not be NULL. If it is NULL, create the queue as follows:

```
if (!pOrderRequestInfo)
{
    // The queue does not exist, so create it
    hr = CoCreateInstance(CLSID_MSMQQueueInfo,
        NULL,
        CLSCTX_ALL,
        IID_IMSMQQueueInfo,
        (void **)&pOrderRequestInfo);
```

```
    if   (FAILED(hr))
    {
        // Generate a COM exception and exit
        return E_FAIL;
    }

    pOrderRequestInfo->put_Path(
        CComBSTR(L"ServerName\\orderrequests"));
    pOrderRequestInfo->put_Label(
        CComBSTR(L"Order Requests"));

    hr = pOrderRequestInfo->Create(
        &CComVariant(VARIANT_TRUE),
        &CComVariant(VARIANT_FALSE));
}
```

Note You should substitute the words *ServerName* in the *put_Path* function with the actual name of the server in your network where the queue is to be created.

6. One way or another (locating an existing OrderRequests queue or creating a new one), you should now have a valid pointer to an IMSMQQueueInfo interface stored in *pOrderRequestInfo*. Open the queue with the *Open* function of this interface. Make sure to open the queue for send access as follows:

```
IMSMQQueue *pOrderRequestQueue;

if (SUCCEEDED(hr))
{
    // Open the queue for sending
    hr = pOrderRequestInfo->Open(MQ_SEND_ACCESS,
        MQ_DENY_NONE,
        &pOrderRequestQueue);
    pOrderRequestInfo->Release();
}
```

7. The *Open* function returns a pointer to the IMSMQQueue interface. The pointer to this interface is now stored in *pOrderRequestQueue*. Put the reference aside as you create the message object that will be sent.
8. The body of the message object will hold a reference to an instance of your persistable object: InvoiceInfo. In preparation for sending the message, create an instance of this object, and then store in the object the parameters that the client program sent when it called the *Send* method, as follows:

```
// Create the persistable object that will contain the
message information
IInvoiceInfo *pInvoice = NULL;
```

```
hr  =  CoCreateInstance(CLSID_InvoiceInfo,
    NULL,
    CLSCTX_ALL,
    IID_IInvoiceInfo,
    (void **)&pInvoice);

if (FAILED(hr))
{
    // Generate a COM exception and exit
    return E_FAIL;
}

pInvoice->put_InvoiceNo(InvoiceNo);
pInvoice->put_FirstName(FirstName);
pInvoice->put_LastName(LastName);
```

9. Create an instance of the MSMQMessage object, and set the body of the message to a variant containing a reference to the pInvoice object. The easiest way to create a variant that will store this reference is to cast the pointer to the IUnknown interface, and use the resulting pointer as the constructor parameter in a CComVariant class instance. In addition, assign a label to the message using the *LastName* parameter as the label, as follows:

```
// Create the message to send
IMSMQMessage *pOrderMsg = NULL;
hr = CoCreateInstance(CLSID_MSMQMessage,
    NULL,
    CLSCTX_ALL,
    IID_IMSMQMessage,
    (void **)&pOrderMsg);

if (FAILED(hr))
{
    // Generate a COM exception and exit
    return E_FAIL;
}

pOrderMsg->put_Label(
    CComBSTR(LastName));
pOrderMsg->put_Body(CComVariant
    (static_cast<IUnknown*>
    (pInvoice)));
```

10. You have just implemented a message object with the body set to a reference to the persistable object. Use the *IMSMQMessage::Send* function to send the message as follows:

```
hr   =   pOrderMsg->Send(pOrderRequestQueue,
    &CComVariant(MQ_NO_TRANSACTION));

// Clean up
pOrderRequestQueue->Release();
pOrderMsg->Release();
pInvoice->Release();
```

11. Build your DLL and test it with the SenderClient.exe program. If you look at the contents of the queue with MSMQ Explorer, you should see each message as it is created. You might need to select Refresh periodically to get an accurate list.

When you are sure messages are being sent properly, continue the lab in Exercise 3, by implementing the *Receive* function of the OrderExchangeObj object.

Exercise 3: Receiving Messages

In this exercise, you will implement the *Receive* function in the OrderExchange-Obj object. This function will set up a callback function to receive messages. Whenever your component receives a message, you will fire an event to the Visual Basic client program that will display the message.

Available on the companion CD in the Labs\Ch08\Clients\Receiver folder, the Visual Basic client program for receiving messages has a visual interface implementation only for invoking a *Receive* function in the OrderExchangeObj object with which you are working.

Figure 8.10 shows the Order Requests (Receiver) dialog box of the Visual Basic client program.

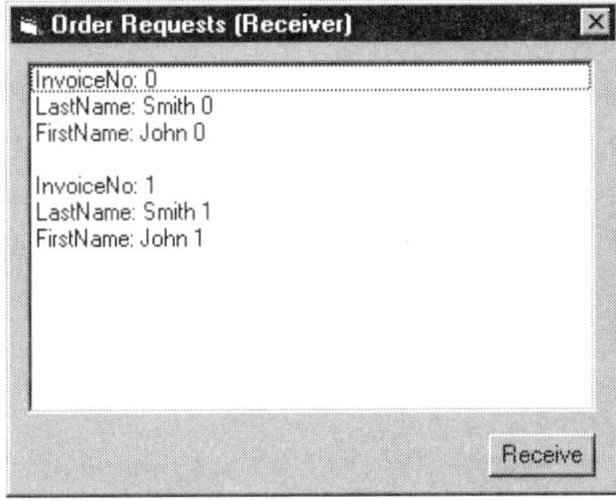

Figure 8.10 Order Requests (Receiver) dialog box

After calling the *Receive* function one time, the Visual Basic program will wait for notifications from your object telling it that a new message has arrived. The OrderExchange project already has an object derived from IDispatch, COrderMsg, that serves as the event sink mentioned in Lesson 2. Your job is to create an instance of the MSMQQueue object and connect the event sink class to it. Next, you will begin the process of receiving messages.

► **Connect the event sink class to MSMQQueue and receive messages**

1. Open the OrderRequests queue for receive access. The code should be identical to the code in steps 4, 5, and 6 in the previous exercise, except that you first do not want to create the queue if it does not already exist; in this case, you should simply exit the function and return E_FAIL. Second, the *Access* parameter in the *Open* function should be set to MQ_RECEIVE_ACCESS. If you are still unsure how to open the queue after reviewing the previous exercise, consult the answer code for Lab 8, which can be found on the companion CD in the Labs\Ch08\OrderExchange\After folder.
2. Create an instance of the COrderMsgReceiver event sink class. This class should be created at the class level, but not at the function level. You want this class to exist for as long as the COrderExchangeObj class exists. Add the following declaration to the OrderExchangeObj.h header file:

   ```
   CComObject<COrderMsg> rcv;
   ```

3. Then in the constructor for COrderExchangeObj, add the following code:

   ```
   rcv.SetParent(this);
   ```

4. This call links the event sink class to the instance of COrderExchangeObj. This is necessary because an event sink class receiving a message needs to notify the COrderExchangeObj class, so that this class can notify the Visual Basic client.
5. Also at the class level, add a declaration for a variable to store the cookie returned by the *Advise* function of the connection point. This cookie is a numeric value that you must use in the *UnAdvise* function to disconnect from the event source. The code for calling *UnAdvise* is left as an exercise for you to do at your leisure. Add the following declaration to the header file:

   ```
   DWORD dwCookie;
   ```

6. In the *Receive* function implementation, add code to create an MSMQEvent object as follows:

   ```
   hr = CoCreateInstance(CLSID_MSMQEvent,
     NULL,
     CLSCTX_ALL,
     IID_IMSMQEvent,
     (void **)&event);
   ```

7. The MSMQEvent object implements the IConnectionPointContainer interface. Use *QueryInterface* to get a pointer to this interface, and then call the *FindConnectionPoint* function to get a reference to the connection point. The GUID of the connection point for which you are searching is stored in DIID__DMSMQEventEvents. When you get a pointer to the particular connection point, you must call the *Advise* function of the IConnectionPoint interface, passing a pointer to the IUnknown interface of your event sink class. The simplest way to accomplish this step is to use the CComQIPtr smart pointer as follows:

```
CComQIPtr<IConnectionPointContainer>
pContainer = event;
if (pContainer)
{
    CComQIPtr<IConnectionPoint> cp;
    pContainer->FindConnectionPoint
    (DIID__DMSMQEventEvents,&cp);
    if (cp)
    {
        cp->Advise(rcv.GetUnknown(),&dwCookie);
    }
}
```

8. As you can see, the code is much simpler than you might have expected. When you find the connection point and connect your event sink class, you must tell the queue that you want to begin receiving messages.

9. Call the *EnableNotification* function in the IMSMQQueue interface as follows:

```
hr = pOrderRequestQueue->EnableNotification(event,
    &CComVariant(MQMSG_FIRST),
    &CComVariant((long)INFINITE));
```

10. Build your DLL and run the receiver client program. You should see the client program receiving messages. You can keep the sender client running to see both programs in action.

After completing this lab, you should have a COM DLL that is able to create a queue (if it has not already been created), send messages to the queue, and receive messages from the queue asynchronously.

Review

The following questions are intended to reinforce key information presented in this chapter. If you are unable to answer a question, review the appropriate lesson and then try answering the question again. Answers to the questions can be found in Appendix B, "Review Questions and Answers," at the back of this book.

1. What are the two main APIs used for programming in MSMQ?

2. In the MSMQ architecture, the enterprise is divided into what?

3. True or false: The IMSMQQueue interface has both *Send* and *Receive* functions for sending and receiving messages.

4. List the three transaction coordinators MSMQ allows you to use.

5. True or false: A queue can be located from a disconnected dependent client using the queue's path.

CHAPTER 9

Using Data Access Services

Lesson 1: Structured Query Language 448

Lesson 2: SQL Server 469

Lesson 3: Data Access Strategies 483

Lesson 4: Using ADO 500

Lesson 5: Using ODBC 524

Lesson 6: Using OLE DB 536

Lab 9: Creating an ADO Application 551

Review 555

About This Chapter

When developing a distributed application, you must be able to identify the most appropriate data access technology. This chapter describes different Microsoft data access technologies—UDA, ODBC, OLE DB, ADO, and RDS—and provides you with guidelines and strategies for choosing the appropriate technology.

Before You Begin

To complete the lessons in this chapter, you must have:

- Installed the Microsoft Visual C++ development tools as described in Lab 2
- Installed Microsoft SQL Server 7 Standard Edition
- Installed the Duwamish Books (Phase 4) database from the Web site at *http://msdn.microsoft.com/library/techart/d4samp.htm*

Lesson 1: Structured Query Language

Structured Query Language (SQL) is the language used for accessing data and querying, updating, and managing relational database systems. This lesson teaches you both the fundamentals and advanced concepts of SQL.

After this lesson, you will be able to:

- Define SQL and list the types of SQL statements
- Write a SQL statement that retrieves data
- Use wildcards in queries
- Write a SQL statement that modifies data
- Write a SQL statement that joins tables and filter the query using fields from each table
- Describe stored procedures and how to create procedures
- Describe triggers
- Create an update and insert trigger
- Create reports that use summary data

Estimated lesson time: 150 minutes

Basic Concepts

SQL is a set of commands that allows you to specify the information that you want to retrieve or modify. With SQL, you can access data and query, update, and manage relational database systems. The American National Standards Institute (ANSI) and the International Standards Organization (ISO) have defined standards for SQL.

Transact-SQL

Transact-SQL is a version of SQL. Microsoft SQL Server uses Transact-SQL as its database query and programming language. Transact-SQL supports the latest ANSI SQL standard published in 1992, called ANSI SQL-92, plus many extensions to provide increased functionality. It is recommended that you write scripts that include only ANSI-SQL standard statements to increase the compatibility and portability of your database.

Transact-SQL Elements

As you write and execute Transact-SQL statements, you will use:

- Data Control Language (DCL) statements, which are used to determine who can see or modify the data

- Data Definition Language (DDL) statements, which are used to create objects in the database
- Data Manipulation Language (DML) statements, which are used to query and modify the data
- Additional language elements, such as variables, operators, functions, control-of-flow language, and comments

DCL Statements

DCL statements are used to change the permissions associated with a database user or role. Table 9.1 describes DCL statements.

Table 9.1 DCL Statements

Statement	Description
GRANT	Creates an entry in the security system that allows a user to work with data or execute certain Transact-SQL statements
DENY	Creates an entry in the security system denying a permission from a security account and prevents the user, group, or role from inheriting the permission through its group and role memberships
REVOKE	Removes a previously granted or denied permission

By default, only members of the sysadmin, dbcreator, db_owner, or db_securityadmin role can execute DCL statements.

The following code grants the public role permission to query the products table:

```
USE northwind
GRANT SELECT ON products TO public
```

DDL Statements

DDL statements define the database by creating databases, tables, and user-defined data types. You also use DDL statements to manage your database objects. Some DDL statements are:

- CREATE object_name
- ALTER object_name
- DROP object_name

By default, only members of the sysadmin, dbcreator, db_owner, or db_ddladmin role can execute DDL statements. In general, it is recommended that no other accounts be used to create database objects. If different users create their own objects in a database, then each object owner is required to grant the proper permissions to each user of those objects. This causes an administrative burden and should be avoided. Restricting statement permissions to these roles also avoids problems with object ownership that can occur when an object owner has been dropped from a database or when the owner of a stored procedure or view does not own the underlying tables.

If multiple-user accounts create objects, the sysadmin and db_owner roles can use the *setuser* function to impersonate another user or the sp_changeobjectowner system stored procedure to change the owner of an object.

The following script creates a table called *customer* in the *northwind* database. It includes cust_id, company, contact, and phone columns:

```
USE Northwind
CREATE TABLE customer
(cust_id int, company varchar(40),contact varchar(30),
phone char(12))
```

DML Statements

DML statements work with the data in the database. By using DML statements, you can change data or retrieve information. DML statements include:

- SELECT
- INSERT
- UPDATE
- DELETE

By default, only members of the sysadmin, dbcreator, db_owner, or db_datawriter role can execute DML statements.

The following code retrieves the category ID, product name, product ID, and unit price of the products in the northwind database:

```
SELECT categoryid, productname, productid, unitprice
FROM northwind..products
```

Retrieving Data

Retrieving data from tables includes using the SELECT statement, which involves specifying columns and rows. The syntax of the SELECT statement is as follows:

```
SELECT [ALL|DISTINCT] <select_list>
FROM {<table_source>} [,...n]
[ WHERE <search_condition> ]
```

Use the SELECT statement to specify the columns and rows that you want returned from a table:

- The select list specifies the columns to be returned.
- The WHERE clause specifies the rows to return. When you use search conditions in the WHERE clause, you can restrict the number of rows by using comparison operators, character strings, and logical operators as search conditions.
- The FROM clause specifies the table from which columns and rows are returned.

You can retrieve particular columns from a table by listing them in the select list. The select list contains the columns, expressions, or keywords to select or the local variable to assign. The options that can be used in the select list include:

```
<select_list>::=

    {   *
        |{table_name|view_name|table_alias}.*
        |   {column_name|expression|IDENTITYCOL|
            ROWGUIDCOL }
            [[AS]column_alias]
        |column_alias=expression
    }   [,  n]
```

When you specify columns to retrieve, keep in mind the following facts and guidelines:

- The select list retrieves and displays the columns in the specified order.
- Separate the column names with commas, except for the last column name.
- Avoid or minimize the use of an asterisk (*) in the select list. An asterisk is used to retrieve all columns from a table.

The following code retrieves the employeeid, lastname, firstname, and title columns of all employees from the employees table:

```
USE northwind
SELECT employeeid, lastname, firstname, title
FROM employees
```

Using the WHERE clause, you can retrieve specific rows based on given search conditions. The search conditions in the WHERE clause can contain an unlimited list of predicates:

```
<search_condition>::=
{[ NOT]<predicate>|(<search_condition>)}
[{AND|OR}[NOT]{<predicate>|(<search_condition>)}]
}[, n]
```

The predicate placeholder lists the expressions that can be included in the WHERE clause.

This example retrieves the employeeid, lastname, firstname, and title columns from the employees table for the employee with an employeeid of 5:

```
USE northwind
SELECT employeeid, lastname, firstname, title
FROM employees
WHERE employeeid = 5
```

WHERE Clause Search Conditions

When you specify the criteria for rows to retrieve in the WHERE clause, use any of the following types of search conditions shown in Table 9.2.

Table 9.2 Types of WHERE Clause Search Conditions

Description	Search condition
Comparison operators	=, >, <, >=, <=, and <>
String comparisons	LIKE and NOT LIKE
Logical operators: combination of conditions	AND, OR
Logical operator: negations	NOT
Range of values	BETWEEN and NOT BETWEEN
Lists of values	IN and NOT IN
Unknown values	IS NULL and IS NOT NULL

There is no limit to the number of search conditions that you can include in a SELECT statement.

You can use the LIKE search condition in combination with wildcard characters to select rows by comparing character strings. When you use the LIKE search condition, consider the following facts:

- All characters in the pattern string are significant, including leading and trailing blank spaces.
- LIKE can be used only with data of the char, nchar, varchar, nvarchar, or datetime data types.

Types of Wildcard Characters

Use the four wildcard characters shown in Table 9.3 to form your character string search criteria.

Table 9.3 Wildcard Characters

Wildcard	Description
%	Any string of zero or more characters
_	Any single character
[]	Any single character within the specified range or set
[^]	Any single character *not* within the specified range or set

Table 9.4 lists examples of the use of wildcards with the LIKE search condition.

Table 9.4 Using Wildcards with LIKE

Expression	Returns
LIKE 'BR%'	Every name beginning with the letters BR
LIKE 'Br%'	Every name beginning with the letters Br
LIKE '%een'	Every name ending with the letters een
LIKE '%en%'	Every name containing the letters en
LIKE '_en'	Every three-letter name ending in the letters en
LIKE '[CK]%'	Every name beginning with the letter C or K
LIKE '[S-V]ing'	Every four-letter name ending in the letters ing and beginning with any single letter from S to V
LIKE 'M[^c]%'	Every name beginning with the letter M that does not have the letter c as the second letter

The following code retrieves companies from the customers table that have the word restaurant in their company names:

```
USE northwind
SELECT companyname
FROM customers
WHERE companyname LIKE '%Restaurant%'
```

On executing the previous code, you get the following sample result:

```
companyname
GROSELLA-Restaurante
Lonesome Pine Restaurant
Tortuga Restaurante

(3 row(s) affected)
```

Modifying Data

You can modify data in existing rows by using the INSERT, DELETE, and UPDATE statements. When you add rows to an existing table, SQL Server can insert default values for you, allowing you to enter partial data.

The INSERT statement adds rows to a table. The syntax for INSERT statement is as follows:

```
INSERT [INTO]
{table_name|view_name}
{[(column_list)]
{VALUES({DEFAULT|NULL|expression}[,...n])
|DEFAULT VALUES
```

Use the INSERT statement with the VALUES clause to add rows to a table. When you insert rows, consider the following facts and guidelines:

- Use the column_list to specify columns that will store each incoming value. You must enclose the column_list in parentheses and delimit it by commas. If you are supplying values for all columns, using the column_list is optional.
- Specify the data that you want to insert by using the VALUES clause. The VALUES clause is required for each column in the table or column_list.

  The column order and data type of new data must correspond to the table column order and data type. Many data types have an associated entry format. For example, character data and dates must be enclosed in single quotation marks.
- An INSERT statement fails if it violates an existing constraint or rule.
- To make your script clearer, you should supply a complete column list.

The following code adds Pecos Coffee Company as a new customer:

```
USE northwind
INSERT customers
    (customerid, companyname, contactname,
    contacttitle, address, city, region,
    postalcode, country, phone, fax)
VALUES ('PECOF', 'Pecos Coffee Company','Michael Dunn',
    'Owner', '1900 Oak Street', 'Vancouver', 'BC',
    'V3F 2K1', 'Canada', '(604) 555-3392',
    '(604) 555-7293')
```

Deleting Data

The DELETE and TRUNCATE TABLE statements remove rows from tables.

DELETE Statement

Use the DELETE statement to remove one or more rows from a table. The syntax for the DELETE statement is as follows:

```
DELETE [from] {table_name|view_name}
WHERE search_conditions
```

When you use the DELETE statement, consider the following facts:

- SQL Server deletes all rows from a table unless you include a WHERE clause in the DELETE statement.
- Each deleted row is logged in the transaction log.

The following code deletes all order records that are equal to or greater than six months old:

```
USE northwind
DELETE orders
WHERE DATEDIFF(MONTH, shippeddate, GETDATE()) >= 6
```

TRUNCATE TABLE Statement

Use the TRUNCATE TABLE statement to delete all rows from a table. The syntax for the TRUNCATE TABLE is as follows:

```
TRUNCATE TABLE [[database.]owner.]table_name
```

When you use the TRUNCATE TABLE statement, consider the following facts:

- SQL Server deletes all rows but retains the table structure and its associated objects.
- The TRUNCATE TABLE statement executes more quickly than the DELETE statement because SQL Server logs only the deallocation of data pages.
- If a table has an IDENTITY column, the TRUNCATE TABLE statement resets the seed value.

The following code removes all data from the orders table:

```
USE northwind
TRUNCATE TABLE orders
```

UPDATE Rows

The UPDATE statement modifies existing data. The syntax for the UPDATE statement is as follows:

```
UPDATE {table_name|view_name}
SET {column_name={expression|DEFAULT|NULL}
    |@variable=expression}[,...n]
WHERE {search_conditions}
```

Use the UPDATE statement to change single rows, groups of rows, or all of the rows in a table. When you update rows, consider the following facts and guidelines:

- Specify the rows to update with the WHERE clause.
- Specify the new values with the SET clause.
- Verify that the input values are the same as the data types that are defined for the columns.
- SQL Server does not update rows that violate any integrity constraints. The changes do not occur, and the statement is rolled back.
- You can change the data in only one table at a time.
- You can set one or more columns or variables to an expression. For example, an expression can be a calculation (like price * 2) or the addition of two columns.

The following code adds 10 percent to the current prices of all the products:

```
USE northwind
UPDATE products
SET unitprice = (unitprice * 1.1)
```

Querying Multiple Tables

A *join* is an operation that allows you to query two or more tables to produce a result set that incorporates rows and columns from each table. You join tables on columns that are common to both tables.

When you join tables, SQL Server compares the values of the specified columns row by row and then uses the comparison results to combine the qualifying values into new rows.

There are three types of joins: inner joins, outer joins, and cross joins. Additionally, you can join more than two tables by using a series of joins within a SELECT statement, or you can join a table to itself by using a self join.

The syntax of a join is as follows:

```
SELECT column_name[,column_name...]
FROM {<table_source>}[,...n]
    <join_type> ::=
    [INNER|{{LEFT|RIGHT|FULL}[OUTER]}]
    [<join_hint>]
    JOIN
    <joined_table> ::=
```

```
<table_source> <join_type> <table_source>
ON <search_condition>
|<table_source> CROSS JOIN <table_source>
|<joined_table>
```

Inner Joins

Inner joins combine tables by comparing values in columns that are common to both tables. SQL Server returns only rows that match the join conditions.

Use inner joins to obtain information from two separate tables and combine that information in one result set. When you use inner joins, keep in mind the following facts and guidelines:

- Inner joins are the SQL Server default. You can abbreviate the INNER JOIN clause to JOIN.
- Specify the columns that you want to display in your result set by including the qualified column names in the select list.
- Include a WHERE clause to restrict the rows that are returned in the result set.
- Do not use a null value as a join condition because null values do not evaluate equally with one another.

The following code returns the buyer_name, buyer_id, and qty values for the buyers who purchased products. Buyers who did not purchase any products are not included in the result set. Buyers who bought more than one product are listed for each purchase.

The buyer_id column from either table can be specified in the select list:

```
USE joindb
SELECT buyer_name, sales.buyer_id, qty
FROM buyers INNER JOIN sales
ON buyers.buyer_id = sales.buyer_id
```

Outer Joins

Left or right *outer joins* combine rows from two tables that match the join condition, plus any unmatched rows of either the left or right table as specified in the JOIN clause. Rows that do not match the join condition display NULL in the result set. You also can use full outer joins to display all rows in the joined tables, regardless of whether the tables have any matching values.

Use left or right outer joins when you require a complete list of data that is stored in one of the joined tables in addition to the information that matches the join condition. When you use left or right outer joins, consider the following facts and guidelines:

- SQL Server returns only unique rows when you use left or right outer joins.
- Use a left outer join to display all rows from the first-named table (the table on the left of the expression). If you reverse the order in which the tables are listed in the FROM clause, the statement yields the same result as a right outer join.
- Use a right outer join to display all rows from the second-named table (the table on the right of the expression). If you reverse the order in which the tables are listed in the FROM clause, the statement yields the same result as a left outer join.
- Do not use a null value as a join condition because null values do not evaluate equally with one another.
- You can abbreviate the LEFT OUTER JOIN or RIGHT OUTER JOIN clause as LEFT JOIN or RIGHT JOIN.
- You can use outer joins between two tables only.

The following example returns the buyer_name, buyer_id, and qty values for all buyers and their purchases. Notice that the buyers who did not purchase any products are listed in the result set, but null values appear in the buyer_id and qty columns:

```
USE joindb
SELECT buyer_name, sales.buyer_id, qty
FROM buyers LEFT OUTER JOIN sales
ON buyers.buyer_id = sales.buyer_id
```

Stored Procedures

Stored procedures are precompiled SQL statements stored on the server. Stored procedures:

- Encapsulate business functionality for use by all applications, ensuring consistent data modification
- Are checked for syntax and compiled the first time they are executed
- Execute faster and are more efficient, because the compiled version is stored in the procedure cache and used for subsequent calls

A stored procedure is a named collection of Transact-SQL statements that is stored on the server. Stored procedures are a method of encapsulating repetitive tasks that executes efficiently. Stored procedures support user-declared variables, conditional execution, and other powerful programming features.

SQL Server supports five types of stored procedures:

- System
- Local
- Temporary
- Remote
- Extended

The following subsections will discuss each of these stored procedures in detail.

System Stored Procedures (sp_)

Stored in the master database, system stored procedures (identified by the sp_ prefix) provide an effective method to retrieve information from system tables. They allow system administrators to perform database administration tasks that update system tables even though the administrators do not have permission to update the underlying tables directly. System stored procedures can be executed in any database.

Local Stored Procedures

Local stored procedures are created in individual user databases.

Temporary Stored Procedures

Temporary stored procedures can be local, with names that start with a single pound symbol (#) or global, with names that start with a double pound symbol (##)—local temporary stored procedures are available within a single user session; global temporary stored procedures are available for all user sessions.

Remote Stored Procedures

Remote stored procedures are a legacy feature of SQL Server. Distributed queries now support this functionality.

Extended Stored Procedures (xp_)

These are implemented as dynamic-link libraries (DLLs) executed outside of the SQL Server environment. Extended stored procedures are typically identified by the xp_ prefix. They are executed in a manner similar to that of stored procedures.

In distributed applications, stored procedures are mostly used for create, retrieve update, and delete operations, and to improve query and common filtering. Most business logic should be kept in Component Object Model (COM) business objects and not stored procedures. However, you can create a stored procedure with business logic in it, as shown in the following code, in which a stored procedure that lists all overdue books in the library database is created:

```
USE library
GO
CREATE PROC dbo.overdue_books
AS
    SELECT *
    FROM dbo.loan
    WHERE due_date < GETDATE()
GO
```

Creating Stored Procedures

You can create a stored procedure in the current database only—except for temporary stored procedures, which are always created in the tempdb database. Creating a stored procedure is similar to creating a view. First write and test the Transact-SQL statements that you want to include in the stored procedure. Then, if you receive the results that you expect, create the stored procedure.

You create stored procedures with the CREATE PROCEDURE statement. Consider the following facts when you create stored procedures:

- Stored procedures can reference tables, views, and stored procedures, as well as temporary tables.
- If a stored procedure creates a local temporary table, the temporary table only exists for the purpose of the stored procedure and disappears when stored procedure execution completes.
- A CREATE PROCEDURE statement cannot be combined with other SQL statements in a single batch.
- The CREATE PROCEDURE definition can include any number and type of Transact-SQL statements, with the exception of the following object creation statements: CREATE DEFAULT, CREATE PROCEDURE, CREATE RULE, CREATE TRIGGER, and CREATE VIEW. Other database objects can be created within a stored procedure and should be qualified with the name of the object owner.
- To execute the CREATE PROCEDURE statement, you must be a member of the system administrators (sysadmin) role, database owner (db_owner) role, or the data definition language administrator (db_ddladmin) role, or you must have been granted CREATE PROCEDURE permission.
- The maximum size of a stored procedure is 128 MB, depending on available memory.

The syntax for creating stored procedure is as follows:

```
CREATE PROC[EDURE] [owner.]procedure_name [;number]
   [({[@] parameter data_type}[VARYING][= default] [OUTPUT])]
```

```
        [,...n]
    [WITH{RECOMPILE|ENCRYPTION|RECOMPILE,ENCRYPTION}]
AS
    sql_statement [...n]
```

Following is an example of creating a stored procedure:

```
CREATE PROC "p_SelectCustomerNames"
AS
SELECT CustomerID,FirstName,LastName
FROM Customers
```

If you are creating a user-defined system stored procedure, you must be logged in as a member of the sysadmin role and use the master database.

Triggers

A *trigger* is a special kind of stored procedure that executes whenever an attempt is made to modify data in a table that the trigger protects. The characteristics of a trigger include the following:

- **Associated with a table** Triggers are defined on a specific table, which is referred to as the trigger table.
- **Invoked automatically** When an attempt is made to insert, update, or delete data in a table and a trigger for that particular action has been defined on the table, the trigger executes automatically. It cannot be circumvented.
- **Cannot be called directly** Unlike standard system stored procedures, triggers cannot be called directly and do not pass or accept parameters.
- **Is a transaction** The trigger and the statement that fires it are treated as a single transaction that can be rolled back from anywhere within the trigger. Trigger definitions can include a ROLLBACK TRANSACTION statement even if an explicit BEGIN TRANSACTION statement does not exist. The statement that invokes the trigger is considered the beginning of an implicit transaction, unless an explicit BEGIN TRANSACTION statement is included. The user that invoked the trigger must also have permission to perform all of the statements on all of the tables.

  If a trigger that includes a ROLLBACK TRANSACTION statement is fired from within a user-defined transaction, the ROLLBACK TRANSACTION rolls back the entire transaction. A trigger that is executed from within a batch that executes a ROLLBACK TRANSACTION statement cancels the batch; subsequent statements in the batch are not executed.

  You should minimize or avoid the use of ROLLBACK TRANSACTION in your trigger code. Rolling back a transaction creates additional work because all of the work that is completed up to that point in the transaction has to be undone. This will have a negative impact on performance. It is recommended that information is checked and validated outside the transaction. Start the transaction after everything is checked and verified.

CREATE TRIGGER Statement

Triggers are created with the CREATE TRIGGER statement. The statement specifies the table on which a trigger is defined, the events for which the trigger executes, and the particular instructions for the trigger.

```
CREATE TRIGGER [owner.] trigger_name
ON [owner.] table_name
[WITH ENCRYPTION]
{FOR {INSERT|UPDATE|DELETE}
AS
[IF UPDATE (column_name)...]
    [{AND | OR} UPDATE (column_name)...]
    sql_statements}
```

When a FOR UPDATE action is specified, the IF UPDATE (column_name) clause can be used to focus action on a specific column that is updated.

When you create a trigger, information about the trigger is inserted into the sysobjects and syscomments system tables. If a trigger is created with the same name as an existing trigger, the new trigger will overwrite the original trigger.

Keep in mind the following parameters when creating a trigger:

- **Requires appropriate permissions** Table owners, as well as members of the db_owner and the sysadmin roles, have permission to create a trigger.

  To avoid situations in which the owner of a view and the owner of the underlying tables differ, it is recommended that the **dbo** user own all objects in a database. Because a user can be a member of multiple roles, always specify the **dbo** user as the owner name when you create the object. Otherwise, the object will be created with your user name as the owner.

- **Cannot contain certain statements** SQL Server does not allow the following statements to be used in a trigger definition:
  - Any CREATE statements (DATABASE, SCHEMA, TABLE, INDEX, PROCEDURE, DEFAULT, RULE, TRIGGER, VIEW)
  - Any DROP statements
  - ALTER (TABLE, DATABASE, PROCEDURE, VIEW, TRIGGER)
  - TRUNCATE TABLE
  - GRANT, REVOKE, DENY
  - UPDATE STATISTICS
  - RECONFIGURE
  - LOAD DATABASE, LOAD TRANSACTION, RESTORE DATABASE, and RESTORE LOG

To determine the tables with triggers, execute the sp_depends <tablename> system stored procedure. To view a trigger definition, execute the sp_helptext <triggername> system stored procedure. To determine the triggers that exist on a specific table and their actions, execute the sp_helptrigger <tablename> system stored procedure.

The following code creates a trigger that generates a contrived customer ID for every row that is inserted into the customer table. The contrived customer ID consists of the identity value from the id column concatenated with the first three letters of the customer's last name and the first letter of the customer's first name. Notice that the identity value is padded with leading zeros to provide a fixed length of the customer ID:

```
CREATE TABLE customer
    (id int IDENTITY(1,1),
        cust_id char(8),
        firstname  char(10),
        lastname   char(20))

CREATE TRIGGER gen_cust_id ON customer FOR INSERT
AS
UPDATE customer SET cust_id=(SELECT
    REPLICATE('0',(4-(DATALENGTH(CONVERT(varchar(10),i.id)))))
        + CONVERT(varchar(10),i.id)
        + SUBSTRING(i.lastname,1,3)
        + SUBSTRING(i.firstname,1,1)
        FROM customer c INNER JOIN inserted I
        ON i.id = c.id)
    FROM customer c INNER JOIN inserted i ON i.id = c.id
```

INSERT Statement

You can define a trigger to execute whenever an INSERT statement inserts data into a table.

The following INSERT statement fires the trigger created in the previous code example:

```
INSERT customer (lastname, firstname)
        VALUES ('Rothenberg', 'Angela')
```

When an INSERT trigger is fired, new rows are added to both the trigger table and the inserted table. The inserted table is a logical table that holds a copy of the rows that have been inserted. The inserted table contains the logged insert activity from the INSERT statement. The inserted table allows you to reference logged data from the initiating INSERT statement. The trigger can examine the inserted table to determine whether or how the trigger actions should be carried out. The rows in the inserted table are always duplicates of one or more rows in the trigger table.

All data modification activity (INSERT, UPDATE, and DELETE statements) is logged, but the information in the transaction log is unreadable. However, the inserted table allows you to reference the logged changes that the INSERT statement caused. Then you can compare the changes to the inserted data to verify them or take further action. You also can reference inserted data without having to store the information in variables.

The trigger in the following example was created to update a derived column (on_loan) in the copy table whenever a book is checked out (whenever a record is inserted into the loan table). Users can quickly search the copy table to determine whether a particular book is available or is already on loan without having to join the copy and loan tables. The syntax to update a derived column is as follows:

```
USE library
CREATE TRIGGER loan_insert
    ON loan
    FOR INSERT
AS
    UPDATE c SET on_loan= Y'
        FROM copy c INNER JOIN inserted i
        ON c.isbn=i.isbn AND c.copy_no = i.copy_no
```

UPDATE Statement

An UPDATE statement can be thought of as two steps: the DELETE step that captures the "before" image of the data, and the INSERT step that captures the "after" image of the data. When an UPDATE statement is executed on a table that has a trigger defined on it, the original rows (before image) are moved into the deleted table and the updated rows (after image) are inserted into the inserted table.

The trigger can examine the deleted and inserted tables, as well as the updated table, to determine whether multiple rows have been updated and how the trigger actions should be carried out.

You can define a trigger to monitor data updates on a specific column by using the IF UPDATE statement. This allows the trigger to isolate activity easily for a specific column. When it detects that the specific column has been updated, it can take proper action, such as raising an error message that says that the column cannot be updated or processing a series of statements based on the newly updated column value. The syntax for an update trigger is as follows:

```
IF UPDATE (<column_name>)
```

The following code prevents a user from modifying the member number:

```
USE library
GO
```

```
CREATE TRIGGER member_update
    ON member
    FOR UPDATE
AS
IF UPDATE (member_no)
BEGIN
    RAISERROR ('Transaction cannot be processed.\
    ***** Member number cannot be modified.', 10, 1)
    ROLLBACK TRANSACTION
END
```

Summarizing Data

You might want to summarize or calculate data when you retrieve it. The following subsections will examine the functions in SQL that support summarizing of data.

Creating a View

CREATE VIEW creates a virtual table that represents the data in one or more tables in an alternative way. Views can be used as security mechanisms by granting permission on a view but not on the underlying (base) tables. The SQL syntax for creating a view is as follows:

```
CREATE VIEW view_name [(column [,...n])]
[WITH ENCRYPTION]
AS
    select_statement
[WITH CHECK OPTION]
```

The CREATE VIEW syntax can contain the following arguments:

- **view_name** The name of the view. View names must follow the rules for identifiers. Specifying the view owner name is optional.
- **column** The name to be used for a column in a view. Naming a column in CREATE VIEW is necessary only when a column is derived from an arithmetic expression, a function, or a constant; when two or more columns can otherwise have the same name (usually because of a join); or when a column in a view is given a name different from that of the column from which it is derived. Column names can also be assigned in the SELECT statement. If a column is not specified, the view columns acquire the same names as the columns in the SELECT statement. In the columns for the view, the permissions for a column name apply across a CREATE VIEW or ALTER VIEW statement, regardless of the source of the underlying data. For example, if permissions are granted on the title_id column in a CREATE VIEW statement, an ALTER VIEW statement can name the title_id column with a different column name, such as qty, and still have the permissions associated with the view using title_id.

- **n** A placeholder indicating that multiple columns can be specified.
- **WITH ENCRYPTION** An argument that encrypts the syscomments entries that contain the text of the CREATE VIEW statement.
- **AS** The actions the view is to take.
- **select_statement** The SELECT statement that defines the view. It can use more than one table and other views. To select from the objects referenced in the SELECT clause of a view being created, it is necessary to have the appropriate permissions. A view does not have to be a simple subset of the rows and columns of one particular table. A view can be created using more than one table or other views with a SELECT clause of any complexity.

  However, there are a few restrictions on the SELECT clauses in a view definition. A CREATE VIEW statement cannot:

  - Include ORDER BY, COMPUTE, or COMPUTE BY clauses
  - Include the INTO keyword
  - Reference a temporary table
- **WITH CHECK OPTION** An argument that forces all data modification statements executed against the view to adhere to the criteria set within select_statement. When a row is modified through a view, the WITH CHECK OPTION guarantees that the data remains visible through the view after the modification has been committed.

Aggregate Functions

Functions that calculate averages and sums are called *aggregate functions*. When an aggregate function is executed, SQL Server summarizes values for an entire table or for groups of columns within the table, producing a single value for each set of rows for the specified columns:

- You can use aggregate functions with the SELECT statement or in combination with the GROUP BY clause.
- With the exception of the COUNT(*) function, all aggregate functions return a NULL if no rows satisfy the WHERE clause. The COUNT(*) function returns a value of zero if no rows satisfy the WHERE clause.

The data type of a column determines the functions that you can use with it. Table 9.5 describes the relationships between functions and data types.

Table 9.5 Relationships Between Functions and Data Types

Function	Data type
COUNT	COUNT is the only aggregate function that can be used on columns with text, ntext, or image data types.
MIN and MAX	You cannot use the MIN and MAX functions on columns with bit data types.
SUM and AVG	You can use only the SUM and AVG aggregate functions on columns with int, smallint, tinyint, decimal, numeric, float, real, money, and smallmoney data types. When you use the SUM or AVG function, SQL Server treats the smallint or tinyint data types as an int data type value in your result set.

The syntax for aggregate functions usage is as follows:

```
SELECT [ALL|DISTINCT]
[TOP n [PERCENT][WITH TIES]] <select_list>
[INTO new_table]
[FROM <table_sources>]
[WHERE <search_conditions>]
[[ GROUP BY [ALL] group_by_expression [,...n]]
[HAVING <search_conditions>]
[WITH{CUBE|ROLLUP}]
]
[ORDER BY{column_name[ASC|DESC]}[,...n]]
[COMPUTE
{{AVG|COUNT|MAX|MIN|SUM}(expression)}[,...n]
[BY expression [,...n]
]
```

The following code calculates the average unit price of all products in the products table:

```
USE northwind
SELECT AVG(unitprice)
FROM products
```

GROUP BY Clause

By itself, an aggregate function produces a single summary value for all rows in a column.

If you want to generate summary values for a column, use aggregate functions with the GROUP BY clause. Use the HAVING clause with the GROUP BY clause to restrict the groups of rows that are returned in the result set.

Use the GROUP BY clause on columns or expressions to organize rows into groups and to summarize those groups. For example, use the GROUP BY clause to determine the quantity of each product that was ordered for all orders.

The following code returns information about orders from the orderhist table. The query groups and lists each product ID and calculates the total quantity ordered. The total quantity is calculated with the SUM aggregate function and displays one value for each product in the result set. The syntax is as follows:

```
USE northwind
SELECT productid, SUM(quantity) AS total_quantity
FROM orderhist
GROUP BY productid
```

Use the HAVING clause on columns or expressions to set conditions on the groups included in a result set. The HAVING clause sets conditions on the GROUP BY clause in much the same way that the WHERE clause interacts with the SELECT statement.

The following code lists each group of products from the orderhist table that has orders of 30 or more units:

```
USE northwind
SELECT productid, SUM(quantity) AS total_quantity
FROM orderhist
GROUP BY productid
HAVING SUM(quantity) >=30
```

Lesson Summary

In this lesson, you were introduced to the basic and advanced concepts of SQL. You looked at the different types of SQL statements. You were also shown how to write SQL statements for retrieving and modifying data in relational database systems, and how to write SQL statements that use wildcards or join tables for querying the database. Finally, you were shown how to create and use stored procedures, triggers, and reports.

Lesson 2: SQL Server

This lesson introduces SQL Server and provides information on the hardware and software requirements of SQL Server and the installation options. It also discusses database objects and data constraints. Finally, it covers the creation and maintenance of indexes.

After this lesson, you will be able to:

- Configure SQL Server
- Create and modify SQL Server tables, fields, field types, default values and constraints
- Create primary and foreign keys to enforce data and referential integrity
- Create and maintain indexes

Estimated lesson time: 180 minutes

Basic Concepts

An understanding of the SQL Server database structure will help you develop and implement your database effectively.

Each SQL Server has two types of databases: *system databases* and *user databases*. System databases store information about SQL Server as a whole. SQL Server uses the system databases to operate and manage the system. User databases are databases that users create. One copy of SQL Server can manage one or more user databases. Both types of databases store data.

System and User Databases

When SQL Server is installed, SQL Server Setup creates four system databases and two sample user databases. The *distribution database* is installed when you configure SQL Server for replication activities. Table 9.6, on the next page, describes each database.

Table 9.6 SQL Server Databases

Details	Description
Master	Controls the user databases and operation of SQL Server as a whole by keeping track of such information as user accounts, configurable environment variables, and system error messages.
Model	Provides a template or prototype for new user databases.
Tempdb	Provides a storage area for temporary tables and other temporary working storage needs.
Msdb	Supports SQL Server Agent and provides a storage area for scheduling information and job history.
Distribution	Stores history and transaction data used in replication.
Pubs	Provides a sample database as a learning tool.
Northwind	Provides a sample database as a learning tool.
User1	Identifies a user-defined database.

Database Objects

Database objects help you structure your data and define data integrity mechanisms. Table 9.7 describes SQL Server database objects.

Table 9.7 SQL Server Database Objects

Database object	Description
Table	Defines a collection of rows that have associated columns.
Data type	Defines the data values allowed for a column or variable. SQL Server provides system-supplied data types. Users create user-defined data types.
Constraint	Defines rules regarding the values allowed in columns and is the standard mechanism for enforcing data integrity.
Default	Defines a value that is stored in a column if no other value is supplied.
Rule	Contains information that defines valid values that are stored in a column or data type.
Index	Is a storage structure that provides fast access for data retrieval and can enforce data integrity. In a clustered index, the logical or indexed order of the key values is the same as the physical, stored order of the corresponding rows that exist in the table. In a non-clustered index, the logical order of the index does not match the physical, stored order of the rows in the table.
View	Provides a way to look at data from one or more tables or views in a database.
Stored procedure	Is a named collection of Transact-SQL statements that execute together.
Trigger	Is a special form of a stored procedure that is executed automatically when a user modifies data in a table.

Installing SQL Server

Knowing the minimum hardware and software installation requirements before you install SQL Server allows you to select the appropriate platform. Table 9.8 describes the minimum hardware and software requirements for a SQL Server installation.

Table 9.8 Minimum Requirements for Installing SQL Server

Minimum requirements	Component
Computer	Intel and compatible systems (Pentium 166 MHz or later). DEC Alpha and compatible systems.
Memory	A minimum of 32 MB additional memory is recommended for large databases and replication. Microsoft Windows NT Server, Enterprise Edition requires a minimum 64 MB.
Hard disk space	Installation only of a new server, with no management tools, requires 72 MB. A typical installation requires 175 MB. Installation of management tools requires 82 MB. These hard disk space requirements do not include upgrading user databases or installing custom installation options.
File system	Microsoft Windows NTFS file system (NTFS) or file allocation table (FAT). NTFS is recommended for server installation due to security and recovery advantages.
Operating system	Windows NT Server 4, Enterprise Edition, with Service Pack 4 or later; Windows NT Server 4 with Service Pack 4 or later; Microsoft Windows NT Workstation 4 with Service Pack 4 or later; or Microsoft Windows 95/98.
Other software	Microsoft Internet Explorer 4.01 with Service Pack 1 or later.

In general, if the hard disk of the computer has a write-caching disk controller, make it unavailable. Unless a write-caching disk controller is designed specifically for a database, it can seriously impact SQL Server data integrity.

Running SQL Server Setup

The Setup program offers these installation types—minimum, typical, and custom. The Setup program runs from the CD-ROM that is packaged with SQL Server or from a shared network directory. Before you can install SQL Server or any component, you must log on to the computer running SQL Server with an account that is a member of the Windows NT Administrators local group.

The Setup program selects a typical installation as the default. If you want to change any installation defaults or add or delete components, perform a custom installation.

Types of SQL Server Installation

Table 9.9 describes the principal differences between the three installation types.

Table 9.9 Comparison of SQL Server Installation Types

Installation option	Minimum	Typical	Custom
Database server	Yes	Yes	Optional
Upgrade tools	No	Yes	Optional
Replication support	Yes	Yes	Optional
Full-text search	No	No	Optional
Client management tools	None	All	Optional
Client connectivity	Yes	Yes	Optional
Online documentation	No	Yes	Optional
Development tools	None	None	Optional
Code samples	None	None	Optional

Microsoft English Query and SQL Server OLAP Services are included on the Microsoft SQL Server 7 CD-ROM and can be installed independently of SQL Server 7.

Configuring SQL Server

After you install SQL Server, you should configure SQL Server Enterprise Manager and SQL Server.

Configuring SQL Server Enterprise Manager

To manage a local or remote server with SQL Server Enterprise Manager, you must register the server with SQL Server Enterprise Manager. The local server is registered automatically when you install SQL Server. To manage a remote server with SQL Server Enterprise Manager, you must register the remote server with SQL Server Enterprise Manager and place it in a server group.

When you register a server, you must be able to connect to that server. You must specify the server name, Windows NT authentication or SQL Server authentication, and a server group. This SQL Server registration information is maintained in the Windows NT registry. SQL Server Enterprise Manager uses this information each time that you connect to a registered SQL Server.

You can register multiple servers with SQL Server Enterprise Manager by using the Register SQL Server Wizard. Registering multiple servers allows you to administer multiple servers from one computer. By default, to administer a server, you must be a member of the Windows NT Administrators local group on the computer on which SQL Server was installed. Windows NT domain administrators are members of the Windows NT Administrators local group.

The default client network library that SQL Server Enterprise Manager uses to connect to a server is Named Pipes. If you cannot connect to a remote server with Named Pipes, you can use the Client Network utility to change the client network library that you use to connect to the remote SQL Server.

When you register a server, you can either place the server within an existing server group or create a new server group. A server group provides a way to organize servers for administration and management tasks.

SQL Server provides an administrative client, SQL Server Enterprise Manager, which is a Microsoft Management Console (MMC) snap-in. MMC is a shared user interface for BackOffice server management. This shared console provides a convenient and consistent environment for administration tools.

Accessing Registration Information

By default, SQL Server Enterprise Manager registry information is specific to each user on each computer. SQL Server Enterprise Manager uses this registration information each time that a user logs on and starts SQL Server Enterprise Manager to display and connect to registered servers. This functionality is similar to the way that Windows NT keeps a separate profile for each user. A Windows NT profile tracks user-specific information, such as user preferences, desktop settings, and messaging profiles.

If you manage multiple SQL Servers on one or more computers and want to configure all computers and users to have the same SQL Servers and groups, you must configure each computer individually by default. However, if the registry information is shared, you can configure all computers and users at one time.

SQL Server allows you to maintain private or shared registration information:

- By default, registration information is private, which prevents others from having access to your configuration.
- Alternatively, registration information can be shared, which allows multiple users to use the same configuration from a local computer, or from a central computer, sometimes referred to as the central store.

Setting Up SQL Server

Before you use SQL Server, you should assign the SQL Server sa logon account password and review configuration options.

When SQL Server is installed, the Setup program does not assign a password for the SQL Server sa logon account. You should assign a password to this account to prevent unauthorized users from using it to log on to SQL Server with SQL Server administrator privileges.

When you assign passwords, consider the following facts and guidelines:

- SQL Server logon IDs and passwords are stored in system tables in the master database and must be modified for each server.
- To assign passwords, use SQL Server Enterprise Manager or the sp_password system stored procedure.

Managing Resources Dynamically

SQL Server manages most SQL Server resources dynamically, based on current system and user requirements. Configuration is primarily automated and dynamic.

However, in some situations, you might need to set server options manually, such as when you want to limit the number of user connections and control the use of memory. You can use SQL Server Enterprise Manager or the sp_configure system stored procedure to configure or view these options.

Implementing a SQL Server Database

Implementing a SQL Server database involves planning, creating, and maintaining a number of interrelated components.

The nature and complexity of a database application, as well as the process of planning it, can vary greatly. For example, a database can be relatively simple, designed for use by a single person, or it can be large and complex, designed to handle all the banking transactions for hundreds of thousands of clients.

Regardless of the size and complexity of the database, implementing a database usually involves the following:

- Designing the database so that your application uses hardware optimally and allows for future growth, identifying and modeling database objects and application logic, and specifying the types of information for each object and type of relationship.
- Creating the database and database objects, including tables, data integrity mechanisms, data entry and retrieval objects (often stored procedures), appropriate indexes, and security.
- Testing and tuning the application and database.
- Ensuring, when you design a database, that the database performs important functions correctly and quickly. In conjunction with correct database design, correct use of indexes, redundant array of independent disks (RAID), and file groups are essential to achieving solid performance.

- Planning deployment, which includes analyzing the workload and recommending an optimal index configuration for your SQL Server database.
- Administering the application after deployment, which includes configuring servers and clients; monitoring server performance; managing jobs, alerts, and operators; and managing security and database backup procedures.

Importing Data into SQL Server

The following procedures demonstrate how to import data into a Microsoft SQL Server database using Microsoft Transact-SQL scripts and external data.

► **To create the Stocks SQL Server Database**

1. On the Start menu, point to Programs and SQL Server 7, and then click Enterprise Manager.
2. In Enterprise Manager, expand the branches for Microsoft SQL Servers, SQL Server Group, and your local computer.
3. Right-click the Databases object. Select New Database from the shortcut menu, and type Stocks in the Name text box. Accept all defaults and click OK.
4. Verify that the Stocks database was created by opening the Databases object and viewing the Stocks database.

► **To create the Pricehistory table in the Stocks database**

1. From the Tools menu of Enterprise Manager, select SQL Server Query Analyzer.
2. From the \Database folder, open the CreatePHTable.sql script that was installed earlier from the companion CD. Using the DB: drop-down list, change the database window to Stocks. Press the F5 key to execute the script, or click the Execute Query button (with a green right arrow icon) on the tool-bar of the SQL Server Query Analyzer. The following message appears: "The command(s) completed successfully."
3. Minimize Query Analyzer.

► **To import data into the Pricehistory table in the Stocks database**

1. Using Enterprise Manager, expand the branches for Microsoft SQL Servers, SQL Server Group, and your local computer.
2. Expand the Databases object and click the Stocks database. On the right side of the screen, click Import Data.
3. When the DTS Import Wizard opens, click Next.
4. From the Sources drop-down list, select Text File. In the File Name box, type the path for the PHImportData.txt file that was installed from the companion CD to the \Database folder, and click Next.

5. In the Select File Format window, verify that Delimited is selected, accept all defaults, and click Next.
6. Verify that Comma is selected as the column delimiter and click Next.
7. In the Destination drop-down box, verify that Microsoft OLE DB Provider for SQL Server is selected. In the Server box, verify that your local server name is displayed. Select Use SQL Server Authentication, type *sa* as the user name, and leave the password blank. Select Stocks as the Database and click Next.
8. In the Select Source Tables dialog box, change Destination Table to [stocks].[dbo].[pricehistory], and click Next.
9. Ensure that the Run Immediately check box is selected and click Next.
10. In the Completing the DTS Wizard dialog box, click Finish.
11. The following message appears: "Successfully transferred 1 table(s) from flat file to Microsoft SQL Server." Click OK.
12. When the Transferring Data dialog box appears, click Done.
13. Open the SQL Server Query Analyzer and click the New Query button on the toolbar. Type the following command: *select * from pricehistory*.
14. Press F5 to execute the script, or click the Execute Query button on the toolbar of the SQL Server Query Analyzer. The data from the table appears in the results window.

Referring to SQL Server Objects

You can refer to SQL Server objects in several ways. You can specify the full name of the object (its fully qualified name), or specify only part of the object name and have SQL Server determine the rest of the name from the context in which you are working.

- **Fully qualified names** The complete name of a SQL Server object includes four identifiers: the server name, database name, owner name, and object name in the following format:

  ```
  server.database.owner.object
  ```

  An object name that specifies all four parts is known as a *fully qualified name*. Each object created in SQL Server must have a unique, fully qualified name. For example, you can have two tables named orders in the same database as long as they belong to different owners. Also, column names must be unique within a table or view.

- **Partially specified names** When referencing an object, you do not always have to specify the server, database, and owner. Intermediate identifiers can be omitted as long as their position is indicated by periods. The valid formats of object names are as follows:

```
server.database.owner.object
server.database..object
server..owner.object
server...object
database.owner.object
database..object
owner.object
object
```

When you create an object, SQL Server uses the following defaults if different parts of the name are not specified:

- Server defaults to the local server.
- Database defaults to the current database.
- Owner defaults to the user name in the specified database associated with the login ID of the current connection.

A user that is a member of a role can explicitly specify the role as the object owner. A user that is a member of the db_owner or db_ddladmin role in a database can specify the **dbo** user account as the owner of an object. This practice is recommended.

The following code creates an order_history table in the northwind database:

```
CREATE TABLE northwind.dbo.order_history
    (orderid int,
    productid int,
    unitprice money,
    quantity int, discount decimal)
```

Most object references use three-part names and default to the local server. Four-part names are generally used for distributed queries or remote stored procedure calls.

System Tables

System tables store information, called *metadata*, about the system and objects in databases. Metadata is information about data.

Each database (including master) contains a collection of system tables that store metadata about that specific database. This collection of system tables is the *database catalog*.

The *system catalog*, found only in the master database, is a collection of system tables that stores metadata about the entire system and all other databases.

System tables all begin with the sys prefix. Table 9.10, on the next page, identifies several frequently used system tables.

Table 9.10 Frequently Used System Tables

System table	Database	Function
syslogins	master	Contains one row for each login account that can connect to SQL Server
sysmessages	master	Contains one row for each system error or warning that SQL Server can return
sysdatabases	master	Contains one row for each database on a SQL Server
sysusers	All	Contains one row for each Windows NT user, Windows NT group, SQL Server user, or SQL Server role in a database
sysobjects	All	Contains one row for each object in a database

Data Integrity

An important step in database planning is deciding the best way to enforce the integrity of the data. Data integrity refers to the consistency and accuracy of data that is stored in a database. The different types of data integrity are as follows:

- **Domain integrity** Domain (or column) integrity specifies a set of data values that are valid for a column and determines whether null values are allowed. Domain integrity is often enforced through the use of validity checking and can also be enforced by restricting the data type, format, or range of possible values allowed in a column.
- **Entity integrity** Entity (or table) integrity requires that all rows in a table have a unique identifier, known as the primary key value. Whether the primary key value can be changed, or whether the whole row can be deleted, depends on the level of integrity required between the primary key and any other tables.
- **Referential integrity** Referential integrity ensures that the relationships among the primary keys (in the referenced table) and foreign keys (in the referencing tables) are always maintained. A row in a referenced table cannot be deleted, nor the primary key changed, if a foreign key refers to the row.

Using Constraints

The preferred method of enforcing data integrity is by using constraints—an ANSI-standard method of enforcing data integrity. Each type of data integrity—domain, entity, and referential—is enforced with separate types of constraints. Constraints ensure that valid data values are entered in columns and that relationships are maintained between tables. Table 9.11 describes the different types of constraints.

Table 9.11 Types of Constraints

Type of integrity	Constraint type	Description
Domain	DEFAULT	Specifies the value that will be provided for the column when a value has not been explicitly supplied in an INSERT statement.
	CHECK	Specifies data values that are acceptable in a column.
	REFERENTIAL	Specifies the data values that are acceptable to update based on values in a column in another table.
Entity	PRIMARY KEY	Uniquely identifies each row—ensures that users do not enter duplicate values and that an index is created to enhance performance. Null values are not allowed.
	UNIQUE	Prevents duplication of alternate (non-primary) keys, and ensures that an index is created to enhance performance. Null values are allowed.
Referential	FOREIGN KEY	Defines a column or combination of columns whose values match the primary key of the same or another table.
	CHECK	Specifies the data values that are acceptable in a column based on values in other columns in the same table.

Defining Constraints

You define constraints by using the CREATE TABLE or ALTER TABLE statement. You can add constraints to a table with existing data, and you can place constraints on single or multiple columns:

- If the constraint applies to a single column, it is called a column-level constraint.
- If a constraint references multiple columns, it is called a table-level constraint, even if it does not reference all columns in the table.

The general syntax for defining constraints is as follows:

```
CREATE TABLE table_name
(column_name data_type
[[CONSTRAINT constraint_name]
       {   PRIMARY KEY [CLUSTERED|NONCLUSTERED]
           |UNIQUE [CLUSTERED|NONCLUSTERED]
           |[FOREIGN KEY] REFERENCES
           ref_table [(ref_column)]
           |DEFAULT constant_expression
           |CHECK (logical_expression)
       }
       ][,...n]

<table_constraint>::=
    |[CONSTRAINT constraint_name]
    {   PRIMARY KEY|UNIQUE}
    [CLUSTERED | NONCLUSTERED]
```

```
        [(column[,...n])]
    |[FOREIGN KEY][(column[,...n])]
        REFERENCES ref_table [(ref_column[,...n])]
    | CHECK (search_conditions)
    }
}[,...n]
)
```

The following code creates an employee table and defines the employee number as the primary key:

```
USE library
CREATE TABLE employee
    (emp_num int NOT NULL CONSTRAINT emp_id PRIMARY KEY,
        emp_lastname char(30) NOT NULL,
        emp_firstname char(30) NOT NULL)
```

PRIMARY KEY Constraints

A PRIMARY KEY constraint defines a primary key on a table that uniquely identifies a row. It enforces entity integrity.

The syntax for defining PRIMARY KEY constraints is as follows:

```
[CONSTRAINT constraint_name]
    PRIMARY KEY [CLUSTERED|NONCLUSTERED]
        {(column[,...n])}
```

The following code adds a constraint that specifies that the primary key value of the member table is the member number and indicates that a clustered index will be created to enforce the constraint:

```
USE library
ALTER TABLE member
ADD
CONSTRAINT PK_member_member_no
    PRIMARY KEY CLUSTERED (member_no)
```

FOREIGN KEY Constraints

A FOREIGN KEY constraint enforces referential integrity. The FOREIGN KEY constraint defines a reference to a column with a PRIMARY KEY or UNIQUE constraint in the same or another table.

The syntax for defining FOREIGN KEY constraints is as follows:

```
[CONSTRAINT constraint_name]
    [FOREIGN KEY] [(column[,...n])]
        REFERENCES ref_table [(ref_column [,...n])].
```

The following code uses a FOREIGN KEY constraint to ensure that any juvenile member is associated with a valid adult member:

```
USE library
ALTER TABLE juvenile
ADD
CONSTRAINT FK_adult_memberno
    FOREIGN KEY (adult_memberno)
    REFERENCES adult(member_no)
```

Creating and Maintaining Indexes

Understanding how data is stored is the basis for understanding how SQL Server accesses data.

How Data Is Stored

A *heap* is a collection of data pages containing rows for a table:

- The data for each table is stored in a collection of 8-kilobyte data pages, which are referred to as extents.
- The data rows are not stored in any particular order, and there is no particular order to the sequence of the data pages.
- The data pages are not linked in a linked list.
- When rows are inserted into a page and a page is full, the data pages split.

How Data Is Accessed

SQL Server accesses data in one of two ways:

- Scanning all the data pages of tables, called a *table scan*. When SQL Server performs a table scan, it:
  - Starts at the beginning of the table
  - Scans from page-to-page through all of the rows in the table
  - Extracts the rows that meet the criteria of the query
- Using indexes. When SQL Server uses an index, it:
  - Traverses the index tree structure to find rows that the query requests
  - Extracts only the needed rows that meet the criteria of the query

SQL Server first determines whether an index exists. Then the query optimizer, the component responsible for generating the optimum execution plan for a query, determines whether scanning a table or using the index is more efficient for accessing data.

Indexing Guidelines

Your business environment, data characteristics, and use of the data determine the columns that you specify to build an index. The usefulness of an index is directly related to the percentage of rows returned from a query. Low percentages or high selectivity are more efficient. Create indexes on frequently searched columns, such as primary keys; foreign keys or columns that are used frequently in joining tables; columns that are searched for ranges of key values; or columns that are accessed in sorted order. Do not index columns that you seldom reference in a query; contain few unique values; or are defined with bit, text, and image data types.

Creating and Dropping Indexes

You create indexes using the CREATE INDEX statement and remove them using the DROP INDEX statement.

The syntax for using the CREATE INDEX statement is as follows:

```
CREATE [UNIQUE][CLUSTERED|NONCLUSTERED]
INDEX index_name ON table (column [,...n])
[WITH
[PAD_INDEX]
[[,] FILLFACTOR = fillfactor]
[[,] IGNORE_DUP_KEY]
[[,] DROP_EXISTING]
[[,] STATISTICS_NORECOMPUTE]
]
[ON filegroup]
```

The following code creates a clustered index on the lastname column in the member table:

```
CREATE CLUSTERED INDEX cl_lastname
    ON library..member (lastname)
```

The syntax for using the DROP INDEX statement is as follows:

```
DROP INDEX 'table.index' [,...n]
```

The following code drops the cl_lastname index from the member table:

```
USE library
DROP INDEX member.cl_lastname
```

Lesson Summary

In this lesson, you were introduced to the process of configuring a SQL Server. This lesson covers details on creating and modifying SQL Server objects such as tables, fields, and field types. It also covers the process of creating keys to maintain referential integrity, and indexing.

Lesson 3: Data Access Strategies

Data Access Strategies provides an introduction to UDA and the tools and technologies you will use to implement UDA.

After this lesson, you will be able to:

- Describe Microsoft's strategy for data access through UDA technology
- Identify the Microsoft Data Access Components (MDAC) features that implement UDA—ADO, OLE DB, ODBC, and RDS
- Evaluate whether a database should be incorporated in the application
- Implement persistence
- Use Sockets
- Implement standard serialization
- Display data using CArchive
- Manage transactions to ensure data consistency and recoverability

Estimated lesson time: 150 minutes

Data Access

The data used for making business decisions often resides in multiple storage areas and formats. Decision makers often have to collate information stored in spreadsheets, relational databases, mainframes, e-mail, and the Internet before making a decision. Because each of these data sources requires its own method of data access, organizational problems can arise.

One solution to such problems is to put all data in a single relational data store, and to use a single data access method. However, this solution would result in data duplication and data integrity issues; to address these issues, Microsoft introduced its UDA technology.

UDA Technology

Microsoft introduced the Microsoft Universal Data Architecture (UDA) technology as a solution to the problems that arise when accessing data from multiple data sources through a single data access method. Using the UDA technology, you can access data in different data stores through a common set of interfaces, regardless of where the data resides. For example, you can use UDA to access data from relational database management systems (RDBMS) such as SQL and Oracle, or from text files.

UDA is a technology for developing multitier enterprise applications that require access to diverse relational or nonrelational data sources across intranets or the Internet. UDA consists of a collection of software components that interact with one another using a common set of system-level interfaces defined by OLE DB.

The strategy of UDA is to allow developers to access diverse types of data, from both relational and nonrelational data sources, although enabling them to work with familiar tools. Nonrelational data sources are data such as document containers (such as Microsoft Internet Explorer), e-mail, and file systems.

The UDA strategy is based on COM. As a result, the UDA architecture is open to programmers and operable with tools or programming languages that support COM. You do not need to use new tools to work with UDA.

UDA Architecture

All interactions among components, shown in Figure 9.1, can occur across process and computer boundaries through network protocols, such as Microsoft Distributed COM (DCOM) or Hypertext Transfer Protocol (HTTP). Transacted interactions among components are possible through MTS.

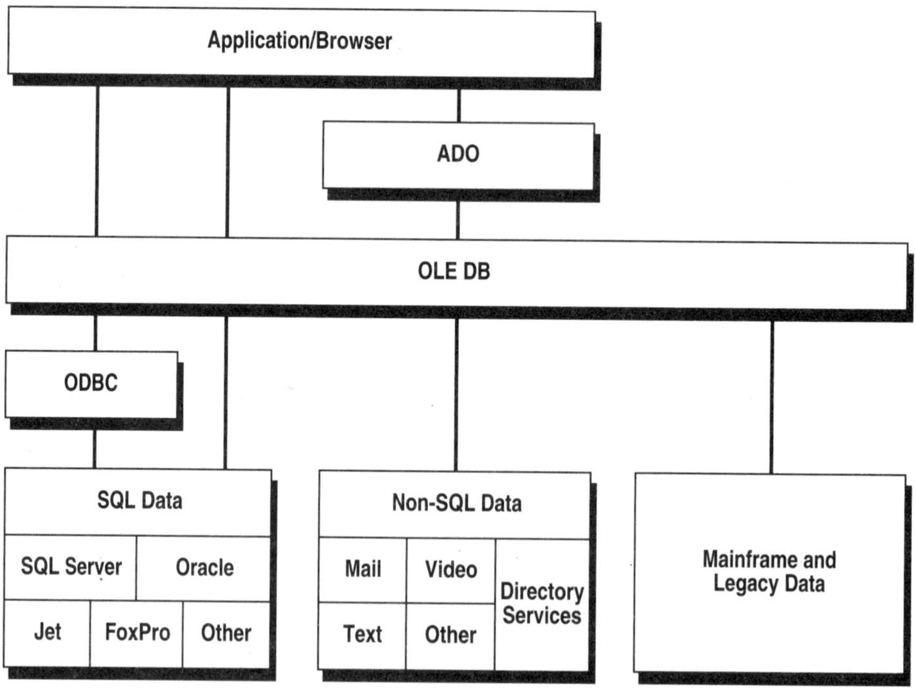

Figure 9.1 UDA architecture and database components

Figure 9.1 shows three general kinds of database components:

- **Data consumers** Components that consume OLE DB data. Examples of consumers include services such as a query processor; high-level data access models, such as Microsoft ActiveX Data Objects (ADO); and business applications written in languages such as Microsoft Visual Basic or Visual C++.
- **Service components** Components that consume and produce OLE DB data. For example, a *cursor engine* is a service component that can consume data from a sequential, forward-only data source to produce scrollable data.
- **Data providers** Components that represent data sources such as SQL databases, indexed sequential files, and spreadsheets. Providers expose information uniformly using a common abstraction known as a rowset.

Fundamental Terms of Data Access

The following sections will examine two types of cursors: client-side and server-side cursors.

Result Sets and Cursors

To retrieve and work with data, you must use a command. That command can be a stored procedure or a SQL query; in either case, a *result set* of data is constructed. A result set is data in the form of rows and columns that results from running a command against a database.

A result set is simply a set of data. A *cursor* stores the result set and provides functionality to allow an application to work directly with the result set. The cursor provides access to the result set through a single record. Thus, at any given time, one record in the result set is current. The cursor allows the application to change the current record by moving through the result set.

Cursor Attributes

Cursors are defined by three attributes: *concurrency*, *scrolling*, and *locking*. The manner in which these three attributes are implemented depends on the cursor's implementer, which is usually the database itself.

- **Concurrency** When you retrieve records from a result set, other users can concurrently make changes to the underlying database tables. Depending on how you use the result set, you might need to view these changes, or you might ignore these changes instead. Cursors can support both options and variations comprising selective viewing and ignoring of different changes within a set of tables. For example, ADO supports the concept of a static cursor, which does not reflect any changes made by other users to the underlying data.
- **Scrolling** Cursors provide access to the result set one record at a time. As a result, the accessed record is always the current record. You can change

which record is current by moving the cursor to a different location. Some cursors support only moving forward through the result set one record at a time, such as the ADO forward-only cursor. This kind of cursor is limited, but allows the database to optimize how the result set is created and used. Cursors that support backwards scrolling or jumping to any point in the result set require more overhead by the implementer to manage them, but they offer more flexibility for how the data is used.

- **Locking** The underlying data can be read-only or updateable. Updateable cursors generally require more overhead than read-only cursors because updateable cursors require complex locking code to ensure consistency. Also, locked data in a database results in an increased risk of other users having to wait to make updates.

Client-Side Cursors

In a *client-side cursor,* the client computer provides the resources required by the cursor and result set. With this type of cursor, all records have to be copied to the client computer before they can be processed. Although this type of cursor consumes a large amount of network resources (depending on the result set's size), a client-side cursor provides quick response when the result set has been downloaded to the client computer. Examples of client-side cursors are the static disconnected recordset in ADO and the snapshot cursor provided by the ODBC client library. In general, you want to avoid using client-side cursors with any large result sets, because copying large result sets across the network is time-consuming and inefficient.

Server-Side Cursors

With a *server-side cursor,* the server computer provides the resources that are required by the cursor and result set. Because the cursor is located closer to the data, it reduces the amount of network traffic and provides greater performance when compared with the client-side cursor.

Server-side cursors support direct positioned updates. This eliminates the risk of collisions when multiple users try to update a single record.

In general, you want to avoid using server-side cursors in scenarios where the result set will be open for a long period of time. Open connections consume server resources and increase the likelihood of a resource conflict with other users. Client-side cursors work more optimally for result sets that will be open for long periods of time.

Microsoft Data Access Components

MDAC is the practical implementation of UDA. MDAC 2.1 supports the following technologies:

- **ADO 2.1** Language-neutral object model that exposes data raised by an underlying OLE DB Provider.
- **OLE DB 2.1** Open specification designed to build on the success of ODBC by providing an open standard for accessing data.
- **ODBC 3.5** Common SQL-based interface for accessing heterogeneous SQL databases as a standard for accessing data.
- **DAO** DAO was added to MFC in version 4. DAO supplies a hierarchical set of objects that uses the Microsoft Jet database engine to access data and database structures.
- **RDS 2.0** Service used to transport ADO recordsets from a server to a client computer. The resulting recordset is cached on the client computer and disconnected from the server.

Incorporating a Database in an Application

A database provides an organization with centralized control over data. A good database is efficient, and can be adapted to meet current and future requirements. A database is incorporated in an application to reduce the redundancy in the data stored, which implies efficient use of storage space. Another reason for incorporating a database in an application is to avoid inconsistency in data. If data stored in multiple tables gets updated in file, the update must be reflected in other files too. This needs to be controlled by a database management system (DBMS). There are many more reasons such as maintaining data integrity, data independence, and so on. Incorporating a database in an application can eliminate all problems when dealing with huge quantities of data in an application.

Implementing Persistence

Application persistence is the act of saving information about the application between program sessions. MFC provides support for persistence through serialization.

Serialization is the process of storing data from the application to a data file or loading data from a data file to the application. Serialization is integrated within the MFC's document/view architecture and can occur as a result of the user explicitly saving or loading a data file. Serialization can also occur as a side effect of modifying the document data. In this case, the MFC application framework will prompt the user to save the data before deleting the data from the document.

The approach to serialization within MFC is that the document object begins the serialization of data. The document object either serializes data directly, or it delegates the task of serialization to the data objects contained within the document. The objects, in turn, implement the functionality to save their data members. Later, these objects can restore their data members by reading, or "deserializing," the data from persistent storage. A key point is that the objects themselves are responsible for reading and writing their own state. For a class to be persistent, it must implement the basic serialization operations.

In the document/view architecture the serialization process starts at the developer's CDocument-derived class where AppWizard has generated a *Serialize* function. From the *Serialize* function, the developer creates application-specific code that transfers the data. The framework passes in a reference to an archive object when the *Serialize* function is called. The archive object acts as an intermediate object between the document and the data file. The document's *Serialize* function uses the archive object directly or, for more complicated document objects, the document will pass the archive object to the document's data objects, which will then serialize themselves.

Serialization in MFC depends upon a number of classes in your application's framework. Table 9.12 lists the primary classes and their purpose.

Table 9.12 Primary Classes and Their Purpose

Class	Purpose
CObject	Serves as a base class for objects that are to be serialized. The member function CObject::Serialize is overridden by the developer to implement serialization for the data object.
CDocument	Contains the information (data and objects) to be serialized. The member function CDocument::Serialize specifies what portion of this information is to be serialized.
CArchive	Provides a context for serialization. CArchive handles process-dependent factors, such as media access and buffering. During construction, a CFile object is attached to the archive. A single CArchive object can be used for either storing or loading data, but not for both.
CFile	Represents the file on a storage device, such as a hard disk. CFile directly provides unbuffered, binary disk input/output services, and it indirectly supports text files and memory files through its derived classes.

The FileNew, FileOpen, and FileSave commands are three common ways to explicitly initiate serialization. This topic describes the MFC classes and functions available to help you implement your serialization code, including the differences between single-document interface (SDI) and multiple-document interface (MDI) applications during the serialization operation.

Serialization and MFC

Important points to remember about serialization support as implemented by MFC are as follows:

- Actual data serialization begins with the *CDocument::Serialize* function.
- All objects are transferred in totality—that is, partial serialization is not allowed.
- Objects are loaded in the same order in which they were saved.
- Synchronize documents by using a schema number.

Opening a New File

When a user clicks the New command on the File menu in an AppWizard-generated application, the default framework behavior is as follows:

1. Checks whether the current document has been modified and, if so, prompts the user to save it. Saves the current document if the user says yes.
2. Removes the contents of the old document.
3. Creates a new document.

Virtual Functions to Manage Document Creation

The CDocument class provides two virtual functions that can be overridden to provide for handling the document-creation process:

- *CDocument::OnNewDocument* is called by the framework as part of the New command. The default implementation of this function calls *DeleteContents* to empty the document, and then marks the document as clean. You can override this function to do per-document initialization instead of placing this code in the constructor for your document class.
- *CDocument::DeleteContents* empties the document without destroying the document object itself. The default implementation of this function does nothing. Commonly, this function is overridden to delete dynamically allocated objects in your document, rather than using the destructor.

Using CSocket

A *socket* is basically an endpoint of network communications. To have communications via a network, each computer must create a socket. These sockets must then be connected to each other. You can think of a socket as a telephone. You pick up the phone and connect to another one somewhere else via the magic of the phone company. In the case of sockets, the magic is handled by your network card, software, and possibly other intermediate computers.

All information sent across this network connection is in binary form. Neither the network nor the sockets interpret the contents of the binary data. It's your responsibility as the programmer to make sense of what comes into a socket. If a client application sends a character string across the network and the server expects an array of integers, the server will interpret the sequence of bytes it receives as an array of integers. This might not cause an error, but it's probably not what the programmer had in mind.

SDK Issues

You need to address three big issues when using sockets and the software development kit (SDK) functions: blocking versus non-blocking, byte ordering, and character sets. The first issue might or might not be a problem depending on the operating system you use. The latter two apply only if you're performing network communications on different platforms or operating systems.

One of the most important things to be aware of is the concept of blocking versus non-blocking. By default, all SDK socket calls are blocking, meaning they don't return until the function is completed. Under the Windows environment, blocking can be devastating. An application that blocks too long doesn't continue to process its messages. Under 16-bit Windows, a non-preemptive environment, blocking applications also don't release control to Windows. The entire system eventually grinds to a halt. In preemptive operating systems, like Windows NT or Windows 95, the problem isn't quite as bad. Your application might run slower or not at all, but the OS should preempt your process and give time to other processes.

Using the SDK, you might want to change your sockets to a non-blocking mode. Calls to a function in non-blocking mode immediately return with a value of WSAEINPROGRESS. You need to check the result of the function constantly and pump Windows messages if the function is still in progress. A fancier implementation of sockets might use multiple threads to manage client connections. If you choose to block in one thread, your process' main thread can continue. If you do decide to go the multithreaded route, remember to limit concurrent access of objects between threads using the Win32 synchronization functions. Both non-blocking and multithreaded methods require about the same amount of code.

Another thing to watch out for is the order in which some platforms store values in memory. Some computer architectures use *big-endian* byte ordering, meaning the high bytes of a value are stored at a higher address in memory. Other computers, like the Intel-based PC, use *little-endian* value, where low bytes are stored at a higher address in memory. Also, some computer architectures store values with their most significant bit (MSB) first. Other computers store the least significant bit (LSB) first. The SDK provides several functions to manage byte ordering: *ntohl*, *htonl*, *ntohs*, and *htons*. Because at the socket level all data is just a series of bits and bytes, it's important to know not only what data is being sent, but also in what format the data is being sent.

Finally, performing network communications across platforms demands an awareness of the differences in character sets. Different computers might have different ways of representing characters. There are at least three different character sets: EBCDIC, ASCII/ANSI (with different code pages), and UNICODE. If you send a particular string across the network in ASCII, the computer on the other end will attempt to interpret the stream of bytes according to its own character set. An "A" in one character set might not be an "A" in another. Be sure to know what character set you're using to send data across the network.

You can solve all three of these problems, but the solution requires a lot of code. Fortunately, MFC contains much of the code you need. As you'll see, using MFC to perform network communications can be as simple as using a file.

MFC Sockets Design

The base class for MFC socket classes is CAsyncSocket. The CAsyncSocket class takes care of message routing and notifications but doesn't take care of anything else. A more usable class for socket communications in MFC is CSocket. It still allows you to take advantage of MFC's message routing and additionally takes care of the three problems mentioned earlier. The default implementation of the CSocket class is adequate for simple communications. If you want to take full advantage of MFC's socket support, you should use CSocket as an abstract base class and derive the implementation classes you need from there. It is usually recommended to create two derived classes for the server side and one for the client side.

On the server side, you should publicly derive one class from CSocket that represents the server socket; let's call it CServerSocket. The only responsibility of CServerSocket is to accept and keep track of client connections. A minimum implementation should have a mechanism to keep track of all connected clients; it is often a good idea to keep a CObList of the clients. First, you should override the *OnAccept* function. *OnAccept* is called when a client socket requests to connect to the server. If the server decides to start communication with the client socket, it should create a new object representing the client socket. The server then should add that client object to a list of all clients. *OnAccept* should look something like this:

```
void CServerSocket::OnAccept(int nErrorCode)
{
    CClientProxy *pClientProxy;

// Create a new proxy and add it to the list
    pClientProxy = new CClientProxy;
    if (pClientProxy)
    {
        Accept(*pClientProxy);
        pClientProxy->Initialize(...);
        m_clientList.AddTail(pClientProxy);
    }
}
```

The other server class is an encapsulation of a connected client. Because a server socket might be connected to one or more client sockets, you need to keep track of all connected clients, for example, observe a client class CClientProxy. The CServerSocket's *OnAccept* function should instantiate one of these classes and add it to its client list. This client proxy is the object that handles communications with each client, not the server socket. All messages that come from a particular client are routed through the message map of the particular proxy socket in the server's list. The MFC application knows which socket a particular communication should be routed to and calls the appropriate object's functions. It is recommended that you override *OnReceive* for the CClientProxy class and take care of reading the socket. Likewise, you should also override the *OnClose* as well. *OnClose* is called when the connected client has disconnected. Usually you want to remove the newly disconnected client from the list of clients.

The client side is a little easier. Because a client socket can connect to only one server, there's just one connection you need to worry about. Truthfully, for a simple socket application the CClientProxy class can be used on the client side as well. CClientProxy should at least override the *OnReceive* member so the socket knows when data is waiting for it. In larger applications, you should generally create a separate socket class called CClientSocket that takes care of specific client-side implementation details. For this simple example, you can allow CClientProxy and CClientSocket to exist as the same class.

Writing MFC Code

In this section, you will observe the steps of writing a simple MFC server and client combination. You need to #include *<afxsock.h>* to get the definitions of the MFC socket classes and functions. One of the first things your application should do is call the *AfxInitSocket* function, usually from your application's *InitInstance* function. This initializes the socket subsystem and lets MFC know that you want to use sockets in your application. To start your application, you need to create a CSocket object on both the server and client sides. You could use MFC's CAsyncSocket class, but that barely wraps the application programming interface (API) calls and doesn't do much to solve the three problems explained earlier. The CSocket class solves these problems in a far easier manner.

As with most MFC objects, there is a two-step construction process. After instantiating the CSocket object, you need to call its *Create* member. The server side needs to pass in a port ID to *Create*. The port ID uniquely identifies which of the possible 64K ports the socket will be using. The first 1K ports are reserved for commonly used utilities such as FTP, TELNET, and finger. The client side might select a particular port ID or specify zero to let MFC select a free port. The client's port really doesn't matter because most of the communication processing will be done on the server side.

The server then needs to call the *Listen* function so it can wait for incoming client connections. After *Listen* has been executed, any incoming connection requests are routed to the server's *OnAccept* function. *OnAccept* is where the server has a chance to start communications or ignore the client.

For the client to attempt connection to the server, the client calls the *Connect* function. The *Connect* function takes at least two parameters. The first parameter is the network address of the server. When using the Microsoft network protocol, this address can be specified in one of two ways. The first way is simply the computer name. The second way is the actual network address of the computer. This address is referred to as Internet Protocol (IP) address. The IP address consists of 4-byte values separated by periods (such as, "123.45.67.89"). Each computer on the network has a unique IP address either entered by the network administrator or generated by a network server.

The second parameter to the *Create* function is the port ID of the server's port. The port that the server specified in its *Create* call needs to be known to all the clients. Without knowing which of the 64K ports to attach to, the client won't be able to establish a connection. For instance, say a particular computer has an IP address of 157.58.125.75 and its computer name is "LACIVITA." If an individual had a client socket and wanted to connect to a server application on the computer, they would call:

```
m_clientSocket.Connect("LACIVITA", PORT_ID)
```

or:

```
m_clientSocket.Connect("157.58.125.75", PORT_ID)
```

The action now shifts back to the server. When a client attempts to connect to a server, the server's *OnAccept* function is called. The server can ignore this client by simply returning from the function. If the server wants to connect to the client, it does two things. First, it instantiates a new instance of the CClientProxy class. This class represents the connection between the two sockets. Second, the server calls its *Accept* function, passing the newly instantiated CClientProxy as a parameter. You don't need to call the CClientProxy variable's *Create* function. The client socket has already been created on the client side. The CClientProxy information gets filled in by the call to *Accept*.

At this point you could use the CSocket's *Send* and *Receive* functions on both the client and server sides to communicate. This process isn't object-oriented—*Send* and *Receive* both take a void pointer and a length as parameters. You basically send a buffer of bytes. It would be much more preferable if you could send actual C++ objects across the connection.

Using CSocketFile and CArchive

In addition to using the generic *Send* and *Receive* functions for the CSocket objects, MFC allows you to encapsulate communications a little more. MFC has a class called CSocketFile, which is derived from CFile. This means almost anywhere you use a CFile you can use a CSocketFile. This inheritance makes it easy for existing MFC applications to become network-aware. You can simply replace any occurrence of CFile with CSocketFile. The CSocketFile takes at least one parameter in the constructor. This parameter is the instantiation of the CSocket-derived class that you want the file to be associated with. On the server side, you would pass the CClientProxy object you created in the *OnAccept* function. On the client side, you would use the only socket class you have, CClientSocket. You can now use the CFile functions, *Read* and *Write*, to get information in and out of the socket. This still doesn't use the object-oriented paradigm as nicely as it could, so you can take this one step further and use MFC's CArchive class.

You create a CArchive object the same way you normally would, simply instantiating it or using the new operator. Pass the newly-created CSocketFile object as the first parameter and specify whether you want the archive to be loading or storing as the second parameter. Because a CArchive can only serialize data in one direction, you'll probably want to create two CArchive objects, one for sending and one for receiving.

With the CArchive created, you can now use the *insertion* and *extraction* operators (<< and >>) to communicate via the sockets. Because CArchive can only be used with classes derived from CObject, you probably want to override your class' *Serialize* member function. Remember to use the DECLARE_SERIAL and IMPLEMENT_SERIAL macros in the header and implementation files. You can optionally overload the insertion and extraction operators for your class as well. One important thing to remember about the CArchive class is that it buffers data. If you need to send data to a client socket immediately, you should call CArchive's *Flush* member.

There are two additional situations you need to be familiar with when using sockets and CArchives. The first situation appears when using sockets under a multitasking operating system. It's occasionally possible for a client socket to close before it notifies the server socket that it's closing. In this case, the server attempts to send data to a socket that's already closed. To fix this situation, you need to encompass the code that sends your data inside a TRY/CATCH block. Inside the CATCH portion of the block you should simply close the CArchive object. The socket should eventually close itself. Consider the following code:

```
TRY
{
// Flush the data because the client needs it now
    (*pArchive) << theBall;
    pArchive->Flush();
}

// If we catch an exception shut down the client
CATCH(CFileException, e)
{
    pClientProxy->ShutDown();
}
END_CATCH
```

The second situation is specific to using CArchive. If a client socket isn't quick enough to read messages as they come in, some messages will become backed up in the socket's message queue. When this situation occurs, *OnReceive* won't be called until all pending messages have been read. The CArchive class has a member function called *IsBufferEmpty* specifically for this purpose. You can simply read in all pending data until the buffer is empty. In MFC, the read loop can be implemented this way:

```
// Get all pending information from the socket
do
{
    (*m_pSocketArchive) >> (*m_pBallWnd);
}
while (!m_pSocketArchive->IsBufferEmpty());
```

Managing Transactions

Transactions and transaction management are important parts of MTS. A transaction is a collection of changes to data. When a transaction occurs either all of the changes are made (committed) or none of them are made (rolled back). MTS can automatically enlist objects and their associated resources into transactions, and manage those transactions to ensure that changes to data are made correctly.

In Figure 9.2, three business objects work together to transfer money from one account to another. The Debit object debits an account and the Credit object credits an account. The Transfer object calls the Debit and Credit objects to transfer money between accounts. Both the Debit and the Credit objects must complete their work for a transaction to succeed. If either object fails to complete its task, the transaction is not successful and any work that was done must be rolled back to maintain the integrity of the accounts.

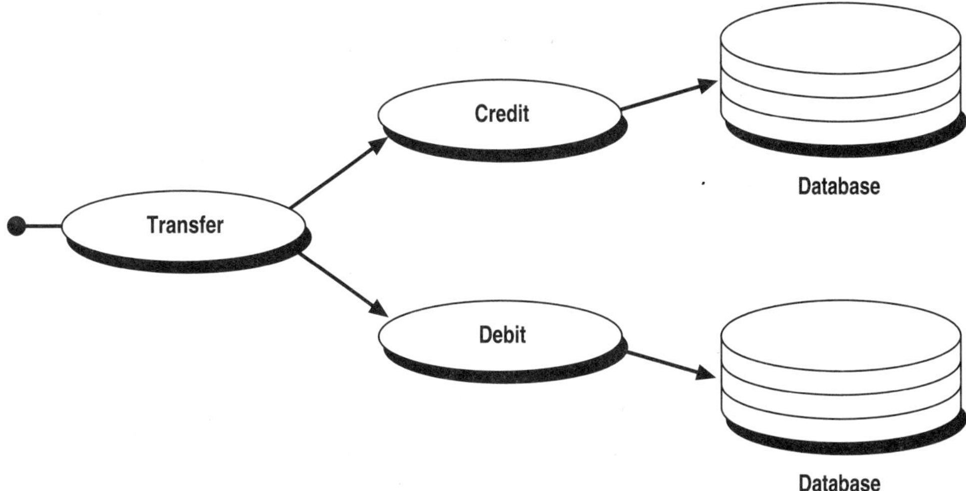

Figure 9.2 Example on transaction processing

Choosing the Right Data Access Technology

Almost all applications require some form of data access. For stand-alone desktop applications, local data access is typically easy to implement with little or no programming effort. For enterprise applications, data access is considerably more complex, often involving remote data sources with different data formats and storage mechanisms.

Developers often ask the question, "Which data access technology should I use to build this enterprise application?" To answer this question, developers need to keep two critical points in mind: the importance of code reuse and developers' ability to implement the chosen interface. Often, developers implement an exotic data access solution in a quest for better performance or more control, only to create an application that is an expensive maintenance burden. The newer data access technologies typically reduce development time, simplify code, and yet still provide high performance and expose all required functionality.

Developers can effectively use virtually all of the Microsoft data access technologies in most situations. Nevertheless, each data access technology has its relative strengths. If their applications require data access, developers will want to understand the unique data access implementation and usage issues specific to each data access method.

When to Use ADO

ADO is Microsoft's premier data access technology. The ADO data access technology and its partner OLE DB comprise the recommended solution for all data access. If a team is developing a new application, developers should definitely use ADO.

If the team is considering migration to ADO, they have to decide if characteristics and benefits of ADO are enough to justify the cost of converting existing software. Older code written in Microsoft Remote Data Objects (RDO) and DAO will not automatically convert to ADO code. However, whatever solutions developers previously developed using other data access strategies can definitely be implemented using ADO. In the long run, ADO should be used.

When to Use RDO

If the team has an RDO application that works well today, there's no reason to change it. If the application needs to be extended to access other kinds of data, consider reengineering to use ADO. As mentioned previously, new applications should use ADO.

When to Use ODBCDirect

ODBCDirect is an acceptable choice if the application must run queries or stored procedures against an ODBC relational database, or if your application needs only the specific capabilities of ODBC, such as batch updates or asynchronous queries. However, every feature in ODBCDirect is also available in ADO.

If developers have a working knowledge of ODBCDirect and have large amounts of existing ODBCDirect code, or just need to extend an existing application that already uses it, ODBCDirect will still work for the application. The drawback is that ODBCDirect cannot provide all data access if the application requires other types of non-ODBC data sources. Eventually, the team could take advantage of design, coding, and performance benefits provided by ADO.

When to Use DAO

DAO is the only data access technology that supports 16-bit operations. If the application must run within a 16-bit environment, DAO is the only logical choice.

If the application must access both native Microsoft Jet and ODBC resources, DAO will work; however OLE DB or ADO will provide faster access and require fewer resources.

If the team is experienced in using DAO and has large amounts of existing DAO code, or just needs to extend an existing application that uses a Microsoft Jet database, DAO might still work for the application. Again, the drawback comes as an application requires other types of data sources, and DAO cannot provide data access. Eventually, the team will want to take advantage of ADO.

When to Use ODBC

Several factors influence choosing the ODBC approach, including a requirement of high performance, more granular control over the interface, and a small footprint.

The ODBC API is considerably harder to code than the object-based interfaces, but provides a finer degree of control over the data source. Unlike other data access technologies (such as ADO, RDO, or ODBCDirect), the ODBC API has not been made "bullet proof." Although it's fairly easy to create ODBC errors during development, the ODBC API provides excellent error handling with detailed error messages. In general, developing, debugging, and supporting an ODBC API application requires a tremendous amount of knowledge, experience, and many lines of code. As a general rule, developers prefer to access data by using a simpler, higher-level object interface such as ADO.

ODBC is not suitable for nonrelational data such as Indexed Sequential Accessed Method (ISAM) data because it has no interfaces for seeking records, setting ranges, or browsing indexes. ODBC simply was not designed to access ISAM data. Although you can use the Microsoft Jet ODBC driver to handle ISAM and the native Microsoft Jet engine data, what is really happening is that the Microsoft Jet database engine converts the ISAM data to relational data and then provides limited ISAM functionality. Performance in this situation is slow due to the extra layer imposed by the Microsoft Jet engine.

If the application requires very fast access to existing ODBC data, and if developers are willing to write many lines of complex code (or already have a log of ODBC code available for reuse), ODBC can be a good choice.

Choosing a Data Access Strategy

A project team needs to consider the following questions before choosing a data access technology:

- **Is the development team creating a new design, or modifying an existing application that uses obsolete data access technology?** For a modification, it's tempting to continue with the application's former data access methods, which in the short term seems like a reasonable and cost-effective decision. However, the downside involves programming difficulty as the application stretches toward new and different data sources. For a new design, developers should use ADO.
- **Where is the data? Is it on the Web, on a remote server, or simply stored locally on user's systems?** If the data is simply stored on users' local systems, the need to build a separate server to manage the data might be overkill. If the data is remote, what about connection management? What happens when the application cannot connect? Should the application be using an asynchronous data access technology such as ADO or RDO?
- **What are the developers trained to use?** Do they already have experience with ADO, RDO, DAO, or ODBC? Is it worth the modest one-time cost and effort to train the entire staff to use ADO? If the team begins using ADO, can developers reasonably anticipate a maintenance cost reduction in the near future?
- **Does an application require data access to both relational and nonrelational data sources? Do developers have an OLE DB provider for each?** If so, use ADO.
- **Are developers planning to use MTS?** If this is the case, developers need to choose one of the data access technologies that can be executed on the server and act as a *resource manager* (an MTS term for a component that implements its set of resource manager interfaces). For example, ADO, RDO,

and ODBC can act as MTS resource managers. The DAO interface is not capable of being a resource manger. The team should also consider if the component must be thread safe, such as with ADO and RDO, because this is a requirement for most MTS-managed components if developers expect reasonable resource use and performance.

- **Does every application already use the ODBC API?** If developers continue with ODBC, how will their applications access other kinds of data sources in the future?

Lesson Summary

In this lesson, you were introduced to UDA and MDAC, the tools and technologies you will use to implement ADO, OLE DB, ODBC, and RDS. This lesson provided you with the guidelines for choosing the right technology for data access. It also covered the concepts of persistence, sockets, serialization, and managing transactions.

Lesson 4: Using ADO

This lesson introduces the objects in the Microsoft ActiveX Data Objects (ADO) object hierarchy and the role of ADO in applications that require database access. It also covers the creation and usage of ADO objects.

After this lesson, you will be able to:

- Describe the ADO architecture and the role of the objects that comprise the architecture
- State the guidelines for choosing ADO as the data access technology
- Connect to a data source, execute a command through ADO objects
- Create an ADO recordset and manipulate records in a recordset
- Identify the various cursor types and locking strategies
- Call stored procedures
- Execute SQL parameterized commands

Estimated lesson time: 160 minutes

Basics of ADO

The ADO object model is designed as an easy-to-use application-level interface to OLE DB. ADO is easy to use because it exposes automation objects that abstract the OLE DB interfaces, allowing the programmer to focus on the tasks to accomplish rather than on the complexity of OLE DB.

Features of ADO

ADO provides the following features:

- **De-emphasized object hierarchy** DAO required the programmer to navigate a deep object hierarchy to access and maintain data. ADO provides a simpler model that allows you to access data from top-level objects. This model results in fewer objects and a smaller working set. You track and create only the relevant objects.
- **Support for use on the Web** ADO scripts can be used from within ASP by using Microsoft VBScript. ADO provides support for free-threaded objects, which makes programming Web server applications more efficient.

ADO recordset objects can also be remoted. *Remoting* is the process of passing parameters between two different processes, usually across a network. ADO recordsets can be used to retrieve data from a Web server, across an intranet, or even across the Internet.

- **Support for batch processing and stored procedures with in/out parameters and return values** ADO also supports retrieval of multiple recordsets by stored procedures and batch statements.

ADO Architecture

The ADO 2.1 object model consists of a number of objects and collections of objects. Each of these objects has a number of properties and methods associated with them. Figure 9.3 presents a diagram of the ADO object model architecture.

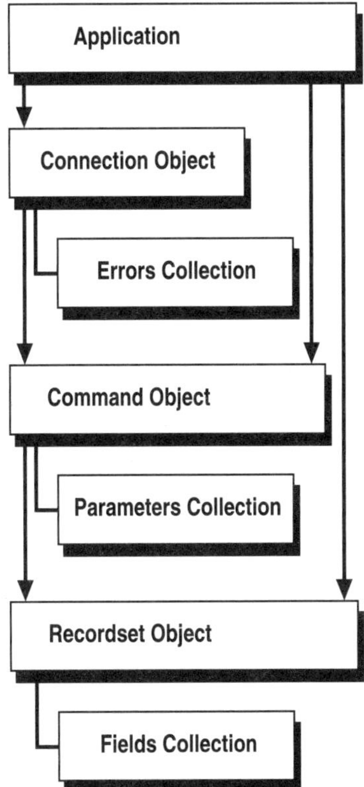

Figure 9.3 ADO object model architecture

Connection Object

The Connection object represents an open connection to a data source. It contains information on the data provider and the underlying schema. To perform any operation on a data source using ADO, you must have an open connection to the data source. Associated with the Connection object is an Errors collection. A *collection* is a group of similar objects owned by another object. The Errors collection contains details about data access errors pertaining to a single operation involving a provider.

Command Object

The Command object defines a command that is to be executed on a data source. A command can be a SQL statement, a stored procedure, or a table name. Use the Command object to retrieve records or manipulate the content of the data source. If the Command object is used without a Connection object, it will create an intrinsic Connection object on the fly. Therefore, if you use several Command objects, they will each create separate intrinsic Connection objects. You can optimize performance by creating a single Connection object and setting each Command object to use this Connection object.

The connection and recordset objects can also execute commands, allowing flexibility with how you choose to execute commands. The best use for command objects is to execute parameterized queries. You can specify these parameters by using the Parameters collection.

The Parameters collection consists of parameter objects. A Parameter object represents a parameter or argument associated with a command.

Recordset Object

The Recordset object represents a set of records retrieved from a table in a database or the result of an executed command. If a Recordset object is opened without using a Connection object, the Recordset object will create an intrinsic Connection object. Again, multiple Recordset objects will each create different intrinsic Connection objects. Therefore, when working with multiple Recordset objects, create a single Connection object and set each Recordset object to use the Connection object.

The Recordset object has a Fields collection comprised of Field objects. Each Field object represents a column in the recordset. You can use the Value property of the Field object to access the data.

Guidelines for Choosing ADO as Your Data Access Technology

ADO is the most appropriate technology for data access, under the following situations:

- **When ease of programming is important** Applications that use ADO are easier to program and modify than those that use OLE DB templates. When writing applications that are subject to frequent change, it might be easier to use ADO than OLE DB templates.

  However, if speed is more important to you than ease of programming, you should use OLE DB templates. Although ADO is easier to use, it can be less flexible. OLE DB is more powerful and allows you the ability to customize the interfaces that are available.

- **When disconnected recordsets are used** ADO recordset objects are unique in that they can be disconnected from the data source. When these objects are in this state, you can pass them to other applications, and make updates to the data in the recordset without requiring any network trips or connections to the data source. This is particularly useful in Web-based applications. When you have made all of the changes to the recordset, you can reestablish the connection to the data source, and post the updates to the data source as needed.

- **When scripting languages are used** Scripting languages rely on Automation to communicate with COM objects. OLE DB contains COM interfaces that are not Automation compatible. However, all ADO interfaces are Automation compatible. Therefore, scripting languages will always use ADO to work with data. You will need to use ADO recordset objects in any applications or components passing data to and from scripting languages.

  If you use multiple programming languages to develop a data access solution, you can also use ADO as a common data access technology.

- **When data-bound controls are used** Data-bound controls are designed to bind to ADO recordsets. If you plan to use data-bound controls on your dialog boxes, you will need to use ADO to create the appropriate recordset objects.

Working with ADO Objects

Next you will learn how to create an ADO Connection object and open a connection to a data source; create an ADO Command object and execute a command; and create an ADO Recordset object and navigate a recordset.

Connecting to a Database

A Connection object represents an open connection to a data source. You can use the Connection object to run commands or queries on the data source. When you retrieve a set of records from the database, the set of records is stored in a Recordset object. The first step in establishing a connection with a data source is to create a Connection object.

► **To connect to a database**

1. Import the Msado15.dll using the #import directive, as shown in the following code:

   ```
   #import "C:\PROGRAM FILES\COMMON FILES\
       SYSTEM\ADO\MSADO15.DLL"
       no_namespace rename("EOF", "EndOfFile")
   ```

   This code allows your application to use the ADO interfaces and methods. When importing Msado15.dll, you need to replace the name of the actual EOF property with EndOfFile to avoid a conflict with the EOF global constant in Visual C++. You can use any name other than EndOfFile, but whenever you refer to the actual EOF property you will have to use the new name. For example, if you renamed EOF to TheEnd, you will have to use TheEnd to refer to the property EOF.

2. Declare a smart pointer to the Connection object.
3. Invoke the *CreateInstance* function to create a Connection object.

   Before using the connection, you should check the HRESULT of *CreateInstance* or verify that the value of the pointer returned by *CreateInstance* is not NULL.

4. Invoke the *CreateInstance* function to create a Connection object.

   You can also call the constructor of the smart pointer to create an instance of a Connection object, as shown in the following code:

   ```
   ConnectionPtr pCon(_uuidof(Connection));
   ```

Specifying Connection Information

After you create a Connection object, the next step is to specify which data source provider to use and which connection parameters to connect to that provider. The connection parameters include the user ID (UID) and the password with which to connect to the data source, the name of the database server, and the database from which data is to be retrieved. Make these specifications by setting the properties of the Connection object.

► **To specify connection information**

1. Specify an OLE DB provider by setting the Provider property. ADO uses the OLE DB ODBC data provider by default. You can change this to another provider by setting the Provider property. For example, to use the SQL Server OLE DB Provider, set the Provider property to SQLOLEDB.
2. Specify connection information by setting the Connection object's ConnectionString property by using the *User ID*, *Password*, *Data Source*, and *Initial Catalog* parameters. You can use additional parameters such as Integrated Security and ConnectionTimeout to control security, timeouts, and other data provider properties.

Opening a Connection to a Data Source

Use the *Open* method to establish a connection to the data source. The syntax for the *Open* method is as follows:

```
Open(BSTR ConnectionString, BSTR UserID, BSTR Password,long Options)
```

When you invoke the *Open* function, you can pass the connection string, UID, and password as the first, second, and third parameters respectively. However, if the ConnectionString property already contains these parameters, pass empty strings to the *Open* function. The fourth parameter determines whether the connection is opened synchronously or asynchronously. The value adConnect-Unspecified indicates that the connection type is not being specified and is used if the connection information has already been set.

After the *Open* method succeeds in connecting with the data source, you can run commands or queries across the connection. You can use the Connection object's *Execute* method to execute a command, as shown in the following code:

```
m_pCon->Execute(
    L"Insert Shippers (CompanyName,Phone)
    Values ('Stupendous Shippers','(555) 555-5555')",
        &vRecordsAffected, adCmdText);
```

The second parameter stores the number of records affected by the query and the third parameter informs the provider that the command being executed is a text command. To the OLE DB provider for SQL Server, the third parameter in this example indicates that the first argument should be interpreted as a SQL command.

Handling Transactions

ADO applications use the Connection object to implement transaction processing. Use the *BeginTrans* method to begin a transaction, as shown in the following code:

```
pCon->BeginTrans();
```

Changes are not written back to the data source until you invoke the *Commit-Trans* method, as shown in the following code:

```
pCon->CommitTrans();
```

To abort a transaction and rollback the data to its state at the last commit, you invoke the *RollbackTrans* method, as shown in the following code:

```
pCon->RollbackTrans();
```

Closing a Connection to a Data Source

When you have finished working with the database, call the *Close* method of the Connection object to close the database connection and free any associated system resources.

Closing a connection also closes any active recordsets associated with the connection. Using the *Close* method does not remove the Connection object or any associated Recordset objects from memory. You can change the object's properties and then use the *Open* method to open it again. To completely remove an object from memory, set the reference count to zero. When using smart pointers, the reference count will be handled automatically, as soon as the smart pointer goes out of scope. To free an ADO object prior to the smart pointer going out of scope, set the smart pointer equal to NULL.

Creating a Command Object

The Command object contains a definition of a command that you want to run against a data source. For a data source that supports SQL, this is a SQL statement. For example, you can execute a SQL statement that returns a recordset, updates a database, calls a stored procedure, or manipulates the structure of the database.

When using ADO, you do not have to create a Connection object before using the Command object. However, if you do not associate the new Command object with an active connection, a new implicit Connection object is created automatically. If you have multiple Command objects, consider creating a single Connection object to associate with all of them. Otherwise each has a separate implicit Connection object, using additional server resources. If multiple commands are to be part of the same transaction, they must use the same Connection object.

Setting Command Properties

The CommandType property adCmdText evaluates the CommandText as a textual definition of a command or stored procedure. You can use the CommandType property to optimize evaluation of the CommandText property. For example, if you set the CommandType property to adCmdUnknown, ADO has to make calls to the provider to determine if the property CommandText is a SQL statement, a table name, or a stored procedure. If the CommandText is a SQL statement, you will achieve greater optimization by setting the CommandType property to adCmdText.

Because the wrapper functions that the #import statement generates do not support optional parameters, all ADO object method calls must include values for all method parameters.

Table 9.13 lists possible values and a brief description for each value of the CommandType property.

Table 9.13 CommandType Property Values

Value	Description
adCmdText	Evaluates CommandText as a textual definition of a command.
adCmdTable	Evaluates CommandText as a table name in a generated SQL query returning all columns.
adCmdTableDirect	Evaluates CommandText as a table name whose columns are all returned.
adCmdStoredProc	Evaluates CommandText as a stored procedure.
adCmdUnknown	Default. The type of command in the CommandText property is not known.
adCommandFile	Evaluates CommandText as the file name of a persisted recordset.
adCmdUnspecified	Indicates that the CommandText property is unspecified.

The items in the table are mutually exclusive. However, if the command text does not return a result set, the command can be optimized for greater performance by logically ORing any of the items with *adExecuteNoRecords*, in which case the Command object will not create or return a Recordset object reference.

Executing a Command

The *Execute* method of the Command object is used to execute a command. The *Execute* method takes three parameters. The first parameter is the address of a VARIANT variable to store the number of records affected as a result of executing the command text. The second parameter is a VARIANT array that stores the parameters that are passed to a stored procedure, if CommandText being executed is a stored procedure. The third parameter is the command type to be executed. If you have already set the CommandType property to a specific command type, you can pass adCmdUnspecified, which directs the *Execute* method to use the value in the CommandType property.

However, if you do not want to store the number of affected records, or there are no parameters to pass, you can pass an empty variant for the first and second parameters. To produce an empty variant, first create a variant and set its type to VT_ERROR and the value to DISP_E_PARAMNOTFOUND, as shown in the following code:

```
VARIANT vEmpty = {VT_ERROR,0,0,0,DISP_E_PARAMNOTFOUND};
```

You can also pass vtMissing, which is defined as an empty variant by the #import statement. This code is the standard way of passing empty parameters to Automation methods. This code will also work on other methods in ADO, in which passing empty parameters is allowed.

If CommandText returns a result set and *adExecuteNoRecords* was not specified in CommandType, then the *Execute* method returns a pointer to an open Recordset object. If CommandText returns a set of records, the Recordset pointer returned by Execute can be used to access the result set.

If CommandText returns a result set but *adExecuteNoRecords* was specified in CommandType, then the *Execute* method returns a NULL pointer.

If the CommandText does not return a result set and *adExecuteNoRecords* was not specified in the CommandType, then the *Execute* method returns a pointer to a closed Recordset object. Attempting to access results through this Recordset object will result in an error.

Creating an ADO Data-Bound Dialog Box

The Enterprise Edition of Visual C++ 6 provides the ADO Data-Bound Dialog Wizard to create skeletal code for a data-bound dialog box-based ADO application. However, if you are using the Professional Edition, this wizard is not available, and you will have to write MFC AppWizard-generated code manually.

► **To create an ADO data-bound dialog box using the ADO Data-Bound Dialog Wizard**

1. Create a dialog box-based application by using MFC's AppWizard.
2. Add the ADO data-bound dialog box from the Components and Controls Gallery, to invoke the ADO Data-Bound Dialog Wizard.
3. In Step 1 of 4 of the wizard, specify a connection string with which to connect to the data provider.
4. In Step 2 of 4 of the wizard, specify the data source as a SQL statement, table name, view, or stored procedure.
5. In Step 3 of 4 of the wizard, specify the cursor location and type.
6. In Step 4 of 4 of the wizard, click Finish to create the dialog box.
7. Modify the *InitInstance* function to display the ADO data-bound dialog box, instead of the default dialog box.

Creating a Recordset Object

The Recordset object allows your application to access data returned from a SQL query or stored procedure. Using the Recordset object, you can navigate through the records that have been returned and, provided the Recordset object is modifiable, edit their values.

You can create a recordset by using three methods. The first is to call the *Open* method of the Recordset object. The second is to call the *Execute* method of the Connection object, which returns a reference to a Recordset object and the third is to call the *Execute* method of the Command object, which returns a reference to a Recordset object.

When you want to retrieve records for a data source into a recordset, perform the following actions:

- Use the *Open* method of the Recordset object when the command has parameters and you need a modifiable Recordset, or when you require more control over the recordset properties, such as the cursor type and type of record locking.
- Use the *Execute* method of the Connection object when the command to be executed has no parameters and you need a forward-only, read-only recordset.
- Use the *Execute* method of the Command object when the command has parameters and you need a read-only recordset.

Like the Command object, you do not have to create a Connection object before using the Recordset object. However, if you do not explicitly associate the new Recordset object with an active connection, a new implicit Connection object is created automatically. If you have multiple Recordset objects, consider creating a single Connection object to associate with all of them. Otherwise, each has a separate implicit Connection object, using additional server resources.

The following code declares a smart pointer to a recordset and creates a Recordset object:

```
RecordsetPtr pRs;
HRESULT hr = pRs.CreateInstance(_uuidof(Recordset));
```

If the Recordset object creation is successful, the returned HRESULT will be zero. Otherwise, it will contain an error code indicating the cause of the failure. You can test HRESULT by using a built-in C++ macro as follows:

```
if (SUCCEEDED(hr))
{
    // Use the Recordset object
}
else
{
    // Handle the error
}
```

Setting Recordset Properties

Before you open a recordset, you must first decide the type and location of the cursor, and the locking strategy that you want to use.

Using Cursors

The functionality of the recordset you create is determined by the values specified for the CursorLocation and CursorType properties. Server-side cursors are the default in ADO. If the data source to which you are connecting does not support server-side cursors, a client-side cursor must be created. To explicitly specify the creation of a client-side cursor, set the CursorLocation property of the Recordset object to *adUseClient*, as shown in the following code:

```
pRs->CursorLocation = adUseClient;
```

If your recordset is created as a result of executing a command from a Connection or a Command object, then you must specify the cursor location that you require before you execute the command. You can specify the cursor location by setting the CursorLocation property of the Connection object.

Cursor Types

When you open a recordset, you can request a specific type of cursor from a provider by passing one of the following cursor-type constants to the *Open* method:

- ***adOpenStatic*** Creates a static cursor. This cursor type provides you with a static copy of data that you can use to search or generate reports. Additions, changes, or deletions by other users are not visible. If you specify *adUseClient* as the CursorType, the cursor type will always be static regardless of what you set it to explicitly.
- ***adOpenDynamic*** Creates a dynamic cursor. The cursor allows all types of movement through the recordset and makes visible users' insertions, updates, and deletions.
- ***adOpenKeyset*** Creates a keyset cursor. Creates a set of keys, which are used to retrieve the records from the data source. This cursor type is similar to a dynamic cursor, except that you cannot see records inserted by others. Also, records deleted by others become inaccessible from your recordset, although you can view data changes made by other users.
- ***adOpenForwardOnly*** Creates a forward-only cursor. This is the default type of cursor. If this option is used with the SQL Server provider, then no cursor is created. Instead, the result set is returned row by row from SQL Server. You can only move forward through the result set. This cursor type offers the best performance because it involves little overhead. This cursor should be used only in situations when you need to make a single pass through the result set.

Lock Types

The Recordset object's default locking type is read-only. You can specify the locking strategy that you want the provider to implement by passing one of the following mutually exclusive constant values to the *LockType* parameter of the *Open* method:

- ***adLockReadOnly*** Places a read-only lock on the records you access. You cannot alter the data.
- ***adLockPessimistic*** Implements pessimistic locking. Records are locked at the data source immediately upon editing.
- ***adLockOptimistic*** Implements optimistic locking. Records are locked only when you call the *Update* method. Client-side cursors only support optimistic locking.
- ***adLockBatchOptimistic*** Implements optimistic locking when performing batch updates.

In general, try to avoid using pessimistic locking, because it places the most restrictions on data and can reduce throughput in the data source. If you do not intend to modify the data, specifying the read-only lock type can increase performance.

Opening a Recordset

Before you open a recordset, you must first set the connection string to connect to the data source and the text of the command to be executed.

Connection String

The *connection string* stores connection parameters about the type of provider being used, the data source, and the mode in which the data source is to be opened. The following code specifies the connection string to a SQL Server database:

```
strConnection = L"Provider=SQLOLEDB.1;Integrated
Security=SSPI;Persist Security Info=False;Initial
Catalog=MyDatabase;Data Source=(local)";
```

The connection string contains the same parameters as would be specified for the ConnectionString property on the Connection object.

Command Text

The *command text* can be the name of a table, view, stored procedure, or SQL statement, as shown in the following code:

```
strCmdText = L"Employees";
```

or:

```
strCmdText = L"Select * from Employees";
```

Opening a Recordset with an Existing Connection

Every time you open a Recordset object, a new connection is established with the database. If you have already opened a connection to the database, you can use this connection to open a Recordset object.

► **To open a recordset by using an existing connection**

1. Get an interface pointer to the Connection object, as shown in the following code:

```
_variant_t vConDisp = pCon.GetInterfacePtr();
```

2. Open the Recordset object by passing the interface pointer to the Connection object as the second parameter to the *Open* method, as shown in the following code:

```
pRs->Open(strCmdText,vConDisp,adOpenDynamic,
adLockOptimistic, adCmdUnspecified);
```

Binding C++ Classes to a Recordset

When you retrieve data from recordset Field objects, the data is returned as a VARIANT data type, which has to be converted to C++ data types before it can be used. This retrieval process is not only cumbersome, but also inefficient. ADO 2 provides the IADORecordBinding interface that allows you to retrieve recordset data into a C++ class.

► **To implement record binding for a C++ class**

1. Include the icrsint.h header file, which contains the necessary declarations for CADORecordBinding and IADORecordBinding.
2. Create a CADORecordBinding-derived class and declare public member variables for each database column. In addition, a variable of type ULONG should be declared for each column to test the status of the field value before it is accessed.

   The data types of the member variables should match the data types of the fields in the database table, as shown in the following code:

```
class CCustomRs : public CADORecordBinding
{
public:
    LONG m_lCustomerID;
    ULONG lCustomerIDStatus;
    ...
};
```

3. Specify how the member variables defined in the previous step are to be bound to the fields in the database table by using the preprocessor macro BEGIN_ADO_BINDING, as shown in the following code:

```
BEGIN_ADO_BINDING(CCustomRs)
    ADO_FIXED_LENGTH_ENTRY(1, adInteger,
    m_lCustomerID, lCustomerIDStatus, FALSE)
    ...
END_ADO_BINDING()
```

4. Create an object of the CADORecordBinding-derived class:

```
CCustomRs CustomRs;
```

5. Retrieve a pointer to the IADORecordBinding interface of the Recordset object, as shown in the following code:

```
IADORecordBinding *piAdoRecordBinding = NULL;
pRs->QueryInterface(__uuidof(IADORecordBinding),
                (LPVOID *)&piAdoRecordBinding);
```

6. Invoke the BindToRecordset method of the IADORecordBinding interface:

```
piAdoRecordBinding->BindToRecordset(&CustomRs);
```

Binding a DataGrid Control to a Recordset

You can display the contents of a Recordset object by using the DataGrid control. To do so, set the DataSource property of the DataGrid control to the DataSource of the Recordset object. You can then set the properties of the DataGrid control to allow inserting, deleting, and editing records in the grid. However, to perform these operations, the underlying Recordset object should be updateable.

Navigating a Recordset

Of all the ADO objects, only the Recordset object allows users to navigate through a set of records. Only one record within a recordset is current at a given time. Therefore, the Recordset object supports a number of properties and methods that allow users to navigate through the recordset. Table 9.14 describes these Recordset object properties.

Table 9.14 Recordset Object Properties Used to Navigate a Recordset

Property	Description
AbsolutePage	Sets or returns the absolute page in which the current record exists.
AbsolutePosition	Sets or returns the absolute position of the current record (this can be affected by record additions or deletions).
BOF	Indicates if the record pointer has moved before the first record.
Bookmark	Returns a unique identifier for the current record. Setting this property to a specific record's bookmark moves the record pointer to that record.
EndOfFile	Indicates if the record pointer has moved past the last record.

Table 9.15 describes Recordset object methods used to navigate through a recordset.

Table 9.15 Recordset Object Methods Used to Navigate Through a Recordset

Method	Description
Move	Moves a specified number of records forward or back.
MoveFirst	Moves to the first record.
MoveLast	Moves to the last record.
MoveNext	Moves to the next record.
MovePrevious	Moves to the previous record.

The Recordset object is normally used to manipulate data from a provider. However, you can also use the Recordset object to build in-memory tables. You can work with such a recordset in much the same manner as you work with a recordset that contains data from a data source.

Finding Records in a Recordset

Use the *Find* method to search a recordset for records that satisfy the specified criteria. When you find a record that satisfies the search criteria, it becomes the current record. If none of the records in the recordset satisfy the search criteria, the current position is set to the end of the recordset. Only one field can be used in the *Find* method.

To find a record based on a criterion that involves more than one field, the *Filter* method must be used. Although you can find a record by using the *Find* method, it is a good practice to retrieve the records you require by using the most appropriate restriction for the SQL query.

The following code shows how you can search for records within a recordset:

```
m_pRs->Find("LastName like 'M*'",0,adSearchForward);
```

The *Find* function takes the following arguments:

- A string containing the search criteria.
- An optional long value that defines the starting record of the search operation. Specify the starting location relative to the current record. For example, if you specify 0, the search skips 0 records from the current record, or starts at the current record.
- The search direction, which can be either adSearchForward or adSearchBackward.
- An optional *bookmark,* which identifies a record. If you specify a bookmark, it will be used as the starting position for the search. You use the *get_Bookmark* method to return a bookmark for the current record, as shown in the following code:

  ```
  variant_t vtBookMark;
  pRs->get_BookMark(&vtBookMark);
  ```

  You can later specify the bookmark stored in vtBookMark as the starting point for the search.

Filtering Records in a Recordset

You can set the Filter property of the recordset to filter records in the recordset that satisfy a search criterion. When constructing the search criteria, you can use comparison operators such as > (greater than), < (less than), = (equal), or *like* (pattern matching). The comparison *like* operator can be used in conjunction with the asterisk (*) wildcard, which represents zero or more characters.

The following code selects all records in which an individual's last name starts with "M" in the database:

```
pRs->Filter = L"LastName like 'M*'";
```

You can also use logical operators such as AND and OR in the filter criteria, as shown in the following code:

```
pRs->Filter = L"LastName like 'M*' OR LastName
like 'S*'";
```

There is no precedence between AND and OR. Clauses can be grouped within parentheses. However, you cannot group clauses joined by OR with another clause by using AND. For example, you cannot group clauses as follows:

```
pRs->Filter = L"(LastName like 'S*' OR LastName
like 'M*') AND FirstName like 'D*'";
```

Instead, you would construct this filter as shown in the following code:

```
pRs->Filter = L"(LastName Like 'S*' AND FirstName like
'D*') OR (LastName like 'M*' AND FirstName like 'D*')";
```

To reset the filter, and view all the records in the recordset, set the Filter property to *adFilterNone,* as shown in the following code:

```
pRs->Filter = (short)adFilterNone;
```

You can also set the Filter property to one of the constants listed in Table 9.16.

Table 9.16 Constants Used to Set the Filter Property

Constant	Description
adFilterNone	Removes the current filter and restores all records to view.
adFilterPendingRecords	Allows you to view only records that have changed, but have not yet been sent to the server. Applicable only for batch update mode.
adFilterAffectedRecords	Allows you to view only records affected by the last Delete, Resync, UpdateBatch, or CancelBatch call.
adFilterFetchedRecords	Allows you to view the records last retrieved from the database.
adFilterConflictingRecords	Allows you to view the records that failed the last batch update attempt.

Adding Records to a Recordset

You can add records to an updateable recordset by calling the *AddNew* method. This method creates and initializes a new record. The method takes two arguments, both of which are safe arrays of VARIANTs. The first argument contains the names of the columns for the new record. The second argument contains the data values for each column.

► **To add records to a recordset**

1. Create two safe arrays of VARIANTs to store the list of field names and values that will be inserted into the corresponding fields of the recordset, as shown in the following code:

```
VARIANT rgf; // Stores field names
VARIANT rgv; // Stores field values
SAFEARRAYBOUND bound;

// Set the type of data the VARIANT will hold
rgf.vt=VT_ARRAY|VT_VARIANT;
rgv.vt=VT_ARRAY|VT_VARIANT;
bound.cElements=3;
bound.lLbound=0;
```

```
// Create a safe array of VARIANTs to store the field
values
rgv.parray=::SafeArrayCreate(VT_VARIANT,1,&bound);
if(rgv.parray==NULL)
    AfxThrowMemoryException();

// Create a safe array of VARIANTs to store the field
names
rgf.parray=::SafeArrayCreate(VT_VARIANT,1,&bound);
if(rgf.parray==NULL)
    AfxThrowMemoryException();
```

2. Store the field names and values to be inserted in the safe array of VARIANTs, as shown in the following code:

```
_variant_t fld[3], val[3];
long rgIndices[1];

fld[0]=L"EmployeeID";
val[0]=m_lDlgID;
fld[1]=L"Name";
val[1]=m_strDlgName;
fld[2]=L"Address";
val[2]=m_strDlgAddress;

for (int i = 0; i < 3; i++)
{
    rgIndices[0]=i;
    ::SafeArrayPutElement(rgf.parray, rgIndices,
    &fld[i]);
    ::SafeArrayPutElement(rgv.parray, rgIndices,
    &val[i]);
}
```

3. Invoke the *AddNew* method, passing the safe array of VARIANTs containing the field names as the first parameter and the safe array of VARIANTs containing the field values as the second parameter, as shown in the following code:

```
pRs->AddNew(&rgf,&rgv);
```

Editing and Deleting Records

The procedure for updating a recordset is similar to adding a new record to a recordset. First, create two safe arrays of VARIANTs to store the list of fields to be updated and the new field. Next, invoke the *Update* method, passing the safe arrays containing the names of the fields to be updated and the new values as parameters.

Use the *Delete* function to delete the current record of a recordset. You can also delete a group of records using this function.

The Delete function takes a single argument. The value of this argument can be *adAffectCurrent*, *adAffectGroup*, *adAffectAll*, or *adAffectAllChapters*. The default, *adAffectCurrent*, deletes only the current record; *adAffectGroup* deletes the records that satisfy the current filter property setting; and *adAffectAllChapters* deletes records in all chapters of the recordset.

To use *adAffectGroup*, you must set the filter property to a filter condition or one of the valid predefined constants—*adFilterPendingRecords*, *adFilterAffectedRecords*, *adFilterFetchedRecords*, or *adFilterConflictingRecords*.

Creating a Disconnected Recordset

An advanced feature of ADO is the *disconnected recordset*. A disconnected recordset contains a recordset that can be viewed and updated, but it does not carry with it the overhead of a live connection to the database. This is a useful way to retrieve data that will be used for a long time. While you work on the data, the database server is not tied up with any open connections.

You can make changes to the disconnected recordset by editing the records directly, or adding or deleting them using ADO methods such as *AddNew* and *Delete*. All of the changes are stored in the disconnected recordset.

When you want to save the changes, reconnect to the database by setting the ActiveConnection property of the Recordset object to an open connection and invoking the *UpdateBatch* method.

To create a disconnected recordset, you must create a Recordset object that uses a client side, static cursor with a lock type of *adLockBatchOptimistic*.

The ActiveConnection property determines if the recordset is disconnected. If you explicitly set it to NULL, you will disconnect the recordset. You can still access the data in the recordset, but no live connection to the database exists. Later, you can explicitly set ActiveConnection to a valid Connection object to reconnect the Recordset object to the database.

► **To create a disconnected recordset**

1. Create a Recordset object and set the CursorLocation property to *adUseClient*, as shown in the following code:

```
pRs.CreateInstance(__uuidof(Recordset));
pRs->CursorLocation = adUseClient;
```

2. Open the recordset, setting the cursor type to *adOpenStatic* and the lock type to *adLockBatchOptimistic*, as shown in the following code:

```
pRs->Open(strCmdText, strConnection,
    adOpenStatic, adLockBatchOptimistic, adCmdText);
```

3. Set ActiveConnection to NULL by invoking the *PutRefActiveConnection* method, and passing NULL as the parameter:

```
pRs->PutRefActiveConnection(NULL);
```

► **To submit batch updates**

1. Open a connection to the database.
2. Set the ActiveConnection property of the Recordset object to the open connection, as shown in the following code:

```
pRs->PutRefActiveConnection(pCon);
```

3. Invoke the *UpdateBatch* method of the Recordset object passing *adAffectAll* as the parameter, as shown in the following code:

```
pRs->UpdateBatch(adAffectAll);
```

When you perform batch updates, conflicts could arise between the records that you are updating and those that have already been updated, by other users, in the data source. For example, if you had edited a record in the disconnected recordset set, and another user has deleted the record, conflicts would arise when you try to update the record in the data source by using the *UpdateBatch* method.

Executing Parameterized Queries with ADO

Next you will learn how to call stored procedures and execute SQL parameterized commands by using the Parameters collection.

Executing a Stored Procedure

As mentioned earlier, stored procedures are compiled collections of SQL statements and control-of-flow language constructs that execute quickly. Executing a stored procedure is similar to executing a SQL command except that the stored procedure exists in the database as an object even after execution has finished. Stored procedures hide potentially complex SQL statements from the components that use them. Also, SQL Server compiles and stores stored procedures, which makes stored procedures run much faster than submitting the SQL statements as separate SQL queries.

SQL queries are compiled the first time they are executed and stored in a cache of execution plans. If the query is executed again, the execution plan is retrieved from the cache, thereby improving the speed of execution. However, there is no guarantee that the execution plan for a query will exist in the cache, even if the query has been executed before; SQL Server occasionally flushes the cache.

You can execute a stored procedure from a Connection, Command, or Recordset object. However, if the stored procedure accepts or returns parameters, you must use the Command object to send or receive the parameter data.

► **To execute a stored procedure**

1. Set the CommandType property to *adCmdStoredProc*.
2. Set the CommandText property to the name of the stored procedure.

   If you are using a Recordset object to call the stored procedure, you can also specify the command text as the first argument to the *Open* method.
3. Call the *Execute* method to execute the stored procedure from a Command or a Connection object, as shown in the following code:

```
m_Rs = m_Cmd->Execute(&vtEmpty, &vtEmpty,
adCmdStoredProc);
```

4. If you use a Recordset object to call the stored procedure, call the *Open* method, as shown in the following code:

```
m_pRs->Open((LPCTSTR)m_strCmdText,
            (LPCTSTR)m_strConnection, adOpenStatic,
               adLockReadOnly, adCmdStoredProc);
```

Passing Parameters to a Stored Procedure

Stored procedures might require that one or more parameters be passed to them. For each required parameter, a Parameter object should be created and appended to the Parameters collection of the Command object.

► **To fill the parameter collection**

1. Create separate Parameter objects and fill in the correct parameter information for the stored procedure call, as shown in the following code:

```
ParameterPtr pParam;
pParam = pCmd->CreateParameter(L"Cust_ID",adChar,
   adParamInput, 5, lCustID);
```

   The syntax for *CreateParameter* is as follows:

```
CreateParameter (Name, Type, Direction, Size, Value)
```

   Table 9.17 lists optional parameters and a brief description for each.

Table 9.17 Optional Parameters for Stored Procedures

Parameter	Description
Name	A BSTR representing the name of the Parameter object. Must be unique for each parameter.
Type	A Long value specifying the data type of the Parameter object. Use one of the DataTypeEnum enumeration constants for this parameter
Direction	A Long value specifying the direction—input, output, input/output, or return—of the Parameter object. Use one of the ParameterDirectionEnum enumeration constants for this parameter.
Size	A Long value specifying the maximum length for the parameter value in characters or bytes.
Value	A Variant specifying the value for the Parameter object.

For number data types (numeric, decimal, money), the Precision and NumericScale attributes must be set before executing the command.

2. Append each Parameter object to the collection using the *Append* method, as shown in the following code:

```
pCmd->Parameters->Append(m_pParam);
```

For multiple parameters, you must append the parameters in the order that they are defined in the stored procedure.

3. Execute the stored procedure by invoking the Command object's *Execute* method, as shown in the following code:

```
pCmd->Execute(&varEmpty, &varEmpty, adCmdStoredProc);
```

Handling Return Codes and Output Parameters

Stored procedures might contain input and output parameters and return values. For example, consider a stored procedure named *CreateOrderID* that accepts two parameters. The first is an output parameter named *@Order_ID,* which returns a new Order ID. The second is an input parameter named *@Order_Date,* which contains a unique date used to create and then retrieve a new Order record and its unique ID. Also, if *CreateOrderID* successfully creates the new Order record and ID, it returns a code of 0. Otherwise, it returns a code of 1.

Just as you can specify input parameters for a stored procedure through the Parameter object, you can also specify output parameters and return values.

You create an output Parameter object by passing *adParamOutput* as the parameter type, and a return value by passing *adParamReturnValue* as the parameter type, to the *CreateParameter* method.

You must append the return Parameter object to the Parameters collection first. You can read the return code just like any other parameter because it is the first parameter in the Parameters collection. Be aware that the return code parameter is at index 0, instead of 1.

If you execute a stored procedure that returns a recordset and you assign the returned recordset to a Recordset object, you must close the Recordset object before you can read any return or output parameters.

If a stored procedure does not have a return value, SQL Server will return an integer value called a return status. This status indicates that the procedure completed successfully, or it indicates the reason for failure. SQL Server has a defined set of return values, shown in Table 9.18.

Table 9.18 Return Values Defined by SQL Server

Value	Meaning
0	Procedure was executed successfully
–1	Object missing
–2	Data type error occurred
–3	Process was chosen as deadlock victim
–4	Permission error occurred
–5	Syntax error occurred
–6	Miscellaneous user error occurred
–7	Resource error, such as lack of space, occurred
–8	Non-fatal internal problem encountered
–9	System limit was reached
–10	Fatal internal inconsistency occurred
–11	Fatal internal inconsistency occurred
–12	Table or index is corrupt
–13	Database is corrupt
–14	Hardware error occurred

Lesson Summary

In this lesson, you looked at the roles of the objects that comprise the ADO architecture—Connection, Command, and Recordset. You learned how to connect to a data source through an ADO Connection object, execute a command through an ADO Command object, create an ADO Recordset object, and navigate a recordset.

In addition, this lesson identified the different cursor types and the locking strategies possible for a Recordset object. You learned how to add, edit, and delete records in the recordset. Finally, you learned how to call stored procedures and execute SQL parameterized commands by using the Parameters collection.

Lesson 5: Using ODBC

This lesson covers the ODBC architecture, how the classes CDatabase, CRecordset, CFieldExchange, and CRecordView wrap the ODBC API to make it easier to work with ODBC. It also discusses the methods for debugging and handling errors in an ODBC application.

After this lesson, you will be able to:

- Describe the ODBC architecture
- Identify the various MFC ODBC classes and describe their purposes
- Add, edit, and delete records in ODBC recordsets
- Debug and handle errors in an ODBC application

Estimated lesson time: 160 minutes

ODBC Architecture

ODBC is a universal API used for accessing data from a variety of databases and computer types, ranging from personal computers to networks. With ODBC, an application developer can create applications that use a single interface to access, view, and modify databases from various databases and DBMSs. Figure 9.4 shows ODBC's architecture and database components.

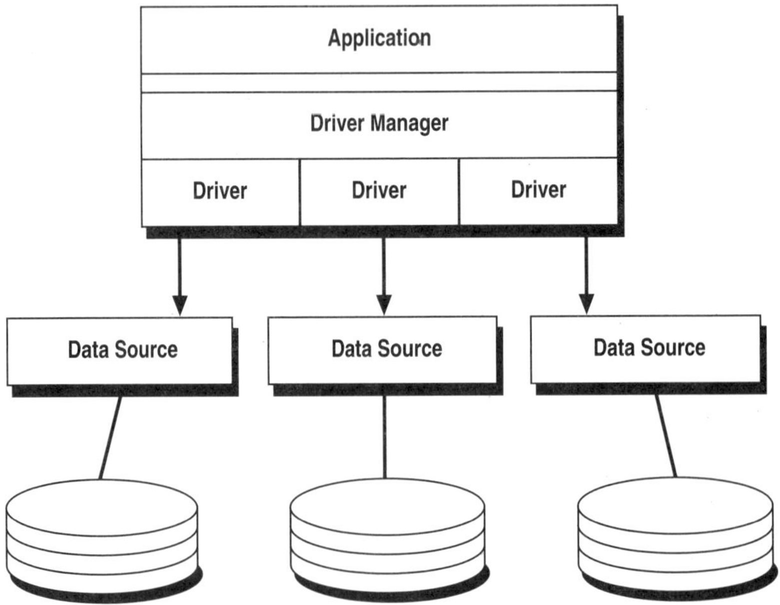

Figure 9.4 ODBC architecture and database components

An ODBC application consists of the following components:

- **Application code** Performs processing and calls ODBC functions to submit SQL statements and retrieve results.
- **ODBC API** Consists of functions that provide precise control over a database and its transactions. This API is used in two places: between the ODBC application and Driver Manager, as well as between the Driver Manager and ODBC drivers. The application code makes calls to the various functions that make up the ODBC API to perform tasks such as opening a database and retrieving records.
- **ODBC Driver Manager** The ODBC Driver Manager intercepts the ODBC API function calls and determines whether a new driver type needs to be loaded, or whether the function calls can be passed to a driver already loaded. If a new driver needs to be loaded in response to an open database call, the driver manager will locate the driver DLL, load it, and then pass connection information to the driver. One of the many tasks of the ODBC Driver Manager is to load a driver when an application calls the *SQLBrowseConnect*, *SQLConnect*, or *SQLDriverConnect* function. Because the driver manager can manage multiple drivers at once, the application can have multiple data sources of different types open at one time. When the driver is loaded, most ODBC function calls are passed through the Driver Manager to the driver.

  The Driver Manager also checks several function calls, arguments, state transactions, and other error conditions before passing the call to the driver associated with the connection. This reduces the amount of error checking that the driver has to perform.

  The Driver Manager also implements some of the ODBC API functions that are not specific to any particular database. These functions include *SQLGetFunctions*, *SQLDataSources*, and *SQLDrivers*.
- **ODBC cursor library** Implemented as a DLL and operates between the driver manager and the driver. This library only supports forward-only or static-scrollable cursors. If you want to create other types of cursors, you will have to use the database-specific driver.
- **ODBC drivers** Middle components that make open, consistent interfaces possible. These components' general role is to translate a logical ODBC request from the application into database commands that a specific DBMS can process. ODBC drivers reside in DLLs that implement ODBC function calls and interact with a data source. The drivers' specific role is threefold:
  - Process ODBC function calls.
  - Submit SQL requests to a specific data source. The drivers sometimes modify the syntax of the application's request to conform to the syntactical requirements of the associated DBMS.
  - Return the results to the application.

ODBC drivers need to meet certain levels of conformance in the areas of API function support and SQL grammar support. To claim support for a particular level of conformance, ODBC drivers must support all requirements of that level of conformance, even if the database server for which the ODBC driver is written does not support that functionality. For details about the functionality to which a driver must conform for each level, see "ODBC API Usage" in the MSDN Library.

- **Data sources** Are generalizations of targeted data. Data sources usually consist of the actual data, the driver that interfaces to the DBMS that manages that data, and information about where that data resides. Each data source must be given a unique name when it is registered. Through this name, the application accesses the data.

MFC ODBC Classes

The MFC database programming model provides a collection of classes that allow you to retrieve data from a data source and display it by using the document-view data presentation mechanism. The classes that you use depend on the data access technology. For ODBC, the following classes are used:

- **CDatabase** Encapsulates a connection to a data source. Through that connection, you can operate on the data source.
- **CRecordset** Encapsulates a set of records selected from a data source. Recordsets allow you to scroll from record to record; add, edit, and delete records; qualify the selection with a filter; sort the selection; and parameterize the selection with information obtained or calculated at run time.
- **CRecordView** Provides a form view directly connected to a Recordset object. The Microsoft Dialog Data Exchange (DDX) mechanism exchanges data between the recordset and the controls of the record view. Like all form views, a record view is based on a dialog template resource. Record views also support moving from record to record in the recordset, updating records, and closing the associated recordset when the record view closes.
- **CFieldExchange** Supplies context information that supports record field exchange (RFX). RFX exchanges data between the field data members and parameter data members of a Recordset object and the corresponding table columns on the data source.
- **CDBException** Represents exceptions that result from failures in data access processing. This class serves the same purpose as other exception classes in the exception-handling mechanism of the MFC Library.

These classes are defined in the file afxdb.h. If you want to use these classes, you must implement #include in this header file in your application.

CDatabase

The MFC ODBC class CDatabase is used to establish a connection to an ODBC data source. To open a connection to a data source, you must first create a CDatabase object. Use the *OpenEx* member function to open a connection to a data source. The syntax for the *OpenEx* function is as follows:

```
CDatabase::OpenEx (LPCTSTR lpszConnectString,
    DWORD dwOptions = 0);
```

The *lpszConnectString* parameter is the connection string that specifies the data source name (DSN), UID with which to log on to the data source, and password. If you pass NULL as the connection string, a dialog box will appear at run time that will prompt you to type the DSN, UID, and password. Table 9.19 lists *dwOptions* values that can be passed to *CDatabase::OpenEx*:

Table 9.19 ***CDatabase::OpenEx dwOptions*** **Values**

Value	Description
CDatabase::openReadOnly	Opens the data source in a read-only mode
CDatabase::useCursorLib	Loads the ODBC cursor library
CDatabase::noOdbcDialog	Does not display the ODBC connection dialog box irrespective of whether insufficient information was provided in the connection string
CDatabase:: forceOdbcDialog	Always displays the ODBC connection dialog box

The following code demonstrates how to call *OpenEx* to open a connection to the Pubs database:

```
CDatabase database;
database.OpenEx("DSN=Pubs;UID=sa;PWD=MyPassword",0);
```

You can also use the *Open* member function to establish a connection to a data source. The syntax for the *Open* function is as follows:

```
CDatabase::Open (LPCSTR lpszDSN, BOOL bExclusive =
FALSE, BOOL bReadOnly = FALSE, LPCSTR lpszConnect =
    "ODBC;", BOOL bUseCursorLib = TRUE);
```

The parameter *lpszConnect* is a string that specifies the DSN, UID, and authentication string (password). If the information in the Connect string is insufficient to make the connection, the ODBC driver displays a dialog box requesting more information.

CRecordset

A *recordset* is where the data from the data source is held. A recordset is comparable to a document in the document/view architecture. A recordset holds the data that CRecordView displays. A recordset can contain data from the source database, tables, or fields within tables.

Recordsets allow scrolling from record to record, updating records (adding, editing, and deleting records), qualifying the selection with a filter, sorting the selection, and parameterizing the selection with information obtained or calculated at run time.

To retrieve data from a data source, the first step is to call the *Open* member function of the CRecordset class, as shown in the following code:

```
CRecordset rsAuthors;
rsAuthors.Open(CRecordset::dynaset,
    "Select * from Authors",
    CRecordset::none);
```

In the previous code, the first parameter determines the type of cursor that will be created for the returned data from the Authors table.

The values that this parameter can take are as follows:

- **CRecordset::forwardonly** Creates a read-only recordset that can be scrolled only in the forward direction. The forward-only cursor is the most used, most efficient, and least memory consumptive cursor. This cursor is useful for database tasks that involve making a single pass through the result set.
- **CRecordset::snapshot** Creates a recordset that does not display the changes made by other users to the data source. This recordset can also be scrolled in both directions. Snapshots are useful when you need to ensure the result set does not change while you are using it—for example, when you are generating reports.
- **CRecordset::dynamic** Creates a recordset that is truly dynamic in nature. The recordset can be scrolled in both directions and is reordered every time a user makes a change to the data source content. The dynamic cursor is the least used cursor because it consumes the most overhead.
- **CRecordset::dynaset** Creates a recordset that is dynamic in nature and scrollable in both directions. However, unlike as in the CRecordset::dynamic value, the ordering of data is determined when the recordset is opened. Dynasets are useful for situations where the result set must be constantly up-to-date. Dynasets are also useful for most database operations because they require little memory to store the keys from the result set, and they show most updates by other users. The only updates that are not visible are record insertions.

The *Open* function's second parameter is a SQL command string. The last parameter is a *bitmask*. The bitmask value determines whether the recordset is append-only or read-only, if the recordset allows processing of multiple rows of records, and so on. The value CRecordset::none indicates that none of the options have been set.

If you have already established a connection to a data source by using a CDatabase object, you can use the connection to open the CRecordset object. To open a recordset with an existing connection, pass the address of the open CDatabase object to the constructor of the CRecordset object, and then call *Open*, as shown in the following code:

```
CRecordset *pRsAuthors;
pRsAuthors = new CRecordset(&database);
pRsAuthors->Open(CRecordset::dynaset,"Select *from Authors",
    CRecordset::none);
```

When you have finished with a recordset, you must call the *Close* member function to free the ODBC statement handle and memory allocated to the recordset by the framework.

ODBC uses a cursor to maintain a pointer to the current record. The contents of the current record, whatever that record happens to be, are stored in the recordset.

CRecordView

The CRecordView class provides the means for displaying the data in a recordset. CRecordView is derived from CFormView, which is derived from CView. CFormView provides a dialog box-based client area, often referred to as a form-based application. CRecordView adds the ability to connect to a recordset.

The DDX mechanism exchanges data between the current record of the recordset and the controls of the *record view*. Like all form views, a record view is based on a dialog template resource. Record views also support moving from record to record in the recordset, updating records, and closing the associated recordset when the record view closes.

CFieldExchange

The CFieldExchange class provides support for the type-safe RFX mechanism by binding parameters and data field members. RFX exchanges data between field and parameter data members of a recordset object and the corresponding table columns on the data source.

The RFX mechanism works in conjunction with the recordset. When the recordset is opened, the RFX mechanism associates the columns of data being read with its corresponding variable defined in the CRecordset derived class. Whenever a call is made to update the recordset using a CRecordset function, the RFX mechanism makes the appropriate call to the ODBC API to send update, delete, or insert instructions to the ODBC driver.

In addition to managing the transfer of data between the columns and the CRecordset variables, the RFX mechanism also manages binding parameters.

AppWizard and ClassWizard generally handle the RFX routines automatically. However, these routines must be manipulated manually when either of the following conditions is true:

- The application uses parameterized queries.
- The application dynamically binds with the data-source columns.

CDBException

CDBException serves the same purpose as other exception classes in the exception-handling mechanism of the MFC Library. You can trap database errors by using the *try...catch* mechanism provided in Visual C++, as shown in the following code:

```
try
{
    rsAuthors.Open();
}
catch(CDBException *e)
{
    // Error handling code goes here
    e->Delete();
}
```

Working with ODBC Recordsets

Next you will see the procedure sfor adding new data to a recordset and how to edit and delete unwanted information from a recordset.

Editing Recordsets

Editing records in a recordset is a three-step process. The first step is to call the *Edit* function to prepare the recordset for editing, as shown in the following code:

```
m_pSet->Edit();
```

Calling the *Edit* function allows you to change the values of the member variables of the CRecordset-derived class. You cannot call *Edit* if you have implemented bulk row fetching. Bulk row fetching is available by passing

CRecordset::useMultiRowFetch as the last parameter to the CRecordset *Open* member function. The CRecordset class does not provide a mechanism for updating bulk rows of data.

Next, call the *Update* function, as shown in the following code:

```
m_pSet->Update();
```

Update completes an *AddNew* or *Edit* operation by saving the new or edited data to the data source. You can call the *Requery* function to refresh the recordset's records, as shown in the following code:

```
m_pset->Requery();
```

However, this procedure depends on the type of cursor used. To view changes made by other users, you must call *Requery* to refresh static cursors.

► **To add records to a recordset**

1. Call the *AddNew* function of the CRecordset class, as shown in the following code:

   ```
   m_pSet->AddNew();
   ```

   The *AddNew* function adds a new blank record to the recordset's edit buffer.
2. Display the blank record on the form view by calling the *UpdateData* function and passing FALSE to it.
3. After the user has filled in the new record information, call *UpdateData* passing TRUE to transfer the new record information into the recordset.
4. Call the *Update* function to save the new record to the data source.
5. You can call the *Requery* function to refresh the recordset's data. This depends on the type of cursor used. To view changes made by other users, static cursors must be refreshed by calling *Requery*.

Deleting Records from a Recordset

To delete a record in a recordset, call the CRecordset class's *Delete* member function. When you have deleted the record, you must explicitly scroll to another record, as shown in the following code:

```
m_pSet->Delete();
m_pSet->MoveNext();
if(m_pSet->IsEOF())
    m_pSet->MoveLast();
if(m_pSet->IsBOF())
    m_pSet->MoveLast();
```

Debugging and Error Handling in ODBC Applications

In this section, you will learn how to debug and handle errors in your ODBC application.

Types of ODBC Errors

ODBC errors are of two types: ODBC driver-generated errors and database-generated errors. ODBC driver errors occur when the driver does not support a certain functionality that the ODBC API requests. For example, if the *Open* call requests a dynaset cursor and the driver does not support the creation of a dynaset cursor, the driver returns an error.

Database errors occur when the ODBC driver makes a request to the DBMS, and the DBMS cannot service the request. For example, if the client application tries to insert a value into a column that conflicts with a constraint, a database error will occur.

Most DBMSs also provide a mechanism for returning user defined error codes. For example, SQL Server allows you to return a user defined error message to a client application by using the Transact-SQL (T-SQL) command RAISERROR. You can also specify a severity level whenever you raise an error. ODBC applications can only trap errors of a severity level higher than 10.

Retrieving Error Information

The CDBException object can be used to trap errors that occur in MFC ODBC applications. You can use the CDBException object with either the MFC exception-handling macros or the C++ exception-handling code, as shown in the following code:

```
try
{
    database.OpenEx("DSN=Pubs");
}
catch(CDBException *e)
{
    AfxMessageBox(e->m_strError);
    e->Delete();
}
```

Exceptions are best handled by using C++ exception handling. You can also call the *ReportError* base class member function to display the error message.

Many operations involving the MFC database classes cause exceptions that are caught by the CDBException object. When you use the MFC database classes, be sure to use extensive exception handling.

The CDBException object has three data members that you can use to retrieve information about the ODBC error that occurred. Table 9.20 lists the data members of CDBException.

Table 9.20 Data Members of CDBException

Data member	Purpose
m_nRetCode	Contains an ODBC return code of type RETCODE.
m_strError	Contains a string that describes the error in human-readable terms.
m_strStateNativeOrigin	Contains a string describing the error in terms of the error codes returned by ODBC.

The *m_nRetCode* member stores the ODBC error code that is returned by the ODBC API whenever an error occurs. The *m_nRetCode* member can store two types of error codes: error codes that are returned by ODBC, which are prefixed with SQL_; and error codes that are returned by the database classes, which are prefixed with AFX_SQL_.

Table 9.21 lists some of the error codes that can be returned and a brief explanation for each.

Table 9.21 Error Codes and Descriptions

Error code	Description
AFX_SQL_ERROR_CONNECT_FAIL	Connection to the data source failed.
AFX_SQL_ERROR_DATA_TRUNCATED	You have tried to retrieve more data than you have provided for memory. This error occurs when you retrieve data from a large data column into a CByteArray or CString variable.
AFX_SQL_ERROR_ILLEGAL_MODE	You have called the CRecordset update function without previously calling Edit or Insert.
SQL_ERROR	Function failed. The error message returned by ::SQLError is stored in the m_strError data member of the CDBException object.
SQL_INVALID_HANDLE	Function failed due to an invalid environment handle, connection handle, or statement handle.

Retrieving Diagnostic Information

An ODBC driver returns diagnostic information every time it executes an ODBC API function call. The information it returns is of two types: *error codes,* which help determine the success or failure of a command; and *diagnostic records,* which contain detailed information about the failure. Diagnostic records are, in turn, of two types: *header records* and *status records.* Header records are returned for all function calls, even if the call succeeds. Status records are returned whenever a function call fails.

You can use the *SQLGetDiagRec* function to retrieve diagnostic records whenever a function call returns a failure code. Using *SQLGetDiagRec*, you can scroll through the diagnostic information that is returned, as shown in the following code:

```
while ((iErrStatus = ::SQLGetDiagRec(SQL_HANDLE_STMT,
       hstmt,iIndex, strSqlState,
       &iNativeError, strMessage,
              sizeof (strMessage),
              &iMsgLength)) != SQL_NO_DATA)
{
   ...
}
```

The *SQLGetDiagRec* function takes eight arguments as follows:

- The handle type for which diagnostic information is required. The values that this argument can take are SQL_HANDLE_ENV, SQL_HANDLE_DB, SQL_HANDLE_STMT, and SQL_HANDLE_DESC.
- A handle for the diagnostic structure. This handle depends on the handle type passed as the first parameter. In the previous code, *hstmt* is a handle to a statement.
- The number of the status record from which the application seeks information. This number starts from 1.
- A pointer to a buffer in which the SQL STATE code pertaining to the diagnostic record is to be returned.
- A pointer to a buffer in which the native error code pertaining to the diagnostic record is to be returned.
- A pointer to a buffer in which the diagnostic message string is to be returned.
- The length of the message text buffer.
- A pointer to a buffer in which to store the length of the diagnostic message text. This excludes the number of bytes required for the null-termination character. If the length of the message is longer than that specified in argument seven, then the message is truncated to the size specified by the length of the message text buffer.

Lesson Summary

In this lesson, you looked at the components of ODBC architecture. The ODBC architecture consists of application code that makes calls ODBC functions; the ODBC API that provides functions to control the database and its transactions; ODBC Driver Manager, which manages ODBC drivers; the ODBC Cursor Library, which provides forward-only or static-scrollable cursor functionality; and data sources.

MFC provides a set of ODBC Classes—CDatabase, CRecordset, CRecordView, CFieldExchange, and CDBException, which encapsulate the ODBC driver functions. The CDatabase class provides member functions to connect to a data source. The CRecordset class provides member functions for adding, editing, and deleting records in a recordset. The CRecordView and CFieldExchange classes provide the functionality to display data from the recordset. The CDBException class allows you to retrieve driver and database error information in ODBC applications. You can also retrieve diagnostic records, which are returned by ODBC drivers by using *SQLGetDiagRec*.

Lesson 6: Using OLE DB

This lesson discusses the OLE DB architecture and the role of the OLE DB Consumer Template classes. It also teaches you how to use the CDynamicAccessor class to retrieve data from a data source, and how to use the CDynamicParameterAccessor class to create and execute parameterized queries.

After this lesson, you will be able to:

- Identify the components of the OLE DB architecture and describe their role in data access
- Identify the components of OLE DB Consumer architecture
- Explain the role of OLE DB Consumer Template classes
- Retrieve data from a data source by using the CDynamicAccessor class
- Execute parameterized queries by using the CDynamicParameterAccessor class

Estimated lesson time: 200 minutes

Basics of OLE DB

OLE DB aims to remedy the need for a technology that businesses can use to access data from diverse data sources. The industry standard for data access interfaces, ODBC requires data to be stored in a tabular format. However, a vast amount of critical information necessary to conduct day-to-day business is found outside traditional databases. A more generic and efficient strategy for data access than ODBC, OLE DB is designed to handle such information.

Some key features of OLE DB include:

- **Component feature set** An ODBC driver must adhere to conformance levels. Currently, three conformance levels exist in ODBC: Core, Level 1, and Level 2. Thus, if a driver needs to support a feature in Level 2, it must also support all other Level 2 features, in addition to Level 1 and Core features.

  OLE DB factors features and functionality into more than 50 different interfaces. Relatively few of these interfaces are mandatory. The rest are optional, allowing a provider to implement only the functionality it needs. Thus OLE DB allows providers to more appropriately match and expose database functionality.
- **Extensibility** Defining new interfaces can extend the OLE DB interfaces. This allows providers to expose custom functionality that cannot be exposed through ODBC.

- **Support for diverse data sources** OLE DB makes it easy for applications to access data stored in relational and nonrelational data sources. ODBC requires a driver to expose data through SQL. This procedure works well for relational data sources such as DB2, Oracle, and SQL Server. However, nonrelational data sources (such as spreadsheets or files) are not easily exposed through SQL. OLE DB providers are not required to support SQL to expose data.

Types of OLE DB Applications

OLE DB application types can be classified broadly into two classes: *consumers* and *providers*.

Consumers

A consumer is any piece of system or application code that consumes an OLE DB interface. Examples of consumers are Visual C++ and Visual Basic applications that access an Oracle or Microsoft Access database.

Providers

Two types of providers exist, *data providers* and *service providers*:

- **Data providers** A data provider is any component that owns data. Data providers expose their data in a tabular format, regardless of the format in which they store data. Examples of data providers are RDBMSs, spreadsheets, ISAM files, and e-mail.
- **Service providers** A service provider does not have its own data, but it facilitates data access between a data provider and a consumer. Examples of service providers are query processors and cursor engines. Service providers act both as consumers and providers. In its role as a consumer, a service provider retrieves data from the base tables owned by the data provider. In its role as a provider, the query processor creates a rowset from the retrieved data and returns it to the consumer.

OLE DB Architecure

OLE DB architecture comprises many COM components, including the following:

- Enumerators
- Data source objects
- Resource pooling
- Sessions
- Command objects
- Rowset objects
- Errors

Enumerators

An *enumerator* is a COM object that can locate available data sources and other enumerators. Consumers that are not customized for a particular data source use enumerators to find a data source to use.

The OLE DB SDK includes a *root enumerator* that traverses the registry looking for data sources and other enumerators. Other enumerators traverse the registry or search in a provider-specific manner. For example, the MSDASQL enumerator will search for ODBC data sources.

Data Source Objects

Data source objects contain the code to connect to a data provider's underlying data store, such as a file or a DBMS. To access an OLE DB provider, a consumer must first create an instance of that OLE DB provider's data source object. The data source object exposes IDBInitialize, which the consumer uses to connect to the data source.

When a data source object has been successfully initialized, the consumer can call methods of IDBProperties to query the capabilities of a provider. These capabilities include rowset properties, such as scrolling ability, and transaction properties, such as supported isolation levels.

Resource Pooling

OLE DB supports *resource pooling,* which is conceptually similar to ODBC connection pooling. Through resource pooling, data source objects are pooled based on connection information. The pool is on a per-process basis and is maintained by the provider. A client must maintain a reference to a data source object, IDataInitialize, or IDBPromptInitialize to maintain the pool.

Sessions

The primary function of a *session* is to provide a context for transactions. A data source object creates one or more sessions. A session can be in one of the following modes:

- **Manual-commit mode** If you call the *ITransactionLocal::StartTransaction* function to start an explicit transaction, the session is in manual-commit mode. You must explicitly commit or abort any work done in the session. You can call *StartTransaction* only after the session has been successfully created. If you do not explicitly commit a transaction, the transaction is aborted when the application terminates.
- **Auto-commit mode** If transactions are not supported or if the call to *StartTransaction* is not made, the session is in auto-commit mode. Any work done in the session is automatically committed; it cannot be aborted.

  For providers that support nested transactions, calling *StartTransaction* within an existing transaction begins a new nested transaction beneath the current transaction. Calling the *Commit* or *Abort* method commits or aborts the transaction at the lowest level, respectively. You can access the nested transactions through transaction objects, which are obtained through the *ITransactionObject::GetTransactionObject* function.

Command Objects

A *Command object* is a container for a text command. In OLE DB, a text command is a string to be passed from a consumer to a provider for execution by the provider's underlying data store. Most commonly, the text command is a SQL SELECT statement.

Executing a command such as a SQL SELECT statement creates a rowset, whereas executing a command such as a SQL UPDATE or CREATE TABLE statement does not create a rowset.

Text commands are expressed in a provider-specific language, which is typically ANSI SQL92. Microsoft SQL Server supports ODBC SQL, SQL-92, and T-SQL syntax.

Rowset Objects

The rowset object allows OLE DB data providers to expose data in tabular form. A *rowset* is a set of rows in which each row has columns of data. Base table providers (for example, databases) present their data in the form of rowsets. Query processors present the result of queries in the form of rowsets.

Rowsets can be created in one of the following ways:

- **As a result of a query, such as calling *ICommand::Execute*** Simple providers, such as those built over a base table, index, file, or in-memory structure, generally do not support this method.
- **By calling *IOpenRowset::OpenRowset*** All providers support this method.

Types of Rowsets

Besides the default rowsets, OLE DB supports the following additional types of rowsets that have additional features for working with specialized data:

- **Schema rowsets** DBMS objects that contain structural information, or metadata, about a database. You can use schema rowsets to obtain table information, column information, and other forms of metadata from a database.
- **Index rowsets** A DBMS object that provides access to data in the rows of a table, based on key values. Providers for ISAM data typically support index rowset objects. Index rowsets contain index information.
- **View objects** In OLE DB, defines a subset of the rows and columns from a rowset. A view object contains no data of its own.

Accessing a Rowset

To access a rowset, the consumer must create one or more *accessors*. An accessor specifies how data in a row will be transferred to and from a data buffer structure in the consumer. Multiple accessors can be created on the same rowset.

Errors

Each OLE DB method provides an HRESULT return code that indicates the success or failure of the method. Two types of return codes exist:

- **Success or warning codes** Begin with S_ or DB_S_ and indicate that the method successfully completed
- **Error codes** Begin with E_ or DB_E_ and indicate that the method failed completely and was unable to do any useful work

When an error is returned from a function in OLE DB, you can obtain an *error object* to get more information about the errors that occurred. You can call *QueryInterface* for the ISupportErrorInfo interface on any provider object to determine if it returns errors. Also, if a provider supports the IErrorRecords interface, you can retrieve a collection of error records that describe errors that occurred. For more information, see "OLE DB Error Objects" in the Microsoft Data Access SDK documentation.

OLE DB Physical Architecture

Each OLE DB method provides an HRESULT return code that indicates the success or failure of the method. Two types of return codes exist—success and warning codes, and error codes.

OLE DB providers are COM DLLs that are loaded into a consumer application's memory space. OLE DB interfaces do not work across process boundaries. Thus you cannot pass a rowset pointer from your application to another.

Depending on the provider, communication with the underlying data store is either direct or through interprocess communication (IPC). The SQL Server Provider communicates with SQL Server using IPC. The Text File Read Only provider sample in MSDN directly reads a file.

The SQL Server Provider is named SQLOLEDB.1 in the Registry. SQLOLEDB.1 is the name used to refer to the provider in a connection string. The provider is a native API, meaning that it does not communicate through a separate API to access the database. This provider communicates directly to SQL Server, which offers excellent performance. The ODBC driver for SQL Server is also a native API, but the SQLOLEDB provider offers greater performance.

OLE DB Consumer Templates

OLE DB Consumer Templates are a set of classes that help you develop OLE DB applications with minimal effort. You can use these classes to implement many of the commonly used OLE DB object interfaces.

OLE DB Consumer Templates are provided in the form of a template library that is similar to ATL. The classes in this template library can be grouped into the following:

- **Provider classes** Use these classes to implement a database provider application.
- **Consumer classes** Use these classes to implement a database consumer application.

The OLE DB provider templates support the OLE DB 2 specification. Using these templates, you can implement simple read-only provider applications that support commands. You can also implement read/write providers using these templates, but you need to add code manually. The provider applications might or might not support commands.

OLE DB Consumer Templates Architecture

OLE DB Consumer Templates simplify the process of developing consumer applications. These templates provide the following features:

- Support for ATL and MFC developers to use the OLE DB interfaces
- Support for native C/C++ data types, such as int and char, for OLE DB programming
- An easy-to-use binding model for database parameters and columns
- OLE DB features, such as provider-owned memory for improved performance and multiple accessors on a rowset

Using these templates, you can create applications that execute parameterized queries to retrieve records selectively, and retrieve records from a data source for further processing. Figure 9.5, on the following page, shows the hierarchy of classes and rowsets in the templates.

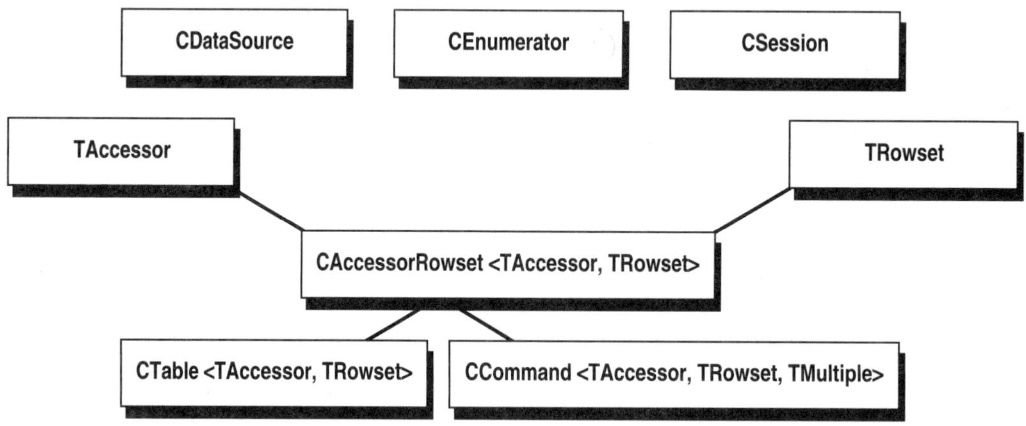

Figure 9.5 Hierarchy of classes and rowsets in OLE DB Consumer Templates

The classes in the top layer of OLE DB Consumer Templates conform to the OLE DB specification as closely as possible. Each class mirrors an existing OLE DB component. For example, the CDataSource class corresponds to the data source object in OLE DB, which represents a connection through a provider to a data source. The CEnumerator class calls an OLE DB Root Enumerator object, which exposes the ISourcesRowset interface. ISourcesRowset returns a rowset describing all data sources and enumerators visible to the root enumerator.

The CSession class represents a single database access session. One or more sessions can be associated with each data source, represented by a CDataSource object.

You can access data by using one of the four types of accessors. Each type of accessor is implemented by one of the following classes:

- **CAccessor** Supports multiple accessors on a rowset and is used when a record is statically bound to a data source. This accessor offers the best performance.
- **CDynamicAccessor** Dynamically creates an accessor at run time based on the column information of the rowset. Use this class to retrieve data from a data source when you do not know the structure at compile time.
- **CManualAccessor** Represents an accessor type designed for advanced use. This class offers functions that can handle both columns and command parameters. This accessor also offers good performance.
- **CDynamicParameterAccessor** Performs the same actions as CDynamicAccessor but is used for handling unknown command types. Use this class to get parameter information from the ICommandWithParameters interface. This accessor is not supported with all providers, so you should use this accessor only if you know your provider supports it. Otherwise, you can use CAccessor or CManualAccessor to pass parameterized queries.

Rowsets are represented by one of the following classes:

- **CRowset** Encapsulates an OLE DB IRowset object and several related interfaces, and provides manipulation methods for rowset data.
- **CBulkRowset** Extends CRowset by overriding methods that retrieve and manipulate rows to work on data in bulk.
- **CArrayRowset** Extends a rowset by allowing access to elements of the rowset using array syntax.

Accessing an OLE DB Provider from a Consumer Application

Next, you will learn about the generic procedure for accessing an OLE DB provider from a Consumer application.

Opening a Data Source

The sequence of commands that an OLE DB consumer application needs to execute to access a data source is almost identical for every OLE DB provider. The only exception to this command sequence is that different properties must be set on the Data Source and Rowset objects.

► **To open a data source with the OLE DB Consumer templates**

1. Create CDataSource, CSession, and CDBPropSet variables.

   The CDataSource variable represents the data source object. The CSession variable will maintain a specific session with the data source. CDBPropSet is a helper class that helps define properties that are to be passed to an OLE DB template function. The following code shows how these variables might be declared:

   ```
   HRESULT hr;
   CDataSource db;
   CDBPropSet dbInit(DBPROPSET_DBINIT);
   CSession session;
   ```

   You must include the header file atldbcli.h in your application if you want to use OLE DB Consumer Template classes.

2. Add connection properties to CDBPropSet.

   The connection properties include the UID, password, and server location. The following code shows how properties would be specified to open the Northwind database on SQL Server:

   ```
   dbInit.AddProperty(DBPROP_AUTH_PASSWORD, L"");
   dbInit.AddProperty(DBPROP_AUTH_USERID, L"sa");
   dbInit.AddProperty(DBPROP_INIT_CATALOG, L"Northwind");
   dbInit.AddProperty(DBPROP_INIT_DATASOURCE,
         L"servername");
   ```

3. Call an *Open* method on CDataSource.

   Several implementations of the *Open* method exist. Calling *Open* with no parameters will force OLE DB to display a dialog box allowing the user to type connection information. Calling *OpenWithServiceComponents* will activate services, such as resource pooling, in addition to opening the data source. The following code shows how to open a data source using properties specified in a CDBPropSet class:

   ```
   hr = db.OpenWithServiceComponents("SQLOLEDB.1", &dbinit);
   ```

4. Call the *Open* method of the CSession template class, as shown in the following code:

   ```
   hr = session.Open(db);
   ```

Opening a Rowset

After you have opened a data source and established a session, you can begin retrieving rowsets.

► **To retrieve a rowset**

1. Define acccssor and rowset classes.

   Before you can retrieve a rowset, you must define how you will access the rowset and what kind of rowset you will retrieve. Specify this information using the accessor and rowset classes.

2. Add rowset properties to CDBPropSet.

   After you have defined the accessor and rowset classes, determine what properties the rowset will have and add them to an instance of the CDBPropSet class. For example, you can set properties so that the rowset you create is scrollable and updateable. The following code shows how to define properties to create a fully functional rowset:

   ```
   CDBPropSet propset(DBPROPSET_ROWSET);
   propset.AddProperty(DBPROP_CANFETCHBACKWARDS, true);
   propset.AddProperty(DBPROP_IRowsetScroll, true);
   propset.AddProperty(DBPROP_IRowsetChange, true);
   propset.AddProperty(DBPROP_UPDATABILITY,
       DBPROPVAL_UP_CHANGE|
       DBPROPVAL_UP_DELETE);
   ```

   Depending on the type of provider, OLE DB uses these properties to create a server-side cursor. With SQL Server, OLE DB creates a cursor by calling the stored procedure *sp_cursoropen,* and passes it the parameters that have been set.

3. Retrieve the rowset by calling the *Open* method on the CCommand class or the CTable class.

   These classes inherit from the accessor and rowset you are using, so you can call any necessary accessor or rowset functions through them. The following code shows how you can open a rowset by executing a simple SELECT statement through a CCommand class:

   ```
   hr = cmd.Open(session, "SELECT CustomerID FROM
   Customers", &propset);
   ```

4. Use the CCommand class if you want to execute a command, such as a SQL command, or if you want to execute a parameterized query. If you want only to open a simple rowset, you can use the CTable class.

Using the CDynamicAccessor Class

Use the CDynamicAccessor class to retrieve data from a data source when, at design time, you do not know the schema of the rowset that will be returned. This class creates an accessor at run time, based on the column information of the rowset. This class also creates and manages a buffer for the data. Because information about the rowset has to be retrieved at run time, the CDynamicAccessor is slower than the CAccessor and CManualAccessor.

Table 9.22 lists some member functions of the CDynamicAccessor class that provide information about the data in the dynamic accessor's buffer.

Table 9.22 Member Functions of the CDynamicAccessor Class

Function	Description
GetColumnCount	Returns a count of the number of columns in the rowset.
GetColumnType	Returns the data type of a specific column in the data source table. For example, the code *DynamicAccessor.GetColumnType(1,&mType);* stores the data type of column 1 in the variable mType, which is of type DBTYPE, an enumerated data type.
GetOrdinal	Retrieves the column index given a column name.
GetColumnName	Retrieves the name of a specified column.
GetLength	Retrieves the maximum possible length of a column in bytes.
SetLength	Sets the length of the column in bytes.
GetValue	Returns the data from a specific column in the current record.
SetValue	Sets the data value of a specific column.

You can use the CRowset member functions *MoveFirst*, *MoveNext*, *MoveLast*, and *MovePrev* to scroll through the records in the rowset. You can retrieve data from the rowset by using the member functions of the CDynamicAccessor class.

► **To use CDynamicAccessor to retrieve data from a rowset**

1. Create and open a data source object.
2. Create and open a session object.
3. Create a Command object that inherits CDynamicAccessor, as shown in the following code:

```
CCommand<CDynamicAccessor> dynaccessorCmd;
```

4. Set the properties that you want the rowset to possess, as shown in the following code:

```
CDBPropSet propset(DBPROPSET_ROWSET);
propset.AddProperty(DBPROP_CANFETCHBACKWARDS, true);
propset.AddProperty(DBPROP_IRowsetChange, true);
propset.AddProperty(DBPROP_UPDATABILITY,
DBPROPVAL_UP_CHANGE);
```

5. Open the command object by passing the session object, SQL string, and CDBPropSet object to the *Open* function, as shown in the following code:

```
dynAccessorCmd.Open(session, strSQLCmd, &propset)
```

   In the previous code, strSQLCmd contains the dynamic SQL command.

6. Create a variable of type DBTYPE and retrieve the data type of the column from which you want to retrieve a data value, as shown in the following code:

```
DBTYPE colType;
dynAccessorCmd.MoveFirst();
dynAccessorCmd.GetColumnType(nColumnNumber, &colType);
```

7. Depending on the data type of the column, retrieve the column value into a variable of appropriate data type by using the *GetValue* function, as shown in the following code:

```
switch (colType)
{
   case DBTYPE_I2:   short *columnValue = (short int*)
         dynAccessorCmd.GetValue(nColumnNumber);
               break;
   case DBTYPE_I4: int *colVal = (int *)
         dynAccessorCmd.GetValue(nColumnNumber);
               break;
   ...
   ...
}
```

Creating Parameterized Queries Using CDynamicParameterAccessor

The CDynamicParameterAccessor class is similar to the CDynamicAccessor class. Like the CDynamicAccessor class, the CDynamicParameterAccessor class maintains the buffer for data that is retrieved as a result of executing a command on the data source. In addition, the CDynamicParameterAccessor class allows you to execute parameterized queries. The CDynamicParameterAccessor stores parameter information and substitutes the values for each parameter when the parameterized command is executed. Calling the ICommandWithParameters interface sets the parameter information. The CCommand class exposes the interface's methods, such as *SetParameterInfo* and *GetParameterInfo*. Keep in mind that not all providers support the dynamic parameter accessor.

The first step in creating and executing a parameterized query is to create the Command object.

► **To create a parameterized command that uses a dynamic accessor**

1. Create and open a data source object.
2. Create and open a session object.
3. Declare a Command object that inherits the CDynamicParameterAccessor class, as shown in the following code:

```
CCommand<CDynamicParameterAccessor> dynParamAccCmd;
```

4. Generate the dynamic query string using "?" as a placeholder for the values of each parameter.
5. Invoke the *Create* method of the CCommand class to create a command, as shown in the following code:

```
dynParamAccCmd.Create(m_session,strCommand);
```

In the previous code, *strCommand* contains the parameterized query string. The *Create* function invokes the *CreateCommand* function that creates a command for the specified session. When you have created a command, you can then set information such as the data type and size for the parameters of the command.

Setting Parameterized Information

When a consumer application executes a parameterized query and passes parameter values to a provider, it must supply type information for each parameter to the provider. The provider uses this information to convert each parameter value from the data type supplied by the consumer to the data type supported by the data source.

Data type information is passed to the provider by using the *SetParameterInfo* method of the ICommandWithParameters interface. The CCommand class exposes ICommandWithParameters interface methods such as *SetParameterInfo* and *GetParameterInfo*.

► **To send parameter information to a provider**

1. Create an array of type DBPARAMBINDINFO, as shown in the following code:

   ```
   DBPARAMBINDINFO* pBindInfo = new
   DBPARAMBINDINFO[ulParams];
   ```

   The DBPARAMBINDINFO stores information about each parameter in the parameterized query. The number of parameters determines the number of elements in the array.

2. Populate the DBPARAMBINDINFO structure with values for each parameter. Table 9.23 lists the data members of the DBPARAMBINDINFO structure, and provides a brief description for each.

Table 9.23 Data Members of the DBPARAMBINDINFO Structure

Data Member	Description
pwszDataSourceType	Stores the data type of the parameter data supplied by the consumer.
PwszName	Stores the name of the parameter. If the provider supports named parameters, this variable can be used; otherwise, it is set to NULL.
UlParamSize	Stores the parameter size.
BPrecision	Stores the numeric precision.
BScale	Stores the scale.
DwFlags	Stores the parameter type, either DBPARAMFLAGS_ISINPUT or DBPARAMFLAGS_ISOUTPUT.

3. Invoke the *SetParameterInfo* method to tell the provider how to convert the data from the type supplied by the consumer to that supported by the data source. For example, the consumer might pass the parameter value "01/01/99" of a data column as a character string. The provider makes use of the information supplied by *SetParameterInfo* to convert the string into a DBTYPE_DBTIMESTAMP value that is understood by SQL Server.

4. Invoke the *BindParameters* function to bind the parameters supplied by the consumer to the data types of the columns in the data source, as shown in the following code:

```
dynParamAccCmd.BindParameters
    (&dynParamAccCmd.m_hParameterAccessor,
    dynParamAccCmd.m_spCommand, &ptr)
```

The *BindParameters* function takes three parameters. The first parameter is of type HACCESSOR and is a handle to the parameter accessor. The second parameter is a smart pointer to the ICommand interface that is encapsulated by the CCommand template class. The third parameter is a void pointer to the parameter information. This parameter has been set to NULL because the parameter information has already been set.

5. Prepare the command for execution by invoking the CCommand member function *Prepare*, as shown in the following code:

```
dynParamAccCmd.Prepare();
```

The values that you set using the *SetParameterInfo* method should closely resemble the data types that the data source supports. If this criterion is met, the provider will convert the data type of the parameter value specified by the consumer to that supported by the data source.

Setting Parameter Values and Executing the Command

After you have informed the provider about the type of data conversion that must be performed on each parameter, by using the *SetParameterInfo* method, you can then set the value of each parameter and execute the parameterized query.

To set the value of a parameter, you must first get a pointer to the buffer that stores the parameter's value by using the *GetParam* template function. You can then assign a value to this memory location, as shown in the following code:

```
lstrcpy((TCHAR*)dynParamAccCmd.GetParam(nParamNo),
    pstrParamValue);
```

The *GetParam* method requires the data type of the value that is to be stored so that it can return a pointer of appropriate data type. The final step is to execute the parameterized query by invoking the *Open* method, as shown in the following code:

```
dynParamAccCmd.Open();
```

You do not have to pass any arguments to the *Open* function, because the command string and session to be used have already been specified. If you want the rowset that is returned to possess certain properties, you can set these properties in a CDBPropSet object and pass it to the *Open* function as the sole argument.

Lesson Summary

In this lesson, you looked at the types of OLE DB applications—providers and consumers. You also examined the roles of the components of OLE DB architecture—enumerators, data source objects, resource pooling, sessions, command objects, rowset objects, and errors. You learned about the components of

OLE DB Consumer Template architecture, including classes, accessors, and rowsets.

This lesson outlined the procedure for accessing an OLE DB provider from a Consumer application, using the OLE DB Consumer Templates. Additionally, you learned how to use the CDynamicAccessor class to retrieve data from a data source. Finally, you learned how to use the CDynamicParameterAccessor class to create and execute parameterized queries.

Lab 9: Creating an ADO Application

In this lab, you will create an ADO-based application that allows employees of the Duwamish bookstore to update personal information in the Employees table. The application accepts a user alias and password, and retrieves the employee's record. The employee can modify the password, cell phone number, emergency contact, and emergency contact's phone number. Startup code for this application is provided in the Labs\Ch09\Startup folder on the companion CD.

Estimated lab time: 45 minutes

This lab requires the installation of Visual C++ 6.0, SQL Server 7 Standard Edition, and the Duwamish Books (Phase 4) database. Following are the broad-level steps that need to be performed to create the ADO application.

1. Connect to the data source.
2. Set the command information.
3. Set parameter information to execute the parameterized query.

These steps are described in more detail in the following exercises.

► Connect to the data source

1. In the *OnInitDialog* function of the CRsCgDlg class, create an instance of the Connection object by calling the *CreateInstance* method of the smart pointer m_Conn, which is defined in the class CRsCgDlg:

```
m_Conn.CreateInstance(__uuidof(Connection));
```

2. Set the Provider property to the OLE DB Provider for SQL Server (SQLOLEDB):

```
m_Conn->Provider = L"sqloledb";
```

3. Set the Cursor location to *adUseClient,* to create a client-side cursor:

```
m_Conn->CursorLocation = adUseClient;
```

4. Open a connection to the data source using an appropriate user logon and password:

```
m_Conn->Open(L"Data Source=(Local);Initial
Catalog=DbP4Data;",L"sa",L"",0);
```

The Data Source has been set to the local computer and can be replaced with the name of your SQL Server. DbP4Data is the name of the Duwamish database.

► **Set the command information**

1. Create a Command object and set the active connection to the connection m_Conn:

```
m_Cmd.CreateInstance(__uuidof(Command));
m_Cmd->ActiveConnection = m_Conn;
```

   The Command object has been defined in the class CRsCgDlg, and is part of the startup code.

2. Set the CommandText property to the parameterized query to be executed:

```
m_Cmd->CommandText = "Select * from Employees where Alias = ? and
Password = ?";
```

► **Set parameter information to execute the parameterized query stored in m_strCmdText**

1. Create a variable of type CPwdDlg. The class CPwdDlg defines a dialog box that accepts the user alias and password:

```
CPwdDlg pwdDlg;
```

2. Create two smart pointers to the Parameter object, to store the parameters of the query:

```
_ParameterPtr pParam1, pParam2;
```

3. Create two variables of type VARIANT to store the alias and password retrieved from the password dialog box:

```
_variant_t vAlias, vPassword;
```

4. Create a Parameter object called Alias as shown in the following code:

```
pParam1.CreateInstance(__uuidof(Parameter));
pParam1 = m_Cmd->CreateParameter("Alias", adChar,
adParamInput, 5, vAlias);
```

5. Append the Parameter object to the Parameters collection:

```
m_Cmd->Parameters->Append(pParam1);
```

6. Create another Parameter object named Password and append it to the Parameters collection as follows:

```
pParam2.CreateInstance(__uuidof(Parameter));
pParam2 = m_Cmd->CreateParameter("Password", adChar,
adParamInput, 8, vPassword);
m_Cmd->Parameters->Append(pParam2);
```

► Execute the query and retrieve the recordset

1. Create a Recordset object:

```
m_pRs.CreateInstance(__uuidof(Recordset));
```

2. Execute the query by using the *Execute* method of the Command object:

```
m_pRs=m_Cmd->Execute(&vEmpty, &vEmpty,adCmdText);
```

   VEmpty is a variant of type VT_ERROR and value DISP_E_PARAMNOTFOUND.

3. If the query is successful, bind the recordset to the class CRsCgDlg; otherwise, close the connection to the data source, and then close the dialog box:

```
if(m_pRs->GetRecordCount()==1)
{
if (FAILED(hr = m_pRs->QueryInterface
    {
        (__uuidof(IADORecordBinding),
        (LPVOID *)&piAdoRecordBinding)))
            _com_issue_error(hr);
        if (FAILED
        (hr = piAdoRecordBinding
        ->BindToRecordset(this)))
            _com_issue_error(hr);
        RefreshBoundData();
    }
    else
    {
        MessageBox("Invalid User ID or Password",
        "Logon Failed",MB_OK);
        m_Conn->Close();
        CDialog::OnCancel();
    }
}
```

► Implement the Save button

1. In the *OnSave* command handler, delete the two existing Parameter objects in the Parameters collection.

```
vIndex = "Alias";
m_Cmd->Parameters->Delete(&vIndex);
vIndex = "Password";
m_Cmd->Parameters->Delete(&vIndex);
```

   The variant vIndex is used to store the identifiers of the parameters to be deleted.

2. Create a parameterized query to update the Employees table.

```
m_Cmd->CommandText = "Update Employees set Password =
?, CellPhone = ?, EmergencyContact = ?, EmergencyPhone
= ? where Alias = ? and Password = ?";
```

3. Invoke *UpdateData(TRUE)* to transfer the contents from the dialog box to the member variables.
4. Create parameter objects to store the values for the update query, and append each parameter to the Parameters collection:

```
pParam1.CreateInstance(__uuidof(Parameter));
pParam1 = m_Cmd->CreateParameter("NewPassword",
    adChar, adParamInput, 256,
    _variant_t(m_strDlgPassword));
m_Cmd->Parameters->Append(pParam1);
pParam2.CreateInstance(__uuidof(Parameter));
vCellPhone=m_strDlgCellPhone.GetBuffer
    (m_strDlgCellPhone.GetLength());
pParam2 = m_Cmd->CreateParameter("CellPhone", adChar,
    adParamInput, 256, vCellPhone);
m_Cmd->Parameters->Append(pParam2);
pParam3.CreateInstance(__uuidof(Parameter));
vEmergencyContact=m_strDlgEmergencyContact.GetBuffer
    (m_strDlgEmergencyContact.GetLength());
pParam3 = m_Cmd->CreateParameter("EmergencyContact",
    adChar, adParamInput, 256,
    _variant_t(m_strDlgEmergencyContact));
m_Cmd->Parameters->Append(pParam3);
pParam4.CreateInstance(__uuidof(Parameter));
vEmergencyPhone=m_strDlgEmergencyPhone.GetBuffer
    (m_strDlgEmergencyPhone.GetLength());
pParam4 = m_Cmd->CreateParameter("EmergencyPhone",
    adChar, adParamInput, 256,
    _variant_t(m_strDlgEmergencyPhone));
m_Cmd->Parameters->Append(pParam4);
pParam5.CreateInstance(__uuidof(Parameter));
pParam5 = m_Cmd->CreateParameter("Alias", adChar,
    adParamInput, 256, m_wszAlias);
m_Cmd->Parameters->Append(pParam5);
pParam6.CreateInstance(__uuidof(Parameter));
pParam6 = m_Cmd->CreateParameter("OldPassword",
    adChar, adParamInput, 256, m_wszPassword);
m_Cmd->Parameters->Append(pParam6);
```

5. Execute the query and call *OnOK* to close the dialog box:

```
m_Cmd->Execute(&vEmpty, &vEmpty,adCmdText);
CDialog::OnOK();
```

Review

The following questions are intended to reinforce key information presented in this chapter. If you are unable to answer a question, review the appropriate lesson and then try answering the question again. Answers to the questions can be found in Appendix B, "Review Questions and Answers," at the back of this book.

1. Which recordset properties must be set to create a disconnected recordset?

2. You want to execute several commands as part of the same transaction. How would you ensure that each command object executes as part of the same transaction?

3. Which type of accessor would you use to retrieve information from a data source that has an unknown schema?

4. A theoretical application has to display a list of cities from a table; the list of cities does not change. Which type of ODBC cursor would you choose to display this list?

5. Which function would you call to retrieve diagnostic records whenever a function call returns a failure code?

6. What is a cursor?

7. Which OLE DB component helps you search for data sources?

CHAPTER 10

Exception Handling

Lesson 1: Exceptions 558

Lesson 2: Handling Exceptions and Errors 565

Lesson 3: Error-Handling Strategies 579

Lab 10: Exception Handling in Duwamish Books 593

Review 598

About This Chapter

This chapter describes how an application can intelligently respond to many types of errors that can occur during program execution. You will learn about specific types of error events called exceptions, and how to write programs that are more stable because they monitor exceptions.

When developing a distributed application, you must consider errors that can occur in several areas—the client program itself, its auxiliary components, COM, data providers, database management system (DBMS) servers, and the operating system on which you are planning to run your application. This chapter discusses various strategies that you can implement in your application to anticipate and cope with errors, regardless of where they occur.

Before You Begin

To complete the lessons in this chapter, you must have:

- Installed the Microsoft Visual C++ development tools as described in Lab 2.
- Read Chapter 8.
- Installed the Duwamish Book database as described in Chapter 9.

Lesson 1: Exceptions

An *exception* is any condition that is considered an error by the operating system or an application. When an application causes (or *raises*) an exception, the system attempts to notify the application that an error occurred by making a call to the application's exception handler code (if it exists). If the application does not provide an exception handler, the operating system resolves the problem itself, often by terminating the application abruptly with a terse message to the user that reads something like this: "This program has performed an illegal operation and will be shut down."

After this lesson, you will be able to:

- Understand the system service known as structured exception handling
- Implement exception handling in a C++ application to handle errors as they occur during execution

Estimated lesson time: 15 minutes

Anticipating Program Errors

The best way to handle exceptions might be to write code that would never encounter an unexpected error. Such ideal code would not need to incorporate exception-handling code because exceptions—or at least fatal exceptions—cannot occur.

Experienced programmers take a conservative approach when allocating memory, adding code that checks the value that the *new* operator returns and using the pointer exclusively if it holds a non-zero value. For example, if *new* returns a null pointer—meaning that the allocation failed—code can react appropriately. The result looks similar to the following:

```
int *ptr = new int[BLOCK_SIZE];
if (ptr)
{
    .
    .  // Memory successfully allocated, so use it
    .
    delete[] ptr;
}
else
{
    // Allocation failed - Take appropriate steps
}
```

Because this code anticipates the potential problem of insufficient heap space, it forestalls any attempt to write to unowned memory, which would cause a fatal fault. Thus, the application has no need for contingency code to handle the exception error because such an error cannot occur. This code is often referred to as *robust,* which means it is stable in the face of adversity and therefore less prone to fail.

Preventing errors by continually checking return values can sometimes make code difficult to read and maintain due to constant interruptions of the program's logic flow. The result often leads to a long series of nested *if-else* blocks, in which the *if* blocks contain the code as it is intended to run, and the *else* blocks contain the code as it is intended to deal with errors. Following is a pseudocode illustration of how such nested tests can creep closer to the right edge of the screen, making the intended line of flow difficult to track:

```
if (condition1 == TRUE)
{
    if (condition2 == TRUE)
    {
        if (condition3 == TRUE)
        {
            .
            .   // Other nested conditions
            .
        }
        else
        {
            // condition3 failed
        }
    }
    else
    {
        // condition2 failed
    }
}
else
{
    // condition1 failed
}
```

Microsoft Windows and the C++ language offer another approach, *exception handling,* to handling potential errors. Exception handling allows developers to separate a function into two sections, one for normal execution and the other for errors. Code in the first section seems oblivious to potential errors, does not check return values, and executes as though no errors can occur. The other section of code traps errors as they occur.

Structured Exception Handling

Two levels of exception handling exist. *Structured exception handling* (SEH) is a service provided by the operating system, while *C++ exception handling* refers to a feature of the C++ language implemented by the compiler.

The two levels are often confused, though they are quite distinct. This chapter focuses mostly on C++ exception handling, but also covers SEH for two reasons. First, an understanding of SEH ensures a more solid grasp of C++ exception handling at the application level. Second, applications written in the C language cannot use C++ exception handling. To incorporate exception handling, C language applications must instead use SEH techniques.

All exception handling is based on the SEH mechanism. SEH initiates the beginning of a communication chain that winds its way to the application level. An application incorporates SEH through the *__try*, *__except*, and *__finally* keywords. A *__try* block must be matched with either an *__except* block or a *__finally* block—but not both—using a syntax such as the following:

```
__try
{
    // Normal code goes here
}
__except(filter)
{
    // Errors that occur in __try block are trapped here
}
```

Notice that SEH keywords are preceded by two underscores, not one. The *__except* block executes exclusively if code in the *__try* block causes an exception. If all goes well and the *__try* block successfully finishes, execution resumes at the next instruction following the *__except* block, thus bypassing the *__except* block entirely.

Through its *filter* parameter, the *__except* block specifies whether or not it is able to deal with the exception. The *filter* parameter must evaluate to one of three values, shown in Table 10.1.

Table 10.1 Catch Block Parameters

Value	Meaning
EXCEPTION_CONTINUE_SEARCH	The *__except* block declines the exception and passes control on to the handler with the next highest precedence.
EXCEPTION_CONTINUE_EXECUTION	The *__except* block dismisses the exception without executing, forcing control to return to the instruction that raised the exception.
EXCEPTION_EXECUTE_HANDLER	The body of the *__except* block executes.

The EXCEPTION_CONTINUE_EXECUTION filter apparently renders the *__except* block useless, and might elicit questions of why an exception handler exists at all if it never executes, but merely requests the statement that caused the exception to be repeated. The answer to such questions lies in the way an *__except* block often uses a helper function that returns a value for the *filter* parameter, as demonstrated in the following:

```
__except(GetFilter())
{
    // Body of __except block
}
.
.
.
long GetFilter()
{
    long iFilter;
    .
    .  // Determine appropriate filter for error
    .
    return iFilter;
}
```

The helper function's task in this instance is to analyze current conditions and attempt to fix the problem that triggered the exception. If it succeeds, the helper function returns EXCEPTION_CONTINUE_EXECUTION, thus causing the control to bypass the *__except* block and return to the original instruction in the *__try* block for another attempt.

Keep in mind that such techniques must be employed with care. If the helper function does not truly fix the problem, the program enters an infinite loop in which the statement in the *__try* block continually executes, repeatedly raising an exception that is never properly resolved.

Although nominally part of SEH, the *__finally* keyword has little to do with the operating system. Rather, *__finally* defines a block of instructions that the compiler guarantees will execute when the *__try* block finishes. Even if the *__try* block contains a return statement or a GOTO statement that jumps beyond the *__finally* block, the compiler ensures that the *__finally* block executes before returning or jumping. The *__finally* keyword does not take a parameter.

C++ Exception Handling

After examining the fundamentals of SEH, you are more aptly prepared to understand exception handling at a general level. C++ exception handling is at the other end of the command chain that SEH initiates. Whereas SEH is a system service, C++ exception handling is the code that you (and the compiler) write to take advantage of that service. C++ exception handling is more sophisticated and offers more options than SEH. In fact, using the low-level *__try* and *__except* keywords of SEH is discouraged for C++ applications.

As with SEH, a C++ application provides exception handler code that executes in response to an error that the system detects. The exception handler can choose to resolve the problem and retry the instruction that caused the error, ignore the problem completely, or pass the notification to the next handler (if it exists) in the chain of handlers. C++ provides the *try, catch,* and *throw* keywords for this purpose. Unlike their SEH counterparts, these keywords do not have an underscore prefix.

To see a simple example of C++ exception handling, reconsider the scenario described in the first section of this lesson, in which a program allocated memory using the *new* operator. The first section demonstrated how an application could prevent failure by testing the value of the pointer that the *new* operator returns. Exception handling offers a somewhat more elegant alternative, in which code is separated into a *try* and *catch* block, instead of a potential series of nested *if-else* blocks, as shown in the following sample:

```
try
{
    int *iptr = new int[BLOCK_SIZE];
    .
    .   // If reach here, allocation succeeded
    .
    delete[] iptr;
}
catch(CMemoryException* e)
{
    // Allocation failed, so address the problem
    e->Delete();
}
```

If the *new* operator fails to allocate the requested memory, it triggers an exception that causes the *catch* block to execute. In the example shown, the *catch* block accepts as its parameter a pointer to an MFC CMemoryException object, which contains information about the out-of-memory condition that the *new* operator encountered.

C++ programs that do not use MFC can design their own class for this purpose or even use a pointer to a standard type, such as a pointer to a string containing an error message. (The lab at the end of this chapter shows how to handle *new* operator exceptions in a program that does not use MFC.) The block's parameter list can also be an ellipsis (...), which tells the compiler that the *catch* block handles any kind of exception, not just memory exceptions.

If the *catch* block can fix the problem, it retries the instruction that caused the exception by executing the *throw* command. Notice that this option is much more flexible than using the EXCEPTION_CONTINUE_EXECUTION filter of SEH because it allows the *catch* block to execute. If the *catch* block does not retry (or rethrow) the exception, program flow continues to the next statement following the *catch* block. In this case, the code in the *try* block does not execute at all.

Benign Exceptions

Some exceptions are *benign* and do not show up as errors in an application. An example of a benign exception occurs when a program accesses an uncommitted page of its stack memory. The operating system deals with this situation transparently by trapping the invalid access, committing another page to the stack, and then allowing the access to continue using the committed page. The application is not even aware that the exception has occurred. The only external evidence is a momentary delay while the operating system sets up the new page.

Visual C++ Exception Handling Support

Visual C++ supports exception handling only if the /GX command line switch is included. For projects created using the services of a wizard such as MFC AppWizard, this switch is made available automatically; therefore, you do not need to worry about exception support in your project. However, for projects not created with a wizard and that use exception handling, this switch must be added to prevent a compiler error. The lab at the end of this chapter demonstrates how to make the /GX switch available through an option in the Project Settings dialog box.

Lesson Summary

This lesson provides a basis for upcoming lessons of this chapter. You learned two methods, return value testing and exception handling, in which an application can anticipate and respond to errors as they occur during execution. Exception handling offers several advantages over testing return values as follows:

- Cleaner code that is often easier to maintain
- More flexibility in the way an application can respond to errors
- A wider net guaranteed to catch all errors that occur in a *try* block, even those that arise from a completely unanticipated source

The disadvantages of exception handling are that it increases overhead and code size, and can be overkill in many situations where simply checking a value works just as well.

The operating system's structured exception handling mechanism is a system service activated through the *__try*, *__except*, and *__finally* keywords. The *__try* keyword defines a block of "optimistic" code that does not concern itself with errors. The *__except* block contains "pessimistic" code that handles errors if and when they occur. SEH is the foundation on which C++ exception handling is built. Visual C++ implements C++ exception handling through the *try*, *catch*, and *throw* keywords.

If the philosophy of error handling were to be summed up in four words, those words would be "Don't make any assumptions." Errors have a habit of occurring when least expected. Proper error-handling techniques allow your program to appropriately respond to unexpected events without terminating—or worse, continuing to execute in an unstable state.

Lesson 2: Handling Exceptions and Errors

This lesson concentrates on how an application can apply the exception-handling techniques described in the previous lesson. First this lesson focuses on MFC, describing how and when the framework raises exceptions to inform an application about errors. Next this lesson examines error handling in COM programs, and describes how COM influences the way both servers and clients deal with errors.

Further adding to the subject of error handling are distributed applications that consist of modules communicating over a network. In these applications, one module often needs to handle exceptions caused by another module. In this lesson, you will learn how exceptions can propagate from one module to another, even across a network.

After this lesson, you will be able to:

- Write code that effectively handles errors as they occur in a running program
- Understand how COM components, such as Microsoft ActiveX controls and data providers, notify clients about errors
- Describe how handlers in one module of a distributed application can respond to exceptions raised in another module of the same application

Estimated lesson time: 15 minutes

Exceptions and MFC

Exception handling has become an integral part of MFC, though it is by no means supported consistently throughout the MFC library. As a general rule, MFC library classes that wrap system services, such as CWnd and CDC, do not throw exceptions when they encounter errors, whereas many other classes, such as CFile and CDaoRecordset, do. It is not possible to handle all MFC errors through exceptions.

Fortunately, most MFC functions—even those that support exceptions—return an error code. Developers often have a choice in how their code responds to errors that the framework encounters, by either monitoring return values or providing exception-handler code as *catch* blocks.

When the MFC framework raises an exception, it creates a CException object that describes the error. Because CException is an *abstract base class*—meaning that it provides declarations for member functions, but does not supply implementation code—an exception object must be created from one of eleven derived classes, such as CMemoryException, COleException, and CFileException. The next section provides examples of how a *catch* block in an MFC application receives an object derived from CException.

Handling Errors in MFC Applications

The CFile class offers a good model for learning how an application can respond to errors in the MFC framework either by checking return values or by handling exceptions. CFile is only one of many MFC classes that support exception handling; however, by examining how this particular class uses exceptions to report errors, you will be more thoroughly prepared to apply exception handling to other MFC classes as well.

Creating an empty CFile object and opening a file does not generate an exception if the *open* operation fails. In this case, the application can recognize an error by monitoring the Boolean value that the *CFile::Open* function returns, as shown in the following:

```
CFile file;

if (file.Open("somefile.txt", CFile::modeRead))
{
    .
    .   // File successfully opened
    .
}
else
{
    .
    .   // Failed to open file
    .
}
```

CFile::Open is somewhat unusual in the fact that it accepts a pointer to a CFileException object. This option offers the best of both worlds, allowing an application to conveniently recover information about an error through an exception object without actually providing a *catch* block to handle the error. The example fragment now resembles the following:

```
CFile         file;
CFileException e;

if (file.Open("somefile.txt", CFile::modeRead, &e))
{
    .
    .   // File successfully opened
    .
}
else
{
    CString str;
    switch(e.m_cause)
    {
```

```
        case CFileException::fileNotFound:
            str = "Cannot locate the requested file";
            break;

        case CFileException::tooManyOpenFiles:
            str = "Too many files already opened";
            break;

        default:
            str = "Unknown error";
    }

    AfxMessageBox(str, MB_ICONEXCLAMATION);
}
```

Other CFile functions such as *Read* and *Write* do not offer this type of flexibility and provide no means for turning off exceptions. If an application does not handle an exception generated inside CFile, the framework displays a generic message such as that shown in Figure 10.1 on the next page, and then terminates the program. Rarely is this desirable behavior, so an application should always place file handling code inside a *try* block when using the CFile class.

Following is an example fragment that uses exception handling. The code no longer calls the *Open* function but instead creates the CFile object and opens the file in one step through a class constructor that accepts the same parameters as *Open.* The constructor does not return a value, so placing the call inside a *try* block is the only means of trapping any errors, as demonstrated in the following:

```
try
{
    CFile file("somefile.txt", CFile::modeRead);
    .
    .   // Read the file
    .
}
catch(CFileException* e)
{
    CString str;
    switch(e->m_cause)
    {
        .
        .   // Initialize str with the error message
        .
    }

    AfxMessageBox(str, MB_ICONEXCLAMATION);
    e->Delete();
}
```

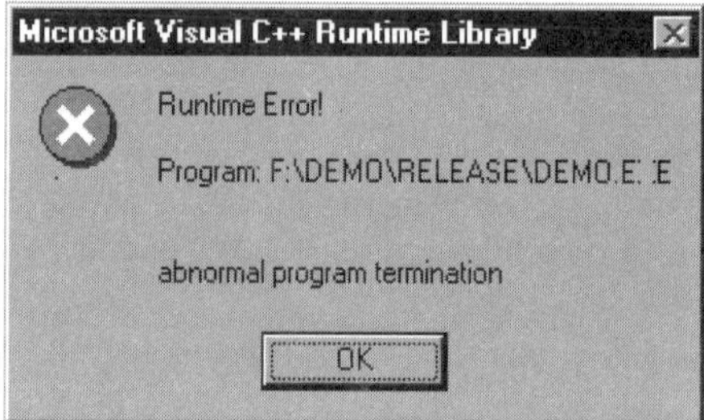

Figure 10.1 Generic termination message displayed when an unhandled exception occurs in MFC

Some MFC functions create more than one kind of exception object, depending on the error. For example, when it encounters an error, *CDaoRecordset::Open* returns either a CDaoException or CMemoryException object, whichever is appropriate for describing the error. An application can provide separate *catch* blocks to field both types of exceptions, as shown in the following:

```
CDaoRecordset rs(&m_db);

try
{
    rs.Open(dbOpenDynaset, szQuery, dbReadOnly);
    .
    .   // Successful open, so use the recordset object
    .
    rs.Close();
}

// Handle DAO errors here
catch(CDaoException *e)
{
    AfxMessageBox(e->m_pErrorInfo->m_strDescription,
        MB_ICONEXCLAMATION);
    e->Delete();
}

// Handle memory errors here
catch(CMemoryException *e)
{
    .
    .   // Respond to the memory error
    .
    e->Delete();
}
```

If the *Open* function in this example attempts to revise or delete a locked database record, it throws a CDaoException error. Notice that, unlike the CFileException class shown earlier, the CDaoException class contains a string that describes the error. The class's *m_pErrorInfo* member points to an error message supplied by the underlying DAO COM object that generated the error. Lesson 3 provides more information about recovering error messages from server objects.

The first *catch* block simply displays the string in a message box. If the *Open* function instead attempts to access invalid memory, it throws a CMemoryException error. In this case, the second *catch* block in the example fragment gains control and takes appropriate action for a memory access error.

MFC Exception Macros

Early versions of MFC provided macros as substitutes for the C++ exception handling commands, naming them as uppercase TRY, CATCH, and THROW. For various reasons, the macros have fallen out of favor, and since MFC 3, have become simply aliases for the original C++ keywords *try, catch,* and *throw*. Thus, while MFC still supports the uppercase macro names, they are no longer recommended, nor are they advantageous.

COM Errors

COM brings its own style to the problem of detecting and dealing with execution errors. COM applications and components can use the following three methods for reporting and monitoring the success of an operation:

- **HRESULT codes** Distributed programs must deal with COM's preferred method of communicating error information through values known as HRESULT codes.
- **Exceptions** As a language-independent standard for binary objects that interoperate, COM is in a delicate position when it comes to exception handling. Exceptions thrown in one object must be catchable in another, regardless of the language used to create each object or how the objects are distributed across a network. Visual C++ provides the _com_error support class to facilitate the transferal of language-independent COM error information through exceptions.
- **Events** ActiveX controls can indicate errors immediately by firing an event. COM provides the Error stock event for this purpose.

This section describes all three reporting methods, and points out various pitfalls to avoid when dealing with COM errors. Keep in mind that, for COM, success and failure are not always black and white concepts. COM allows for the idea that success and failure might be only partial, not complete.

HRESULT Codes

In COM, interface methods return HRESULT codes to report success or failure. Despite its H prefix, an HRESULT code is not a handle, but merely a 32-bit value indicating a success or failure condition.

COM predefines many HRESULT values such as S_OK for success, S_FALSE for partial success, and various failure codes such as E_INVALIDARG and E_NOTIMPL. The E prefix stands for error. The S prefix identifies the first two codes as SCODE (or *status code*) values. Under 32-bit Windows, HRESULT and SCODE are synonymous with each other.

Although COM allows your programs to define new HRESULT values, as the next section will reveal, you should use COM's predefined values whenever appropriate. For example, the E_OUTOFMEMORY code, which the COM library has already defined, communicates a common error condition without ambiguity. You can find a list of predefined HRESULT values and their meanings in the WinError.h include file under the heading "OLE Error Codes."

Anatomy of an HRESULT Code

An HRESULT code consists of four bit fields, as illustrated in Figure 10.2 and as described in Table 10.2 following the figure.

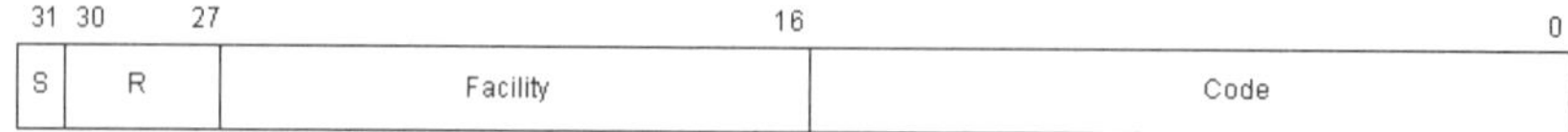

Figure 10.2 Bit fields of an HRESULT value

Table 10.2 Bit Fields in HRESULT Code

Field ID	Bits	Meaning
S	31	Severity code. A value of 0 indicates success, and a value of 1 indicates an error. Because the severity bit is also the value's sign bit, a severity value of 1 makes the HRESULT code a negative number.
R	27-30	Reserved bits of the facility code. Should be zero.
Facility	16-26	Facility code that indicates a general category to which the error code belongs.
Code	0-15	A 16-bit WORD value that identifies the condition. For custom HRESULT codes, this field should hold a value of 0x200 or higher to prevent confusion with COM's predefined values.

COM defines several facility codes that must be universally unique. When defining your own HRESULT codes, use the FACILITY_ITF manifest constant as shown in the following:

```
#define MY_SUCCESS_CODE ((0 << 31) | \
    (FACILITY_ITF << 16) | 0x200)
#define E_MY_ERROR_CODE ((1 << 31) | \
    (FACILITY_ITF << 16) | 0x201)
```

The WinError.h file defines FACILITY_ITF as 4, so the first code line in the previous example creates a positive value of 0x00040200. The second code line in the previous example produces a negative value of 0x80040201. WinError.h also defines the MAKE_HRESULT macro to simplify forming HRESULTs on the fly, such as that shown in the following example:

```
// Set HRESULT value 0x80040202
HRESULT hr = MAKE_HRESULT(SEVERITY_ERROR, FACILITY_ITF,
    0x202);
```

Testing HRESULT Codes

Another aspect to keep in mind when dealing with HRESULT codes is that COM assumes zero means success, not failure. For instance, the manifest constant S_OK has a value of zero. As the previous table illustrates, COM assumes that a value of zero or greater indicates success, though perhaps a qualified success.

To save developers the trouble of memorizing the rules outlined in the previous table, COM provides two macros, SUCCEEDED and FAILED, which are often used to test HRESULT codes. The macros are not a required addition to your COM programs, but they help make code more readable and less ambiguous, as the following code demonstrates:

```
HRESULT hr;

hr = pUnk->QueryInterface(IID_SomeObject,
    (PVOID*) &pObj );
if (SUCCEEDED(hr))
{
    .
    .   // Use the pObj value
    .
    pObj->Release();
}
```

The macro definitions in the WinError.h header file show how SUCCEEDED returns TRUE for any expression that evaluates to zero or greater, and how FAILED returns TRUE for any negative expression, as shown in the following:

```
#define SUCCEEDED(Status) ((HRESULT)(Status) >= 0)
#define FAILED(Status) ((HRESULT)(Status) < 0)
```

The S_FALSE manifest constant is defined as 1. Thus, SUCCEEDED(S_FALSE) actually evaluates to TRUE, contrary to what you might expect. This explains why S_FALSE is not often used in COM programming.

When dealing with an HRESULT that you have not created, be careful how your code interprets it. Generally, you can rely on any constant with an E prefix to have a negative value; otherwise, you have no assurances. When unsure, you should consult the appropriate header file to determine a defined constant's true numeric value.

Client Access to HRESULT Codes

You might be disappointed to learn that many client applications cannot even receive HRESULT codes that a server's methods return. Thus, your carefully constructed and expressive codes can often go to waste. The problem can be traced to the manner in which many popular development tools, such as MFC and Microsoft Visual Basic, implement the IDispatch interface.

For example, the MFC client applications discussed in Chapters 5 and 6 do not receive HRESULT codes from their embedded COM components, because the wrapper class that Visual C++ creates for a component communicates through the IDispatch interface rather than calling component methods directly through a v-table. During its circuitous connections with a server, MFC's IDispatch implementation loses a method's HRESULT value before returning to the client. The MFC client using IDispatch can only infer when an error occurs in a COM server because a negative HRESULT value returned from a method generates an exception. By couching access to the server in *try-catch* blocks, the client can respond in a general manner to errors, though it often cannot determine precisely what error occurred. Without the code field of the HRESULT return value, the client is in the dark.

However, some C++ clients properly receive HRESULT return codes. Whether it uses MFC or not, a C++ application does not need to rely on IDispatch. Instead, the C++ application can receive a server's return values by bypassing the wrapper class that Visual C++ creates. However, such a technique is beyond the scope of this discussion.

A C++ client can also receive negative HRESULT codes through the _com_error class, which is discussed in the next section.

COM Exceptions

Visual C++ provides the _com_error support class, which encapsulates an HRESULT code and an associated IErrorInfo object. The _com_error class has several member functions that retrieve information about the encapsulated error, the most important of which are listed in Table 10.3.

Table 10.3 Member Functions in the _com_error Class

Member function	Return value
Error	The HRESULT code from which the _com_error object is constructed.
ErrorInfo	A pointer to an associated IErrorInfo object, or NULL if IErrorInfo is not supported. The caller must call *Release* on the returned IErrorInfo object when finished using it.
WCode	The HRESULT minus 0x80040200 if the HRESULT uses FACILITY_ITF. Otherwise, the function returns zero.
ErrorMessage	A TCHAR pointer to a system message describing the error. If no system message is available, the returned string is "Unknown error" followed by the hexadecimal HRESULT value.

If the encapsulated HRESULT has an associated IErrorInfo object, _com_error can access the contextual error information that the object contains. For example, the *HelpFile* and *HelpContext* member functions access the IErrorInfo object and return information about context-sensitive help pertaining to the error, which the caller can then display to the user through the familiar Windows Help system.

Passing a _com_error Object to a Catch Block

Because _com_error represents an exception condition, it often serves as the object passed to a *catch* block. This practice illustrates how to trap errors with _com_error, using the E_OUTOFMEMORY error code as an example.

The steps in this practice create a simple console-based program named Test that represents both a client application and its component server. To keep the illustration to a manageable length, the program does not load an actual COM module, but simply throws its own E_OUTOFMEMORY error and catches it.

► **To create and run the Test program**

1. In Visual C++, click New on the File menu.
2. Select the Win32 Console Application icon in the Projects tab of the New dialog box.
3. Type *Test* in the Project Name box to name the project, and then click OK.
4. Select the radio button labeled A Simple Application.
5. Click Finish, and then click OK.

6. Open the Test.cpp file in the text editor and add two #include statements as follows:

```
#include <comdef.h>
#include <stdio.h>
```

7. Add code to the main block. The final result should look like the following:

```
#include "stdafx.h"
#include <comdef.h>
#include <stdio.h>
int main (int argc, char* argv[])
{
    try
    {
        // Construct object and force exception
        _com_error e(E_OUTOFMEMORY);
        throw(e);
    }
    catch(_com_error &e)
    {
        printf("Error   = %08lx\n", e.Error());
        printf("Wcode   = %04x\n", e.WCode());
        printf("Meaning = %s\n\n", e.ErrorMessage());
    }
    return 0;
}
```

8. Press F7 to build the project.
9. When the project compiles and links correctly, press Ctrl+F5 to execute the Test application. The program displays the lines as follows:

```
Error   = 8007000e
WCode   = 0000
Meaning= Not enough storage is available to
    complete this operation.
```

A genuine client application would not throw its own error (unless it had good reasons for doing so), so under actual conditions, the *try* block contains code that calls the component. In the simplified example provided, the lines inside the *try* block actually represent code that would be found in the component, not in the client itself, as demonstrated in the following:

```
_com_error e(E_OUTOFMEMORY);
throw(e);
```

Error Events

When a COM component method returns an HRESULT code to the client application, the notification is *synchronous* because it forms part of the normal flow of communication between a server and client. The client calls the server; the server detects an error and returns an HRESULT code explaining the problem; and then the client reacts to the error. These steps occur one after the other in ordered progression; the client learns of the error only after the server component ceases work and returns.

However, COM components such as ActiveX controls do not need to cease work to notify a client when an error occurs. Such components can simply fire an event to immediately inform the client about any interesting conditions, and then continue working.

In another scenario, an ActiveX control might have worker threads operating simultaneously with the client. If a worker thread detects an error, its only means of directly notifying the client is by firing an event. COM defines a stock event named Error that allows this type of *asynchronous* error notification.

COM assigns to the Error event the predefined dispatch identifier DISPID_ERROREVENT, which has a negative value of -608. An ActiveX control derived from MFC's COleControl class can call the *FireError* member function to fire the Error event.

► **To add the Error event to an MFC ActiveX control**

1. Create a project using MFC ActiveX ControlWizard, as described in Chapter 4.
2. On the View menu, click ClassWizard to invoke the MFC ClassWizard dialog box.
3. On the ActiveX Events tab, click the Add Event button.
4. Select Error from the External name drop-down list as shown in Figure 10.3.

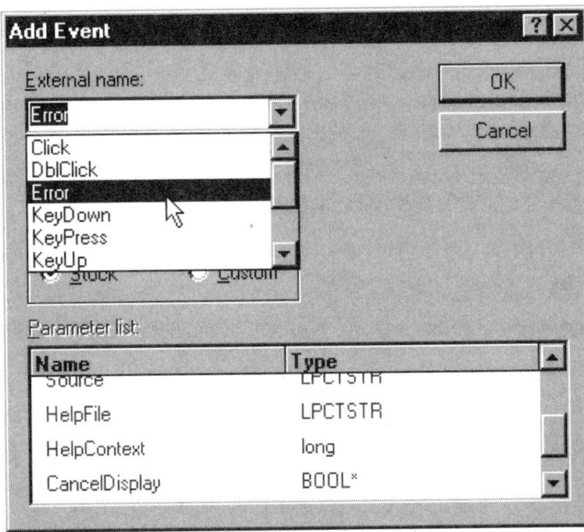

Figure 10.3 Adding the Error stock event to an MFC ActiveX control project

5. Leave the Stock radio button selected and click OK.

Because Error is a stock event, no other code or settings are required. To fire the event at any time, the control needs only to call *COleControl::FireError,* and provide an HRESULT code, a pointer to a string containing the error description, and an optional Help identifier:

```
HRESULT hr = MAKE_HRESULT(SEVERITY_ERROR, FACILITY_ITF,
    0x202);
FireError(hr, "A suitable error message goes here",
    HELP_ID);
```

The MFC framework provides default handlers for stock events like Error, so if a client application does not handle the Error event, the framework calls *COleControl::DisplayError* to display the string that the ActiveX control passes to the *FireError* function. The preceding lines of code result in a message box as shown in Figure 10.4.

Figure 10.4 Default handling of the Error stock event

While the message notifies users that an error has occurred, it does not inform the client application. To respond properly to an error in one of its components, the client must provide a handler function to receive notification that the Error event has been fired.

The client's Error event handler receives seven parameters, including a pointer to the string message, and another pointer to the appropriate Help file location. The *CancelDisplay* parameter points to a Boolean value that, when set to TRUE, prevents the framework from displaying the message box shown in Figure 10.4. The following fragment shows what a typical Error handler function looks like in an MFC client, and demonstrates how the client suppresses the framework's message box by setting the **CancelDisplay* flag:

```
BEGIN_EVENTSINK_MAP(CContainerDlg, CDialog)
    //{{AFX_EVENTSINK_MAP(CContainerDlg)
    .
    .
    .
    ON_EVENT(CContainerDlg, IDC_MYCTRL1, -608 /* Error */, \
        OnError, VTS_I2 VTS_PBSTR VTS_SCODE VTS_BSTR \
        VTS_BSTR VTS_I4 VTS_PBOOL)
    //}}AFX_EVENTSINK_MAP
```

```
END_EVENTSINK_MAP()

void CContainerDlg::OnError(short Number, BSTR FAR* Description,
SCODE Scode, LPCTSTR Source,
    LPCTSTR HelpFile, long HelpContext,
    BOOL FAR* CancelDisplay)
{
    .
        // Respond to the error
    .
    *CancelDisplay = TRUE; // Suppress the message box
}
```

Exceptions and Distributed Applications

As you can imagine, the error reporting mechanisms for distributed applications are fairly complicated. When a remote module encounters an error, COM and the operating system must cooperate to transfer the exception or event information back to a client that is most likely running on a different computer and perhaps under a separate platform. Fortunately, this transfer takes place beneath the surface. You do not need to provide special error-handling code for exceptions raised in other parts of the network; you can usually treat all events and exceptions as local phenomena.

Like any information that must traverse a network, errors communicated back to a client on another computer can be relatively slow to arrive. This is particularly true for nested modules in which one component contains another. (See Chapter 5 for a discussion of containment and aggregation.) Contained modules must fire events or send exceptions up a chain of handlers until control reaches the client. The client should not, therefore, make assumptions about exactly when an error occurred.

Error handling for distributed applications, especially large multitiered programs, requires increased developer attention. Such applications can encounter seemingly impossible errors of the most cryptic origins, arising when least expected. The next lesson describes some common errors that can occur when using MTS, MSMQ and Data Access Components (DAC), and discusses how an application can effectively deal with such errors through exception handling.

Lesson Summary

The MFC library does not consistently support exception handling. The member functions of many common classes such as CWnd and CDC do not throw exceptions, and indicate success or failure by returning an error code. However, some MFC classes, such as CFile and CDaoRecordset, do support exceptions. When they encounter an error condition, the member functions of such classes create an object from one of eleven classes derived from CException. The application receives a pointer to the exception object as the parameter of a *catch* block.

This lesson described COM error codes, and explained how to create and use HRESULT codes in server components such as ActiveX controls. HRESULT codes are not handles, but simply 32-bit values containing four fields. The fields describe an error's severity, facility category, and code within a category. Negative HRESULT codes indicate failure and generate exceptions in MFC and Visual Basic clients. The type definitions HRESULT and SCODE are interchangeable under 32-bit Windows programming.

By encapsulating an HRESULT value, the _com_error support class can help make dealing with COM errors easier. A _com_error object is often passed as the exception parameter to a *catch* block. This process provides a way for MFC clients to receive HRESULT codes (albeit only negative failure codes) that are otherwise lost through MFC's IDispatch implementation.

Although developers of COM servers have an obligation to ensure their products return accurate and meaningful error codes, many client applications cannot or do not receive those codes.

The stock Error event allows a COM component to immediately notify the client when an error occurs. However, the Error event should be used sparingly, if at all. The component has no assurance that a client application will ever see the event because the client might not provide a handler function for Error. When practical, a COM server, such as an ActiveX control, should rely on returned HRESULT values to indicate errors.

Lesson 3: Error-Handling Strategies

Lessons 1 and 2 outlined some of the ways an application can handle errors. This lesson discusses the strategy behind error handling, helping you to decide on the best technique for a given situation. The chosen strategy usually depends on factors such as the likelihood of an error, available support code such as MFC and ATL, the context in which the application operates, and personal programming style.

A monolithic application must handle errors without significant aid from the operating system other than exception passing, whereas a program using MTS or ADO can take advantage of the system's rich error-reporting services. Error handling in multitiered applications is somewhat complicated by the fact that errors can arise in other modules, even errors not caused by the application. For example, errors might occur if a network connection suddenly fails, or if another application unintentionally corrupts a shared data store.

After this lesson, you will be able to:

- Create a log of program behavior by using either the MFC TRACE macro or logging messages to a text file
- Handle errors in applications and components that use MTS, MSMQ, or ADO

Estimated lesson time: 25 minutes

Working with Error Logs

The first two lessons of this chapter described how a program could handle and solve errors as they occur. This lesson presents another technique in which an executing program simply compiles a record of errors without stopping to deal with them. You can then read through the resulting *error log* after the program terminates, and revise the code to ensure that these errors do not occur again.

TRACE Macro

MFC programs can use the TRACE macro and its variations to achieve this "offline" approach to error handling. Many C programmers employ a similar technique by liberally sprinkling *printf* statements throughout their code, providing a running commentary on the code's progress by displaying brief messages such as these:

```
Entering Function1
Allocating memory block
Block successfully allocated
.
.
.
Leaving Function1
```

The TRACE macro accomplishes the same goal, displaying messages at the location specified by *afxDump*, which by default is the Debug tab of the Visual C++ Output window. TRACE operates only for a project's debug build; for release builds, the macro does nothing and thus does not increase the size of a program's final version. (Debug and release configurations are described in the next chapter.)

TRACE accepts the same string formatting commands as *printf,* so you can display variables in a TRACE line like this:

```
int  iFileSize = 10;
char sz[]  = "kilobytes";

// Display the string "File size is 10 kilobytes"
TRACE("File size is %d %s\n", iFileSize, sz);
```

The maximum string length after formatting cannot exceed 512 characters, including the terminating NULL. MFC also offers the macros TRACE0, TRACE1, TRACE2, and TRACE3, but these variations offer no advantages over TRACE except that they expand into code that is a bit more compact.

Logging Messages to a Text File

The TRACE macro has two potential disadvantages: it works only when the debugger is active and the messages it writes to the Output window disappear the next time you debug the application. MFC provides an alternative that solves both of these problems. The MFC library's CDumpContext class allows an application to conveniently write messages to a text file rather than the Output window, thus forming a permanent record of the application's execution that can be examined at leisure. In addition, CDumpContext does not require the program to execute within the debugger.

To use CDumpContext, a class derived from CObject must override the *CObject::Dump* member function. Most MFC classes already implement an override for *Dump,* as do the document and view classes that AppWizard generates. The application creates a dump object by passing the CDumpContext constructor a pointer to a CFile. The CFile object identifies the text file, known as the *log file*, to which messages are written. The application then writes a string to the dump object using the class's insertion operator (<<), which accepts both strings and variables.

The following code fragments demonstrate how this is done, illustrating with a log file named Dump.txt that receives the messages. Because the *Dump* function is not defined for release builds, the code is placed inside #ifdef blocks that compile only when the _DEBUG constant is defined. The application first creates a CFile object for the log file. Usually, this is done only once, as shown in the following code for the initial update of a class derived from CView. For the sake of simplicity, the code does not check for errors.

```
void CDemoView::OnInitialUpdate()
{
    CView::OnInitialUpdate();
    #ifdef _DEBUG
        m_file.Open("f:\\temp\\Dump.txt",
            CFile::modeCreate | CFile::modeWrite);
    #endif
}
```

After the log file has been created, the application can dump a message to the file using a CDumpContext object. Each time it executes, the code shown here writes a new string that records the current value of the hypothetical *iCount* variable:

```
#ifdef _DEBUG
    CDumpContext   dc(&m_file);
    // Create a dump object
    CString strMessage;
    // Message string

    strMessage.Format("\nCurrent counter value = %i\n",
        iCount);
    dc << (LPCTSTR) strMessage;  // Write the string
    dc.Flush();                  // Commit to file
    Dump(dc);                    // Dump the message
#endif
```

Log files created this way can become unexpectedly large because the *Dump* function that an MFC class implements usually includes additional information along with the logged message. In the preceding example, the *CView::Dump* function not only writes the string to the file, but also includes data pertaining to the view such as its window handle, current size, parentage, and so on. The following code shows a single log record in which the first line holds the message passed to CDumpContext and the remaining lines have been added by *CView::Dump:*

Note The function writes ASCII 10 linefeeds, which can be properly viewed in the Visual C++ text editor.

```
Current counter value = 103
a CDemoView at $771C00
m_hWnd = 0x940 (permanent window)
caption = ""
class name = "AfxFrameOrView42d"
rect = (L 136, T 198, R 728, B 521)
parent CWnd* = $771E10
style = $50000000
id = 0xE900
with document: a CDemoDoc at $770120
m_strTitle = Untitled
m_strPathName =
m_bModified = 0
m_pDocTemplate = $770310
```

Trace Statements in ATL

ATL provides its own means of logging messages for those programs that do not use MFC. Like MFC's TRACE macro, the ATLTRACE macro accepts a string and sends it to the current dump device, which is usually the Visual C++ Output window. ATLTRACE accepts formatting instructions in the manner of *printf,* making it easy to add variable values to strings. Like TRACE, the ATLTRACE macro works only for debug builds, and does not add code to a program's release build.

ATL also supports a global function named *AtlTrace,* which is not used often. *AtlTrace* accepts the same type of string parameter as the ATLTRACE macro, but unlike the macro, a call to *AtlTrace* becomes a permanent part of the program, both for debug and release builds. However, the function takes no action when compiled under release configuration, so the result is merely added code with no benefit.

OutputDebugString Function

Applications that use neither MFC nor ATL can call the *OutputDebugString* API function to display messages to the Debug window. However, *OutputDebugString* accepts only a pointer to a string and is less flexible than the TRACE and ATLTRACE macros. For example, each call to the function becomes a permanent part of your code unless placed inside an #ifdef block. Furthermore, *OutputDebugString* does not support *printf*-style string formatting; thus, including data values in the string requires extra work.

Working with MTS

Because a client application that uses the services of MTS communicates through COM interfaces, the error-handling techniques discussed in Lesson 2 of this chapter pertain to MTS programming. In particular, the base client application should scrupulously consult returned HRESULT values and use the SUCCEEDED and FAILED macros to test the results of each method call.

Components that execute inside the MTS environment require additional considerations beyond those for the client, to both prevent errors and handle errors that do occur. For example, an MTS object must not assume that its state data (if it has any) persists from one call to the next. MTS destroys an object after each call and instantiates it again at the next access. Although it seems to the client that it is communicating with a single object instance, an MTS object in reality only exists long enough for a method to execute and return to the caller.

The root object—that is, the first object created in a transaction—should monitor errors that occur in other objects that it creates. If an error occurs anywhere in a transaction, the root object should usually throw an exception back to the base client describing the error and suggesting a solution.

How MTS Handles Errors

MTS performs extensive internal integrity and consistency checks. If MTS encounters an unexpected internal error condition, it immediately terminates the process. This policy, called *failfast*, facilitates fault containment and results in more reliable and robust systems.

For example, if MTS determines that one of its data structures has been corrupted, it immediately terminates the client process. The rationale behind this action is that both the cause and magnitude of the corruption are unknown, and MTS cannot determine how far the damage has spread. Like any other DLL, MTS is hosted in a process environment and shares a single address space with the main program. Therefore, the safest course is to assume that the entire process has become unstable. Terminating the process prevents it from spreading potentially corrupted information to other processes or, worse yet, allowing incorrect data to be committed and made durable. When a failfast error occurs, you should inspect the Windows NT Event Viewer Application Log for information pertaining to the failure.

MTS does not allow exceptions to propagate outside of a context. If an exception occurs when executing inside an MTS context and the application does not catch the exception, MTS terminates the process as dictated by the failfast policy. In this case, MTS assumes that the exception has placed the process into an indeterminate state; it is thus not safe to continue processing.

MTS does not change negative HRESULT codes, such as E_UNEXPECTED or E_FAIL, which a root object returns. However, if the root object incorrectly returns a positive HRESULT code, such as S_OK or S_FALSE, MTS can convert the value into an MTS error code before returning to the caller. For example, this conversion can happen when the root returns S_OK after calling *SetComplete*. If another object in the transaction has failed to commit, MTS changes the returned HRESULT to CONTEXT_E_ABORTED. When MTS changes an error code, it clears the method's output parameters. Returned references are released, and the returned object pointer values are set to NULL.

MTS Explorer

MTS provides a tool named MTS Explorer that provides a way to monitor your program's transactions. MTS Explorer is a snap-in for the Microsoft Management Console (MMC). Through MTS Explorer, you can observe activity inside the MTS environment as your application executes. MTS Explorer can also assist in packaging and deploying an MTS application.

For monitoring an application's transaction activity, MTS Explorer offers three views named Trace Message, Transaction Statistics, and Transaction List. Together these views can provide valuable information about the status of transactions managed by MS DTC.

MTS Explorer's transaction activity monitor can also reveal transaction failures. The Duwamish Books project provides a way to trigger such a failure, as described in the following practice.

Using MTS Explorer to Observe Transactions

For testing purposes, Duwamish Books intentionally cancels the transaction when users attempt to include *The Iliad* (ID: 748) as part of a sale or purchase order. The procedures that insert the details of the sale or order check for this key value and return an error when this value is detected. The error causes the data access layer's *ExecQuery* method to invoke *SetAbort* instead of *SetComplete,* which rolls back the entire sale or order operation.

This practice demonstrates how to use MTS Explorer to monitor a failed transaction as it occurs. Initially this practice explains how to invoke MTS Explorer and view the transactions that Duwamish Books issues. The final step involves selecting *The Iliad* as a sales order and observing the results of the failed transaction in MTS Explorer.

► **To launch MTS Explorer**

1. Click Start, point to the Programs menu, Microsoft Windows NT 4.0 Option Pack, and then Microsoft Transaction Server.
2. Click Transaction Server Explorer on the submenu as shown in Figure 10.5.

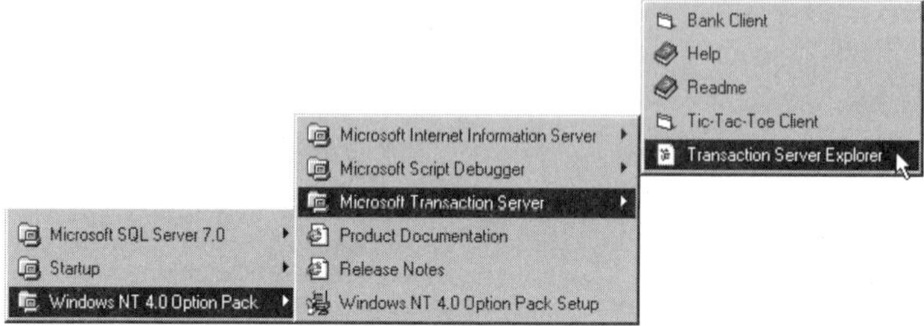

Figure 10.5 Starting MTS Explorer

► **To observe a Duwamish Books transaction**

1. Expand the tree in MTS Explorer's left pane and select the computer hosting the transactions. (When running under Microsoft Windows 98, MTS Explorer shows only one pane.)
2. Double-click the Transaction Statistics icon.

3. In Microsoft Internet Explorer, navigate to the Duwamish Books Entry page at http://*host*/D4_Entry, where *host* represents your server's name.
4. Select the application page appropriate for your browser. For example, click the Client 3 Start button if you are using Internet Explorer 5.
5. Click Categories in the navigation bar at the top of the page.
6. On the Category Search page, click English and then click Books.
7. Select a book as described in the instructions included with Duwamish Books and add it to the shopping cart. Figure 10.6 shows an example title.

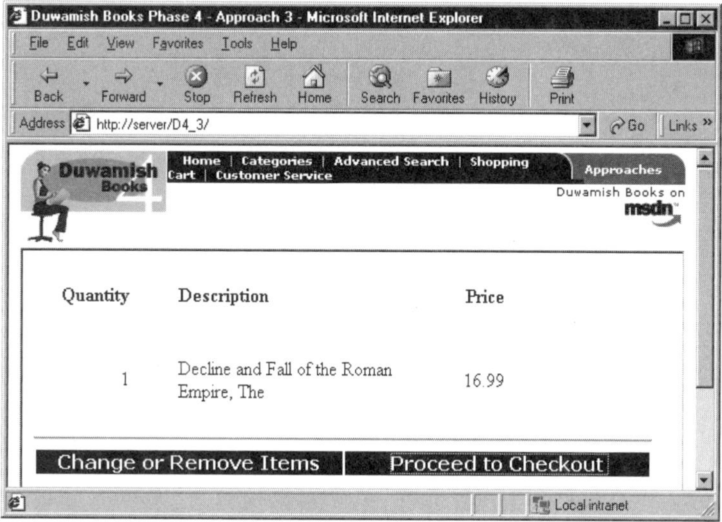

Figure 10.6 Book added to the shopping cart

8. Click Proceed to Checkout.
9. Create a new customer account if you have not already done so. (See the Duwamish Books instructions for information on how to create a new account.) Otherwise, select an existing account. Once a customer account is specified, a Continue to Payment Site link should be visible.
10. Click Continue to Payment Site.
11. Type a fictitious bankcard number and billing name. Any random text will satisfy the page requirements for this information.
12. Click the Submit button to purchase the book.

13. Note the successful transaction in MTS Explorer's Transaction Statistics view, which should appear as in Figure 10.7.

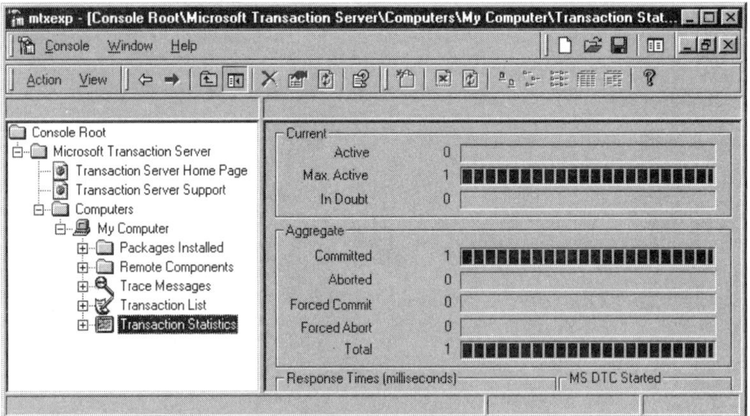

Figure 10.7 Successful transaction in MTS Explorer

► To observe a transaction failure

1. In Internet Explorer, click Advanced Search in the navigation bar at the top of the Duwamish Books page.
2. In the Title Search box, type *Iliad, The* and click the Go button to the immediate right.
3. Select and purchase the book as you did before. When you click the Continue to Payment Site link when checking out, the following error message appears in the browser window, explaining why the transaction failed:

```
BusinessLogicAPI error '80040e14'

[Microsoft][ODBC SQL Server Driver][SQL Server]Item 748 is
designated to fail so that transactional integrity might be tested.

/D4_Common/d4wfl1a.inc, line 394
```

Figure 10.8, on the next page, shows the MTS Explorer Transaction Statistics window that appears after your attempt to purchase *The Iliad*. The view indicates that two transactions have occurred, corresponding to the two purchases made in this practice session. The Aggregate box shows that one transaction was successful (or committed) and the other transaction failed.

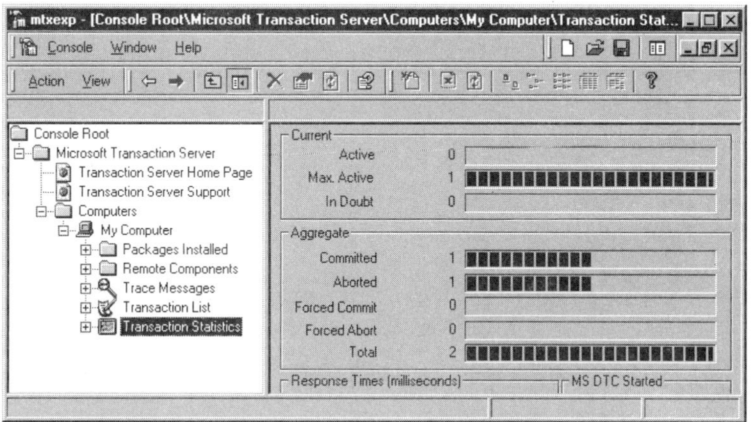

Figure 10.8 Monitoring a failed transaction in MTS Explorer

Working with MSMQ

When MSMQ detects an error, it returns an HRESULT value to the calling application. Errors pertaining to properties are also recorded in the optional *aStatus* member of the MQQUEUEPROPS, MQMSGPROPS, and MQQMPROPS property structures. The *aStatus* member is entirely optional. If an application sets the field to NULL, MSMQ does not record property errors. Otherwise, *aStatus* should point to an array of HRESULT values, as shown in the following code, for a typical call to *MQSendMessage:*

```
MQMSGPROPS    MsgProps;
QUEUEHANDLE   hQueue = NULL;
ITransaction *pTransaction = NULL;
HRESULT       hr, hrArray[NUMBER_OF_PROPERTIES];
.
.
.
MsgProps.aStatus = hrArray;     //Error reports

try
{
    hr = MQSendMessage(hQueue, &MsgProps, pTransaction);
    if (FAILED( hr ))
    throw hr;
}
catch( HRESULT hr )
{
    .
    .       //Read error reports in MsgProps.aStatus
    .
}
```

Notice that MSMQ functions such as *MQSendMessage* do not generate an exception if an error occurs, so this sample fragment throws its own error when the returned value is anything other than a success code.

If provided, the *aStatus* array must hold as many HRESULT values as there are properties. This is because there is a one-to-one correspondence between the *aStatus* elements and the property list. The first error code in *aStatus* pertains to the first property, the second error code pertains to the second property, and so on. Common errors can stem from an illegal property tag or insufficient access rights. If MSMQ detects no error for a property, it sets the corresponding value in *aStatus* to MQ_OK.

The HRESULT value that MSMQ functions return is for the error of the highest severity encountered in processing the call. If no errors occur, MSMQ returns MQ_OK. If property errors are detected, the return value identifies only the most serious error but offers no other information. To determine which properties caused errors (and why), the caller must examine the property status array.

Working with ADO

ADO offers you assistance in handling and reporting errors. When a provider encounters an error, ADO stores the information in a collection named Errors, which contains any number of Error objects, and one object for each error. The purpose of the Errors collection is to list additional warnings exposed by the underlying provider. The set of Error objects in the Errors collection describes all errors encountered in response to a single statement. As the provider encounters each error, the provider notifies the ADO run time, which then constructs an Error object and adds it to the Errors collection associated with the connection. ADO maintains only a single Errors collection; if another operation generates an error, ADO clears the Errors collection to make way for the new set of Error objects.

Each Error object exposes the properties shown in Table 10.4.

Table 10.4 Properties of an Error Object

Property	Description
Description	Error description
HelpContext	Help context for the given Help file
HelpFile	Path to the provider's Help file (if it exists)
NativeError	An error code specific to the provider
Number	OLE DB error constant
Source	A string identifying the provider that raised the error
SQLState	Indication of the SQL state for the error

The ADO Errors collection is available only after an ADO Connection object has been instantiated. Besides errors raised by the underlying provider, the Errors collection might contain information about errors arising in components that the provider uses. When a component throws an exception back to the provider, the provider passes it on to ADO.

For example, errors that ODBC encounters are passed to the OLE DB Provider for ODBC, and then passed to ADO where they join the Errors collection. Errors that ADO itself encounters are also placed in the collection; an application's error-handling routines must therefore check the ADO Errors collection as well as trap exceptions raised by the component. The next section demonstrates how this is done.

Handling Exceptions in an ADO Application

This section illustrates how a client application should handle an ADO exception. The example code interprets both the _com_error object (passed to the exception's *catch* block) and the Error objects contained in the associated Errors collection. The code purposely causes an exception by attempting to open an illegal connection.

The following steps create a console-based client program named AdoDemo, included on the companion CD, in the Labs/Ch10/AdoDemo folder. The source code for this practice is a bit longer than usual, so if you create the project as outlined here, you might prefer to cut and paste from the original AdoDemo.cpp file. To simplify the code as much as possible, the AdoDemo program uses the #import directive to load ADO, as explained in Chapter 9. If the MSADO15.dll file registered on your system does not exist in the path given here to the #import command, revise the command for the correct path.

► **To create and run the AdoDemo program**

1. In Visual C++, click New on the File menu.
2. Select the Win32 Console Application icon on the Projects tab of the New dialog box.
3. Type *AdoDemo* in the Project name box to name the project, and then click OK.
4. Select the radio button labeled *A simple application.*
5. Click Finish and then click OK.
6. Open the AdoDemo.cpp file and modify the code to look like the following:

```
#include "stdafx.h"
#include <windows.h>
#include <stdio.h>
```

```
#include <adoint.h>
#import \
"C:\Program Files\Common Files\System\ADO\msado15.dll" \
rename("EOF", "EndOfFile")

void Interpret_com_error(_com_error &e)
{
    _bstr_t bstrSrc(e.Source());
    _bstr_t bstrDsc(e.Description());
    printf("Interpretation of _com_error:\n");
    printf("---------------\n");
    printf("Code        = %08lx\n", e.Error());
    printf("Meaning     = %s\n", e.ErrorMessage());
    printf("Source      = %s\n", (LPCTSTR) bstrSrc);
    printf("Description = %s\n", (LPCTSTR) bstrDsc);
}

void InterpretErrorsCollection(
ADODB::_ConnectionPtr pConn)
{
    ADODB::ErrorsPtr  pErrors= NULL;
    ADODB::ErrorPtr   pError = NULL;
    HRESULT    hr      = S_OK;
    long           i, nCount;

    pErrors = pConn->GetErrors();
    nCount  = pErrors->GetCount();
    for(i=0; (SUCCEEDED(hr)) && (i < nCount); i++)
    {
        hr = pErrors->get_Item((_variant_t) i,
        &pError);
        _bstr_t bstrSrc(pError->GetSource());
        _bstr_t bstrDsc(pError->GetDescription());
        _bstr_t bstrFile(pError->GetHelpFile());
        _bstr_t bstrSQL(pError->GetSQLState());
        int iNumber      = pError->GetNumber();
        int iHelpContext = pError->GetHelpContext();
        int iNativeError = pError->GetNativeError();

        printf("\n");
        printf("Interpretation of Errors");
        printf("Collection:\n");
        printf("-------------------");
        printf("\n");
        printf("Number      = %08lx\n", iNumber );
        printf("Source      = %s\n",(LPCTSTR)bstrSrc);
        printf("Description = %s\n",(LPCTSTR)bstrDsc);
        printf("HelpFile    = %s\n",(LPCTSTR)bstrFile);
        printf("HelpContext = %ld\n",iHelpContext);
        printf("SQLState    = %s\n",(LPCTSTR)bstrSQL);
```

```
        printf("NativeError = %ld\n", iNativeError);
    }

    if (pErrors)
        pErrors->Release();
    if (pError)
        pError->Release();
}

int main (int argc, char* argv[])
{
    HRESULT        hr = ::CoInitialize(NULL);
    ADODB::_ConnectionPtr pConn;

    if (SUCCEEDED(hr))
    {
        hr = pConn.CreateInstance(
            __uuidof( ADODB::Connection));
        if (SUCCEEDED(hr))
        {
            try
            {
                // Cause an exception
                pConn->Open("", "", "", -1);
                pConn->Close();    // Never executed
            }
            catch(_com_error &e)
            {
                Interpret_com_error(e);
                InterpretErrorsCollection(pConn);
                pConn = NULL;  // Clean up
            }
        }
    }

    ::CoUninitialize();
    return 0;
}
```

7. Press F7 to build the project.
8. Press Ctrl+F5 to execute the AdoDemo application. When the program runs, it displays the following lines:

```
Interpretation of _com_error:
---------------
Code        = 80004005
Meaning= Unspecified error
Source      = Microsoft OLE DB Provider for ODBC
              Drivers
Description = [Microsoft][ODBC Driver Manager] Data
```

```
                  source name not found and no default
                  driver specified

Interpretation of Errors Collection:
-------------------
Number      = 80004005
Source      = Microsoft OLE DB Provider for ODBC
              Drivers
Description = [Microsoft][ODBC Driver Manager] Data
              source name not found and no default
              driver specified
HelpFile    = (null)
HelpContext= 0
SQLState    = IM002
NativeError= 0
```

Lesson Summary

Usually created only for debugging purposes, an error log contains a running record of an application's behavior that you can peruse after the application has finished. At strategic positions in the code, place instructions that write information to the log such as milestones (for example, function entry and exit), current data values, system times, and additional information that you consider important. The result forms a written history of execution that serves to verify whether the application is performing as expected, and that can provide clues for tracking down the source of a program error.

To facilitate error logging, MFC provides the TRACE macro. This macro writes a string to the Debug tab of the Visual C++ Output window, where it can be viewed during and after program execution. TRACE works only when the debugger is active, and the generated error log is overwritten by the next debugger session. The MFC CDumpContext class creates a more permanent error log. CDumpContext accepts a CFile pointer that identifies a log file, then writes specified strings to the file.

For error handling in applications and components that use MTS, MTS provides a tool, MTS Explorer, through which you can receive trace messages, view statistics of a transaction, and observe the effects of a transaction failure. The Duwamish Book project provides a "back door" method to trigger such a failure.

As one of the Microsoft DAC technologies, ADO offers a rich error handling service through its Errors collection. The Errors collection contains information pertaining to all errors that occur in a single ADO statement. If ADO raises an exception, the client application can examine both the _com_error object passed to the client's *catch* block as well as the individual Error objects contained in the Errors collection associated with the connection. Each Error object exposes properties that identify and describe a single error.

Lab 10: Exception Handling in Duwamish Books

In this lab, you will add exception-handling code to the D4Cache module. Currently, the CCache.cpp file allocates memory using the *new* operator without verifying the success of the allocation. Although unlikely, the Duwamish Books application will generate a fault if the module's free store becomes so depleted that it cannot provide the requested memory. The changes you make in this lab will help prevent such failure, making the program more robust under conditions of low memory.

However, these changes are exclusively for demonstration purposes, and do not necessarily represent an improvement to the D4Cache component. D4Cache eschews exception handling to reduce code size, an important consideration for any COM component. The exception handling code you will add to the component in this lab requires the services of the C run-time library, which D4Cache currently does not use. The revised code must link to the C run-time library to gain access to the *_set_new_handler* function. This function allows a program to set up a callback function that executes whenever *new* fails to allocate memory.

Linking to the C run-time library adds a lot of overhead to the component. As a result of the added library code, the revised component created in this lab—while technically more stable under rare conditions—is considerably larger than the original component.

This lab requires the installation of the Duwamish Books project source folders. If you have not yet installed the source folders, do so now as described in Chapter 9.

Estimated lab time: 15 minutes

Exercise 1: Adding Exception Handlers

In this exercise, you will add exception handlers for two memory allocations in the D4Cache module. In the unlikely event that free store memory becomes insufficient, the handlers will gain control and ensure that functions properly return the E_OUTOFMEMORY value to describe the error.

► **Open the D4Cache project in Visual C++**

1. On the Visual C++ File menu, click Open Workspace.
2. Browse to the folder containing the D4Cache project files, and double-click the D4Cache.dsw file. By default, the project files are located in Program Files\Duwamish\Phase4.0\servers\vc\d4cache\src.

► **Revise the CCache.cpp source file**

1. Open the CCache.cpp file and scroll down to the *CCache::get_NewEnum* function. The Visual C++ WizardBar can help you locate the function.

2. Edit the following lines:

```
enumvar* p = new enumvar;
ATLASSERT(p);
```

to add exception handling as follows:

```
enumvar* p;
try
{
    p = new enumvar;
}
catch(std::bad_alloc)
{
    ATLTRACE("Allocation failed in get_NewEnum\n");
    return E_OUTOFMEMORY;
}
```

The ATLASSERT statement is no longer needed because the exception handler guards against a failed allocation. Moreover, the handler works for both release and debug builds, whereas ATLASSERT works exclusively for debug builds.

3. Scroll further down the file until you see the implementation code for the *CCache::GenerateErrorInfo* function. This function also uses *new* to allocate memory without verifying whether or not the allocation is successful. Change the function's first line to the following:

```
HRESULT hRC = S_OK;
```

4. Add exception handling by replacing the following lines:

```
    bstrTemp1 = new CComBSTR(pBuffer);
    sMsg = ::SysAllocString(bstrTemp1->m_str);
    delete bstrTemp1;
}

// set ErrorInfo with info
hRC = Error(sMsg,__uuidof(ICache), hRes);
```

with the following lines:

```
    try
    {
        bstrTemp1 = new CComBSTR(pBuffer);
        sMsg = ::SysAllocString(bstrTemp1->m_str);
        delete bstrTemp1;
    }
    catch(std::bad_alloc)
    {
        ATLTRACE("bstrTemp1 allocation failed");
```

```
            hRC = E_OUTOFMEMORY;
        }
    }

    // set ErrorInfo with info
    if (SUCCEEDED(hRC))
        hRC = Error(sMsg,__uuidof(ICache), hRes);
```

5. At the bottom of the CCache.cpp file, add the following function:

```
int BadAllocation(size_t)
{
    throw std::bad_alloc();
    return 0;
}
```

The *BadAllocation* function serves as a callback for the *new* operator, and is responsible for triggering an exception whenever *new* fails to allocate a requested block of memory. When *BadAllocation* executes, control proceeds to the first available *catch* block to handle the exception. However, *BadAllocation* must first be installed as the *new* operator callback by using the *_set_new_handler* function; this procedure is done as the last step in this exercise.

► **Revise the CCache.h file**

1. Open the CCache.h file and add the following #include statements as follows:

```
#include <new>
#include <new.h>
```

2. Add a declaration for *BadAllocation* near the top of the file outside the CCache class declaration as follows:

```
int BadAllocation(size_t);
class ATL_NO_VTABLE CCache :
.
.
.
```

3. To set *BadAllocation* as the *new* operator callback, add a call to *_set_new_handler* in the CCache constructor as follows:

```
public:
    CCache()
    {
        .
        .
        .
        _set_new_handler((_PNH) BadAllocation);
    }
```

Exercise 2: Rebuilding the D4Cache Project

The D4Cache project requires two changes to its Visual C++ configuration. As mentioned earlier, the added exception handlers rely on the services of the C run-time library. In this exercise, you will remove the preprocessor definition that currently prevents linkage to the C run-time library. You will also add a switch that enables compiler support for exception handling.

Because rebuilding the D4Cache project overwrites the original D4Cache.dll file, the following steps can be completed only when the Duwamish Books program is not executing. Unfortunately, Duwamish Books currently does not correctly release the D4Cache object, so simply exiting the program may not unlock the DLL file. If you encounter a link error saying that D4Cache.dll cannot be overwritten, reboot your computer to unlock the file and then link again.

► **Revise settings and rebuild the D4Cache project**

1. On the Build toolbar, select the Win32 Release MinSize active configuration.
2. On the Visual C++ Project menu, click Settings to display the Project Settings dialog box.
3. Click the C/C++ tab and select C++ Language in the Category box.
4. Select the check box labeled Enable exception handling, as shown in Figure 10.9.

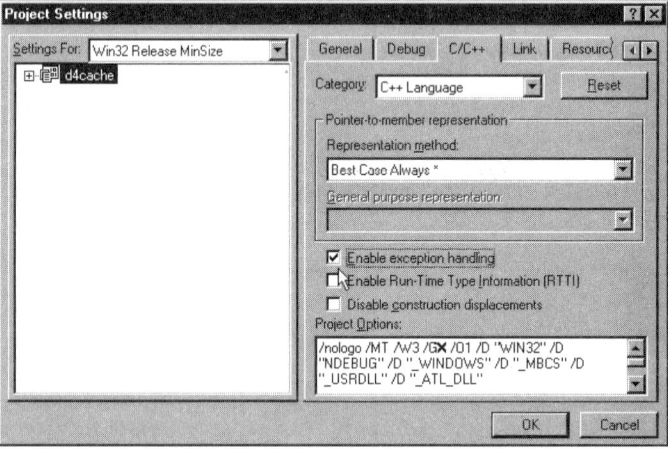

Figure 10.9 Making exception handling available in the D4Cache project

5. On the C/C++ tab, select Preprocessor in the Category box.
6. Select and delete the definition _ATL_MIN_CRT in the Preprocessor Definitions box (Figure 10.10). This deletion removes the block that prevents linkage to the C run-time library.

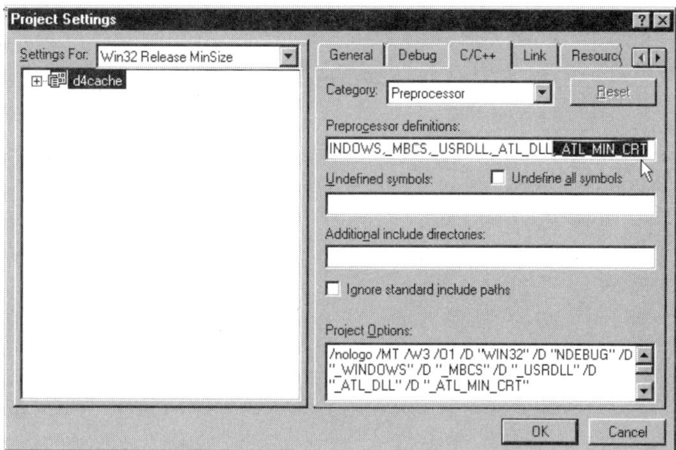

Figure 10.10 Removing the _ATL_MIN_CRT preprocessor definition from the D4Cache project

7. Click OK to close the Project Settings dialog box.
8. Press F7 to rebuild the D4Cache module with its new exception handlers. Visual C++ automatically registers the new component.

Review

The following questions are intended to reinforce key information presented in this chapter. If you are unable to answer a question, review the appropriate lesson and then try answering the question again. Answers to the questions can be found in Appendix B, "Review Questions and Answers," at the back of this book.

1. What is SEH?

2. Does Visual C++ always support exception handling?

3. What is an HRESULT?

4. Name two ways that an application can determine when an error occurs in the MFC framework.

5. Name three ways in which a COM server can communicate an error to a client. Discuss pros and cons of each.

6. What is an error log, and when should it be used?

7. How does MTS prevent errors from corrupting data?

8. What is MTS Explorer?

9. Your client application establishes a connection using ADO to access a provider. In turn, the provider makes use of other components, several of which detect errors. How can your client (1) determine how many errors occurred; (2) receive a description of each error; and (3) learn which modules detected the errors?

CHAPTER 11

Debugging and Testing

Lesson 1: Introduction to Debugging 600

Lesson 2: Using the Integrated Debugger 605

Lesson 3: Debugging COM Objects 614

Lesson 4: Dependency Walker 628

Lesson 5: Spy++ 631

Lesson 6: Testing a Distributed Application 636

Lab 11: Debugging a COM Object 640

Review 651

About This Chapter

In this chapter, you will learn about the second half of the software development process, which comprises the steps of debugging and testing. These final steps should be viewed as an essential part of development; they merit as much attention as that given to the designing/coding phase, or more. Generally viewed as less glamorous or interesting than actual coding, debugging and testing often receive inadequate attention due to budget and schedule constraints. However, this lack of attention is almost always false economy; a poorly tested application can cost you in lost revenue, wasted productivity, and strained relations with users.

Before You Begin

To complete the lessons in this chapter, you must have installed the Microsoft Visual C++ development tools as described in Lab 2 of Chapter 2. The lab at the end of this chapter requires access to two separate computers on a LAN system, configured for either peer-to-peer or client/server networking.

Lesson 1: Introduction to Debugging

This lesson presents a general introduction to the Visual C++ integrated debugger. The extensive subject of debugging is most aptly approached through an overview rather than through an intensive and overly rigorous discussion of the debugger. After attaining a solid foundation about the debugger's purpose, advantages, and limitations, you will be sufficiently prepared to use the debugger, which is described in more detail in the next lesson.

The sections that follow speak of programs only in a general sense. As you read, bear in mind that discussions apply equally to both client programs and their components.

After this lesson, you will be able to:

- Understand the fundamentals of how a debugger works
- Understand specific features of the Visual C++ integrated debugger
- Use various Microsoft Foundation Classes (MFC) macros that facilitate the task of debugging

Estimated lesson time: 15 minutes

What Is a Debugger?

Debugging is a general term used to describe the process of finding and correcting program errors. The term "bug," used to describe a problem in a program, dates back to the early days of computers when, according to legend, a mysterious error was found to be caused by a moth caught between the contacts of a relay. A *debugger* is an application designed to assist in the debugging process. The debugger runs a program under tight control and can freeze operation at any point to allow you to check the program's status during execution. Because of this extremely useful ability, it is now nearly impossible to write a distributed application for Microsoft Windows without the aid of a debugger.

The Visual C++ debugger is incorporated into the development environment with its own menu and toolbar commands. Before using the debugger, you must create a *debug build* for your project, compiling the program into a form that the debugger can read. Thus, you cannot begin using the debugger until your code compiles cleanly enough to create an executable file.

► **To create a debug build**

1. On the Build toolbar, select the Win32 Debug build context from the drop-down list as shown in Figure 11.1. A project can include a context named Unicode Debug or similar; if your project uses Unicode, select that context instead of Win32 Debug.
2. On the same toolbar, click the Build button to compile and link the project.

Figure 11.1 Select Win32 Debug on the Build toolbar prior to creating a debug build

A debug operation consists of several steps, typically beginning in the text editor. First, identify in the source code a section of a failing program where you suspect the problem arises, and then mark the instruction that begins the section. (Lesson 2 describes how to mark an instruction.) Next, start the debugger, which executes the program until control reaches the mark at the start of the questionable section. When the debugger stops the program's execution, you can then single-step through each instruction. This procedure gives you the opportunity to check current data values while the program is suspended and to ensure that the flow of control is proceeding along an expected path.

Debug vs. Release

You use the debug version of an application during the final stages of development and throughout testing to ensure that the program is error-free. The release version of an application is the final product, which is distributed to your customers. The debug version contains symbol information that the compiler places in the object file. By reading both the original source files and the symbol information, the debugger can associate each line of the source code with the corresponding binary instructions in the executable image. The debugger runs the executable but uses the source code to show the program's progress.

The release version contains only executable instructions optimized by the compiler, without the symbol information. You can execute a release version inside the debugger, but without symbols, the debugger can only display the code in its disassembled form. You can also execute the debug version of a program normally, without the debugger.

Running a debug version without the debugger has practical consequences because of a Visual C++ feature known as Just-In-Time (JIT) debugging. If the program raises an unhandled exception, the system's structured exception handling (SEH) mechanism causes control to wind its way back to Visual C++, which then executes the debugger. The debugger shows the instruction that caused the fault, and displays data values as they existed when the program ceased to operate.

MFC Debug Macros

MFC provides several macros that serve as debugging aids. The previous chapter introduced the TRACE macro and its variations and described how a program can use TRACE to record an error log of milestones, as well as the application's current state. This section examines several other MFC macros, including ASSERT, VERIFY, and DEBUG_NEW. Two of these macros, ASSERT and DEBUG_NEW, work only for debug builds and have no effect on a program's release version.

ASSERT Macro

The ASSERT macro offers a convenient way to test assumptions during development without adding permanent error-checking code. For example, say you want to check a pointer for a non-zero value before using it in your program. One way to check this pointer is to add a specific *if* test, as demonstrated in the following code for a function that accepts a CButton pointer as its parameter:

```
void SomeFunction(CButton* pbutton)
{
    if (pbutton)
    {
        .
        .   // Use the pbutton pointer
        .
    }
}
```

Although such checks represent solid programming practice and help avoid potential problems, these checks may no longer be warranted in a program's release version when it finishes and operates consistently. Hundreds of these checks throughout a program can add unnecessary code to the finished product. This unneeded code can be avoided by replacing each explicit code check with an ASSERT statement such as that shown in the following:

```
void SomeFunction(CButton* pbutton)
{
    // Make sure that pbutton is not NULL
    ASSERT(pbutton);
    .
    .   // Use the pbutton pointer
    .
}
```

If the expression passed to ASSERT evaluates to FALSE, the program halts with a message alerting you of the problem. As shown in Figure 11.2, the message gives you the choice of terminating the application or debugging the application to learn more about the problem.

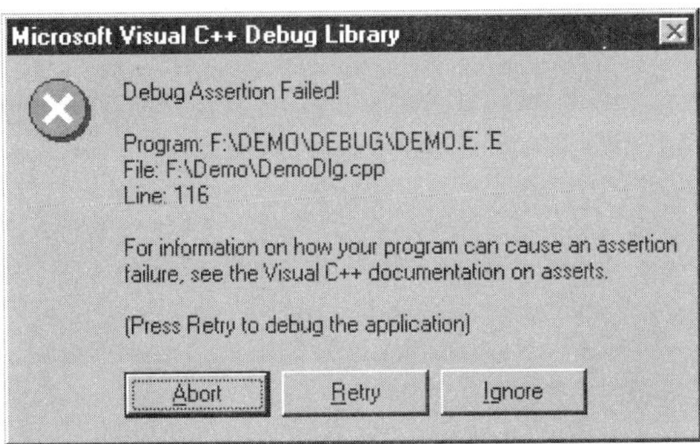

Figure 11.2 Message resulting from an ASSERT failure

Because the ASSERT macro evaluates to nothing in release builds, you can insert hundreds of ASSERT statements in your code without increasing the size of the final product. If you prefer to leave a check in place for both debug and release builds, use the VERIFY macro instead, which functions regardless of the build configuration.

ASSERT accepts any Boolean expression, such as ASSERT(x < y) and ASSERT (i > 10), but its variants are more specialized. For example, the similar ASSERT_VALID macro accepts only pointers to an object derived from MFC's CObject class. This macro does everything ASSERT does, but also calls the object's *AssertValid* member function to verify that the object is ready for use.

Like ASSERT_VALID, the ASSERT_KINDOF macro applies only to pointers to objects derived from CObject. ASSERT_KINDOF tests that the pointer represents an object of a specified class, or is an object of a class derived from the specified class. For example, this line verifies that *pDoc* does indeed point to an object derived from CDocument as follows:

```
ASSERT_KINDOF(CMyDocument, pDoc)
```

DEBUG_NEW Macro

The DEBUG_NEW macro helps you find memory leaks that result when a block allocated using *new* is not released by a matching *delete* statement. The macro is extremely easy to use, and requires only the addition of a single line to your source code as follows:

```
#define new DEBUG_NEW
```

With this definition in place, the compiler interprets every *new* statement in your code as DEBUG_NEW, and MFC takes care of the rest. For debug builds, DEBUG_NEW keeps track of the file name and line number in which each *new* statement occurs. Your program can then call the *CMemoryState::Dump AllObjectsSince* member function which displays, in the Visual C++ Output window, a list of all *new* allocations that have not been released. For release builds DEBUG_NEW simply resolves to *new*.

Lesson Summary

This lesson introduced the important process of debugging, in which you locate and correct program errors. This lesson also described in general terms how a debugger works, the differences between release and debug versions of a project, and some of the macros that MFC provides as aids to debugging.

Debugging represents an important part of software development. Visual C++ can create a debug version of a program that contains symbol information, allowing the debugger to match computer instructions in the program's executable file with the program's source code and variable names. The debugger thus serves as a liaison between two worlds and is able to understand equally your own source code and the CPU's computer code. You interact with the debugger in terms of familiar functions and variables name, which the debugger applies to the executable image.

MFC provides several macros for debugging, the most common of which is the ASSERT macro. ASSERT provides an effective means of alerting you to errors without becoming a permanent part of your program's release version. Its variants ASSERT_VALID and ASSERT_KINDOF are used with pointers to objects derived from MFC's CObject class.

The DEBUG_NEW macro is useful for finding cases in which memory is allocated from the free store but not properly released. The macro replaces the *new* operator in debug builds, helping you find bugs that result when a *new* statement is not matched with a corresponding *delete* statement.

Lesson 2: Using the Integrated Debugger

Armed with the general overview of debugging provided in the first lesson, you are now ready to use the Visual C++ debugger. As you will see in this lesson, the debugger greatly facilitates the debugging process and can help you find most of the bugs you are likely to encounter when developing a distributed application for Windows.

After this lesson, you will be able to:

- Use the Visual C++ integrated debugger and understand the information presented in the debugger windows
- Monitor a running program and set breakpoints to interrupt the program's execution
- Single-step through a program
- Use the debugger's Edit and Continue feature to correct code on-the-fly while debugging

Estimated lesson time: 30 minutes

Breakpoints

The debugger does not interrupt the program being debugged. Rather, the program interrupts itself when it hits the marker set in the text editor. The marker is called a *breakpoint*.

As the program executes, the debugger sleeps. The debugger regains control only when the executing program triggers a breakpoint. The debugger recognizes two different types of breakpoints, one based on location in the code and the other based on program data.

A *location breakpoint* is a marker attached to a particular instruction in your source code, similar to a bookmark in the text editor. A *data breakpoint* depends on data instead of code. Use a data breakpoint when you suspect a variable is being incorrectly altered in an unknown area of your program. The data breakpoint tells the debugger to break execution when the variable changes or becomes a certain value, for example, when a pointer is reassigned or when the variable x exceeds a value of 500.

Setting Breakpoints

Location breakpoints are by far the most commonly used breakpoints, and are easy to set in the Visual C++ debugger. You need only to have some prior idea where you think your program is going wrong.

► **To set a location breakpoint**

1. Open the program's source file in the Visual C++ text editor and find the line in which you want to interrupt execution when the program runs.
2. Click anywhere on a line to place the cursor, and then press F9 to set a location breakpoint. The editor marks the line by placing a small red dot in the selection margin to the left of the line.
3. To remove a location breakpoint, press F9 again to toggle the breakpoint off.
4. You can also set or remove a location breakpoint by clicking the right mouse button on the line. On the shortcut menu that appears, select the Insert/Remove Breakpoint command to clear or set a breakpoint, as shown in Figure 11.3.

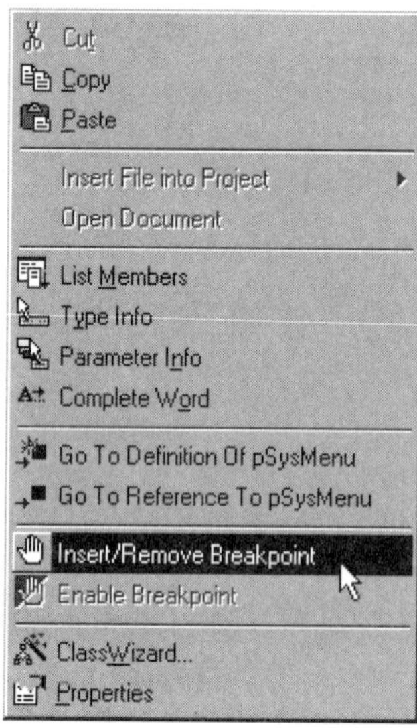

Figure 11.3 Selecting Insert/Remove Breakpoint from the shortcut menu

You can also set a location breakpoint using the Breakpoints dialog box. This dialog box provides the only means for setting data breakpoints and two other variations, conditional breakpoints and message breakpoints, which are described below.

Breakpoints Dialog Box

To display the Breakpoints dialog box shown in Figure 11.4, press Ctrl+B or click the Breakpoints command on the Edit menu. You can use the options in the dialog box to set location, data, conditional, and message breakpoints.

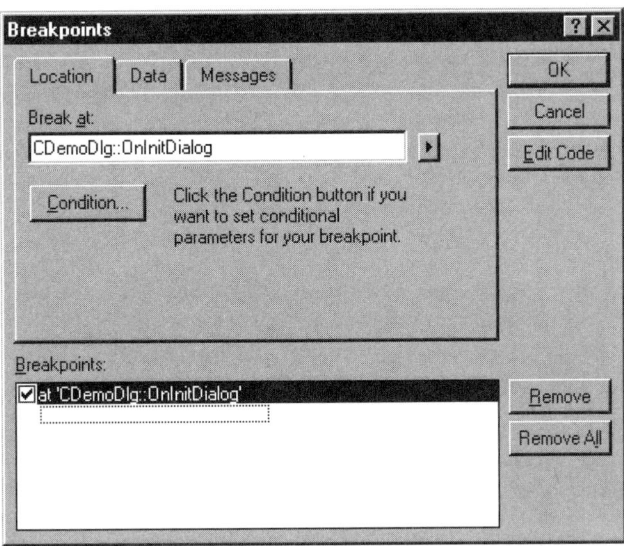

Figure 11.4 Breakpoints dialog box

Location Breakpoints

The Breakpoints dialog box provides several useful enhancements for location breakpoints. For instance, you can type the name of a function in the Break At control to set a location breakpoint at the first line of the function; typing the name of a label sets a breakpoint at the labeled line. Letter case in the Break At control must match the function name or label, and a C++ function name must include the class name and scope resolution operator. Thus, the entry *OnInitDialog* does not specify a valid breakpoint location, but *CDemoDlg::OnInitDialog* does.

Data Breakpoints

The Breakpoints dialog box provides the only means for setting a data breakpoint. Expose the Data tab in the Breakpoints dialog box, click the small arrow button, and choose Advanced. In the Advanced Breakpoint dialog box, type the function name, the source file, and the name of the variable or the expression you want the debugger to monitor. Type an expression in the form of a standard C/C++ conditional expression, such as *i == 100* or *nCount > 25*.

The debugger can monitor a range of variables identified by a pointer, such as an array or structure name, provided that you dereference the pointer in the expression.

► **To set a data breakpoint for an array or structure**

1. Click the Data tab of the Breakpoints dialog box.
2. For an array, type the array name in the Enter The Expression To Be Evaluated text box followed by *[0]* to dereference the pointer—*iArray[0]*, for example.

   To set a data breakpoint for a structure, precede the pointer variable with the asterisk dereference operator, such as **pStruct*.
3. To monitor more than just the first element of the array, set the number of elements in the smaller control labeled Enter The Number Of Elements. Notice that this is the number of elements, not the number of bytes.

Your program's execution speed can slow significantly when debugging with data breakpoints, especially if you set data breakpoints for variables with automatic storage class. Such data exists on the stack, and forces the debugger to perform much more work when monitoring it with breakpoints.

Conditional Breakpoints

The debugger responds to a *conditional breakpoint* only if a specified condition is true when control reaches the marked instruction. Each time a marked instruction executes, the debugger evaluates the breakpoint expression and interrupts program flow only if the expression is non-zero.

► **To set a conditional breakpoint**

1. Expose the Location tab of the Breakpoints dialog box.
2. Specify the location at which to set the breakpoint.
3. Click the Condition button, as previously shown in Figure 11.4, to display the Breakpoint Condition dialog box.
4. At the top of the dialog box, type the breakpoint condition in the form of a C/C++ conditional expression.

Message Breakpoints

A *message breakpoint* attaches to a window procedure, breaking execution when the procedure receives a specified message. Message breakpoints aren't of much use in MFC programs because window procedures lie buried inside the MFC framework. To trap a specific message in an MFC program, set a location breakpoint for the function that handles the message, which is identified in the class's message map.

Running the Debugger

When you have created a debug build and established where and under what conditions you want your program to stop, you are ready to execute the debugger. To simplify discussions, this section assumes the program being debugged is a stand-alone application—that is, a program with an .exe extension. (Lesson 3 describes how running DLL and OCX executable components under the debugger abides by nearly the same procedures described as follows.)

► **To start the debugger**

1. On the Build menu, select the Start Debug option, which presents you with four choices: Go, Step Into, Run To Cursor, and Attach To Process.
2. Select the Go command when you have set at least one breakpoint in the source code. The debugger runs the program normally, halting when the flow of execution in your program reaches a location breakpoint or triggers a data breakpoint.
3. Select the Step Into command to start the program and stop at the first statement.
4. Select the Run To Cursor command to run the program and break at the source line on which the cursor rests. If no source file is open in the text editor, the Run To Cursor command is unavailable. Otherwise, it gives you a convenient means of quickly jumping into a program without setting a breakpoint.
5. Select the Attach To Process command to launch the debugger and attach it to a program that is currently executing. Later in this chapter, you will learn how to use this feature to debug a COM component.

The debugger provides shortcut keys for the first three Start Debug commands, so you don't have to display the Build menu to begin debugging. The shortcut keys are F5 for Go, F11 for Step Into, and Ctrl+F10 for Run To Cursor.

Note These debug commands are discussed in more detail later in this lesson, in the section "Stepping Through Code."

Debugger Windows

When the program you are debugging stops at a breakpoint, the debugger updates its windows with information about the program's current state. The most important of the debugger windows is the source window, which shows the source code where the program stopped. A small yellow arrow called the instruction pointer appears in the selection margin to the left of the interrupted instruction. The arrow identifies the next instruction to be executed when the program resumes running.

The Debug toolbar appears on the screen when the debugger has control. The six buttons labeled Debugger windows in Figure 11.5 act as toggles that expose or hide dockable windows containing information about the current state of the program. Table 11.1 describes the type of information that each debugger window displays.

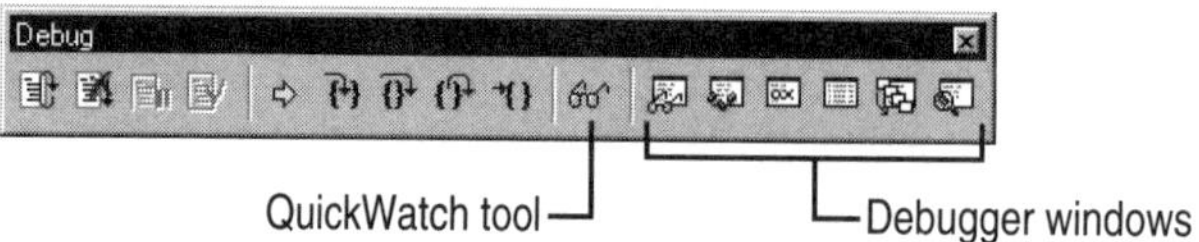

Figure 11.5 Tool buttons that toggle Debugger windows on and off

Table 11.1 Six Debugger Windows Activated by Buttons on the Debug Toolbar

Window	Information Displayed
Watch	Current values of variables and expressions tracked by the debugger
Variables	Current values of variables accessed at or near the break location
Registers	Current contents of the CPU registers
Memory	Memory contents at a specified address
Call Stack	List of called functions that have not yet returned
Disassembly	Assembly language translation of the compiled code that supplements the source window on the screen

Variables and Watch Windows

The Variables window displays information about variables relevant to the point where the program flow has been interrupted. Variables referenced by the instruction that last executed, and usually one or two previous instructions, appear in the Variables window. You can change the value of a variable by double-clicking it in the Variables window and typing a new value.

The Watch window shows the current values of specified variables no matter where they are referenced in the program. To add a variable to the Watch window, double-click the dotted new-entry box in the window and type the variable name. The QuickWatch tool, which can be opened by clicking the QuickWatch button shown in Figure 11.5, lets you query for a current value without adding the variable to the Watch window. If the variable name appears on the screen, the debugger offers an even more convenient way to query for its current value.

Simply pause the mouse cursor over the variable name in the source window to see a pop-up tooltip showing the current value.

Memory and Registers Windows

The Memory window shows the contents of memory at a given address. The window is useful for examining buffers not shown in the Variables window. Determine the value of the buffer pointer by locating it in the Variables window or Watch window, then type or paste the address into the text box in the Memory window and press Enter.

The Registers window shows the state of processor registers as they existed when the program was suspended. The window is generally used only when the Disassembly window is active, showing the code in assembly language.

Call Stack Window

The Call Stack window shows the route program flow has traversed to reach the point you are examining. It answers the question, "How did I get to this place?"

A *call stack* is a list of nested functions, each of which have been called and none of which have yet returned. The list begins with the current function that contains the point of interruption, and continues in reverse order toward the oldest parent function. MFC programs often wind through many nested functions hidden in the framework, so the call stack for these programs can be fairly lengthy.

Stepping Through Code

The Debug toolbar holds a group of four buttons shown in Figure 11.6 that let you step through a suspended program. You can recognize the Step tools by the arrows and curly braces on them. In the order shown, the buttons activate the Step Into, Step Over, Step Out, and Run To Cursor commands. The Run To Cursor command has already been discussed, but the other three need a little more explanation.

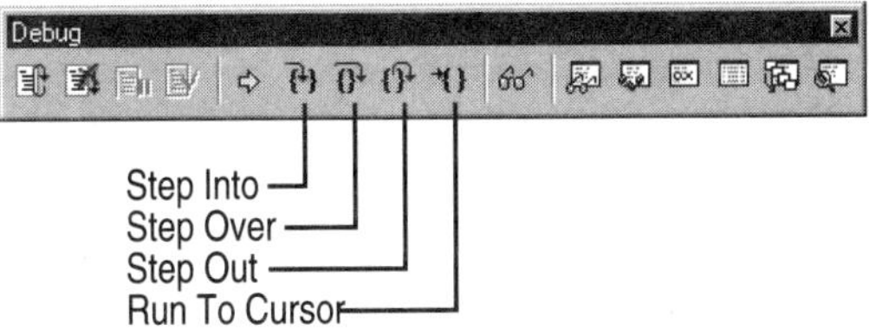

Figure 11.6 Four Step tools on the Debug toolbar

The Step Into and Step Over commands let you single-step through the program. When you select Step Into or Step Over, the debugger allows the program to resume execution, but only for one instruction. After the instruction finishes, the debugger again suspends execution. If the Disassembly view is available, the Step tools act on individual assembly instructions instead of the high-level C/C++ instructions. If applied to an instruction that calls a function, Step Over halts at the instruction following the call, whereas Step Into (as its name suggests) halts at the first instruction of the called function. For instructions that do not call a function, Step Into and Step Over have the same effect.

The Step Out command is useful for leaving a function. The command executes the rest of the current function, then stops at the next statement following the function call. In other words, when applied to a function call the Step Into and Step Out commands together have the same effect as Step Over.

Edit and Continue

Through its Edit and Continue feature, Visual C++ lets you permanently fix many problems right in the debugger's source window without having to exit the debugger and recompile. When you resume running the program after editing the source, Visual C++ compiles the revised code and replaces the affected module with the corrected version.

Edit and Continue has certain limitations. The feature does not recognize source changes that are impossible, impractical, or unsafe to compile while debugging, such as:

- Alterations to exception handler blocks
- Wholesale deletions of functions
- Changes to class and function definitions
- Changes to static functions
- Changes to resource data in the project's RC file

Attempting to resume execution through Edit and Continue after making any of these changes causes the debugger to display an error message in the status bar that explains the problem. You have the option of continuing to debug using the original code or closing the debugger and recompiling the revised code normally.

Lesson Summary

This lesson described the Visual C++ debugger, an invaluable tool for locating and solving program errors. The debugger greatly facilitates the debugging process by its ability to interrupt a running application at selected breakpoints positioned in the source code.

You learned how to set both location and data breakpoints using the Breakpoints dialog box, how to launch the debugger, and how to single-step through code when the debugged program halts at a breakpoint. The lesson also described the debugger's Edit and Continue feature, which allows you to edit source code and recompile without having to first exit the debugger.

A debugging session typically begins in the text editor, where you set breakpoints at positions in the source code at which you want execution to halt. The debugger automatically starts the project's program and gains control when execution flow reaches a breakpoint. The debugger displays six dockable windows:

- **Watch** Displays the values of selected data
- **Variables** Displays information pertaining to the current instruction
- **Call Stack** Contains a list of nested function calls
- **Registers** Displays the current contents of the CPU registers
- **Memory** Displays any area of accessible memory
- **Disassembly** Translates source code into equivalent assembly instructions

Lesson 3: Debugging COM Objects

Debugging COM objects can present you with certain challenges, depending on whether source code is available and on how the client, its server objects, and the debugger are distributed on a network. Some parts of a distributed application might not be accessible at all to the debugger, and can only be debugged through more indirect means such as compiling an error log. For example, the Visual C++ debugger can offer little help debugging an application's client side if the client is a third-party Web browser reading ASP scripts.

This lesson focuses on how to debug the COM components that form an application's server objects. This lesson also considers two main development scenarios, listed as follows in the order of difficulty they present for debugging:

- **Local objects** In this scenario, the client, server, and debugger all run on the same host computer and do not communicate across a network. This case is the easiest to debug because it involves (at most) local process communication between client and server. ActiveX controls are typical examples of objects that can be debugged locally.
- **Remote objects** In this scenario, the client and debugger run on one computer, whereas server objects run elsewhere on the network. Typical of multitier applications, this case can require more debugging effort because modules execute in separate processes located at different network nodes.

The sections that follow examine these scenarios in greater depth. The discussions are intended to prepare you for the lab at the end of this chapter, which demonstrates how to use the debugger to examine both local and remote server objects.

After this lesson, you will be able to:

- Debug local components on a single computer
- Debug remote components communicating over a network
- Use the Test Container utility to activate and examine Microsoft ActiveX controls
- Troubleshoot Microsoft COM errors
- Search the error log maintained by the Microsoft Windows NT Event Viewer

Estimated lesson time: 30 minutes

Debugging Local Objects

This section explains how to use the Visual C++ debugger to debug local COM servers such as ActiveX controls. As described in Chapter 5, such components can run in the same process as the client, or execute as separate processes linked through stub and proxy DLLs. This discussion assumes that both client and component execute on the same computer and do not communicate across a network.

Debugging In-Process Servers

The Visual C++ debugger easily accesses in-process COM servers, though such components require a client application to run them. If you have written the component's client as another project, it doesn't matter where you begin debugging, whether in the client's project or in the component's project. The debugger crosses the boundary between projects transparently when execution flows from client to server and back again.

To begin debugging in the component's project, first specify the client application in which you want to embed the component. In the Debug tab of the Project Settings dialog box, type the client's path and file name in the text box clicking the arrow next to the text box. This displays a small menu of choices, one of which is ActiveX Control Test Container.

ActiveX Control Test Container

The Test Container utility shown in Figure 11.7 is just what its name suggests: a general-purpose container utility for ActiveX controls. Visual C++ provides the Test Container so that you can debug and test ActiveX controls without having to write a corresponding container for them.

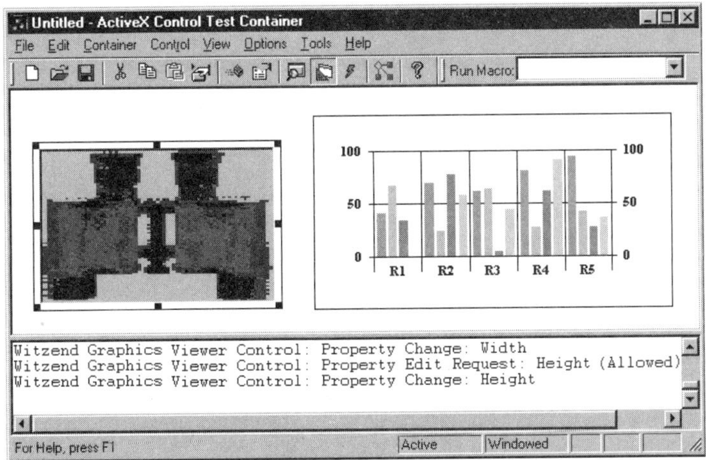

Figure 11.7 Test Container utility running two typical ActiveX controls

The first step, as usual, is to set breakpoints in your project's source files. If you have chosen the Test Container to embed your component during debugging, the debugger launches the utility automatically, as it would any other container. When a breakpoint in the method triggers, focus returns to the Visual C++ debugger, and you can begin or continue to single-step through your source code.

You can also execute the Test Container without the debugger, as demonstrated in the following practice session.

Executing ActiveX Controls in the Test Container

In this practice session, you will launch the Test Container utility manually without starting the debugger. The steps show how to open an ActiveX control in the Test Container and program it through its methods and properties.

► **To start the Test Container**

1. In Visual C++, click the ActiveX Control Test Container command on the Tools menu.
2. When the Test Container appears, click the New Control command on the toolbar, which displays a list of registered ActiveX controls.
3. If you have built your own ActiveX control and it has been properly registered, locate it in the list. Otherwise, double-click any control in the list, such as the Calendar control that comes with Microsoft Internet Explorer, to activate it.
4. When the control appears in the Test Container window, click the Invoke Methods tool to display the Invoke Methods dialog box.
5. Click the Method Name list box to expose a list of methods that the control exports. If you have activated the Calendar control or a similar object, select the BackColor (PropPut) property method in the list. A method identified as PropPut indicates that it writes a control property; a PropGet method reads a property.
6. Input the new property value in the Parameter Value box. To set a color, select VT_I4 in the Parameter Type box and input the decimal equivalent of an RGB value, such as 255 for bright red.
7. Click the Invoke button to call the method with the new value. If the property affects the control's appearance (as does the BackColor property), you should see the control change accordingly.
8. Click Close to close the Invoke Methods dialog box.
9. Press the Del key to delete the selected control, and then close the Test Container.

Debugging Out-of-Process Servers

Out-of-process ActiveX controls and other COM servers can run as stand-alone programs, and so do not technically require an executing container. However, because the server's methods and events execute only when activated by a client, you should specify a path to the client in the Debug tab of the Project Settings dialog box. Set breakpoints in the server's source code as desired, then launch the debugger, which automatically starts the client application. When both the client and server are active, switch to the client and invoke the commands necessary to activate the server's functions that contain the breakpoints. As with an in-process server, the Visual C++ debugger becomes active when execution reaches a breakpoint. You can then examine the server's code.

Visual C++ also allows you to begin a debugging session in the client itself. When the client calls into the out-of-process server module, you can continue debugging in the server's code. Visual C++ steps across the intervening marshalling code from the client into the server using JIT debugging. This feature automatically activates a separate instance of the debugger to run the server.

Because Visual C++ automates most of the work, starting a debugging session in the client project is similar to starting the debugger in the component's project. The main differences are that you need not specify the starting program in the Project Settings dialog box (since the client *is* the starting program), and you must work in two separate instances of the debugger. An overview of the necessary steps follows.

► **To start a debugging session in the client project**

1. Begin by opening the client project in Visual C++ and creating a debug build. Make sure the JIT feature is available by clicking the Options command on the Tools menu and exposing the dialog box's Debug tab. The check boxes labeled Just-In-Time debugging and OLE RPC Debugging should both be selected.

Note When running under Microsoft Windows NT, you must have administrator privileges to allow OLE RPC debugging.

---

2. Set a breakpoint at the line that calls the server, and then start the debugger to execute the client.
3. When execution reaches the breakpoint, use the debugger's Step Into command to step into the call. If your application links to MFC, execution proceeds into the framework code, for which Visual C++ automatically opens the correct source file.
4. Use the Step Over command to single-step through MFC until execution reaches a series of assembly instructions, marking the beginning of the client's stub DLL. (For a description of how a stub and proxy link to both client and server, see Chapter 5.)

5. Continue single-stepping through the stub and proxy. When the point of execution finally reaches the called method in the out-of-process server, Visual C++ automatically starts another instance of the debugger to run the server. You can now switch between the two debugger sessions, setting breakpoints as desired in both client and server.

MSDN describes these same steps in somewhat more detail, demonstrating with the well-known Scribble program. To locate the article, select the Search Titles Only check box in MSDN and search for "HOWTO: Debug OLE Applications."

Debugging the Message ActiveX Control

This practice demonstrates how to use the Visual C++ debugger to peer inside an ActiveX control named Message. Shown in Figure 11.8, Message is a simple control created by the MFC ActiveX Control Wizard, and merely displays a message when the mouse is clicked inside its window or when a key is pressed. Though it performs little useful work, Message is adequate for demonstrating how to debug an ActiveX control.

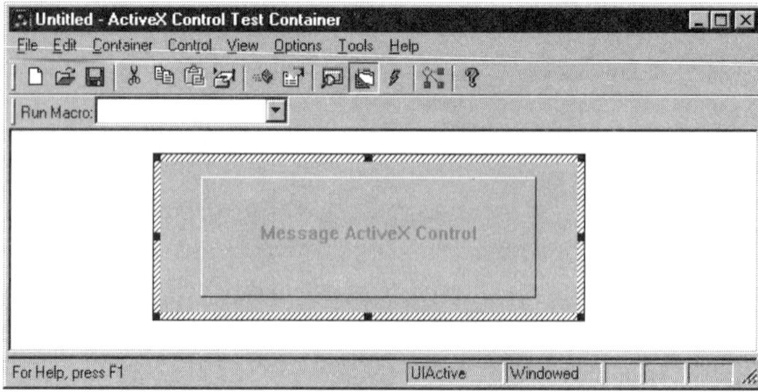

Figure 11.8 Message ActiveX control

► **To build the Message control on your computer**

1. If you have not already done so, copy the Message project files to your hard disk from the Labs\Ch11\Message folder on the companion CD.
2. Open Message.dsw in Visual C++.
3. In the configuration box located on the Build toolbar, select Win32 Debug as shown earlier in Figure 11.1.
4. On the same toolbar, click the Build button to compile the project.
5. After finishing the link step, Visual C++ automatically registers the control.

► To debug the Message ActiveX control

1. With the Message project still open in Visual C++, expose the Projects menu and choose the Settings command.
2. In the Debug tab of the Project Settings dialog box, click the small arrow button adjacent to the box labeled Executable For Debug Session.
3. Click ActiveX Control Test Container from the list and click OK. This selection tells the Visual C++ debugger to automatically launch the Test Container when the debugging session begins.
4. Open the MsgCtl.cpp file and set breakpoints at the first lines of the *OnLButtonDown* and *OnKeyDown* message handlers. These functions appear at the bottom of the MsgCtl.cpp file.
5. Press F5 to start the debugger. The debugger displays a message informing you that the Test Container does not contain debugging symbol information.
6. Click OK to close the message.
7. When the Test Container appears, click the New Control command on the toolbar.
8. Double-click the Message Control entry in the list of registered controls. If the entry does not appear in the list, it means that the control has not yet been properly registered. In this case, check the compiler messages in the Output window's Build tab. If the project compiled correctly but Visual C++ did not register the control, register the control manually by running the RegSvr32 utility at the command line:

   ```
   regsvr32 path\message.ocx
   ```

   where *path* represents the path to the Message.ocx file. RegSvr32 displays a message indicating success after registering the control.
9. When the Message control appears in the Test Container window, place the mouse cursor anywhere inside the window and press the left mouse button. This triggers the breakpoint set at the *OnLButtonDown* function, causing the debugger to update its windows to show the control's current state.
10. Single-step through the instructions to observe their effects, and then press F5 to continue execution.
11. You can also press a letter key to trigger the breakpoint for the *OnKeyDown* handler function. Again, press F5 to continue execution.
12. To examine the control's *AboutBox* method, set a breakpoint at the function's first instruction, switch back to the Test Container, and click the Invoke Methods tool button to expose the Invoke Methods dialog box.
13. Using the same steps as outlined in the previous practice, select *AboutBox* from the list of exported methods and click the Invoke button. When the Test Container calls the *AboutBox* method, execution stops at the breakpoint.

14. Each time you press the F5 key, execution continues and returns to the Test Container client. Close the Invoke Methods dialog box if it is open and press the Del key to delete the Message control. You can now exit the Test Container.

Debugging Remote Objects

This section focuses on debugging a remote object that executes on a separate computer, and communicates with its client across a network through the services of DCOM. For the sake of simplicity, the discussions in this section focus on COM components that execute as DLLs, not as stand-alone programs with an .exe extension. This simplification is easily justified, because most remote components exist as DLLs. Currently, MTS cannot create an object in any other form, so a component that supports MTS must be a DLL.

Before learning how to view a remote object in the Visual C++ debugger, you must first examine the remote object's execution context to see how it differs from that of a local object. The difference has to do with a program known as a surrogate host.

Surrogate Hosting

This book has referred to DLL components as in-process servers, meaning that they run in the same process as their clients. However, remote objects seem to introduce a paradox. Because the object and its client do not execute on the same computer, the two actually do not share one process, as would normally be expected for an object and its client.

Instead, a remote object runs in the address space of a *surrogate host*, which is a program that provides a process for an object but otherwise does not interact with the object. Through aggregation (described in Chapter 5), the surrogate exposes all of the object's interfaces as its own. Some surrogates are passive shell applications that do no more than load and aggregate components, whereas others offer sophisticated services well beyond simple hosting. Perhaps the most well-known surrogate host is MTS.

In a strict technical sense, a surrogate is an object's true client because it supplies the context under which the object runs. However, DCOM takes great efforts to ensure that the relationship between surrogate and object remains hidden from the object, the client application, and you. The transparency is so complete that when you are developing a calling application, you can usually forget that the surrogate even exists and continue to consider the program you are writing—that is, the application that calls the component's methods—as the client. The application communicates normally with its component and can even be unaware that the object is running elsewhere on the network.

However, when you begin debugging a component, you will often find it necessary to deal with the surrogate instead of the client application. The next section explains how to view a surrogate—and the remote components it executes—in the Visual C++ debugger.

Attaching the Debugger to a Remote Process

Each instance of the debugger controls only a single process. Therefore, you cannot begin debugging a client application and step across a network connection into a remote object the way you can step into the code for a local object. You've seen how Visual C++ solves the problem of debugging across local process boundaries by launching another instance of the debugger, but the JIT feature cannot automatically start the debugger on a remote computer. It is often easier to develop a component first to run locally on the client's computer, and then install it on another computer only after it has been thoroughly debugged and tested. If you want to use the debugger to peer inside a remote component as it executes, you must first install Visual C++ on the same computer on which the object runs. You then would start the debugger manually.

Note You should examine the terms of your Visual C++ license to ensure compliance before installing the product on separate computers.

The secret to debugging a remote object is to debug the surrogate process, rather than the object itself. This procedure is best accomplished by connecting the debugger to the running program using the Attach To Process command. Later in this section, the practice exercise, "Attaching the Debugger to the Object," outlines the steps required for using Attach To Process to investigate a remote object, but first you will practice how to debug an executing component.

Debugging an Executing Component

This practice demonstrates how the debugger can hook into an executing process, allowing you to debug a program that is already running. The following steps make use of the Message ActiveX control created in the previous practice session; if you have not already built the Message control project, do so now.

Although the Message control is not a remote component, it serves well for this introduction to the Attach To Process command. A discussion on using the command to debug a remote COM object is deferred until the lab at the end of the chapter.

► **To attach the debugger to the executing Message control**

1. Make sure that no workspace is open in the Visual C++ environment. If the Message project is open, click the Close Workspace command on the File menu to close the workspace.

2. Click the ActiveX Control Test Container command on the Tools menu to launch the Test Container utility, and then load the Message control as outlined in the previous practice session.
3. Switch back to Visual C++ and click the Attach To Process command, as shown in Figure 11.9.

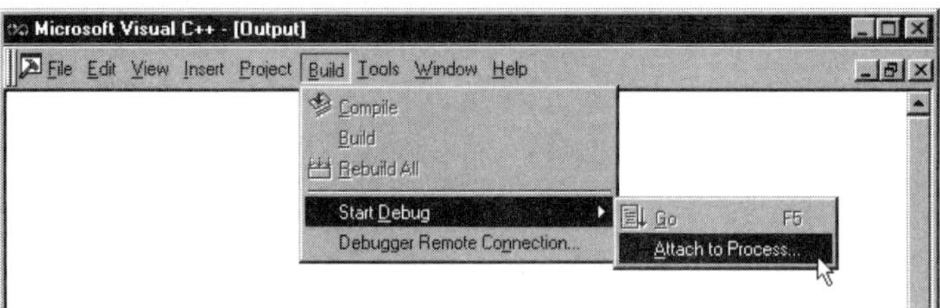

Figure 11.9 Selecting the Attach To Process command in Visual C++

4. In the Attach To Process dialog box, select TSTCON32 in the list of running processes and click OK. (TstCon32 is the name of the Test Container executable file.)
5. Because the Message ActiveX control shares the Test Container's address space, hooking the Test Container process allows the debugger to set breakpoints in the Message control. In Visual C++, select Open from the File menu. Locate and open the MsgCtl.cpp source file in the text editor and set a breakpoint at the *OnLButtonDown* function, as done in the previous practice.
6. Press the left mouse button inside the Message control window to trigger the breakpoint.

When the debugger is attached to the control's process, debugging works exactly the same way as in the previous practice session. The only difference between the two exercises is that in one case the debugger started before the Message control and in the other case it started after.

Attaching the Debugger to the Object

Now that you understand surrogate hosting and are familiar with the Attach To Process command, you can more easily use the Visual C++ debugger to view an object running remotely. This section summarizes the steps you should follow to attach the debugger to the object.

The procedure outlined in the following steps requires you to move back and forth between the client's computer and the server's computer; therefore, the procedure is practical only when the computers are near one another. Ideally the computers should be arranged in the same room so that you can conveniently reach the keyboard and mouse of each.

► **To attach the debugger to the object**

1. Open the client application's project and set a breakpoint at or before the call to the object's method in which you are interested. You should set the breakpoint somewhere after the instruction that instantiates the object. MFC programs usually call a component's *Create* function to instantiate the object; other programs call *CoCreateInstanceEx* or *IClassFactory::CreateInstance*.
2. Execute the client in its debugger until the breakpoint is triggered. Assuming the object has been successfully instantiated, it is now running in its own process on a remote computer but has not yet been accessed by the client (other than the call to the component's class factory).
3. Start Visual C++ on the component's computer and activate the Attach To Process command. In the list of running processes, double-click the component's program or its surrogate to attach the debugger to the object's process. The lab at the end of this chapter illustrates how to attach to an object running in a surrogate host.
4. Open the component's source files in the Visual C++ text editor and set breakpoints as desired.
5. Return to the client's computer and press F5 to resume execution. When the program flow reaches a breakpoint in the remote object, execution halts and you can then examine the object's behavior when running under its remote context.

Installing and Registering a Remote Component

As mentioned, development of a remote component is best done locally—that is, on the same computer as the client—until the code performs as expected. After debugging and testing, install the component on its intended host computer in two steps as follows:

► **To install and register a remote component**

1. Copy the component's executable file to the server on which it will run. Although the operating system can load a component from any node on the network, load time is improved when the system can locate the file on a local hard disk.
2. Register the component on the server using the RegSvr32 utility. If the component runs as an out-of-process executable, specify the server computer in the RemoteServerName registry key. If the component runs as an in-process DLL in the context of a surrogate host, add registry information to identify the surrogate. Both of these techniques are discussed in more detail in the next two sections.

Whether you should leave the component registered on the development computer depends on the registry information and on how the client application instantiates the component. Consider the following sequence, in which a client calls *CoGetClassObject* to access a component's class factory:

```
IClassFactory* pcf = NULL;
CoGetClassObject(CLSID_MyComponent, CLSCTX_ALL, 0,
                 IID_IClassFactory, (PVOID*) &pcf);
```

The CLSCTX_ALL parameter instructs COM to first search the local registry for the component's CLSID information. If the registry entry is found, COM loads the component from the local hard disk. The client can therefore continue to use the local component, even though you have installed a copy on a remote server.

Specifying the Remote Computer for an Out-of-Process Component

If your component executes as an out-of-process .exe program, the registry on the client's computer can contain the name of the remote computer on which the component should execute. To instruct COM to load a copy of the component at a specific location on the network, the CLSID entry in the local registry should include the RemoteServerName key to specify the name of the remote host.

Adding or removing the RemoteServerName key from the registry allows you to switch between local and remote instances of the component without recompiling the client. The lab at the end of this chapter describes another method by which a client can specify a remote server using the COSERVERINFO structure.

Specifying the Surrogate for an In-Process Component

To identify the surrogate for an in-process component, the registry for the remote computer (on which the surrogate executes) requires two entries in addition to the component's normal registry data. The first registry entry is a value named *AppID* in the component's CLSID folder. AppID contains a GUID string that refers to the second registry entry, which is in HKEY_CLASSES_ROOT\AppID. The second entry contains a value named *DllSurrogate*, which specifies the surrogate. If the value of DllSurrogate is an empty string, DCOM provides a default surrogate program named DllHost.exe.

Following is a summary showing the required registry entries for a typical in-process component that executes in the DllHost surrogate. Keep in mind that these entries are in the registry belonging to the remote computer on which the component runs. HKCR is a standard abbreviation for HKEY_CLASSES_ROOT:

```
HKCR\AppID\{xxxxxxxx-xxxx-xxxx-xxxxxxxxxxxx}
DllSurrogate = ""
 .
 .
 .
HKCR\CLSID\{yyyyyyyy-yyyy-yyyy-yyyyyyyyyyyy}
AppID = "{xxxxxxxx-xxxx-xxxx-xxxxxxxxxxxx}"
```

Although this scheme might seem a bit involved, it is easy to implement and needs to be done only one time. The lab at the end of this chapter demonstrates these steps, showing how to set up a surrogate host for a remote in-process component.

Troubleshooting COM Objects

This section lists a few troubleshooting tips that can help diagnose the cause of a problem related to remote COM objects:

- Make sure that MS DTC is running on all servers.
- Check network communication by first testing it on a local computer to verify that the application works across the network. If you are running TCP/IP on your network, use the Ping utility to verify that the computers are attached to the network.
- When utilizing ODBC data sources, make sure that SQL and MS DTC are located on the same computer or that the DTC Client Configuration program specifies that MS DTC is on another computer. If not, *SQLConnect* returns an internal error when called from a transactional component.
- For MTS transactions, set the timeout period to a higher number than the default 60 seconds. After the transaction timeout has elapsed, the system terminates the transaction. All subsequent calls to the component return immediately with a value of CONTEXT_E_ABORTED.
- Make sure that the ODBC drivers are thread-safe and do not have thread affinity.
- If you have difficulty getting an application to work over several servers, reboot the client and verify that the domain controller is configured properly.

Debugging File-Locked Server Modules

You might encounter a sharing violation when rebuilding a Web-based server project immediately after exiting the debugger. Such a violation occurs because IIS usually loads a component into the same address space as all the other IIS services. Instead of immediately unloading the component when the client has finished with it, IIS artificially raises the component's release count to prevent it from dropping to zero. This caches the module in memory where it can be quickly restored should the client need it again, thus improving performance. However, caching the component also prevents Visual C++ from rebuilding the project, because the linker cannot overwrite the existing file while IIS retains a lock.

An initial solution to this problem is to restart the Web server, thereby flushing all components from the IIS object cache. Though this technique unlocks the file and allows the linker to overwrite it, it is inconvenient to restart the Web server before installing every new build.

A more efficient solution is to use the IIS *process isolation* feature. Available in IIS versions 4.0 and higher, process isolation allows you to load a component into a separate process that can be shut down independently of the rest of the Web server. Unfortunately, setting up process isolation involves additional work and requires you to address several issues such as security, fault isolation, and performance. For more information, see the MSDN article titled "Simplify Development with Process Isolation."

Using the Windows NT Event Viewer

When a component fails or causes unexpected behavior, the first task of debugging is to determine in which module the error occurs. Often, this information is encapsulated in an error object returned to an exception handler, as described in Chapter 10. For alternate sources of error information, you should look for clues in the Windows NT Event Viewer log. The Windows NT Event Viewer is a utility that tracks events originating from application, security services, and Windows NT. However, keep in mind that, although the Event Viewer records many transparent errors, it does not list every possible error.

You should first refer to the Application Log in the Event Viewer to check the application associated with the event message. The Event Viewer archives event records that form a history of events, including errors. Double-clicking an entry in the log activates an Event Detail, which provides more information about the system event.

Lesson Summary

Because in-process ActiveX controls are DLLs, they are debugged with the same ease as normal DLLs. A single instance of the debugger can follow execution flow as it passes from the client into the control and back again. An out-of-process component requires its own debugger session. Thus, it is possible to simultaneously debug the client in one debugger instance and the component in a separate debugger instance. Visual C++ creates a new instance automatically when you single step from the client into an out-of-process object.

The Test Container utility included with Visual C++ serves as a general-purpose container application for running ActiveX controls. The Test Container allows you to debug and test your ActiveX control without having to develop a separate container for it.

Because a remote object runs on a different network node than its client, it cannot share the client's process. An invisible application known as a surrogate host must load a remote component cast as a DLL. This surrogate aggregates the component and exposes its interfaces to clients operating elsewhere on the network. It is usually not necessary for the client to be aware that the object does not share its process or its computer resources.

During development, a component should run locally if possible. Keeping the client and server on the same computer greatly facilitates development and debugging. You should move a component intended to run as a remote server to another computer only after you have thoroughly debugged and tested that component on the client's computer. When you have moved the component to its intended host computer, you should retest the component to check its behavior and ensure that performance remains within acceptable tolerances.

If you must view an object in the debugger during remote operation, install Visual C++ on the component's computer and follow these steps:

► **To view an object in the debugger during remote operation**

1. Select an instruction in the client application that executes after the component is loaded and set a breakpoint there. Execute the client in the debugger until the breakpoint is reached.
2. Move to the component's computer, invoke the Attach To Process command, and then select the component's process from the list.
3. Open the component's source file in the text editor and set breakpoints as desired.
4. Returning to the client's debug session, press F5 to invoke the Go command to resume. When execution reaches a breakpoint in the component's debug session, execution again halts.

Lesson 4: Dependency Walker

Visual C++ provides other utilities besides the debugger that can help you peer inside an application or DLL component. In this lesson, you will learn how to use the Dependency Walker utility, sometimes referred to by its file name, Depends.exe.

After this lesson, you will be able to:

- Explain why Windows programs depend on other modules to run
- Execute the Dependency Walker utility to examine a program's dependencies

Estimated lesson time: 15 minutes

What Is a Dependency?

A Windows program is not as self-sufficient as it might appear on the surface. Even the simplest "Hello, world" program requires the presence of several DLLs provided by the system, such as Kernel32 and GDI32. An MFC program depends on the help of even more module files such as MFC42.dll. MFC in turn cannot run without additional files, such as the C run-time library, MSVCRT. This list of required modules must be available to the operating system before a program can execute. Together, these modules form a program's *dependencies*.

Each executing Windows module, whether an application or a DLL, stores a list of its dependencies in a header area of the executable file. When the operating system loads a module, it reads the list of dependencies and loads each required module. Only when all dependencies are loaded does the original program run.

Dependency Information

Ordinarily, a program's dependencies are invisible to users. A dependency usually makes itself known to users only when it is missing. In other words, Windows displays a message explaining that the program in which a user wants to work cannot run, because a required file cannot be found.

The Dependency Walker utility reads the dependency table located in a program's header and displays information about each dependency. The results are shown in Figure 11.10, which lists the dependencies for a typical program named Demo.exe.

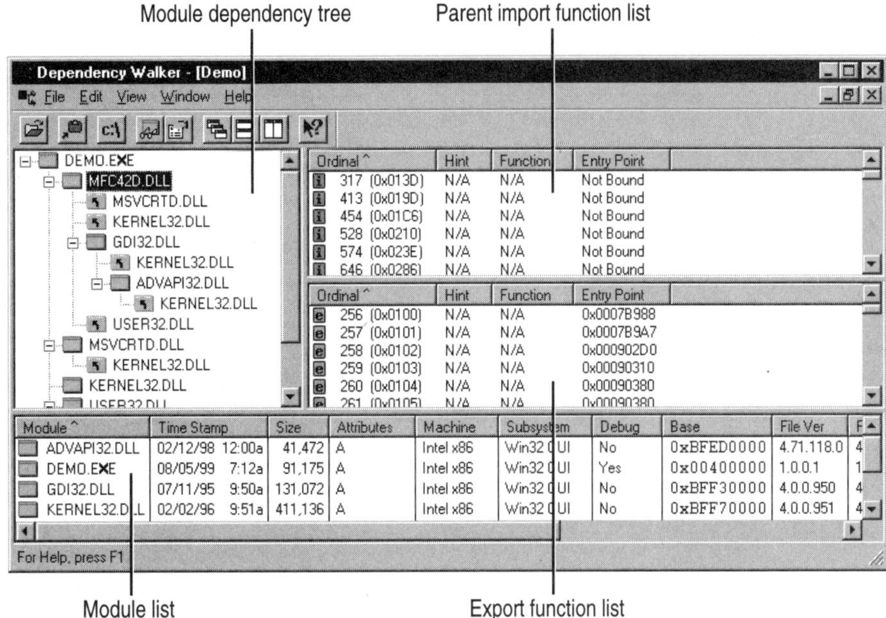

Figure 11.10 Dependency Walker utility

The Dependency Walker utility shows information such as the following:

- Files required to run an application or DLL and their locations
- Base address of each dependency module
- Version information about each dependency module
- Whether or not each dependency module contains debug information

► To start the Dependency Walker

1. Click the Start button and display the Programs menu.
2. Select Microsoft Visual Studio 6.0, Microsoft Visual Studio 6.0 Tools, and then click Depends on the submenu. As with any utility, you can also add a command to the Visual C++ Tools menu to invoke the Dependency Walker.
3. When the Dependency Walker window appears, select the Open command on the File menu, and browse to the application or DLL you want to examine.

The Dependency Walker is an MDI application, so you can open several views, each showing the dependencies for a different executable file. The Dependency Walker displays four panes separated by splitter bars, as previously shown in Figure 11.10. Table 11.2, shown on the next page, describes the four panes identified in Figure 11.10.

Table 11.2 Four Panes Displayed in the Dependency Walker

Pane	Description
Module Dependency Tree	A hierarchical tree showing the program's dependencies. The tree often contains duplicate names because several modules might have the same dependencies.
Parent Import Function List	A list of parent import functions for the module selected in the Module Dependency Tree. Parent import functions are those functions that are called in the selected module by the module's parent module. The selected module must export every function that the parent is importing from it. If the selected module does not export one of the functions that the parent module expects to call, an unresolved external error occurs when the module is loaded.
Export Function List	A list of functions exported by the module selected in the Module Dependency Tree. Export functions are functions that a module exposes to other modules.
Module List	A list of all required dependencies for the opened program. This list defines the minimum set of files needed for the program to execute.

Lesson Summary

This lesson introduced the Dependency Walker, a utility that provides information about the modules a Windows program requires to run. Such modules are known as dependencies. The Dependency Walker displays the following:

- Tree view of modules forming a program's dependencies
- List of import functions called by a module's parent
- List of functions that a module exports
- List of a program's dependencies

Lesson 5: Spy++

In this lesson, you will learn how to use another Visual C++ utility named Spy++. This popular and useful utility can display information about all current processes, their threads, and all open windows—even hidden windows.

After this lesson, you will be able to:

- Execute the Spy++ utility and use it to display a graphical tree of relationships among system objects, including processes, threads, and windows
- Use Spy++ to search for specified windows, threads, processes, or messages
- View the properties of selected windows, threads, and processes
- Use the Spy++ Finder Tool to select a window for monitoring
- View a real-time record of messages that a window sends and receives

Estimated lesson time: 15 minutes

Spy++ Views

Start Spy++ the same way you start the Dependency Walker, by selecting it from the Microsoft Visual Studio 6.0 Tools submenu. The utility displays four main views:

- **Windows** Shows a list of open windows
- **Processes** Lists current processes
- **Threads** Lists all current threads
- **Message Log** Lists the messages that a window receives

These four views are activated by commands in the Spy menu, or by the first four buttons on the toolbar. Each time a command is invoked, it creates a view as a new child window; the tool buttons do not toggle between existing views. You should thus create a view only one time, and thereafter switch between views by making a selection in the Window menu. Like the Dependency Walker, Spy++ is an MDI program, so you can tile views within the client area.

Figure 11.11, on the next page, shows how the Windows and Processes views might look when arranged in the Spy++ window. The views show that Visual C++ is currently running (named MSDEV in the Processes view) and has created several child windows.

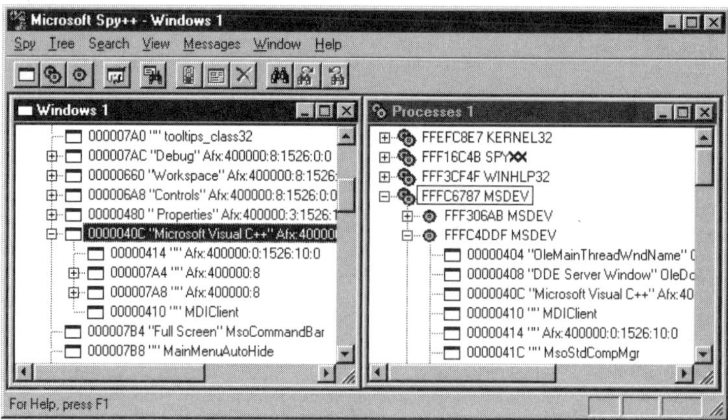

Figure 11.11 Spy++ utility, showing a list of open Windows and Processes

A Spy++ view represents a snapshot, so applications that begin running after Spy++ are not automatically added to the lists. Conversely, applications that terminate during Spy++ execution are not automatically removed from the list. To update a view, give the view focus and click the Refresh command on the Window menu.

Windows View

The Windows view displays a list of all windows currently open. It does not matter if the window is hidden, and indeed many open windows in a typical Windows session are invisible, serving their various applications only as message receivers. When Spy++ begins or when the view is refreshed, the utility compiles a list of all windows and displays the list in the Windows view.

The list is a normal tree view with small plus and minus icons that collapse or expand the list into levels. The tree's hierarchy indicates window parentage—that is, the relation between windows in which one window can create others as child windows. Click any plus icon adjacent to a window to expand the list to include that window's children. If a plus icon does not appear next to a window, it means that the window does not have any children.

A typical list in the Windows view can include many windows, so it's sometimes difficult to locate the entry for a particular window. In these cases, use the Window Finder tool.

► **To use the Window Finder Tool**

1. Arrange the screen so that Spy++ and the window you want to investigate both are visible on the screen.
2. Click the Find Window button on the Spy++ toolbar.
3. Drag the Finder Tool icon, as shown in Figure 11.12, out of the Find Window dialog box.

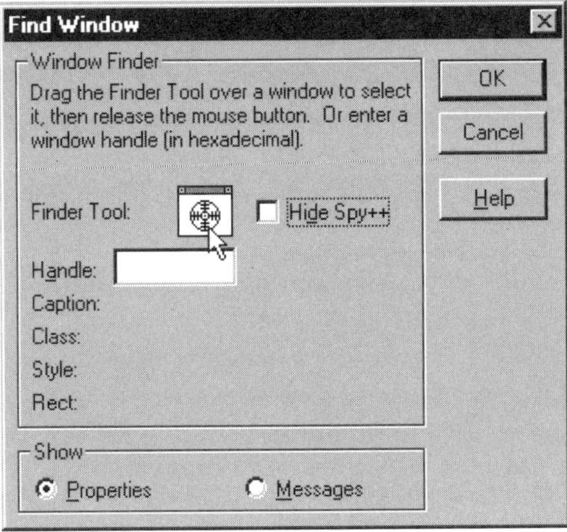

Figure 11.12 Using the Window Finder Tool in Spy++

As the dragged icon passes over an exposed window, the window appears framed in thick black lines and the Find Window dialog box notes the window's handle. Release the dragged icon over the desired window and close the Find Window dialog box. You can then locate the window's entry in the list by scanning for its window handle.

Processes View and Threads View

Each process running in the Windows multitasking environment creates one or more threads, and each thread can create any number of windows. Use the Processes view to examine a particular process, which usually corresponds to an executing program. Processes are identified by module names, or designated as *system processes*.

The Threads view lists all currently executing threads along with the names of their owner processes. Expand a thread entry to see a list of its associated windows.

Message Log View

The message log view is very useful for debugging purposes. The message log keeps a record, in real time, of all messages that a window sends or receives. This record allows you to examine a list of messages to see in what order they arrive, which is particularly useful for capturing window initialization messages.

A convenient way to begin message logging for a window is by using the Window Finder tool described earlier. Drag and drop the Finder Tool icon over a target window as before, but this time, click the Messages radio button at the bottom of the Find Window dialog box before closing the dialog box.

As you work in the target window, Spy++ compiles a list of messages the window sends and receives, as shown in Figure 11.13.

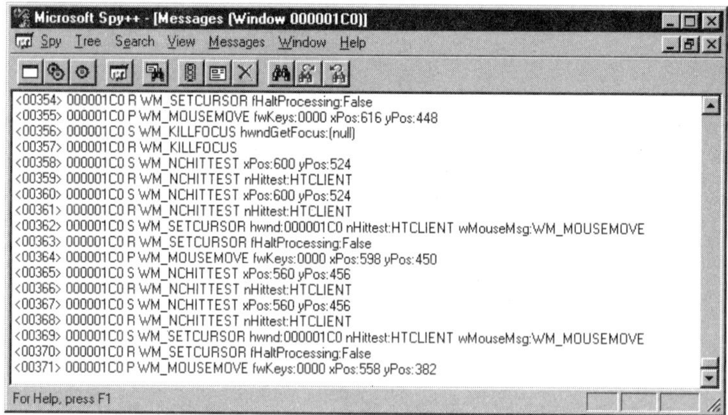

Figure 11.13 Spy++ message log

The Spy++ message log is divided into four columns as shown in Table 11.3.

Table 11.3 Columns of Spy++ Message Log

Column	Description
1	Index number showing the message count
2	Window handle
3	Message code, either S (sent), R (received), P (posted), or s (message was sent, but security prevents access to the return value)
4	Message, parameters, and return values

By default, the list includes all messages, including mouse movement and keystroke messages such as WM_KEYDOWN and WM_KEYUP. This means the list can quickly become crowded, but Spy++ can filter the log to include only those messages that most interest you. Click Options in the Messages menu and select the Messages tab. Click the Clear All button to clear all the check boxes, and then select only those check boxes for the messages you want to investigate.

End message tracking either by clicking the button with the stoplight icon on the Spy++ toolbar, or by selecting the Stop Logging command from the Messages menu.

Viewing Window Messages in Spy++

In this practice session, you will launch the Spy++ utility and use it to spy on another application. By turning on the utility's message logging feature, you can view in real time the messages belonging to a selected window.

▶ **To start Spy++**

1. Click the Start button and display the Programs menu.
2. Select Microsoft Visual Studio 6.0, Microsoft Visual Studio 6.0 Tools, and then click Spy++ on the submenu.
3. When the utility appears, click the Find Window tool on the toolbar and drag the Finder Tool icon and drop it onto another window. If no other application is running, drop the Finder Tool icon onto the desktop. (You cannot use Spy++ to spy on itself.)
4. Click the Messages radio button at the bottom of the Find Window dialog box, and then click OK.
5. Experiment by moving the mouse cursor over the selected window. You will see the many messages that the window sends and receives pertaining to mouse movement, such as WM_MOUSEMOVE and WM_SETCURSOR.
6. Select Exit in the Spy menu to close Spy++.

Lesson Summary

This lesson described Spy++, a Visual C++ utility that reports information about executing programs. Spy++ can provide invaluable insight into an application's behavior not available through the Visual C++ debugger.

Spy++ displays four main views that show a list of windows, processes, threads, and messages pertaining to a particular window. Its Window Finder tool aids in associating any exposed window with the list of windows that Spy++ displays. The useful message tracking feature intercepts and logs all messages that enter and leave a window, showing chronological order and values of message parameters. The message log can be filtered to monitor only messages of particular interest.

Lesson 6: Testing a Distributed Application

When your application is nearly complete and reasonably stable, testing to detect errors and debugging to fix them should begin in earnest. This lesson examines some of the techniques of testing.

As much as possible, testing should be conducted under widely different scenarios that mimic the real-world conditions under which an application might have to function. For example, a program designed to run under Microsoft Windows 95/98 and Windows NT should be tested under all three operating systems. The tester's job is to try to "break" the application, whereas your job, as the developer, is to ensure that the application cannot be broken. If you must wear both hats, you should bring equal zeal to each task.

After this lesson, you will be able to:

- Design an effective test plan
- Understand terminology pertaining to testing
- Employ common techniques for testing your application

Estimated lesson time: 15 minutes

Glossary of Testing Terms

Testing has become a rigorous process, and many organizations correctly take testing seriously. Like any field, testing has its own lexicon. This section defines some of the terms that pertain to testing, making subsequent discussions in the lesson more meaningful. The glossary is arranged by level, starting with the simplest test and proceeding to tests that are more involved.

- *Unit testing* verifies a discrete piece of code, such as a loop, block, subroutine, or event. In formal terms, a unit test applies to the smallest piece of code for which a practical test can be conducted.
- *Integration testing,* the next highest level, confirms that no problems arise from combining units of code into more complex processes. For example, two functions might test successfully as units, but the effects of providing one function with the output of the other should also be considered. Threads must be subjected to stringent integration testing to ensure that they perform as expected when running simultaneously.
- *System testing* focuses on the full build of an application. At this level, the emphasis is less on bug hunting per se and more on checking that the various parts of the application interact with one another correctly.
- *Stress testing* verifies how an application behaves under adverse conditions such as low memory, high network traffic, insufficient disk space, and so on.

- *Regression testing* repeats previous tests after changes have been made to the source code. The purpose of regression testing is to verify that the application still works as expected and that new bugs have not been introduced by the code revisions.
- *Beta testing* is a means of testing by which you distribute an application to a group of selected users. You should generally choose users for their familiarity with past versions of a product, their willingness to use the new version under a wide variety of conditions, and a demonstrated ability to communicate what they like and dislike about a product.

Creating a Test Plan

A *test plan* is a written version of the entire test suite for an application. Done correctly, the test plan completely describes all of the testing that needs to be done, and what constitutes the success of any particular test. Test plans should be written as though they provide directions on how to test an application to someone other than the test plan author. The primary criterion for a successful test plan is whether or not a person unfamiliar with the testing protocol for the application can pick up the test plan halfway through a project and continue the testing cycle.

Custom applications can be effectively tested through three methods:

- Testing by you and the testing/quality assurance team
- Beta testing by selected users
- User acceptance testing

Elements of a Test Plan

A test plan provides a formal basis from which to develop repeatable regression tests. When systems evolve or when new builds are created during the debug cycle, it is essential that the existing stability of the application has not been damaged. A test plan also provides a basis from which the test strategy can be inspected and discussed by all interested parties.

A solid test plan starts with a description of the application to be tested, which is followed by a brief discussion of the test objectives. The plan should include the following elements:

- A description of how the tests should be performed, explaining the various degrees of reliance that should be made on key testing components such as test scripts, manual checklists, and user involvement.
- A description of the environment in which the test should occur, including the operating system and, if relevant, its version number. For example, the original release of Windows 95 has slightly different characteristics than the same operating system with Service Pack 1 installed. A test plan might need to consider these differences.

- A listing of the test data that must be made available for the tests to be valid.
- A discussion of any restrictions placed on the test team that might affect the reliability of the test results. For example, if you are testing an application designed for hundreds of users accessing a large central database, a small organization would probably not be able to simulate this volume of usage.
- A declaration of the relative orders of importance placed on different criteria (for example, your concern for robustness compared to that of performance).
- A list of features that are not tested, with a commentary explaining your reasons, such as known issues or errors.
- An intended test schedule that shows milestones. This schedule should tie into the overall project plan.
- Objectives of the test exercise.

Test Scenarios

After designing a test plan, the next step is to list each test scenario, using the same breakdown of functionality as presented in the design specification. Each scenario should include the following:

- References to the items being tested
- Expected results
- Commentary that describes how the test results confirm or deny that the tested items are functioning as expected

Creating a Test Harness

When developing a COM component, you should almost always allocate time during the test process to develop a *test harness*. A test harness is a client program designed to load and run the component, but which is not intended to ship as part of the final product. The purpose of the test harness is to subject the component to a battery of planned tests. These tests should represent the types of operations, both typical and atypical, you expect your component will be called upon to perform when released to the world.

Do not underestimate the time and thought that should be dedicated to developing a test harness. The test harness should be modularized to facilitate expansion, because you will almost certainly conceive of new tests as development proceeds. A test harness should automate as many parts of the test plan as possible so that conducting a new regression test, for example, is merely a matter of running the test harness. Many test harnesses read script files, thus making it unnecessary to rebuild the test harness every time a new test is devised.

Endowed with a UI and perhaps a Help file, test harnesses can often grow into full-fledged evaluation programs that are released to prospective customers or made available on a Web site for downloading. In this way, some of the development costs can be defrayed as advertising.

Lesson Summary

This lesson defined some of the common terminology pertaining to software testing, and described how to write an effective test plan. A test plan is an important part of developing any Windows program intended for the market or for widespread distribution. A test plan outlines an intended program of testing procedures, including the following:

- **Unit testing** Examines small sections of code
- **Integration testing** Verifies how code sections operate together
- **System testing** Verifies the overall stability of the entire program
- **Stress testing** Determines how the program reacts to conditions of limited system resources
- **Regression testing** Ensures that a revision to the code does not introduce new errors
- **Beta testing** Gathers user input

Small development teams of less than four or five people usually have to serve as both programmers and testers. In larger organizations with more personnel, developers and testers often form two distinct teams. Even in this case, programmers can benefit from the information in this lesson, because the entire development process runs more smoothly when both teams understand each other's work.

When you are writing a COM component, a significant portion of development time should be dedicated to the simultaneous development of a test harness program. A test harness facilitates testing, especially regression testing, by subjecting the component to the tests listed in the test plan. The test harness is generally for in-house use only, and is not released to users of the final product.

Lab 11: Debugging a COM Object

In this lab, you will gain hands-on experience debugging a COM object using the Visual C++ debugger. The lab is divided into three exercises:

- Debugging a local component
- Debugging a remote component
- Debugging an MTS component

All three exercises implement the same component and client application. The component, named Beeper, exports a single method that merely beeps the computer speaker. The resulting sound indicates unambiguously on which computer the component is executing. Beeper can execute inside the MTS environment, although it does not support transactions. A simple console-based application, named Client, loads and calls the Beeper component. Both the Beeper and Client projects are kept as simple as possible, making it easy to locate pertinent code in the debugger.

Estimated lab time: 20 minutes

Exercise 1: Debugging a Local Object

If you have not already done so, run the Setup program on the companion CD to copy the project files for the Beeper and Client projects to your hard disk. The project files are in the Labs\Ch11\Beeper and Labs\Ch11\Client folders. When the files are installed, you are ready to create debug builds for both projects.

► **To create debug builds for the Beeper and Client projects**

1. Begin with the Beeper project. In Visual C++, select Open Workspace on the File menu.
2. Browse for the Beeper project folder on your hard disk and double-click the Beeper.dsw file.
3. On the Build toolbar, make sure the Win32 Debug build context is selected, as shown at the beginning of this chapter in Figure 11.1.
4. Click the Build button on the Build toolbar to compile a debug version of the Beeper component. The Beeper source code was created using the ATL COM AppWizard. The only addition to the project is the *Beep* method located in the BeepCtl.cpp file. (BeepCtl is the name given to the object in ATL Object Wizard when the project was created.) The function accepts a parameter specifying the number of beeps desired, and then calls the *MessageBeep* API function to sound the speaker as the code on the following page demonstrates.

```
STDMETHODIMP CBeepCtl::Beep(long iNumber)
{
    for (long i=0; i < iNumber; i++)
    {
        ::MessageBeep(-1L);   // Sound the speaker
        ::Sleep(250);  // Pause 1/4 sec between beeps
    }

    return S_OK;
}
```

5. Close the workspace and select the Open Workspace command again.
6. Browse to the Client project folder and open the Client.dsw file.
7. Repeat the steps listed previously to create a debug build for the Client application. Be sure to select the Win32 Debug build configuration before compiling. Following is the source code for the Client.cpp file:

```
///////////////////////////////////////////////////////////////////////
//
// Client.cpp  Console-based client for the Beeper component
//
///////////////////////////////////////////////////////////////////////

#define  _WIN32_DCOM
#include "stdio.h"
#include "ole2.h"
#include "beeper.h"

int main()
{
    IUnknown*  pUnk    = NULL;
    IBeepCtl*  pbeep   = NULL;
    COSERVERINFO   si  = {0, L"server", 0, 0};
    MULTI_QI       mqi = {&IID_IUnknown, NULL, 0};
    HRESULT    hr;

    CoInitialize(NULL);
    hr = CoCreateInstanceEx(CLSID_BeepCtl, 0,
              CLSCTX_INPROC_SERVER,
              &si, 1, &mqi);
    if (SUCCEEDED(hr))
    {
        pUnk    = mqi.pItf;
        hr  = pUnk->QueryInterface(IID_IBeepCtl,
                    (PVOID*) &pbeep);
        if (SUCCEEDED(hr))
        {
            // Beep twice
            pbeep->Beep(2L);
```

```
                pbeep->Release();
            }
            else
                printf("\n\nQueryInterface returned %08X", hr);
            pUnk->Release();
        }
        else
            printf("\n\nCoCreateInstanceEx returned %08X", hr);

        CoUninitialize();
        return 0;
    }
```

Because Beeper is an in-process COM component, Client and Beeper both execute in the same process on the local computer. Therefore, it does not matter which project is open when you begin debugging the Beeper component. The following steps assume that debugging begins in the Beeper project.

► **To debug the Beeper component on a single computer**

1. Reopen the Beeper project if necessary by selecting Recent Workspaces from the Visual C++ File menu and clicking Beeper on the submenu.
2. Select Settings from the Project menu.
3. In the Debug tab of the Project Settings dialog box, click the small arrow button adjacent to the box labeled Executable For Debug Session.
4. Select Browse on the shortcut menu and navigate to the Client\Debug folder. Double-click the entry for the Client.exe file. This action tells the debugger to start the Client program when you begin debugging the Beeper component.
5. Click OK to close the Project Settings dialog box.
6. Open the BeepCtl.cpp file in the text editor.
7. Right-click the first line of the *Beep* function and select Insert/Remove Breakpoint to set a breakpoint. A red dot appears in the selection margin to the left of the line.
8. Press F5 to start the debugger. The debugger automatically launches the Client application, which calls the *Beep* method in the Beeper component.
9. When execution reaches the breakpoint, repeatedly click the Step Over button on the Debug toolbar to single step through the *Beep* function.
10. When the yellow instruction pointer reaches the function's closing bracket, click the Step Over button again to step out of *Beep* and into the Client source code. Although the Beeper project is still open, Visual C++ can locate the correct source file belonging to another project.
11. When you press F5 to continue execution, both the Client application and the debugger terminate, returning control to the Visual C++ environment.

Exercise 2: Debugging a Remote Object

In the preceding exercise, the computer speaker proved incontestably on which computer the Beeper component executed. In this exercise, you will install Beeper on another network node and register it so that it runs remotely rather than in the address space of Client.exe.

This exercise requires a separate installation of Visual C++ on each of two networked computers. To make discussions easier to follow, assume that the computers have the names LocalSys and ServerSys. The LocalSys node is your normal development computer on which the Client application is already installed. This is the computer used in Exercise 1. ServerSys is the remote computer on which both the Beeper project and a separate copy of Visual C++ must now be installed. If you have not already done so, and assuming your license allows multiple copies, install Visual C++ on the ServerSys computer.

Note You will encounter fewer problems if you log on to LocalSys and ServerSys under the same user name and have administrator privileges on both computers.

It is not necessary to register the second copy of Beeper on ServerSys because the following steps recompile the project. The new installation of Beeper requires the same registry information as on LocalSys, but with added AppID information to identify a surrogate host program. (See the section, "Installing and Registering a Remote Component," for a description of the AppID registry data.) The following steps explain how to add the new registry information to ServerSys, specifying the default DllHost program as Beeper's surrogate.

► **To install the Beeper project on the remote ServerSys computer**

1. Make a new Beeper folder on ServerSys and copy the Beeper project files to it. It is not necessary to copy the contents of the Debug folder.
2. Start Visual C++ on ServerSys and open the Beeper project.
3. Set the build context to Win32 Debug, and then build the Beeper project.
4. After the project compiles and links correctly, add registry information to specify the DllHost surrogate. The easiest way to do this is by using the RegEdit registry editor program. Run the RegEdit program and choose the Import Registry File command from the Registry menu, as shown in Figure 11.14 on the next page. Browse for the Beeper project folder and double-click the Surrogat.reg file. This file contains the required AppID values in a form that the RegEdit can automatically copy to your registry.

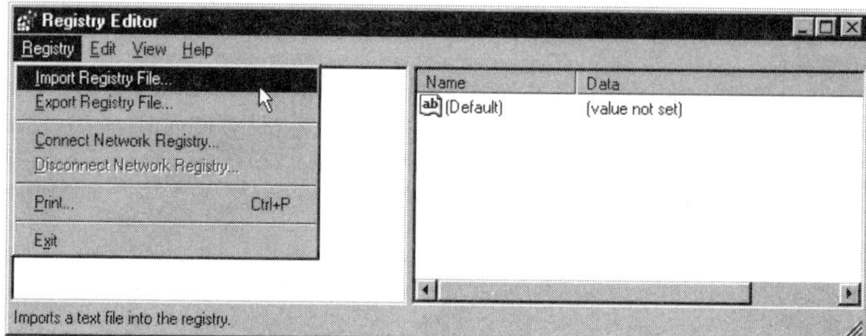

Figure 11.14 Selecting the Import Registry File command in the RegEdit utility

5. RegEdit displays a message saying that the information in Surrogat.reg has been successfully entered into the registry. Close the message, and then close RegEdit.

Now that the Beeper component is registered on ServerSys, it might be necessary to set access and launch permissions so that it can be accessed from another computer. Unless you have Administrator privileges on both LocalSys and ServerSys, follow these steps.

► **To set access and launch permissions**

1. Run the DcomCnfg utility (usually located in the Winnt\System32 or Windows\System folder), and select BeepCtl in the list of registered components. Figure 11.15 shows BeepCtl selected in DcomCnfg's Applications tab.

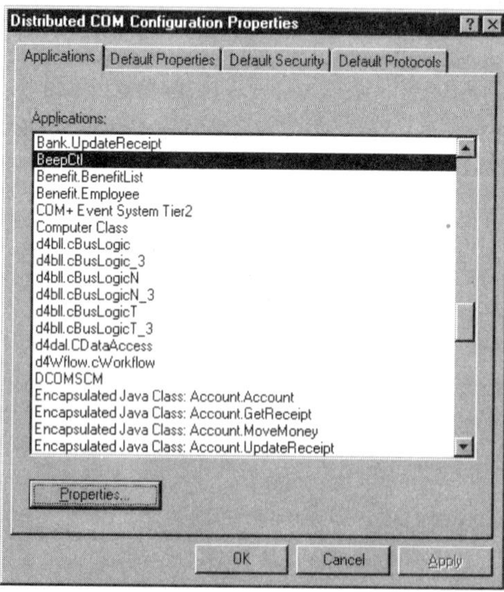

Figure 11.15 Selecting the BeepCtl object in the DcomCnfg utility

2. With BeepCtl selected, click the Properties button to invoke the BeepCtl Properties dialog box.
3. Display the Security tab.
4. Select the radio button labeled Use Custom Access Permissions, and then click the adjacent Edit button.
5. In the Registry Value Permissions dialog box, click the Add button. The Add Users And Groups dialog box appears, as shown in Figure 11.16.

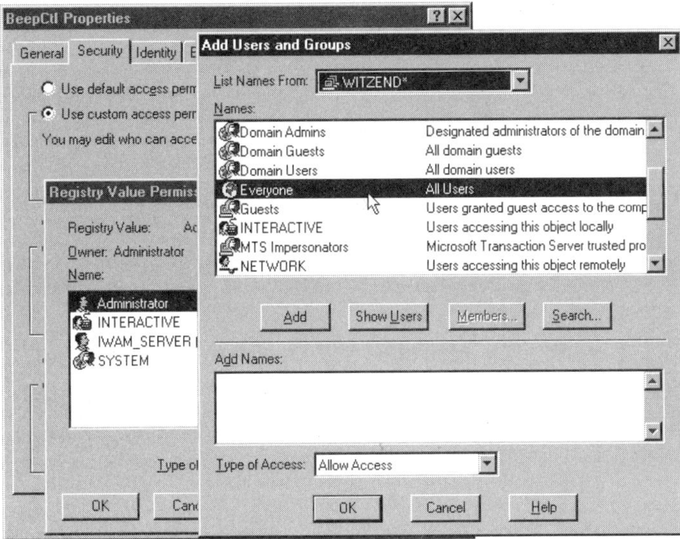

Figure 11.16 Setting user access permission in the Add Users And Groups dialog box

6. Select the appropriate user name in the list, click Add to add the name to the Add Names list, and then click OK.
7. Click OK to close the Registry Value Permissions dialog box.
8. Return to the BeepCtl Properties dialog box and select the Use Custom Launch Permissions radio button. Click the adjacent Edit button. Following the same steps as just outlined for access permissions, select your user name to establish launch permission.
9. Return a third time to the BeepCtl Properties dialog box and select the Use Custom Configuration Permissions radio button. Click the adjacent Edit button and grant your user name Full Control permission.
10. Click OK to close the BeepCtl Properties dialog box, and then click OK to exit the DcomCnfg program.

You are now ready to debug the Beeper component as it runs on the ServerSys computer.

► **To debug the remote Beeper component**

1. Return to the LocalSys computer and open the Client project in Visual C++.
2. Open the Client.cpp file in the text editor and edit the line shown as follows:

   ```
   COSERVERINFO   si  = { 0, L"server", 0, 0 };
   ```

   The *si* structure must contain the true name of the ServerSys computer. Change the placeholder "server" to ServerSys's true name.
3. The third parameter of the call to *CoCreateInstanceEx* indicates on which computer the BeepCtl object should be loaded. The preceding exercise used a value of CLSCTX_INPROC_SERVER for the parameter, causing the operating system to load BeepCtl on the LocalSys computer. You must change the parameter to CLSCTX_REMOTE_SERVER, which informs DCOM that BeepCtl should be instantiated on the remote computer named in the COSERVERINFO structure of step 2. The revision should look like this:

   ```
   hr = CoCreateInstanceEx(CLSID_BeepCtl, 0,
           CLSCTX_REMOTE_SERVER, &si, 1, &mqi);
   ```

4. Press F7 to rebuild a debug version of the Client project.
5. In the Client.cpp file, set a breakpoint at the line as follows:

   ```
   pUnk = mqi.pItf;
   ```

   This breakpoint causes execution to break after Beeper is correctly instantiated on ServerSys but before the client calls the *Beep* method to sound the speaker.
6. Press F5 to start the Client application in the debugger. Execution should stop at the breakpoint. If the Client application runs without stopping at the breakpoint, the BeepCtl object was not successfully instantiated.
7. Move to ServerSys and open Visual C++. Close any open projects by selecting the Close Workspace command from the File menu.
8. Invoke the Attach To Process command by selecting the Build menu, pointing to Start Debug and selecting Attach To Process, as shown earlier in Figure 11.9. In the Attach To Process dialog box select the DllHost process in the list. Figure 11.17 shows DllHost selected in the Attach To Process dialog box.

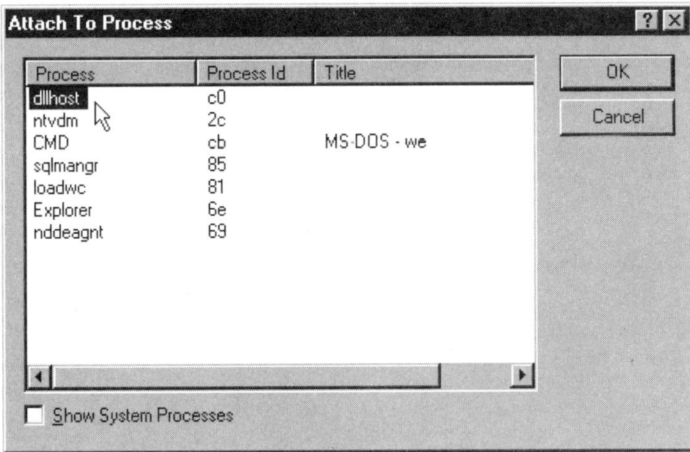

Figure 11.17 Attaching the debugger to the DllHost Surrogate program

9. Click OK to attach the debugger to DllHost.
10. Still working in the Visual C++ session on ServerSys, select Open from the File menu. In the Open dialog box, locate and open the BeepCtl.cpp file. In the BeepCtl.cpp file place a breakpoint at the first line of the *Beep* method. It's important to open the file located on ServerSys, not the copy located on LocalSys.
11. Return to the LocalSys computer and press F5 to resume execution of Client.exe. When Client.exe calls the *Beep* method, DCOM marshals the call across the network to the DllHost process running on ServerSys. The marshalling proxy calls the *Beep* method, triggering the breakpoint set in the preceding step. You can now single-step through the code. Notice that when *Beep* calls *MessageBeep*, the sound is heard on ServerSys, not LocalSys, proving that the BeepCtl object is indeed executing on the remote computer.
12. When you single-step to the end of *Beep*, press F5 to resume execution. Control returns back to the Client application, which then releases the BeepCtl object before exiting. The debugger sessions on both LocalSys and ServerSys terminate automatically when the program ends.
13. Click the Close Workspace command to close the workspace in Visual C++ running on ServerSys.

Exercise 3: Debugging an MTS Object

This exercise shows how to debug a remote object as it runs under MTS. The procedure is similar to the steps taken in Exercise 2 with two exceptions:

- The object executes inside the MTS host environment instead of DllHost.
- The object must be installed on the remote system using MTS Explorer.

The following steps again make use of the Client application and the Beeper component, and discussions continue to refer to the two computers involved as LocalSys and ServerSys. You must have completed the preceding exercise before continuing because both the Beeper project and Visual C++ must be installed on ServerSys.

The first step is to create an MTS *package*, which is a collection of one or more related objects that run in the same MTS process. In this case, the package contains only one object, BeepCtl. A package forms a unit of deployment for MTS components, a subject discussed in more detail in Chapters 7 and 8.

► **To add the Beeper component to an MTS package**

1. On ScrverSys computer, start MTS Explorer as described in the section, "Using MTS Explorer to Observe Transactions," in Chapter 10.
2. Expand the tree in MTS Explorer's left pane and right-click the Packages Installed entry listed under the host computer.
3. Select New, and click Package, as illustrated in Figure 11.18.

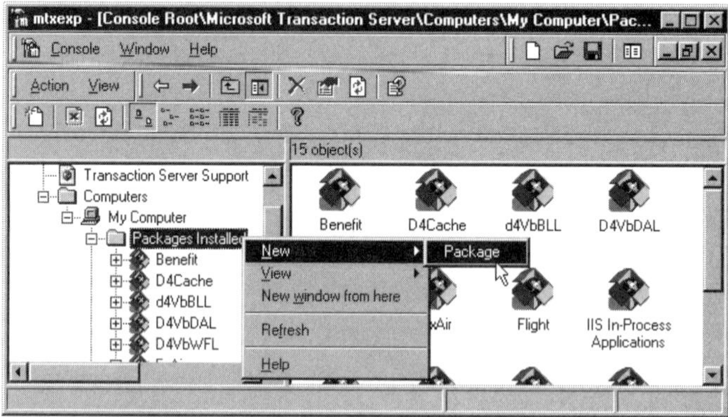

Figure 11.18 Creating a new package in MTS Explorer

4. When the Package Wizard appears, click the large button labeled Create An Empty Package.
5. Type Beeper as the name of the new package and click the Next button.

6. At the wizard's next step, titled Set Package Identity, accept the default account setting of Interactive User. Click the Finish button to close the wizard.
7. In MTS Explorer, click the plus icon to the left of the new Beeper package to expand the entry, and then right-click the Components folder directly beneath the Beeper entry.
8. Select New and click Component, as shown in Figure 11.19.

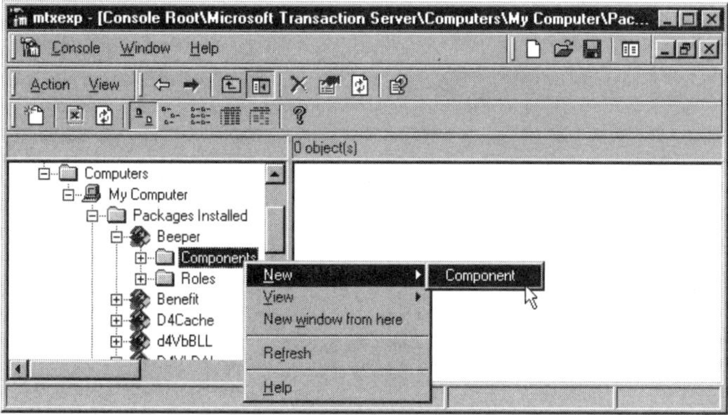

Figure 11.19 Adding a component to an MTS package

9. When the Component Wizard appears, click the button labeled Import Component(s) That Are Already Registered.
10. The wizard momentarily pauses while it reads data from the registry, and then displays a list of programmatic identifiers for all registered COM components. Scroll down the list and select the identifier for Beeper, which is Beeper.BeepCtl.1.
11. Click the Finish button to close the wizard. The component appears in MTS Explorer's object view.

The package has been successfully created, but do not close MTS Explorer yet. Because the utility monitors objects that are active inside MTS, it will provide additional evidence that the BeepCtl object is operating correctly on the ServerSys computer.

▶ **To debug the Beeper component executing inside MTS**

1. Return to the Client Visual C++ project on LocalSys computer. The breakpoint set in Exercise 2 should still be in place at the following line:

```
pUnk = mqi.pItf;
```

2. Press F5 to launch the debugger and the Client application.

3. When the breakpoint interrupts execution, return to the ServerSys computer. Notice that the icon for Beeper is now rotating in MTS Explorer, indicating that the object has been successfully instantiated and is running inside MTS.
4. Switch to Visual C++ on ServerSys and attach the debugger to the Mtx process. Mtx.exe is the surrogate host in which all MTS objects execute.
5. Select Recent Files in the Visual C++ File menu and open the BeepCtl.cpp file as in Exercise 2.
6. Set a breakpoint at the first line of the *Beep* method.
7. Return to the debugger session on LocalSys and then press F5 to resume execution.
8. As before, DCOM marshals execution flow to ServerSys, where it triggers the breakpoint in *Beep*.
9. Press F5 to continue on ServerSys, after which the Client application terminates. The debugger session on ServerSys remains running, however, because Mtx is still active. Click the Stop Debugging command on the Debug menu to close the debugger.

Review

The following questions are intended to reinforce key information presented in this chapter. If you are unable to answer a question, review the appropriate lesson and then try answering the question again. Answers to the questions can be found in Appendix B, "Review Questions and Answers," at the back of this book.

1. How does a debug version of a program differ from its release build?

2. Describe the ASSERT, VERIFY, and DEBUG_NEW macros in MFC.

3. How does a debugger cause a running program to interrupt itself?

4. What utility does Visual C++ provide for running and testing ActiveX controls?

5. What is a dependency?

6. What information is contained in the four lists that Spy++ can display?

7. What is regression testing?

8. What are some of the differences between debugging a local component that runs on the same computer as its client, and a remote component that runs on another computer?

CHAPTER 12

Deploying Distributed Applications

Lesson 1: Setup Programs 654

Lesson 2: Using InstallShield 668

Lesson 3: Packaging COM Components 674

Lesson 4: Installing COM Components 682

Lesson 5: Deployment Methods 686

Lesson 6: Zero Administration for Windows 690

Lab 12: Packaging and Deploying a Distributed Application 694

Review 710

About This Chapter

After your application has been debugged and has passed every test, one further task remains: *deployment*. Deployment combines *distribution*, getting an application into the hands of the users; and *configuration*, correctly updating registry settings on a user's computer so that the application can run. Deployment is usually not as simple a task as you might first imagine, especially for distributed applications that must be deployed to several—or several hundred—networked computers.

In this chapter, you will learn some of the ways that a Windows application created with Microsoft Visual C++ can be efficiently deployed. Lesson 1 presents an overview of deployment methods, focusing on how to write an installation program that copies required files to the user's hard disk. Lesson 2 discusses InstallShield, a tool that helps automate the creation of installation programs for Visual C++ projects.

Lessons 3 and 4 describe how to prepare COM components so that they are correctly recognized on a user's computer by Windows services such as MTS and Microsoft SQL Server. Lesson 5 describes three specific methods for deploying an application, ranging from standard diskettes to the Web. Lesson 6 examines the Microsoft Zero Administration for Windows (ZAW) initiative and discusses how it will affect program installation in the future.

Before You Begin

To complete the lessons in this chapter, you must have set up InstallShield, which is part of the Visual C++ 6 Professional Edition or Enterprise Edition installation. Neither the Learning Edition of Visual C++ 5 nor the Standard Edition of Visual C++ 6 includes InstallShield. (InstallShield is also available separately.) If you don't have InstallShield you can still benefit from the information in this chapter, but you will not be able to complete the exercises in Lesson 2 or Lab 12.

Lesson 1: Setup Programs

Deployment is divided into two stages. In the first stage, all necessary files are transferred to the user's hard disk. The second stage can be much more complicated, as it involves configuring the host system so that it recognizes and correctly runs the installed application. Proper deployment includes software, known as a *setup program* or *installation program*, that automates installation as much as possible. Windows applications today generally include a setup program to help the user get an application up and running.

After this lesson, you will be able to:

- Describe how an application can be installed and uninstalled on a user's system
- List the services provided by a typical setup program
- Describe the registry entries created by a setup program
- Create cabinet (.cab) files and registry (.reg) files
- Understand how a setup program adds a command to the taskbar's Programs menu to launch a new application

Estimated lesson time: 20 minutes

Writing a Setup Program

An installation program should be named Setup for two reasons:

- To conform with convention
- To be recognizable to the Add/Remove Programs applet in Control Panel

Because it has become a standard, the Setup name minimizes the chance of causing confusion among users. Nearly every Windows user has learned what a program named Setup is for, even though setup programs can differ in individual style and methods. This lesson describes installation programs in a generic sense. For purposes of discussion, this lesson assumes that the installation program is named Setup.

If your application is distributed on several disks or CD-ROMs, the setup program should be located in the root directory on the first disk or CD-ROM of the series. This ensures that the Add/Remove Programs applet correctly locates the program. Typically, the setup program provides a number of services for the user:

- Prompts for selected program options.
- Creates folders on the user's hard disk as required.
- Copies files from the distribution media to the hard disk.
- Adds registry information for shared DLLs.
- Registers an application's ActiveX controls and other COM components.
- Adds information to the system registry specifying the command needed to uninstall the application. This allows the Add/Remove Programs applet to identify the application's uninstall program.
- Records in the system registry the extension used for the application's document files. This allows users to launch the application from Windows Explorer by double-clicking a document in a file list.
- Adds an entry to the system's Programs menu.
- Executes "run-once code." This minimizes installation size if the setup program is not copied to the hard disk.

The user simply has to select an installation option and insert disks or CD-ROMs into the drive as prompted. Microsoft recommends that setup programs include the following four installation options:

- **Compact** For systems with limited disk space, such as laptops
- **Custom** To give the user control over what is installed
- **Typical** To provide a common default suitable for most users
- **Silent** For unattended installation

The silent installation option is provided for systems managers who want to install an application across a large network. While running in silent mode, the setup program should not query for input or display error messages, and must assume intelligent default settings for all cases.

Guidelines for Writing a Setup Program

Keep the following points in mind when you plan a setup program for your application's deployment. An intelligent setup program should:

- Store private initialization (.ini) files in the application directory if the application is running locally, or in the directory returned by the *GetWindowsDirectory* API function if the application is shared.
- Avoid inappropriately copying files to the Windows, WinNT, System, or System32 directories. If an application package includes font files, for example, the files should be placed in the system Fonts folder.
- Check that a file does not already exist on the hard disk before copying it. If it finds a conflict, the setup program should decide which file is most recent and avoid overwriting a newer file.
- Supply defaults. In particular, the setup program should provide a common response to every option so the user need only press the Enter key at each prompt.
- Avoid asking the user to insert a disk more than once.
- Inform the user about required disk space.
- Display a progress indicator.
- Use the Temp directory for storing intermediate files. However, if the setup program must restart Windows before reading intermediate files, it should confirm that the Temp directory resides on a hard disk and not on a RAM disk. This ensures that the files will still exist after rebooting.
- Give the user a chance to cancel before finishing. The setup program should keep a log of files that have been copied and settings that have been registered so that it can clean up canceled installations.

A user can install your application either by running the setup program directly or by running the Add/Remove Programs applet in Control Panel. Add/Remove Programs automatically checks the floppy or CD-ROM drive for an installation program, searching for the Setup.exe filename. If the file is found and the user confirms that they want to proceed with the installation, Add/Remove Programs starts the setup program and exits. The setup program is responsible for guiding the user through the rest of the installation process.

Uninstall Program

An installed product should be able to safely and as completely as possible remove all traces of itself. This operation, known as *de-installing* or *uninstalling*, is typically carried out by a separate program with a descriptive name such as Uninstall or Uninst. Alternatively, the setup program itself can be written to act as the uninstaller. You have much more flexibility when choosing a name for your uninstall program, because during installation the setup program registers the location and filename of the uninstall program. This assures that Add/Remove Programs locates the correct uninstaller executable regardless of its name.

Uninstalling is an important feature for users and is one of the prerequisites for an application marked with the Windows compliance logo. Uninstalling includes deleting application files (but not documents) and removing entries added to the system registry.

Because distributed applications share resources and make modifications throughout a network, deleting an application is rarely a matter of deleting files in a single subdirectory. Users must be able to uninstall cleanly and reinstall to correct problems, change configurations, or upgrade applications. The uninstall feature also allows users to free disk space and to abide by licensing agreements when deleting an application from one computer before installing it on others.

Uninstalling a Windows application must be done carefully. A potential problem arises when deleting a program's dependency modules such as dynamic link libraries, ActiveX controls, and other COM servers. The uninstall operation must not delete modules on which other applications depend. For more information on dependencies, see Lesson 4 of Chapter 11.

An uninstall program cannot directly determine whether a module serves other programs, but it can infer whether a module is shared by consulting a usage count stored in a common area of the registry. Usage counts are described in the next section.

Adding and Removing Registry Information

An installation program adds to the registry all necessary information about your application. You should write user preference data to the registry's HKEY_CURRENT_USER\SOFTWARE folder. This is information that application vendors used to write to the Win.ini file. For information specific to the application, add entries to the HKEY_LOCAL_MACHINE\SOFTWARE registry key, using this format:

```
HKEY_LOCAL_MACHINE\SOFTWARE\CompanyName\ProductName\
Version
```

Substitute names for the italicized placeholders that are appropriate for your application.

PATH Environment Variable

Each running application has its own PATH environment setting containing a list of paths to various folders. The list specifies paths that the operating system should search when looking for executable modules that the application requires. By default, Windows searches certain system folders in an effort to locate files required for loading an application. Because most applications are installed to unique directories, the path to the application's components must be specified in an application-specific PATH setting.

For example, consider an application in the MyApp folder that uses a dynamic link library located in the MyDLL folder. Assuming normal linkage—that is, assuming the application does not call the *LoadLibrary* API function to load the DLL—the application cannot run unless MyDLL appears in the PATH list. This is because the operating system searches for DLL files only in prescribed folders, including those specified in the PATH variable. If a DLL is not located, the system refuses to run the application. The application's installation program must therefore specify a PATH setting that includes the MyDLL folder where the required DLL file resides.

To register a PATH environment variable, the setup program should write the desired value in the HKEY_LOCAL_MACHINE root under the key SOFTWARE\Microsoft\Windows\CurrentVersion\App Paths. This is the same string contained in the REGSTR_PATH_APPPATHS text macro defined in the Regstr.h file. Notice that the last nested key, App Paths, is two words.

The setup program should create a new registry key having the same name as the application's executable file, and then insert a Path value containing the desired path. Here's an example of how the Path registry value might look for the NewApp program located in the MyApp folder of the preceding example:

```
HKEY_LOCAL_MACHINE\SOFTWARE\Microsoft\Windows\
CurrentVersion\App Paths\NewApp.exe
Default=D:\MyPrograms\MyApp\NewApp.exe
Path=D:\MyPrograms\MyDLL;D:\MyPrograms\MyApp\Utilities
```

The Default value specifies the full path to the executable file. The operating system refers to this value when the user types the application name into the Run dialog box without specifying a full path to the executable file. Windows locates the requested executable by searching the App Paths key, then reads the full path from the Default value.

The Path value contains NewApp's PATH environment, which includes a reference to the MyDLL folder. When the operating system loads NewApp, it searches the specified locations for the dynamic link library that NewApp needs.

By including the MyDLL folder in the application's PATH, the setup program ensures that the system can always locate the required DLL file when running NewApp.

Usage Counts for Shared Modules

For each shared module that it installs, the setup program should consult the registry and increment the module's usage count. When the application is removed, the uninstall program must decrement the usage count. If the count drops to zero, the uninstaller can delete the module. If every setup program followed this procedure, dependency modules could be safely removed. Unfortunately, not every developer creating installation programs conforms to this convention; thus, it is customary to query users for permission before removing a file for which the reference count has reached zero. At worst, the usage count will be artificially high, in which case an unused file will remain on the user's system.

Usage counts for shared modules are stored in the HKEY_LOCAL_MACHINE\SOFTWARE\Microsoft\Windows\CurrentVersion\SharedDLLs key. Figure 12.1 shows an example using the RegEdit utility, in which the usage count is currently 2 for an ActiveX control named MSInet.ocx.

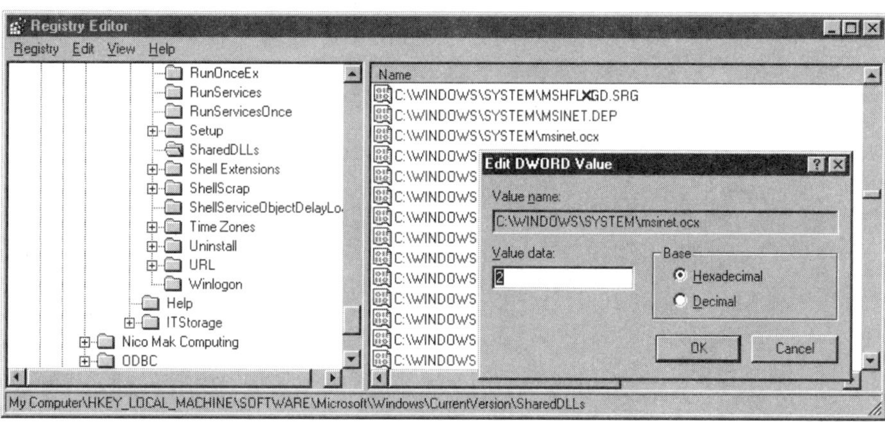

Figure 12.1 Viewing a control's usage count in the RegEdit utility

Cabinet Files

A *cabinet file* contains other files in compressed form, resulting in a single file that serves as a file library. Cabinet files, recognizable by their .cab extensions, are often used when deploying large applications because they reduce the number of disks or CD-ROMs required. The application's setup program reads the

.cab files, decompresses their contents into the original files, and writes the original files to the user's hard disk.

A .cab file is similar to a .zip file in that it serves as a compressed archive for a group of files. A .cab file can have a digital signature, which identifies the creator of the file and ensures that the file has not been maliciously or accidentally altered. Digital signatures are described in more detail in Lesson 5.

Creating a .cab file requires a program such as the MakeCab or CabArc (Cabinet Archiver) utilities. Both programs are part of the Cabinet SDK, available as a free download from msdn.microsoft.com/workshop/management/cab/cabdl.asp. MakeCab creates compressed disk images containing a product's files, and is designed to work with setup programs. CabArc is a console-based program that can both read and write .cab files. To run CabArc, type a list of options, the name of the .cab file, and a list of files to compress or decompress. For example, the line

```
cabarc n images.cab \myapp\images\*.jpg
\myapp\images\*.gif
```

creates a file named Images.cab, which contains in compressed form all the JPG and GIF graphics files in the MyApp\Images folder. The *n* option tells CabArc to create a new file. The Cabinet SDK contains examples and documentation for the CabArc and MakeCab programs.

Registry Files

Setup programs sometimes use registry files to write entries into the system registry. Recognizable by its .reg extension, a registry file serves as a script that lists keys, values, and locations to be added to the registry. You have already encountered a registry file in this book—Lab 11 made use of a file named Surrogat.reg to add registry data required by the Beeper component.

Because a registry file is in ASCII format, it can be viewed and edited in a text editor. For example, here is what a registry file that specifies the program's PATH environment looks like for the NewApp program mentioned earlier:

```
REGEDIT4
[HKEY_LOCAL_MACHINE\SOFTWARE\Microsoft\Windows\
CurrentVersion\App Paths\NewApp.exe]
@="D:\\MyPrograms\\MyApp\\NewApp.exe"
"Path"="D:\\MyPrograms\\MyDLL;D:\\MyPrograms\\MyApp\\
Utilities"
```

Although long lines in the script are broken here to fit on the printed page, each entry must occupy a single unbroken line. There is no continuation character for registry scripts.

The example given assumes that the NewApp program is located in the MyPrograms\MyApp subdirectory, and demonstrates a potential problem with registry files—the setup program must ensure that any paths specified in the script correspond to the location where the user ultimately decides to install the application. This means that the setup program must be prepared to alter a .reg file before using it.

The RegEdit utility can both read and write registry files. A setup program can use RegEdit to read (or *import*) the script into the user's system registry, supplying a registry file in the command line like this:

```
regedit newapp.reg
```

This command copies the contents of the NewApp.reg file to the system registry. You can use the */e* switch to cause RegEdit to write (or *export*) a section of the registry to a specified file. For example, here's how to create a file named IEpath.reg, which contains a copy of the path information for Microsoft Internet Explorer:

```
regedit /e IEpath.reg
"HKEY_LOCAL_MACHINE\SOFTWARE\Microsoft\Windows\
CurrentVersion\App Paths\IEXPLORE.exe"
```

Again, the command is actually a single line, although it is broken into three lines in the previous code. Including the registry key information in double quotation marks is necessary only when the key contains a space, as in "App Paths." Otherwise, the quotation marks are not required.

As demonstrated in Lab 11, the RegEdit utility provides a simple Windows user interface, so you do not have to run it from the command line. Lab 11 used the utility's Import command to read a registry file. The following steps demonstrate how to use the corresponding Export command to write data from the registry to a file.

► To create the IEpath.reg file

1. Start the RegEdit utility by clicking the Start button, selecting Run, and typing *regedit.*
2. Beginning with the HKEY_LOCAL_MACHINE root, expand the tree view and select the IExplore.exe key shown in Figure 12.2. The full path to the IExplore.exe key is shown at the bottom of the RegEdit window in the figure.

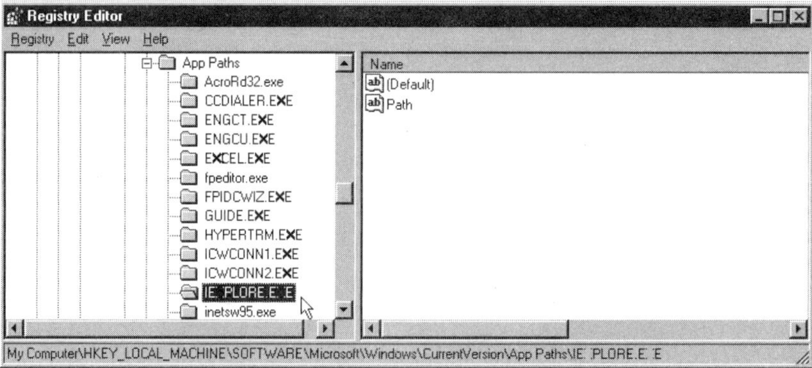

Figure 12.2 Selecting Internet Explorer's PATH entry in the system registry

3. Click the Export Registry File command in the Registry menu.
4. Select the desired folder and type *IEpath* in the File Name text box.
5. Click the Save button, then exit RegEdit.

Start a text editor such as Notepad and open the new IEpath.reg file. The script shows that like many programs, Internet Explorer includes its own application folder as part of its PATH environment.

A registry file is most useful when a large amount of registry data is being manipulated or when the data is transitory and the setup program must load and then unload the information again. A setup program can also use the RegEdit utility to create a backup copy of selected registry information. The uninstall program can then restore the original settings if the user chooses to delete the application.

Adding a Command to the Programs Menu

A setup program often adds a command to the taskbar's Programs menu, thus providing a convenient way for the user to launch the installed application. Updating the Programs menu is only one of many issues a typical setup program must address. This section is intended to give you a brief hands-on feel for the obstacles that a typical setup program faces when installing an application.

To add a command to the Programs menu, the setup program completes four steps:

1. Queries the Windows shell for a pointer to an IShellLink object. The Windows shell is responsible for managing the system desktop and taskbar.
2. Determines the location of the Startmenu\Programs folder, which is a special system folder that holds shortcut files listed on the Programs menu.

3. Creates a shortcut file for the application being installed.
4. Obtains a pointer to an IPersistFile object and calls *IPersistFile::Save* to save the shortcut.

The SetPad example program demonstrates these four steps. SetPad is a simple console-based program that adds to the Programs menu an entry for the WordPad utility, as shown in Figure 12.3.

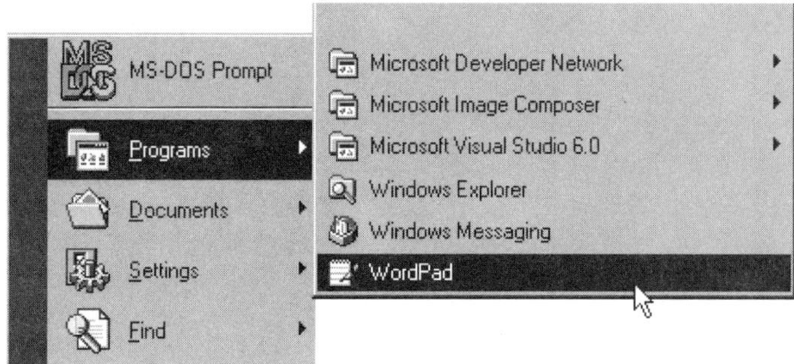

Figure 12.3 Command added to the Programs menu to launch the WordPad utility

Updating the Programs menu is only a small part of a typical setup program's capabilities, yet as the following example shows, even this simple task involves complex code.

```
SetPad.cpp
///////////////////////////////////////////////////////////////////
//
// SetPad.cpp  Example console-based setup program for
WordPad
//
///////////////////////////////////////////////////////////////////

#include <windows.h>
#include <shlobj.h>

int main()
{
    HRESULT     hr;
    IShellLink*     psl;
    IPersistFile*  ppf;
    LPITEMIDLIST   pidl;
    TCHAR          szPath[MAX_PATH];
    WCHAR          wszPath[MAX_PATH];

    hr = CoInitialize(NULL);
    if (SUCCEEDED(hr))
```

```
{
    // Get an IShellLink pointer
    hr = CoCreateInstance( CLSID_ShellLink, NULL,
        CLSCTX_INPROC_SERVER, IID_IShellLink,
        (PVOID*) &psl);

    if (SUCCEEDED(hr))
    {
        // Point the shortcut to WordPad.exe.
        For simplicity, code assumes WordPad is
        in the Program Files folder.
        psl->SetPath("c:\\Program
        Files\\Accessories"\
            "\\WordPad.exe");

        // Get path to system Startmenu\Programs
        folder
        hr = SHGetSpecialFolderLocation(NULL,
        CSIDL_PROGRAMS,
            &pidl);
        if (SUCCEEDED(hr))
        {
            hr = SHGetPathFromIDList(pidl,
            szPath);
            if (SUCCEEDED(hr))
            {
                // Make
                "...\startmenu\programs
                \WordPad.LNK"
                lstrcat(szPath,
                "\\WordPad.lnk");

                // Convert to WCHAR
                MultiByteToWideChar(CP_ACP,
                0, szPath, -1,
                    wszPath, MAX_PATH);

                // Get IPersistFile ptr and
                save the shortcut
                hr = psl-
                >QueryInterface
                (IID_IPersistFile,
                    (PVOID*) &ppf);
                if (SUCCEEDED(hr))
                {
                    // Call
                    IPersistFile::Save
                    to save link
                    ppf->Save(wszPath,
                    TRUE );
```

```
                ppf->Release();
            }
        }

        // SHGetSpecialFolderLocation
        allocates memory for the item ID
        list by using the calling process's
        task allocator. You are responsible
        for freeing the allocation using
        the task allocator's IMalloc.

        LPMALLOC pMalloc;
        hr = SHGetMalloc(&pMalloc);
        if (SUCCEEDED(hr))
        {
            pMalloc->Free(pidl);
            // Free item ID list
            pMalloc->Release();
            // Free task allocator
        }
    }
    psl->Release();
  }
  CoUninitialize();
 }
 return 0;
}
```

This example also illustrates one of the steps that will be discussed in Lesson 2. Lesson 2 uses a setup program created by InstallShield to add to the Programs menu a command for the NotePad utility. The demonstration in this section shows precisely what the setup program is doing behind the scenes.

▶ To create and run the SetPad program

1. If you have not already done so, run the Setup program on the CD-ROM to copy the sample projects to your hard disk. Alternatively, you can simply copy the project files from Labs\Ch12\SetPad on the CD-ROM to a folder on your hard disk.
2. In Visual C++, click Open Workspace on the File menu and browse for the SetPad project.
3. Double-click the entry for SetPad.dsw.
4. For the sake of simplicity, SetPad assumes that the WordPad.exe file is in the C:\Program Files\Accessories folder. If this is not the case for your system, edit the following line in SetPad.cpp to specify the path:

```
psl->SetPath("c:\\Program Files\\Accessories\\WordPad.exe");
```

5. Set the active configuration on the Build toolbar to Win32 Release.

6. Press the F7 key to build the SetPad.exe program.
7. Press Ctrl+F5 to run the SetPad program.
8. When SetPad finishes, click the Start button on the taskbar and expose the Programs menu. The menu should have a new entry for the WordPad program, similar to that shown in Figure 12.3.

► **To delete the WordPad command from the Programs menu**

1. Click the Start button, select Settings, and choose Taskbar.
2. Expose the Start Menu Programs tab in the Taskbar Properties dialog box.
3. Click the Remove button.
4. Double-click the new WordPad entry in the list. This causes Windows to delete the shortcut file that the SetPad program created.

Lesson Summary

This lesson presented a general overview of the installation process in which a program, commonly named Setup, configures a user's computer to run an application. The installation program typically:

- Queries the user for preferences
- Decompresses stored files and copies them to the user's system
- Adds information to the user's registry that the application requires when executing
- Writes a log detailing everything it has done so that the application can be cleanly uninstalled
- Copies an uninstaller program to the user's hard disk
- Records the uninstaller's location in the registry, enabling the Add/Remove Programs applet to find the uninstaller and execute it if the user decides to remove the installed application

A setup program should at a minimum provide installation options labeled Compact, Custom, Typical, and Silent. Silent installation allows administrators to run the setup program unattended when installing the application across a network. Professional-quality setup programs seek to make the installation process as easy for the user as possible. To this end, a setup program should:

- Place fonts, help text, and other system files in appropriate folders rather than in the already-crowded Windows and System folders
- Scan file dates to avoid overwriting newer files with older versions
- Organize installation efficiently so that the user handles each disk or CD-ROM only once

- Keep the user informed by displaying a progress indicator and timely messages
- Allow the user to cancel installation before finishing

If the application requires a custom PATH environment variable, the setup program should record the desired value in the registry. This specifies the PATH setting that Windows makes current when the application runs. A setup program should also consult the registry when installing shared modules such as dynamic link libraries and COM components, incrementing usage counts for the modules. During program removal, the uninstaller program should decrement the counts and offer to delete any file for which the usage count drops to zero.

This lesson included an introduction to cabinet and registry files. Cabinet files serve as archives that contain other files in compressed form. Microsoft makes available utilities such as MakeCab and CabArc for creating and using cabinet files. Registry files are scripts that can be inserted into the system registry using the RegEdit utility.

To illustrate some of the complex issues a typical setup program must address, a practice session at the end of the lesson showed the correct technique for adding a command to the taskbar's Programs menu. Updating the Programs menu is only a small part of a setup program's many capabilities.

Lesson 2: Using InstallShield

As a shortcut for developing setup and uninstall programs, the Professional and Enterprise Editions of Visual C++ include a scaled-down version of Stirling Software's InstallShield. This lesson introduces the InstallShield toolkit, which allows you to write a script that specifies the steps you want performed during installation. InstallShield then builds a setup program that installs your product on a user's computer.

With InstallShield, you don't have to write a separate script for uninstallation. InstallShield creates an uninstall program named Uninst that reads a log file created during the setup process. The log file allows Uninst to reverse the steps performed during setup.

InstallShield creates a setup program for your project that looks and acts much like the Setup.exe program you used to install Visual C++. Microsoft creates installation programs for many of its own products using InstallShield.

An exhaustive description of InstallShield is well beyond the scope of this lesson, which is intended only as an introduction to the product. As described in Lesson 1, setup programs today must be capable of handling a wide variety of file types, accommodating different operating systems, and dealing with a bewildering number of potential problems. Setup programs must work not only with traditional distribution media such as disks and CD-ROMs, but also over networks and the Internet. InstallShield is not difficult to use, but it offers a wide array of options designed to address many installation issues. Further, complete control over the product requires learning its script language, named InstallScript. As with most programs, practice is the only true teacher.

InstallShield treats your setup program as a *project*, the same term applied to normal Visual C++ projects. To avoid confusion, this lesson employs the phrases *setup project* or *installation project* when referring to work done inside InstallShield, and *application project* when referring to the Visual C++ program files that the setup program deploys in their compressed state.

Note The Learning and Standard Editions of Visual C++ do not include the InstallShield tool.

After this lesson, you will be able to:

- Set up InstallShield to run as a Visual C++ tool
- Step through the InstallShield tutorial
- Create a simple setup program using InstallShield

Estimated lesson time: 15 minutes

Installing InstallShield

If you selected the InstallShield option when installing Visual C++, the environment's Tools menu already contains a command for starting the InstallShield Wizard. If the command does not appear on the Visual C++ Tools menu and you own the Professional Edition or the Enterprise Edition of Visual C++ 6, install InstallShield now.

► **To install InstallShield**

1. Place the Visual C++ CD-ROM #1 in your CD-ROM drive.
2. Start the Add/Remove Programs applet in Control Panel.
3. Browse for the IShield folder on the CD and double-click Setup.

The Setup program installs InstallShield, places a command on the taskbar's Programs menu, and adds the InstallShield Wizard command to the Visual C++ Tools menu.

Running the InstallShield Tutorial

The InstallShield program provides a good tutorial that introduces you to the product and demonstrates how to develop a sample setup program for the familiar NotePad utility. The tutorial walks you through various steps, eventually creating a setup program that places an icon and command on the taskbar's Programs menu. When selected, the command invokes NotePad. The setup program that InstallShield generates is thus similar to the SetPad program demonstrated in the preceding lesson, which added a command for WordPad to the Programs menu. However, the setup program that InstallShield creates is much more polished and user-friendly than SetPad.

The InstallShield tutorial shows how InstallShield categorizes your application files into different groups, allowing you to work on different parts of an installation project. Each *file group* contains files that have similar characteristics, such as system DLLs, executable files, and help files.

► **To run the InstallShield tutorial**

1. Click the Start button and display the Programs menu. Click InstallShield for Microsoft Visual C++ 6.
2. When InstallShield appears, click Getting Started on the Help menu.
3. In the Help Topics dialog box, expand the list by double-clicking Welcome to InstallShield, Tutorials, and Use the Project Wizard.
4. Double-click the first entry, Outline: Use the Project Wizard.
5. Move through the six steps, following the tutorial's instructions.

After running the completed Setup demonstration, be sure to uninstall it by running the Add/Remove Programs applet, as suggested in the tutorial's last step.

The preceding example shows how to start InstallShield from the taskbar's Programs menu, activating the Project Wizard to create a new project or to open an existing project. You can also run InstallShield from inside Visual C++ by clicking the InstallShield Wizard command on the Tools menu. This alternative is convenient when creating a setup program for an existing Visual C++ application project, because it fills in information that you would otherwise have to type manually. When you click the InstallShield Wizard command, the wizard appears as shown in Figure 12.4. Select the desired Visual C++ project, click Next, and follow the wizard's remaining instructions.

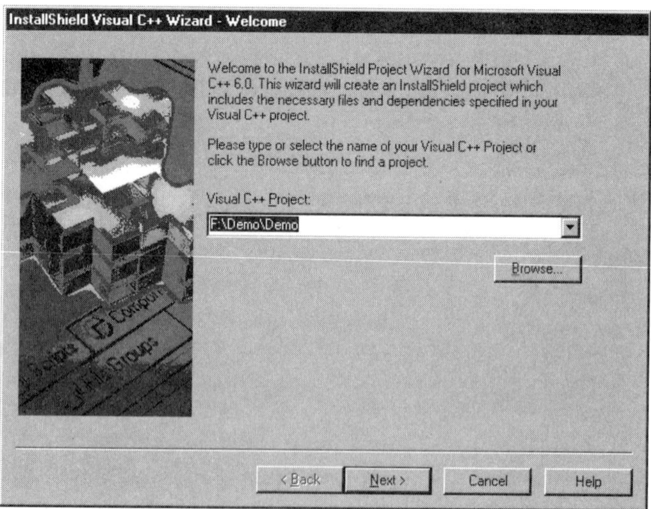

Figure 12.4 The InstallShield Wizard, invoked from the Visual C++ Tools menu

Including and Removing Program Files

InstallShield scans the application folder and locates all necessary executable files, adding them to the installation project. Figure 12.5 shows how the wizard's third step lists the application's dependency files. In this case, the Demo application links dynamically to MFC, so InstallShield adds MFC42.DLL to the setup project. Because MFC42.DLL in turn uses the C runtime library, the MSVCRT.DLL module is also added to the installation project.

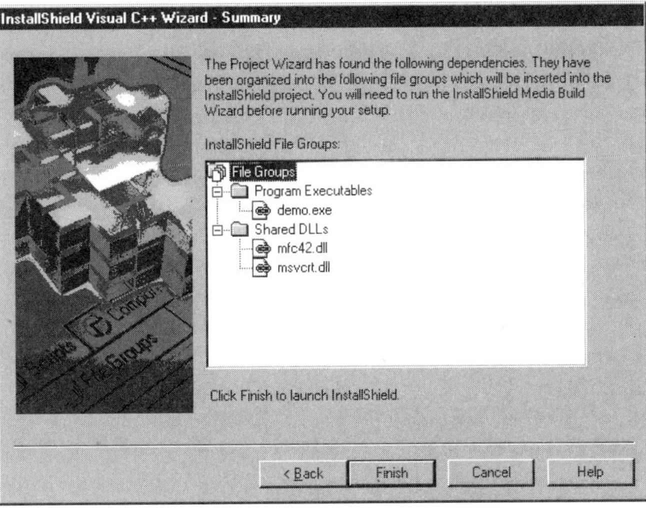

Figure 12.5 Listing an application's shared files in the InstallShield wizard

If you intend to distribute your application only to sites where you know the files already exist, you may not want to include dependencies such as MFC42.DLL and MSVCRT.DLL in your setup program. The InstallShield wizard does not allow you to alter the list, but you can remove the files from the installation project later. After the wizard finishes, it starts InstallShield automatically.

Creating the Setup.exe Program

After your installation project compiles and runs correctly, the last step is to build the project. This step is where you create the Setup.exe program and the associated .cab files distributed to your users. InstallShield provides the Media Build Wizard to walk you through the six steps of creating the Setup program. The following outline assumes you have created an installation project and are ready to build a setup program for it. The outline gives a general description for each of the wizard's steps; Exercise 5 of Lab 12 applies these steps to an actual project.

► **To create a setup program**

1. Click the Media Build Wizard command on InstallShield's Build menu.
2. In the wizard's first step, type the name of the application project in the Media Name box.
3. In the second step, choose the type and size of the media you intend to use for your application's deployment. The wizard offers the choice of various disk formats, CD-ROM, a customizable size, and an option named InstallFromTheWeb that creates a setup program that can be installed over the Internet.

4. In the third step, choose either Full Build or Quick Build. The Full Build option creates the compressed files required for distribution to users. The Quick Build option is intended only for testing purposes, allowing you to quickly build a setup project and test it without creating actual compressed files. The Quick Build option creates disk images that contain links to the application files instead of compressed data. A Setup program created with the Quick Build option will run only on the development computer where the application project is stored.
5. The wizard's third step includes an Advanced button. Click this button to expose a dialog box that allows you to enter various settings and to establish a password for the setup program. You can also specify the folder to which the setup files will be written. If you do not specify a folder, the wizard writes the disk image files to C:\MyInstallations*project*\Media*project*, where *project* represents the name of the installation project.
6. Confirm the information displayed in the wizard's fourth step, titled Tag File.
7. In the wizard's fifth step, select the operating systems under which your application can run. InstallShield includes files required for the selected operating systems.
8. The wizard's sixth and final step is titled Summary. Click the Finish button to build the setup program.
9. InstallShield shows the Building Media dialog box, in which an animated display tracks its progress. When the build is complete, click the Finish button again.

You now have a folder named Disk Images in your chosen installation project folder. The Disk Images folder contains a nested folder named Disk1 that holds the disk image for the first disk of the series. If the setup requires additional disks, their images are contained in folders Disk2, Disk3, and so forth. The contents of each Disk folder must be copied to disks or other media of the type selected in the Media Build Wizard's second step. If the installation creates more than one Disk folder, each receiving medium must be labeled with the disk number to ensure that the user is able to insert disks in the correct order when prompted to do so.

As a final test before shipping your application, run the Setup package on a computer other than your development computer. Test the installed application to ensure that all components have been correctly copied and registered.

Lesson Summary

This lesson introduced the InstallShield program, a tool that creates sophisticated installation programs for Visual C++ projects. InstallShield largely automates the entire process of building a setup program, scanning for dependencies, generating cabinet files, and creating disk images. InstallShield even provides an uninstaller program named Uninst.

Through its Media Build Wizard, InstallShield is accessible from inside the Visual C++ environment where it automatically reads information for the current application project. InstallShield encourages the sorting of project files into distinct categories referred to as file groups, allowing you to specify different characteristics for each group. InstallShield generates a script that governs the installation process, using its own InstallScript language. Complete control over installation is possible by editing the script.

Lesson 3: Packaging COM Components

The simple InstallShield project demonstrated in Lesson 2 is fine for a monolithic application like NotePad that does not use remote COM components. But a setup program for a distributed application must include some means of configuring both the client systems and the remote servers on which the application will run. This section discusses some of the issues involved when creating a setup program that installs a distributed application over a network. Such applications rely on COM server components that in all likelihood execute on computers other than the one on which the client runs.

As you read this lesson, bear in mind that the discussions often refer to two different execution venues: your development system and your customer's network. The former is where packaging takes place, and the latter is where your application and COM components must be installed—in effect, "unpackaged." The text makes clear which venue is being described, so you will have no trouble following the discussions.

After this lesson, you will be able to:

- Describe why the name of the server on which a remote component runs must be stored on the client's host computer
- Create and deploy a group of MTS components combined as a package
- Describe how to configure a network system for MSMQ applications by creating queues, either automatically in a setup program or manually by using MSMQ Explorer
- Describe load balancing

Estimated lesson time: 15 minutes

Determining Remote Server Names

Before a distributed, multitiered application can run, the client program must have some way of determining at runtime the names of server computers that host the application's remote components. In Lab 11, for example, the client application passed a COSERVERINFO structure to *CoCreateInstanceEx* that specified the name of the target server computer.

DCOM offers another method for remote instantiation in which a client program does not need to be directly aware of a server's identity. This approach relies instead on the presence of a special registry key named RemoteServerName, which is associated with a component's class identifier. Storing the host server name in the RemoteServerName key means that the client can use a component without worrying about its location, as DCOM takes care of establishing the remote link. When the client program instantiates a component, DCOM consults the RemoteServerName value to locate the server on which the component executes. DCOM then forwards a request to that server to load the component, and transparently establishes a connection across the network between the client and the component.

A setup program must contend with the problem of correctly identifying server computers. If the setup program can discover this information during installation, it should store the information to make it available to the application. Adding a RemoteServerName key to the client system's registry is the preferred method for storing a server name, but other methods can work just as well. For instance, the setup program might write the server name to a file that the application reads at startup.

If you are developing an application for use within your own company or a subsidiary firm, you can often determine the names of server systems on which your components will execute after deployment. With this information you can create an installation program that configures a client system to instantiate COM objects on the correct server, thus making installation—at least on the client side—completely automated.

In most cases, however, you cannot know server names beforehand. You must then write your setup program to identify the correct computers during installation, usually by querying the user. Lab 12 demonstrates another technique for passing a server name to an application at startup.

MTS Components

COM components that execute as an MTS transaction form a *package*, which is a collection of components that run in the same process and are therefore bound by the same security restrictions. Physically, a package consists of the component executable file (or files) and a *package file*, which contains information about the package's security and support configurations. A package file allows your MTS components to take their configuration settings with them when deployed to another network. This ensures that the components work the same on your customer's system as they do on your development system.

Deploying MTS components requires three separate steps:

1. Use the MTS Explorer management tool to create a package file for your components. A package file is recognizable by its .pak extension.
2. Distribute to your customers the component executables and their associated PAK file.
3. Install the packages on the customer's network, again using MTS Explorer.

The first two steps are the responsibility of you, the developer. The third step is often left to the system administrator who oversees the customer's network. Setting up a distributed multitiered application is thus rarely a completely automated process. Installing MTS components usually requires human intervention in which a system administrator performs the following tasks:

- Copies the packages to the desired servers on the network.
- Registers the components. (Lesson 4 explains how COM components are registered during installation.)
- Runs MTS Explorer to read each package file and register the components that form the package. The administrator can deploy packages to any desired servers from a single instance of MTS Explorer.
- Makes a setup program available on a public share so that users can install the client application and correctly configure their computers.

Creating an MTS Package for Distribution

This section describes how to create a package file from a set of MTS components. The text assumes that you have already configured a component package as explained in Lab 11. The instructions in this section are divided into two parts. The first part applies only if you know the name of the target server—that is, the server on which your components will execute when deployed to your customer's network. The second part applies in all cases, whether the server is known or not.

If you do not know the server names for your customer's network, skip to the second set of instructions.

► **To configure an MTS package for installation on a known server**

1. Start MTS Explorer as described in Lab 11 and expand the tree in the left pane.
2. Right-click the My Computer folder and choose Properties on the shortcut menu to invoke a property sheet.
3. Click the Options tab.
4. In the Remote Server Name text box, type the name of the server computer on which your components will execute. This is the name of the server on your customer's network, not the server on your network.
5. Go to Step 2 in the next set of instructions.

► **To create an MTS package for installation on an unknown server**

1. Start MTS Explorer and expand the tree in the left pane.
2. Select the Components folder beneath the package you want to deploy.
3. Ensure that all components appear in the right pane. If you wish to add other components to the package, drag and drop the desired component files from Windows Explorer onto the right pane.

4. Select the package name in MTS Explorer's left pane and click the Action button. You can also right-click the package name to expose the same menu.
5. Click Export to invoke the Export Package dialog box shown in Figure 12.6.

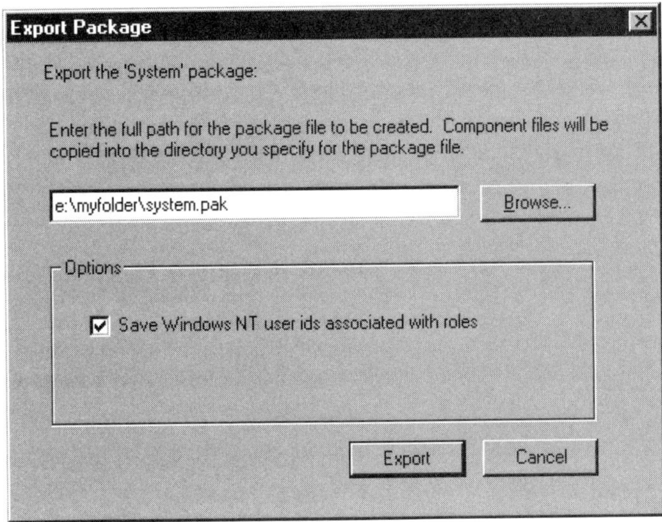

Figure 12.6 Specifying the path and name of a package file

6. Type a path and filename for the PAK file, choosing a folder such as the Release folder in your Visual C++ project to which you want to export the package. If you do not add a .pak extension to the filename, it will be added for you.
7. Click the Export button. MTS Explorer writes the designated PAK file to the target folder, copies the packaged component files to the same location, and displays a message saying that the package was successfully exported.
8. Dismiss the message and close MTS Explorer.

Besides generating a PAK file for the component, MTS Explorer also creates a new subfolder named Clients at the same location as the PAK file. The Clients subfolder contains a single executable that installs necessary files and registry keys for the component. The executable is designed to run on computers that host the client application using your components, allowing the client to remotely access the MTS package and the COM servers it contains. The next section describes the generated executable file, referred to here as the *client configuration utility*.

MTS Client Configuration Utility

The client configuration utility generated as part of MTS Explorer's export procedure assumes only that the host computer supports DCOM; MTS itself need not be installed. The client configuration utility performs a useful service in readying a user's computer on a network, but is not intended for registering the components themselves on a server computer. That task is best left to the administrator.

Note The client configuration utility should not be run on the server computer that hosts the MTS components, as doing so removes registry entries required to run the server package. The mistake can be rectified by running the Add/Remove Programs utility to delete the program's registered data, and then using MTS Explorer to remove and re-install the component package.

When run on a client computer, the configuration utility completes the following steps:

1. Locates the system Temp directory and extracts necessary client-level files, including type libraries and proxy-stub DLLs.
2. Transfers the type libraries and proxy-stub DLLs for the component to the Remote Applications directory in the Program Files subfolder. Each remote component resides in its own folder, which is given the name of the component's class identifier GUID.
3. Updates the system registry with entries that allow clients to use the COM server components remotely. The entries include class identifiers, programmatic identifiers, library identifiers, and RemoteServerName keys. If a server name is known beforehand when creating the configuration utility, the RemoteServerName key for the package contains the server name specified in MTS Explorer's Remote Server Name option. (See Step 4 of the first set of instructions in the preceding section.)
4. Registers an uninstallation procedure in the Windows\CurrentVersion\Uninstall registry folder, and adds an INF file to the Windows\Inf (or Winnt\Inf) folder. Together, these additions allow the user to remove all traces of the installation by running the Add/Remove Programs utility.
5. Cleans up by deleting all temporary files.

Uninstalling the Client Configuration Utility

As mentioned in the preceding section, the client configuration utility registers an uninstallation procedure for itself. The procedure is invoked through the Add/Remove Programs applet, where it appears in the list of removable programs prefaced with the words "Remote Application," followed by the name of the installed client. Your customers can conveniently uninstall the setup by selecting the entry from the list and clicking the Add/Remove button.

Limitations of the Client Configuration Utility

The client configuration utility has the potential to become a valuable part of the installation process for applications that use remote MTS components. However, the utility currently suffers from several limitations. Although the documentation claims that the client configuration utility registers all data that a client needs to run the packaged components, this claim is not yet strictly true. The client configuration utility does not register interfaces that a component exposes, preventing a client application from successfully instantiating a remote object by calling *CoCreateInstanceEx*.

The documentation also refers to a method for customizing the client configuration utility. This method involves a simple text file named Clients.ini, which must be prepared prior to using the Export command to generate the configuration utility. Currently, the customization feature does not work correctly.

Using MSMQ

A distributed application using MSMQ requires the services of at least one queue manager. A single queue manager running on a remote server can both accept messages from a client and disburse messages to a receiver. More often, however, a separate queue manager runs on the client's computer and communicates with another manager running on the server. This arrangement takes full advantage of queued messages because it allows the client to operate normally without being connected to the network. The client interacts with its queue manager, which then takes on the responsibility of forwarding messages—either immediately or at a later time—to the queue manager running on the server.

To install a client and its components so that they communicate via queued messages, a setup program that installs an MSMQ application should:

- Copy the client application to its designated computer
- Copy the required components to the server and register them
- Create the required queues

To create a queue, a setup program has two choices. It can query for a target computer and then create a queue "on the fly" by calling the *MQCreateQueue* function, and setting appropriate security and properties. The advantage of this technique is that it assures proper queue naming and represents more convenience for the user.

Alternatively, the setup program can delegate the task of creating queues to the system administrator, usually providing a text file that contains a clear set of instructions. The administrator can then create queues using MSMQ Explorer, as demonstrated in Chapter 8. This approach might seem to work against the goal of automating the installation process as much as possible, yet there can be good reasons for enlisting manual aid when creating queues. A system administrator might prefer to install components and set up queues manually to assure optimum load balance for the network.

Load Balancing

A distributed application serving many users simultaneously can create a large number of objects. If the objects are all instantiated on a single network server, the server's performance can suffer as its resources are taxed. Even the computing power of the fastest hardware is often not enough to keep up with demand. The solution to this problem is to distribute the application's components among multiple server computers, thereby sharing the load. This technique is known as *parallel deployment* or *load balancing*. DCOM does not automatically provide load balancing as is sometimes asserted, but simply makes load balancing possible.

Load balancing schemes fall into two classifications: static load balancing and dynamic load balancing. In *static load balancing*, decisions regarding the deployment and use of components are preset by the network administrator, who can monitor network usage and decide how best to balance load. Each user is assigned a server, and the installed application always connects with components on the assigned server. Server usage patterns are generally difficult to predict with perfect accuracy, so static load balancing represents only the administrator's best guess.

In contrast, *dynamic load balancing* determines at runtime to which server a client's request should be routed. This technique requires an operating system service that, by continually monitoring server load, can instantly pick the least-worked server at any given moment. Dynamic load balancing provides much more flexibility and accuracy than static load balancing, but currently neither the Windows operating system nor MTS implements dynamic load balancing.

Lesson Summary

Before it can instantiate objects on remote servers, the client level of a distributed application must first be able to identify those servers. DCOM recognizes the special RemoteServerName registry key for this purpose. RemoteServerName is associated with a component's class identifier, and contains the name of the server computer on which the component executes. When the client application calls *CoCreateInstanceEx* to instantiate the object, DCOM transparently establishes the required link between the client and the remote object.

When you deploy a group of transaction components to another network system, you must deploy the group's security and support configurations as well. MTS

Explorer refers to each transactional group of components as a package, and can create a package file that contains the group's configuration settings.

As part of its export feature, MTS Explorer also constructs a client configuration utility designed for a specific package. The utility installs registry information for host computers on which the client application runs. The registry information includes a server identifier stored in a RemoteServerName key for each component in an MTS package. The client configuration utility has considerable potential for facilitating MTS installations, but currently suffers from several defects that limit its effectiveness.

A setup program that installs an MSMQ application can also create required queues as part of its installation tasks. Queues allow a client and its components to communicate via queued messages. To create a queue, the setup program allows you two choices:

- Query for a target computer and then call the *MQCreateQueue* function, setting appropriate properties and security flags.
- Delegate the task to the system administrator, who can use MSMQ Explorer to create the queues.

Lesson 4: Installing COM Components

During installation, a setup program must register on the user's computer any local COM components that the application requires to run. For example, the registry entry for an ActiveX control includes:

- The control's class identifier GUID
- The location of the control's executable file
- Characteristics such as the component's threading model
- Various flags that specify how the component operates—for example, whether the control is visible or invisible, whether it can be activated inside a container's window, and so forth

Most COM servers are *self-registering*, meaning they contain their own registry information and are able to write that information to the system registry. By taking on the task of registering themselves, ActiveX controls and other COM servers remove most of the burden from the setup program.

After this lesson, you will be able to:

- Describe the self-registration feature possessed by many COM components, including ActiveX controls
- Describe how exported functions add COM information to the registry and remove the information from the registry
- Configure an InstallShield project to correctly install self-registering COM components on the user's system

Estimated lesson time: 10 minutes

Self-Registering Components

To update the user's system registry for installed COM components, a setup program can use registry files as described in Lesson 1. However, self-registering components do not require registry files because they contain all the necessary registration information within their own code.

An in-process self-registering COM component exports a function named *DllRegisterServer* that, when called, writes to the registry all the information the component requires. The only obstacle is that some other application must load the control and specifically call the *DllRegisterServer* function.

For an ActiveX control, this task often falls to a Web browser, which must register any control that is downloaded as part of a Web page. Before executing a script on the page that uses the control, the browser loads the object, calls its

DllRegisterServer function, and then unloads it. With the registry information correctly copied, the script can then load the control again by supplying to COM the control's class identifier. A setup program follows the same procedure as the Web browser: it loads a component, calls *DllRegisterServer*, and then unloads the component. Because users generally acquire COM components only over the Internet or by installing an application, registration takes place invisibly and most users do not ever have to worry about registering COM server components.

Control files that are acquired through other means—via e-mail, for example—require manual registration before they can operate. Windows provides a utility named RegSvr32 that handles this task. RegSvr32 simply loads a requested ActiveX control or any other self-registering COM component and calls the component's *DllRegisterServer* function:

```
regsvr32 path\MyComponent.ocx
```

The italicized *path* represents the location where the component is stored. The command

```
regsvr32 /u path\MyComponent.ocx
```

causes the program to instead call the component's *DllUnregisterServer* function, which removes from the registry everything that *DllRegisterServer* wrote. The */u* switch included in the command stands for uninstall.

Adding Self-Registering Components to an InstallShield Project

To install a self-registering component, a setup program can either launch RegSvr32 or simply load the component and call its *DllRegisterServer* function. When setting up a distributed application, there are no hard rules regarding component registration. It depends on whether your setup program can determine at runtime where the components are to execute. Components such as ActiveX controls that execute in-process with the client application should be copied to the same computer on which the client is installed and registered there. A setup program should keep a list of any components that it registers. If the user decides later to remove your application, the uninstaller program can consult the list, load each component in turn, and call the component's *DllUnregisterServer* function to unregister it.

InstallShield can create Setup and Uninst programs that automatically register and unregister your application's COM components. To configure your installation project to correctly handle self-registering components, you must create a file group that contains the component files and then specify the Self Registered property for the group. The script must also be modified to allow the self-registering feature. The entire process is somewhat involved, and requires attention to detail in order to succeed. Lab 12 demonstrates how to add a self-registering component to an InstallShield project.

Registering Remote COM Servers

Distributed multitier applications can be difficult to install correctly, particularly on the server side. During installation of multiple server components, a sophisticated installation program should be prepared to:

- Query the customer for the names of the network host computers that will receive the servers
- Confirm the availability of program requirements
- Deploy components to specified network nodes and register them correctly
- Store a permanent record of the installation, so that the components can be later uninstalled if the customer desires

These are only the requirements for installing an application's servers; the section "Writing a Setup Program" in Lesson 1 included installation steps for the client side as well.

As you have seen by installing Duwamish Books, the setup program runs on the server and can therefore create the MTS packages that Duwamish Books requires. Yet the program does not automate installation completely. (The Duwamish Books setup program was not created using Visual C++, but by modifying the Setup1 project in the PDWizard folder of the Microsoft Visual Basic Setup toolkit. Setup1 is a product of Visual Basic's Package and Deployment Wizard.) The user is called upon to perform several tasks manually, including:

- Confirming that the correct versions of MTS and SQL Server exist
- Confirming that MDAC 2.1 exists
- Confirming the presence of Microsoft Internet Explorer 5 or another source for Microsoft XML Parser
- Configuring MS DTC and RPC Locator services to start automatically
- Adjusting IIS security settings
- Creating IIS virtual directories

The fact that the Duwamish Books installation procedure has so many manual steps only highlights the many types of problems that a setup program for a distributed database application must confront and deal with, if only to instruct the network administrator what steps to take.

Lesson Summary

Many in-process COM components contain their own registry information. These components export a function named *DllRegisterServer*, which writes the component's information to the system registry, and a second function named

DllUnregisterServer, which removes the same information from the registry. These functions make COM components self-registering and self-unregistering.

Users typically acquire COM server components by installing applications that use the servers, in which case registration takes place behind the scenes when the setup program calls the component's *DllRegisterServer* function. To allow users to manually install or uninstall a component such as an ActiveX control, Windows provides the RegSvr32 utility.

An InstallShield project that automatically registers components for a distributed application requires two extra steps. First, a file group must be added to the project with its Self-Registering property set to Yes. Second, all self-registering components used by the application must be manually added to the new file group. The second step is necessary because InstallShield cannot recognize COM components as dependencies until specifically instructed to do so. When the resulting setup program executes, it calls the *DllRegisterServer* function for each self-registering component in the file group.

Lesson 5: Deployment Methods

When the setup program is created and working properly, you are ready to deploy your application. This lesson discusses how best to get your application into the hands of users, and addresses some issues that you should consider when releasing your application.

Today, the three most common means of deploying a Windows program are:

- On media such as floppy disks or CD-ROMs
- Over a network
- Over the Internet

After this lesson, you will be able to:

- Describe the advantages and disadvantages of deployment via disk-based media, network, and Web site
- Describe digital signing and explain its purpose

Estimated lesson time: 10 minutes

Media-Based Deployment

For smaller applications, disks and CD-ROMs provide a cost-effective and convenient means of deployment. In their 3.5-inch form, disks also have the advantage of ubiquity, as nearly all users have access to a floppy disk drive that can read the media.

Disk media are often used for the distribution of application upgrades, which can take the form of simple bug corrections or completely new versions. The upgrade package should include a setup program that installs only the files that have been revised for the upgrade, making the installation as quick and convenient as possible.

Network-Based Deployment

Deployment via a network is the least expensive method of distribution, and is ideal if your application is intended to serve only a set of users within a company or group of companies. Such users are generally linked through a local area or wide area network. Your disk images can be placed on a share accessible by all intended users, who can then install the client application by running the setup program over the network. The task of installing COM components on one or more server computers can be undertaken by the network administrator. This scheme might involve two separate installation programs, one for the users and another for the administrator.

Deployment of applications with a *site license* (a purchase agreement for using more than one copy of a software product) usually involves two steps. First, an organization receives a single set of disks and copies the disk images and setup program to a server. The users covered by the site license can then install the application over the network.

Web-Based Deployment

Deployment over the Web has become increasingly common in the last few years. Web-based deployment offers several compelling advantages:

- No packaging costs
- No distribution costs other than the normal maintenance of a Web site
- No reseller costs, as the software manufacturer can also fill the role of vendor
- More efficient distribution to international markets, allowing customers in other countries to access a Web site written in their native languages and download only the application files localized for their languages
- The opportunity for distribution of evaluation copies

The disadvantages of Web-based deployment must also be considered:

- Potential inconvenience exists in that the user might be forced to download many megabytes of data over a poor-quality connection.
- Customer base is restricted to only users with Internet access.
- Care must be taken to ensure that site passwords are given only to licensed users.

The following is typical HTML code that creates a link to a setup program on a Web server:

```
<a href="XYZSetup.exe">Click here to install the XYZ
application.</a>
```

In most browsers, clicking on a link like this one displays a dialog box asking if the file should be downloaded to the user's computer or run from its current location. The first option is practical only for self-extracting executables that contain all required files, including .cab files. Generally, your Web page should include instructions telling your users to select the "Run from current location" option.

Time-Trial Evaluations

A popular method of deploying software on the Web is to give away a free copy that is functional for a limited period of time. If you want the software beyond that time, you have to purchase it. At the expiration of the evaluation period, the program politely refuses to run until the user purchases a license. The license arrives via e-mail in the form of a keyword, which the application recognizes as proof of a valid license. When the keyword is installed, the user continues using the application as before, but now without time restraints.

Distributing Application Updates

The Web also serves as an excellent means of distributing application updates. The developer can place files in a common area, perhaps protected by a password known only to users. Registered users can be notified by e-mail that an upgrade has been posted. SQL scripts for an application update can contain new stored procedure definitions, database table changes, and data manipulation operations required to update the application database. Client program executables typically contain updated functionality and bug fixes.

Digital Signing

Through their security settings, browsers can require that downloadable software such as setup programs have a digital signature. A *digital signature* provides a way to verify that:

- The file is identical to when it was signed
- The file comes from a responsible source

Without a digital signature, most modern browsers display a warning when the user selects the "Run from current location" option to run a setup program. The warning tells the user that the program is from an unknown source. Signing helps assure your users that the setup program is indeed from you or your company, and hasn't been tampered with. The signature verifies the source by identifying the legal entity that created the software. When you include a digital signature with a setup program or any other file, you are the legal entity. The legal entity might be held responsible for any destruction caused by signed software when it is downloaded or run.

You provide a digital signature by purchasing a certificate from a *certificate authority*. A certificate authority is a company that validates your identity and issues a certificate to you. The certificate contains your digital signature and is a verification of your credentials. In the event of any problems, the certificate authority becomes a witness to your identity.

Deployment Checklist

This section provides a short checklist of miscellaneous items you should consider when deploying a distributed application:

- Make sure the application and all components have been built under their release configuration, not their debug configuration. Although Visual C++ by default optimizes the release version for speed, most programmers prefer to optimize for size. This is especially important for COM server components.
- Before including dependencies with your application, make sure the dependencies are legally distributable. Microsoft allows you to distribute both the MFC and the C run-time library modules MFC42.DLL and MSVCRT.DLL along with your Visual C++ application, but other vendors might impose restrictions.
- Users do not require licenses for ActiveX controls. Therefore, do not include control license information in the installation package.
- Make sure your application's help files are included in the installation package. It is not necessary to distribute the Windows Help Viewer WinHlp32.exe with the Help files, since every Windows system already has the Help Viewer installed.
- Test your setup program thoroughly under different scenarios and operating systems. Ensure that it reacts correctly when encountering duplicate folder or filenames, and under conditions of insufficient disk space and low memory.
- Apply the same tests to your uninstaller program, and make sure it correctly deletes files and cleans the registry.

Lesson Summary

Windows applications are commonly distributed to users through one of three methods:

- As a series of disks or CD-ROMs
- As a setup program running on a network
- As a downloadable file over the Internet

This lesson described these three methods and discussed some of their advantages and disadvantages. Besides offering the advantage of low maintenance and distribution costs, a Web site makes an ideal medium for distributing evaluation copies to interested users.

As a final checklist for deployment, you should verify that:

- Your application has been built under its release configuration
- Dependency files are legally distributable to users
- All auxiliary files such as dynamic link libraries, Help files, and font files are included
- Your setup and uninstaller programs have been tested and work as expected

Lesson 6: Zero Administration for Windows

ZAW is a Microsoft initiative designed to reduce costs associated with using networked personal computers in a corporate environment. The initiative's core technologies greatly facilitate the management of users, software, and hardware within an organization, and are intended to eliminate the need for an administrator to touch individual desktops on a network.

This lesson first presents a broad overview of ZAW. It then narrows its focus to concentrate on ZAW's Windows Installer and Microsoft Systems Management Server (SMS), two key technologies that pertain directly to application deployment.

After this lesson, you will be able to:

- List the key features of the ZAW initiative
- Understand the basics of Windows Installer technology
- Understand SMS

Estimated lesson time: 15 minutes

Features of ZAW

The ZAW initiative is part of the Microsoft Windows Client Strategy. ZAW exists in some measure today within Microsoft Windows NT Server 4, but is slated to become a major part of Microsoft Windows 2000. Some of ZAW's capabilities are:

- Automatic system update and application installation
- Persistent caching of data and configuration information
- Central administration and system lockdown

Automatic System Update and Application Installation

Software installation and maintenance today is typically a labor-intensive and error-prone process. Under ZAW, this process becomes much simpler through automation. When a system component, device driver, or a new version of the operating system becomes available, Windows can automatically update itself with the new components. The system can be configured to boot in a minimal network configuration and check for any updates on the Internet. If an update is found, the system can update itself without user intervention.

Persistent Caching of Data and Configuration Information

Previous lessons in this chapter showed how installation programs store state and configuration information in a host's registry. This means of storage can be problematic in a networked or mobile environment, in which users who are primarily away from their desks cannot access their applications or tools from other locations.

Under ZAW, the local host's data can be automatically reflected to servers, allowing users to log on to different computers on the network and work within the configuration and data of their host computer located elsewhere. This idea of data and configuration information following a user to another computer is known as *persistent caching*.

Central Administration and System Lockdown

To prevent users from installing hardware and software on their computers as they please, ZAW allows the network administrator to hide devices such as disk drives, presenting the user with a single drive letter that represents their home directory.

Windows Installer

Perhaps the most important part of ZAW for application deployment is the Windows Installer, which automates application installation across a network. The Windows Installer offers many benefits over the conventional installation procedures described in previous lessons, including:

- The ability to automatically repair an installed application. For example, if an application's component file is accidentally deleted, the Windows Installer ensures that it is transparently replaced when the application starts.
- Automatic installation on an enterprise-wide system with thousands of users.
- Installation on demand, in which COM components are installed only when they are first accessed by a client application. This speeds installation and prevents unnecessarily cluttering the disks of users who have no need for the components.

The Windows Installer is not a program, but rather a set of services. Setup programs will still exist under ZAW and will interact with the user as before. Nor does the Windows Installer replace installer products like InstallShield. Rather, such products will undoubtedly become even more important under ZAW as installation becomes more intricate and technology more sophisticated.

New releases of InstallShield and other installer products can generate setup programs that incorporate the features and services of the Windows Installer. You can download an evaluation version of InstallShield for Windows Installer from the MSDN Web site at *http://msdn.microsoft.com/downloads/tools/Installshield/Installshield.asp.*

Systems Management Server

SMS is a ZAW service that continually inventories computers on a network. The software and hardware detected on each computer is then listed in a SQL database. Through SMS, a network administrator has instant access to an up-to-date inventory of all computers on the network, without the expense and disruptions of a manual inventory.

SMS makes software deployment more efficient, because it provides query functions by which an installation package can gain access to the SMS database. This access allows a setup program to automatically test each computer before deployment, and install only on computers that meet a specified set of criteria. When it detects a computer that does not qualify for installation, the setup program can suggest to the administrator any required changes, such as hardware upgrades.

Zero Administration Kit

ZAW is an integral part of Windows 2000, but many of its features are available for Windows NT 4 today. Microsoft provides the Zero Administration Kit for installing ZAW on NT 4. You can download the kit from *http://www.microsoft.com/windows/zak/zakreqs.htm.*

The entire Zero Administration Kit is a self-extracting file roughly 6 MB in size. If you prefer to receive only the documentation, a separate file in Microsoft Word format (415 KB) is also available for downloading.

Lesson Summary

The ZAW Initiative is designed to reduce the labor and costs associated with operating a Windows-based network. ZAW's features include:

- Automatic updating of both the operating system and application files. At regular intervals the system checks data sources such as Web sites, and as new files become available downloads them automatically.
- Persistent caching, which allows a computer's data and configuration to follow a user to other locations.
- Central administration and system lockdown, allowing an administrator to protect individual systems by hiding devices from users.

The Windows Installer provides services to installation programs running on a network, making application installation faster and more efficient in its use of disk space. As a system service, the Windows Installer is at work even when no setup program is running. Because it is always active, the Windows Installer is able to repair applications as needed by automatically replacing files that have been accidentally deleted or moved.

ZAW's SMS maintains an inventory of hardware and software on a network, storing the information in a SQL database. Installation programs can query SMS for a computer's configuration before deployment, and install only on workstations that meet the application's requirements.

Lab 12: Packaging and Deploying a Distributed Application

This lab demonstrates how to bundle a simple distributed application into an installation package, and how to deploy the package to another network system. The installation package consists of two parts:

- An installation program named Setup, created as an InstallShield project
- An MTS component and its associated PAK file

When executed on the client's system, the setup program decompresses data stored in .cab files, copies executable files to specified computers on a network, and registers the component's single interface. Although the Visual C++ edition of InstallShield is less capable than the commercial version, the program nevertheless offers many advantages over writing your own setup procedure. The resulting interface is attractive, behaves professionally, and automatically provides an uninstall program.

The MTS component must be installed manually on a server computer. Distributed files should normally include a Readme file that instructs a network administrator how to install components using MTS Explorer; however, this lab does not include such a file.

The Client and Beeper projects introduced in Chapter 11 serve as the distributed application that is packaged and deployed in the following exercises. The source code for the client program has been slightly modified for this lab, and the new project is named Client2. In Chapter 11, a server name was hard-coded into the program, but this technique is not workable for programs deployed to other networks using different server names. Client2 therefore accepts a server name as a command-line argument, allowing the program to work normally for any system on which it is installed.

In this lab, you will:

- Create release versions of Client2 and Beeper
- Generate an MTS package file for Beeper
- Create an InstallShield project for the installation program
- Create a disk containing the Setup program, required .cab files, the component file, and a package file for the component
- Test the installation package

As mentioned at the beginning of the chapter, the Learning and Standard editions of Visual C++ do not include InstallShield, though you may purchase the tool separately. If you do not have access to InstallShield, you should follow along in the text although you will not be able to complete all of the exercises.

Estimated lab time: 20 minutes

Exercise 1: Building Release Versions of Client2 and Beeper

The Beeper.dll component created in Chapter 11 should not be distributed to customers because it is a debug version. This exercise builds release versions of both the Client2 and Beeper projects. A release version of an executable file is smaller and faster than a debug version because the compiler does not add symbol information to the object files, and because the compiler optimizes the code to make it more efficient. In accordance with good programming practices, this exercise configures the compiler to reduce code size rather than increase execution speed.

► **Create a release build of Client2.exe optimized for size**

1. Open the Client2 project in Visual C++.
2. On the Build toolbar, select the Win32 Release build context as shown in Figure 12.7.

Figure 12.7 Select Win32 Release on the Build toolbar prior to creating a release build

3. Click the Settings command on the Project menu.
4. In the Project Settings dialog box, expose the C/C++ tab and select Minimize Size in the Optimizations box.
5. Click OK to close the dialog box.
6. Click the Build button on the Build toolbar to build a release version of the Client2 application.

► **Create a release build of Beeper.dll optimized for size**

1. Open the Beeper project in Visual C++. Chapter 11 required two copies of the Beeper project files, one project located on the local computer (named

LocalSys) and the other project copied to the remote server computer (named ServerSys). The setup program requires only the Beeper.dll file, so it does not matter which Beeper project you work with.

2. Select the Win32 Release MinDependency configuration to make the component independent of the Atl.dll library file. Do not choose Win32 Release MinSize. Although this selection would result in a smaller executable file, it also adds Atl.dll as a dependency to the setup program.
3. Ensure that the Minimize Size option is selected in the Project Settings dialog box, as described in Step 4 for the Client2 program.
4. Build the Beeper project.

Exercise 2: Creating a Package File for the Beeper Component

Part of Lab 11 called for using MTS Explorer to create a package for the Beeper component. Although this package refers to Beeper's debug version instead of its new release version, it is not necessary to delete the package and recreate a new one. This is because both the debug and release versions of a component use the same class identifier, and the same package file can therefore serve for both. You need only be careful to distinguish between the component's new release file and its original debug version when adding the component to the InstallShield project.

► **Create a package file for the Beeper component**

1. Move to the server computer on which Beeper executes, and start MTS Explorer.
2. Expand the tree list in the left pane to expose the list of installed packages, and then right-click the entry for the Beeper package.
3. Click the Export command on the shortcut menu.
4 Type the path and desired filename for the new package file. You can export the package file anywhere, but do not specify the ReleaseMindependency folder that contains Beeper's release build to avoid overwriting the new Beeper.dll file with the debug version.
5. Click the Export button. After a moment, a message box appears saying that the package was successfully exported.
6. Click OK to dismiss the message box and close MTS Explorer.

At the location specified in Step 4, MTS Explorer generates a new package file with a .pak extension, and creates a subfolder named Clients. The Clients subfolder contains an executable file named Beeper.exe, which is the client configuration utility described in Lesson 3. You can delete the Beeper.exe file, because it is not used in the exercises that follow.

Exercise 3: Creating the InstallShield Project

Now that all the files are prepared, the next step is to create an InstallShield project for the distributed application. The InstallShield project builds the required setup program that deploys the Client2 application.

► **Create an InstallShield project for Client2**

1. Click the Start button, select the Programs menu, and click InstallShield For Visual C++ 6 to launch InstallShield.
2. Double-click the Project Wizard icon.
3. Fill in the wizard's first step as shown in Figure 12.8. For the entry at the bottom of the dialog box, either type in the complete path to the Client2.exe program or click the Browse button (marked by three dots) and browse for the file.

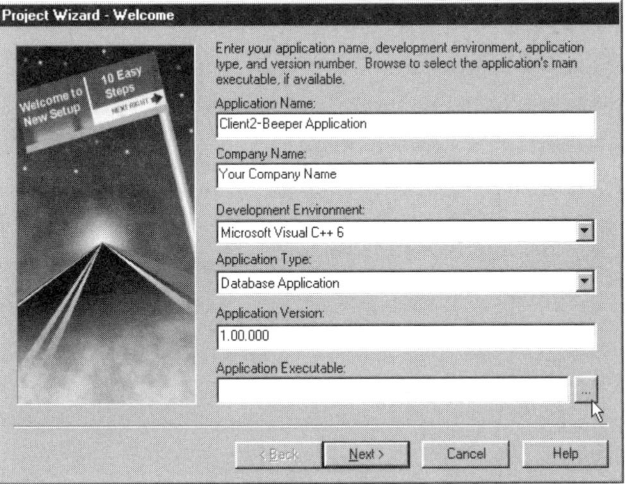

Figure 12.8 Project information in InstallShield's Project Wizard

4. In the wizard's second step, clear all the check boxes except Welcome Message, Choose Destination Location, and Setup Complete. The result should look like Figure 12.9.

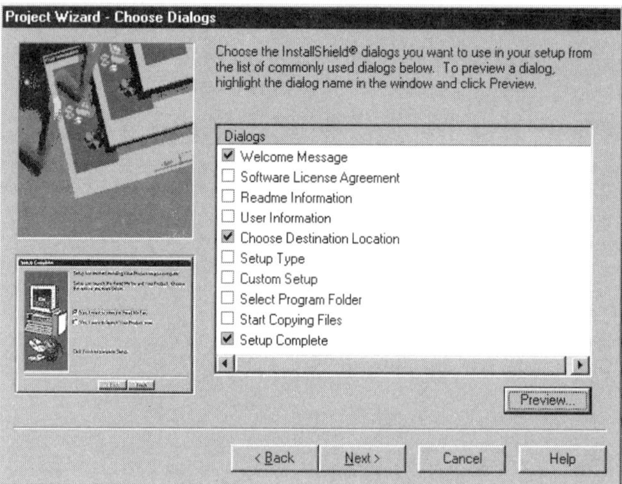

Figure 12.9 Selecting installation dialog boxes in Project Wizard

5. In the third step, titled Choose Target Platform, select the operating system under which the Client2 program will execute. If you are using Windows 98, select Windows 95 in the list. It is not necessary to also select the operating system that hosts the Beeper component.
6. Click the Next button twice to skip over the Specify Languages step.
7. In the step titled Specify Setup Types, click anywhere in the white area to clear all entries in the list. None of the setup types should be selected, as shown in Figure 12.10.

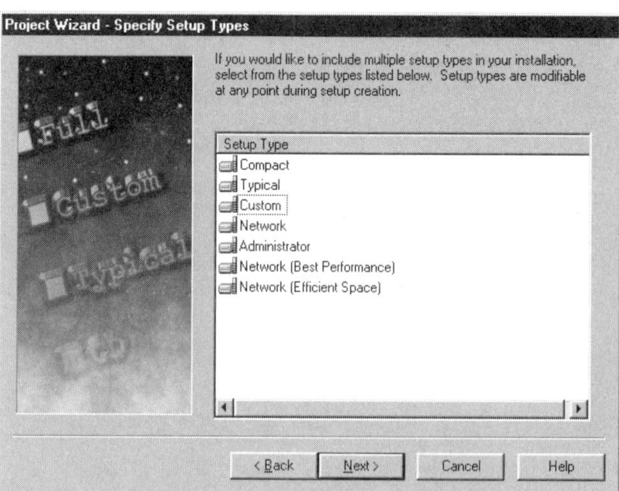

Figure 12.10 Clearing setup types

8. The Project Wizard's next step lists project components, including program files, example files, help files, and shared DLLs. Select each entry except the first entry and use the Delete button to remove it from the list. Only the Program Files entry should remain, as shown in Figure 12.11.

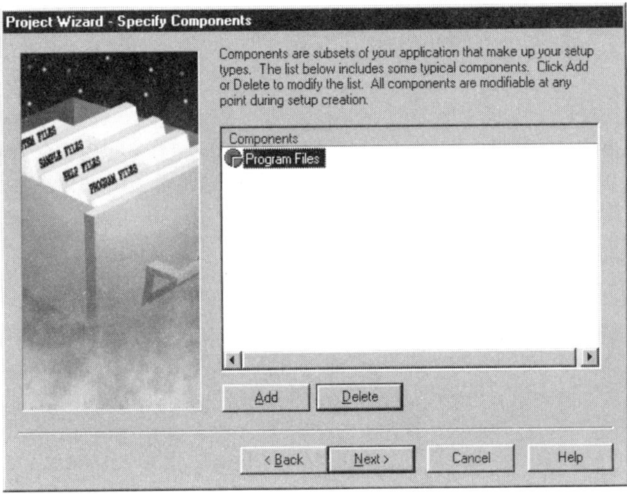

Figure 12.11 Selecting project components

9. Click the Next button to advance to the next step. Of the five file groups that the Project Wizard displays, delete the bottom three. Only the Program Executable Files and Program DLLs groups should remain, as shown in Figure 12.12.

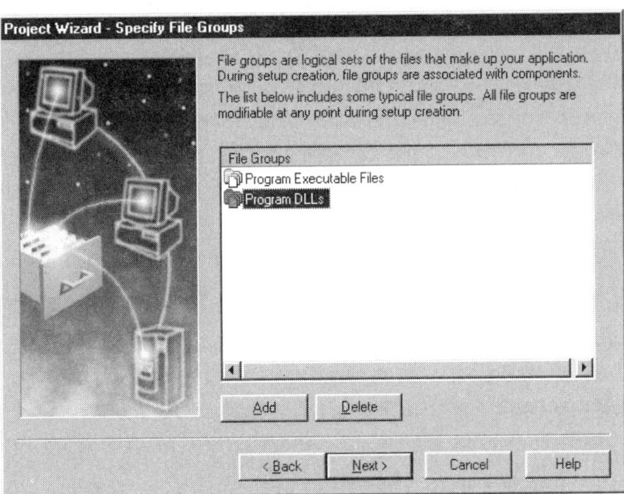

Figure 12.12 Selecting file groups

10. Click Next to advance to the wizard's summary page, and then click Finish.

InstallShield creates the new project according to the selections made in the preceding exercise, and then automatically opens the project. You are now ready to modify the project so that it correctly builds a setup program for the Client2 application.

Had Client2.exe required normal dependencies—for example, if it used ActiveX controls or the MFC library—the wizard summary page would have listed the names of dependency files. The wizard is able to glean the information from the project's DSW file and from the list of DLL dependencies stored in the program's header. However, COM components such as Beeper.dll do not appear listed in either location, so InstallShield at this point does not know that Beeper is a dependency of Client2.

You might wonder why InstallShield can recognize ActiveX controls as project dependencies but not other COM server components like Beeper. The reason has to do with how ActiveX controls are added to a Visual C++ project. When you add an ActiveX control using the Add To Project command and the Gallery (as described in Chapter __), Visual C++ writes the control's class identifier to the project's DSW file. When it creates a setup project, InstallShield reads the list of controls in the DSW file and looks up class identifiers in the registry to find information about a control, including the path and name of the control's executable file. Server components like Beeper are not added to a Visual C++ project using the Gallery, and so are not listed in the project's DSW file. In such cases, you must specify dependency files manually. The next exercise shows how to add Beeper.dll as a dependency to the setup project.

Exercise 4: Modifying the InstallShield Project

Technically, Beeper.dll is not required on the client system because it executes on a remote server, not on the local host. However, including the file in the setup program makes the installation procedure completely automatic on the client side. To understand the reason for this, recall from Chapter 11 that the client system's registry must include an entry for the IBeepCtl interface to allow the client to instantiate the BeepCtl object. A registry file could provide this information, but would have to be imported into the RegSvr32 utility. However, the Visual C++ edition of InstallShield cannot create setup programs that can launch other programs like RegSvr32 during installation, so using a registry file would require the user to perform the step manually. A common theme running throughout this chapter is that manual operations during installation should be avoided whenever possible.

Fortunately, another option is available, one that avoids enlisting the aid of the user. Although the setup program cannot launch RegSvr32, it can automatically register Beeper.dll—and thus the IBeepCtl interface—by calling the component's *DllRegisterServer* function. The only disadvantage is that more information is placed into the registry than the Client2 program requires.

Modifying the InstallShield project requires four steps:

1. Add the Client2.exe and Beeper.dll files to file groups.
2. Set the Self-Registering property for the file group that contains Beeper.dll.
3. Incorporate the file groups into the list of project components.
4. Make the self-registration feature available by modifying the project script.

Follow the steps carefully in this exercise, as leaving out a single step prevents the component from being properly registered at runtime. If registration fails, the InstallShield setup program gives no indication that an error occurred, nor does it offer clues about what went wrong.

► **Add the Client2.exe and Beeper.dll files to their respective file groups**

1. Select the File Groups tab in InstallShield's project workspace and expand the list of file groups. The project has two groups, named Program DLLs and Program Executable Files.
2. Select the Links node beneath the Program Executable Files folder in the workspace area.
3. Right-click anywhere in the area to the right of the workspace pane. From the shortcut menu shown in Figure 12.13, choose the Insert Files command.

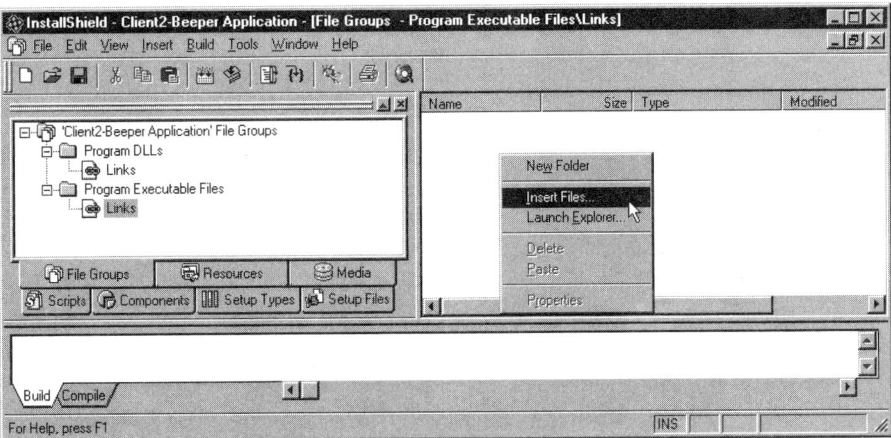

Figure 12.13 Inserting a file into a selected file group

4. In the Insert File Links dialog box, navigate to the Client2\Release folder, select Client2.exe, and click the Open button. The file is added to the list of files contained in the Program Executable Files group.
5. Select the Links entry beneath the Program DLLs folder in the workspace area.
6. Right-click in the right pane and again choose the Insert Files command.
7. Navigate to the Beeper\ReleaseMindependency folder, select Beeper.dll, and click Open. The file is added to the Program DLLs file group.

It is now necessary to set the Self-Registering property for the Program DLLs file group. The Self-Registering property affects every file in a group, which explains why Client2.exe and Beeper.dll must be placed into separate file groups. Of the two files, only Beeper.dll exports *DllRegisterServer*, so it must occupy its own group.

▶ Set the self-registering flag for the Program DLLs file group

1. Select the Program DLLs entry in the workspace to expose the group's property list in the right-hand pane.
2. Double-click the Self-Registered field in the property list.
3. Select the Yes radio button in the Properties dialog box, as shown in Figure 12.14. This choice marks the group as containing only self-registering components.

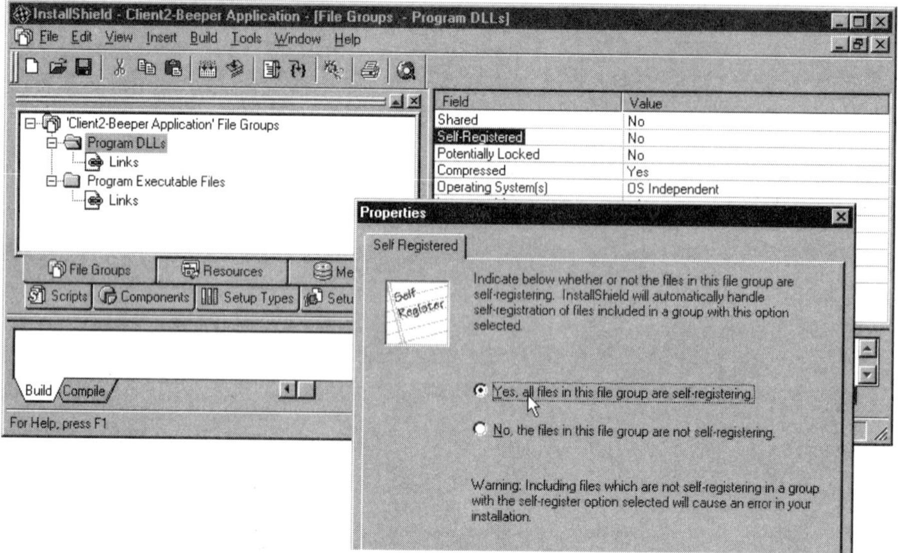

Figure 12.14 Marking the Program DLLs file group for self-registering files

4. Click OK to close the Properties dialog box. The value of the Self-Registered field changes to Yes.
5. Double-click the Shared field in the display area.
6. Select the Yes radio button and close the Properties dialog box. The value of the Shared field changes to Yes.
7. Double-click the Potentially Locked field.
8. Select the Yes radio button and close the Properties dialog box. The value of the Potentially Locked field changes to Yes.

These changes signal InstallShield to create a setup program that loads the Beeper.dll file, calls its *DllRegisterServer* function to register the component, and then unloads the file. You must now add the two executable files to the list of project components. Note that InstallShield uses the term *component* to mean any executable module, not just COM components.

► **Add the file groups to the project components**

1. Click the Components tab in the workspace window.
2. Select Program Files in the workspace pane to expose a list of component properties in the right pane.
3. Double-click the Included File Groups value located at the bottom of the property list.
4. In the Properties dialog box, click the Add button.
5. Select Program DLLs from the list of file groups shown in Figure 12.15 and click OK.

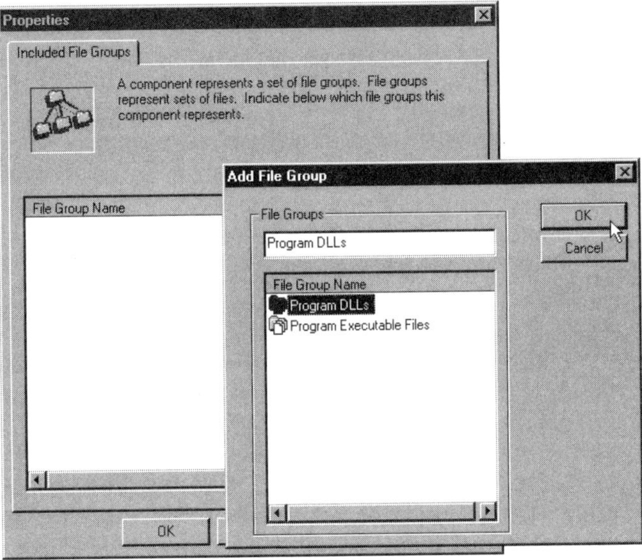

Figure 12.15 Adding a file group to the list of project components

6. Click the Add button again, and add the remaining group, Program Executable Files.
7. With both file groups listed in the Properties dialog box, click OK to close the dialog box.

By default, InstallShield assumes the self-registering feature is unavailable. It is therefore necessary to add to the project script two lines of code that cause the setup program to call Beeper's *DllRegisterServer* function.

► **Make the self-registering feature available**

1. Select the Scripts tab in the project workspace to expose the script window.
2. Scroll down to locate the *MoveFileData* function. InstallShield provides a Find command on the Edit menu that can help you locate the *MoveFileData* source code.
3. Just before the line that calls *ComponentMoveData*, add a call to the *Enable* function, passing it the SELFREGISTERBATCH value. Immediately after the line that calls *HandleMoveDataError*, add a line that passes the SELFREGISTRATIONPROCESS value to the *Do* function. The result after these two additions should look like this:

```
Enable(SELFREGISTERBATCH);
nResult = ComponentMoveData(MEDIA, nDisk, 0);
HandleMoveDataError(nResult);
Do(SELFREGISTRATIONPROCESS);
```

InstallShield provides a Function Wizard that can save you the effort of typing these lines and that helps ensure accuracy. To invoke the Function Wizard, create a blank line in the script by pressing the Enter key, right-click the blank line, and choose the Function Wizard command from the shortcut menu. Select a function name such as *Enable* in the list to the right and click Next. You can then select the SELFREGISTERBATCH parameter value from the combo box list.

Exercise 5: Building the Setup Program

You are now ready to create the setup program using the Media Build Wizard. After the wizard walks you through several steps, it compresses all executables into .cab files and generates the Setup.exe program.

► **Create the setup program**

1. Click the Media Build Wizard command on InstallShield's Build menu.
2. In the wizard's first step, type *Client2-Beeper* in the Media Name box shown in Figure 12.16 and click the Next button.

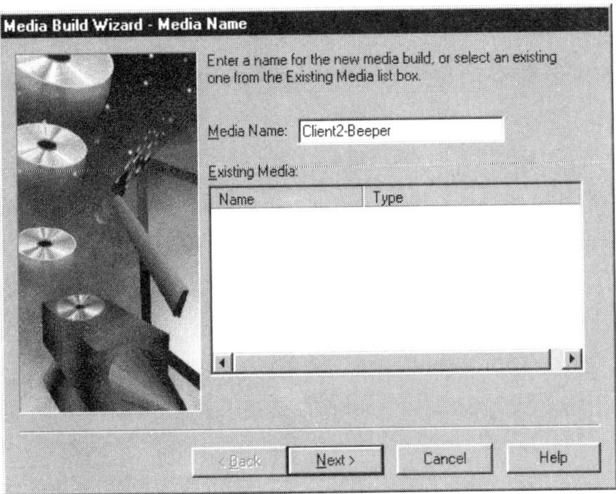

Figure 12.16 The first step of the Media Build Wizard

3. In the second step, accept the default choice specifying 3.5-inch disk and click Next.
4. In the third step, accept the default Full Build setting and click the Advanced button.
5. In the Build Location tab of the Property Sheet dialog box, specify the folder to which you want InstallShield to write the setup files, as shown in Figure 12.17.

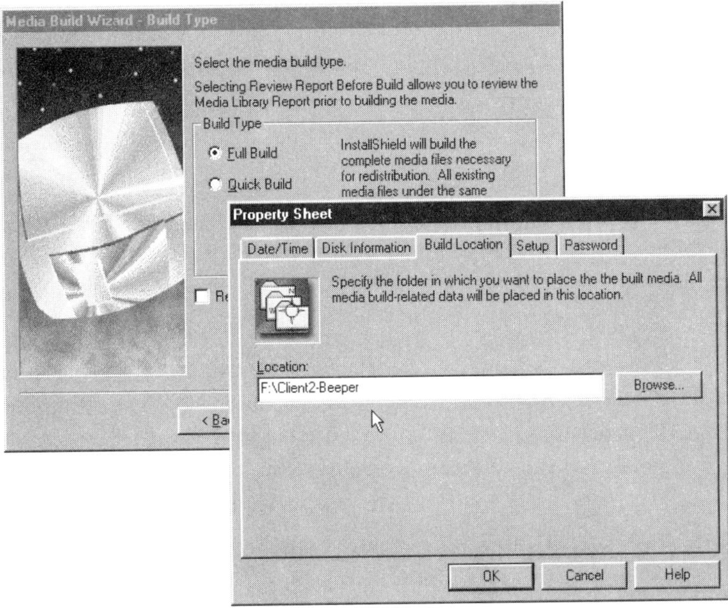

Figure 12.17 Specifying the build location for the setup program

6. Click OK to close the Property Sheet dialog box.
7. Click Next twice to skip over the wizard's fourth step and advance to the summary page.
8. Click the Finish button to build the setup program.
9. When the build is complete, click the Finish button again.

Exercise 6: Deploying and Testing the Setup Program

The folder specified in the Build Location tab contains a subfolder named Disk Images\Disk1, which holds files that can be copied to a single 3.5–inch floppy disk. In this final exercise, you will distribute the disk to a fictitious customer, who will install the Client2 program and the Beeper component on another network. A second network is not necessary for this exercise, as instructions are included for unregistering the Beeper component from your development network. Your own network can then represent your customer's network to which the application is deployed.

▶ **Unregister the Beeper component from your network**

1. Execute MTS Explorer on your server, expand the tree view, and right-click the Beeper package listed in the left pane.
2. Click Delete on the shortcut menu to delete the package. When MTS Explorer prompts for confirmation, click OK.
3. Run RegSvr32 on both your network server and on your workstation to uninstall the Beeper component, using the */u* switch in each case. The switch causes RegSvr32 to call Beeper's *DllUnregisterServer* function, which removes all information from the registry. The correct command-line sequence looks like the following, where *path* represents the path to the Beeper.dll file:

   ```
   regsvr32 /u path\beeper.dll
   ```

   It does not matter whether you specify the debug or release version of the file, because both versions use the same class identifiers. If you are not certain whether Beeper is still installed, run RegSvr32 anyway, as calling *DllUnregisterServer* for an uninstalled component does no harm. Remember to run the utility on all computers on which Beeper is present.

When the registries have been cleaned of Beeper's settings, you can then test the setup by installing both Client2 and Beeper on your network. Copy the installation files to a diskette if you wish, although this step is not necessary if you are re-installing to your development computer. The files required for installation include:

- The release version of the Beeper.dll file created in Exercise 1
- The Beeper.pak file exported from MTS Explorer in Exercise 2
- All contents of the Images\Disk1 folder that InstallShield created in Exercise 5

The first part of the exercise describes the tasks that normally would fall to a system administrator. A real installation program would include a set of instructions for the administrator modeled after the following steps.

► **Install the Beeper MTS component to a server**

1. Copy Beeper.dll and Beeper.pak to any location on the server's hard disk.
2. Run RegSvr32 to register Beeper.dll, typing the following command:

   ```
   regsvr32 path\beeper.dll
   ```

   (As before, *path* represents the path to the Beeper.dll file.) RegSvr32 displays a message saying that *DllRegisterServer* succeeded; if any other message appears, it most likely indicates that the path has not been entered correctly. Reenter the command, carefully typing the full path and filename.
3. Start MTS Explorer.
4. Expand the tree list in the left pane and select the Packages Installed folder under My Computer.
5. On the Action menu, select New, and click Package.
6. When the Package Wizard appears, click the large button labeled Install Pre-built Packages as shown in Figure 12.18.

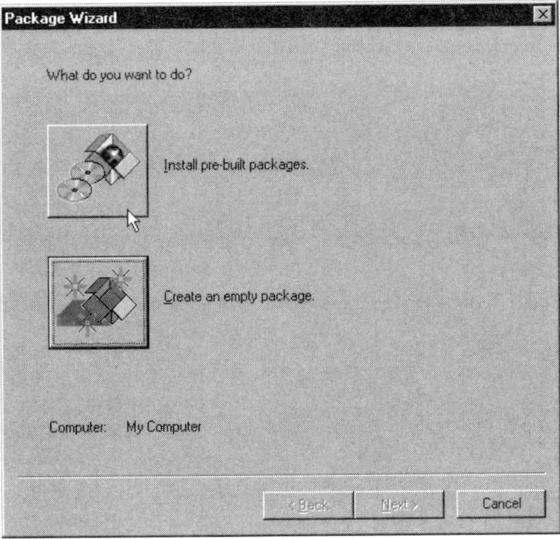

Figure 12.18 Installing a pre-built package in MTS Explorer

7. When the Select Package Files dialog box appears, click the Add button.
8. In the Install From Package File dialog box, browse for the Beeper.pak file, select it, and click Open. The Beeper.pak file appears in the Select Package Files dialog box.

9. At the next step, accept the setting for interactive user.
10. The next step shows the default installation path as Program Files\Mts\Packages. Accept the default path and click the Finish button. The list of installed packages in MTS Explorer now includes an entry for the Beeper component.
11. Right-click the new Beeper entry in the list and choose Properties from the shortcut menu.
12. Expose the Security tab in the Beeper Properties dialog box. Notice that the current authentication level is the same as when you created the package. The Beeper.pak file contains all information pertaining to the component, including its security settings.
13. Click Cancel to close the dialog box.
14. Close MTS Explorer.
15. Move to the workstation on which you intend to install the Client2 application. If you copied the setup files to a diskette, place the diskette in the disk drive.
16. In Control Panel, double-click the icon for the Add/Remove Programs utility.
17. Click the Install button and click Next.
18. If you have not inserted a diskette, the Run Installation Program dialog box prompts you to browse for the Setup.exe program. Click the Browse button and navigate to the Disk Images\Disk1 folder created in Exercise 5. Select Setup.exe and click Open, then click the Finish button.
19. The Setup program begins, first displaying the prototype splash screen shown in Figure 12.19, which is followed by the Welcome dialog box.

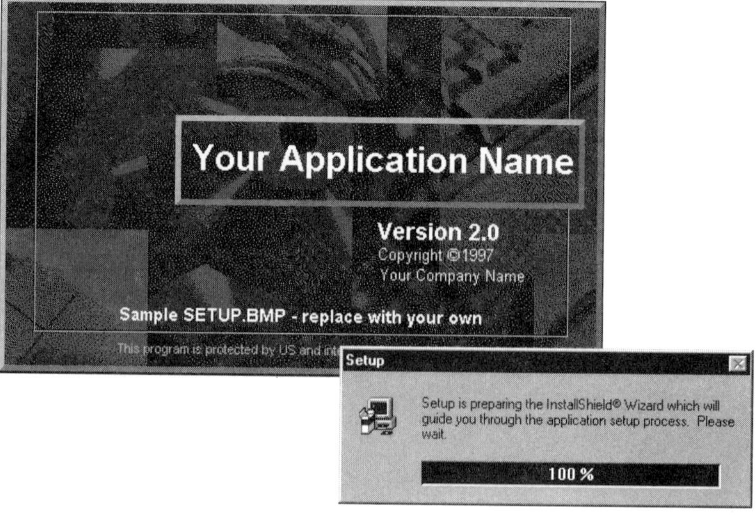

Figure 12.19 Starting the Setup program

20. At the next screen, click the Browse button and navigate to the location where you want the Client2.exe program installed. If you specify a folder that does not exist, the Setup program asks if you want it to create the folder for you.
21. Click Next and then click Finish.

    The Setup program registers the Beeper.dll component and then terminates. The Client2 program is now ready to execute. Run the program and specify on the command line the name of the server that hosts the Beeper component, as illustrated here:

    ```
    client2 serversys
    ```

    The Client2 program does not appear in the taskbar's Programs menu because the required code for this feature was not added in Exercise 4. If you wish to place a command in the Programs menu, follow the procedure outlined in the InstallShield tutorial described in Lesson 2, and then rebuild the project.

One of the advantages to using InstallShield to create the Setup program is that it automatically provides a professional-quality uninstallation feature. To remove the Client2 program, start the Add/Remove Programs utility, select Client2-Beeper Application in the list of installed programs, and click the Add/Remove button. After confirming that you want to delete files, the uninstall procedure first calls Beeper's *DllUnregisterServer* function to clean the registry. Before deleting the Beeper.dll file, it notifies you that the shared file is no longer used by any programs and queries for permission to delete it. Click the Yes button, after which both the Client2.exe and Beeper.dll files are deleted.

Review

The following questions are intended to reinforce key information presented in this chapter. If you are unable to answer a question, review the appropriate lesson and then try answering the question again. Answers to the questions can be found in Appendix B, "Review Questions and Answers," at the back of this book.

1. What are the two stages of deployment?

2. What are cabinet files and registry files?

3. What is the purpose of the InstallShield tool?

4. Must a COM server be registered on a system before it can operate? If so, what examples can you give of a server's registry information?

5. Name three modes of application deployment.

6. How does MTS Explorer facilitate the deployment of components?

7. You have written a distributed application that uses MSMQ. What steps can you take to ensure queues are properly created on your customer's computers?

8. What is load balancing?

9. What is ZAW?

APPENDIX A

Application Design Concepts

Lesson 1: Architecture Descriptions 712

Lesson 2: Design Process 724

About This Appendix

In this appendix, you will learn about application design principles, which can be used as a road map for creating successful applications, including distributed applications. Along with learning ways to describe an application's design, you will learn about additional development life-cycle processes that your development team can use in structuring an application's development process. Additionally, you will learn about a detailed design approach that you can use to define an application architecture. This approach, the Microsoft Solutions Framework (MSF) design process, can provide your development team with a means to identify and design the application's classes and components. This book advocates a slightly modified version of the traditional MSF design process, expanded to include certain concepts from the Unified Software Development Process (Unified Process or UP) and the Unified Modeling Language (UML).

Although the concepts discussed in this appendix are not specifically addressed in Exam 70-015, they are an important part of application development in general, and are particularly important for the development of distributed applications. This appendix cites several useful texts that will provide a good foundation as you study for Exam 70-015.

Before You Begin

To complete the lessons in this appendix, you must have a basic understanding of the application development life cycle.

Lesson 1: Architecture Descriptions

Any architectural plan is only as good as the depth of its detail and the breadth of its coverage. The construction plan for a house that didn't include the electrical or plumbing subplans would be seriously flawed, as would a plan that included all necessary drawings but lacked any strategy for obtaining and storing the building materials. A complete design architecture includes both application design and plans for execution.

This lesson discusses various approaches that address the need for architecture descriptions and processes. You will take a brief look at UML, a popular language for describing and modeling both processes and software. What follows is an introductory discussion of design patterns and antipatterns, intriguing ways of examining problems and solutions that lend themselves to design and component reuse.

Both the Unified Process and the MSF are examples of development life cycle approaches to creating applications. This lesson explores both MSF and Unified Process, showing each framework's various models that are pertinent to design and execution tasks.

After this lesson, you will be able to:

- Describe techniques to define application architectures
- Describe architecture models that aid in application design

Estimated lesson time: 40 minutes

Architecture Definitions

One of the difficulties involved in developing an application architecture is finding a common terminology to express new concepts and apply existing concepts. Ways of overcoming communication difficulties are not addressed in Exam 70-015, but because these difficulties can exist on both the development and organization levels, tools for addressing them are discussed in this section.

Unified Modeling Language

One of the most important factors in delivering successful applications is the ability to communicate process, business, and technical information to everyone involved on a project. UML can provide the common language with which to communicate and build this information.

A complete description of UML is beyond the scope of this book. However, because it is often used to help organizations visualize, specify, create, and document the artifacts of a software solution, its key features are discussed briefly here.

The current version of UML evolved from several primary modeling languages that were prevalent in the late 1980s and 1990s. Further additions and approval by the Object Management Group (OMG) have increased UML's status as a strongly supported, industry-standard modeling tool.

UML can be separated into four sections:

- **Modeling elements** These elements are categorized into four primary groups:
  - Structural
  - Behavioral
  - Grouping
  - Other
- **Relationships** These elements are also categorized into four groups:
  - Dependency
  - Association
  - Generalization
  - Realization
- **Extensibility mechanisms** These elements provide a mechanism for adding capabilities to models.
- **Diagrams** These elements provide graphical representations of an application solution. Each diagram is represented in either a static or dynamic view. (See Table A.1 on the following page.) Different views provide different perspectives of a problem, and a specific model within UML represents each view.

Table A.1 Static and Dynamic UML Diagram Views

View	Model	Characteristics
Static	Use case	Built in the early stages of development to capture an application's functionality as seen by users. The purpose of use case is to specify an application's context, capture its requirements, validate its architecture, drive implementation, and generate test cases. Typically generated by analysts or experts in a particular problem or industry domain.
	Class	Captures an application's vocabulary. After it is built, it is continually refined throughout the application's development. Classes exist to name and model solution concepts, specify collaborations, and specify logical database schemas. Generated by systems analysts, designers, and implementers.
	Object	Shows specific instances and links to other objects. Created during the analysis and design phase. Illustrates data and object structures and provides specific snapshots of system occurrences. Typically generated by systems analysts, designers, and implementers.
	Component	Captures the physical structure leading to implementation. Created as part of the architectural process before development, thus the architecture-driven approach. Components exist to organize and structure source code, lead the construction of an executable release, and specify a physical database structure. Created by the systems architects and programmers.
	Deployment	Captures the actual topology of an application's installation and hardware. Deployment specifies component distribution and identifies application performance bottlenecks. Created as part of the architectural process by systems architects, network engineers, and systems engineers.
Dynamic	Sequence	Captures time-oriented, dynamic behaviors. Sequences represent an application's flow controls. Describes what the application does in typical scenarios.
	Collaboration	Captures message-oriented dynamic behavior. Also represents flow controls and demonstrates the object structures' coordinated behavior.
	Statechart	Captures event-oriented behaviors. Can represent objects' life cycles and reactive nature. Often used to help model the user interface (UI), as well as devices.
	Activity	Captures movement-oriented behaviors. Primarily used to model the business workflow, the application's interaction with business workflows, and general operations.

An understanding of UML can be helpful in developing and communicating successful application architectures. Several textbooks provide more information about UML, including *The Unified Modeling Language User Guide* (Addison-Wesley, 1998) by Grady Booch, Ivar Jacobson, and James Rumbaugh; and *Tried and True Object Development: Practical Approaches with UML* (Cambridge University Press, 1999) by Ari Jaaksi, Juha-Markus Aalto, Ari Aalto, and Kimmo Vatto.

Design Patterns

Another approach to describing and communicating complex application architectures involves using *design patterns*. The principles of design patterns were first applied to building architecture by Christopher Alexander, Sara Ishikawa, and Murray Silverstein in *A Pattern Language: Towns, Buildings, Construction* (Oxford University Press, 1977). In 1995, Erich Gamma, Richard Helm, Ralph Johnson, and John Vlissides applied these principles to software engineering in their foundation book *Design Patterns: Elements of Reusable Object-Oriented Software* (Addison-Wesley, 1995), where the authors stated that the pattern technique:

> *...identifies the key aspects of a common design structure that make it useful for creating a reusable object-oriented design.*

The term *design patterns* has achieved buzzword status. Anything and everything must follow a pattern, and all architectural designers have identified their designs as a pattern. In an article in the *Theory and Practice of Object Systems* journal, Dirk Riehle and Heinz Zullighoven provide a definition that represents the practices of the design pattern community:

> *A pattern is instructive information that captures the essential structure and insight of a successful family of proven solutions to a recurring problem that arises within a certain context and system of forces.*

This definition provides some clues on how to identify a pattern. As noted in *Pattern Languages of Program Design* by James O. Coplien, Douglas C. Schmidt (Editor), Jim Coplien (Addison-Wesley, 1995), a design pattern has the following characteristics, which you can use to identify a design pattern:

- Solves a problem, and the solution to this problem is not obvious
- Is a proven concept
- Describes a relationship
- Has a significant human component

Another way to identify a design pattern is to remember that it is a recurring phenomenon and is subject to the *rule of three*; that is, it can be identified in at least three separate systems or solutions within the same problem domain.

Design patterns can be either generative or nongenerative. *Generative* patterns can be used to solve engineering problems, whereas *nongenerative* patterns are merely observed. In his book *The Timeless Way of Building* (Oxford University Press, 1979), Christopher Alexander discusses the difference in these terms (we've added the term in brackets):

> *...in one respect they are very different. The patterns* [nongenerative] *in the world merely exist. But the same patterns in our minds are dynamic. They*

have force. They are generative. They tell us what to do; they tell us how we shall, or may, generate them; and they tell us too, that under certain circumstances, we must create them. Each pattern is a rule which describes what you have to do to generate the entity which it defines.

Fortunately for those of us who wish to reuse them, a number of generative patterns can be applied to solve common application problems. These patterns typically are defined within a template. Some patterns focus on a particular industry segment, while some address specific technical design problems. Although an organization can identify its own patterns for its applications, it should first follow the patterns that have successfully provided solutions within the software industry.

To apply a pattern to an application, you must identify technical and business requirements for your application. After you have set requirements, you can select the design pattern that best fits the needs of your application. A good generative design pattern supplies the rationale for the solution's requirements as well as the solution itself. However, most software development design patterns stop at the architectural level and do not suggest specific code implementations. In this respect, design patterns get to the heart of reusability, because they enable entire system architectures to be reused.

As with any science, disagreement can abound on what should be included in a properly defined pattern. However, several common elements exist among many patterns. The general consensus regarding these elements has been summarized by Brad Appleton in his paper *Patterns and Software: Essential Concepts and Terminology* (*http://www.enteract.com/~bradapp/docs/patterns-intro.html*); these elements are outlined in the following:

- **Name** A meaningful single word or short phrase that identifies the pattern and the structure it describes. (In some cases, patterns are identified by their classifications in addition to their names.) Solid pattern names form a vocabulary for discussing conceptual abstractions. When more than one name has been assigned to a single pattern, the alternative names are documented as aliases.
- **Problem** A statement of the predicament that describes the goals and objectives you want to reach within the given context and forces. Often the forces oppose these objectives as well as one another.
- **Context** The preconditions under which the problem and its solution occur and for which the solution is desirable. You can consider the context as the initial configuration of the application before the pattern is applied.
- **Forces** A description of all the relevant pressures and constraints, and how they interact or conflict with one another and with the goals to be achieved. Forces reveal the intricacies of a problem and define the kinds of tradeoffs that must be considered.

- **Solution** A description of how to realize the desired outcome. Instructions can provide pictures, diagrams, and text to show how the problem is solved. The solution should describe not only the static structure (the pattern's form and organization) but also the dynamic behavior, which can provide guidelines as well as pitfalls to avoid when attempting a concrete implementation of the solution.
- **Examples** One or more sample applications of the pattern that illustrate a specific initial context; how the pattern is applied to and transforms that context; and the resulting context left in its wake. Easy-to-comprehend examples from known systems are usually preferable.
- **Resulting context** The state of the application after the pattern has been applied, including the consequences (both positive and negative) of applying the pattern, and other problems and patterns that can arise from the new context. When a pattern is just one step toward accomplishing a larger task or project, the resulting context of the pattern is often correlated with the initial context of other patterns.
- **Rationale** A justifying explanation of steps or rules in the pattern, and also of the pattern as a whole, in terms of how and why it resolves its forces in a particular manner to be aligned with desired goals, principles, and philosophies. The rationale provides insight into the deep structures and key mechanisms of the system and explains how the pattern works, why it works, and why it is beneficial.
- **Related patterns** The static and dynamic relationships between this pattern and others within the same pattern language. Related patterns often share common forces and have compatible resulting or initial contexts, provide alternative solutions to the same problem, or become codependent.
- **Known uses** The known occurrences of the pattern and its application within existing systems. Known uses verify that the pattern is a proven solution for a recurring problem. Known uses of the pattern often serve as instructional examples.

A typical design pattern has a brief abstract that summarizes all these elements, and presents a clear picture of the forces and the solution that the pattern addresses.

Design Antipatterns

Generative design patterns provide complete solutions to business and technical problems. These patterns are primarily geared toward "green field," or new, designs. Design antipatterns are geared toward solving problems for which an inadequate solution is already in place. The best way to differentiate patterns and antipatterns is to follow the lead of William Brown, Raphael Malveau, Hays McCormick III, and Thomas Mowbray in their book *AntiPatterns: Refactoring Software, Architectures, and Projects in Crisis* (John Wiley & Sons, 1998):

> *Patterns lead to an original solution for a set of criteria and forces. Antipatterns lead to a new solution when the current design is not working.*

In other words, you should use patterns when starting from scratch, and antipatterns when fixing an incomplete or nonfunctional solution. Figure A.1, also taken from *AntiPatterns: Refactoring Software, Architectures, and Projects in Crisis,* illustrates the differences between design patterns and antipatterns.

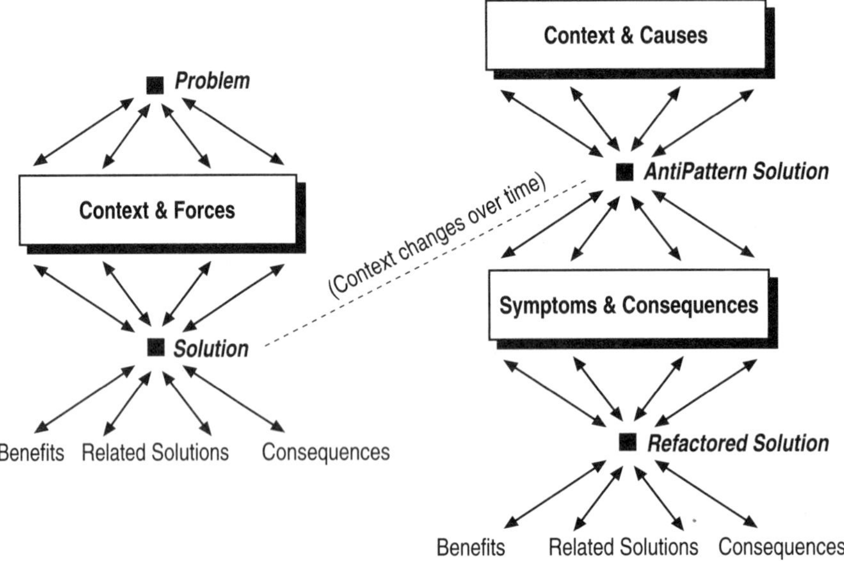

Figure A.1 Differences between design patterns and antipatterns

Design patterns and antipatterns are similar in their structures and underlying principles. Thus, like design patterns, antipatterns:

- Have a structured description that provides a common language for communicating with everyone involved in an application development project
- Require the rule of three
- Begin with a recurring problem

Existing antipattern definitions can be leveraged as solutions, or as starting points for the process of creating organization-specific antipatterns. Antipatterns can provide a structured way for new or novice software developers to learn how to solve complex application development problems that they will encounter.

Unified Software Development Process

The information in this section is primarily based on *Software Project Management: A Unified Framework* (Addison-Wesley, 1998) and on *The Unified Software Development Process* (Addison-Wesley, 1999). Although we try to summarize this model accurately, this brief discussion nevertheless reflects our interpretation of the Unified Process, which is based on our development experience. For a strict definition of Unified Process, refer to the source texts mentioned above.

One commonly used model for the analysis, design, and implementation of enterprise applications is the Unified Process. The Unified Process, which requires extensive use of UML modeling, is:

- Use-case driven
- Architecture-centric
- An iterative and incremental development process
- Risk-confronting
- An object-oriented and layered-design approach
- A repository for object-oriented system development patterns, objects, and code

Workflows

At the heart of Unified Process are five core workflows that are continually executed during the four phases of the development process (discussed below) until the application is completed. Each completion of the five workflow steps is called an *iteration;* each iteration culminates in an internal product release. The workflows' names are descriptors that simplify communication. The core workflows are:

- **Requirements** Gathers business, application, and technical requirements
- **Analysis** Provides business and application modeling derived from requirements
- **Design** Uses object-oriented design techniques to complete the application architecture
- **Implementation** Executes designed work, including prototypes
- **Testing** Verifies that the work has been done properly

Subsequent iterations restart the cycle with the Requirements Workflow.

Project Phases

Unified Process is based primarily on the traditional Spiral Model for application development, and like that model, it divides the development process into four phases: Inception, Elaboration, Construction, and Transition. Each phase strives to achieve specific goals as follows:

- **Inception** Focuses on producing the business case
- **Elaboration** Is responsible for developing the baseline architecture
- **Construction** Focuses on creating the product with incremental releases of product builds and features
- **Transition** Ensures that the product is ready for release to users

Requirements and the analysis, design, and implementation architecture represent the majority of work within the Inception and Elaboration Phases. The completion of each phase describes the application in detail using Unified Process models.

In addition, movement from one phase to the next is the result of reaching goals and milestones for the initial phase. At each phase's major milestone, a critical go/no-go business decision is made about whether the project should continue, thus approving the next phase's requirements for budget and schedule. These major milestones are the synchronization points between the technical and business portions of the project.

Iterations

As development of the product continues through its phases, each workflow iteration brings the product closer to its final release. Iterations are continued within a specific phase until the goal for that phase has been reached. The emphasis of each iteration changes as time progresses through the four phases. Over time, the amount of detail displayed within each Unified Process model grows; thereafter, the models are gradually completed.

Microsoft Solutions Framework

MSF is a collection of models, principles, and practices that helps organizations become more effective in their creation and use of technology to solve their business problems. MSF helps project teams by providing measurable progress and rigorous guidance that is flexible enough to meet an organization's changing needs. The core building blocks for this solution's guidance are the six major MSF models, as follows:

- Enterprise Architecture Model
- Risk Management Model
- Team Model for Application Development

- Process Model for Application Development
- Application Model
- Design Process Model

This section describes each model briefly and elaborates further on its specific uses.

MSF Enterprise Architecture Model

The MSF Enterprise Architecture Model provides a consistent set of guidelines for rapidly building enterprise architecture through versioned releases. The model aligns information technology with business requirements through four perspectives: Business, Application, Information, and Technology. Using this model helps shorten the enterprise architecture planning cycle.

MSF Risk Management Model

The MSF Risk Management Model provides a structured and proactive way to manage project risks. This model sets forth a discipline and environment of proactive decisions and actions to continuously assess potential problems, determine what risks are important to confront, and implement strategies to deal with those risks. Using this model and its underlying principles and practices helps teams focus on the most important aspects of a project design, make sound decisions, and be more thoroughly prepared for when the unknown future becomes known.

MSF Team Model for Application Development

The MSF Team Model for Application Development (MSF Development Team Model) provides a flexible structure for organizing project teams. This model emphasizes clear roles, responsibilities, and goals for team success, and increases team member accountability through a team-of-peers approach. The Development Team Model's flexibility allows for adaptation depending on project scope, team size, and team member skills. Using this model and its underlying principles and practices helps produce more engaged, effective, resilient, and successful teams.

MSF Process Model for Application Development

The MSF Process Model for Application Development (MSF Development Process Model) provides structure and guidance through a project's life cycle that is milestone-based, iterative, and flexible. This model describes the phases, milestones, activities, and deliverables of an application development project, and these elements' relationship to MSF Development Team Model roles. Using this model helps improve project control, minimize risk, improve quality, and shorten delivery time.

MSF Application Model

The MSF Application Model provides a logical, multi-layer, services-based approach to designing and developing software applications. The implementation of user, business, and data services allows for parallel development of application code, efficient use of technology, easier maintenance and support, and optimal flexibility in distribution. The services that make up the application can reside anywhere from a single desktop to servers and clients around the world.

MSF Design Process Model

The MSF Design Process Model provides a three-phase, user-centric continuum that allows for a parallel and iterative approach to design for the greatest efficiency and flexibility. Three design phases—Conceptual, Logical, and Physical—provide three different perspectives for three unique audiences: users, project teams, and developers. Moving through the three design phases shows the translation of user-based scenarios to services-based components so that application features can be traced back to user requirements. Using this model helps ensure that applications are created to meet business and user requirements.

Presentation of MSF, Unified Process, and UML in this Book

Throughout this book, some of the basic concepts of MSF, the Unified Process, and UML provide a foundation for discussions of application design and implementation. The MSF models and their key principles originate within the MSF team at Microsoft; the Unified Process originates with the Rational Corporation; and an industry-based committee controls UML. This book draws upon materials provided by the Microsoft MSF team, as well as publications on the Unified Process and UML.

This book also uses other resources and application development experiences to round out these concepts and show how they can be applied in practical ways within an organization. This book attempts to maintain integrity in its discussions of MSF, Unified Process, and UML concepts. However, you should refer to the MSF material for a specific and complete treatment of MSF. For details on Unified Process and UML issues, you should consult *The Unified Software Development Process* and *The Unified Modeling Language User Guide* (Addison-Wesley, 1998). For additional information, you can also read *Analyzing Requirements and Defining Solution Architectures: MCSD Training Kit* (Microsoft Press, 1999).

Lesson Summary

One of the most important factors in delivering successful applications is being able to communicate process, business, and technical information to all individuals involved in a project design. UML can provide the common language with which to communicate application designs and build an understanding of these designs with the project's customer, users, and the application team. UML's primary purpose is to help organizations visualize, specify, create, and document the artifacts of a software solution.

Another approach to describing and communicating complex application architectures involves the use of design patterns. A design pattern identifies the key aspects of a common design structure that make it useful for creating a reusable object-oriented design. Such a pattern is instructive information that captures the essential structure and insight of a successful family of proven solutions to a recurring problem that arises within a certain context and system of forces.

Generative design patterns provide complete solutions to business and technical problems. They are primarily geared toward "green field" or new designs. Design antipatterns are geared toward solving problems for which an inadequate solution is already in place. As cited in the lesson, the best way to differentiate patterns and antipatterns is found in the following quote from *AntiPatterns: Refactoring Software, Architectures, and Projects in Crisis*:

> *Patterns lead to an original solution for a set of criteria and forces.*
> *Antipatterns lead to a new solution when the current design is not working.*

Also discussed is the need for a systematic approach to the task of design and execution. One commonly used application life cycle framework for the analysis, design, and implementation of enterprise applications is the Unified Process. Requiring extensive use of UML, the Unified Process is use-case driven; architecture-centric; risk-confronting; and representative of an iterative and incremental development process, an object-oriented and layered design approach, and a repository for object-oriented application development patterns, objects, and code. One of the key components of the Unified Process is its use of models for showing both an application's design and the processes used to design and build such an application.

MSF is a collection of models, principles, and practices that help organizations become more effective in their creation and use of technology to solve their business problems. MSF helps the project team by providing measurable progress and rigorous guidance that is flexible enough to meet an organization's changing needs. The core models of MSF that are applicable to the scope of this book are:

- Process Model for Application Development
- Risk Management Model
- Design Process Model
- Application Model

In addition to these four models, the MSF Enterprise Application Model provides insight into the various viewpoints and layers of large, complex enterprise systems; and the MSF Team Model for Application Development discusses the roles often used to successfully complete a development project.

Lesson 2: Design Process

As a developer, you must answer two fundamental questions before beginning any project:

1. Will you use a systematic process to do your work?
2. If so, which process will you use?

The answer to the first question should almost always be "Yes." All except the smallest and simplest projects will benefit from a systematic approach to your application's design and implementation tasks. A well thought-out design process ensures that all user requirements are known and that an implementation plan is in place before beginning work on development. Using a standardized process for designing and building your applications will ultimately save development time and reduce your stress level, because you're more confident that you will build the application your customer wants.

The answer to the second question is somewhat more problematic, because multitudes of possibilities exist when designing an application. Although various design systems have been formulated over the years, this book endorses, as an ideal approach for application design and planning, a slightly modified version of the MSF design process. As mentioned, this modified design process is expanded to include certain concepts from the Unified Process and UML, discussed later in this appendix.

After this lesson, you will be able to:

- Understand the three-phase MSF design process
- Understand the Use Case Model
- Understand the Class Model

Estimated lesson time: 90 minutes

Introduction to the Design Process

The design process consists of three distinct phases of design work: conceptual, logical, and physical. Each of these phases generates a model of the same name, approaches the design task from a different perspective, and defines the solution differently, shown in Table A.2.

Table A.2 Approaches of Three-Phase Design Process

Phase	Perspective	Action
Conceptual	Views the problem from the perspective of the user and business	Defines the problem and solution in terms of use cases and scenarios
Logical	Views the solution from the perspective of the project team	Defines the solution as a set of cooperating services
Physical	Views the solution from the perspective of the developers	Defines the solution's services and technologies

Each phase consists of a starting and ending point. In practice, these phases are not executed in a strict, linear fashion, with each phase's completion signaling the beginning of the next phase. As noted later in this lesson, the design phases are instead overlapped; in other words, logical design can begin before conceptual design is completed. After enough information is gathered for a phase, a baseline of that phase's model is created. Each model contains the outputs of the work performed during a particular phase. This baselined output is used as the input for the succeeding phase, as Figure A.2 illustrates.

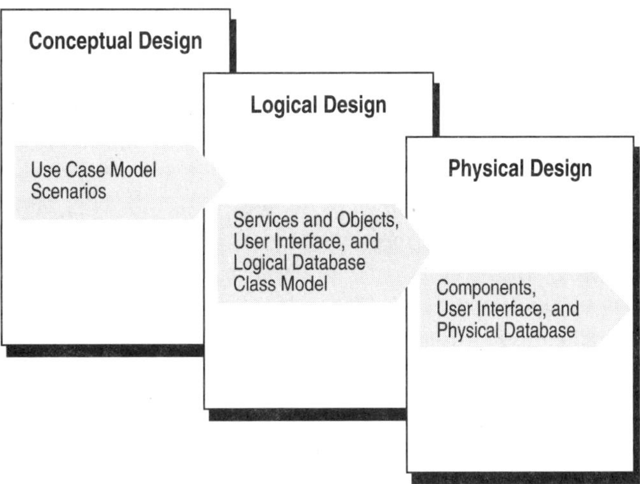

Figure A.2 Outputs of the three interdependent design process models

The goals of the three models are as follows:

- **Conceptual Design** Identify business needs and understand what functions users perform, and what they require the application to do. Conceptual Design produces the baselined Use Case Model and scenarios that reflect complete and accurate requirements by involving the customer, users, and other stakeholders in the application's development. It also begins the creation of the Class Model.

- **Logical Design** Organize the solution and the communication among its elements. Logical Design takes the business problem identified in Conceptual Design Use Case Model and scenerios and formulates an abstract model of the solution. Following the workflow in Figure A.2, Logical Design takes the scenarios from Conceptual Design and produces services and objects, UI prototypes, and a logical database design. Additionally, the Class Model detail is improved along with updating the Use Case Model to reflect any changes.
- **Physical Design** Apply real-world technology constraints, including implementation and performance considerations, to the outputs of Logical Design by specifying solution details. The outputs of Logical Design are used to produce components, UI specifications, and physical database design. This also signifies the baseline of the Class Model with the Use Case Model once again receiving updates as needed.

Within the application life cycle, the Design Process begins whenever enough user requirements have been gathered to begin Conceptual Design. The design work continues throughout the application's planning phase, culminating in a design document. This design document then serves as the basis for the actual developing phase of the project. Note that the phase and model names are provided to help show some steps and documentation for an application design. The names are not the important thing to remember, but the actual work and workflow being described.

Conceptual Design

The first phase of the design process, Conceptual Design, is the process of acquiring, documenting, validating, and optimizing business and user perspectives of the problem and solution. The purpose of Conceptual Design is to capture and understand business needs and user requirements in their proper contexts. The output of Conceptual Design is a set of information models, use cases, and usage scenarios that document the current state of existing systems and the future state of the solution that you will develop.

Conceptual Design can be compared with the first stage of designing a house, when both the client and architect collaborate on a rough sketch and a short list of needs and requirements. Using the Conceptual Design Model facilitates the gathering of complete and accurate requirements by involving the customer, users, and other stakeholders. Without a solid conceptual design, the project team might end up with a wonderful solution to the wrong problem, thus not helping the customer and/or users.

In application design and development, it is critical that products are *user-centric*, or attuned to users' true requirements. User-centric means having an awareness of how users view the current environment and what they would like to see in a new product. Whereas gathering requirements has traditionally meant compiling a list of desirable features, your aim in Conceptual Design is to understand and document the relationships among the users, the application, and the organization. It is vital that you uncover what users truly care about when you begin to develop an application.

The goals for Conceptual Design are as follows:

- **A design based on real data from the customer and users** This data represents the organization's needs and user requirements for the solution.
- **A coherent, integrated picture of the product** The project team needs to understand exactly how the proposed application affects the application's intended organization and users.
- **Useful levels of abstraction or classification** Conceptual Design uncovers information about the organization itself. Understanding users and their requirements in the context of organizational activities eliminates unnecessary or extraneous requirements, and increases the visibility of the critical requirements that remain.
- **A common set of expectations among the customer, users, and the project team** Agreement is important early in the process, not only because divergent expectations (which can only increase with time) can be dangerous, but also because these three parties are all important to the product's success.
- **Group consensus in design** Consensus ensures the implemented solution's success.
- **Synchronization with the enterprise architecture** Conceptual Design represents one of the earliest opportunities for the customer, users, and project team to validate the application architecture, and also to validate the proposed application against the business models included in the enterprise architecture.
- **A basis for team communication** Including the customer and users as project participants fosters open communication, and in turn reduces the possibility of future design changes, due to an ongoing understanding of the evolving solution.

The Conceptual Design phase consists of three subphases, or steps: *research, analysis,* and *rationalization*.

Research

To begin research, you must first determine the focus of your investigation. For example, you might start by describing the core operational processes of the appropriate organizational area, rather than the organizational function. Your descriptions might address:

- Core organizational processes and their boundaries, along with the functional elements of the organization
- High-level details about organizational transactions within these processes
- The customer and users

More specific details can include organizational process maps and their interdependencies, information structure and usage, and measurements and metrics (such as revenue per unit, expenses, operational locations, forecasts, and projections). Much of this information can be obtained from the enterprise architecture documentation, if it is available. When using UML or the Unified Process Model, these activities can be related to the use case, activity, and collaboration models.

The project team should conduct a high-level evaluation of existing organizational processes and activities in the context of enterprise strategy, goals, and objectives in the focus area. It should identify core corporate processes that support the organization's objectives and goals. These objectives and goals can represent product, service, or managerial processes, and in most cases, they are cross-functional in nature and move horizontally across the organization rather than vertically within its traditional departments or *silos*.

A core process:

- Runs the organization
- Directly addresses strategic directions and competitiveness
- Contains identifiable owners and customers
- Has a definition that makes as much sense to external customers or suppliers as it does to internal staff
- Depends discretely and minimally on other core processes

After you have identified and prioritized organizational processes and activities, you should conduct additional investigations to complete your understanding, such as tapping into the organizational culture, gathering artifacts, and so on. You should strive to gain a complete, accurate picture, prioritizing quality of information over quantity of data. Examples of these processes can be an organization's sales, marketing, accounting, production, customer service, human relations, inventory, distribution, services, or other processes that form the core of the organization.

In addition to researching organizational processes, you can also conduct research on users and user groups. The first step is to identify as many groups as possible, including the organization's owner, users within the organization, and users outside the organization such as suppliers and consumers. After the various constituencies have been identified, a user profile must be created for each one, detailing the group's role in the organization, as well as the group's department, location, and involvement in specific activities. Any background data appropriate to the project scope should be included. Finally, user roles must be related to the activities and processes documented earlier.

You are ready to move to application requirement analysis when you have performed the following tasks:

- Identify input to Conceptual Design, including appropriate enterprise architecture information, organizational processes and activities, and users and user profiles.
- Gather data, including business and user requirements.

Analysis

The first task of analysis is to validate research results, usually at a group debriefing. After a data-gathering activity is completed, the interviewer's findings, which might include diagrams and notes, are presented to your team. Comments from team members help the interviewer interpret the results, and the session helps your team to more thoroughly understand user requirements.

When the research is deemed credible, the next task is to build information models to capture context, workflow processes, and task sequences. Two types of information models exist: use cases and scenarios.

Use Cases

A *use case* is a behaviorally related sequence of interactions performed by an actor in a dialogue with a system to provide some measurable value to the actor. An *actor* can be a person, a group of people, another solution, or even a piece of equipment. The defining characteristic of an actor is a role, or set of roles, performed in relation to the organization or system.

Use cases serve the following purposes:

- To identify the organizational process and all activities, from start to finish
- To document the context and environmental issues
- To trace a path between organizational needs and user requirements
- To describe needs and requirements in the context of usage
- To focus users and your project team on solving the right problem

For many applications, the amount of information that can be gathered by the design team can be overwhelming. By breaking the information into smaller, manageable chunks, you can simplify the information set that your team members must maintain to move forward with the application's development. Use cases help provide this simplification. In addition, use cases have the following benefits:

- They provide the context for all business and user requirements.
- They facilitate a common understanding of the application.
- They provide the basis for user workflow scenarios.
- They facilitate objectivity and consistency in evaluating user suggestions.
- They provide organization for the Functional Specification, which describes in developer's terms what the application will do.
- They enable paths to be traced between user needs and logical design.

Scenarios

A *scenario* is defined as a single sequence of interactions between objects and actors. A scenario describes a particular instance of a use case and can show either the current state of the process or a desired future state of the application.

Four types of information are captured within a scenario:

- **Context** This includes cultural norms, policies, procedures, rules, regulations, and standards that constrain and support the organization and the user.
- **Workflow process** This process depicts the flow of products and information within an organizational process, and among departments and customers. Note that organizational processes can cut across organizational boundaries.
- **Task sequence** This sequence documents the activities and tasks within a discrete part of a process. Included in the task sequence are the tasks that trigger the sequence; the activities, tasks, and steps involved in the task sequence; any decisions and loops within the sequence; and both typical and atypical paths.
- **Physical environment** This illustrates the physical, environmental, and ergonomic conditions that constrain or support the work. The physical environment could include geographic maps of sites; personnel or other resources; work area schematics or floor plans; or photographs showing equipment, computers, furniture, and lighting.

Scenarios document the sequence of tasks performed by a specific role. Because each scenario represents only one particular instance of the use case, many scenarios are needed to document all the tasks comprising the workflow process in a given use case. Scenarios can be easily documented in narratives, pseudocode, and task sequence diagrams; they also provide an excellent basis for creating prototypes for verification with users.

As mentioned earlier, you must understand the current state of existing organizational processes and systems before creating the new solution. To demonstrate and communicate this understanding among your development team and project stakeholders, use cases and scenarios of the current state are often created. Building current-state scenarios has both positive and negative aspects. On the positive side, current-state scenarios can:

- Provide reference points for proposed development
- Educate users and project team members on the current environment
- Reveal additional justification for the new solution, as well as reveal inter-system dependencies

On the negative side, however, current-state scenarios can also:

- Consume time, resources, and money
- Fail to provide added value if the solution is small or already well understood
- Be irrelevant, meaning the new application will not be related to the current applications or workflow processes

On every project, you must evaluate the negative and the positive aspects of creating the project's current-state scenarios, considering the resources required to construct them. Risk assessment brings a degree of objectivity to this process, by asking the questions "What is the risk of taking the time to create scenarios versus not doing so?" and "What is the risk of misunderstanding if we don't create scenarios?"

Analysis is complete when you have performed the following tasks:

- Synthesize organizational and user data, integrating the four categories of information—context, workflow process, task sequence, and physical environment—needed for scenarios.
- Create scenarios, to whatever extent you have deemed appropriate.

Rationalization

As discussed, use cases and scenarios are based on the current state of existing systems. Use cases and scenarios can also document what users would like to see in the solution. The final step in Conceptual Design is to rationalize the scenarios and use cases to develop the actual future state of the application you are developing.

In rationalization, the goals are to include organizational processes as part of the design process and to make improvements wherever possible. Often, design patterns and antipatterns can help you understand which streamlining methods can be used for any processes determined to be inefficient.

The scope of Conceptual Design includes not only the system under evaluation, but also the broader context of organizational processes, information, and goals that a new solution will support. The project team might not implement all the improvements themselves but might coordinate with other efforts already underway, or coordinate with organizational consultants hired specifically for reengineering work. Depending on the project's scope and the depth of your organizational understanding, you might be able to optimize one or more processes without any outside help.

As the final step of Conceptual Design, you should determine which processes should be optimized. The goal in making these decisions is to eliminate as many of the following as possible:

- Inefficiencies
- Bottlenecks and unnecessary steps
- Redundant and ineffective practices and processes
- Unnecessary paperwork
- Dysfunctional policies
- Transport and delay time

To eliminate these hindrances, you should begin by asking how you can improve productivity, which areas you can optimize, and in which areas (if any) you can integrate entire processes. It's not enough to simply identify weaknesses; you must also be able to imagine and describe the desired future state. After the desired future state has been clearly visualized and described, you can build appropriate new scenarios.

When your team wants to optimize the processes involved in the project, you can use the following design basics:

- **Break the rules** Question assumptions. For example, ask why principles and rules such as mandatory unit, departmental, and divisional approval for travel requests exist.
- **Align with performance goals** Ensure that goals chosen at the outset are genuinely aligned with projected results. Think of performance as meeting long-term customer requirements rather than simply meeting short-term needs.
- **Design work around products and services** Design a person's job around the goals and objectives of the process as a whole, not around a single, discrete task.

- **Eliminate bureaucracies and other obstacles** Replace bureaucratic hierarchies with self-organized teams working in parallel.
- **Improve productivity** Move away from task fragmentation and specialization of work roles, and move toward task compression and integration of work roles.
- **Ask where technology can facilitate and support** Consider the availability of appropriate technology that will support and facilitate the redesigned process. Suggest replacing activities and roles that simply relay information with ones that can be handled more efficiently with technology.
- **Be aware of the risk of taking on too complex a process at the outset** Break the process into subprocesses that can be addressed sequentially.

After the new future-state use cases and scenarios are created, the final step in rationalization is to validate the new scenarios to assure that they solve the business problem. You accomplish this by completing these steps:

- Build a proof-of-concept version of the application.
- Use the proof-of-concept version to represent the UI design.
- Get usability and organizational feedback.
- Repeat until both customer and users are satisfied.

Early in the design process, proof-of-concept solutions should show only the main features, UI design, and overall structure of the application. With this proof-of-concept, you are open to quickly reworking the design, because you have not invested a lot of effort into one solution. Proofs-of-concept at this stage can take some of the following forms:

- Applications displaying basic functionality
- Storyboards (either paper-based or screen-based)
- Paper prototypes of the overall structure and user interaction
- Microsoft PowerPoint slides that illustrate the main elements of the application, and demonstrate navigation through the application for one or more tasks

As the design process progresses, prototypes should become more detailed and automated, allowing you to evaluate visual style and some design details, particularly the UI and high-risk technical decisions.

Validation using scenarios is generally preferable to producing a generic requirements document, as a scenario contains the larger context of the requirements. It's much easier to validate a scenario with a walk-through, role-play, or proof-of-concept. One objective of validation is to uncover, before user sign-off, any missing pieces or incorrect interpretations of the design goals. Divergent views among users over any aspect of the solution will also become starkly apparent and should immediately raise concerns.

You should not try to reengineer the entire organizational process with the initial releases of the application. Later product releases can introduce more future-state scenarios that provide additional streamlining of the modeled organizational processes. Often, users will be hesitant to change how they do everything with one application release, and the phasing of future states into the application can be a compromise for the user community.

Rationalization is complete when you have performed the following tasks:

- Build future-state scenarios that will improve the work.
- Validate desired future-state scenarios with an update to the organization's enterprise architecture.

Modeling as Part of Design

Modeling organizational concepts provides value by allowing you to graphically describe elements that contribute to the effectiveness and efficiency of an organization. For example, you can use models to describe resources, roles, workflow, activities, and business rules. Furthermore, models provide you with insight into the manner in which an organization runs; thus, they are helpful in locating, diagnosing, and solving technical problems related to performance, system automation, and service integration. Additionally, models provide a means for solving project management problems, such as forecasting resources required for implementation and estimating application development costs.

In reality, understanding systems, processes and user roles can be difficult. Modeling helps to simplify reality by creating levels of abstraction that can be separated from the system. This simplification and separation can be easier to understand for the implementation team, as well as other project stakeholders such as the customer and users.

UML is rapidly becoming the *de facto* standard for modeling systems throughout the design process. A complete discussion of UML is outside the scope of this book; however, we will briefly examine certain aspects of UML as part of this book's discussion of the design process.

One aspect of UML that is important to define is its use of diagrams. In UML terms, a *diagram* is a single drawing of a particular type, such as a class or use case diagram. A *model* is a collection of similar diagrams that shows the relationships among them. Models usually include all diagrams for a given *domain*, or area of knowledge.

Starting the Class Model

Although the primary model for Conceptual Design is the Use Case Model (to be discussed later), you might find it helpful to begin your modeling work by making a high-level first cut at the class model. In design work, a *class* is a category or group of items with similar attributes, behaviors, and relationships. In a bookstore, for example, your research might reveal classes that include salespersons, books, and customers. A complete *class diagram* shows the name of the class, its *attributes* or properties, and its *operations* or methods. For example, a class diagram for a salesperson might resemble the one in Figure A.3.

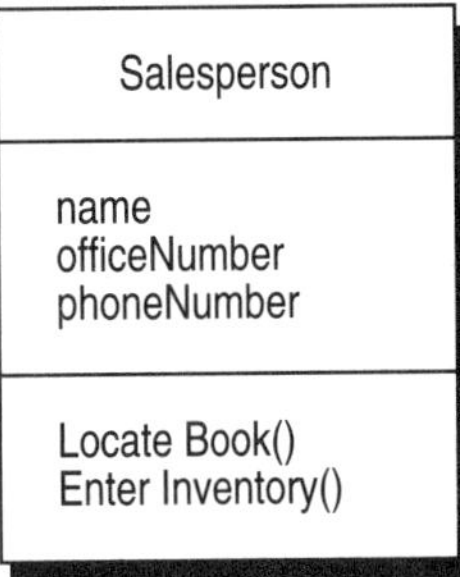

Figure A.3 Example of a class diagram

When you first begin your research work, it is unlikely that you will be able to complete class diagrams such as this. Your goal at this phase is simply to discover as many *candidate* (tentative) classes as possible. To accomplish this, you interview users and clients and listen for nouns they might use as they describe various organizational processes. The end result will be a first attempt at a class model that shows potential classes only by name. For example, several candidate classes from a class model for the bookstore might resemble the one in Figure A.4.

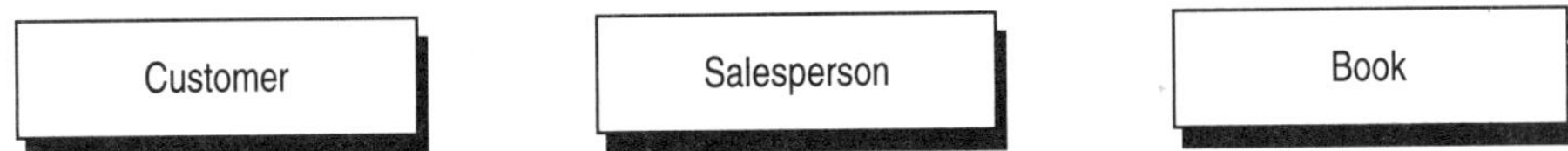

Figure A.4 First cut at a candidate class model

Beginning with the class model helps ensure that you know the domain terminology well enough to proceed with use cases. The act of discovering candidate classes allows you and the users to begin thinking conceptually about the organizational processes that make up the current system. The concepts that result from your candidate classes will eventually be replicated or added into the software.

Developing the Use Case Model

After you have identified the candidate classes, you are ready to begin building use cases. As defined in *The Unified Software Development Process*, a use case "specifies a sequence of actions, including variants, that the system can perform and that yields an observable result of value to a particular actor." One actor initiates a use case, which returns a result to either the actor who initiated the use case or a different actor.

For example, a common use case within a bookstore might be the Locate Book use case. This use case would include all steps involved in finding a book for a potential customer. The Locate Book use case diagram is shown in Figure A.5. This use case diagram shows the initiating actor on the left, the use case in the middle, and the receiving actor on the right. As mentioned, the receiving actor can be the same as the initiating actor.

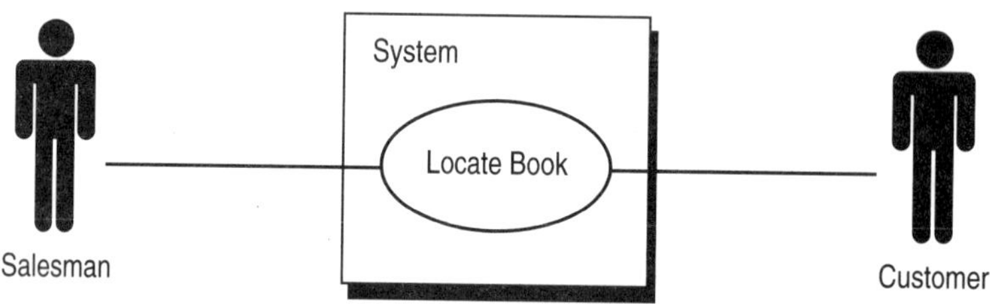

Figure A.5 Example of a use case diagram

Within a given use case is the scenario, or sequence of tasks, that make up the use case. A use case should be described by at least one scenario, but will often contain more, depending on outside circumstances, or conditions that occur or change during the use case's lifetime.

For instance, you might include three scenarios within the Locate Book use case: one for locating a book still in print, another for locating a book currently out of print, and a third for showing the steps of finding a book on the bookstore's shelves.

All three scenarios can begin with the same steps: a customer finds a salesperson, the customer requests a book, and the salesperson gathers information from the customer. To prevent unnecessary duplication of steps, you could take these three steps out of the Locate Book use case and make a separate use case called Prepare To Locate. You would then include the Prepare To Locate use case in your Locate Book use case.

The use case diagram does not show the scenarios, much less the steps in the scenarios. The scenarios and their respective steps are delineated in a separate design document, which is eventually approved by both the customer and the design team. For all scenarios in each use case, you outline the following:

- A brief description of the scenario
- Any assumptions for the scenario
- Steps in the scenario
- The conditions that exist when the scenario is complete
- The actor who initiates the use case
- Any preconditions for the use case
- The receiving actor who benefits from the use case

The example in Table A.3 shows the task sequence of a sample scenario and the services within it.

Table A.3 Example of a Usage Scenario

Use Case: Locate Book

Actor: Salesperson

Receiving Actor: Customer

System: Inventory Management

Pre-Conditions: Book is in print; author's name is known

Post-Conditions: Customer knows location of book within the store

Scenario: In-Print with Author's Name

Task sequence	**Exceptions**
1. Prepare to Locate	
2. Type Author Last Name	
3. Type Author First Name	
4. Query for Author	
5. Select Complete Author Name	Author is not found Identical author names are displayed
6. Query for Author's Titles	Appropriate Title is not displayed
7. Select Complete Title	
8. Book location is displayed according to sections within the store	Book is out of stock

Rationalizing the Use Case Model

A key concept in developing any model of a solution is the *level of abstraction*. What is the appropriate level of detail to include? How extensively do you want to analyze, or how abstract do you want to be? Often you can combine similar objects into a more abstract parent object in a process called *generalization*. Conversely, you can break an object into its constituent child objects in another process known as *rationalization*.

An important step at this point in your design process is to rationalize the Use Case Model you have just developed. Your software application must at least mimic, if not improve upon, the processes that your users commonly follow. Rationalizing the Use Case Model is a critical step in ensuring that you have faithfully and accurately captured those organizational processes at an appropriate level of abstraction.

Note You might position your design at the wrong place on the abstraction continuum. If you have too broad or general a scope, your models will be useless as design tools. In contrast, if your design is too convoluted with detail, your models will also be useless, as they will be cluttered and unreadable. However, if you must err, err on the side of detail.

Key to this step is the fact that most systems do not have a simple hierarchy for use case scenarios–task sequences hierarchy. Instead, you will find, upon closer examination, that some of the individual tasks should actually be separate use cases in their own right. A careful assessment will often reveal new use cases that you need to add to your model.

For example, suppose you have a use case called Sell Product, containing as one of its scenarios the In Store scenario. A task in this scenario is Validate Credit Card. This task can easily become a use case of its own with various scenarios, such as credit card swipes in credit card authorization machines, or phone-based validation (with exceptions for declined authorizations or busy signals). The UML term for this use case hierarchy is *includes*, as in *the In Store scenario includes the Validate Credit Card use case*.

Developing the Activity Model

Use case diagrams and models are valuable, but primarily static. As noted earlier, the use case diagram shows the transfer of control from initiator to use case to receiver, but does not show the individual steps in the process. One way to show these steps is to use an *activity diagram.*

A UML activity diagram resembles the program flowcharts with which many developers are already familiar. These diagrams show the flow from activity to activity, as well as any decision points and resulting branches. A single diagram, such as that shown in Figure A.6, has a start point (represented by a filled-in circle), one or more activities, and an end-point (represented by a bull's eye). Diamonds represent decision points.

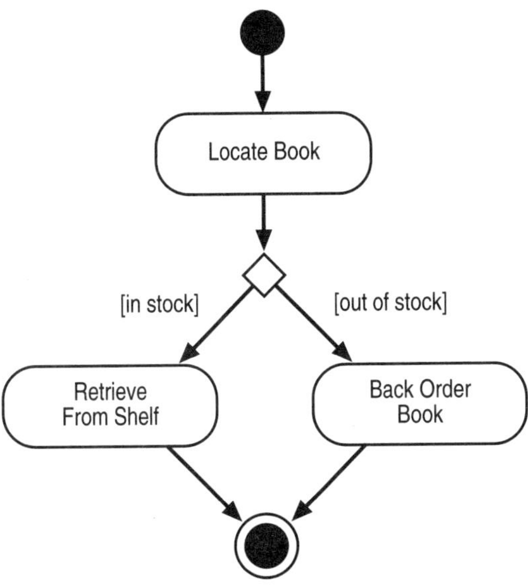

Figure A.6 Example of a simple activity diagram

One of the most helpful attributes of activity diagrams is the ability to indicate which role or actor performs which steps in the sequence. You accomplish this by using *swim lanes*. Each role is assigned a lane, and the lane lists the role's activities in the order in which they are performed. Figure A.7, which appears on the following page, shows an example of an activity diagram without swim lanes, and Figure A.8, on page 31, shows the same diagram redrawn with swim lanes.

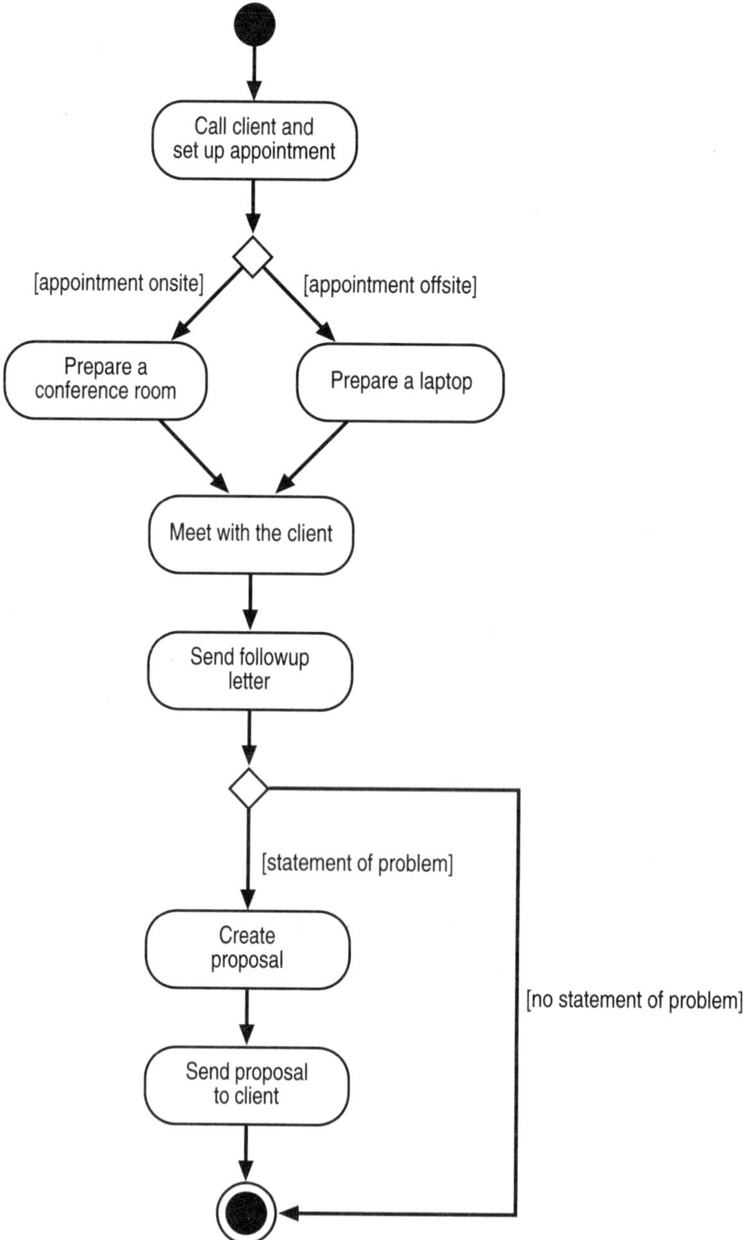

Figure A.7 Example of an activity diagram without swim lanes

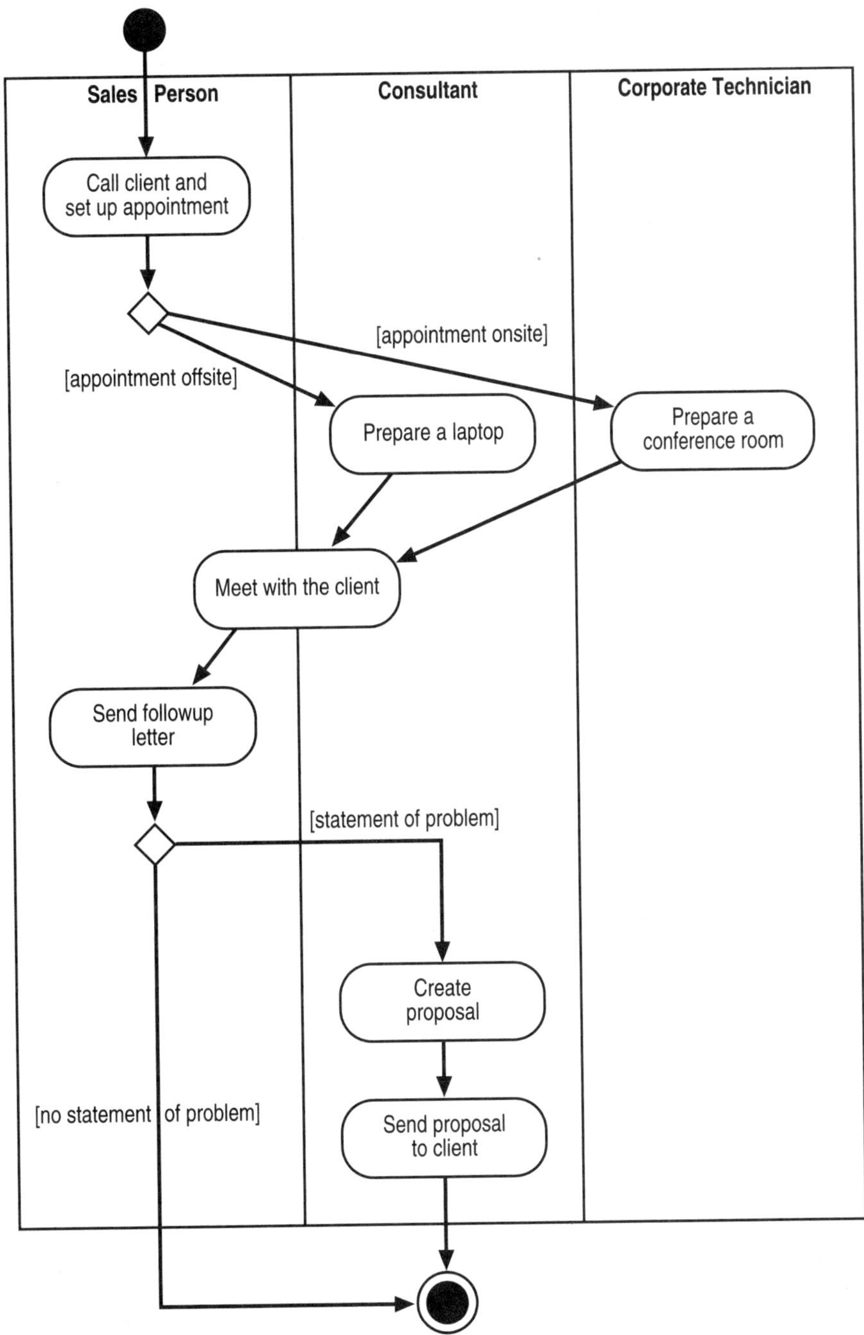

Figure A.8 Example of an activity diagram with swim lanes

If you develop a complete set of use cases with their respective scenarios, followed by a complete set of activity diagrams, you can be fairly sure that you have captured the essence of the current processes. You are then ready to move into Logical Design.

Logical Design

Logical Design is defined as the process of describing a solution in terms of its organization, structure, syntax, and the interaction of its parts from your project team's perspective.

The purpose of Logical Design is to apply basic, services-based organizing principles and to lay out the solution's structure and the relationships among the solution's parts. The outputs of Logical Design are: a set of business objects with corresponding services, attributes, and relationships; a high-level UI design; and a logical database design.

Logical Design can be likened to the second stage of designing a house, during which an architect concentrates on creating the floor plan and elevation. In designing a house, architectural elements such as doors, windows, roofs, patios, rooms, and spatial relationships are organized into a harmonious whole.

Logical Design is your view of the solution. It paints a picture of the solution's behavior and logical organization, which is required for Physical Design. Logical Design helps you refine the requirements specified in Conceptual Design and manage the complexity of the whole solution.

In the Logical Design phase, you should accomplish the following:

- Manage and reduce complexity by defining the solution's structure, describing its components, and describing how these components interact to solve the problem.
- Set boundaries and describe interfaces to provide an organizational structure for interaction among multiple groups.
- Uncover any errors and inconsistencies in Conceptual Design.
- Eliminate redundancy and identify potential reuse.
- Improve operations among the various components of the solution, as well as the solution itself.
- Articulate a common view of the solution among your project team members.
- Provide a foundation for Physical Design.

Logical Design is independent of physical implementation. You should focus primarily on what the solution needs to do, as described by an organized set of cooperating elements. It is important to understand the solution completely before making a commitment to specific technologies.

Logical Design has two steps: analysis and rationalization. (Logical Design has no research step, because the output of Conceptual Design is the input to Logical Design.) Analysis involves identifying business objects, services, attributes, and relationships. Rationalization involves verifying business objects and identifying implied business objects and scenarios.

Analysis

The goal of analysis in Logical Design is to convert the use cases and scenarios from Conceptual Design into modules for use in Logical Design. *Modules* are the core use cases of the system, the services or activities that occur within these use cases, and the hierarchical relationships among them. A module is a logical unit that is an abstraction of the use cases and scenarios created in Conceptual Design.

For each module, you should identify the services, objects, attributes, and relationships. To identify these elements, refer to the workflow and task sequence information of the scenarios, which are contained in both documentation and activity diagrams. Each of these elements has its own focus:

- Services focus on actions (verbs)
- Business objects focus on people or things (nouns)
- Attributes focus on properties
- Relationships focus on methods

Services

A *service* is a unit of application logic that implements an operation, function, or transformation. Services can be relatively straightforward and can provide algorithmically simple functions—such as *Create*, *Read*, *Update*, and *Delete*—or algorithmically complex calculations or transformations—such as Pay, Validate, and Reserve.

The capabilities and responsibilities of a service should be stated as generally as possible, using only active verbs. A service should be identified by a clear, unambiguous name. Difficulty identifying and naming a service often indicates that its functionality or purpose isn't clear, and that additional Conceptual Design investigation might be necessary.

The example in Table A.4, on the following page, shows a sample task sequence and the services within it.

Table A.4 Sample Task Sequence and Its Services

Sample task sequence	Candidate services
Customer looks for a book	View books
System retrieves books reserved for customer	Retrieve reservations Reserves books
Salesperson sells a product	Sell product

Business Objects

A *business object* is an encapsulation of services and data used to organize the solution and reduce its complexity. Business objects are people or things described in scenarios. These objects become the anchor points for attributes and relationships.

Note This definition is different from that of an object from a COM perspective, which is the instance of a class definition.

Some business objects might not be specifically stated in a scenario, though they might be necessary to complete the organizational activities (often noted as non-functional requirements) that the scenario describes. To identify business objects, you should look for structures, other solutions, devices, things, or events not actually present in the scenario; roles played; operational procedures; locations or sites; and organizational units. To identify missing objects, you must look for behaviors that have no apparent object associated with them.

The example in Table A.5 shows the same sample task sequence as that of Table A.4 with its business objects.

Table A.5 Sample Task Sequence and Its Business Objects

Sample task sequence	Candidate business objects
Salesperson looks up customer reservation	Salesperson, Customer reservation
System retrieves book reserved by a customer	System, Book, Customer
Salesperson issues a receipt	Receipt

Attributes

An *attribute* (called a *property* in COM) is an element of a business object that an organization must know and track. Attributes are definitions of data values held by a business object. Each instance of a business object maintains its own set of values based on the corresponding attributes. For example, an attribute might be First Name; the value that this attribute takes in a certain instance might be John. Attributes can also show ownership of one business object by another. The set of values for a business object's attributes at a given point is its *state*.

As you attempt to discover attributes, you must be sure to note any attributes derived—that is, computed—from other attributes. The derivation of this type of attribute becomes a service of the object, and the calculation or manipulation is maintained as part of the interface contract for that service. Also, you must examine the total set of attributes for a business object. If some attributes are unrelated to other attributes, you might need to create a new business object.

Table A.6 shows the same sample task sequence as that of the two preceding tables with some candidate attributes. Examples of irrelevant attributes for this sample are age, height, religion, ethnicity, and Social Security number. Note that the same object can have many states.

Table A.6 Sample Task Sequence and Its Attributes

Sample narrative	Candidate attributes	Values at one state
Customer has a name and address	First Name Last Name Address	Dan Shelly 100 Microsoft Way
Customer must have a type of reservation	Type	Preferred
Depending upon type of reservation, a customer can belong to an company	Company	Microsoft
Books can be in print or out of print	Availability	In-Print

Relationships

A *relationship* is a logical association among business objects. Recognizing relationships is required for determining effective design and assembly of an application's parts.

Relationships illustrate the way in which objects are related or linked to one another. Relationships fall into one of three types: whole or part; interaction; or generalization or specialization. As you look for relationships, you should consider any whole or part relationships that you can identify, any interactions that you must identify to maintain context, and any generalizations or specifications that you can make.

As the example in Figure A.9 demonstrates, the *customer* business object can be a specialization of the more generic *person* object; a *customer* can be part of a *company list*; and a *customer* can purchase a *book*.

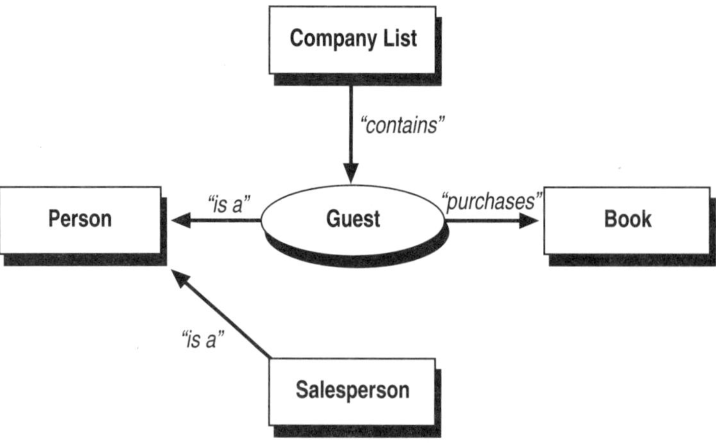

Figure A.9 Example of identifying relationships

To summarize, analysis is concerned with identifying the objects, services, attributes, and relationships comprising the scenarios. The diagram in Figure A.10 illustrates this process. Note that this process is also known as *noun-verb analysis*.

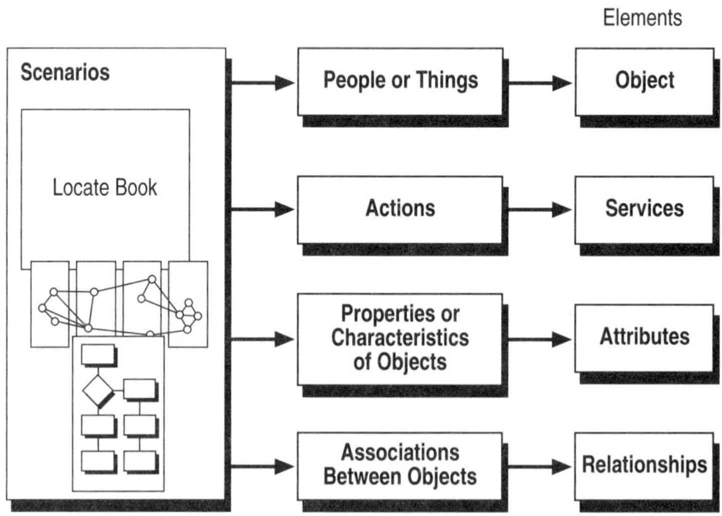

Figure A.10 Process of noun-verb analysis

Logical Design analysis is complete when you have performed the following tasks:

- Identify and prepare a list of services.
- Identify and prepare a list of objects.
- Identify and prepare a list of attributes.
- Identify and prepare a list of relationships.

Rationalization

The first task of Logical Design rationalization is to create any needed services and objects that have not yet been created but whose existence is implied or needed for control. You then refine and verify the Logical Design.

Creating Implied Services and Objects

This stage consists of creating business objects and services that seem to be missing from Logical Design. For example, a customer might have a company affiliation. Business objects represent both customers and their company affiliations. However, a relationship might not exist between these business objects. For example, customers might or might not use company credit cards for discounted rates. Creating a new *type of purchase* business object effectively handles the missing, implied object, and records the relationships among customers, their purchases, and their companies, if they exist.

Creating Services and Objects Needed for Control

At this point, you should concern yourself with matters of *control*. Control means ensuring that services are conducted in the correct sequence at the proper time. In distributed applications, you can use transactions, such as MTS transactions as a means of determining effective sequencing and the dependency relationships of objects. Otherwise, you can create control objects to ensure the transactional integrity of a scenario, coordinate services across multiple objects, or manage cross-object dependencies.

For example, the Reserve book scenario is a business transaction or a collection of objects that has dependency and sequencing relationships. You would need to create an object or service to ensure that those relationships are honored, and to take corrective action (such as canceling the reservation) if one of the relationships is broken.

You must always consider the need for additional business objects to handle control, sequencing, and dependency. You can also isolate unstable services from stable ones.

Iterating and Refining Objects

After you have identified the objects, you need to refine the design by:

- Eliminating objects that are irrelevant or out of scope
- Combining redundant objects
- Refining vague or implicit objects
- Distinguishing between attributes and objects
- Considering transactional control
- Distinguishing actors and roles from objects

The first attempt at specifying objects using noun-verb analysis usually requires some refinement. Not all of the nouns will be relevant for describing the solution. The remaining candidates might consist of physical entities such as customers, employees, and pieces of equipment; as well as concepts that indicate business transactions such as room assignment, payment authorization, or promotion.

As part of the refinement process, you can also use services to discover objects. For each service identified during analysis, you might ask, "What does this service act upon?" and "Is there an entity, individual, or organization that has the responsibility of carrying out this service?" Any objects with no services or only one service defined might need further investigation.

Verification

Verification refers to the testing of the functional completeness and correctness of the design at the object level. The objects are tested in both an individual and cooperating context. Verification of independent objects makes the task of integration much easier because the independent parts have been rigorously tested prior to assembly. Verification of cooperating objects ensures that the work specified in the scenario is accomplished as a whole.

For individual objects, you should examine the pre-conditions feeding into the object and the post-conditions coming out of the object. The question to ask is, "For a given set of pre-conditions, do the post-conditions match the scenario's requirements?"

However, this testing will not uncover assembly issues. You also need to look at the combination of objects that can solve the higher-level problems captured in the scenarios. A collection of modules that solve a problem interdependently can be complex. A simple way to verify multi-object scenarios is to conduct a full walk-through of the scenario, ensuring that all the needs of the scenario are met by a combination of objects.

You can walk through a scenario and determine which object's services are required in which sequence to complete the scenario's tasks successfully. From a starting trigger object, you must determine what other objects' services are needed for the scenario to be complete.

Logical Design rationalization is complete when you have performed the following tasks:

- Identify implied objects and services
- Refine control
- Verify objects and services
- Refine the class model

Developing the Class Model

One of the most important models you will build during the design process is the *Class Model*, which comprises all the class diagrams developed during research and design. Earlier this book suggested making a first cut at a class model by simply analyzing your research results to discover as many potential or candidate classes as possible. You achieved this by listening for the nouns used by both the customer and users to describe the business and its processes.

At this point we are talking about logical classes, not programming classes. In the next phase of the design process (Physical Design), we will translate many of these logical classes into programming classes and components. As you build your class model, remember that you should include classes for every entity that interacts with the application you are modeling, as well as all objects created by those entities.

Remember that a class is a set of objects that share the same attributes, operations, and relationships. You should model a class using a *class diagram*, such as the one shown in Figure A.11.

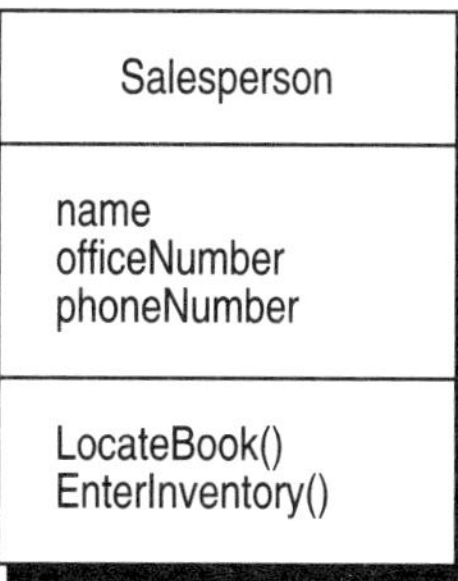

Figure A.11 Example of a class diagram

The first (top) section of the diagram shown contains the class name. The second section contains the attributes or properties of the class. The third section shows the class *operations*, or the actions that the class can perform. (These operations correspond to the services identified earlier in the noun-verb analysis.)

The lists of attributes and operations for the Salesperson class could grow quite large. In fact, if you were to attempt to include every attribute and operation for this class, the class diagram would become much too large to be useful. You should include only those attributes and operations pertinent to your current design problem. In some models, you might also want to leave out, or *elide*, some of the attributes and operations included in the base class diagram. Such elision is indicated by an ellipsis, shown in Figure A.12.

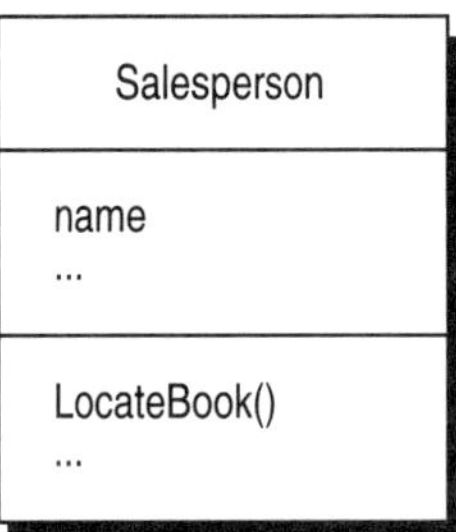

Figure A.12 Class diagram with elision

Classes can be part of larger classes, or they can include smaller classes. For example, in the case of a bookstore, the class called Salesperson is also part of a larger class called Employee. This parent-child relationship is identified by connecting the *subclass* or child class (Salesperson) to the *superclass* or parent class (Employee) with a solid line and an open arrowhead, shown in Figure A.13. This relationship is called *generalization*. A class with no parents is a *root* class, and a class with no children is a *leaf* class.

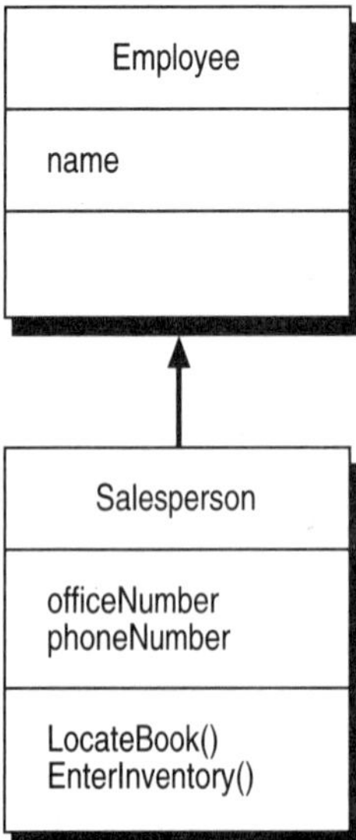

Figure A.13 Two class diagrams showing generalization

Following this chain upward, the class called Employee is part of a larger class called Citizen, which is part of a larger class called HumanBeing, which is part of a yet larger class called Lifeform. Following the chain downward, the class called Salesperson can contain two classes called Parttime and Fulltime. Whether to pursue such extension of detail is a subjective decision that is driven by your project's specific needs. You have to decide the level of abstraction that makes sense for your project.

An *association* is a relationship that shows that one class is related to another in a manner other than parent-to-child. Associations will be the most common relationships in a class model, and they are shown as simple solid lines. You can also include certain *adornments* with the basic association line to show additional information about the association. The *name* of the association typically shows the nature of the relationship, such as "Works for." Each class in the association plays a specific *role* in the relationship.

You can also show *multiplicity* in the association, indicating how many objects of the class might be connected across an instance of the association. (In database design, multiplicity is often referred to as *cardinality*.) Multiplicity is designated by a number or range of numbers (including ∞ for "many") at one end of the association line. The number indicates how many of the objects at that end on the line are connected to each object of the class at the opposite end. All of these adornments are shown in Figure A.14.

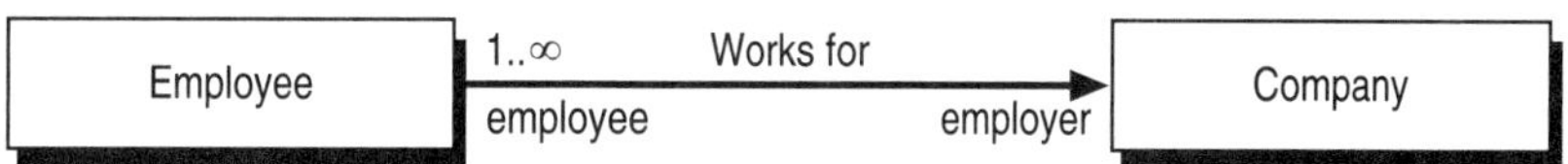

Figure A.14 Example of an association between two classes

The class model is the primary place where business object information is stored. The business objects themselves become classes; their attributes are shown as attributes of the class; their services are shown as operations; and their relationships are shown as either parent-to-child or as associations among classes.

A useful additional step to take at this time is to distribute the logical classes into the three service tiers (user, business, and data) to the extent possible. This distribution will facilitate designing the physical distribution, which is part of Physical Design.

The book *The Unified Modeling Language User Guide* states that a well-structured class diagram:

- *Is focused on communicating one aspect of a system's static design view*
- *Contains only elements that are essential to understanding that aspect*

- *Provides detail consistent with its level of abstraction, with only those adornments that are essential to understanding*
- *Is not so minimalist that it misinforms the reader about important semantics*

Note A class diagram shows the static design view of one part of a system. In other words, the class diagram shows the state at a given time. To model how a system changes over time, use state diagrams.

Developing the State Model

A *state diagram* shows the states an object can be in, in sequence, including the transitions among the states. In other words, a state diagram shows a single instance of a single class over time. Thus, the State Model is a collection of the state diagrams for a given system or subsystem.

As shown in Figure A.15, a state diagram resembles an activity diagram in that it has a start point (indicated by a solid circle), a series of states (indicated by rounded rectangles), transitions among states (represented by arrows with open arrowheads), and an endpoint (represented by a bull's eye). Each state rectangle has a name; optionally, the states can show state variables and state events. Common state events are: *entry* (what happens when the application enters the state), *do* (actions and events occurring during the state), and *exit* (what happens when leaving the state). Joseph Schmuller's simple state diagram of a computer Graphical User Interface (GUI) illustrated in *Teach Yourself UML in 24 Hours* (Sams Publishing, 1999) demonstrates that the state of the GUI changes at a high level.

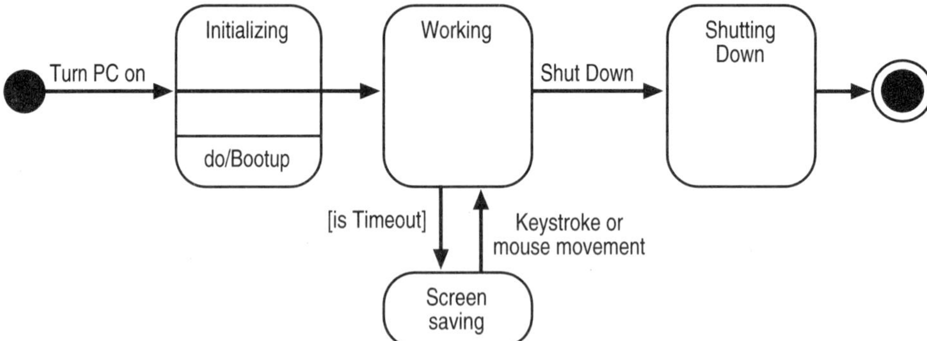

Figure A.15 Example of a state diagram

Through the state drawings, you can identify what happens to various objects throughout a scenario. Each state diagram graphically illustrates the text description of the scenario, so if you build a state diagram for every object in every scenario of a given use case, the resulting model shows the state of the entire solution at each step along the way, including values of all the variables and activities occurring in every object. A well-developed state model can communicate, quickly and effectively, information that would otherwise take pages to describe.

Completing the Logical Design

The beginning of this section noted that the output of Logical Design is a set of business objects with corresponding services, attributes, and relationships; a high-level UI design; and a logical database design. The Class Model, supplemented by the State Model, shows the set of business objects. At this point, you still need to develop a UI and a logical database design.

The UI design is an intentionally high-level, logical design rather than a prototype or screen shot, because no technology has been chosen for implementation at this point. The UI design is simply a document whose purpose is to show what objects and services will be part of the UI. You must determine which services will be apparent to users when they interact with the application. A simple bulleted list (such as "Locate Book" and "Reserve Book") will often suffice.

Similarly, the logical database design is not a complete listing of all tables and fields needed for the application. The logical database design is simply a model, taken from the Class Model, showing the classes that need to be part of one or more permanent data stores. Obviously, the attributes of the classes will probably become fields in a table, but for now, you simply want to document the information you want to capture, as well as the relationships within that information.

Physical Design

Physical Design is the process of describing the components, services, and technologies of the solution from the perspective of your development team. The purpose of Physical Design is to apply real-world technology constraints to Logical Design, including implementation and performance considerations. The output of Physical Design is a set of components, a UI design for a particular platform, and a physical database design.

Physical Design can be likened to the third and final stage of designing a house. After the basic architectural plan is complete, contractors create wiring plans, plumbing plans, heating and ventilation plans, and so on, which are the internal "components" of the house.

In the Physical Design stage, you should aim to:

- Break down the solution's requirements to simplify segmenting and estimating the work needed to create the application, and to provide focus and clarity for development.
- Provide a bridge between Logical Design and implementation, by defining the solution in terms of implementation.
- Evaluate implementation options.
- Provide a flexible design based on services.
- Seek compatibility with the organization's enterprise architecture.
- Trace use cases and scenarios back through Logical Design.

The Physical Design represents the last chance to validate the design before writing the code. After you have begun code development, you can still make design changes, but the cost to the project in time and resources will be much higher than if you make them during this planning phase.

The Physical Design baseline can be established when enough information is available for you to start developing the application. Thus, you can begin development before the baseline is frozen. The Physical Design baseline can be frozen well into actual development, allowing you to take advantage of opportunities for refinement, but the baseline must be frozen before the solution can be deployed.

The Physical Design segment of the design process consists of four steps: research, analysis, rationalization, and implementation. (The research step is required to identify possible technologies to be used in the application.) Each step ends with its own baseline except for implementation, the baseline of which is included in the overall Physical Design baseline.

Research involves:

- Determining physical constraints of the infrastructure
- Determining physical requirements of the solution
- Managing risks from this conflict between physical constraints and requirements

Analysis involves:

- Selecting candidate implementation technologies
- Drafting a preliminary deployment model composed of network, data, and component topologies

Rationalization involves:

- Determining a packaging and distributing strategy
- Decomposing objects into services-based components
- Distributing components across topologies
- Refining packaging and distribution

Implementation involves:

- Determining the programming model
- Specifying the component interface
- Specifying the components in the development language
- Understanding component structure considerations

The Physical Design baseline includes the implementation baseline, and constitutes the culmination of research, analysis, rationalization, and implementation.

Research

The goals during research in Physical Design are as follows:

- Determine the infrastructure's physical constraints and the application's physical requirements.
- Manage the risks from conflict between the infrastructure's physical constraints and the application's physical requirements.

By this point, the physical requirements of the application should be well known in a general sense—the application must serve a given number of people, it must carry out a given number of transactions per day, and so on. These types of requirements are often referred to as non-functional requirements, as they are important to the application development, but do not describe specific functionality or how work is being done by the application. You might have to conduct fairly specific research to determine detailed physical requirements, including building and testing proof-of-concept trial applications.

On the other hand, the infrastructure's physical constraints are rooted in the organization's enterprise architecture. It is entirely possible that the organization's enterprise architecture might not be formally documented. If it isn't, this is an opportunity for you to establish its baseline.

As you list both the requirements of the application and its matching constraints, beginning with the application will yield one list, while beginning with the infrastructure might yield a somewhat different list as you may consider different types of tasks. Building the list from both viewpoints ensures that nothing is missed. Examples of the list's requirements and constraints might include the following:

- Performance metrics
- Cost versus benefit
- Deployment costs
- Support infrastructure and costs
- Technology choices
- Reliability of the data
- Availability of the application
- Security concerns

One means of examining the current physical infrastructure is through *topologies*, which are maps showing an aspect of the infrastructure. For purposes of planning an application at the physical level, it is helpful for you to produce network, data, and component topologies. (Graphic examples of these items are included in the following section on analysis.) Infrastructure topologies produced during the research step of Physical Design represent the current state of the infrastructure.

During analysis, you will develop preliminary versions of the proposed state (what the topologies *might* resemble after the solution is built and deployed). Finally, in the rationalization step, you will develop final versions of the proposed state (what the topologies *will* resemble after the solution is built and deployed).

It is important for you to do the current state topologies, even though it might take time, so that your development team is aware of what components, data stores, and network capabilities are already present. Because a fundamental goal of modern development work is reuse, it makes little sense to build a component or data store from scratch when a functioning one already exists that, with a little tweaking, would be perfectly useable.

After the physical requirements and constraints are listed, the next task is to manage the risks presented by any conflicts or gaps that have been identified among the three topologies. This is a five-step process as follows:

1. **Identify where infrastructure constraints conflict with application requirements** When the infrastructure's physical constraints and the application's physical requirements are compared, some constraints and requirements will be in conflict, some will not be in conflict, and some will be immaterial. For example, the infrastructure might require use of TCP/IP across the enterprise. The application might require some other protocol

(conflict or gap), might require TCP/IP (no conflict or gap), or might be indifferent as to which protocol it uses (immaterial).

2. **Perform a preliminary assessment to highlight the gaps or conflicts** You need to identify whether a gap (a deficiency that could possibly be overcome) or a conflict (some sort of choice or crossroads) is involved. You also need to establish the size of the gap or conflict.
3. **Prioritize the tradeoffs to determine which aspects are more important** You need to establish which requirements are absolutely necessary and which constraints are the result of enterprise architecture decisions. When prioritizing, you must be sure to examine the business case, if any, for either requirements or constraints.
4. **Brainstorm initial solutions with your team** Fundamentally, you can perform only two actions with a gap or conflict:
   - Accept it without doing anything (move ahead and see what happens later).
   - Change either the requirements or constraints, possibly both.
5. **Identify associated risks branching from the original list** When mitigating any risks, you should make sure you avoid introducing any new and unforeseen issues into your design.

Research in Physical Design is complete when you have performed the following tasks:

- Determine constraints and requirements.
- Identify the current network, data, and component topologies, as well as physical application requirements.
- Manage risks resulting from conflicts or gaps between constraints and requirements.
- Produce a risk assessment and mitigation plan.

Analysis

When performing analysis in Physical Design, you should focus on selecting candidate technologies for implementation, based on your understanding of the application requirements. Note that these technologies are merely candidates; you will make the final choice among them during code development. After the potential technologies have been chosen, you can draft a preliminary deployment model, taking into consideration these technologies.

In evaluating candidate technologies, you should first address business considerations, then take enterprise architecture considerations into account, and finally address technology considerations. You should not evaluate the technologies on their technological merits until you have completed the first two steps.

Business considerations include the following:

- **Ability** The technology must meet business needs.
- **Product cost** The complete product cost must be understood. Consider developer, server, and reseller licenses, as well as upgrade costs.
- **Experience** Lack of experience can have a large impact on the project. Evaluate what experience is available, in terms of training (costs or time), consultation (costs or availability), and comfort level.
- **Maturity or innovation** Maturity is hard to quantify, and decisions must be made based on risks. A *mature* product is accepted in the market, well understood, stable, or revised from something done before; a mature product also has knowledgeable resources available. An *innovative* product is the "latest and greatest" or is "ahead of the curve." The ideal product will be mature but will cycle quickly to stay as current as possible with new technologies.
- **Supportability** The technology must be supported, just as the solution built with it must be supported. You need to consider the implications of that support for the project and the enterprise. A supportable product has options such as vendor, outsourcing, and help desk support, and also accumulates support costs such as incidental costs and maintenance.

Other points you should consider include deployment, competitive advantage, time to completion, and industry perception.

Enterprise architecture considerations include the following:

- **Alignment with enterprise architecture goals** The application must fit within the goals and principles outlined by the enterprise architecture. These goals will be based on the four perspectives of enterprise architecture: Business, Application, Information, and Technology.
- **Adherence to the enterprise architecture** The enterprise architecture identifies the current state and future state plans. Specifically, the application should fit within the detail architectures of the application, information, and technology models of the enterprise architecture.
- **Opportunity for growth** Scalability of the application must fit with the growth plans for the organization, including the addition of people and markets through acquisition.
- **Interoperability** The application must work with the other systems within an organization. Not only must the application not interfere with other sys-

tems, but a communication interface must be defined so that other applications can easily interact with the new application.

Technology considerations include the following:

- **Languages** When selecting a language for component development, you should consider using different languages for different tasks within a project. You should also evaluate whether a language supports the design and implementation of loosely coupled components that can be replaced and upgraded as necessary.
- **Component interaction standards** Platforms and interaction standards are related. When selecting a component interaction standard (how components connect and communicate with one another), you should weigh cross-platform integration against power and performance. More than one technology should be considered for the component communication.
- **Data access methods** When selecting a data access method (how components interact with data stores), you should consider performance, standardization, and future direction, as well as the diversity of supported data stores and data access management. When selecting a data store, you should consider more than one type, and base your decision on structure and location of information.
- **System services** When selecting system services, you must identify the types of services required by the solution, as well as which of those services can be provided natively by application software.
- **Operating systems** When selecting the operating system, you should evaluate the services provided by the operating system, which can significantly reduce the application's coding requirements. Additionally, you must consider whether the operating system can meet security and scalability needs, bearing in mind that different operating systems provide varying methods of access to their services.

With the candidate technologies in mind, you can now draft a preliminary deployment model consisting of network, data, and component topologies. At this stage in Physical Design, you propose these topologies but do not yet select them.

The *network topology* is an infrastructure map that indicates hardware locations and interconnections. A current-state version of the infrastructure map was developed during research, but during this stage of Physical Design, this infrastructure map might require changes to support the new Physical Design. A sample network topology diagram is shown in Figure A.16, on the following page.

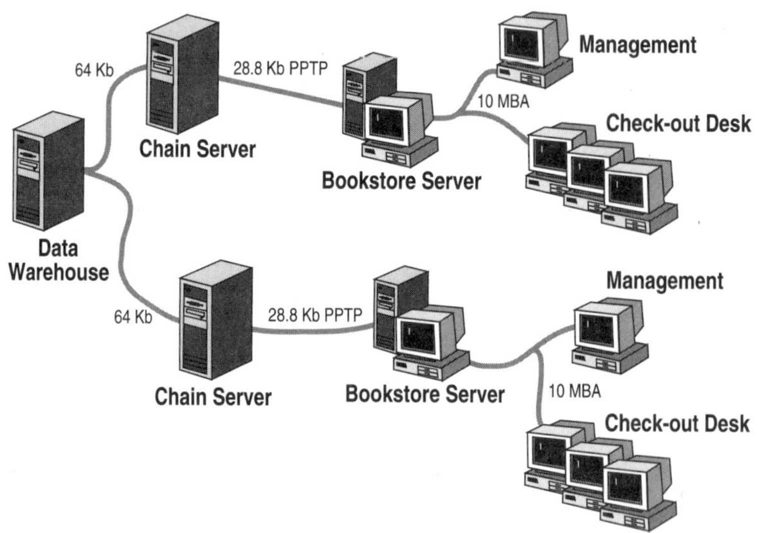

Figure A.16 Example of a network topology

The *data topology* is a data distribution map that indicates data store locations in relation to the network topology. Again, you constructed a current-state version during research, but you might need to consider a new data distribution strategy or new data technologies to support the new Physical Design.Figure A.17 shows a sample data topology.

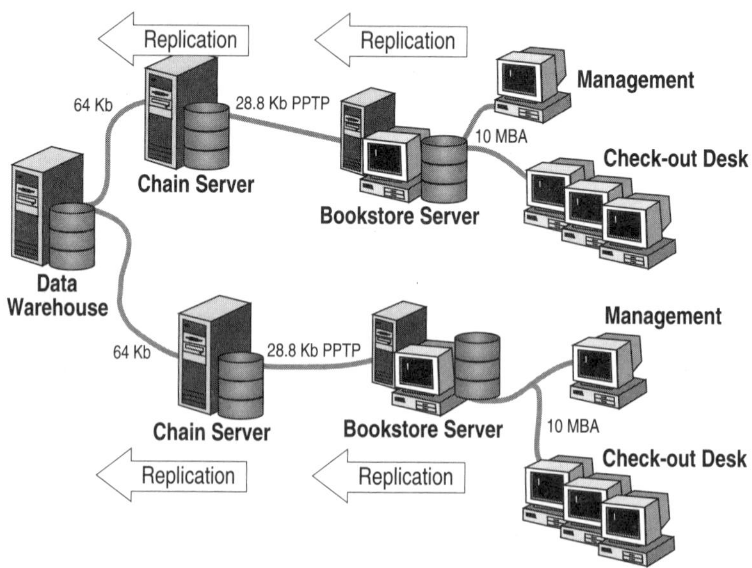

Figure A.17 Example of a data topology

The *component topology* is a component distribution map that indicates the locations of components and their services in relation to the network topology. The current-state version should already exist from work in the research step. You should now add any new components and services required by the new application, and make any updates as required to reflect changes in the data and network topologies. Figure A.18 shows a diagram of a sample component topology. Each box represents a component and in this figure identical components across the topology are labeled with the same letter.

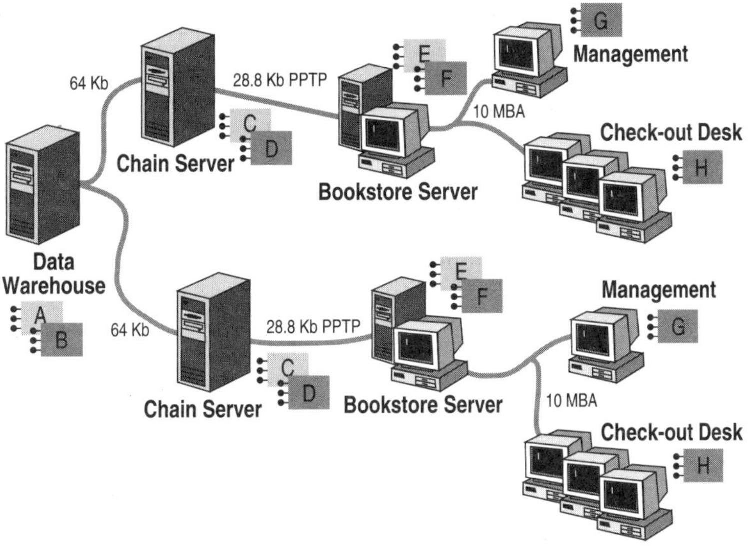

Figure A.18 Example of a component topology

Determining Methods and Properties

A prerequisite for building the preliminary component topology is drafting a preliminary component model. Although you can draft this model using many methods, this book recommends that you base your first attempt at the component model on the MSF Application Model's three logical service layers: user, business, and data.

Using the Logical Model (especially the Class Model) defined in the Logical Design phase, you should decide which logical classes and their associated services should become physical classes with associated methods. The value of the Conceptual Design and Logical Design now becomes apparent; if you have done a thorough job in those phases, you will find it fairly easy to move logical classes to physical classes, logical attributes to physical properties, and logical services to physical methods. In this way, you rationalize the Logical Class Model, packaging the classes together based on which service layer—user, business or data—the class interacts with. You can then distribute these packaged classes to the computer systems that support the particular service layer.

Physical Design analysis is complete when you have performed the following tasks:

- Select and list candidate implementation technologies.
- Draft a preliminary deployment model to include the proposed network, data, and component topologies.

Rationalization

After conducting research and analyzing it, you should begin solidifying your design. Determining a packaging and distribution strategy is part of this process.

Obviously, you can't plan for packaging and distribution when you haven't yet finalized the component model. However, you cannot complete the component model without a firm packaging and distribution plan. The tasks involved in Physical Design rationalization are both interactive and iterative. In some cases, you might want to begin with the component model; in others, you might decide that packaging considerations take precedence when you perform rationalization. One possible guideline is to begin with the task that seems most complex or critical.

Packaging the Classes

The primary focus of rationalization is distributing objects and services to components. To begin rationalization, you must package and distribute candidate components to provide a bridge between logical objects and service distribution. After you have distributed the initial candidate components as a component topology, you might want to use various packaging and distribution strategies to further optimize the components.

To determine the initial candidate components, you can begin with a simple packaging strategy by following these steps:

- Identify objects and services by category of service (user, business, or data). This identification method will assist you in making sure that all components are identified properly.
- Package objects together into components that exist in the same category of services.

After the objects and services have been packaged into components, you must distribute the components across the network and data topology. Combining the network and data topology into a single drawing will simplify the distribution process.

To start the distribution process, you can identify categories of services (user, business, and data) for the combined network and data topologies. The following guidelines will start the distribution process, and later will be revised:

- Distribute data services to the data locations identified in the data topology. These locations could be database servers or other locations where the data services will reside.
- Distribute user services to Web servers or client computers.
- Distribute business services to application servers or Web servers.
- Distribute components, which were previously identified with a category of service, to the location where that category of service resides on the combined network and data topology. This distribution represents the initial component topology.

You are now ready to finalize the component model. As shown in Figure A.19, services are distributed throughout the topology. As a result, you can package candidate components from the same logical service located in the same place in the topology.

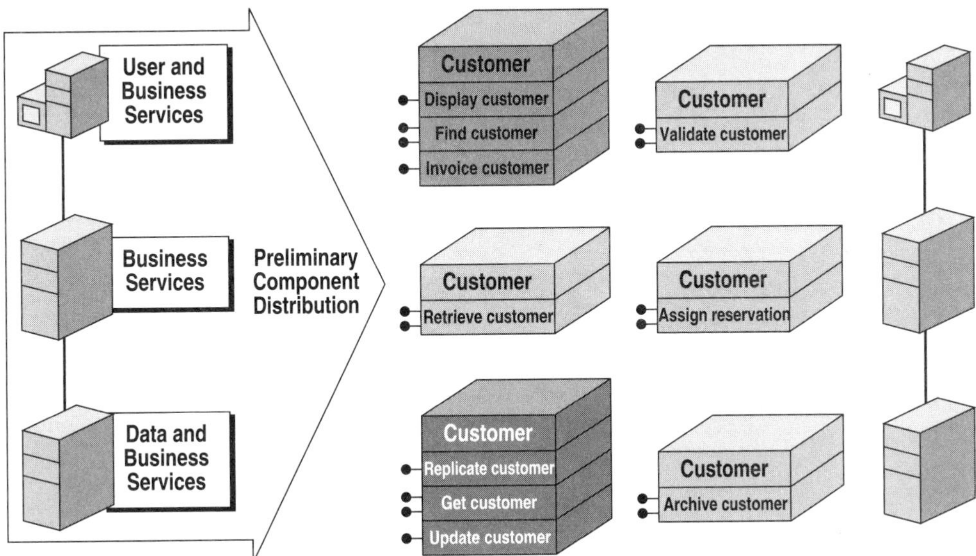

Figure A.19 Example of a component model

When the component model is complete, you are ready to finalize the distribution of those components. Again, the first cut at distribution should have been based on the user, business, and data service layers. Note, though, that the use of three logical service layers does not in any way imply a distribution of three physical locations. It is entirely possible to build an n-tier application that runs on a single computer. By the same token, a distribution strategy for a multi-site, complex application might involve 10, 20, or more physical locations.

When determining the packaging and distribution strategy, you should follow three basic steps. The first is to consider various packaging rationales, or reasons, to choose a particular strategy. These rationales could include any of the following:

- **Service** Categories based on service layers, as previously discussed
- **Scalability** The ability to quickly and easily extend the solution to handle more transactions or more use
- **Performance** The response time of the system and the speed with which it performs application tasks
- **Manageability** The ease with which an application can be managed on all levels
- **Reuse** The ease with which components can be reused by other applications
- **Business context** The separate business functions, such as accounting or sales
- **Granularity** The number of services and objects packaged in a component

In addition to these strategies, the components should also be packaged and distributed based on the application's programming model.

The second step is to align the strategy with the programming model. Because the programming model is not firm at this point, this step is inherently interactive in nature.

The third step is to determine the design tradeoffs that impact the strategy, based on the rationales used in the first step. For example, you might have based the strategy primarily on the performance needs of the application. In doing so, you might have compromised any necessary scalability, and if you have, you will need to decide what to do about this tradeoff.

Throughout rationalization, you should validate the proposed components and their packaging and distribution. Issues to consider include whether the components fit the packaging strategy, whether you are meeting the design goals and application requirements outlined earlier, whether the components you have derived actually match up with the logical design, and whether everything fits with the enterprise architecture.

One way to validate the design is to build prototypes and proof-of-concept test applications. As you define more and more components, you should include them in these trial applications and observe the results.

Although you have been performing validation work throughout rationalization, you should carry out formal component refinement and validation at the conclusion of this Physical Design step. These tasks should be performed by people qualified to perform testing. In some cases, you might find it worthwhile to schedule a formal quality assurance review of the component design, to be carried out by an outside expert with component design expertise. Following are several attributes of a solid component plan to be implemented by such an expert:

- The identified components contain all the services identified in the Logical Design Model.
- All component and service dependencies have been taken into account.
- Distribution of components across topologies matches rationales on which the distribution is supposedly based.
- Services are grouped into components based on a solid balance of physical location, packaging rationale, and technology constraints.
- The component plan demonstrates high cohesion and loose coupling.
- The component plan addresses both upward and downward scalability.

Cohesion and Coupling

One of the design goals noted earlier is high cohesion and loose coupling. *Cohesion* is the relationship among different internal elements of a component, whereas *coupling* is the relationship of a component to other components.

A component in which its internal elements—primarily its services—are closely related has high cohesion. Cohesion can be both beneficial and non-beneficial, depending on the cause of the cohesion.

Beneficial types of cohesion include the following:

- **Functional** A component does one and only one thing. This is the strongest type of cohesion.
- **Sequential** A component contains operations that must be performed in a specific order and must share the same data.
- **Communicational** Operations in a component use the same data but aren't related in any other way. This type of cohesion minimizes communication overhead in the system.
- **Temporal** Operations are combined because all of them are performed at the same time.

Non-beneficial types of cohesion include the following:

- **Procedural** Operations are grouped together because they are executed in a specific order. Unlike sequential cohesion, the operations do not share any of the same data.
- **Logical** Several operations are grouped into a single unit that requires some control flag, such as a large or highly nested IF or CASE statement, to be passed to select the appropriate operation. The operations are related only by artificial selection logic.
- **Coincidental** Operations are grouped without any discernible relationship to one another.

Metrics that can be used to determine the amount of coupling include the following:

- **Size** Minimize the number of connections and the complexity of interfaces.
- **Intimacy** Use the most direct connection.
- **Visibility** Define all connections explicitly.
- **Flexibility** Use cohesive, loosely-coupled interfaces.

Ultimately, the flexibility goal means the interfaces should have high cohesion and loose coupling. High cohesion provides a clearer definition of the component's function and behavior. An example would be arranging services by organizational function so that each component has only the services that pertain to its function.

Loose coupling provides more flexibility and independence, and leads to better-defined and simpler interfaces. An example would be organizing relationships among components by business function so that each component interfaces with the minimum number of other components for access to data.

Though you would carry out a formal refinement process at the end of rationalization, you can expect refinement to continue during development and deployment. Packaging and distribution will change as you test for the results of the determining criteria, such as performance. Thus, if the solution fails to meet performance objectives during testing, you might have to revisit the packaging and distribution plan that was supposed to provide the expected performance levels.

Physical Design rationalization is complete when you have performed the following tasks:

- Determine a packaging and distribution system.
- Transform objects into services-based components to create a services-based component model.
- Distribute components across topologies to produce a final deployment model that includes the future network, data, and component topologies.
- Use strategies and prototypes to refine packaging and distribution, resulting in a baseline deployment model.

Implementation

The last step of Physical Design is implementation. During this step, you specify the programming model that you will use, the interfaces for each component, and the internal structure of each component.

The programming model, or the programming *specifications* or *standards*, achieves the following:

- Prescribes how to use the selected technologies
- Sets design guidelines for component specifications, which helps to ensure consistency across the project
- Uses different considerations to address different aspects of the solution, such as asserting that all business services will be stateless whereas client-side services will be stateful

You must consider several aspects when building a programming model, some of which are highlighted in Table A.7 on the following page.

Note An application typically has more than one programming model, and some applications have many programming models, depending on the different requirements of the various components.

Although not a part of the programming model itself, an important consideration is the skill set and experience of the technical people who will implement the programming model.

When the programming model has been outlined, you are ready to specify the external structures of the components. These are outlined in the component interface, which:

- Is a contract that represents the supplier-consumer relationship between components.
- Is a means to access the underlying services.
- Represents one or more services.
- Includes underlying object attributes.

The specification of the component interface must include all the different manners in which the component can be accessed, and if possible, should also include examples of how the component can be used for each manner in which it is accessed. The interface must be documented and understandable to the developers who will use the components and is typically written using IDL or the development language the team has chosen.

Table A.7 Programming Model Aspects

Aspect	Considerations
Implementation technologies	Programming language; application programming interface (API); servers and server technologies; and other technologies affecting implementation. Implementation technologies are a consideration because some technologies require a specific programming model to take full advantage of them. For example, MTS requires single-entrant, single-threaded, in-process components.
Stateful vs. stateless objects	A *stateful* object holds private state accumulated from the execution of one or more client calls. A *stateless* object does not hold private state. Typical issues to be addressed include where state will be kept and tradeoffs such as scalability, complexity, and performance.
In-process vs. out-of-process function calls	In-process is fast and direct. Out-of-process on the same computer is fast and offers secure interprocess communications. Out-of-process across computers is secure, reliable, and offers a flexible protocol based on Distributed Computing Environment, Remote Procedure Calls (DCE-RPC).
Connected vs. connectionless modes	In connected application/component environments, the various components participating in the service of a task must have real-time, live connections to each other to be able to function. If the connection is severed because of problems at run time, the components involved in the interaction fail. Real-time applications typically must be run in connected mode. Applications/components that are written to run in a connectionless environment are able to reestablish a connection as and when needed.
Synchronous vs. asynchronous programming models	A synchronous programming model blocks the calling component from proceeding with other work until the called interface completes the requested service and returns control to the calling component. An asynchronous programming model allows components to send messages to other components and continue to function without waiting for a reply. A component designed to use an asynchronous programming model is harder to program, but it lends itself to more scalability. A component isn't blocked and doesn't have to wait for a spawned process to complete before proceeding.
Threading model	Choosing the threading model for a component is not a simple matter because it depends on the function of the component. A component that does extensive input/output (I/O) might support free-threading to provide maximum response to clients by allowing interface calls during I/O latency. On the other hand, an object that interacts with the user might support apartment threading to synchronize incoming COM calls with its window operations.
Error handling	Certain programming and deployment model decisions will constrain the number of error handling options available.
Security	A given component or service has four security options: component-based, at either the method level, the interface level, or the component level; database-based; user-context based, in either an interactive method using system security, or a fixed security within the application; or role-based, such as a sales clerk or general manager.
Distribution	Having three logical tiers does not necessarily translate into three physical tiers. The logical tiers will be spread among the physical tiers. For example, some business services reside on the client.

You should consider three implications when creating component interfaces:

- A published interface is an interface contract and should be considered permanent.
- A modification of an existing interface should be published as either a new component or an entirely new interface.
- The data types of published attributes must be supportable by the service interface consumer.

The interface contract defines the parameters, the data types, any interaction standards, and a description of the interface. The degree of specificity depends on user needs—ultimately, the degree of reuse.

Finally, you are ready to specify the internal structure of the components. (Note that internal structure is important only when building the component itself. When assembling components, the public interface is the important factor.)

Many factors come into play when defining the internal structure of a component. The most significant factor is the language or tool used to implement the component. The other factors are used as criteria to determine the component's internal structure. For example, when writing the first n-tier application for a large organization that plans to develop other applications that will use many of the same services, the internal structures of the components should be designed so as to enhance their reusability.

When the internal structures have been specified, the baseline for the implementation step is established. This baseline is merged into the overall Physical Design baseline.

Physical Design implementation is complete when you have performed the following tasks:

- Determine a programming model.
- Specify the external structures of components, including interfaces, attributes, and services.
- Specify the internal structures of components.

Completing the Physical Design

As noted at the beginning of this section, the output of Physical Design is a set of components, a UI design for a particular platform, and a physical database design. At this point, the set of components, including packaging and distribution, is complete. The remaining two outputs of Physical Design still need to be completed.

The details of solid UI database design are beyond the scope of this chapter; however, you should be aware of the following.

- **UI design applies to a particular platform or platforms** The most efficient application design might combine both a Web-based interface for some functions and a Win32 client for other functions. The details of choosing various technologies for the UI and user services layer are discussed in the following section.
- **Adequate Conceptual and Logical Design paves the way for database design** If you did a thorough job in Conceptual and Logical Design, including a fully rationalized class model and logical database design, completing the physical database design is much easier. In addition, you can be fairly confident that the database design is closely aligned with both user needs and with reality, and should need only minor changes throughout the actual development work. Again, time spent in early attention to detail in Conceptual and Logical Design winds up actually saving time over the life of the project.

Lesson Summary

To create a solid application, you should design the application in such as way that the developers responsible for code implementation have the appropriate guidance. Working through Conceptual, Logical, and Physical Design can help you move from nebulous concepts to a concrete application that can be implemented efficiently. The use case model, class model, and state model provide different views and descriptions of the application. The use case model describes what the application must do from the user's perspective and how these actions are interrelated. The class model moves the project from the language of the user and customer into the language of the developers. Additionally, the class model guides you in creating a modularized application that can be packaged and deployed as needed. Finally, the state model describes the properties and actions of the application at specific points in time. The fidelity of these models is refined throughout the design process.

APPENDIX B

Review Questions and Answers

Chapter 1

Review Questions

1. What is the value of a services-based approach to solution design?

   A services-based approach to solution design provides a modular and distributed approach to design solution components. This modularity allows for the use of resources, skills, and assets to help benefit the solution development process.

2. What are the service layers of the MSF Application Model?

   The service layers of the MSF Application Model are user, business, and data.

3. What is the purpose and value of conceptual design?

   The purpose and value of conceptual design is to capture, understand, and prioritize business and user requirements in their proper context. It increases the value of the requirements gathered. It provides a vehicle for building stakeholder consensus about the solution.

4. What role can data services provide within a distributed application?

   Data services (DS) can provide the standard Create, Retrieve, Update, Delete (CRUD) data component. This component interfaces with the business services layer, providing that layer with the DS that it needs to carry out business functions. In many applications, the DS component or service will also need to provide data manipulation, access security, and data connection pooling.

5. What is the purpose of physical design?

   The purpose of physical design is to apply real-world technology constraints to a logical design, create a view of the solution from your perspective, and provide the roadmap for the implementation team.

Chapter 2

Review Questions

1. List the four stages of the production channel and the purpose of each stage.

   The four stages of the production channel are:

   - **Development** Used by developers to make all changes to code
   - **Testing** Used by the testing team to check basic functionality
   - **Certification** Used by the certification team for extensive testing, including integration testing with other applications and the actual production environment
   - **Production** Product or application put into actual use in the real-world environment

2. What are the two overall areas of change control?

   The two overall areas of change control are the source code itself and all other artifacts of a project.

3. What are some examples of change control systems?

   Some examples of change control systems are word processors, electronic mail and groupware systems, and version control applications.

4. What is VSS?

   VSS is a version-control system consisting of a central database application on a server, as well as client applications that access the central database. VSS is tightly integrated with all of the Visual Studio 6 products, including Visual C++.

5. What are sharing, branching, and merging in VSS?

   In VSS, one file can be *shared* among multiple projects. Changes to the file from one project are automatically seen by other projects sharing the file.

   Branching is the process of taking a file in two directions (that is, branches or paths) at once. VSS keeps track of these branches by tracking the different paths as a project.

   Merging is the process of combining differences in two or more changed copies of a file into a single, new version of the file.

6. Where in VSS do you make project-based security available?

   You make project-based security available using the Administrator tool, which you can access by clicking the Options command on the Tools menu.

7. What does an E/R diagram show?

   An E/R diagram shows entities, attributes of entities, relationships among various entities, cardinality required within a relationship, and existence required by a relationship.

8. What is Visual Modeler used for?

   Visual Modeler is used to develop the class and component models for an n-tier application.

9. What is Dcomcnfg.exe?

   Dcomcnfg.exe is a utility used to configure various COM-specific settings in the registry that relate to COM activity over a network.

10. What is OLEView?

    OLEView is an administration and testing tool that duplicates many functions of Dcomcnfg.exe in a Microsoft Windows Explorer-style window.

Chapter 3

Review Questions

1. What is the MFC document/view architecture?

   MFC's document/view architecture makes it easy to support multiple views, multiple document types, splitter windows, and other valuable UI features. At the heart of document/view are four key classes:

   - CDocument (or COleDocument), an object used to store or control your program's data
   - CView (or one of its many derived classes), an object used to display a document's data and manage user interaction with the data
   - CFrameWnd (or one of its variations), an object that provides the frame around one or more views of a document
   - CDocTemplate (or CSingleDocTemplate or CMultiDocTemplate), an object that coordinates one or more existing documents of a given type and manages creating the correct document, view, and frame window objects for that type

   The CDocument class provides the basic functionality for programmer-defined document classes. A document represents the unit of data that the user typically opens with the Open command on the File menu and saves with the Save command on the File menu. The CView class provides the basic functionality for programmer-defined view classes. A view is attached to a document and acts as an intermediary between the document and the user: the view renders an image of the document on the screen and interprets user input as operations upon the document. The view also renders the image for both printing and print preview.

2. How can the OnDraw member function be used with Printing and Print Preview?

   For basic printing and print preview, you can override the view class's *OnDraw* member function. That function can draw to the view on the screen, to a printer DC for an actual printer, or to a DC that simulates your printer on the screen. You can also add code to manage multipage document printing and preview, paginate your printed documents, and add headers and footers to them.

3. Within thread management, what is an apartment?

   An apartment is a basic unit of thread safety. Two types of apartments exist: STA and MTA.

4. Within thread management, what is an STA?

   An STA can have only a single thread executing within an apartment. Method calls to objects in an STA are automatically serialized, or kept in sequence as they come in.

5. Within thread management, what is an MTA?

   An MTA can have multiple threads executing within the apartment. Method calls to objects in an MTA are not serialized.

6. Within memory management, what is a stack?

   The stack is an area of memory automatically allocated whenever a function is called. The stack is used for a number of purposes, including holding the values of variables used by the function and storing the memory address of the next execution point of the code that called the function. The stack is a Last-In/First-Out mechanism, meaning that normally the last values pushed onto the stack must be popped off the stack in sequence.

7. Within memory management, what is a heap?

   The heap is reserved for the memory allocation requirements of the application, and is separate from the program code and the stack. The total size of objects allocated on the heap is limited only by the computer system's available virtual memory. You use the built-in operators *new* and *delete* to allocate and deallocate objects in heap memory. Although the *malloc* and *free* functions exist, they should be abandoned in favor of the *new/delete* combination in almost every instance.

8. What are some common problems that cause memory leaks within an application?
   - **Forgetting to allocate memory at all** For instance, you create a pointer, but don't then use *new* to actually create a memory-based object to which the pointer can point.
   - **Going out of bounds on an array** For example, an array has 10 elements, and you try to get the value of element 20. Forgetting that the first element in an array is number 0 often causes this mistake.
   - **Forgetting to walk the "chain of destruction" that occurs whenever an object is destroyed** If the object has members that are also objects, their destructors will also be called, sometimes leading to unwanted results.
   - **Going out of bounds when putting something into a variable or buffer** For instance, you dimension a char with a size of 5, and then try to load "Hello!" into it.
   - **Assuming that memory actually got allocated** It is just good practice to include exception handling code to deal with an allocation that fails.

Chapter 4

Review Questions

1. Which function adds menu commands to a cascading menu?

   The *AppendMenu* function adds menu commands to a cascading menu.
2. To create a dockable toolbar, which steps must you complete?

   You must complete all three of the following steps: enable docking for the frame; enable docking for each toolbar you want to be dockable; and dock the toolbar to the frame.
3. How do you invoke modal and modeless dialog boxes?

   You invoke modal dialog boxes with *CDialog::DoModal*, and invoke modeless dialog boxes with *CDialog::Create*.
4. Which function adds controls to a rebar?

   The *AddBar* function adds controls to a rebar.

Chapter 5

Review Questions

1. What is a coclass?

   A coclass is a named implementation of one or more COM interfaces. A coclass is named using a class identifier (CLSID), which is a type of GUID. Like interface identifiers (IIDs), CLSIDs are guaranteed to be unique, but are difficult to use. Therefore, coclasses can also have string names, called programmatic identifiers (ProgID).

2. What is a COM object?

   COM objects are run-time instances of a particular class, with the class representing a real-world entity. For example, based on their characteristics, classes could define a Customer, Order, or SalesTaxCalculator object. Thus, each Customer object would represent a specific instance of a real-world customer; each Order object would represent a specific instance of an order; and so on. An object usually contains an identity, a state, and a type of behavior. Identity is the unique name or label distinguishing one object from another; state represents data associated with a particular object; and behavior is a set of methods called to query or manipulate an object's state.

3. What is a COM component?

   A COM component is a binary unit of software you can use to create COM objects. For a given CLSID, a component will include the COM class, the code to implement the class object, and usually the code needed to create appropriate entries in a system registry.

4. What are the four interfaces that every COM class must implement?

   IUnknown, *QueryInterface*, *AddRef*, and *Release* are the standard interfaces developed by Microsoft for use with COM, as opposed to any custom interfaces that you develop within your own code.

5. True or false: allocating and deallocating instances of an exported class is the job of the client; it should not be left to the server.

   False. It is actually the job of the server. If the client allocates and deallocates the exported class, the client will not work properly when the DLL memory requirements change.

6. What method do C++ programmers use to separate the interface declaration from the implementation?

   C++ programmers use abstract classes with all the methods being pure virtual.

7. Regarding inheritance, what primary advantage is offered by template classes?

   Template classes allow you to use both implementation inheritance and interface inheritance at the same time.

8. What are the four entry points to a COM DLL?

   The four entry points to a COM DLL are *DllGetClassObject*, *DllCanUnloadNow*, *DllRegisterServer*, and *DllUnregisterServer*.

9. True or false: *AddRef* and *Release* must always return an accurate count of an object's outstanding references.

   False. *AddRef* and *Release* can return arbitrary values if the object was not allocated on the heap.

10. Can ATL be used only to create in-process servers?

    No. ATL can also produce boilerplate code for an out-of-process server.

Chapter 6

Review Questions

1. Which function is used to create a mutex synchronization?

   The function used to create a mutex synchornization is *CreateMutex*.

2. Which files does Dcom95.exe install on a computer?

   The files that Dcom95.exe installs on a computer are Dcomcnfg.exe, Rpcss.exe, and Dllhost.exe.

3. Which class forms the base for creating Windows NT services?

   The class that forms the base for creating Windows NT services is CNTService.

4. To register a server for remote access, what part of the registry do you need to modify?

   You need AppID to register a server for remote access.

Chapter 7

Review Questions

1. What are the four rules that all transactions must follow?

   The four rules are known as the ACID rules—transactions must be atomic, consistent, isolated, and durable.

2. What is the technique that the context wrapper uses to do preprocessing and postprocessing of every call into an object?

   The technique is interception.

3. In MTS 2, can two objects created by two separate base clients ever take part in the same transaction?

   No. Two base clients (clients outside of MTS) creating two MTS objects would result in different activities. In MTS 2, objects have to be in the same activity to participate in a transaction.

4. What are the four stages of an MTS object's life cycle?

   The four stages of an MTS object's life cycle are creation, activation, deactivation, and destruction.

5. True or false: two MTS components in different computers cannot be part of the same activity because you must use *IObjectContext::CreateInstance* to do so, and you cannot specify a remote computer name with this function.

   False. Although it is true that *IObjectContext::CreateInstance* does not allow you to create a component in a different computer, you can declare the component to be a remote component in MTS Explorer; *CreateInstance* would then create the object remotely. Both the creator and created object would exist in the same activity.

6. True or false: if you call *SetAbort* within a method call, the transaction is doomed immediately, and nothing can be done to make it succeed.

   False. The transaction is not doomed until the method call ends and passes back through the context wrapper. Within the method call, you can call *SetComplete* again.

Chapter 8

Review Questions

1. What are the two main APIs used for programming in MSMQ?

   The two APIs are a C API and a COM API. This chapter focuses on using the COM API.

2. In the MSMQ topology, the enterprise is divided into what?

   The enterprise is divided into sites.

3. True or false: the IMSMQQueue interface has both *Send* and *Receive* functions for sending and receiving messages.

   False. The sending of a message is done through the IMSMQMessage interface. Receiving messages is done through the IMSMQQueue interface.

4. List the three transaction coordinators that MSMQ allows you to use.

   The three transaction coordinators are the internal coordinator, MS DTC, and MTS.

5. True or false: a queue can be located from a disconnected dependent client using the queue's path.

   False. Disconnected dependent clients do not have access to MQIS, which is what MSMQ uses to translate the path into the queue's ID number. MSMQ needs the ID number to locate a queue.

Chapter 9

Review Questions

1. Which recordset properties must you set to create a disconnected recordset?

   You must set the cursor type to adOpenStatic and the lock type to adLockBatchOptimistic.

2. You want to execute several commands as part of the same transaction. How would you ensure that each command object executes as part of the same transaction?

   You would open a connection to the data source; call the *BeginTrans* method of the connection object; and set the ActiveConnection property of each Command object to the open connection before executing the command.

3. Which type of accessor would you use to retrieve information from a data source that has an unknown schema?

   You would use CDynamicAccessor.

4. A theoretical application has to display a list of cities from a table; the list of cities does not change. Which type of ODBC cursor would you use to display this list?

   You would use ForwardOnly.

5. Which function would you call to retrieve diagnostic records whenever a function call returns a failure code?

   You would call *SQLGetDiagRec*.

6. What is a cursor?

   A cursor stores the result set and provides functionality to allow an application to work directly with the result set.

7. Which OLE DB component helps you search for data sources?

   Enumerators.

Chapter 10

Review Questions

1. What is SEH?

   SEH is a Windows service responsible for locating and calling handler code in an application when an error occurs. An application using SEH encloses within a *__try* block the code that can cause an error, and identifies the associated error handler code by placing it inside an *__except* block. Only if code in the *__try* block causes an error does program control proceed to the *__except* block; otherwise, the *__except* block does not execute.

2. Does Visual C++ always support exception handling?

   Not always—it depends on the presence of the /GX switch. Wizards such as MFC AppWizard add the switch automatically. A project that does not use exception handling should make the switch unavailable to reduce overhead. The C/C++ tab in the Project Settings dialog box provides access to the switch.

3. What is an HRESULT?

   As used in COM programming, an HRESULT is a defined type for a 32-bit long integer containing an error code. COM components such as Microsoft ActiveX controls and database providers export functions (or methods) that return HRESULT codes. An HRESULT integer contains bit fields that specify severity, facility, and a code descriptor. HRESULTs are signed integers; zero or a positive value indicates success, whereas a negative HRESULT indicates failure and usually causes an exception to occur.

4. Name two ways that an application can determine when an error occurs in the MFC framework.

   Member functions of MFC classes indicate an error by either returning a specified value (such as NULL or FALSE), or throwing an exception. An application can determine when an error occurs by either testing return values or, for those functions that support exception handling, placing function calls inside a *try* block and providing an associated *catch* block to trap any exceptions. Many MFC functions return both error values and throw exceptions, giving you a choice in how to handle potential errors.

5. Name three ways in which a COM server can communicate an error to a client. Discuss pros and cons of each.

   When a COM server detects an error, it can indicate the condition by doing one of the following:

   - Returning an HRESULT code
   - Raising an exception
   - Firing an event such as the Error stock event

An HRESULT code represents the simplest and most traditional way for a server to report an error; all server methods should return an HRESULT value even if they throw exceptions or fire events. However, not all clients correctly receive returned HRESULT values. Such clients can recognize exceptions, but only if they provide code to trap the error. The same problem pertains to events because the server has no guarantee that clients include event handler functions. A potential advantage of events is that they offer a way for the server to notify the client asynchronously of an error and then continue working.

6. What is an error log, and when should it be used?

   An error log is a running record of an application's state. As it executes, the application writes selected information to the log, such as the current value of variables and return codes received from functions. The log thus provides a paper trail that you can later scan to verify the program's behavior or to track down the origin of errors. To facilitate error logging, MFC provides the TRACE macro, which writes a string to the Debug tab of the Visual C++ Output window. An error log can also exist as a file, making it a more permanent record.

   An error log has several uses. It can help demonstrate that an application is behaving as expected, or simply serve as a notification to you that something unexpected has taken place. An error log can also be a valuable ally in tracking down mysterious errors that seem to arise exclusively in release builds, but not in debug builds.

7. How does MTS prevent errors from corrupting data?

   MTS implements a policy known as failfast, in which unhandled exceptions lead to immediate termination of the offending process. The rationale behind failfast is that unexpected errors indicate an unstable state that must be abruptly halted before the client has the opportunity to unknowingly commit the transaction, thus adding potentially corrupted data to the store.

   MTS also monitors values returned from a transaction's root object, preventing the object from returning a spurious success code when the transaction has failed. This process ensures that the client is not mistakenly advised of success in the event of an error.

8. What is MTS Explorer?

   MTS Explorer is an MMC snap-in that allows you to manage MTS components. Primarily intended as a management tool for system administrators, MTS Explorer can also act as a transaction viewer that allows developers to spy into the otherwise closed world of transaction processing. This feature of MTS Explorer can help you test program behavior and track down errors.

9. Your client application establishes a connection using ADO to access a provider. In turn, the provider makes use of other components, several of which detect errors. How can your client (1) determine how many errors occurred; (2) receive a description of each error; and (3) learn which modules detected the errors?

   The ADO Errors collection provides all three pieces of information. An Errors collection contains one or more Error objects, the number of which can be determined by calling the collection's *GetCount* method. This method informs the client of how many errors occurred.

   The application then loops through the collection contents, accessing each Error object in turn through the collection's get_item property. Each Error object provides methods that return the second and third pieces of required information. The *GetDescription* method returns a pointer to a string describing the error, and *GetSource* returns a pointer to a string that identifies the module in which the error occurred.

Chapter 11

Review Questions

1. How does a debug version of a program differ from its release build?

   Debug and release builds differ in two main characteristics. First, a program's debug build contains symbol information placed in the object code by the compiler, whereas the release code does not. Second, code in a debug build is not optimized, ensuring that the generated object code closely matches the original source code. Release code is almost always optimized.

2. Describe MFC's ASSERT, VERIFY, and DEBUG_NEW macros.

   ASSERT and VERIFY are very similar, differing in only one respect. Both macros take an expression as a parameter and cause an exception if the expression evaluates to FALSE. The only difference is that ASSERT does nothing in release builds, whereas VERIFY works in both debug and release code.

   DEBUG_NEW replaces calls to the new operator, performing the same service but also recording the filename and line number where each new statement occurs. This can help locate the cause of memory leaks resulting from a failure to match a new statement with a delete statement.

3. How does a debugger cause a running program to interrupt itself?

   The debugger places breakpoint code at designated locations in the program. When the running program encounters a breakpoint, execution freezes and the debugger gains control. There are two types of breakpoints: location and data. Visual C++ also allows conditional and message breakpoints, but these are simply special cases of location breakpoints.

4. What utility does Visual C++ provide for running and testing ActiveX controls?

   Visual C++ provides the ActiveX Control Test Container, a general-purpose container program that can embed any ActiveX control. The Test Container can call methods, set and read properties, activate the control's property sheet, and monitor events.

5. What is a dependency?

   A dependency is an executable module, usually a DLL or ActiveX control, that an application requires to execute. Dependencies themselves can have dependencies, forming a hierarchy of modules. For example, an MFC application might make no direct use of the C run-time library, yet nevertheless is dependent on the library because MFC itself requires the C run time.

6. What information is contained in the four lists that Spy++ can display?

   Spy++ can display views of current windows, processes, and threads. It can also display a log of messages that a window sends or receives.

7. What is regression testing?

   In regression testing, an application is again submitted to the same battery of tests it has already passed. Regression testing takes place after changes are made to an application, and ensures that the changes do not introduce new bugs or unexpected behavior.

8. What are some of the differences between debugging a local component that runs on the same computer as its client, and a remote component that runs on another computer?

   Debugging is easier and more convenient when both component and client run on the same computer. This is particularly true for components that run in-process—that is, components that have a DLL or .ocx extension and that share a client's address space. In this case, a single instance of the Visual C++ debugger can track execution as it flows between the two modules. An out-of-process component requires its own instance of the debugger, which Visual C++ starts automatically when execution reaches a breakpoint in the component.

   Debugging a remote component requires a separate installation of Visual C++ on the component's computer, forcing you to move between two different computers when debugging. To avoid this inconvenience, developers generally develop, debug, and test a component first as a local object, and relocate it to a remote computer only after the component passes all tests.

Chapter 12

Review Questions

1. What are the two stages of deployment?

   The first stage of deployment is the transfer of all necessary files to a user's hard disk. The second stage involves configuring the host system so that it recognizes and correctly runs the installed application.

2. What are cabinet and registry files?

   Recognizable by its .cab extension, a cabinet file contains a collection of files in compressed form. A registry or .reg file holds a script that can be merged into the system registry using the RegSvr32 utility.

3. What is the purpose of the InstallShield tool?

   Given a Visual C++ project, InstallShield creates an installation package consisting of a setup program, cabinet files, and miscellaneous information files. When run on another computer, the installation package installs the application and automatically configures the computer to run it.

4. Must a COM server be registered on a system before it can operate? If so, what examples can you give of a server's registry information?

   A COM server must be registered on a system before it can be used. Usually, this process is hidden from the user because it is performed automatically by an installation program. ActiveX controls, which are COM servers, are automatically registered by a Web browser when downloaded from a Web page. Most COM servers are self-registering, meaning that they export a function named *DllRegisterServer* that, when called, registers the information that the server requires.

   The registry information for any COM server must include the server's class identifier and its location on the system's hard disk. A COM server that runs remotely usually requires an AppID setting that specifies a surrogate host application for the component.

   Networked computers that host the client side of a distributed application also require additional registry information pertaining to the application's server components, even remote components that reside and execute on other computers. The RemoteServerName registry key holds the name of the server computer on which a remote component executes. The RemoteServerName key allows a client application to create a component object as though it were local, without regard for which computer on which the component actually runs.

5. Name three modes of application deployment.

   Applications can be deployed on media such as disks and CD-ROMs, over a network, and over the Internet through a Web site.

6. How does MTS Explorer facilitate the deployment of components?

   MTS Explorer can export a package file for any group of installed components, whether transactional or not. The package file, recognizable by its .pak extension, contains the security and configuration settings for all components in the package. Creating and deploying a package requires three steps:

   - Create the package file using MTS Explorer.
   - Copy the package file and component DLLs to a second computer.
   - Use MTS Explorer to install the package on the second computer.

   The package file ensures that properties for the package installed on the second computer exactly match properties for the original package on the first computer.

7. You have written a distributed application that uses MSMQ. What steps can you take to ensure that queues are properly created on your customer's computers?

   If your setup program can determine the name of the server computer that hosts the MSMQ component, the program can create a queue programmatically by calling the *MQCreateQueue* function. Otherwise, you should include instructions for the network administrator to create any required queues using MSMQ Explorer.

8. What is load balancing?

   Load balancing is the reduction of overall load on a single server computer by distributing remote components among multiple networked computers. Load balancing falls into two categories: static and dynamic.

   In static load balancing, a network administrator decides in advance how to distribute the components, and configures the network to assign groups of users to certain servers. Thus, of 100 users running the same distributed application, 50 users can run a component on server A whereas the other 50 users can run the same component on server B.

   Dynamic load balancing defers linking decisions until run time. This scheme requires the operating system to continually monitor server loads so that client requests can be routed to the least-worked server. Currently, neither the Windows operating system nor MTS implements dynamic load balancing.

9. What is ZAW?

   ZAW is a Microsoft initiative designed to reduce the cost and labor associated with administering a Windows-based network. ZAW incorporates two key technologies that pertain directly to application deployment: Windows Installer and SMS.

Glossary

A

ActiveX All component technologies built on Microsoft COM, other than OLE technology.

ActiveX control An embeddable, reusable COM object that exposes interfaces such as IOleObject and IDataObject. ActiveX controls are embedded in client applications known as containers, and can serve multiple containers at once, depending upon licensing restrictions. An ActiveX control can interact with the user either through its own windows or by using window services provided by the client application. Many ActiveX controls do not create windows at all and remain invisible during operation.

ActiveX control container An application that supports the embedding of ActiveX controls by implementing the IOleControlSite interface. *See also* ActiveX control.

aggregation A composition technique by which a COM object exposes the interfaces of other COM objects. With aggregation, a new object can reuse one or more existing objects. This reuse is achieved by exposing one or more of the interfaces in the original object. *See also* containment.

ambient property A run-time property that is managed and exposed by a container application. Typically, an ambient property represents a characteristic of a form, such as background color, that is communicated to a control so the control can assume the look and feel of its surrounding environment.

apartment-model threading A threading model for COM components that groups one or more threads into collections known as apartments. The apartment model further specifies that only threads within an apartment can interact directly with a COM object created by one of the apartment threads. Calls to the object from outside the apartment must be marshaled. *See also* free threading model, marshaling, MTA model, single threading model, and STA model.

application class Derived from the MFC class CWinApp, the class that encapsulates the initialization, running, and termination of a Windows-based application. An application must have exactly one object of an application class.

application framework Or framework. A library of C++ classes (such as the MFC Library) that provides the essential components of a Windows application. The application framework defines the basic operational structure of an application, and supplies standard UI implementations that can be incorporated into the application.

assertion A Boolean statement in a program's debug version that tests a condition that should evaluate as true, provided the program is operating correctly. If the condition is false, an error has occurred; thus, the program will typically issue an error message that gives a user the option to abort the program, activate the debugger, or ignore the error.

asynchronous operation In programming for Windows, a task that proceeds in the background, allowing the thread that requested the task to continue to perform other tasks.

ATL Active Template Library. A set of compact, template-based C++ classes that simplify the programming of COM objects. ATL provides a mechanism to use and create COM objects.

Automation A technology based on COM, which enables interoperability among ActiveX components. Formerly referred to as OLE Automation.

B

backward compatibility Ensuring that existing applications will continue to work in a new environment. Also, ensuring that the new release of an application will be able to handle files created by a previous version of a product.

bitmap Or pixel image, pixel map. An array of bits that contains data describing the colors found in a rectangular region on the screen (or the rectangular region found on a page of printed paper).

browser A program used to view formatted Web documents. *See also* WWW.

C

call stack An ordered list of functions that have been called, but have not returned, with the currently executing function listed first. Each call is optionally shown with the arguments and types passed to it. During a debug session, you can view the functions that have been called, but have not returned.

CGI Common Gateway Interface. A mechanism that allows a Web server to run a program or script on the server and send the output to a Web browser. *See also* ISAPI.

child window A window that has the WS_CHILD or WS_CHILDWINDOW style, and is confined to the client area of its parent window, which initiates and defines the child window. Typically, an application uses child windows to divide the client area of a parent window into functional areas. *See also* parent window.

class factory An object that creates one or more instances of an object identified by a given CLSID. A class factory object implements either the IClassFactory or IClassFactory2 interface. A class factory is one of the most frequently used types of class objects in COM.

client An application or process that requests a service from an in-process server or another process.

client area Or client rectangle. The portion of a window where an application displays output, such as text or graphics.

clipboard An area of storage, or buffer, where data objects or their references are placed when a user carries out a cut or copy operation.

CLSID Class identifier. A UUID that identifies a COM component. Each COM component stores its CLSID in the registry, allowing the operating system to locate a particular component by scanning the list of class identifiers. *See also* IID, GUID, UUID.

collection class In object-oriented programming, a class that can hold and process groups of class objects or groups of standard types. A collection class is characterized by its *shape* (the way the objects are organized and stored) and by the types of its elements. MFC provides three basic collection shapes: lists, arrays, and maps (also known as *dictionaries*).

COM Component Object Model. An open architecture for cross-platform development of client/server applications based on object-oriented technology as agreed upon by standards initiated by Digital Equipment Corporation and Microsoft Corporation. COM predefines certain interfaces but allows applications and components to define their own interfaces. COM dictates that every COM interface must be derived from the predefined interface IUnknown.

command message In Windows, a notification message from a UI object, such as a menu, toolbar button, or accelerator key.

compound document Or container document. A document within a container application that contains data of different formats, such as sound clips, spreadsheets, text, and bitmaps.

connection point In OLE, a mechanism consisting of the object calling the interface, referred to as the *source,* and the object implementing the interface, referred to as the *sink*. The connection point implements an outgoing interface that can initiate actions, such as firing events and change notifications, on other objects. By exposing a connection point, a source allows sinks to establish connections to the source.

container application *See* ActiveX control container.

containment A composition technique for accessing one or more COM objects via a single interface. Containment allows one object to reuse some or all of the interface implementations of one or more other objects. The outer object manages requests to other objects, delegating implementation when it uses the services of one of the contained objects. *See also* aggregation.

control A discrete element of a UI that allows a user to interact with application data.

critical section A segment of code that is not reentrant; that is, the code segment does not support concurrent access by multiple threads. Often, a critical section is used to protect shared resources.

D

DBMS Database management system. A layer of software between the physical database and the user. The DBMS manages all requests for database action (for example, queries or updates) from a user.

DC Device context. A data structure maintained by the operating system that defines the graphic objects, their associated attributes, and the graphic modes affecting output on a device.

DDV Dialog data validation. In MFC, a method for checking data as it is transferred from the controls in a dialog box. DDV is an easy way to validate data entry in a dialog box. *See also* DDX.

DDX Dialog data exchange. In MFC, a method for transferring data between the controls of a dialog box and their associated variables. DDX is an easy way to initialize dialog box controls and gather user data input. *See also* DDV.

deadlock A state in which every process in a set of processes waits for an event or resource that only another process in the set can provide. For example, in data communications, a deadlock can occur when both the sending and receiving sockets are waiting on each other, or for a common resource.

debugger A program designed to help find errors in another program by allowing the programmer to step through the program, examine data, and check conditions.

debug version A version of a program built with symbolic debugging information.

default window procedure A system-defined function that defines certain fundamental behavior shared by all windows.

device driver A low-level software component that permits device-independent software applications to communicate with a device such as a mouse, keyboard, monitor, or printer.

dialog editor A resource editor that allows you to place and arrange controls in a dialog box template and to test the dialog box. The editor displays the dialog box exactly as a user will see it. While using the Visual C++ dialog editor, you can define message handlers and manage data gathering and validation with ClassWizard. *See also* dialog template.

dialog template A template used by Windows to create a dialog box window and display it. The template specifies the characteristics of the dialog box, including its overall size, initial location, style, and types and positions of its controls. A dialog template is usually stored as a resource, but templates can also be stored directly in memory. *See also* dialog editor.

dispatch interface In Automation, the external programming interface of a grouping of functionality exposed by the Automation server. For example, a dispatch interface might expose an application's mouse clicking and text data entry functions. *See also* type library.

dispatch map In MFC, a set of macros that expands into the declarations and calls needed to expose methods and properties for Automation. The dispatch map designates internal and external names of object functions and properties, as well as data types of function arguments and properties.

DISPID Dispatch identifier. A 32-bit attribute value for identifying methods and properties in Automation. All accessor functions for a single property have the same DISPID.

document object An object that defines, stores, and manages an application's data. When a user opens an existing or new document, the application framework creates a document object to manage the data stored in the document.

document template In MFC, a template used for the creation of documents, views, and frame windows. A single application object manages one or more document templates, each of which is used to create and manage one or more documents (depending on whether the application is SDI or MDI). *See also* MDI, SDI.

document/view architecture A design methodology that focuses on what a user sees and needs, rather than on an application or what the application requires. This design is implemented by a set of classes that manage, store, and present application-specific data.

DSN Data source name. The name of a data source that applications use to request a connection to the data source. For example, a DSN can be registered with ODBC through the ODBC Administrator program.

dual interface An interface that derives from IDispatch and supports both late-binding via IDispatch and early-binding (vtable binding) via direct COM methods for each of its Automation methods.

dynaset A recordset (or set of records) with dynamic properties that is the result of a query on a database document. A dynaset can be used to add, change, and delete records from the underlying database table or tables. *See also* recordset, snapshot.

E

edit control Or edit box, text box. A rectangular control window in which a user can type and edit text.

entry point A starting address for a function, executable file, or DLL.

environment variable A symbolic variable that represents an element of a user's operating system environment, such as a path, directory name, or configuration string. For example, the environment variable PATH specifies the directories in which the operating system searches for executable files.

event Any action or occurrence, often user-generated, to which a program can respond. Typical events include keystrokes, mouse movements, and button clicks.

In ActiveX, a notification message sent from one object to another (for example, from a control to its container) in response to a state change or a user action.

event object A synchronization object that allows one thread to notify another that an event has occurred. Event objects are useful when a thread needs to know when to perform its task. For example, a thread that copies data to a data archive would need to be notified when new data is available. By using an event object to notify the copy thread when new data is available, the thread can perform its task as soon as possible.

external name In Automation, an identifier that a class exposes to other applications. Automation clients use the external name to request an object of this class from an Automation server.

F

file I/O File input/output. The mechanism for making data persistent among program work sessions by creating files, reading from files, and writing to files.

frame window In MFC, the window that coordinates application interactions with a document and its view. The frame window provides a visible frame around a view, with an optional status bar and standard window controls such as control menus, buttons to minimize and maximize the window, and controls for resizing the window.

free threading model A model in which an instance of a COM object can be safely accessed by any thread at any time without marshaling. Free threading is also known as the MTA model. *See also* apartment-model threading, MTA model, STA model.

FTP File Transfer Protocol. A method of retrieving files to a home directory or directly to a computer using TCP/IP.

G

GDI Graphics Device Interface. A set of operating system services that process graphical function calls from a Windows-based application, and pass those calls to the appropriate device driver, which performs the hardware-specific functions that generate output.

GIF Graphics Interchange Format. A form of graphics compression.

GUID Globally unique identifier. Another name for UUID. *See also* IID, UUID.

H

Help context A string and a number (Help context ID) that an application passes during a call to Windows Help to locate and display a Help topic. *See also* Help project file.

Help project file A project file that controls how the Windows Help Compiler creates a Help (.hlp) file from topic files. Microsoft Help Workshop is used to create a Help project file. The file name extension of a Help project file is .hpj. *See also* Help context.

Help topic The primary unit of information in a Help (.hlp) file. A topic is a self-contained body of text and graphics, similar to a page in a book. Unlike a page, however, a topic can hold as much information as required. If more information exists in a topic than the Help window can display, scroll bars appear to let a user scroll through the information.

HTML Hypertext Markup Language. Derived from SGML, a markup language that is used to create a text document with formatting specifications that inform a browser how to display the page or pages included in the document.

HTTP Hypertext Transfer Protocol. The Internet protocol used by Web browsers and servers to exchange information. The protocol makes it possible to use a client program to enter a URL (or click a hyperlink) and retrieve text, graphics, sound, and other digital information from a Web server. HTTP defines a set of commands and uses ASCII text strings for a command language. An HTTP transaction consists of a connection, request, response, and close.

hyperlink A link used to jump to another Web page. A hyperlink consists of both the display text and the URL of the reference.

I

IDL Interface Definition Language. The platform-independent standard language for specifying the interface for remote procedure calls. *See also* MIDL.

IID Interface Identifier. A globally unique identifier associated with an interface. Some functions take IIDs as parameters to allow the caller to specify which interface pointer should be returned. *See also* GUID, UUID.

in-process server A COM server implemented as a DLL that runs in the process space of an object's client. *See also* local server, remote server.

interface In COM, a set of related functions; a description of an abstract type. An interface translates directly into a pure abstract C++ base class, in which virtual functions are defined but not implemented.

Internet A global, distributed network of computers. *See also* intranet, WWW.

intranet A network within an organization, usually connected to the Internet via a firewall, that uses protocols such as HTTP or FTP to enhance productivity and share information. *See also* Internet, WWW.

ISAPI Internet Server Application Programming Interface. A set of functions for Internet servers, such as a Windows NT Server running IIS.

ISAPI extension A DLL that can be loaded and called by some HTTP servers. Used to enhance the capabilities of applications that extend a Web server.

ISAPI filter An Internet server filter packaged as a DLL that runs on ISAPI-enabled servers.

L

licensing A COM feature that provides control over object creation. Licensed objects can be created only by clients that are authorized to use them. Licensing might afford different levels of functionality, depending on the type of license.

list-box control In Windows, a child window that contains a list of items that can be selected by a user. List-box controls can permit the selection of one item or multiple items.

local server A COM server implemented as an executable file that runs on the same computer as the client application. Because the server application is an executable file, the local server runs in its own process. *See also* in-process server, remote server.

locking mode A strategy for locking records in a recordset during update. A record is locked when it is read-only to all users except the one currently entering data into it. *See also* optimistic locking, pessimistic locking.

M

marshaling In COM, the process of packaging and sending interface parameters across process or thread boundaries.

MDI Multiple document interface. The standard UI architecture for Windows-based applications. An MDI application enables a user to work with more than one document at the same time. Each document is displayed within the client area of the application's main window. *See also* child window, client area, SDI.

message A structure or set of parameters used for communicating information or a request. Messages can be passed between an operating system and an application, different applications, threads within an application, or windows within an application.

message box A window that displays information to a user. For example, a message box can inform the user of a problem that the application has encountered while carrying out a task.

MFC Microsoft Foundation Classes. A set of C++ classes that encapsulate much of the functionality of applications written for Windows operating systems.

MIDL Microsoft Interface Definition Language. Microsoft's implementation and extension of IDL. Processed by the MIDL compiler. *See also* IDL.

modal A restrictive or limiting interaction created by a given condition of operation. Modal often describes a secondary window that restricts a user's interaction with other windows. A secondary window can be modal with respect to its primary window or to the entire system. The user must close a modal dialog box before the application can continue operations. *See also* modeless.

modeless Not restrictive or limiting interaction. A modeless secondary window does not restrict a user's interaction with other windows. A modeless dialog box remains on a user's screen, available for use at any time, but also permits other user activities. *See also* modal.

mutex object In interprocess communication, a synchronization object which has a signaled state when the mutex is not owned by a thread, and has a nonsignaled state when it is owned. Only one thread at a time can own a mutex.

MTA model Multithreaded apartment model. Another name for the free threading model. *See also* free threading model.

O

optimistic locking A recordset locking strategy in which records are left unlocked until explicitly updated. The page containing a record is locked only while the program updates the record, not while a user is editing the record. *See also* pessimistic locking.

P

parent window A window that creates a child window, thereby providing the coordinate system and boundaries used to position the child window. *See also* child window.

persistent Lasting between program sessions, or renewed when a new program session is begun.

pessimistic locking A recordset locking strategy in which a page is locked when a user begins editing a record on that page. While the page is locked, no other user can change a record on that page. The page remains locked until records are updated or the editing is canceled. *See also* optimistic locking.

pixel The smallest addressable picture element (that is, a single dot) on a display screen or printed page.

platform The hardware and operating system that support an application. A platform sometimes is considered as the hardware alone, as in the Intel x86 platform.

primary key In a database program, a field or group of fields that uniquely identifies a record in a table. No two records in a table can have the same primary key value.

property The variable associated with an object that can contain data values.

property page A grouping of properties presented as a tabbed page of a property sheet.

property sheet A type of dialog box that is often used to modify the attributes of an external object, such as the current selection in a view. A property sheet has three main elements: the containing dialog box, one or more property pages shown one at a time, and a tab at the top of each page that a user clicks to select that page. An example of a property sheet is the Project Settings dialog box in Visual C++.

proxy An interface-specific object that packages parameters for methods in preparation for a remote method call. A proxy runs in the address space of the sender and communicates with a corresponding stub in the receiver's address space. *See also* stub, marshaling, unmarshaling.

Q

query A request for records from a data source. For example, a query can be written that requests "all invoices for Joe Smith," where all records in an invoice table with the customer name "Joe Smith" would be selected. *See also* recordset.

R

radio button In graphical UIs, a round button operated by a user to toggle an option or choose from a set of related but mutually exclusive options.

raw data Unprocessed, typically unformatted data. Raw data is a stream of bits that has not been filtered for commands or special characters. More generally, it is information that has been collected but not evaluated.

read-only Describes information stored in such a way that it can be played back (read) but cannot be changed (written).

record A collection of data about a single entity, such as an account or customer, stored in a table row. A record consists of a group of contiguous columns (sometimes called *fields*) that contain data of various types. *See also* recordset.

recordset A set of records selected from a data source. The records can be from a table, query, or stored procedure that accesses one or more tables. A recordset can join two or more tables from the same data source, but not from different data sources. *See also* record.

record view In form-based data-access applications, a form view object in which controls are mapped directly to the field data members of a recordset object, and indirectly to the corresponding columns in a query result or table on the data source.

reference count A count of the number of pointers that access, or make reference to, an object, allowing for multiple references to a single object. This number is decremented when a reference is removed; when the count reaches zero, the object's space in memory is freed.

referential integrity In database management, a set of rules that preserves the defined relationships between tables when records are entered or deleted. For example, enforcing referential integrity would prevent a record from being added to a related table when no associated record in the primary table exists.

registry In 32-bit Windows, the database in which configuration information is registered. This database takes the place of most configuration and initialization files for Windows and new Windows-based applications.

registry key A unique identifier assigned to each piece of information in a registry.

relational database A type of database or DBMS that stores information in tables and conducts searches by using data in specified columns of one table to find additional data in another table.

remote server A COM server application, implemented as an executable file, that runs on a different computer from the client application using it. *See also* in-process server, local server.

RFX Record Field Exchange. The mechanism by which MFC ODBC classes transfer data between the field data members of a recordset object and the corresponding columns of an external data source. *See also* DDX.

RGB Red-green-blue. A mixing model, or method of describing colors, in light-based media such as color monitors. RGB mixes percentages of light-based colors (red, green, and blue) to create other colors. Windows defines these percentages as three 8-bit values called RGB values. Zero percentage of all three colors, or an RGB value of (0,0,0), produces black; and 100 percent of all three colors, or an RGB value of (255,255,255), produces white.

rich edit control In MFC, a window in which a user can type new text, and edit existing text. The text can contain character and paragraph formatting and include embedded ActiveX objects.

root In a hierarchy of items, the single item from which all other items are descended. The root item has nothing dominating it in the hierarchy.

S

scrolling The process of moving a document in a window to permit viewing of any desired portion.

SDI Single document interface. A UI architecture that allows a user to work with just one document at a time, although the document might be displayed through any number of views. Windows Notepad is an example of an SDI application. *See also* MDI.

SEH Structured Exception Handling. A mechanism for handling hardware-generated and software-generated exceptions that gives developers complete control over the handling of exceptions, provides support for debuggers, and allows use across all programming languages and computers.

semaphore A synchronization object that maintains a count between zero and a specified maximum value. A semaphore's state is signaled when its count is greater than zero and nonsignaled when its count is zero. The semaphore object is useful in controlling a shared resource that can support a limited number of users. This object counts the threads as they enter and exit a controlled area, and limits the number of threads sharing the resource to a specified maximum number.

serialization Also known as object persistence. The process of writing or reading an object to or from a persistent storage medium, such as a disk file. The basic idea of serialization is that an object should be able to write its current state, usually indicated by the value of its member variables, to persistent storage. Later, the object can be recreated by reading, or deserializing, the object's state from storage.

server An application or a process that responds to a client request.

In a network, any device that can be shared by all users.

server object An object that responds to a request for a service. A given object can be a client for some requests, and a server for other requests.

shell A piece of software, usually a separate program, that provides communication between a user and an operating system. For example, the Windows Program Manager is a shell program that interacts with MS-DOS.

single threading model A model in which a single object instance serves one or more client threads. All calls to the object must be marshaled except those from the thread that created the object. The concept of apartments does not exist in single threading, which should not be confused with the STA model. *See also* apartment-model threading, free threading model, MTA model, STA model.

smart pointer In C++, an object that implements the functionality of a pointer and additionally performs some action whenever an object is accessed through it. Smart pointers are implemented by overloading the pointer-dereference (->) operator.

snapshot In MFC, a recordset that reflects a static view of the data as it existed at the time the snapshot was created. *See also* dynaset, recordset.

SQL Structured Query Language. A programming language often used by DBMSs to query, update, and manipulate databases.

STA model Single-threaded apartment model. The simplest form of apartment-threading, in which an apartment contains only a single thread. By creating its own instance of a COM object, each apartment can interact directly with the object without marshaling. This contrasts with the single threading model, which allows only a single object instance to serve all threads. *See also* free threading model, marshaling, single threading model.

STL Standard Template Library. A set of template classes that provide programmable solutions to common tasks such as sorting and searching.

status bar A control bar at the bottom of a window, with a row of text output panes. The status bar is usually implemented as a message line (for example, the standard menu help message line) or as a status indicator (for example, the CAP, NUM, and SCRL indicators).

stub An interface-specific object that unpackages the parameters for that interface after they are marshaled across the process boundary, and makes the requested method call. The stub runs in the address space of the receiver, and communicates with a corresponding proxy in the sender's address space.

A function without an empty body used as a placeholder.

synchronization object An object in which the handle can be specified in one of the *wait* functions to coordinate the execution of multiple threads. The state of a synchronization object is either signaled, which can allow the *wait* function to return, or nonsignaled, which can prevent the function from returning. More than one process can have a handle of the same synchronization object, making interprocess synchronization possible. *See also* mutex object, semaphore.

T

tab control A common control used to present multiple pages of information or controls to a user; only one page at a time can be displayed.

tab order The order in which the TAB key moves the input focus from one control to the next within a dialog box. Usually, the tab order proceeds from left to right in a dialog box, and from top to bottom in a radio group.

thread The basic entity to which the operating system allocates CPU time. A thread can execute any part of the application's code, including a part currently being executed by another thread. All threads of a process share the virtual address space, global variables, and operating system resources of the process.

toolbar A control bar based on a bitmap that contains a row of button images. These buttons can act like pushbuttons, check boxes, or radio buttons. *See also* status bar.

ToolTip A tiny pop-up window that presents a short description of a toolbar button's action. ToolTips are displayed when a user positions the mouse over a button for a period of time.

type library A file or resource within a component that contains type information about a component's exposed objects. Type libraries are created using either the MkTypLib utility or the MIDL compiler, and can be accessed through the ITypeLib interface. *See also* dispatch interface.

U

UDA Universal Data Access. A Microsoft strategy for providing access to all types of information across the enterprise. UDA provides high-performance access to a variety of information sources.

UI thread User-interface thread. In Windows, a thread that handles user input and responds to user events independently of threads executing other portions of the application. UI threads have a message pump and process messages received from the system. *See also* worker thread.

UNC Universal naming convention. The standard format for naming resources throughout a network. Often associated with paths that include a local area network file server, as in *\\servername\sharename\directoryname\filename*.

unmarshaling In COM, the process of unpacking parameters that have been sent across process or thread boundaries.

URL Uniform Resource Locator. The address of a resource on the Internet. URL syntax is in the form *protocol://host/localinfo,* where *protocol* specifies the means of fetching the object (such as HTTP or FTP), *host* specifies the remote location where the object resides, and *localinfo* is a string (often a file name) passed to the protocol handler at the remote location.

UUID Universally unique identifier. A 32-digit number (128 bits) generated through an algorithm designed to never produce the same number twice. Because all UUIDs are (in theory) unique no matter where or when they are created, they are used to identify entities such as COM components and interfaces. *See also* CLSID, IID, GUID.

V

variant In Automation, an instance of the VARIANT datatype that can represent values of many different types, such as integers, floats, Booleans, strings, pointers, and so on.

view A window object through which a user interacts with a document.

vtable A table of pointers to virtual functions in a C++ class. The pointers in the vtable point to the members of the interfaces that an object supports. *See also* dual interface.

W

Win32 platform A platform that supports the Win32 API. These platforms also include Intel Win32s, Windows NT, Windows 95, Windows 98, MIPS Windows NT, DEC Alpha Windows NT, and Power PC Windows NT.

window class A set of attributes that Windows uses as a template to create a window in an application. Windows requires that an application supply a class name, the window-procedure address, and an instance handle. Other elements can be used to define default attributes for windows of the class, such as the shape of the cursor and the content of the menu for the window.

window handle In the Win32 API, a 32-bit value (assigned by Windows) that uniquely identifies a window. An application uses this handle to direct the actions of functions to the window. A window handle has the HWND data type; an application must use this type when declaring a variable that holds a window handle.

window procedure A function, called by the operating system, that controls the appearance and behavior of its associated windows. The procedure receives and processes all messages to these windows.

wizard A special form of dialog box that guides a user through a difficult or complex task. For example, a database program can use wizards to generate reports and forms. In Visual C++, AppWizard generates a skeleton program for a new C++ application.

worker thread A thread that handles background tasks while a user continues to use an application. Worker threads do not process messages, making them suitable only for tasks such as recalculation and background printing that do not require interacting with a user. *See also* UI thread.

WWW World Wide Web. The portion of the global Internet that uses hypertext links to connect pages and resources in a way that lets a user reach any page from any other page. *See also* browser, Internet, intranet.

Index

A

abstract base class, 565
abstract classes, 251, 255
abstraction, level of, 738
access, 19
  permissions, setting, 644
ACID rules, 351
ACL, 229
activation security, 229
Active Directory Services Interface. *See* ADSI
active documents, 333–35
Active Server Pages. *See* ASP
Active Template Library. *See* ATL
ActiveX
  COM and, 218
  control, Message, 618
  MFC and, 86
ActiveX controls, 21, 109, 176, 196, 210, 575
  adding custom property pages to, 193
  adding to property pages, 191
  adding support to, 185
  advanced features of, 188
  COleControl class, 189
  Component Gallery and, 176
  containers, 190
  creating, 180–84
  data exchange with property pages, 191
  debugging, 615
  DLLs, 178
  downloading to a UI, 195
  events, 190
  HTML Help, 136
  .ocx files, 178
  property pages, 191
  registry entries for, 682
  signing, 194
  subclassing, 188
  using event handlers, 179
  worker threads and, 575
ActiveX Control Test Container, 615, 616
ActiveX Data Objects. *See* ADO
ActiveX DLLs, COM DLLs as, 304
activities, 360
activity diagrams, 739
activity models, 738
actors, 729, 736
AddRef function, 262, 326
administration, remote, 390
administration objects in MTS, 365
Administrator tool in VSS, 49
ADO, 27, 31, 592
  applications, creating, 551
  architecture, 501
  command type property values, 506
  Connection Object, 502
  as data access technology, 502
  data-bound dialog box, creating, 508
  error handling and, 579, 588
  Errors collection, 589
  exception handling, 589
  executing parameterized queries with, 519
  features, 500
  Recordset object, 502
  when to use, 496
  working with, 503
ADSI, 26
AfxBeginThread function, parameters, 312
AfxEndThread, 314
aggregate functions, 466
aggregation, 326, 620
allocation of memory, 122–24
alpha product releases, 7
American National Standards Institute. *See* ANSI
ampersand symbol, 150
Analysis Workflow, 719
ANSI, MFC and, 88
antipatterns, 717, 732
apartment-model objects, 109
apartments, 114
APIs, 6, 26
  MSMQ and, 412
  OutputDebugString function, 582
  RegisterTypeLib API, 233
  vendor-neutral, 26
AppendMenu function, 152
AppIDs, 231, 624
application architecture, n-tier, 34
application development
  ADO and, 27
  architecture-first, 2, 4
application development *(continued)*
  parallelism, 13
  plan-while-building, 3
  Web browser considerations, 20
application model, 10
application programming interfaces. *See* APIs
applications
  architecture, 2
  benign exceptions and, 563
  Calendar control, adding, 178
  COM errors, 569
  component-based, 6, 216
  context-sensitive help for MFC, implementing 139
  DCOMCNFG, 69
  debug version, 601
  design, 4, 6, 10
  development. *See* application development
  dialog box–based, 96
  dialog boxes, implementing, 206
  distributed. *See* distributed applications
  distribution flexibility, 13
  dockable toolbars and, 155
  enterprise, data access and, 30
  exception and error handling, 565
  exception handler code and, 562
  exception handling in ADO, 589
  exceptions and, 558
  features, implementing, 96
  framework, 86
  HTML Help file links, adding to the Web, 141
  Internet-based, 17
  interoperable, 10, 13
  logic, 34
  MFC and error handling, 566
  MFC Help, 137
  MTS-based, creating 386
  multithreaded, 113
  multitier, designing, 12
  n-tier, 223
  native, 15, 16
  in OLE DB, 537
  operating system client support, requiring, 15
  porting between platforms, 88
  release version, 601
  requirements, 18
  reusability, 13
  robust code, 559

applications *(continued)*
scalable, 34
scaling with MTS, 389
SEH and, 560
service-layered, 223
services, 11
sharing of classes, 235
three-tier, 10
uninstalling, 657
user interface, 14
using CNTService in, 321
Web-based, advantages, 18, 19
wizards, 133
WYSIWYG, 105
AppWizard, 88
creating form views, 170
MFC ActiveX ControlWizard, 184
toolbar creation and, 154, 155
WinHelp and, 137
architecture, 712
application, 2
document/view, 92–95
MDI, 142
messages and commands, 89
MFC, 89
ODBC, 524
OLE DB, 537
print preview, 107
SDI, 142
architecture-first design, 2, 4, 5
archiving, in VSS, 51
arguments, 247
array of bytes, 123
arrays, setting data breakpoints, 607
ASP, 17
browser capability, 20
ASSERT macro, 602
ASSERT_KINDOF macro, 603
ASSERT_VALID macro, 603
AssertValid member function, 603
associations of classes, multiplicity, 751
asynchronous
communication, applied to MSMQ, 404
error notifications, 575
messages, receiving with ATL Object Wizard, 424
ATL, 86, 109, 270, 290
advantages, 111
aggregation, implementing, 327
AppWizard, 182
AtlTrace function, 582
ATL *(continued)*
ATLTRACE macro, 582
creating a DLL in-process server, 270
creating ActiveX controls, 180
creating multithreaded components, 318
creating out-of-process components, 304
creating persistable objects, 434
declarative security, 306
error logs and, 582
features, 110
global threading model, 319
interfaces, 180
limitations, 110
vs. MFC, when to use, 110
properties and methods, adding to objects, 276
support of STA and MTA threading models, 318
ATL COM AppWizard, 272
ATL Object Wizard
receiving messages asynchronously, 424
replicating features, 369
ATLTRACE macro, 582
atomic, 351
Attach function, 151
Attach to Process command, 621
attributes, 60. *See also* individual attributes.
authentication, 306–8
Authoring Guide, HTML Help, 136
authorization, 307, 308
Automation
IDispatch and, 227
MFC and, 87
oleautomation attribute and, 258
parameter types, 258

B

backup site controllers. *See* BSCs
balancing loads, 384
base classes, 240
inheritance and, 250
base clients, 360
BaseCtl framework, 183
baseline, 44
Beeper component, 695, 696, 706, 707
Beeper.dll, adding to setup project, 700
BEGIN_INTERFACE_MAP macro, 284
BEGIN_INTERFACE_PART macro, 283
BEGIN TRANSACTION statements, 461
benign exceptions, 563
beta product releases, 7
Beta testing, 636
big-endian byte ordering, 490
binary standard, 215, 218, 233
bitmap files, 135
blocks. *See* individual blocks
.bmp files, 135
branching, in VSS, 48
Break At control, 607
breakpoints, 605–8
BSCs, 405
bugs, 600
fixing in debugger's source window, 612
indicated in debugger windows, 609
removing from programs, 599
removing using MFC debug macros, 602
business
code, 235
components, building, 255
goals, alignment with, 5
objects, 744–45
rules for data access, 28
services, 11, 22–24
business service layer, 22, 23

C

C Point class, 100
C run-time library, 87
C++, 7, 27
compilers, sharing and, 236
easier integration with other languages, 235
exception handling, 560–64
interfaces, 221
libraries, 86, 109
objects, 220
C++ classes, 215
binding to a recordset, 512
template-based, 109
cabinet files, 659, 660
Call mtstran1::Begin button, 400
call security, 229
call stacks, 611
Call Stack window, 610, 611
CancelDisplay parameter, 576

candidate
classes, 735
components, packaging, 762
technologies, 757, 758
CArchive, 493, 494
cardinality of entities, 60, 61
cascading menus, 146
cascading style sheets, 17
catch keyword, 562, 563, 566, 568
CBitmap class, 100
CBrush class, 100
CChildView class, 96
CClientDC class, 99
CCmdTarget class, 91, 97, 284
CCmdUI, 149
CColorDialog class, 100
CComClassFactory, 276
CComCoClass, 276
CComGlobalsThreadModel, 319
CComModule, 273
CComModule class, 272
CComObjectThreadModel, 319
CDaoException object, 568
CDaoRecordset, 565
CDAORecordset function, 568
CDatabase in MFC ODBC, 527
CDataExchange, 172
CDBException, 530
CDC class, 99, 565
CDC objects, 101
CDialog class, 87, 90, 163, 166
CDocTemplate class, 93
CDocument class, 93
CDocument object, 97
CDocument::UpdateAllViews function, 95
CDumpContext class, 580
CDumpContext object, 581
CDynamicAccessor class, 545
CDynamicParameter Accessor, creating queries with, 547
central administration, 691
certificate authority, 688
certification, 40
CException, exception handling and, 565
CFieldExchange, 529
CFile class, 565–67
CFileException object, 566
CFile function, 566, 567
CFile object, 580
CFont class, 100
CFontDialog class, 100
CFormView class, 169–70, 529
CFrameWnd class, 90, 93
CGdiObject class, 100
CGI, ISAPI and, 336
change control, 38, 43–45
check marks, setting and clearing, 149
CHtmlStream, 337, 338
CHttpFilter, 337
CHttpFilterContext, 337, 338
CHttpServer, 337
CHttpServerContext, 337, 338
classes, 247, 255, 735. *See also* individual class names
abstract, 251
abstract base, 565
associating with a dialog template, 166
association, 751
attributes, 735
base, 240
business code, 235
C++, 215
candidate, 735
characteristics, 250
_com_error, 572
consumer, 541
derived, 240
diagrams, 62, 735, 749
document, programmer-defined, 93
document/view, 93
exported, 243, 246
factories, 263
graphic-object, 98
implementation, 254
implementation inheritance and, 240
interfaces, 250
MFC, 88, 99, 100
operations, 735, 749
parent, 280
pure virtual functions, 250
shared, 235, 236
template, 252
view, programmer-defined, 93
ClassFactory, 268
class model, 735, 749
ClassWizard
associating a dialog template with a class, 166
event handlers, adding, 179
handler functions, adding to menu commands, 147
property pages, adding, 191
DDV and, 171, 173
DDX and, 171
Client2, building release versions, 695
client programs, 236, 247
creating, 241
ensuring same directory as DLL, 243
modifying to use COM, 268
clients
access to HRESULT codes, 572
base, 360
configuration, 677–79
creating, 329
dependent, 406
fat, 352
independent, 406
project, debugging and, 617
client-side COM components, 21
client-side cursors, 486
client-side objects, 19
CLSIDs, 219, 222, 266
CMDIChildWnd class, 90
CMDIFrameWnd class, 90
CMemoryException class, 565
CMemoryException error, 569
CMemoryException object, 562, 568
CMemoryState, 604
CMenu class, 151, 162
CMetaFileDC class, 99
CMultiDocTemplate class, 93
CMyService class, 322
CNs, MQIS and, 406
.cnt files, 135
CNTService class, 321–25
CoADO Command object, 502
CObject class, 97, 603
CDumpContext and, 580
CObject function, 580
coclasses, 219, 233, 266, 358
CLSIDs and, 219
enhancing type library, 259
functions, 259
GUIDs and, 219
vs. language-based classes, 219
in type libraries, 368
CoCreateInstance function, 327, 358
CoCreateInstanceEx function, 219
codes
exception handler, 562
HRESULT, 570
MFC, writing, 492
shared classes, 235
stepping through, 611
code segments, COM, 216
coding, manual, advantages/disadvantages, 110

CoCreateFreeUnusedLibraries function, 267
CoGetClassObject function, 219, 358
cohesion, 765, 766
COINIT_APARTMENT-THREADED, 115
CoInitialize, 115, 116
CoInitializeEx, 115, 116
COINIT_MULTI-THREADED, 115
COleControl class, 189, 190, 575
COleControl function, 576
COleDocObjectItem class, 333
COleDocument class, 93
COleException class, 565
collections, Errors, 588
COM, 15, 215
- ActiveX and, 218
- ActiveX controls, 176
- business server layer and, 23
- APIs, 262
- authorization, 307
- availability, 19
- basics, 216
- as binary standard, 215, 218
- calls, remote, 22
- call security, 229
- classes, 23
- clients, creating, 305, 346
- coclasses, 219
- _com_error class, 572
- COM errors, 569–78
- components, 216, 222, 674, 682
- creating ActiveX controls with ATL, 180
- DLL component structure, 223
- DLL entry points, 265
- exceptions, 573
- executables, 304
- facility codes, 571
- functions, 267
- HRESULT, 570–73
- identifiers, 223, 224
- IDL and, 218
- interface pointers, 220
- interfaces, 23, 109, 225–28, 412
- IUnknown and, 278
- language independence, 217
- marshaling, 232
- MSMQ APIs, 412

COM *(continued)*
- object lifetime management, 221
- object reuse with containment, 329
- objects, 109, 614
- OLE and, 218
- SCODE, 570
- security, 229, 306
- server types, 304
- settings, configuring, 64
- specifications, 216
- support in distributed environments, 232
- transactions and, 352

COM API functions, 266
COM components, 24
- building with ATL, 270
- building with IUnknown, 226
- client-side, 21
- COM objects and, 222
- COM support in distributed environments, 232
- creating using ATL, 304
- DLL entry points, 223
- as DLLs, 223
- DLL structure of, 223
- errors and, 575
- extending existing, 326
- packaging methods, 24, 222
- registry settings, 231
- self-registering, 21

COM DLLs, 304
_com_error class, 572, 578
_com_error object, 589, 592
- passing to a catch block, 573

COM in-process server, converting components, 256
COM objects, 23, 219, 290
- AddRef method, 226
- coclasses, 219
- COM components and, 222
- debugging, 640
- lifetime management, 221
- location transparency and, 228
- pointers and, 220
- QueryInterface method, 226
- Release method, 226
- sending messages and, 420
- troubleshooting, 625

COM programming model, 23
COM reliance on the registry, 230
COM security, 229–34

COM servers, 291
- compiling, 277
- creating, 277, 286, 304, 344
- registering, 308, 309
- registering a DCOM component, 308
- self-registering, 682
- types, 304

command line switches, 563
Command objects, 502, 506, 539
Command properties, setting, 506
commands
- adding to the Programs menu, 662
- executing, 507
- handlers, 90
- IDs, 91
- messages, 89, 90
- objects and, relationships, 91
- targets, 92
- text, 512
- UI handler functions, 148, 150
- update handlers, creating, 160

commits, two-phase, 351
Common Gateway Interface. *See* CGI
Common Object Request Broker Architecture. *See* CORBA
compiled programs, problems with large size, 235
compiling
- debug errors, 245
- IDL files, 260

component-based approach, 6
component development, middle-tier, 235
Component Gallery, 176, 178
component interfaces in type libraries, 368
components, 6
- as objects, 217
- assigning roles to, 382
- categories, 24
- in applications, challenges 216
- COM, 24, 216
- building, goals, 236
- data access, 30
- DCOM, accessing, 22
- debugging, 621, 642
- distributing, 762
- executing, debugging, 621
- existing, 326
- in-process, interactions among, 117

components *(continued)*
in-process, specifying the surrogate, 624
interface, 767
making security available, 380
of MTS, deploying, 675
multithreaded, creating, 311
packaging, 762
remote, installing/registering, 623
self-registering, 682
services, 6
sharing by compiled programs, 236
switching between local and remote, 624
component topology, 761
computer inventory, SMS, 692
Conceptual Design, 726–33, 742
conceptual design phase, 724
conditional breakpoints, 606, 608
connected networks. *See* CNs
Connect function, 493
connection
to data source, 505, 506
information, specifying, 504
points, 109
string, 511
types, 22
Connector Server, MSMQ, 404
consistent transactions, 351
constants, _DEBUG, 580
constraints, 478–80
Construction Phase, 720
constructors, 120
ConstructStream function, 338
consumer classes, 541
consumers, 537
containers, 190
active documents, 333
containment, 329–33
context, MTS components and, 359
context wrapper, 359
context-sensitive help, 132, 139
controlling unknown, IUnknown as, 327
control notifications, 90
controls, 21, 747
ControlService function, communicating with services, 324
ControlWizard, 184
coordinating transactions, 351
CORBA, 23
core processes, 728
COSERVERINFO structure, 624
costs
of changing requirements, 34
reducing, 690
coupling, 765, 766
coverage testing, 40
CPaintDC class, 99
CPaintDC objects, 101
CPalette class, 100
CPen class, 100
CPreviewDC class, 107
CPreviewDC object, 108
CPrintDialog class, 100
CPrintInfo structure, 103
CPropertySheet, 168
CreateAndDestroy method, 394
Create function, 165
CreateInstance function, 219, 360, 386
Create member, 492
CreateMenu function, 151
Create mtstran1 button, 400
CreateMutex function, 316
Create, Retrieve, Update, Delete. *See* CRUD
CREATE TRIGGER function, 462
CREATE TRIGGER statements, 462
creating an in-process COM server, 286
creating in-process COM servers, 269
CRecordset, 527
CRecordView, 529
CRect class, 100
CRectTracker class, 100
CRgn class, 100
CRUD, 28
CSingleDocTemplate class, 93
CSize class, 100
CSocket, 489, 491
CSocketFile, 493
CStatusBar class, 161, 162
CString class, 173
CTestCtrl class, 186
CTestPropPage class, 186
CToolBar class, 154, 162
current-state scenarios, 731
cursors, 423, 485–86, 510
custom events, 190
custom property pages, adding, 193
CView class, 90, 93, 100, 102, 171, 580
CWinApp class, 89, 97
CWindowCD class, 99
CWinThread, 314
CWnd class, 87, 90, 151, 565

D

DA, 27–30, 483
for enterprise applications, 30
fundamental terms of, 485
strategies, 483, 498
technology, choosing, 32, 496, 502
DAO, 27, 31
MFC and, 86
when to use, 497
data
access. *See* DA
breakpoints, 605, 607
deleting, 454
display, 93
document, accessing, 94
duplicate, eliminating from database, 62
exchange, 171–72
integrity, 29, 478
modeling, 59, 62
modifying, 453
processing, 171
providers, 537
retrieving, 450
rules, 28
services. *See* DS
sources, 506, 543
storing, 26, 481
structures, memory allocation, 124
summarizing, 465
topologies, 760
types, relationship to functions, 466
validation, 171–75
writing to persistent storage, 93
data access. *See* DA
database management systems. *See* DBMSs
database objects, 470
databases
components of, 485
connecting to, 503
duplicate data, eliminating, 62
in VSS, archiving, 51
in VSS, logging in to new, 51
incorporating in applications, 487
MQIS, 405
DataGrid control, binding to recordsets, 513
data service design, 25
data service layer, 25
data source objects, 538

DBMSs, 25
DCE-RPC, 23, 257
DCL statements, 449
DCOM, 19, 215, 302, 310, 620
  availability, 19
  components, accessing, 22
  COM support in distributed environments, 232
  configuring, 302
  registering a component in, 308
  security, 306
  Windows and, 302, 303
DCOMCNFG, 64–67
Dcomcnfg.exe, 230–31, 303, 307–8, 310
DCs, 97, 99
DDL statements, 449
DDV, 163, 171–75
DDV_ValidateAge function, 175
DDX, 163, 171–75, 191
DDX_Text function, 172
dead letters queues, 422
deallocation of memory, 123, 244, 255
DebugBreak function, 322
_DEBUG constant, 580
debuggers, 245
  integrated, Visual C++, 600
  monitoring a range of variables, 607
  running, 609
  windows, 609, 610, 612
debugging, 599–601
  ActiveX controls, 615
  in the client project, 617
  COM objects, 614, 640
  components, on a single computer, 642
  in debugger's source window, 612
  errors while compiling, 245
  executing components, 621
  file-locked server modules, 625
  in-process servers, 615
  local objects, 614, 615, 640
  Message ActiveX Control, 618
  in ODBC applications, 532
  out-of-process servers, 617
  remote objects, 614, 620, 621, 643
  surrogate hosts and, 621
  using MFC debug macros, 602
  with Visual C++ integrated debugger, 605
  without adding permanent code, 602
DEBUG_NEW macro, 602, 603
DEC Alpha, 88
declarative programming, 354
declarative security, 306
default
  handlers, MFC, 576
  printing, 101
  properties, DCOMCNFG, 66
  security, DCOMCNFG, 65
degrading gracefully, 21
delete operator, 120, 121, 125
DELETE statements, 454
dependencies, 628
Dependency Walker, 628, 629
dependent clients in MSMQ, 406
Depends.exe. *See* Dependency Walker
deployment, 686–88, 706
derived classes, 240, 250
design, 4
  architecture-first, 2, 4
  business server, 23
  data service, 25
  modeling, 734
  multilayer, 10, 34
  multitier, 12, 13
  patterns/antipatterns, 715–17, 732
  phases, 724. *See also* individual phases
  process, 724
  user service, 15
  within context of enterprise, 6
Design Workflow, 719
desktop operating system, constraints, 19
destructors, 121, 250
Detach member function, 98, 151
developers, necessary skills, 37
development
  changes, on development computers, 39
  environment, 37, 38
  essentials, 85
  parallelism, 13
  process, software, 4
  stage, 39
  tools, 57
device contexts. *See* DCs
device-independent bitmap. *See* DIB
DHTML, Web-based interfaces, 17
diagnostic information, retrieving, 533
diagrams, 734
  activity, 739
  UML, 713
dialog box in ADO, data-bound, 508
dialog box–based applications, 96
dialog boxes, 163–68, 175
  creating property page resources, 193
  Help Topics, 133
  implementing into an application, 206
Dialog Data Exchange. *See* DDX
Dialog Data Validation. *See* DDV
dialog template, 165, 166, 201–3
DIB, 210
digital signatures, 688
direct caller vs. original caller, 383
DirectX multimedia, 15
DisableCommit method, 387
Disassembly window, 610, 611
disconnected recordset, creating, 518
disks, use in deployment, 686
DISPID_ERROREVENT, 575
distributed applications
  designing, 62
  exceptions and, 577
  installing, 684
  packaging and deploying, 694
  testing, 636
Distributed COM. *See* DCOM
Distributed Computing Environment, Remote Procedure. *See* DCE-RPC
distributed design application, 10
distribution flexibility, 13
DllCanUnloadNow function, 267, 273
DllGetClassObject class, 368
DllGetClassObject function, 266, 273, 358
DllRegisterServer function, 265, 272, 682
DLLs, 24, 110, 340
  ActiveX controls as, 178
  allocating and destroying exported classes, 246
  as COM components, 223
  COM, 265, 304
  component structure in COM, 223
  debugging, 615

DLLs *(continued)*
- ensuring same directory as client programs, 243
- entry functions, 254
- inheritance and, 250
- ISAPI, 336
- location, 368
- memory, 244
- MFC, 340
- middle-tier, 255
- proxy/stub, 260
- recompiling, 245
- registering, 178
- regular, MFC, 340
- sharing source files and, 235
- unloading, 267

DllSurrogate, 624
DllUnregisterServer function, 265, 272
DML statements, 450
dockable toolbars, 155
documentation of changes, 44
documents
- active, 333–35
- classes, programmer-defined, 93
- data, accessing, 94
- pages, vs. printer pages, 105
- templates, 94
- views and, relationship, 93

document/view architecture, 92–95
DoDataExchange function, 172, 175, 192
domain controller, authentication, 307
domains, 734
DoModal function, 164
DoPreparePrinting function, 104
drawing, 99
DS, 11, 28
DTC Client Configuration, 625
dual interfaces, 109
durable transactions, 351
dynamic
- changes to menu text, 150
- cursors, 510
- load balancing, 384, 680

dynamic HTML. *See* DHTML
Dynamically Linked Library. *See* DLLs

E

early-binding, 227
ECMA, 20
Edit and Continue, 612
editing
- records, 517
- recordsets, 530

editor, programming, 57
Elaboration Phase, 720
EnableCommit method, 387
Enable function, 149
encapsulation, 87
encryption, 19
END_INTERFACE_MAP macro, 284
END_INTERFACE_PART macro, 283
EndDoc member function, 102
EndPage member function, 102
enterprise applications, and data access, 30
enterprise development teams, 235
entities, 59–61
entity-relationship diagram. *See* E/R diagram
enumerators, 538
E_OUTOFMEMORY, 570, 573, 593
E/R diagram, 59, 61
error codes, 533
- E_OUTOFMEMORY, 573

error events, 574–78
error handling
- ADO and, 588
- COM programs and, 565
- failfast and, 583
- MFC applications and, 566
- strategies, overview, 579

error logs, 579, 582–83, 592
error notifications, 574–75
Error object, properties exposed by, 588
errors, 540
- ADO and, 579, 588
- anticipating, 558
- applications and, 565
- CMemoryException, 569
- COM, 569
- COM components and, 575
- debug, 245
- exception handling and, 559
- exceptions, 558
- MTS error handling, 583
- networks and, 577
- in ODBC and OLE DB, 589
- in programs, finding, 599
- remote modules and, 577
- retrieving information, 532
- root objects and, 582
- types of, in ODBC, 532
- Windows NT Event Viewer and, 626
- Windows NT Event Viewer Application Log, 583

Errors collection, 588, 589, 592
Errors object, 588
Escape member function, 102
European Computer Manufacturers Association. *See* ECMA
evaluation software, 687
event handlers, 179
events, 190, 575
EXCEPTION_CONTINUE_EXECUTION filter, 561
exception handling, 559–566
exception macros, 569
exceptions, 557, 558, 578
- ADO and, 579
- applications and, 565
- benign, 563
- CException, 565
- COM, 573
- distributed applications and, 577
- error handling code in networks, 577
- error logs, 579
- fatal, 558
- handling in ADO, 589
- macros, 569
- MFC and, 565, 577
- MTS and, 579, 582, 583
- new operator, 562
- in non-MFC programs, 562
- objects for, 562
- raising, 558
- trapped by ADO, 589
- turning off, 567

__except keyword, 560, 562
ExecQuery method, 584
executables, sharing source files and, 235
executing
- commands, 507, 549
- components, debugging, 621
- parameterized queries in ADO, 519
- stored procedures, 519

export direction, switching, 242
exported classes, allocating and destroying, 246
Export Function List, 629
exporting packages, 377
extended stored procedures, 459
Extensible Markup Language. *See* XML

F

FACILITY_ITF, 571
FAILED macro, 571, 582
failfast, 583
Fail function, 174
fatal exceptions, 558
fat clients, 352
faults, fatal, 559
file-locked server modules, debugging, 625
file management, in VSS, 46
files
  cabinet, 659
  program, including/removing, 670
  registry, 660
  in VSS, 46–51
filtering records in recordsets, 515
filter objects, HTTP, 337
filters
  creating, 339
  setting, 516
__finally keyword, 560, 561
firewalls, 19
folders in VSS, 47, 51
footers, 106
FOREIGN KEY constraints, 480
form views, creating with AppWizard, 170
forms, 163
forward-only cursors, 510
frame windows, making docking available in, 155
free function, 120, 125
free store. *See* heaps
free-threaded model objects, 109
functions, 247, 254. *See also* individual function names
  access, 149
  aggregate, 466
  command UI handler, 148
  handler, 90
  leaving, with Step Out command, 612
  overriding, 248
  relationship to data types, 466
  service callback, 320
  signature in classes, 250
Function Wizard in InstallShield, 704

G

GDI, 89, 97, 98, 107
GDI32, 628
GDPro, 63
generalization, 738
generative patterns, 715
GetControlling Unknown function, 327
GetDocument function, 94
GetExitCodeThread function, 315
GetExtensionVersion function, 337
GetFromPage function, 103
GetMaxPage/SetMaxPage function, 103
GetMessage/DispatchMessage, 116
GetMinPage/SetMinPage function, 103
GetToPage function, 103
global threading model, 319
graphical device interface. *See* GDI
graphical user interface. *See* GUI
graphic objects, creating in a DC, 98
GROUP BY clause, 467
GUI, 311
Guidgen.exe, 224
GUIDs, 219
  CLSIDs, 266
  COM identifiers and, 224
  Guidgen.exe, 224
/GX command line switch, 563

H

handler functions, 147, 148, 150, 151
handlers, 90, 160
handles
  hInstance, 272
"happy" flags, 387
HAVING clause, 467
header files, creating, 242
headers and footers, printing, 106
heaps, 119
  insufficient space, 559
help, 132–141,
  adding handler functions to menu commands, 147
  MFC ActiveX ControlWizard, 185
  ToolTips, 156
HelpContext function, 573
HelpFile function, 575
hierarchy, implementation inheritance, 253
hInstance handle, 272
history, viewing, in VSS, 51
HKCR. *See* HKEY_CLASSES_ROOT
HKEY_CLASSES_ROOT, 624
.hlp files, 135
.hm files, 135
.hpj files, 135
HRESULT value, 261, 269
HRESULT codes, 570–78, 582, 583
HTML, 62, 338
HTML 3.2, 21
HTML Help, 136–141
HTML pages, ActiveX controls and, 218
HTTPExtensionProc function, 337
HTTP filter objects, 337
HTTP servers, 338
HWND handle, 90
Hypertext Markup Language. *See* HTML
Hypertext Transfer Protocol. *See* HTTP

I

IClassFactory, 263, 267, 269
IClassFactory2 interface, 109
IClassFactory class, 368
IClassFactory::CreateInstance method, 368
IClassFactory interface, 109, 219, 228, 263
iCount variable, 581
IDE, 57
IDispatch, automation and, 227
IDispatch interface, 109, 227, 572
IDL, 269
  COM and, 218
  compiling an IDL file, 260
  creating an IDL file, 256
IDs, command, 91
IErrorInfo object, HRESULT and, 573
if-else blocks, 559
IIDs, compared to CLSIDs, 219
IIS, 17, 356
  ISAPI and, 336, 338
IIS process isolation, 626
illegal operations. *See* exceptions
Image Editor, HTML Help, 136
impersonation-level authentication, 307
implementation, 250
implementation inheritance, 240, 252–55
Implementation Workflow, 719
#import directive, 589
importing packages, 378
[in] attribute, function of, 258
in-process components, 24
  interactions among, 117
  specifying the surrogate, 624
in-process COM servers, 269

in-process servers. *See* DLLs
in-process threads, 116
Inception Phase, 720
includes, 738
independent clients, in MSMQ, 406
Indexed Sequential Access Method. *See* ISAM
indexes, 137, 481–82
inheritance, 240
  hierarchy, 253
  interface, 247
  primary benefit, 250
  problems, 250
  template classes and, 252
.ini file, 20
InitInstance member function, 97
inner joins, 457
inner objects, implementing, 329
InsertMenu function, 152
INSERT statement, 454
INSERT triggers, 463
installation programs, 654
installations
  automated, 690
  manual tasks, 684
  options for, 655
installer products, new releases, 692
InstallScript, using, 668
InstallShield, 668–70, 683, 709
InstallShield project, 697, 700, 701
integrated development environments. *See* IDE
integration testing, 636
integrity data, 478
interception, and MTS, 353, 369
INTERFACE_PART macro, 284
interfaces, 250, 259. *See also* individual interface names
  advantages of using, 254
  assigning roles to, 382
  attribute structure, 257
  COM, 109, 225
  DCE-RPC, 257
  declarations, 256, 260
  dual, 109
  inheritance, 247, 255
  interface pointers, 220, 229
  navigation, 225
  supporting, 279
  tear-off, 109
  template classes and, 252
  versioning, 225, 228
  viewing with OLEView, 69
  Visual Basic, 221
InternalAddRef function, 284
InternalQueryInterface function, 284
InternalRelease function, 284
internal transaction coordinator, 430
Internet
  connection types, 22
  programming, MFC and, 86
  ready-to-use ActiveX controls and, 195
Internet Component Download, 195
Internet Information Server. *See* IIS
Internet Protocol. *See* IP
Internet Server Application Program Interface. *See* ISAPI
interoperable applications, 10, 17, 13
Intranet connections, 22
IObejcetContext interface, 386
IP, 19
ISAM, 32
ISAPI, 336–39
IsCallerInRole method, 382
ISecurityProperty interface, 383
isolated transactions, 351
IsSecurityEnabled method, 382
iteration, 719
IUnknown, 256, 267, 269, 278, 280
  aggregation and, 326
  as controlling unknown, 327
  implementing, 261
IUnknown interface, 23, 109, 180, 225, 226, 233, 256, 280

J

Java, 7
  ease of use in projects, 235
  HTML Help applet, 136
JIT, 355, 601, 617, 621
  in MTS 2, 370
joins, inner/outer, 457
Just-In-Time activation. *See* JIT
Just-in-Time debugging. *See* JIT

K

Kernel32, 628
keys, registering a DCOM component, 308
keyset cursors, 510
keywords, 564. *See also* individual keyword names

L

LAN, 232
language independence, 217
Last-In/First-Out, 119
late-binding, IDispatch and, 227
launch permissions, setting, 644
legacy systems, 35
libraries
  C run-time, 87
  C++, 86
  MFC, 99
  static, 235
  template vs. standard C++, 109
  Visual C++ run-time library, 89
library blocks, 259
library packages, 357, 375
licensing, 185
lifetimes, managing, 221
LIKE search condition, 452
little-endian value, 490
load balancing, 384, 680
LoadMenu function, 151
local
  components, 24
  objects, debugging, 614, 615, 640
  queue storage. *See* LQS
location breakpoints, 605, 607
location transparency, 228, 302
lock types, 511
log files, 581
logic, application, 34
Logical Design, 742, 743, 747, 753
logical design phase, 724
Logical Model, 761
logical services layers of MSF, 761
LQS, 414

M

macros. *See also* individual macro entries
  MFC, 283, 569, 602
  switching export direction, 242
main STA, 117
MAKE_HRESULT macro, 571
malloc function, 120, 125
managing
  resources, dynamically, 474
  transactions, 495
Manipulate function, 28
manual merge, 49

MAPI, 26
marshaling, 116, 118, 232–34, 368
m_bContinuePrinting member, 106
MDAC, 27, 487
MDI, 142
Media Build Wizard, creating setup programs, 704
member functions. *See* individual member function names
member variables, creating, 244
memory
  allocation, 121–24, 244, 245
  areas, 119
  blocks, 125
  leaks, 122–26
  management, 119, 121, 125
  problems, 126
  unowned, 559
Memory window, 610, 611
menu commands, 147, 152
menu resource, creating menus with, 144
menus, 142–152, 162
merge conflicts, resolving, 49
merging files, in VSS, 48, 49
Message ActiveX control, 618, 621
message-handler functions, 90
messages, 89–91, 404
  breakpoints, 606, 608
  handlers, 90
  log, 633, 634
  maps, 89, 91
  purging, 428
  receiving, 422, 443
  sending, 419, 438, 439
  sending/receiving within transactions, 430
  transactional messaging, 429
  transactional queues and, 429
  window, viewing in Spy++, 634
Message log view, in Spy++, 631
Messaging API. *See* MAPI
METHOD_PROLOGUE macro, 285
methods. *See also* individual method names
  adding to objects, 276
  determining, 761
MFC, 86, 290
  active document containers and, 333
  active document servers, implementing, 334
  ActiveX ControlWizard, 184
MFC *(continued)*
  advantages/disadvantages, 110
  ANSI and, 88
  architecture, 89
  vs. ATL, when to use, 110
  classes, 88, 99, 100, 565, 577. *See also* individual class names
  creating ActiveX controls, 184
  creating COM servers, 277
  creating ISAPI DLLs, 336
  creating ISAPI server extensions/filters, 339
  creating secondary threads, 311
  DDV/DDX, 171
  debug macros, 602
  default handlers, 576
  error handling in applications, 566
  exception handling and, 565
  exception macros, 569
  exception objects, 562
  exceptions and, 565
  features, 87
  functions, exception support, 565
  libraries, 99
  limitations, 87
  macros, 283
  multithreading and, 311
  platforms, 88
  property page functions, 192
  regular vs. extension DLLs, 340, 341
  serialization and, 489
  stock events, adding, 190
  TRACE macro and, 579
  UI objects, updating 92
  UNIX and, 88
  writing code in, 492
MFC applications
  adding help-file links to the Web, 141
  implementing context-sensitive help in, 139
  toolbars, 155
  types of help in, 137
MFC AppWizard, 97, 334, 563
MFC ClassWizard, 89
MFC library, 86
MFC sockets design, 491
Microsoft ActiveX controls and user service layer, 15
Microsoft ActiveX Data Objects. *See* ADO
Microsoft Data Access Components. *See* MDAC
Microsoft Distributed Transaction Coordinator. *See* MS DTC
Microsoft Exchange, 27
Microsoft Index Server, 27
Microsoft Internet Information Server. *See* IIS
Microsoft Jet, 32
Microsoft JScript, 20
Microsoft Message Queuing Services. *See* MSMQ
Microsoft Open Database Connectivity. *See* ODBC
Microsoft Solutions Framework. *See* MSF
Microsoft Transaction Services. *See* MTS
Microsoft Universal Data Architecture. *See* UDA
Microsoft Visual Basic, 7, 16, 235
Microsoft Visual Component Manager, 62
Microsoft Visual J++, 16
Microsoft Visual Modeler, 59, 62–64
Microsoft Windows, 27
Microsoft Windows DNA, 15
Microsoft Windows Graphics Device Interface. *See* GDI
Microsoft Windows Sockets, MFC and, 86
middle-tier component development, 235
MIDL
  compiler, 233, 257
  interface declarations, 260
m_nCurPage function, 103
modal dialog boxes, 163, 164
modeless dialog boxes, 164
modeling
  data, 59
  as part of design, 734
  UML, 719
models, 63, 734
  activity, 738
  class, 749
  programming, 767
  state, 752
  thread, combinations, 115
  UI threading, 114
  use case, 736
ModifyMenu function, 152
Module Dependency Tree, 629
Module List, 629
modules, 628, 743
most-recently used, 96

m_pErrorInfo member, 569
MQIS, 405, 406, 411–16
m_rectDraw member, headers and footers and, 107
MS DTC, 430–32, 583, 625
MSF, 712, 720, 722, 761
MSF Application Model, 11, 722
MSF Design Process Model, 722
MSF Enterprise Architecture Model, 721
MSF Process Model for Application Development, 721
MSF Risk Management Model, 721
MSF Team Model for Application Development, 721
MSMQ, 356, 404, 410, 679
  APIs and, 412
  architecture, 405
  asynchronous communication and, 404
  client computers, types, 406
  clients, dependent/independent, 406
  Connector Server, 404
  cursors, creating, 423
  enhanced, 404
  enterprise, 405
  Explorer, 410
  Information Store. *See* MQIS
  installing, 406
  interfaces for writing applications, 412
  internal transaction coordinator, 430
  LQS and, 414
  messages, receiving, 422
  messages, sending, 419
  peeking, 422
  private queues and, 414
  queues, creating, 413
  queues, deleting, 427
  queues, locating, 416
  queues, opening, 418
  Rel parameters and their values, 417
  sites, 405
  standard, 404
  transactional queues and, 429
  transaction coordinators, 429, 432
  versions, 404
MSVCRT, 628
MTA, 115
MTA model, 116
MTA threading model, ATL support in, 318
MTS, 17, 349, 625, 747
  activities/transactions, understanding, 392
  administering server programmatically, 365
  administration objects, 365
  advanced techniques, 380
  benefits of using, 353
  client configuration utility, 677
  components, 359, 675
  configuring, 362, 363
  defined, 353
  designating objects for, 367
  designing with, 389
  developing objects for, 367
  DLLs and, 620
  error handling and, 579, 583
  exceptions and, 582
  failfast and, 583
  forbidding exceptions, 583
  interception and, 353, 369
  managing activities, 395
  negative HRESULT codes and, 583
  objects, 367, 376, 648
  operation, 392
  packages, 676
  packaging objects for, 371
  scaling applications, 389
  sending messages with transactions, 432
  structures, 357, 361
  as surrogate host, 620
  techniques, advanced, 380
  transactional messages and, 430
  transactions and, 350
MTS-based applications, creating, 386
MTS Explorer, 355, 583, 592
MTS Spy, 392
multilayer design, 10, 34
multiple
  document types, 93
  page, printing/previewing, 101
  tables, querying, 456
  views, 93, 95
multiple-document interface. *See* MDI
multiple-file change control systems, 45
multiplicity of class associations, 751
multithreaded, 113
  applications, 113
  components, 311, 318
multithreading, 311, 319
multitier design, 12, 13
multitiered programs, error handling in. *See* distributed applications
mutexes, 316, 317

N

n-tier
  application architecture, 34
  applications, 223
  design, 28
  distributed applications, designing, 62
native applications, 15, 16
navigation, 142, 161
networks, handling exceptions in, 577
network topology, 759
new
  files, opening, 489
  operator, 120, 121, 125, 558, 562
  statements, tracking, 604
nongenerative patterns, 715
nonsignaled mutexes, 317
normalization of data model, 62
Notepad, 669

O

object identity, 225
object lifetime management, 221, 225
Object Management Group. *See* OMG
object-oriented frameworks, 6
object request broker. *See* ORB
objects, 109. *See also* individual object names
  activating, 229
  adding, 372
  COM, 219
  COM vs. MSF, 744
  Command, 506, 539
  commands and, 91
  as components, 217
  constructor, 120
  for control, 747
  data source, 538
  database, 470
  destructor, 121
  graphic, creating in a DC, 98
  identity, 225
  implied, 747
  inner, 329
  inviting into same activity, 387
  iterating, 748

objects *(continued)*
- life of, 120
- lifetime management, 221, 225
- memory allocation, 124
- MTS and, 367, 371, 376
- outer, 327, 330
- pooling, 371
- properties and methods, adding, 276
- properties of, 375
- refining, 748
- reusing with containment, 329
- rowset, 539
- surrogate hosts and, 620
- UI, 91, 92
- viewing, with OLEView, 69

.ocx files, 178
ODBC, 15, 26, 31, 525–532, 625
- API, 497
- errors, 589
- MFC and, 86
- when to use, 497

ODBCDirect, 31, 497
ODL, 260
OLE
- COM and, 218
- MFC and, 86, 87

oleautomation, 258
OLE DB, 27, 31, 536–543, 589
OLE DB for Data Access, 15
OLE RPC Debugging, 617
OLEView, 68–69
OMG, 713
OnBeginPrinting function, 102
OnColors function, implementing, 199
OnDraw member function, 100
OnDraw methods, 184
OnEditClearAll function, 91
OnEndPrinting function, 102
online help, HTML Help, 136
OnOptionsStdcolors function, 199
OnPrepareDC function, 102
OnPrepareDC member function, 104
OnPreparePrinting function, 102, 109
OnPreparePrinting member function, 104
OnPrint function, 102
OnPrint member function, 104, 106
OnUpdateEditClearAll command handler, 92
OnUpdateItem function, 150
Open Database Connectivity. *See* ODBC
open windows in Spy++, listing, 632
operating systems, exception handling and, 558
operations, class, 735, 749
operators, new, 558, 562
ORB, 353
original caller vs. direct caller, 383
[out] attribute, function of, 258
outer joins, 457
outer objects, 327, 330
out-of-process components, creating using ATL, 304
out-of-process servers, 304, 344
out-of-process threads, 117
OutputDebugString function, 582
output parameters, handling, 521

P

packages
- adding objects to, 372
- creating roles for, 381
- exporting, 377
- importing, 378, 393
- library, 357, 375
- load balancing, 384
- in MTS, 357, 676
- properties, 374
- security, making available, 380
- server, 357, 375

packaging COM components, 674
packaging and deploying, distributed applications, 694
pages, printer vs. document, 105
pagination, 103, 106
parallel deployment, 680
parallelism in application development, 13
parameterized information, setting, 547
parameterized queries
- creating with CDynamicParameter Accessor, 547
- executing with ADO, 519

parameters
- attributes of, 258
- CancelDisplay, 576
- filter, 560
- passing to a stored procedure, 520
- TRUE/FALSE, 423
- types, limiting to Automation, 258
- values, setting, 549

parent classes, 280
Parent Import Function List, 629
ParseStandardArgs function, 322
PATHs, 658
patterns, 715, 716
PECs, 405
peeking, 422
performance testing, 40
permissions
- access/launch, setting, 644
- security, 307
- specifying for launching a server, 308

persistable objects, creating, 434
persistence, implementing, 487
persistent caching, and ZAW, 691
phases of UP, 720
Physical Design, 753
- analysis, 754, 757
- completing, 769
- implementation, 755, 766
- output, 769
- rationalization, 755, 762
- relationship to Logical Design, 742
- research, 754, 755
- steps, 754

physical design phase, 724
Ping utility, 625
plan-while-building approach, 3
platform-neutral UI framework, 20
platforms, 88
Platform SDK, 269, 277, 291
- building COM servers with, 268
- Guidgen.exe, 224

pointers. *See* individual pointer names
pooling objects, 371
pop-up help windows, 134
portability, 88
primary enterprise controllers. *See* PECs
PRIMARY KEY constraints, 480
primary site controllers. *See* PSCs
primary threads, 311
printer pages, vs. document pages, 105
printf statement, 579
printing, 99–101
- allocating GDI resources and, 107
- headers and footers, 106

print preview, 99–101, 107–8
print-time pagination, 106
private queues, 414
process isolation. *See* IIS process isolation

processes, 43
core, 728
priority values, 313
processors, 88
Processes view in Spy++, 631, 633
product evaluations, 7
production, 39–43
production stage, 41
product mindset, 6
ProgIDs, 219, 266
program errors, 558
programmatic security, 306
programming
declarative, 354
editor, 57
model, 767
programs
client, creating, 241
debugging, 599, 609, 621
errors, 599, 602, 626
evaluation, 639
files, including/removing, 670
stepping through, 611
testing, 599
uninstall, 657
Programs menu, 662, 663
project-based security, 50
projects, 46
aligning with business goals, 5
phases, languages for, 6
in VSS, 46, 51
project settings, resetting, 311
proof-of-concept, 7, 17, 733
properties
adding to objects, 276
default, DCOMCNFG, 66
determining, 761
of objects, 375
of packages, 374
property pages, 168, 191–93
property sheets, 168, 169
[propget], 258
[propput], 258
prototypes, 7
provider classes, 541
providers, 537
proxy/stub DLLs, 233, 260
proxy/stub technology, 232
PSCs, 404
pure virtual classes, 255
pure virtual functions, 250
purging messages, 428

Q

QueryInterface, 261
QueryInterface function, 261, 262, 267, 278, 326
queues
creating, 413, 679
dead letters, 422
defined, 404
deleting, 427
local, 406
locating, 416
LQS, 414
opening, 418
private, 414
transactional, 429
QuickWatch tool, 610

R

rationalization
of Logical Design, 747
in use case model, 738
Rational Rose, 63
RDO, 27, 31, 496
realloc function, 125
rebars, 157
records, 514–17, 531
Recordset objects
in ADO, 502
creating, 508
recordsets, 509–518, 530, 531
reference counting, 221
reference help, 133
referential integrity, 29
Regedit utility, 661
Regedit.exe, 308, 310
RegisterServer function, 272
Registers window, 610, 611
RegisterTypeLib API, 233
RegisterTypeLib function, 266
registry
COM, 230
files, 660
information, 473, 657
RegisterTypeLib API, 233
settings, configuring, 64
settings, in COM, 231
regression testing, 636
Release function, 262, 326
Release mtstran1 button, 400
ReleaseMutex function, 317
release versions, 601, 695
Rel parameters, values, 417
remote
access, 308
administration, 390
COM calls, 22
components, 24, 623
computer, specifying for an out-of-process component, 624
COM servers, registering, 684
modules, errors and, 577
objects, 614, 620, 621, 643
process, attaching debugger to, 621
remote server names, determining, 674
servers, usage, 302
stored procedures, 459
Remote Data Objects. *See* RDO
Remote Procedure Calls. *See* RPC
RemoteServerName key, 624
RemoteServerName value, setting in registry with Dcomcnfg.exe, 231
RemoveMenu function, 152
requirements, changes, 34
Requirements Workflow, 719
resource manager. *See* RM
resource pooling, 538
resources, adding to menus, 142
result sets, cursors and, 485
retrieving, guidelines, 451
return codes, handling, 521
return on investment. *See* ROI
return value testing, 559, 563
[retval] attribute, function of, 258
reusability in application development, 13
rich-text format files, 135
risk management, 7, 756
RM, 352
robust code, 559
ROI, 5, 13, 43
role-based security, 354, 380
roles, 361, 381, 382
ROLLBACK TRANSACTION statement, 461
root objects, 582, 583
routing servers, 405
rowsets, 539–544
RPC, 22
.rtf files, 135
rule of three, 715
rules, business, for data access, 28
Run member function, 89, 324
Run to Cursor command, 611

S

SaveStatus function, 322
SayHello method, 394, 398
scalable applications, 34
scenarios, 730, 731
SCM, 229, 263, 266
SCODE, 570
SDI, 142
SDK, 183, 490
secondary help windows, 134
secondary threads, 311
security, 19
  activation, 229
  affecting programmatically, 382
  authentication, 307
  call, 229
  COM, 229, 306
  data access, 29
  DCOM, 306
  declarative, 306
  default, DCOMCNFG, 65
  options, configuring, 68
  packages and component, 380
  permissions, 307
  programmatic, 306
  project-based, 50
  protection, 302
  role-based, 354, 380
  testing for, at method level, 382
  in VSS, 50
SEH, 560, 562, 564
SELECT statement, 450
self-registering components, 682, 683
serialization, 487, 489
Serialize function, 488
server packages, 357, 358, 375
servers
  active documents, 333, 334
  COM types, 304
  extensions, creating, 339
  in-process, debugging, 615
  out-of-process, debugging, 617
  registering, 473
  specifying permissions for launching, 308
server-side cursors, 486
service-layered applications, 223
service layers of MSF, 761
service providers, 537
services, 743
  16-bit programming, MFC and, 88
  business, 22
  callback functions, 320
  communicating with, 324
  component, 6
  for control, 747
  ControlService function and, 324
  creating, 320
  data, 25, 28
  implied, 747
  initializing, 323
  installing/removing, 325
  main function, implementing, 322
  major functions of, 320
  managing, 325
  of MSF Application Model, 11
  running, 324
  writing code, 323
services-based approach, 10
sessions, 538
SetAbort method, 388, 584
SetCheck function, 150, 583, 584
SetComplete method, 388
SetHeight function, 155
SetMaxPage, 104
_set_new_handler function, 593
SetPad, 663, 665
setting
  Command properties, 506
  parameterized information, 547
  parameter values, 549
  recordset properties, 509
Setup.exe program, creating, 671
setup programs, 654–56, 666, 704, 706
shared classes, 236
shared modules, usage counts for, 659
sharing, 235, 236
  violations, 625
  in VSS, 48, 51
shortcut menus, 150, 151
shortcuts, 147
signaled mutexes, 317
single-document interface. *See* SDI
single-file change control system, 45
single-threaded, 113
single-threaded objects, 109
site licenses, 687
sites, MSMQ, 405
SMS, computer inventory, 692
sockets, closing without notifying server, 494
software
  development process, shifting, 4
  installation and maintenance, 690
  licensing, 687
  deployment, 692
software development kit. *See* SDK
source files, sharing among projects, 235
splitter windows, 93
Spy++, 631–34
SQL, 448, 625
SQLConnect, 625
SQL queries, 519
SQL Server, 405, 469–476
SQL Server Enterprise Manager, 472
STA, 115, 117
STA threading model, ATL support in, 318
stacks, 119
stack unwinding, 120
standard marshaling, 368
Standard Template Library. *See* STL
StartDoc member function, 102
StartPage member function, 102
StartService function, 322
statements. *See* individual statement names
state model, 752
static cursors, 510
static libraries, solving sharing problems, 235
static load balancing, 384
status bars, 158–160
StdAfx.h, global threading model, 319
Step Into command, 611, 612
Step Out command, 611, 612
Step Over command, 611, 612
stepping through code, 611
Step tools, 611
STL, 111
stock events, 190
stock property pages, 193
stored procedures, 458–460, 519, 520
storing data, 481
strategic value, 5
strategies, data access, choosing, 498
stress testing, 636
structure definitions, VARIANT, 258
structured exception handling. *See* SEH

Structured Query Language. *See* SQL
structures. *See also* individual structure names
  of MTS, 357
  setting data breakpoints for, 607
stub and proxy system, 232
subkeys, AppID, 309
submenu commands, inserting, 146
SUCCEEDED macro, 571, 582
Summarize function, 28
surrogate process, 24
surrogate processes for components, 354
surrogates, 620, 621, 624
SuspendThread function, 314
switches, 563
synchronization, mutex object, 316
synchronizing threads, 315, 319
synchronous error notifications, 574
systems, 43
  services, 119
  lockdown, 691
  tables, 477
  testing, 636

T

table of contents, 135, 137
tables system, 477
task-oriented help, 132
tear-off interfaces, 109
technology, candidate, 757, 758
templates
  classes, 252, 255
  documents, 94
  libraries, vs. standard C++, 109
temporary stored procedures, 459
terminating threads, 314
test assumptions, without adding permanent code, 602
Test Container. *See* ActiveX Control Test Container
test harness, 638, 639
testing, 599
  components in separate packages, 396
  distributed applications, 636
  for security, at method level, 382
  HRESULT codes, 571
  methods, 637
  packages in different computers, 397
  return values, 559
  scenarios, 636
testing *(continued)*
  stage, 40
  terminology, 636
Testing Workflow, 719
test plans, 637
test scenarios, 638
text editor, 57
THIS pointer, 262, 278
Threading Model, combinations, 117
threading models, 318, 319
Threading Model value, 116
threads, 113–17, 311–15
Threads view, in Spy++, 631, 633
three-tier applications, 10
throw keyword, 562
time-trial evaluation software, 687
toggle switches, 149
Toolbar Editor, 153
toolbars, 152–57
tools, 57, 62
ToolTips, 156
topologies, 756
  component, 761
  data, 760
  network, 759
TP, 353
TRACE macro, 579–582, 592
TrackPopupMenu function, 150
Transact-SQL, 448
Transaction Statistics, 399
transactional messages, 433
transactional messaging, 429
transactional queues, 429–433
transactions, 350
  activity monitor, 584
  atomic, 351
  COM and, 352
  consistent, 351
  controlling flow of, 386
  coordinators, 429–433
  coordination, 351, 356
  criteria, 351
  determining longevity of, 386
  durable, 351
  handling, 505
  isolated, 351
  managing, 397, 495
  MTS and, 350
  MTS Explorer and, 584
  processing. *See* TP
  understanding in MTS, 392
Transition Phase, 720
triggers, 461
troubleshooting COM objects, 625
TRUE, returning, 239
TRUE/FALSE parameters, 423
TRUNCATE TABLE statement, 455
try block, 574
try C++ keyword, 562, 567
try-catch blocks, 572
__try keyword, 560, 562
try keyword, 562, 567
two-phase commits, 351
type libraries, 259, 266
type library marshaler, 258, 260
type library marshaling, 368

U

UDA, 27, 483, 484
UIs, 14
  command handler functions, 148
  creating, 197
  design, 753
  framework, platform-neutral, 20
  native and Web-based, 18
  navigation in, 142
  objects, 89–92
  threading model, 114
  threads, 114
  ToolTips, 156
  Web-based, 16
UML, 6, 63, 712, 722, 728
  activity diagram, 739
  diagrams, 713, 734
  includes, 738
  Visual Modeler and, 62
"unhappy" flags, 387
Unified Modeling Language. *See* UML
Unified Process, 712, 719, 720, 722, 728
Unified Software Development Process. *See* Unified Process
uninstall programs, 657
unit testing, 636
universal storage approach, 25, 26
UNIX, MFC and, 88
UpdateAllViews member function, 95
UPDATE statements, 455, 464
UPDATE triggers, 464
upgradability, 250
UnregisterServer function, 272
UpdateData function, 173

usage
  counts for shared modules, 659
  scenario, 41
  testing, 40
use case models, 41, 736, 738
use cases, 41, 729, 738, 743
user interface. *See* UIs
user service design, 15
user service layer, 15, 16, 18
user services, 11
users, input, 94
UUIDs, 257

V

validation, 171–75
VALUES clause, 454
variables, member, creating, 244
Variables window, 610
VARIANT, 258
verification, 748
VERIFY macro, 602, 603
version control, 45, 47
versioning interfaces, 228
views, 93–95, 632
virtual functions, 255
  and managing document creation, 489
  introduced, 249
  lack of, 238
  pure, 250
  using, 250
virtual storage access method. *See* VSAM
Visio, 63
visual
  data modeling, 59
  tools, using, 62
Visual Basic, 27
  ActiveX controls and, 218
  interfaces, 221
Visual C++, 16
  integrated debugger, 600, 605, 615, 621, 622
  libraries, 86
  Watcom C++ and, 250
Visual C++ run-time library, 89
visual display, 21
visual merge, 49
Visual SourceSafe. *See* VSS
Visual Studio, dialog template in, 165
VSAM, 29
VSS, 45–51
vtables, 220, 249, 255

W

WaitForSingleObject function, 317
WAN, 19
Watch window, 610
Watcom C++, Visual C++ and, 250
Web
  adding HTML Help file links for applications, 141
  browsers, 20, 21
  deployment over, 687
  development, 38
  distributing application updates, 688
  pages, visual display, 21
  servers, 336, 337
  sites, HTML Help, 136
Web-based applications, 18, 19
Web-based deployment, 687
Web-based interfaces, with dynamic HTML, 17
Web-based user service layer, 16
what you see is what you get. *See* WYSIWYG
WHERE clause, 451, 452
wide area network. *See* WAN
wildcard characrters, 452
Win32 API, 15
Window Finder Tool, 632, 633
Windows
  applications, MFC classes and, 88
  help systems, 133
  HTML Help, 136
  messages, 90
windows
  messages, viewing in Spy++, 634
  splitter, 93
Windows 2000, authentication in, 306
Windows 95, 303
Windows 98, DCOM support for, 302
Windows Distributed interNet Application. *See* Windows DNA
Windows DNA, 10, 24
Windows Installer, ZAW, 691
Windows NT, 306, 320–25, 583
Windows NT 4
  testing DCOM with, 303
  installing ZAW, 692
Windows NT Directory Service API, 26
Windows NT Directory Services, 27
Windows NT Event Viewer, 626
Windows NT Event Viewer Application Log, errors and, 583
Windows program deployment, 686
Windows Scripting Host. *See* WSH
Windows view, in Spy++, 631, 632
WinError.h file, 571
WinError.h header file, 572
WinHelp, 137, 141
WinHelp files, 135, 138
WizardBar, 89
wizards, 133
WM_COMMAND messages, 89, 90
WM_PAINT message, 101, 108
WordPad, 158, 666
worker threads, 114, 575
workflows, 719
working folders in VSS, 47, 51
World Wide Web. *See* Web
WSH, 363
WYSIWYG, 142
WYSIWYG applications, 105

X

XML, 16

Z

ZAW, 690–92
Zero Administration for Windows. *See* ZAW

The manuscript for this book was prepared and submitted to Microsoft Press in electronic form. Text files were prepared using Microsoft Word. Pages were composed by Online Training Solutions, Inc. (OTSI) using Adobe PageMaker 6.5, with text in Times and display type in Helvetica Narrow.

Project management, author management, editing, production, and graphic services for this book were provided by OTSI. The hard-working project team included:

R.J. Cadranell
Joyce Cox
Leslie Eliel
Michelle Kenoyer
Steve Lambert
Rachel Moorhead
Gale Nelson
Gabrielle Nonast
Joan Lambert Preppernau
Mary Rasmussen

Online Training Solutions, Inc.
http://www.otsiweb.com

MICROSOFT LICENSE AGREEMENT

Book Companion CD

IMPORTANT—READ CAREFULLY: This Microsoft End-User License Agreement ("EULA") is a legal agreement between you (either an individual or an entity) and Microsoft Corporation for the Microsoft product identified above, which includes computer software and may include associated media, printed materials, and "online" or electronic documentation ("SOFTWARE PRODUCT"). Any component included within the SOFTWARE PRODUCT that is accompanied by a separate End-User License Agreement shall be governed by such agreement and not the terms set forth below. By installing, copying, or otherwise using the SOFTWARE PRODUCT, you agree to be bound by the terms of this EULA. If you do not agree to the terms of this EULA, you are not authorized to install, copy, or otherwise use the SOFTWARE PRODUCT; you may, however, return the SOFTWARE PRODUCT, along with all printed materials and other items that form a part of the Microsoft product that includes the SOFTWARE PRODUCT, to the place you obtained them for a full refund.

SOFTWARE PRODUCT LICENSE

The SOFTWARE PRODUCT is protected by United States copyright laws and international copyright treaties, as well as other intellectual property laws and treaties. The SOFTWARE PRODUCT is licensed, not sold.

1. **GRANT OF LICENSE.** This EULA grants you the following rights:

   a. **Software Product.** You may install and use one copy of the SOFTWARE PRODUCT on a single computer. The primary user of the computer on which the SOFTWARE PRODUCT is installed may make a second copy for his or her exclusive use on a portable computer.

   b. **Storage/Network Use.** You may also store or install a copy of the SOFTWARE PRODUCT on a storage device, such as a network server, used only to install or run the SOFTWARE PRODUCT on your other computers over an internal network; however, you must acquire and dedicate a license for each separate computer on which the SOFTWARE PRODUCT is installed or run from the storage device. A license for the SOFTWARE PRODUCT may not be shared or used concurrently on different computers.

   c. **License Pak.** If you have acquired this EULA in a Microsoft License Pak, you may make the number of additional copies of the computer software portion of the SOFTWARE PRODUCT authorized on the printed copy of this EULA, and you may use each copy in the manner specified above. You are also entitled to make a corresponding number of secondary copies for portable computer use as specified above.

   d. **Sample Code.** Solely with respect to portions, if any, of the SOFTWARE PRODUCT that are identified within the SOFTWARE PRODUCT as sample code (the "SAMPLE CODE"):

      i. **Use and Modification.** Microsoft grants you the right to use and modify the source code version of the SAMPLE CODE, *provided* you comply with subsection (d)(iii) below. You may not distribute the SAMPLE CODE, or any modified version of the SAMPLE CODE, in source code form.

      ii. **Redistributable Files.** Provided you comply with subsection (d)(iii) below, Microsoft grants you a nonexclusive, royalty-free right to reproduce and distribute the object code version of the SAMPLE CODE and of any modified SAMPLE CODE, other than SAMPLE CODE, or any modified version thereof, designated as not redistributable in the Readme file that forms a part of the SOFTWARE PRODUCT (the "Non-Redistributable Sample Code"). All SAMPLE CODE other than the Non-Redistributable Sample Code is collectively referred to as the "REDISTRIBUTABLES."

      iii. **Redistribution Requirements.** If you redistribute the REDISTRIBUTABLES, you agree to: (i) distribute the REDISTRIBUTABLES in object code form only in conjunction with and as a part of your software application product; (ii) not use Microsoft's name, logo, or trademarks to market your software application product; (iii) include a valid copyright notice on your software application product; (iv) indemnify, hold harmless, and defend Microsoft from and against any claims or lawsuits, including attorney's fees, that arise or result from the use or distribution of your software application product; and (v) not permit further distribution of the REDISTRIBUTABLES by your end user. Contact Microsoft for the applicable royalties due and other licensing terms for all other uses and/or distribution of the REDISTRIBUTABLES.

2. **DESCRIPTION OF OTHER RIGHTS AND LIMITATIONS.**

   - **Limitations on Reverse Engineering, Decompilation, and Disassembly.** You may not reverse engineer, decompile, or disassemble the SOFTWARE PRODUCT, except and only to the extent that such activity is expressly permitted by applicable law notwithstanding this limitation.
   - **Separation of Components.** The SOFTWARE PRODUCT is licensed as a single product. Its component parts may not be separated for use on more than one computer.
   - **Rental.** You may not rent, lease, or lend the SOFTWARE PRODUCT.
   - **Support Services.** Microsoft may, but is not obligated to, provide you with support services related to the SOFTWARE PRODUCT ("Support Services"). Use of Support Services is governed by the Microsoft policies and programs described in the

user manual, in "online" documentation, and/or in other Microsoft-provided materials. Any supplemental software code provided to you as part of the Support Services shall be considered part of the SOFTWARE PRODUCT and subject to the terms and conditions of this EULA. With respect to technical information you provide to Microsoft as part of the Support Services, Microsoft may use such information for its business purposes, including for product support and development. Microsoft will not utilize such technical information in a form that personally identifies you.

- **Software Transfer.** You may permanently transfer all of your rights under this EULA, provided you retain no copies, you transfer all of the SOFTWARE PRODUCT (including all component parts, the media and printed materials, any upgrades, this EULA, and, if applicable, the Certificate of Authenticity), **and** the recipient agrees to the terms of this EULA.
- **Termination.** Without prejudice to any other rights, Microsoft may terminate this EULA if you fail to comply with the terms and conditions of this EULA. In such event, you must destroy all copies of the SOFTWARE PRODUCT and all of its component parts.

3. **COPYRIGHT.** All title and copyrights in and to the SOFTWARE PRODUCT (including but not limited to any images, photographs, animations, video, audio, music, text, SAMPLE CODE, REDISTRIBUTABLES, and "applets" incorporated into the SOFTWARE PRODUCT) and any copies of the SOFTWARE PRODUCT are owned by Microsoft or its suppliers. The SOFTWARE PRODUCT is protected by copyright laws and international treaty provisions. Therefore, you must treat the SOFTWARE PRODUCT like any other copyrighted material **except** that you may install the SOFTWARE PRODUCT on a single computer provided you keep the original solely for backup or archival purposes. You may not copy the printed materials accompanying the SOFTWARE PRODUCT.

4. **U.S. GOVERNMENT RESTRICTED RIGHTS.** The SOFTWARE PRODUCT and documentation are provided with RESTRICTED RIGHTS. Use, duplication, or disclosure by the Government is subject to restrictions as set forth in subparagraph (c)(1)(ii) of the Rights in Technical Data and Computer Software clause at DFARS 252.227-7013 or subparagraphs (c)(1) and (2) of the Commercial Computer Software—Restricted Rights at 48 CFR 52.227-19, as applicable. Manufacturer is Microsoft Corporation/One Microsoft Way/Redmond, WA 98052-6399.

5. **EXPORT RESTRICTIONS.** You agree that you will not export or re-export the SOFTWARE PRODUCT, any part thereof, or any process or service that is the direct product of the SOFTWARE PRODUCT (the foregoing collectively referred to as the "Restricted Components"), to any country, person, entity, or end user subject to U.S. export restrictions. You specifically agree not to export or re-export any of the Restricted Components (i) to any country to which the U.S. has embargoed or restricted the export of goods or services, which currently include, but are not necessarily limited to, Cuba, Iran, Iraq, Libya, North Korea, Sudan, and Syria, or to any national of any such country, wherever located, who intends to transmit or transport the Restricted Components back to such country; (ii) to any end user who you know or have reason to know will utilize the Restricted Components in the design, development, or production of nuclear, chemical, or biological weapons; or (iii) to any end user who has been prohibited from participating in U.S. export transactions by any federal agency of the U.S. government. You warrant and represent that neither the BXA nor any other U.S. federal agency has suspended, revoked, or denied your export privileges.

DISCLAIMER OF WARRANTY

NO WARRANTIES OR CONDITIONS. MICROSOFT EXPRESSLY DISCLAIMS ANY WARRANTY OR CONDITION FOR THE SOFTWARE PRODUCT. THE SOFTWARE PRODUCT AND ANY RELATED DOCUMENTATION ARE PROVIDED "AS IS" WITHOUT WARRANTY OR CONDITION OF ANY KIND, EITHER EXPRESS OR IMPLIED, INCLUDING, WITHOUT LIMITATION, THE IMPLIED WARRANTIES OF MERCHANTABILITY, FITNESS FOR A PARTICULAR PURPOSE, OR NONINFRINGEMENT. THE ENTIRE RISK ARISING OUT OF USE OR PERFORMANCE OF THE SOFTWARE PRODUCT REMAINS WITH YOU.

LIMITATION OF LIABILITY. TO THE MAXIMUM EXTENT PERMITTED BY APPLICABLE LAW, IN NO EVENT SHALL MICROSOFT OR ITS SUPPLIERS BE LIABLE FOR ANY SPECIAL, INCIDENTAL, INDIRECT, OR CONSEQUENTIAL DAMAGES WHATSOEVER (INCLUDING, WITHOUT LIMITATION, DAMAGES FOR LOSS OF BUSINESS PROFITS, BUSINESS INTERRUPTION, LOSS OF BUSINESS INFORMATION, OR ANY OTHER PECUNIARY LOSS) ARISING OUT OF THE USE OF OR INABILITY TO USE THE SOFTWARE PRODUCT OR THE PROVISION OF OR FAILURE TO PROVIDE SUPPORT SERVICES, EVEN IF MICROSOFT HAS BEEN ADVISED OF THE POSSIBILITY OF SUCH DAMAGES. IN ANY CASE, MICROSOFT'S ENTIRE LIABILITY UNDER ANY PROVISION OF THIS EULA SHALL BE LIMITED TO THE GREATER OF THE AMOUNT ACTUALLY PAID BY YOU FOR THE SOFTWARE PRODUCT OR US$5.00; PROVIDED, HOWEVER, IF YOU HAVE ENTERED INTO A MICROSOFT SUPPORT SERVICES AGREEMENT, MICROSOFT'S ENTIRE LIABILITY REGARDING SUPPORT SERVICES SHALL BE GOVERNED BY THE TERMS OF THAT AGREEMENT. BECAUSE SOME STATES AND JURISDICTIONS DO NOT ALLOW THE EXCLUSION OR LIMITATION OF LIABILITY, THE ABOVE LIMITATION MAY NOT APPLY TO YOU.

MISCELLANEOUS

This EULA is governed by the laws of the State of Washington USA, except and only to the extent that applicable law mandates governing law of a different jurisdiction.

Should you have any questions concerning this EULA, or if you desire to contact Microsoft for any reason, please contact the Microsoft subsidiary serving your country, or write: Microsoft Sales Information Center/One Microsoft Way/Redmond, WA 98052-6399.

PN 097-0002296

Proof of Purchase

0-7356-0926-8

Do not send this card with your registration.
Use this card as proof of purchase if participating in a promotion or rebate offer on *Distributed Applications with Microsoft® Visual C++® 6.0 MCSD Training Kit*. Card must be used in conjunction with other proof(s) of payment such as your dated sales receipt—see offer details.

Distributed Applications with Microsoft® Visual C++® 6.0 MCSD Training Kit

WHERE DID YOU PURCHASE THIS PRODUCT?

CUSTOMER NAME

mspress.microsoft.com

Microsoft Press, PO Box 97017, Redmond, WA 98073-9830

OWNER REGISTRATION CARD

Register Today!

0-7356-0926-8

Return the bottom portion of this card to register today.

Distributed Applications with Microsoft® Visual C++® 6.0 MCSD Training Kit

FIRST NAME | MIDDLE INITIAL | LAST NAME

INSTITUTION OR COMPANY NAME

ADDRESS

CITY | STATE | ZIP

E-MAIL ADDRESS | ( ) PHONE NUMBER

U.S. and Canada addresses only. Fill in information above and mail postage-free.
Please mail only the bottom half of this page.

start
faster
go
farther